The March of
LITERATURE

Literary Criticism from Dalkey Archive Press

Edward Dahlberg ● *Samuel Beckett's Wake and Other Uncollected Prose*

Ford Madox Ford ● *The March of Literature*

Miriam Fuchs, ed. ● *Marguerite Young, Our Darling*

Marie-Lise Gazarian Gautier ● *Interviews with Latin American Writers*

Marie-Lise Gazarian Gautier ● *Interviews with Spanish Writers*

Geoffrey Green, et al., eds. ● *The Vineland Papers*

Jack Green ● *Fire the Bastards!*

William McPheron ● *Gilbert Sorrentino: A Descriptive Bibliography*

Clifford Mead ● *Thomas Pynchon: A Bibliography*

Paul Metcalf ● *Where Do You Put the Horse?*

Leon Roudiez ● *French Fiction Revisited*

Viktor Shklovsky ● *Theory of Prose*

Alain Vircondelet ● *Duras*

The March of
LITERATURE

FROM CONFUCIUS' DAY TO OUR OWN

by

FORD MADOX FORD

THE DALKEY ARCHIVE PRESS

Normal • *1994*

©1938 by Ford Madox Ford. Copyright renewed 1966 by Janice Biala.
Introduction ©1994 by Alexander Theroux
First Dalkey Archive Edition, 1994

Library of Congress Cataloging-in-Publication Data
Ford, Ford Madox, 1873-1939.
  The march of literature : from Confucius' day to our own / Ford Madox
Ford ; introduction by Alexander Theroux. — 1st Dalkey Archive Press ed.
  Originally published: New York : Dial Press, 1938.
  Includes bibliographical references (p.) and index.
  1. Literature—History and criticism. I. Title.
PN523.F6   1994   809—dc20   93-21208
[<Rare Bk Coll.>]
ISBN 1-56478-051-1

Partially funded by grants from the National Endowment for the Arts and the
Illinois Arts Council.

Dalkey Archive Press
4241 Illinois State University
Normal, IL 61790-4241

Printed on permanent/durable acid-free paper and bound in the United States of America.

A DEDICATION WHICH IS ALSO AN
AUTHOR'S INTRODUCTION

TO

JOSEPH HILLYER BREWER AND ROBERT GREENLEES RAMSAY
PRESIDENT AND DEAN OF MEN, OLIVET COLLEGE, MICHIGAN

My dear Mr. President and Mr. Dean,

It is usual for a dedicator to assure his dedicatees that without their help he could not successfully have concluded his labors. That is true in a literal and physical sense, in this case, because, had you not provided me with a room in your admirable library, I should never have been able to finish this book—or not in ten years. But my spiritual obligation to you is no less deep. We have been working together for some time now, I under your presidency and deanship, in the attempt to restore to the youth of this state a lost art—that of reading . . . and in the hope that that art may spread from this state in ever widening practice to the ends of the earth.

Its present condition must be humiliating to every thinking man. The population of your nation is 150,000,000, that of mine over 450,-000,000, every soul of whom is at least taught to read English in the schools. Yet of those six hundred million how many do, after their school days, read any books at all, much less any book that a reasonably cultivated man would not be ashamed to be seen reading? Well, a good—a very good—sale for a book of any literary merit whatsoever would be in my country, 14,000 copies; in yours 40,000. There are also, I have seen it estimated, in our joint vast realms, over 50,000 professors of literature. That means that one professor in a life of conscientious labor induces about 1.08 pupils to become, after tuition, reasonably civilized human beings. . . . And, in addition, there must be in existence hundreds and hundreds of thousands of learned works dealing with literature.

So it occurred to us three that there must be something wrong with the way in which the attractions of literature and the other arts are presented to our teeming populations. The solution of the problem seemed to us to be that that presentation must be in the wrong hands —that, in fact, such tuition, whether by word of mouth or in books, should be, not in the hands of the learned, but in those of artist-practitioners of the several arts—in the hands, that is to say, of men and women who love each their arts as they practice them. For it is your hot love for your art, not your dry delvings in the dry bones of ana and philologies that will enable you to convey to others your strong passion.

So you set up your educational institution in which the professoriate consists solely of practicing artists—amongst whom it was my pride to enroll myself and my pleasure to serve. And having, thus, your corporate assurance that I was an artist, I thought I might undertake this book.

It is the book of an old man mad about writing—in the sense that Hokusai called himself an old man mad about painting. So it is an attempt to induce a larger and always larger number of my fellows to taste the pleasure that comes from always more and more reading. But that imposes on me certain limitations—the first being that, contrary to the habits of the learned, I must write only about the books that I have found attractive: because if I lead my reader up to unreadable books I risk giving him a distaste for all literature. Too many of the classics that the learned still mechanically ram down the throats of their pupils or their readers have lost the extra-literary attractions that once they had and so have become but dry bones, the swallowing of which can only inculcate into the coerced ingurgitators a distaste for all books. At the same time, I have such a distaste myself for writing injuriously about my fellows of the pen, though they may have been dead a thousand years, that I have, as you would say, panned hardly any writer, except for one or two stout fellows whose reputations may be considered as able to take care of themselves. So there may well be here certain omissions that may astonish you until you reflect upon the matter.

I have, in fact, tried to do here, making allowance for the differing nature of the medium, what you do with your students. You turn them loose in your library. You say: "Choose a book. Try it out thoroughly. If, after a sincere trial, you find it distasteful, reject it and try something else. If you like it, study it carefully and study the other books of its author and his circle, observing what you can of his methods as to which we shall afterwards speak to you. Then try other books until you find more to which you are attuned. . . ."

I, of course, have had to dilate upon the methods of authors when recommending readers to read various books, otherwise my method has been the same as yours. I have taken book after book that I liked —and that in so many cases I have liked since my adolescence—and have suggested that if the reader likes the idea of the writer that I present to him, he should try steeping himself in that author's books, and so I have attempted to trace for that reader the evolution from the past of the literature of our own day and our own climes.

In any case, I beg you to accept the assurance of my affectionate thanks, of my hopes for the continued success of your admirable labors, and of the fact that I am

Your humble and, as I hope you have always found me,

Obedient servant,

F. M. F., D.Litt.

Olivet College, Michigan
14 July mcmxxxviii

ACKNOWLEDGMENT

The author must make the usual acknowledgments for the innumerable quotations with which his pages have been beautified; the quotations are acknowledged where they are made. Unless otherwise stated, translations and adaptations are by the author. For the sake of space he has omitted the translation from foreign languages of passages whose interest is purely stylistic.

INTRODUCTION
by ALEXANDER THEROUX

G oethe once said that all writing is confession. It is a truism, if one
at all, that applies here. We tend to learn as much about Ford in
The March of Literature, this compendious tour of worthy writing to
which he is guide, as we do of the work itself. It is, among other things,
a record of his own quaint prejudices and fixed tastes, though, for being
that, no less valuable a book. There is no end to the remarkable
thoughts and theories he brings to world literature. He believed that
Herodotus was the first great prose writer and that Icelandic literature
was highly refined ("one of the few earthly near-paradises that the
world has ever seen") and that the great novels of the world have all
been mystery stories. He was convinced greater material luxury leads to
self-expression. The poorer a race is, he felt, the less will be the number
of its accomplishments. He ignored Tolstoy, judged Leon Daudet "so
great a genius as to be almost alone in the world," and badly overrated
Heine whom he called "the most exquisite of all the world's lyrists" (his
word, though Heine never played the lute) "since the great Greeks."
And while he abused many of our most honored novelists, notably
Fielding and Cervantes—a sentimentalist as profound as his own Ash-
burnham, Ford thought chivalry might have saved Western civilization
and despised Cervantes in bringing it under ridicule for destroying it—
he considered the genre and its practitioners in a way that Thackeray
himself would have approved, when he wrote, "There's no good
novelist who isn't a good gossip."

It was also Ford's belief—and he had the habit by way of testing it of
always turning to page 90 of an author's work and quoting the first
paragraph (which I did in this volume only to find it somewhat basic and
low-flown)—that a passage of good prose is a work of art in itself,
exclusive of context, "with no more dependence on its contents than is a
fugue of Bach, a minuet of Mozart, or the writing for the piano of
Debussy." Along with that he felt that being "slightly mannered" is

ix

characteristic of the work of all great writers, an idea that may come as a blow, constructive, one would hope, to the now popular Less Is More school, the Reporter-As-Novelist, today's undermedicated hack, etc. Ford explained: "In great moments the convention which is a necessity for all works of art must be enhanced by just the merest notion of the screw and the language must, by the merest shade, marmorealize itself."

Ford Madox Ford (1873-1939), although he attended the Praetorius School at Folkestone and the University College School in London, never went to college—as was the case, curiously, with most of the well-read people he grew up with and later respected. He converted to Catholicism at nineteen years old. He entered the army at forty-one as a second lieutenant, writing a poem "Antwerp" that T. S. Eliot once said was "the only good poem he'd met with on the subject of war." (Ford was shell-shocked during the Battle of the Somme in 1916.) He spoke fluent French and German, some Italian and Flemish, and a lot of Greek and Latin. He could quote long passages from memory. He was prolific and in his lifetime wrote eighty-one books, over four hundred articles, and edited two notable literary magazines, the *English Review* and the *Transatlantic Review*. He was the complete writer, brought up to believe that artists were the only serious people, that everyone else was simply "stuff to fill graveyards."

He was a fat man, ponderous, with blond hair that became almost white in old age, bad teeth, rosy cheeks, and a heavy mustache. He was a heavy smoker—Gauloises ("dust and dung," he called them). In 1894 he married Elsie Martindale, who was formally his only wife, and although never divorcing her, for the marriage broke up in 1908, he had many affairs. (Supposedly he had eighteen major relationships with women over the course of his lifetime.) Although a prodigious writer, he was financially strapped all his life. He also had a prodigious memory and once began a French translation of his masterpiece *The Good Soldier* without a copy of the book or a note at hand. Thirty-seven pages of that truncated version survive at Cornell University.

In a sense, the critical book he wrote in 1929, *The English Novel*, prefigures *The March of Literature* in that it is subjective, personal, and unashamedly unacademic, "almost more an after-dinner conversation than a book," according to one biographer, Alan Judd, who observes that "the voice that addresses you is warm and intelligent, its judgements made more definite—for good or ill—by an overwhelming love for its subject." The premise of chatty, open-ended comment is indeed quite the same, though it was a much more laborious undertaking, this last great book which he wrote in his declining years, and in spite of its quirkiness one that represents a much vaster and more comprehensive erudition.

The March of Literature was written over the course of a year. Ford had been staying with his friends Allen and Caroline Tate, and through them met Joseph Brewer, the new president of Olivet College in Michigan. Brewer was impressed enough with Ford to offer him the post of writer-in-residence at the college, a position in which Ford saw an opportunity finally to write a commentary on world literature that had long been on his mind. He managed to interest the Dial Press in the project and began the book during the swelteringly hot summer of 1937 in Clarksville, Tennessee, where, living with the Tates at their house "Benfolly," he made progress though he found the place rackety and complained of "the children and chickens and birds and cows and steamboats and Tennessee voices and doors slamming in the wind." Nevertheless, before leaving for Olivet in the fall he managed to do most of the required reading, often in original texts, and sedulously began cranking out about a thousand words a day, dictating much of the book to Wally Tworkov, the sister-in-law of Janice Biala, his last consort. The poet Robert Lowell, who as a young man was also living there, described the atmosphere as "Olympian and somehow crackling."

Upon arriving at Olivet, he secured an office in the basement room of the college library and by December had completed half the book, some four hundred pages, whereupon he and Janice went off to Paris. He suffered a minor heart attack there and generally was not well. Ford and Janice then returned to Michigan in April 1938 where he resumed work on the book, toiling away often from early morning to evening, as he had promised the publisher that he would finish the book by July, which in fact he did. Results were mixed. It turned out, much to Ford's dismay, that Dial cut out most of the untranslated quotes as being too formidable, the book sold poorly in the end, and even the original manuscript disappeared after being donated by Ford for a Spanish Civil War organization to sell for funds.

It was Ford's strong conviction that the tuition of presenting literature "should be, not in the hands of the learned, but in those of artist-practitioners . . . men and women who love each their arts as they practice them." "Hot love," says Ford, as distinguished from "dry delvings." He had simple premises for what should be included by way of analysis in *The March of Literature*. Is a work readable or not? Is it creative, imaginative, and poetic or just "factual writings"? And while he says it is rash "to set one's private judgements up against the settled opinions of humanity," for contemporary literature the only test, he assures us, is one's personal taste. To him, the working writer was by far the best judge of literature, which is interesting to me, since for twenty years in academic life I myself have often seen constantly preferred to good writers eighth-rate academics on the tenure track—classic examples of 1 Corinthians 3:18—with narrow monographs and mediocre books of criticism dropping out of their insufficiencies like eggs from battery fowl, never failing to call to mind for me those lines from Yeats's "The Scholars":

> Bald heads forgetful of their sins,
> Old, learned, respectable bald heads
> Edit and annotate the lines
> That young men, tossing on their beds,
> Rhymed out in love's despair
> To flatter beauty's ignorant ear.

The envy of scholar for artist, the preposterous idea that a literary critic sees—is capable of seeing—more deeply into a writer's work than he himself can, is a commonplace in American academic life and is, among other things, the driving force behind much modish criticism of recent years, most of it the sort of impenetrable wall of noise we find in university periodicals where costive functionaries with Ph.D.s and prooftexting pencils make sad sallies into the world of the imagination, which for most of them is foreign travel. ("What Poe failed to understand about 'Ulalume' was . . .")

Critics and textual commentators of literature—the "professorio-academic pack"—Ford found hopelessly pompous. Scholars to him tend to kill literature, invariably approaching it in the wrong light, as morticians, untrained psychologists, the kind of deconstructionist theorists of the sort I met with during my years at Yale with their fatuous poses, unbearable jargon, and sophomoric "zones of meaning" ("I've got a secret"). The teacher as expositor is often a complete and utter fake, frequently complicating the obvious and obfuscating what he is paid to clarify. I can't tell you how many professors I've known who pretty much echo Faulkner's overly circumspect Flem Snopes and his cunning reflection, "It can't be right, it isn't complicated enough." One of the leitmotifs of *The March of Literature* is the ruination by formal education of the joy and innocence of reading. With Ezra Pound, Ford quite despised overly pedantic or professional anybodies. "For them the controlled monochrome of reason," he might have said with novelist Patrick White, who also dismissed academic critics in his memoir *Flaws in the Glass*, "for me the omnium gatherum of instinctual color which illuminates the more often than not irrational behavior of sensual man."

The March of Literature, then, taken altogether, is a "massive and idiosyncratic survey from Confucius to Conrad," anecdotal, erudite, observant, mostly unpretentious, full of adventures of the mind and unexpected moments, what the French call *accidenté*. If anything, its fault can be found, not in its quirkiness—for it is often singularly wrongheaded and even outlandish—but in its wordiness. There is a good deal of the "project" in it, the verbal equivalent to my mind of something like handmade furniture, which we value not only because of but in spite of its flaws, a vast and elephantine personal undertaking, at once encyclopedic, unwieldy, overdetermined here, too slight there, something along the lines of, say, the monumental wooden plane called the *Spruce Goose* (it flew only once) built by amateur aviator Howard Hughes, a fellow, curiously enough, whom Ford actually mentions in this book! It was Ford's ambition, in short, not only to take us on this literary tour but to save literature from the corrupt province of the learned.

To make various points in the book, Ford often argues from his own life. He writes that if he had to send a child to school, he "would give the strictest possible orders that he was to be taken through none of the great classics by any teacher," and expressly identifies with a friend of his for whom, he recalls, Jesus and Shakespeare, having been taught in class-rooms, became figures who had the faces of schoolmasters. It is the reason Ford says he could never read Goethe and Kleist, Klopstock and Schiller. "Shakespeare profited above [his contemporaries], no doubt, in the fact that he did not go to university," says Ford, and benefited rather "in running, like De Quincy, the cruel streets of London." The bold and vital unself-consciousness of that period allows for Ford to plead that overintellectualizing Shakespeare is wrong. "The Elizabethan wrote to be ranted. He needed overaction and vast, harsh voices to cow and affright his audiences." It was Ford's belief, therefore, that Shakespeare is intelligible to "any fourth-form schoolboy" or fourteen-year-old. "No teacher can teach Shakespeare," pronounces Ford, who never quite forgave the schools for doing it so poorly. "The most the 'teacher'—and, alas, *quis docebit ipsos doctores?*—can do for a pupil is to perform the functions of an easier dictionary, telling the meaning of a tassel gentle, a hernshaw, a fardel, a bourne."

And with what relish does Ford report Gibbon's dissatisfaction, for example, with his own English education. "To the university of Oxford I acknowledge no obligation," wrote the historian, "and she will as cheerfully renounce me for a son, as I am willing to disclaim her for a mother. I spent fourteen months at Magdalen College; they proved the fourteen months the most idle and unprofitable of my whole life." Gibbon, who was disgusted by the curriculum there, thought that universities from their early beginnings have proved not the advance-ment but the very ruin of learning and the arts, "an assertion," Ford adds significantly, "with which we are not minded to disagree." Surely the echoes of his own bitter memories and lost opportunities under-score Ford's remarks.

The craft of the writer, with "a sort of priestly and lawyer-like respectability attached to the man who could write," was always venerated. And so it is predominantly Ford the writer, not the critic, who takes us from ancient Egypt through the Golden Age of Chinese Literature, the Old Testament, which Ford called "an anthology"—the more lucid if read when "freed from the shadow of unreasonable gloom and almost insane vindictiveness with which one is accustomed to invest the Sacred Writings" (he is quite good on the Psalms)—to solid Aristotle through Cicero and Horace, into the Middle Ages, and beyond. Ford shows great learning in his explanations, in spite of the brief he has with academics. (Even his earnest thumbnail biographies are quite compelling.) He can single out his favorite lines of Ovid, explain Virgil's intricate vowel-coloring, and speak off-handedly about Persian poets of the thirteenth century like Jalal 'U Ddin Ru'Mi and Fari'Da Ddin with ease, never sacrificing as he rambles along an anecdote, a story, or a sudden idea, which of course adds great charm to the book.

We learn in *The March of Literature*, for example, how and where cigarette-smoking was introduced to the West, how Mussolini relied on Ciceronian rhetoric, on what points of poetry he and Pound disagreed, and so forth. And he is always ready to digress or interrupt himself—a digression about World War I, for instance, on page 295, in the middle of a discussion of the Border ballads, lasts *three pages*—a wonderful irony, it might be noted, in light of Ford's blasts against Henry Fielding for his own authorial intrusions.

But as this is not history—Ford, while trying to be reasonable, is not running for mayor—he can be not only unpredictable in his tastes, but positively maddening. He devotes six pages to the Roman poet Tibullus and then doesn't mention Melville. He takes three pages to sing the praises of the "great" Jean Paul Richter, of whom he ludicrously writes "a man is hardly a complete man until he has read a great deal of Jean Paul," and proceeds to dismiss James Joyce in a few lines as a word-juggler, the content of whose books "is of relatively little importance." He vilifies Tasso, pronounces Dryden's dramas to be worse than awful, rejects Ibsen's plays as "almost unreadable," and unequivocally denounces Victor Hugo for being a snob who wanted Paris to be named after himself.

Ford hated snobs. Byron was "odious" and wrote nothing but the "verse and language of a nobleman who considered himself impregnable behind his rank and the fashion of the day." (Ford also blames him for the rise of Marxism!) He is no kinder to the English novelist. Defoe was "an insufferable bore." Jane Austen overdrew her characters. Goldsmith was a materialist and Dickens a loudmouth and Thackeray a despicable misconstruer of plots as well as a snob. ("The dread spectre of the Athenaeum Club was ever in his background.") "Both Thackeray all his life and Fielding in *Tom Jones* were intent first of all on impressing on their readers that they were not real novelists," said Ford, "but gentlemen." *Tom Jones*, in fact, remained for Ford "one of the most immoral books ever written." Dickens was "vulgar" and "excruciatingly bad." "He overwrote; he exaggerated; he was without delicacy; his humor was the humor of a tough in a Putney barroom today. There was no literary fault that he did not blaze out all over his pages all of the time." Paradoxically, while faulting Dickens for vulgarity, it disgusted Ford that Fielding *avoided* certain low details, for it was Ford's contention that the snobbish and self-promoting Fielding claimed to be unfamiliar with such facts. The fact that Ford rated Trollope's *Framley Parsonage* "higher than any other English novel" seems to save him somehow from joining with E. M. Forster in that writer's hair-raising remark, "There has never been a first-class novel written in English." Ford Madox Ford, who ironically wrote one of them, comes perilously close to agreeing.

It may be this hatred of snobbery, at least in part, that gives a distinct anti-English tone to the book, which begins even as he dismisses *Beowulf* as "a rather clumsily constructed sackful of legendary wisdoms, human instances, and *longueurs*." It is a poem, he says significantly, that has "all the imperfections of *clumsiness that has distinguished English workmanship from time immemorial*" (my italics). Can this explain his shocking indifference to Milton? Why he gives nine pages to Lessing and only one each to Jonathan Swift and Alexander Pope, whom he snipes at for his clichés? (Ford seems to have begrudged him the £8000 he received for his Homeric translations, judging him "no scholar.") He calls Dryden a "hack poet" and compares Smollett to Le Sage to the detriment of the former for lacking both sardonic and lambent humor—he finds him "cruel" ("almost the most insensitive of this world's greatest writers") —just as he resents the phony "manly" model *Tom Jones* has become in Britain, a novel he finds "heartless," artlessly digressive, of negligible story, etc. On the other hand, he loves *Clarissa* in spite of its poundage, and goes on to add a rather severe criterion of value for a writer's worth: only Richardson and Henry James among Anglo-Saxon writers are "international-minded." Jane Austen, whom to some degree he condescends to admire, you see, never attained that status.

If he's woeful on the English eighteenth century, he's ruthless to the nineteenth. A dislike of the Victorians harbored by many of his generation lingered long in Ford and seems only to exacerbate his dislike of its many writers. Byron, as we've seen, to him was a prig, Southey "second-rate," and Tennyson tepid. "You will find nowhere in the world such a body of ill-written stuff as in the English nineteenth-century poets; nor so great an inattention to form either of sentences or of stories; nor such tautology; nor yet such limp verbiage," wrote Ford who thought highly of only Browning and Christina Rossetti, whom he inexplicably raises to the empyrean as "the one consummate artist that the English nineteenth-century produced." (Hadn't he heard of Gerard Manley Hopkins, who had been published by 1918?) Nor was it just this or that in poor Tennyson. Ford makes it a sweep: "There was nothing that Tennyson touched, in fact, that he did not water down—to the very day of his death." Ford's favorite pejorative, "backboneless," is repeatedly used in these chapters as he scores off one poet after another.

Ford's quirks are utterly memorable. "The academic critic," he writes, "despises the novel as he dislikes most forms of art," but which of them with Ford would have called Cervantes "a chronically impoverished hack author" with whom, as he says, he had "a complete want of sympathy." Or said this: "I have no intention of increasing, however microscopically, the number of his readers by writing of him." *Don Quixote* he calls "a hideous affair," "a masterpiece of ill-taste, whose sole effect was to go towards rendering the world fit for Big Business." There is often no accounting for his favorites. He thought Captain Marryat to be "the greatest of English novelists" but doesn't mention Tolstoy at all. And where is Proust? He rated the sentimental and moralizing *Paul and Virginia* as "necessary to a world that would be poorer without them." He makes mention at the very end of Dostoevsky (whom he had clearly forgotten) but devotes three or four reverential pages to Alfieri, eight to Chateaubriand. He adores James Fenimore Cooper ("a magnificent prose-writer") and Molière ("no other genius save Jefferson ever lived so completely"), and he especially treasures Dante. Gibbon wrote, he felt, "as if he were throwing at you pieces of his own heart." So much did he admire *The Decline and Fall of the Roman Empire* that, throwing caution to the wind, he wrote "unless a man has read Gibbon he scarcely merits the name of an Englishman, an Anglo-Saxon, or even a man at all."

All in all, then, his criticism is biased, tendentious, and even unfair. But in his defense Ford never wanted to be anything but forthright. His concern is almost always about how writing works—where and why writers fail, where and why succeed. *The March of Literature* is in a sense less a story of literature, a compendium, a college course, than one man's constatation of it, to use one of Ford's favorite words, though it is, as is quite obvious, far, far less dispassionate a presentation than that term denotes. He has worked to pull together what by saving he wants you to know and by knowing to remember and by remembering to treasure against changing fashion and foolery. "It is the book of an old man mad about writing," said Ford. "In the great sense, the supreme art is the supreme expression of common sense," he once wrote, making a rather strange remark about art, but he was a great believer in the practical and the unpretentious and even the odd.

Robie Macauley called Ford "the least academic man who ever taught," duly pointing out that "for him all books in themselves were contemporaneous." I like to think of Ford as believing that, who also humbly knew that glory never happens in the presence of guides or lecturers. Vision, like poetry, resists academic pretension, just as dogma evaporates on contact with the mystery of true spirituality.

BOOK I
Part One

CHAPTER ONE

THE modern English sense of the word "literature" is something very difficult to define. The original Latin word from which it is derived, *"litterae"* (even without the adjective *"humaniores"*), was apparently exclusively applied to what we now call *"belles-lettres"* or "humaner letters." It would be a good thing if the term were today restricted exclusively to those departments of the written, printed or the incised word.

Rather unfortunately, for a century or so, the word has here been applied to two or three other departments of human activity—to records, to catalogues, to tendential works of every kind. People say, for instance, "The literature of the subject comprises," and they will follow with a catalogue of books or pamphlets descriptive of almost any object under the sun, from flowers or women's clothing to astronomic speculations. Thus refreshing my memory as to Ancient Egypt, I might say: The literature of the subject includes Budge's (Wallis) *The Mummy*, Weigall's *The Treasury of Ancient Egypt*, Burrows' *Discoveries in Crete*, Maspero's *Contes Populaires*, Torr's *Memphis and Crete*. And I might continue with a long list of learned works devoted to this subject. Practically none of these compilations will display any imagination, human insight or literary talent—with the possible exception of Professor Maspero's French renderings of early East Mediterranean folklore.

But actually, in the earlier sense of the word, if we wrote the "literature of Ancient Egypt includes," we should have to follow it by "the Messianic prophecy derived from the poem of Ipuwer of the 12th Dynasty; a number of peasant songs dating from the fourth millennium B.C.; the more naïve later literature of the age of Rameses the Second," and so on. We should catalogue, that is to say, the works of imagination or pure literature produced by the Ancient Egyptians themselves. We should completely exclude the works of learned Egyptologists of every nation under the sun who, in the last century and a half, have dug into the sands of the Egyptian deserts and discovered, deciphered and then, not writing anything of human interest, have merely catalogued the objects of every description that they have found.

In the book that follows, we shall confine ourselves exclusively to chronicling the humaner letters of the world. If we succeed in turning out a work of insight and imagination and one couched in clear, uncomplicated and not harsh prose, we may make ourselves see the great stream of literature issuing from its dark and remote sources and broadening through the centuries until it comes to irrigate with its magnificent and shining waters, almost the whole of the universe of today. If we succeed in that, we too shall have produced . . . a piece of literature.

This may appear a contradiction of the paragraph immediately preceding the last one. That would appear to say that history cannot be literature. Actually, whether a history be literature or not depends entirely upon the animation, the perspicacity, the insight, the incisiveness, the poetic qualities—upon, in short, the personality of the writer. Thus Gibbons' *Decline and Fall of the Roman Empire*, or the story of Ruth and Boaz may both be classed as history and also as prose or poetic literature. But Mommsen's *Roman History* or a textbook of geography for the use of high schools would be neither.

The term "literature" even in its strictest sense of *"belles-lettres"* or in the more poetic term, "the humaner letters," does not exclude works on account of their form or their subject. On the face of it, the pamphlets of political propagandists would not appear to come under either heading. But, because of their fire, their close-knit styles, the passion of their invectives, and their lucidity, it would be a bold man who denied that the *Philippics* of Demosthenes, the *In Catalinam* of Cicero or in the lesser rank, the *Impeachment of Warren Hastings*, or the famous oration of Patrick Henry were either *belles-lettres* or humaner letters. In short, the quality that is necessary for the production of the Art of Literature is simply that of a personality of wide appeal. An art is the highest form of communication between person and person. It is nothing more and nothing less. The more attractive the personality making the communication, the wider in extent, the deeper in penetration and the more lasting, will be the appeal. What the subject may be, is of no importance whatever. The famous Greek Idyl of a woman outside a temple carrying a baby and trying to see a procession is as poignant as any of the cantos of the *Divine Comedy*, any of the books of the Bible, any passage from Shakespeare, or from *Le Rouge et le Noir* by Stendhal or any story by Turgenev.

The quality of literature, in short, is the quality of humanity. It is the quality that communicates, between man and men, the secret of human hearts and the story of our vicissitudes.

It is therefore in the sense of creative, imaginative, or poetic work that we shall henceforth employ the word "literature." This, at any rate, in Anglo-Saxondom, is contrary to the existing fashion. The French, the Germans, the Italians, and most other civilized nations differentiate between the two classes of writing by calling all imaginative literature "poetry," and all merely instructional or cataloguing matter, generally prose. Hence the word "prosaic." But in Anglo-Saxondom the tendency has always been to regard instructional writings as being on a higher plane and creative literature as being, at any rate, relatively frivolous. In England it is not unusual for newspapers to list books that they receive for review under the headings "Serious Literature" and "Other Books." Thus I remember having seen in one and the same journal a volume of short biographies of music hall stars and another devoted to recipes for cocktails, classified as "Serious Literature" while Conrad's *Under Western Eyes* and Thomas Hardy's *Collected Poems* were dismissed as "Other Books." American papers seldom go as heroically far as that. But the tendency of the public on either side of the Atlantic is, on the whole, similar. It would, however, be absurd to write a history of factual, scientific or instructional books and call it a History of Literature. Records of facts, statistics and scientific theories are always so swiftly superseded that in a very few years almost no trace of them remains on the public consciousness. We may doubt, for instance, if any lay people today read Darwin's *Origin of Species*, or the book called *Babel and Bible*, works which, some decades ago, shook the civilized world. But a couple of score novels and volumes of poems written since the 1880's are part of the necessary pabulum of every man or woman who passes for educated or who takes pleasure in the written word. And if you consider the number of serious works of the imagination that, since men began to write, have passed a similar test, the disparity is so great as to be farcical. Let us glance backwards. The educated reader needs to know of the literature of ancient Egypt a few folksongs, a few small collections of precepts written by sages, and the few first forms of the legends that are important as showing the solidarity, the permanence that unite humanity throughout all the ages—the first forms of legends of the Deluge, of the Creation, of the Messiah, of the Trinity, or of the stories told by Scheherazade. The same is true of the writings of Babylon or of Crete. Then immediately you come upon the immense mass of propaganda and prophecy that make up the Hebrew Bible.

Contemporaneously, or immediately afterwards, came the great mass of Greek poetry and drama, and later the imaginative works of the Latin writers. As against these, you have on the borderline between the serious and the creative, the dialogues, say, of Plato, a few geographical or historical works like the writing of Thucydides, Herodotus, Xenophon, and possibly Strabo, Pliny, and the *De Bello Gallico* of Caesar. These serious writings that will hold the critical or pleasure-loving intelligence are very rare.

It is here necessary to make an effort to be explicit. The dialogues of Plato or Julius Caesar's *De Bello Gallico* are philosophic or factual works. But Socrates before beginning an argument will mention that there is a hill with trees outside the city wall to which it will be agreeable to retire for discussion. The passage is so brilliantly written that you have at once an addition to your mental picture of Athens. Or Caesar, with the detail as to chariots used by the blue-stained Briton, will make you see an early battle field. That is literature. If a work devoted to the biographies of music hall stars or to cocktails contained a sufficiency of such passages, that also would be literature. Actually there exist innumerable written or incised documents, records of law suits, market accounts, astronomical speculations and codices of the Egyptian, the Babylonian, in addition to the Classical Greek or Roman unreadable matter just mentioned. But they are of a sort that is unlikely, however the taste of mankind may change, ever to bulk very large in the human consciousness, so they could hardly be called literature. There exist, for instance, case-books of Greek and early Arab physicians. In the diagnoses that they contain, even the medical layman may find a certain pleasure. He will discover that, two to three thousand years ago, people had very much the same symptoms as at times are felt by himself. And, the earliest written document in existence, being a Babylonian lawyer's pleading in a law suit, may be equally interesting. For, in the remotest times, testamentary uncertainties were as frequent as they are today. But these things are of importance merely because of their quaintness or because they are evidence of what I have called human solidarity. . . . They show the sameness of the vicissitudes and passions of humanity down the ages. . . .

In the meantime there was being written a great—a very great—stream of literature that, coming from the East, has ever since impinged on the current of our western writings. Actual contact between Chinese, Indian, Persian and other Eastern literatures is not very hard to establish. In Greek philosophic writing, like that of Pythagoras, unmistakable traces of Chinese thought are visible. Pythagoras was a semi-mythical Greek philosopher of the sixth century whose existence is traceable almost solely, as quotations, in writings by his successors. But amongst those traces we discern many of the *Precepts* of Confucius. Thus, even if we didn't know historically the commercial and aesthetic associations uniting Greece to the farthest East, we should have to suspect that some such contact had taken place. Moreover, in the great body of the great literature written in Arabic the influence and even the name of Plato occur very frequently. In any case it will be well if the reader gets into his head the image of a vast panorama of the Eastern world across which shimmered two streams of literary influence. The one descended the Nile, the other came from China, yet both discharged themselves into the Mediterranean to form that Mediterranean civilization which is today our own.

The Far Eastern Chinese stream we may take for the moment as having been more "serious" than the one which descended between Nile banks. Or it would be perhaps more just to put it that the Western world has found more use for the philosophy than for the creative imagination of the East. The names of Oriental works which spring immediately to the mind are those of the *Moral Precepts* or *Canon* of Confucius, the four *Vedas*, the *Mahabharata*, and the *Ramayana*. Against them one may set the *Sakuntala* of Kalidaça, a heroic epic.

Into these things we shall have to go more fully later, but it may help our initial impression to say that, as against Mediterranean literature, Oriental writings have been better preserved. The notorious First Emperor of China made, like Mr. Hitler, a spirited attempt to destroy the records of all Chinese civilizations that had preceded that over which he reigned. But he excepted from this *auto-da-fé* all works on agriculture, medicine and divination; thus, if he had succeeded, the balance might have gone heavily down on the side of "serious" books. But, after his death, hidden copies of the works of earlier poets and philosophers were discovered in plenty. For instance, a copy of the *Canon* of Confucius was found in the ruins of the house he had inhabited. Thus this holocaust is petty compared with the burning of the library at Alexandria and the almost complete rooting out, for eight hundred years or so, of the classic Greek and Roman literature. This last took place at the successive sacks of Rome and of all the littoral cities of the Mediterranean before and during what were known as the Dark Ages. Thus, the view of what we have remaining of Greek and Roman literature may well be unbalanced. The works of many reputedly great writers of whom we have traces only in the quotations made by their admirers have completely disappeared. Thus, of Hesiod almost nothing remains—sixteen hundred lines or so. And even of these it is questionable whether a thousand of them may not have been written by one of his disciples. Yet in his own day—which fell in the eighth or ninth century before Christ—and for hundreds of years later, Hesiod was a poet esteemed as on a level with, or even greater than, Homer. Similarly, almost nothing remains of the writings of Sappho.

Thus when estimating the relative outputs of imaginative or of "serious" writing in the Graeco-Roman classical age we must always remain more or less at fault. But it would seem fairly safe to say that, in what remains to the public consciousness of today, their creative imaginative literature immensely exceeds their factual writings. You might say that for one person who today, outside law schools, reads the *Codices* of Justinian, one hundred thousand delight in the athletic prowess of the heroes of Homer or in Virgil's account of the fate of Laocoön and his sons.

With the re-ascent towards civilization that began after the Dark Ages, the estimation becomes at once much clearer and much easier. Almost none of the "serious" work that was written for a thousand or so years after the fall of the Roman Empire would today be taken seriously or even read for its quaintnesses. You might read an Anglo-Saxon *Bestiary* for philological reasons or in order to discover how much knowledge of natural history was possessed by tenth or eleventh century Anglo-Saxons. But you would hardly read it either for pleasure or to improve your knowledge of the habits of beasts or birds. Similarly you would not read the fourteenth century *Travels of Mandeville* to help your geography. Nor yet would you read Culpepper's *Herbal* for its botany, nor Malory's *Morte d'Arthur* to add to your knowledge of history. But there at once we come upon a snag. For it is quite possible to read Culpepper because of the quaintnesses of his conceits and language and Malory must, with his words, his imagination and the beauty of his point of view, have given inconceivable delight to uncounted millions since his day. There exists, however, another branch of science—if theology be indeed a science—that must give serious pause to anyone wishing to classify what the pen has produced. Where exactly would you place the *Imitation of Christ?* Yet only a few years ago a German firm of international booksellers declared—and there is no reason to doubt their veracity—that the masterpiece of Thomas à Kempis or Gerson or Vercellius or whoever wrote it, was the most read book in the world, the number of copies sold exceeding even those of the Bible. This last statement, as an Anglo-Saxon, one may imagine to be an exaggeration. Nevertheless, the sale of the *Imitation* may be taken to be immense. It finds readers of practically entire populations wherever the Roman, Greek or Coptic rites flourish, whereas to read the Bible is not a necessary act of faith for Catholics. And next in sales to the *Imitation of Christ*, comes Bunyan's *Pilgrim's Progress* which must at one time or another have been read by every Protestant child on the globe, an exception being made for the Protestant populations of the Danube and Balkan states. They for their part read an almost exactly similar work, by Comenius. But here again the safest test dividing imaginative from "serious" work must simply be the quality of the execution of the task, the poetic imagination of the writer. And, even at that, there are many books which must fall on either side of the borderline.

How, for instance, would you classify the mystic writings of the great St. Theresa?

Or how, indeed, today—otherwise than by their good or bad writing —would you classify the innumerable romanticized biographies of every imaginable type of historical character from Helen of Troy to Mrs. Harriet Ward Beecher Stowe?

Let us then sum up Literature as that which men read and continue to read for pleasure or to obtain that imaginative culture which is necessary for civilizations. Its general characteristic is that it is the product of a poetic, an imaginative, or even merely a quaintly observant mind. Since the days of Confucius, or the earliest Egyptian writers a thousand years before his time, there have been written in stone, on papyrus, wax, vellum, or merely paper, an immense body of matter—innumerable thousands of tons of it. This matter is divisible into that which is readable and that which is unreadable except by specialists in one or another department of human knowledge. The immediate test for one's self as to what is literature and what is not literature—*biblia a-biblia* as the Greeks used to call this last—is simply whether one does or doesn't find a book readable. But if a book has found readers in great numbers for two thousand or five hundred or merely eighty or ninety years, you would be rash, even though you could not read it yourself, to declare that it was not literature—not, that is to say, a work of art. You may dislike Homer as much as this writer actually dislikes, say, Milton. But neither of us would be wise if we declared that either the *Iliad* or *Paradise Lost* were not literature. We should be unwise because it is foolish to set one's private judgment up against the settled opinions of humanity for generation on generation, and because our tastes may change before the end of our lives. This writer used, for instance, as a boy, very much to despise Ovid, as a poet, mainly, perhaps, because he was forced at school to memorize an immense number of lines from the *Metamorphoses*. But today one of the chief consolations of his existence is that he has still a great number of those lines by heart and can recite them to himself at night when he is unable to sleep.

But for the judging of contemporary literature the only test is one's personal taste. If you much like a new book, you must call it literature even though you find no other soul to agree with you, and if you dislike a book you must declare that it is not literature though a million voices should shout to you that you are wrong. The ultimate decision will be made by Time.

There remains in the settling of these preliminaries the question of what is and what is not poetry. As we have said, the Anglo-Saxon world—the British Empire and the United States—stands alone in considering that verse is the necessary frame of poetry. A fine novel is called in French *poésie*, in Italian *poésia*, in German *Dichtung*, and in almost all other languages the same classification is made. It is to be wished that we did the same because that classification is more reasonable and indeed more scientific. But since insisting on calling the *Morte d'Arthur* or Flaubert's *St. Julian* or Turgenev's *The Singers* or Cunninghame Graham's *Beattock for Moffatt* "poems" though they are written in prose—since to do that would cause confusion—we had better throughout this work use the term "poetry" only for that which is written in verse.

Verse it should be remembered is much the older medium of the two. It served for the expression of the most early and most savage passions. The naked prehistoric savage jumping up and down and yelling "Rah, Rah, Rah, Ho, Ho, Ho," like the university cheerleader during a football game today, was laying the foundations of the verse-poetry that should—and shall—succeed them. These wordless chants, dating from before the time when humanity could communicate its thoughts by words, gradually stereotyped themselves as rhythms, then adopted some sort of musical inflection and later took words to themselves. They expressed rage. They incited to war. They timed the stroke of paddles, as, later, they gave the signal for the hauling of ropes on ships. These primitive, utilitarian developments of verse, particularly on the seas, accompanied humanity, until very late times, in the form of sea chanties. So that, if you could write a history of these chanties from the earliest times until the coming of steam, you would have a very useful epitome of the earlier development of verse in almost all civilizations.

Whilst civilizations remained primitive, whilst men were mainly hunters, nomads or pioneers, their verse retained the quality of primitive chanting. Then as civilization attained to luxury, and the greatest of all luxuries, that of leisure, the thoughts that they thought became less passionate. They passed hours in reverie, in the sports of love, or in loitering in pleasure gardens. They found words to express these moods or occupations, but these moods or occupations, not being rhythmic, they could not express them in verse like that of the chants of the cavemen. So, gradually, out of these non-rhythmic but pleasurable or emotional occupations, was born the more sophisticated and the more difficult art of prose.

Strong emotions, nevertheless, continued to call for rhythmic expression such as distinguishes early Chinese, Arabic or American-Indian odes.

Later again, as in the artificially accented or stressed verse of the Romans, the actual form of the verse itself began to become important. The poet began to take pleasure and to attempt to convey pleasure to his hearers by all sorts of verbal devices from rhymes that would become even puns, to the repetition of whole sentences so as to make verbal patterns. These tricks are innumerable. In nearly all literatures they began with what is called "onomatopoeia"—the expression of an event, of the aspect of a landscape or of a frame of mind, by the actual sound of the word employed. Thus you have the famous *Poluphlisboion* or the *Anerhythmon gelasma* of the Greeks, the one word signifying the sound made by a huge rock when cast into the sea by a hero, or the other expressing the "innumerable smile" of the smooth sea when its surface is broken up into diamond-shaped wavelets. Or the later Romans using recurring vowel sounds attempted to render, in addition to the meaning of the words, the actual exclamation of the emotions expressed. Thus, you had Virgil's *Infandum regina jubes renOvare dOlOrem. Et quOrum pars magna fui quis talia fando. MyridOnum, DOlOpum,* etc., the "o" followed by "o-o" sounds heard during the recitation of the poem giving the effect of lamentation for the fall of Troy. Later rhyme came on the scene to add its incentive for admiration to those already afforded by the ingenuity of verse. And it is to be remembered that for many thousands of years, verse was intended to be recited or read aloud rather than read to one's self. Thus the reader or reciter was to some extent an actor, and the more ingenious his verbal conceits the more the actor would excite his hearers. He did this by all sorts of devices that in no way rendered his meaning clearer or gave more definition to his emotion. Thus, you have the troubadours of mediaeval Provence. Their meanings when their art was at its height became almost completely stereotyped, the verse limiting itself to extolling the perfections of some lady, and recounting the poet's sufferings, or the deeds that he was prepared to do in order to obtain her favor. Thus, you had in their poems not merely what are called "conceits" or "images" but repetitions of the same rhymes going on through the hundreds of lines of a long poem. As for instance:

> Li dous coss*ire*
> Quem don amors sov*en*
> Domnam fas d*ire*
> De vos mas vers plaz*en*
> Pessan rem*ire*
> Vostre cors car é g*en*
> Cui eu des*ire*
> E cui non fasz parv*en,*

a poem which continues with the same *"ire"* and *"en"* rhymes for a great number of lines. Later, you had the ballad form in which the same line would be repeated at the end of every verse to form what was called a "burden;" later still there were developed the more formal symmetrical and stereotyped forms, such as the rondel, the pantoum, the virelai, the ode, or such slightly less artificial forms as the sonnet—a fourteen ten-syllabled line construction in which, given that his end rhymes went A B B A, A B B A, and that he could find a strong couplet end-piece, the poet might express himself how and about what he liked.

But in whatever age, or with whatever race, the history of the development of poetry has always been the same. It begins with the simplest form of expressions of emotion, goes on to express other emotions more simply, less rhythmically. Then it adopts all kinds of tricks and devices until poetic emotion itself almost disappears behind the jewelled blossomings of tricks and conceits. Then, suddenly, humanity and the poets get tired of so much artificiality and so much sameness, and poetry once more returns to being simply an expression of the simpler emotions.

That recurring phenomenon has distinguished all the literatures of all the ages. And not merely in verse. Several times in the course of its history, Egyptian literature became extremely full of tricks, conceits and word-juggling, and then again, as with the coming of the dynasty most distinguished by Rameses the Second, it returned to a complete naïveté. The great Chinese poets—for prose literature of China is relatively undistinguished—showed exactly the same progressions. Never very passionate then, it tended always towards more and more verbal and metrical felicities, and then in reaction came the naturalistic poetry of the Tao-ist Quietists. For the last thousand years or so, it has remained almost entirely a matter of metrical and verbal juggleries. And if we could—which unfortunately we can't—accurately date the writing of the Hebrew scriptures, we should no doubt find exactly the same tendencies: the relatively florid writing of the Song of Solomon giving place to the comparatively unornamented Books of Kings and these once more being succeeded by the impassioned writings of the poet-prophets. These, from the very fact of their passions, developed extraordinarily literary aspects.

But to make the matter exactly clear we had better consider the literature of our own race and language. Thus, not to go too far back, you found in Tudor days the highly ornamented and trick-filled prose and verse of the Euphuist and sonnetteer movements giving place to the relative simplicity of the later Shakespeare or Marlowe, and that in turn waning before the complete but wonderfully lucid simplicities of George Herbert and his contemporaries. This again passed into the hammered prose of Browne and his contemporaries. This again was succeeded by the more hammered prose of Clarendon and the more complicated rhythms of Swift, until you had the complete, bewigged artificiality of Pope and the eighteenth century. There succeeded the possibly exaggerated simplicities of the Lake and Cockney Schools of poets—the Wordsworths, Coleridges, Shelleys and Keats. This tendency once more gradually passed away before the comparative artificialities and pastiches of Tennyson and the pre-Raphaelite poets. Then once more in the first decade of this century you had a striving towards complete simplicity of diction. This tendency was interrupted by the thunders of the guns of Armageddon, and our poetry is again tending towards a sort of mysticism wrapt up in language of some involution and derivativeness.

The fact is that humanity cannot be static in these matters. It requires, by turns, extraordinarily skillful posturings and stage-tricks in the use of words, accompanied by a relative vapidity of meaning. Then, tiring of rhetoric and histrionics which will have grown out of touch with the spirit of the age, nations will cry out for the expression of strong emotions, of simple aspects of life or of great moral truths couched in straightforward or in merely common diction. Whether it is the call of the public that makes for these changes or whether the revolution of the tastes in poets and prose writers themselves forces these changes upon the attention of the reader is a matter that everyone must decide for himself, according as he is by temperament Plutarchian or anti-Plutarchian. It is sufficient for us here merely to recognize and to state the phenomenon. Let us then put it, that in the extreme East, the voluminous literature of the Chinese has remained almost statically artificial, whereas for nearly a century and a half the tendency of Western and Anglo-Saxon literature has been more and more away from technical rules in the construction, and from artificial felicities in the wording, of both its prose and its verse. This, of course, is a merely by-and-large diagnosis of the case, but it is one sufficiently true to be accepted as a rough pattern in the minds of those to whom literature is a matter of importance.

CHAPTER TWO

A<small>T ALL</small> accurately to chart the enormous sea that is the record of human thought and emotion since the earliest days, it is necessary to take the matter in hand as chronologically as possible. As has already been suggested, all national literatures are products, to some extent, of all the literatures that have preceded them. The earliest civilizations of man in his present dispensation stretched in vast disappeared empires or, in the alternative, in small or large nomadic hordes between the Nile and the Hoang-Ho. Actually to trace today the influence of early Egyptian moralists or later Egyptian imaginative writers on, say, Confucius would at the present state of learning be difficult in the extreme and the task would be too technical for a work like this present one.

But let us attempt to have some vague, misty image of the vast matter of the beginnings of human thought. Let us say that the proud and magnificent civilization of Babylon lasted fifteen hundred years from about 2000 to 500 B.C. This civilization influenced with its moral precepts, its theology and its legends, not merely the literature and thought of the Egyptians and the Hebrews, the Phoenicians, the Classical Greeks and Romans, but almost certainly its influence on the Chinese was very great as in turn was the influence of China upon Babylon. You have to consider that all across Asia there was a continual, an unending, going and coming of merchants, of conquerors, of missionaries, of nomads, and that one body of men cannot come into contact with another body of men without maxims, practices, or merely material habits and knowledges getting transferred from the one to the other. Our civilization today is an extraordinary jumble of habits and psychologies derived not merely from our fathers but from the very peoples that our fathers conquered, enslaved, or merely traded with. So it was with the greater, more beautiful, luxuriant, and reasonable civilizations that have preceded this of our own day. I have begun with Babylon, a relatively modern civilization, because such a figure as that of 2000 years B.C. is relatively easily graspable and because relics of Babylonian civilization are fairly numerous and fairly complete. For, when one comes to think that the Old Kingdom in Egypt began at least 8,000 years before our own day, the task for the mind is rather burdensome and appalling. Nor, indeed, does legend begin to play much part in the story of Egypt until 1,500 years or so later than the date of the earliest fragments of the Old Kingdom that have come down to us. That legend dates from about 3,500 years before the Christian era and is that of Memphis, a city with a great civilization founded by a semi-legendary king called Mena, whose solar myth singularly resembles that of our own King Arthur at Camelot. From that to saying that the Arthurian legend is traceable to the similar one in Memphis would, perhaps, be too far a cry. Nevertheless, human conceptions of great kings and Golden Ages must somewhere have had a beginning. The mere image of a great ruler who was also a great civilizer will make itself felt in countries vastly different and after uncounted tales of years. How much influence did not the legends even more than the historic achievements of Alexander, the Macedonian, have upon the mind and thus upon the achievements of Buonaparte, the Corsican? And how much influence have not the legends almost more than the historic achievements of Napoleon not had upon the psychologies of innumerable dictators, newspaper proprietors and owners of dry-goods stores, to the present day, and with what disastrous—or, perhaps in a few cases, happy—results for humanity? So it is not unreasonable to consider that the legendary figure of a good King Mena of the Nile may have had its influence in the creation of the legend of the good King Arthur of the Western Islands.

Be that as it may, the civilization of Mena progressed for, say, 1,500 years until towards 2,000 years before the Christian era. Really great historic kings of Egypt begin to be traceable and with them a literature, that is to say, a record, of human thoughts or imagination begins to be born. As far as we are concerned, the first Egyptian record that appears to be of literary value is Amenemhet I's advice to his son, a record of some bitterness written after an attempt to assassinate that great sovereign had failed. But even before that records were made of primitive literary attempts. Thus, you have incised tablets giving you the folk songs of peasants and fishermen dating well into the third millennium, say 2,200 years, before the Christian era. Or you had the precepts of the ministers of early kings, like the precepts of Ptahketep, prime minister of King Aessa of the Third Dynasty.

The great period of flourishing of Egyptian literature came about a hundred and eighty years after the death of Amenemhet I under Amenhotep III, who died about the year 1801 B.C. (It is to be remembered that Egyptian chronology like all Eastern reckoning of time is very vague and uncertain. Early and indeed late Egyptian, Hebrew, Babylonian and Chinese, like early British, historians numbered time by the births and deaths of dynasties or sovereigns, or from forgotten floods or catastrophes. Nearly all modern historic chronology of these periods is computed from an eclipse which took place in the year 763 B.C. This gives us the fact that Solomon was probably reigning in the year 940 B.C., that the power of the Theban priest kings disappeared at about the same time, or that Ahab was King of Israel in 854. The historian, therefore, has continually to qualify his dates with the word "about," and this word being usually symbolized in the letter "c" from the Latin *"circa,"* we may as well in the future so qualify our dates when they are uncertain.)

Literature then and most of the other arts were at their most flourishing in Egypt under King Amenhotep III, who died as we have seen c 1800 years B.C. and whose reign lasted apparently for about forty-five years. This was a period of great architecture, but of architecture not so florid or of such exaggerated proportions as that of Rameses II, who came about five hundred years afterwards, reigned, say, from c 1290–c 1225 B.C., and carried on his enormous works with indentured labor. Thus, you have the historic captivity of Joseph in Egypt.

Not only were architecture and sculpture of the Amenhotep III era magnificent and sympathetic, but in that age Egypt enormously extended her boundaries and sent voyagers to almost every portion of the known world, but more particularly of course to the waters of the Eastern Mediterranean. And this magnificence and these exploits are fully reflected in the literature of the time. They still show their effect on our imagination today. Thus, the work called the *Voyage of Sinuhe,* the fabulous account of a shipman of the great King who was wrecked on a Mediterranean island four thousand or so years ago, is still echoed faintly in our nurseries in the story of Sinbad the Sailor. And the *Exploits of Thutiy,* the story of a general of Thoumose III who took and sacked the city of Joppa after having introduced part of his army within the walls in grain sacks carried on the backs of asses, is the primitive version of the legend of Ali Baba and the Forty Thieves. . . .

You have to imagine this literature being produced whilst dynasties rose and fell, whilst Egypt spread herself out in great empires or shrank again into the merest strip of territory along the Nile in the sands of the desert. That strip would be invaded by mysterious barbarians who tyrannized the country and were finally expelled, leaving traces of their own civilizations, material or spiritual. . . . Thus, c 1675 B.C. Egypt was invaded by a mysterious Oriental horde called the Hyksos, whose rule lasted only some 75 years or so. Nevertheless, they left behind them horses and wheeled vehicles, forms of transport and warfare that the mightiest of the empires that preceded them had never known. . . . Thebes had latterly replaced Memphis as the splendid center of the country.

Under the great Emperor Thotmose III, the master of Thutiy of the Forty Thieves, Egypt began once more to expand. She went on expanding under the Amenhoteps, the great Tutankhamen—the rifling of whose tomb proved, if it were needed, the magnificence of the Egyptian civilization of that day—and under the Rameses in their earlier days. That stage occupied the periods of what are called the XVIIIIth to the XXXIIId Dynasties and, in time, lasted about 500 years—from the expulsion of the Hyksos about 1600 B.C. to 1090 B.C. when there fell the last of the kings of the name of Rameses.

It is important to notice when it comes to the name of Rameses that here contact is made and maintained between the Egyptian civilization and literature and that of the Hebrews—the period lasting almost exactly 200 years from the birth of Rameses II to the outstanding date of 1090, these dates being pretty firmly established by the eclipse of which we have already spoken.

The Hebrews of that period were made up of a dozen or so of loosely affiliated nomadic tribes, distinguished by the same habits and gradually emerging from a welter of other not very dissimilar Semitic septs. These all inhabited a large quadrangle of territory to the north of Egypt and to the east of the Mediterranean. All these Semitic tribes were known among themselves as Canaanites and to the Greeks as Phoenicians. They displaced eventually a colony of Cretans known as Philistines. And, as far as the Hebrews were concerned, towards the end of the age of the Rameses, they occupied, as a more or less settled federation, Palestine—the land of the promise of Yahweh. This Hebrew occupation lasted from about 1200 B.C., under Joshua, until the year of the destruction of Jerusalem under Titus, in 70 B.C. after a revolt of the Jews against the Roman supremacy. In the year 132-135 A.D. a rising of the Jews of Palestine in the reign of the Emperor Hadrian resulted in the Diaspora—the dispersal of the people. It is curious to consider as a parallel that the occasion of that rising was the establishment of a Roman colony on the site of Jerusalem, more than half a million Jews being massacred in that place, whereas to-day the Arabs are rising against a Jewish recolonization.

What is most immediately interesting to us as students of that history of human thought which is literature, is the Egyptian period from c 1460 B.C. Then Joseph is said to have led his own small sept of the Hebrews across the Nile into Egypt. In c 1025 the power of Egypt was beginning to decline and the Hebrews in a more federated state took to themselves the king, Saul, who was succeeded c 1000 B.C. by David and c 960 by Solomon, when for a short time that federation took on an imperial aspect. What, from our point of view is more important, is that the first six in order of the books of the Bible—the Yahvist Hexateuch which was the Pentateuch plus Joshua—would appear to have been begun under Solomon, about 940. They must have been finished after the division of the Hebrew Empire into the Kingdom of Judah under Rehoboam, who ruled over Judah, Simeon and part of Benjamin and the Levites, and the kingdom of Israel under Jeroboam who was acknowledged by the remainder of the tribes.

During the more or less legendary 360 years from the day of Joseph in 1460 to that of the fall of the Rameses Dynasty and the arising of the Hebrew monarchy between 1090 and 1000 B.C. there occurred the remarkable reigns of the Amenhoteps, of Tutankhamen and, of course, of the Rameses. During that period the first ideas of monotheism in this world rose and temporarily declined under the Amenhoteps I-IV between about 1500 and 1360 B.C. Gradually, that is to say during that period, those monarchs seem to have evolved the ideal of a single deity typified by the sun from whom came all life.

You hear the note in the hymn written by Amenhotep III, who was a mighty man of war, conquering both the Syrians and the Ethiopians in the latter days of the fourteenth century before Christ.

Hymn to the Sun

When thou shinest as Aten by day, the darkness is banished.
When thou sendest forth thy rays, the Two Lands rejoice daily,
Awake and standing upon their feet, for thou hast raised them up.
Their limbs bathed, they take their clothing;
Their arms uplifted in adoration to thy dawning;
Then in all the world, they do their work.

The ships sail upstream and downstream,
Every road is open because thou hast dawned.
The fish in the river leap up before thee,
And thy rays are in the midst of the great sea.

This rather pedestrian poem shows the gradual progress of the monotheistic ideal which had begun to take shape perhaps a hundred years before. Then Amenhotep IV elevated it to the state religion of the Empire. The priests, however, proved too powerful for him and by the reign of magnificent Tutankhamen, all the High Ones of the

Nilotic polytheism ruled once more in the great temples—Isis and Nephtys, the Rescuers; Thot Anubis, the God of the Arts and Letters; and the forty-four Incorruptible Divine Ones presided over by the Great God, Osiris, the All-seeing Eye. . . .

Thus, the Hebrews in bondage must have undergone the influence of all the literary and literary-supernatural legends and tendencies of which we have been talking. They came into contact with the ideal of a Messiah of Ipuwer, with the chants of victory of Thutiy in the days of the great Thotmose III, with hymns inshrining the peculiar doctrines of the immortality of the threefold soul which we shall shortly read, with the primitive folk songs of the first felaheen on the earliest tombs as well as of the more sophisticated but highly monotonous *Complaint of the Peasant*, with the legends of the Creation and the Flood. These themselves were in all probability assimilated by the Egyptians from the mighty Sumerian-Babylonian-Semitic civilizations. At any rate, the Hebrews of the Bondage must have come in contact with Egyptian literature at its greatest. They left the country when, under Rameses II and his successors, it had descended to a very low level. . . . The Ramesian literature, that is to say, was, like the later Chinese poetry of which we have spoken, apparently so stylized and anaemic that now it hardly ranks amongst the great literatures. Nevertheless, owing to a tenacity of both the material in which it was inscribed and of the Egyptian brain, the older and finer literatures of simpler ages persisted and were chanted and sung by the Egyptian peasantry and masons, whilst their feudal and priestly superiors were amusing themselves with the more frivolous poems and tales of the fashion of the day. . . . In much the same fashion, in the Provence of today, the peasantry still chant songs and perform dramas that date back for a thousand or even two thousand years, and are entirely ignored by their French overlords on the Riviera shores. . . . So the Hebrew laborers who took part in the building of the pyramids and temples of Rameses mixed not with the lords and priests but with the laborers and peasants singing at their tasks. They were in the first case brought to Egypt by Joseph and other padrones probably as free indentured laborers, and later, by Rameses II, apparently as prisoners of war, and they shared the hardships of the other laborers of all kinds. Nor was their striking because they were asked to make bricks without straw a solitary insurrection. On the contrary, strikes of almost all the workers in Egypt were of regular monthly occurrence. The conditions in which they lived were terrible, in windowless mazes of huts all under one roof without ventilation or light. And, as their food of millet or chic beans was served out to them on the first day of the month and as it was very insufficient by the end of the month, almost every workman on any given job would be starved into striking. And whilst they struck they chanted endless songs descriptive of their misery—songs which they hoped would reach the ears of the Pharaoh—or chants of defiance for the masters who used them so miserably on the Nile banks beside the great columns of the temples of Osiris of the All-seeing Eye and Isis the Succorer.

So it is not to be wondered at that when the Hebrews finally escaped across the Red Sea they were a people of singers with heads filled with fierce or pitiful legends. . . .

And it is to be remembered that songs and legends are the last comfort and refuge of the destitute. Indeed, from the histories of these great, lost civilizations, one is sorely tempted to make the generalization that the literature of a people will be great, nervous and virile only as long as the people is simple, in poor circumstances and without the spirit of imperialism. But as soon as a people becomes rich, with a luxurious civilization, its talents will expend themselves on the plastic arts, on furnishings, on monuments, on painted tablets displaying the victories and splendors of ancestors, or on temples inscribed with poems to the glory of the avenging or succoring gods. And then, as the victorious and conquering people spreads its territories by force of arms to great distances, the spirit of the heart of the empire will die out; its literature and its arts alike will become degenerate. Until, at last, the whole empire crumbles before the assaults of outer barbarians, and nothing is left but the desert sands whirling in the winds and settling on the ruins of the temples and on the inscriptions recording their forgotten glories. Their legends and tales and chants will far outlive them.

So for eight hundred years or so after the fall of the last king of the name of Rameses—from 1150 B.C. to 330 B.C.—literature itself disap-

pears from Egypt, and the strip of land along the Nile was swept by
invasions from Bubastis, from Ethiopia, from Abyssinia. These invaders each held the land for a little time. The Bubastian King
Shisak founded the XXII Dynasty in 945 B.C. and reigned for twenty-
one years, during the last two of which he took and sacked the
unfortunate city of Jerusalem. Then an Ethiopian incursion founded
the XXV Dynasty in 712 B.C. Not quite fifty years after that, Sarda-
napalus drove out the Negroes, and Egypt became an Assyrian colony
under, usually, native administrators. Eleven years later one of these
consuls made international alliances with a number of Greek and
Semitic tribes, and with the help of their mercenary troops drove
out the Assyrians, made himself King of Egypt, and founded the
XXVI Dynasty. Foreigners of every kind crowded into the Nile
valley, until little by little the Greeks assumed the spiritual, if not
temporal, mastery of the empire. The XXVI Dynasty lasted for about
a century and a half of incessant invasions or expeditions in every
direction. The Egyptian kings fought with the aid of Greek and
Semitic mercenaries who, when they were displeased, captured and
strangled the sovereign. And you have to consider this period of the
lands of the East of the Mediterranean as one perpetual tangle of
mercenary troops fighting for one sovereign or another, with the
Grecian mercenaries as a rule obtaining mastery for whoever had
the luck to employ them. The most celebrated of all these expeditions
was that of Xenophon with his ten thousand Greeks, an expedition
whose chief result was the immortal *Anabasis* of that writer. In 525
B.C. Cambyses defeated Pfantik III at the Battle of Pelusium, and
Egypt became a Persian colony. Then in 332 Alexander the Great
conquered Egypt and for a short space the valley of the Nile lived
under Macedonian rulers. Then came for 300 years the magnificent
Ptolemaic period. Its extraordinary Helleno-Egyptian splendors daz-
zled the Nile itself, and Egyptian temples rose side by side with those
of the Assyrians. Then in the year 31 B.C. came the Battle of Actium;
Cleopatra fell and Egypt became a Roman province notable chiefly
for the immense quantity of grain of all sorts that she exported to
the metropolis of the world. But the main thing for us to remember
is that this Egypt and this already mysterious Orient exported also

to both Rome and Greece an infinite number of legends, creeds, scribes and sorcerers, so that the Graeco-Roman gods became confounded with the deities of the Nile—Astarte being confounded at once with Venus of the Romans and Aphrodite of the Greeks, Diana being confused with Isis, and Jove himself with the great god Osiris. So civilizations spread themselves and the one modifies the other, England, as you might say, blessing the United States with her woolen goods, and the United States returning her Negro jazz melodies and syncopated turns of speech.

But the main thing to be considered is that during all these revolutions and counter-revolutions the craft of the writer—if not his art— was always venerated. Whether he made his letters with the chisel on stone or painted his idiographs on the walls of temples or palaces, whether he wrote with a stylus on tablets of wax or incised them on rolls of clay which were afterwards baked, or whether in the end he wrote much as we write with a split reed upon sheets of papyrus which is the inner fiber of the papyrus plant—always a sort of priestly or lawyer-like respectability attached to the man who could write at all. He recorded laws and judgments given under those laws; he set down histories from the dictation of conquerors; he kept the accounts alike for market people and for the granaries of the Pharaohs. He was, in fact, the priest of the material necessities of life.

And once again we come upon the problem of whether the *Imitation of Christ* is to be considered as literature. And once again we have to answer with a "yes." For the lay literature, like the lay sculpture and the lay architecture of this mighty and luxuriant civilization, fades to nothing beside the immortal effigies and records of polytheistic religion. When you think of Egypt it is not of the exploits of Thutiy or of Sinuhe that you think. Like roots creeping under the earth they have, it is true, made their appearance in our nurseries of today. But Egypt stands for the immense lion gods, hawk gods, and Pharaoh gods—the innumerable effigies of deities in stone that stand forever silent along the banks of the Nile and gaze eternally into distances that no human eye shall ever penetrate. And along with these stone gods goes an immense literature of stone—what M. Mardrus calls "*The Book of Stone.*" It extends for 1,400 kilometers, say 1,000 miles, along the great river from the upper Nile to the sea. Here you have the irrational, the awe-inspiring, the almost ungraspable religion of the Egyptian soul set out in this vast length and in this almost eternally lasting material, as, buried amongst the sands in their immense mausoleums the innumerable mummies lie waiting through the ages till the Triple Soul shall come again to inhabit them, to let them stride once again over the green banks beneath the palm trees.

The reason for the burying of these mummies beneath those immense piles was of course to insure their safety from the riflings of robbers—and the excavators. This was not merely because of the instinctive hatred of humanity for the idea that its dead should be disturbed or its sepulchres violated. It was because the mummy that had once been flesh must again become flesh and in that flesh see the light of the sun and the works of the gods, and because, if it should be mutilated, its reincarnation would be impossible.

On the mystical side it was necessary for the most divine of the dead man's three souls to make a confession of faith and belief in the Truth before the terrible tribunal of the forty-four Incorruptible Gods. For if that soul failed to convince the tribunal of the purity of its belief, it could never again inhabit the mummy that had been its flesh. And the mummy must lie still forever or until its final decay. So inscriptions of that *Great Book of Stone*, when they rise to be literature, consist mainly of the record of confessions of those higher souls before the tribunal of the gods.

When the body died and was preserved by the mummifiers, the three souls took their departure. The first soul—the Human Consciousness—departed and was lost among the winds. The second soul, called the Divine Bird, disappeared into the ether and went from planet to planet for millennium upon millennium until the third soul, Kou, the Luminous, succeeded in gaining the sanction of the gods. The three souls might then enter again into their mummy and their mummy become flesh. The procedure was this:

After purification in an outer chamber the luminous soul was introduced to the Hall of Judgment. It went in supported by its counsel, as a prisoner today goes into our courts. On the one hand were Isis and Nephtys, the comforting and succoring goddesses, and on the other Thot Anubis, the god of writing and painting, who from time to time helped the suppliant with hints.

The suppliant then, before the forty-four Incorruptible Ones presided over by the great god, Osiris, must make his declaration of the Truth. Here is part of one of those declarations:

> Before you all, Gods of the Truth, I invoke in my spirit, my Creator, Him of whom I was born, the Unshakable, son of the Unshakable, conceived and born of Himself in the territory of Stability itself.
> He is called Ineffable.
> He is called the Hidden of the Hidden.
> Everything that has existed, everything that exists, everything that shall exist is His Name.
> He is the One: He is The Three; He remains The One Alone.
> The child in his mother's womb already turns his face towards Him.
> I give homage to this King of Kings:
> For I am of a Mummy that lived in its Day.
> I live in Truth, in this witness of the Light.
> And the Word having been made Truth by my just Voice
> I arrive as a Sparrow-hawk and depart as the Phoenix.
>
> (J. C. Mardrus: *Textes*. Author's translation.)

CHAPTER THREE

The years from 551 to 479 B.C. make up between them an era that was one of the most momentous in the history of mankind. They are the years of the birth and of the death of Confucius. His name is more literally rendered from the Chinese by the sounds *K'ung-Fu-Tsze*, but since to the Western peoples he has been known as Confucius for at least two thousand years it is more convenient for us so to style him.

That man's span of seventy-two years, being partly contemporaneous with the life of the great rival philosopher of China, Lao-Tsze, was remarkable enough merely because it enshrined the thinking careers of those two sages whose rules of life have had a great share in influencing the mentalities of all civilized humanities from their day to ours. But all through the world known to the ancients, which contained all our ancestors in civilization, all through that world that then stretched from Tokio, say, to the Scilly Islands, and from the Danube to the Cape of Good Hope—those seventy-odd years saw periods of great mental activity expressing itself in literature and of great physical activities and excitements expressing themselves in the conquests of ancient civilizations and their replacement, by force of arms, with newer combinations.

In the Egypt that we have just left, this period coincided with the reign of the Pharaoh Amasis (*Ahmose*)—a time of great mental activity, caused by the encouragement that the sovereign gave to foreigners to practice their arts and crafts in Egypt. It was the beginning of the Hellenizing of the country.

It was also the period of the great expansion of the highly civilized Persian Empire. Egypt became a Persian province in 525 B.C., Babylon in 538. In the same year the great Cyrus released the Jews who had been taken into bondage, and the Jews began with his aid the rebuilding of the Temple of Solomon and the re-constitution of their state. The German school of Biblical commentators—notably Delitsch of *Babel and Bible*—dates the Jews' acquaintance with the story of

the Garden of Eden and the Flood from the time of their bondage
in Babylon; and certainly the Babylonians had a story of a composite
single god of many attributes called Marduch. He discomfited the
powers of evil by preventing a deluge that they had called into existence in the marshy country at the end of the Persian Gulf. More
modern authorities believe the Hexateuch was written in the later
years of the reign of Solomon; in that case the Hebrews' acquaintance
with those two stories must have preceded the Captivity by at least
four hundred years and they must, as this writer has always believed,
have heard the stories during their servitude to the Pharaohs. That is,
however, a matter as to which he has no intention of dogmatizing
and it is one to which we shall have to return in due course.

The other great world events which occurred during the lifetime of
Confucius had their being on the north-eastern shores of the Mediterranean in and around the territory we know as Greece. They were
the events of the great struggle between the Greeks and the Persians.
Marathon was fought eleven years before the death of the sage,
Thermopylae and Salamis two years before, and Plataea in the year
of his death itself. Greece had to wait a couple of decades for the Great
Age of Pericles; but all these events gave rise to literature enough in all
conscience . . . to the most glorious literatures of all.

We are for the moment far to the East of the Mediterranean. After
dwelling a little on the exploits of Cyrus and Cambyses, the Persian
conquerors, we will return farther east still and think about Confucius
and his rival Lao-Tsze, the first great Quietist. The Persian conquerors
were mighty men of war before the coming of the Lord. They conquered Babylon; they annexed Egypt; they all but took Carthage; they
invaded Ethiopia; they built the bridge of boats over the Bosphorus
and trampled all over Greece. They had courts of an unexampled
luxury; they constructed military roads and moved innumerable fighting men from end to end of their realms, employing methods of transport that we have not much bettered today. They had even a post office.
They called their ruler Khshayathiya-Khshayathiyanam—the King of
Kings. The feats of Cyrus inspired the Grecian story of Herodotus of

how Cyrus captured Croesus and denuded him of his realms but spared his life and used him as a counsellor, after the Delphic Apollo had miraculously quenched the fire which Cyrus had lit to burn him. . . . According to the Lydians, however, Croesus was about to commit suicide by fire as a sacrifice to the Sun God so that his people might be saved. But the Sun God did not approve of the nature of the sacrifice and extinguished the fire by torrential rains. . . . And again, according to Herodotus, in his work which we may well call both history and literature, Cyrus was at last taken prisoner by the warlike Tamyris, queen of the Massagetes. And she, cutting off his head, put it into a sack of blood . . . so that he might drink his fill. And so, in the end, Darius, the last of the name, falling across Alexander the Great, was slain whilst flying from the Battle of Arbela, and the Persian Empire came to an end. It had produced no very striking writing of its own. The great age of Persian literature was still many hundreds of years ahead. But, Herodotus apart, it had inspired literature enough. . . . As thus:

Thus saith the Lord . . . of Cyrus, He is my shepherd and shall perform all my pleasure: even saying to Jerusalem Thou shalt be built; and to the temple: Thy foundation shall be laid.

Thus saith the Lord to His anointed, to Cyrus, whose right hand I have holden, to subdue nations before him; and I will loosen the loins of kings, to open before him the two leaved doors; and the gates shall not be shut;

I will go before thee, and make the crooked places straight: I will break in pieces the gates of brass, and cut in sunder the bars of iron:

And I will give thee the treasures of darkness, and hidden riches of secret places, that thou mayest know that I, the Lord, which call thee by thy name, *am* the God of Israel.

For Jacob my servant's sake, and Israel mine elect, I have even called thee by thy name; I have surnamed thee, though thou hast not known me.

(Isaiah: 44.28; 45, 1-4.)

Those things, then, were happening in the world whilst Confucius and Lao-Tsze lived and thought. Cyrus released the Hebrews when Confucius was thirteen. The Greeks began their final beating back of the Persians in the year of his death and the years just preceding that event. And, as we have seen, the life of Confucius coincided in part with that of Lao-Tsze; once at least those two type-sages of the world met; and apparently Lao-Tsze was rather rude to Confucius. So that, if we consider all that—all that Hebrew Holy Writ, and Greek Civilization and the teachings and writings of Confucius and the spoken and written Quietism of Lao-Tsze . . . all that all those things mean to our poor wilting civilization of today—we may well see, or imagine ourselves seeing, evidence of design in the Architect of the Universe.

For if the links of our stages of Western civilization have from time to time been broken, erased even, and then slowly again picked up, the chain of that older and greater civilization of the Far East has continued with a sort of equanimity from that era until today. The rule of the Literati, the exponents of Confucian lore, is being challenged and even shaken in China now. But it has been challenged and shaken before—by Buddhism, by the incursion of Western savages—and it has always reëmerged purged and stronger for the trial. And we have no reason to imagine that our Western savagery will prove any more permanent for destruction in the lands of the Quietist Middle Kingdom than were the savageries and superstitions that have preceded our day.

We may permit ourselves to look at the matter in that light, we ourselves, at any rate for the duration of these present investigations, being Literati. So that our sympathies must go out to any spot of the world or system of government where humane wisdom like that of Confucianism inspires the rulers, and the Quietist teachings of Lao-Tsze give tranquillity to the mentalities of the peoples. For you may yourself be a mining engineer or an electrician or in the alternative a Tammany, or a London County Council, candidate for office. But whilst you have this book in hand you are for the moment at once a Confucianist and a follower of Lao-Tsze.

Speaking as broadly as we must speak in a work of this small extent embracing provinces so vast, we may say that Confucius tried by his teachings, his writings and his anthologies to induce men, for the purposes of better government of human affairs, to become "superior"—as who should say "gentle"-men. Man was to make himself superior or gentle by the study of the maxims of—or the chronicles of ancient lore collected by—Confucius. They would thus become Literati, Masters of Arts, Mandarins. . . . And after their knowledge had been proved by examinations, they would become administrators of this or that department of human activities or, beneath the Sacred Emperor, of the small departments or the immense provinces of which the Empire was made up.

Lao-Tszeism, on the other hand, was in its origins, individualist-quietist. "Give me a jade kettle and a store of wine which has the gift of making men see the Spring at all seasons of the year": so writes Ssu-Kung Tu, a Secretary of the Board of Rites and so a Confucianist. But he threw up his job in disgust at the futility of the pursuits of men and officials and became a Lao-Tszeist. "Give me," then he writes

> ". . . a jade kettle with a purchase of spring,
> A shower on the thatched hut
> Wherein sits a gentle scholar,
> With tall bamboos growing right and left,
> And white clouds in the newly-clear sky,
> And birds flitting in the depths of trees.
> Then, pillowed on his lute in the green shade,
> A waterfall tumbling overhead,
> Leaves dropping, not a word spoken,
> The man placid, like a chrysanthemum,
> Noting down the flower-glory of the season—
> A book well worthy to be read."
> (from *History of Chinese Literature,* by Herbert A. Giles.)

And one may quickly make the note that the same poet later records, as realistically as you could wish, the disadvantages of resigning your official salary . . . the days passing without food, the forced acceptance

of offerings of poor meats and poorer wines from peasant neighbors.
. . . He, nevertheless, remained steadfast till his death, in his philosophy
and mode of life!

The Confucian poets, on the other hand, record the joys of official
life, of provincial prefectures or higher mandarinships—but nearly
always in terms of reminiscence or bitter regret.

That, I suppose, is natural. A young mandarin spends his evenings
with the "purchase of spring" in the beloved companionship of other
young or youngish mandarins, sitting amongst illuminated bamboo-
rods under colored lanterns that swing from the boughs of trees overhead, watching gilded girls with their shining nudities slip in or out
of, or play amongst, the waters of fountains to the sound of their
own lutes. And a young mandarin of literary gifts so occupied loses
the time that he might have devoted to pouring out his soul in poems.
But when came the loss of his job and exile—as often as not because
he was reported by spies to have uttered gibes against his superiors or
their wives—in remote solitudes at the bitter ends of the Empire he
may well find time to write many poems voicing his moods. . . . And
his moods will be always those of bitter regret and dispirited longings.

Chinese literature—and in its whole immense three-thousand-year-
old mass of production that literature is almost exclusively poetry, the
novel never having there reached any noteworthy stage of development and plays being left almost unwritten for the actors to gag un-
limitedly—Chinese literature, then, is always a literature of soberness
of thought and almost always one of remembrance and regret, a literature of forsaken wives, concubines or lovers, of Emperors mourning
murdered queens, of exiles because of politics or because of the exigencies of war. So that, as it were through a diminishing mirror, you
look at scenes sometimes of great luxury and splendor, or, in the case
of the war-exiles, of great hardships and even horror. But even the
hardships and the horrors you will seem to see through a veil of
translucent and shimmering glass, since almost always the salient
points of the narrative will be in the past.

A poem may begin: "Here we are digging the last fern-roots," and
present you vividly enough with the picture of bowmen exiled as a
guard at the extreme northern limits of the Empire, almost without

food, conducting endless skirmishes with the barbarians. But the real pull of the poem comes when the poet, if only for a word or two, remembers the softness of his home pillows and the society of his convivial friends.

And the sense of seeing these things through a veil of shimmering glass is added to by the extreme delicacy and brilliance of the shining words and the skill in form of which we have already read. It is really as if the words hung between the reader and the objects or emotions that the poets present.

And so there are thousands—literally thousands and thousands—of the little quatrains called something like "two-ply" poems. Or one might more fancifully translate the name: "come-backs." Here the form is perfectly rigid. You are sitting, say, in an outside café at the bottom of Fifth Avenue in the bright sunshine—or, if you prefer it, on the Boulevard St.-Germain—and you write:

"Here we sit in the brightness sipping the purchase of spring.
All around us are our friends lifting their cocktails (or apéritifs)
     in purple or green or scarlet,
The sun is mirrored in the tops of the gay automobiles. . . .
But we . . . we are remembering the delicate shadows of the plane-
     trees on the Boulevard St.-Germain. . . ."

Or "in Washington Square" according as you choose to consider that you are writing your two-ply on this or the other side of the water. . . . Always, always, you look back—to the women you knew in lands thousands of miles away; to the friends you conversed with thousands of days ago; to the jewels that shone so brightly in your concubine's frontlet in Barbaria when your Chinese blood ran warmer in your veins. . . . Yes, always, always, you ask *"Mais où . . . mais où, sont les neiges d'antan?"*

This writer has read in his time a great many hundreds of Chinese poems, as at one time he made a careful study of Chinese music and songs . . . in which he resembled Confucius. But only one poem with a cheerful ending comes back to him—and, alas, he cannot remember either its name or its author. It is one about a poet who loves two ladies with an equally excruciating passion, both ladies regarding his suit favorably. He goes through agonies at the idea that if he chooses one lady he will lose the other. And material obstacles intervene; we do not remember what they were. But at last they are cleared up; and the poet has a brilliant thought. He will marry both ladies at once. And so he does and they all three live happily ever after.

And, of course, in its immense stream, Chinese poetry, concerning itself with every side of human life—except the glories of ideal love, of Heaven or of war—takes note of a great many things to all appearances passionlessly or with a sub-current of semi-sensuous enjoyment. It lingers on rich silks, shining jewels, willows beside broad and tranquil rivers, and, particularly, on that "promise of spring" which is wine, on the rustlings of bamboos, the moon and sunsets.

But always, even in poems apparently of passive enjoyment and contemplation, there is a note of the ruins of the past. Thus, even in this portion of an eighth-century elegy by Rihaku, quoted and translated by Mr. Pound, that touch must come in:

> The River Song
>
> This boat is of shato-wood . . .
> Musicians with jewelled flutes
> Fill full the sides in rows, and our wine
> Is rich for a thousand cups. . . .
>
> King So's terraced palace
>   is now but a barren hill . . .
>   (from *Lustra*, by Ezra Pound.)

And it will be noted that even there the *strong* note of the poem lies in the line "King So's terraced palace is now but a barren hill"— as if this were a reminder to the then reigning Emperor, to whom Rihaku of course owes allegiance, that some day his glory too may vanish from sight and memory. Even the nightingales, which are referred to later in this same poem, are not permanent for Rihaku, though, as will appear later, for Heraclitus they are.

The Chinese poem is in fact always full of implications, usually bitter or bitterish, lying beneath even an enjoyable surface like water-weeds that encumber the swimmer's feet beneath the mirror-smooth surface of a twilit lake. Even a very mediocre Chinese poet can be so subtle as to make the famous two-ply or come-back of the Japanese Emperor Yoshihito written for the Japanese poetry festival of 1894 seem coarse in texture.

> I went to fetch water from the spring;
> I saw that the honeysuckle had twined its tendrils around the
>   well-rope:
> I went and borrowed water from my neighbour.

Compare that with the "Jewelled Stairs' Grievance" of Rihaku and it will seem a very simple affair. Rihaku, of course, was not a mere technician but one of the relatively rare Chinese poets who was also a poet in our Western sense of the term. He wrote in the eighth century of our era when the Art of Poetry in China was not merely immensely skillful in form, but when the actual poetic content was at nearly its highest and its texture at its most delicate. The "Grievance" is one of the literally innumerable poems recording the grief of a deserted wife or mistress. Later that device became so stereotyped as a subject that the skill of the poet went entirely into playings with words, metres and intonations. But Rihaku, a great poet, was incomparably skillful in the most difficult of all the world-poetic sides of technique. It consists in getting exquisite poetic meaning out of the mere transcription of natural objects, without any comments or ejaculations whatsoever. That is not merely Chinese, it is the supreme achievement in all the poetries of the world. Here is Mr. Pound's translation of the "Jewelled Stairs' Grievance":

> The jewelled steps are already quite white with dew,
> It is so late that the dew soaks my gauze stockings,
> And I let down the crystal curtain
> And watch the moon through the clear autumn.

> (from *Lustra*, by Ezra Pound.)

And Mr. Pound supplies the following explanation of these lines: "Jewel stairs, therefore a palace. Grievance, therefore there is something to complain of. Gauze stockings, therefore a court lady, not a servant who complains. Clear autumn, therefore he has no excuse on account of weather. Also she has come early, for the dew has not merely whitened the stairs, but has soaked her stockings. The poem is especially prized because she utters no reproach."

It will be noticed that the last line of this quatrain is not, as in the usual come-back, a complete antithesis to the sense of the first three lines. It is, rather, a completion of the sense of the whole. It is true that it is as it were a veiled reproach as if to say: "My lover does not come although the weather is so fine," the rest of the poem being as it were a passionless statement as to natural objects. But no doubt in that slight alteration of tone, Rihaku, who was a miracle of delicacy, considered that he had sufficiently supplied his dramatic contrast.

You have thus an epitome of one stage of what happens in a literary progression. You have reached with Rihaku a point at which suggestion is more important than the object or the incident presented in a poem or a piece of imaginative prose. That means that you have reached a high stage of civilization and some measure of imperial tranquillity. And, accordingly, in history you find that Rihaku wrote between 618 and 718 A.D. in what is called the Golden Age of Chinese Literature, which was the Golden Age of the Dynasty of Tang. Thus also, Confucius, whose chief characteristic is not a suave literary quality but a sort of chaotic gathering together of human instances, did his work in an era of wars and anarchy. The greater part of the empire, at its two extremities, was then under the tempestuous rule of greater or lesser feudal chieftains. Only the center of the country, known as the Middle Kingdom, had any semblance of order or imperial government. And even that was shaken almost to pieces under Li Yang, who was ruling at the date of Confucius' birth.

We bring Confucius in again at this point merely to recall him to mind. We must consider the poets a little more before devoting any serious attention to his and Lao-Tsze's prose, but we should here make the note that between the birth of Confucius and the death of Rihaku was a matter of some 1,200 years.

So let us consider the earlier periods. In these, both matter and manner are more harsh and bitter. The most memorable of them are laments over war in which the soldiers hardly indulge even in reminiscences of their homes. The earliest of them would date to about a thousand years before Christ when the West and East Chow Dynasties of the Middle Kingdom struggled not only against their own feudal semi-subject dukes, but against ceaseless hordes of Mongol invaders. Thus, we have the "Song of the Bowmen of Shu," by Bun-No, reputedly of 1100 B.C.

> Here we are picking the first fern-shoots
> And saying: When shall we get back to our country? . . .
> The enemy is swift, we must be careful. . . .
> We are hungry and thirsty,
> Our mind is full of sorrow, who will know of our grief?
> (Ezra Pound's translation, in *Lustra*.)

Nor, eleven hundred years later, do things seem much to have improved if we are to believe the famous poem called "Battle" written between 332 and 295 B.C. by Chu-Yuan. Chu-Yuan himself is one of the poets best known to the Chinese—a sort of more decorous Villon, much addicted like most Chinese poets to the purchase of spring by wine, afflicted with a much too sharp tongue as regards his mandarin superiors . . . so that the most famous of all his poems is called "Getting into Trouble"—and he died at a relatively early age, having for his misbehaviors been sent to the wars. Here is his poem "Battle," as translated by Arthur Waley:

> "We grasp our battle spears: we don our breast-plates of hide.
> The axles of our chariots touch: our short swords meet.
> Standards obscure the sun: the foe roll up like clouds.
> Arrows fall thick: the warriors press forward.
> They menace our ranks: they break our line.

The left-hand trace-horse is dead: the one on the right is smitten.
The fallen horses block our wheels: they impede the yoke-horses!

They grasp their jade drum-sticks: they beat the sounding drums.
Heaven decrees their fall: the dread Powers are angry.

The warriors are all dead: they lie on the moor-field.
They issued but shall not enter; they went but shall not return.
The plains are flat and wide; the way home is long.
Their swords lie beside them: their black bows, in their hand.
Though their limbs were torn, their hearts could not be repressed.
They were more than brave: they were inspired with the spirit of
"Wu."*
Steadfast to the end, they could not be daunted.
Their bodies were stricken, but their souls have taken Immor-
tality—
Captains among the ghosts, heroes among the dead."

(from *A Hundred and Seventy Chinese Poems*, translated by
Arthur Waley.)

Shortly after the time of Chu-Yuan, the great infamous First Emperor, Shi Hwang Ti, founded the dynasty of Chin and burned the
books containing the wisdom and poetry of the earlier reigns of the
Middle Kingdom. Because of that villainy—I had almost called it Hit-
lerism—men averted their minds from his memory and of all the good
or bad emperors who are chosen for mention on the Day of the Celebration of the Imperial Dead, his name alone is never exhibited on the
sacred tablets.

He, nevertheless, extended the Middle Kingdom to the sea; broke
the power of the feudal dukes; defeated the Mongols, and built the
Great Wall of China. His dynasty, however, only lasted for four years
after his death. It was succeeded by those of the East and West Hans
and for over four hundred years—from B.C. 206 to A.D. 220—China flourished at home, and extended her dominions abroad.

It is a matter of constant argument whether literature and the arts
flourish best in periods of peace and plenty or in times of frugality

* i.e., Military genius.

and struggle. We need not propose here to attempt any decision of the matter. We shall notice instances enough of happenings in both directions before we come to the end of this journey and we may then, if we want to, make some sort of summing up. But certainly the upholders of peace and plenty score points in the four hundred years of the Chin and East and West Han Dynasties. For China was then peaceful, and literature—but more particularly commentaries, rituals, and philosophic works such as Confucius had collected and tabulated—literature, then, sprang up in profusion to replace the books that the First Emperor had destroyed.

There ensued four hundred years or so of confusion, civil strife and disasters until another great usurper, Kau-Tsu, in 618 A.D. founded the great Tang Dynasty which lasted nearly three hundred years. That was the most brilliant period of Chinese history and influence, embassies coming from all over the world to the East—from Teheran and Samarkand as from Constantinople; and it is interesting to note that during the Tang Dynasty the Roman Eastern Empire in Constantinople was slowly crumbling away, Rome herself forever fallen before the barbarians. The Persians (who had become Mohammedans) and the Arabs took more and more territory from the Eastern Romans; Charlemagne's Empire rose and fell; Haroun Al Raschid wandered in the night streets of Bagdad; the Moors conquered Spain . . . and perhaps most immediately important of all, Mahomet's Hegira—his flight from Mecca to Medina where he founded Islam—took place in 622. That was four years after Kau-Tsu founded the Tang Dynasty in China; and before that dynasty ended, the Arabs had made great progress with one of the other great literatures of the world—the Arabic.

And it was, as we have seen, the Golden Age of Chinese literature —the suave age of Li-Po and Ssu-Kung-Tu and Rihaku and Po-Chu-I, and of such thousands. They were poets of a luxuriating age. . . . They suggest Omar Khayyam and Firdusi, dividing themselves into Confucian bureaucrats in or out of office and Tao-ist recluses in usually agreeable circumstances. Or, again, they suggest the Villon who never knew whether he was or wasn't in Dutch with his uncle the Canon.

Consider Li-Po who lived from A.D. 705 to 762. Says Mr. Giles:

> Li-Po began wandering about the country, until at length, with five other tippling poets, he retired to the mountains. For some time these Six Idlers of the Bamboo Grove drank and wrote verses to their hearts' content. By and by Li-Po reached the capital, and on the strength of his poetry was introduced to the Emperor as a "banished angel." He was received with open arms, and soon became the spoilt child of the palace. On one occasion, when the Emperor sent for him, he was found lying drunk in the street; and it was only after having his face well mopped with cold water that he was fit for the Imperial presence. His talents, however, did not fail him. With a lady of the seraglio to hold his ink-slab, he dashed off some of his most impassioned lines; at which the Emperor was so overcome that he made the powerful eunuch Kao Li-shih go down on his knees and pull off the poet's boots.
>
> (from *History of Chinese Literature,* by Herbert A. Giles.)

So they idled and revelled and sometimes wrote, these poets, until some disorder or some inopportune jest or a mere change in the disposition of the ruler sent them out of the sunlight of the Presence. Some went to minor posts in the provinces; some became hermits and praised in their verse that life; some went into bitter exile at the verges of the empire where they lived eternally remembering the golden past and eternally hoping against hope for recall; some were sent to the hateful wars . . . and they had no hope and avoided even remembering. Let us once more quote Rihaku, not because he was the greatest of the Chinese poets of the era, that glory being accorded by the Chinese themselves to Li-Po. But he has had the luck to find for translator a poet as great as himself who has done for him what Fitzgerald did for Omar Khayyam or Baudelaire for Edgar Allan Poe. No poet can hope for greater good fortune.

The novelist and writer in prose generally can find a translator whose work will at least serve the turn of conveying his thought and some at least of his rhythm into another language. But to get anything like the verbal texture of your verse, the magic of your language, the subtlety of your rhythms, adapted into another tongue . . . for that you *must* find a poet at least as great as yourself. Such a translator Rihaku and the others have found in Mr. Ezra Pound without whom and his little volume called *Cathay* the English reader could have little idea of the literary magic and quality of the Chinese poets. Other translators can give you the content, the subject, the conceits and above all the quaintnesses of their poetry. And for these we may be grateful enough, since after a good deal of reading of them we may invent for ourselves some of the texture and quality of the originals—or they will filter through to us. But without someone to give us at least some rendering—a rendering as free as you like—of a foreign literature we will never be able to gather what the real magic and aura of that literature may be. . . . For it is not literal translation that is needed for this purpose. The valuable rendering may be full of verbal mis-translations or even of misunderstandings of meanings. . . . But only consider any exactly correct translation of the Bible as against the Authorized Version. It would be more correct to translate the apple that Eve ate as a shaddock but that arboricultural exactitude helps nobody and would bewilder many; or how would we be helped if in the Second Book of Kings we read (X.ɪɪ.): "So Jehu slew all that remained of the house of Ahab in Jezreel and all his great men and his *acquaintances*," instead of "kinsfolk." We would have a relatively commonplace and obviously inexact word instead of one that has a beauty in itself and is probably more true to the fact. For Jehu can hardly have slain every man who had ever said "How do you do" to Ahab, whereas he would take good care to get rid of all the kinsfolk of that ruler for fear pretenders should later arise. So that though the Hebrew word does actually mean something like "acquaintances" the account of the slaughter gains in intensity from the "kinsfolk" of the Authorized Translator. It gives at least an effect nearer in spirit to that of the inspired writer of the original.

Let us return to China and Rihaku. The regrets and remembrances of the bureaucratic exile from office formed, then, one of the conventional motifs of all Chinese emotional poetry. These motifs as we have seen are relatively few. The writers express regrets of abandoned wives or concubines or abandoned husbands or lovers; they express regrets for banishments and remembrances of good times that are gone. Or, if they are banished to wars, they express bitter regrets, and as a rule do not chronicle their memories as being too poignant for expression, since they have no glimmer of hope of return. But once the limited scale of the motifs is accepted, the forms and the conceits that the poet may adopt become almost infinite. So much is recapitulation so that we may not forget it.

But one should emphasize in one's mind that the love song or the song of the glories of war are almost completely absent, along with devotional verse. And one should remember as the reason for this that whether the poet be a superior man moulded by the philosophy of Confucius or a hermit swayed by the teachings of Lao-Tsze, each, like his master, would dislike thinking about war and would almost as much dislike any religious or metaphysical speculations or conjectures as to the future state. The orthodox Chinaman believed in— or, at least, did not deny—the existence of a single deity attended by spirits. But as a rule only the Emperor was qualified to address the Divine Being or to offer Him either prayers or sacrifices—and that only twice a year, at the summer or winter solstices. But the orthodox Chinese subject never addressed prayers to his god and, indeed, practically never thought about Him, or about the future of his soul after death. As Confucius put it: Since we know practically nothing about the life that we have and must manage, why should we waste time with thinking about things over which we have no control? And the attitude of Lao-Tsze was much the same.

As regards the love-trimmings of the Westerner and most other Orientals, the conception of those things, too, simply did not exist for the Chinese superior man. If he could have read

> Bid me to live and I will live thy Protestant to be;
> Or bid me love and I will give a loving heart to thee. . . .
> Or bid me die and I will dare e'en death for love of thee

the great Li-Po would have said that that was mere sound and fury signifying nothing. He would have no conception of what the words meant. . . . The actions of sex were agreeable functions having just as much and no more relation to the mentality than eating food or drinking wine. He would take the two latter functions far more seriously than we usually do, but neither they nor the actions of sex cast any extraneous glow over his existence. None of the three were romantic. So the lover promised to his mistress or the fiancée to her accepted, no glory, no immortality, no deathless deeds—and, indeed, no eternal constancy in song. A husband and wife lived, ate, drank and slept together with, as it were, equanimity; and in place of what we call love they expected friendship and agreeable and stimulating conversation. . . . And, indeed, in his poetic regrets the exiled friend or the deserted husband expresses remembrance of, and yearning most for the interrupted friendship and the conversations with which they sent the moon down the sky.

And as with religion, so with war: the Chinese poet acknowledged that it existed, hoped that he would be kept out of it, regarded the professional soldier as a butcher of a lower order of beings—lower even than the slaughterer of cattle, since his functions helped no one—and so that poet never thought about wars. Certainly he never celebrated their glories in song. He found interests enough in life, in friendship, in his bureaucratic career, in his hermitry—and in the purchase of spring sensations through the ingurgitation of innumerable small cups of wine.

That being said, let us prepare to take leave of the Chinese poetry with quotations from two more poems by the inimitable Rihaku. Both are translated by Ezra Pound and appear in *Lustra*.

Here is a portion of one of Rihaku's poems treating of war when it must be endured:

Lament of the Frontier Guard

By the North Gate the wind blows full of sand . . .
There is no wall left to this village.
Bones white with a thousand frosts,
High heaps covered with trees and grass. . . .

And here is a fragment from his famous

Exile's Letter

And then I was sent off to South Wei . . .
And you to the north of Raku-hoku,
Till we had nothing but thoughts and memories in common.
And then, when separation had come to its worst,
We met, and travelled into Sen-Go. . . .

And what a reception:
Red jade cups, food well set on a blue jewelled table,
And I was drunk, and had no thought of returning. . . .
And the vermilioned girls getting drunk around sunset,
And the water a hundred feet deep reflecting green eyebrows. . . .

But before we can leave Chinese poetry, we must consider one of her most famous popular narrative poems, *The Everlasting Wrong* of Po-Chu-I, who flourished between A.D. 772 and 846—a century, roughly speaking, after Rihaku. We have said that after the Golden Age of Chinese poetry that ended about 800 A.D., this art became a matter of verbal and of metrical ingenuities and tricks and so it has remained until the present day. And we have also said that Chinese prose was always more a matter of records, annals and philosophical speculation than of imaginative or literary writing. The novel has remained, according to our standards, in the lower stage of the connected short story. The Chinese Revolution is, however, changing all these aspects: a strong Russian tinge is infusing itself into imaginative work and innumerable revolutionary pamphlets are being written.

It is, nevertheless, worth while to spend a moment on the Chinese play.

The Western playgoer going into a Chinese theatre is appalled to perceive that, as he supposes, a single play lasts a month or so, going apparently from birth to death of a character at the tempo of the ordinary human life. It is true that a Chinese play proceeds as a rule exactly at the tempo of human life—which is to say that it observes the unities of time and place of the Greek Theatre. The Chinese, like the

Athenians, were—and are—unwilling to make the mental step of letting time pass as it were unseen behind the back-cloths. They refuse to take the trouble to adopt the modern, comparatively uncivilized, convention of letting the first act of a play take place in France in the summer; the second in Dunsinane in autumn; and the third on the Italian Riviera two springs later, the whole year and three-quarters being supposed to elapse between 8:30 and 11:15 of one evening. That would shock their sense of the reasonable. Their play must take place in the Here and the Now. The Here is the scene represented for the moment of the play; the Now is just the amount of time that the action represented needs to take place in. Thus a Chinese evening at the play means attending as many playlets—tiny representations of incidents—as the spectator has the time or the inclination to sit through. But as the playlets have no indication of division between them, no announcements, no curtain, the Western observer is prone to imagine that what he is witnessing is one play of immense length. Actually a hero, say, will be awaited by brigands in ambush; by bravery or by the intervention of spirits the brigands will be foiled. They will be slain; will get up and walk out with the hero. Without any interval the same brigands will be on the stage again, representing quite other brigands. They will abduct a heroine from one side to the other of the stage; the same hero, representing however a quite different player, will enter, rescue the heroine, slay the brigands and they will all go off, returning however a minute later to represent quite different characters in quite another short story or episode. The time effect would, in short, be exactly that of an evening at the modern western cinema—but an evening in which Miss Garbo and Mr. Clark Gable should play in a number of short pieces, each piece without connection, but each being played by those distinguished stars without change of costume or make-up. There are, of course, longer plays in which a series of episodes in the life of the same hero is performed; and such a play might even last through several evenings, so that the effect would be exactly that of attending a serial at the movies—only each evening of the life of the boards would take up just as much time as was occupied by the spectator in his seat. . . . Thus, most Eastern apparent quaintnesses resolve themselves into reasonable conventions not much differing from those of the West—or at any rate easily explicable.

In one way or another, in fact, the narrative occupies as much time in Chinese life as it does in the Occident—and, indeed, more if the listeningo to public story tellers and the theatre are taken into account. So the novel as a form has not much developed itself. The cultured Oriental prefers to take his cultured narrative in verse, because it adds to the romantic effect; his popular fiction he gets through the ear, and the place of the novel is and always was a lowly one.

There are of course novels in Chinese and some of them like the famous *Romance of the Three Kingdoms* have been read with greater or less enthusiasm by limited Western audiences in English or in French. But the novel is not an essentially Chinese form and it will be more convenient to defer our discussion of it until we arrive at its development, in its sixteenth-century western, picaresque form. Specialists of Sinology will object to this—but we are not specialists. Our glass is not big but we must drink out of our own glass.

The Chinese narrative poem, then, recounting incidents, is more popular in *genre* than the reflective or elegiac pieces of the great poets. This came from the sharp divisions between the three classes of Chinese life: public, cultural and religious. Let us consider them cursorily for a minute, since at one period or another of our western histories the Chinese philosophic, and even their political, examples have played a considerable part in our own cultural and political developments—notably in the eighteenth century, when all our political theories and practices and, above all, our ideals were profoundly influenced by the example of the French Revolution and our reactions against French revolutionary ideas.

It would, for instance, not be fantastic to see in Voltaire a public figure like that of Confucius, and in Jean Jacques Rousseau another resembling that of Lao-Tsze the Quietist. And on Voltaire the influence of Confucius was profound; on Rousseau that influence of echoes of the philosophy of Lao-Tsze was as of something continuously whispering in his ear. Says Voltaire:

By what fatality, shameful maybe for the Western peoples, is it necessary to go to the far Orient to find a wise man who is simple, unostentatious, free from imposture, who taught men to live happily six hundred years before our Vulgar era, at a time when the whole of the North was ignorant of the usage of letters, and when the Greeks were barely beginning to distinguish themselves by their wisdom?

This wise man is Confucius, who being a legislator, never wanted to deceive men. What more beautiful rule of conduct has ever been given man since the world began? Let us admit that there has been no legislator more useful to the human race.
(from Voltaire's *Dictionary of Philosophies*.)

And the tendency of Rousseau to see in the Quietism of Lao-Tsze the source of all the gentle and idyllic theorizings of his time was even more pronounced.

There was, however, a third strand in Chinese public life—one much more active, virulent and bloodthirsty: the one which impelled the First Emperor to burn the books of his predecessors and to attempt to wipe out their civilizations. This was the Tao-ist religion, a phenomenon which might stand for the Terror of the French Revolution. It had nothing to do with the philosophy of Lao-Tsze, any more than the executions promoted by Robespierre and the Mountain had to do with the Quietism of Rousseau; but it arose in a fairly similar manner from fairly similar reactions. Voltaire was, like Confucius, an aristocrat trying to restore, by the virulence of his criticisms, virtue and strength to an ancient form of monarchy. Rousseau, like Lao-Tsze, was a person of obscure birth and descent, determined to shake off all the vanities and jealousies of the courts, and to find for himself an hermitage in which he should pass undisturbed days in reflecting on the virtues of sage and primitive peoples like the Chinese.

There remained, however, in each case a third factor—the common people who were neither superior men nor Quietists. And the "common people" of China consisted not merely of the poor. It was made up of every man from the Emperor downwards who was not a philosophic lover of the virtues and rites of the past ages of China.

The superior men of Confucius and the Quietists of Lao-Tsze's following did their best to ignore metaphysical questions and the nature of the supernatural. Thus, the worship of God was left entirely in the hands of the Emperor, and the common people was completely without guidance as to religion. It set itself to supply the want and, importing every sort of superstition from the West, it compounded one that was a religion with a vengeance. Neither Confucianism nor Tao-ism provided for any kind of retribution either here or in the next world for sins committed in this life. The compounders of the new religion borrowed from the Jews the idea of punishment in this life as it is projected in the book of Job; from Christianity it took the idea of Hell—and, particularly, of Purgatory; from the Buddhists it borrowed metempsychosis and the practices of a priestcraft that has hardly elsewhere been equalled for rigidity of practice and superstition. It incorporated devil-worship, the type of patriotic faith that makes for the murder of all foreigners . . . and the idea of a materialistic Nirvana that resembled faintly the idea of the Christian Heaven but included marriage, polygamy and concubinage galore. That accounts for the passages shadowing after-death blisses that occur in the poem of Po-Chu-I, some extracts from which we are about to read, according to the translation of Mr. Giles in his *History of Chinese Literature*. Po-Chu-I was born A.D. 772 and died in 846, and his poem purports to tell the story of the Emperor Ming-Hu-ang who was born A.D. 685 and died just ten years before the birth of Po-Chu-I.

In his youth and early manhood this Emperor, according to the poem, was everything that an Emperor should be. Frugal and industrious, he held his courts and gave audiences in the early hours of the morning. Forever on the frontiers, he kept the barbarians at bay or drove them into their own territories. But one day came the *femme fatale* into Ming-Hu-ang's life.

The Everlasting Wrong

Hair like a cloud, face like a flower, headdress which quivered as
  she walked,
Amid the delights of the Hibiscus Pavilion she passed the soft
  spring nights.

Spring nights, too short alas! for them, albeit prolonged till
dawn,—
From this time forth no more audiences in the hours of early morn.
Revels and feasts in quick succession, ever without a break,
She chosen always for the spring excursion, chosen for the nightly
carouse.
Three thousand peerless beauties adorned the apartments of the
monarch's harem
Yet always his Majesty reserved his attentions for her alone
Passing her life in a "golden house,"* with fair girls to wait on her,
She was daily wafted to ecstasy on the wine fumes of the banquet-
hall.

From that time everything goes wrong with the Empire; the taxes
fail, like the harvests; starvation and oppression stalk through the land;
the fortifications of the frontiers are neglected. . . . And, at last, the
barbarians make such dangerous inroads that the Emperor himself
must march against them at the head of his troops. But the wicked
one goes with him. For her sake the marches cannot be forced; the
Emperor spends hours in her pavilion when he should be on the road.
Indiscipline spreads through the army. Until there comes the crisis:

The soldiers refuse to advance; nothing remains to be done
Until she of the moth-eyebrows perishes in sight of all.
On the ground lie gold ornaments with no one to pick them up,
Kingfisher wings, golden birds, and hairpins of costly jade.
The monarch covers his face, powerless to save;
And as he turns to look back, tears and blood flow mingled
together.

The Emperor is deposed for many years. But at last reascending his
throne, he calls to him a magician who promises to go, like Orpheus,
down into the far Eastern equivalent for Avernus and to report to

---

* Referring to A-chiao, one of the consorts of an Emperor of the Han dynasty. "Ah,"
said the latter when a boy, "if I could only get A-chiao, I would have a golden house
to keep her in."

the Emperor how the soul of the beautiful lady is engaged and whether she is still faithful to her lover. The magician finds the lady in a great hall, much resembling in its splendor those that on earth she had inhabited. So:

Then she takes out the old keepsakes, tokens of undying love,
A gold hairpin, an enamel brooch, and bids the magician carry
    these back.
One half of the hairpin she keeps, and one half of the enamel
    brooch,
Breaking with her hands the yellow gold, and dividing the enamel
    in two.
"Tell him," she said, "to be firm of heart, as this gold and enamel,
And then in Heaven or on Earth below we two may meet once
    more."
At parting, she confided to the magician many earnest messages
    of love,
Among the rest recalling a pledge mutually understood;
How on the seventh day of the seventh moon, in the Hall of
    Immortality,
At midnight, when none were near, he had whispered in her ear,
"I swear that we will fly like the one-winged birds,*
Or grow united like the trees with branches which twine together."
Heaven and Earth, long-lasting as they are, will some day pass
    away;
But the fame of this great wrong shall stretch out forever, end-
    less, forever and aye.

From which it would appear that, outside the circles of the superior men and the Tao-ists, lovers gave pledges and took vows in China, and that love there must have been very much like what it was elsewhere—for the common people.

It is interesting, too, to note that the lady believes that she and her lover will meet whether in heaven or on earth. That is a trace of the Buddhist belief in the transmigration of souls occurring in the Tao-

* Each bird having one wing must always fly with a mate.

ist religion. The Tao-ists, that is to say, believed that souls were promoted to inhabiting other bodies after a certain stage in purgatory, and that if in that reincarnation it behaved very well its next body might be that of a more and more superior being until at last the soul entered for good into Nirvana—or, that failing, was condemned to eternal extinction. . . . And if a woman behaved very well her soul might be promoted to inhabiting the body of a man . . . which might prove disagreeable to the Emperor Ming-Hu-ang.

CHAPTER FOUR

WE COME then by due chronological process to the literature of the Hebrews . . . not that we have by any means really finished with Confucius and the great Lao-Tsze—or even with the writers of the Egyptian *Book of Stone* that is fourteen hundred kilometres long. And indeed so inextricably entangled is the endless rope of human thought that, once the writers of any one civilization have entered into it, we shall never be rid of them. There are of course literary pockets like that of Japan that so isolated themselves that they have contributed little or nothing, in the way either of letters or that quasi-literature that is found in books of philosophy, to the great current of human thought and its written preservations.

I don't mean to say that there is not a great Japanese literature, but it is one that derived from and, as it were, desiccated the more generous and untidy literature of the Chinese, and that because of Japan's millennial self-isolation in no way spread its thought outside the realms of the Island Kingdom. . . . Until indeed a very few years ago under the aegis of Mr. H. G. Wells the Japanese theory of government called Bushido attracted a little attention in the Occident, or, under the aegis of Messrs. Pound and Waley the Japanese play form, called Nô, attracted rather less.*

* The reader who wishes, and there is every reason why he should, to acquaint himself more deeply with the literature of Japan could not do better than to read the *Tale of Genji* by the Lady Murasaki and its five sequels all translated by Mr. Arthur Waley. These books will not merely present him with a series of exciting amours compared with which the adventures of Casanova are dull grossnesses, but in the course of these novels the characters themselves—as we shall later have occasion to find out, indulge in so many speculations as to the technique of not only Japanese literature but of the Chinese from which the Japanese closely descends that the reader will find himself provided with a very good idea of what both literatures represent in the way of technique. He could then proceed to deepen his knowledge by reading W. G. Aston's *Japanese Literature*, and C. H. Page's *Japanese Poetry*. Mr. Waley has also translated a number of Nô plays which are perhaps Japan's most significant literary form, and his admirable and indefatigable labors have presented us with renderings of innumerable other Chinese poetic works, his last volume being a very valuable *Book of Songs* issued in London by Messrs. Allen & Unwin in 1937. The novel of the Lady Murasaki is also obtainable from Houghton Mifflin, Boston.

54

But we have not in a work of this scale either the space or the time to investigate these pockets. We are concerned with the history of human thought as expressed and handed down through generations, in imaginative letters. That confines us to the five or six great literatures, living or dead, that still exercise great influence on us of today or that so influenced our fathers that we still feel the results of those influences. Considering them, initially, in order of time we find, first, the great stone literatures, the Sumerian, the Egyptian, the Babylonian. Overlapping them in its beginnings and continuing to the present day we have the Chinese at which we have just looked. Overlapping the Chinese and equally continuing into our own times we have, next, the Hebrew—both as an influence on the past and as a still written language.

And so we have the great Literatures of Greece and Rome, the one merging into the other. Then, in Europe, came the Dark Ages when the sacred torch was kept alive and its flames handed down in the magnificent and luxuriating literature of the Arabs. That sprang up after the birth of Mahomet, from the very borders of China, through Persia to Bagdad, and from Bagdad all along the North Coast of Africa to Carthage, and from Carthage to Granada and through all Spain to the foothills of the Alps in Provence—and, the other way round, through the Balkans and Greece to the very walls of Vienna. And all that territory produced and still produces literature in Arabic. Then, as Europe at the beginning of the Middle Ages again girded her loins to throw back the Eastern invaders, her varying languages disentangled themselves the one from the other and, amongst the interminable scramblings for each other's territories that God has not yet seen fit to allow to finish, the great modern literatures began their courses that also have not yet seen their earthly closes. It is they that in consequence have become the receptacles and melting pots of all the philosophies and literatures of all the ages that preceded or accompanied those called Dark—the period of universal barbarian flame over Europe, when only in lost monasteries in hidden valleys was the light of former civilizations kept dimly alive, to emerge again with some steadiness in the tenth and eleventh centuries with the *Chanson de Roland*, the miracle plays of the nun Hroswitha, the song of Piers Plowman, the thirteenth and fourteenth century compilations of the *Roman de la Rose*. And their music and traditions, passing across the Channel, gave us the verse of Chaucer, who was the father of our poetry, and the prose of the *Morte d'Arthur*. And that last work, which was completed in 1469, gave us in spite of the first modern novelist, called Cervantes —the poor framework of human conduct which still faintly prevails in such chivalry as you may still see faintly in our school playgrounds and our playing fields.

These interweaving influences it is difficult to trace with certainty in all our complicated fabric of days running back into centuries. They are, indeed, almost untraceable, so many of them running into spheres where we have no immediate business. How, for instance, should we trace the influence of Confucius and Lao-Tsze, which—very much exciting the curiosity of the Greeks of the classical age—passed, as an influence, right back again under Alexander of Macedon, with the Greek-Bactrian Empire, into the very shadow of the Himalayas? So that today the lives and habits of thought of the inhabitants of the Punjab are still influenced by the habits and thoughts of the Greeks who were the companions of Alexander the Great three hundred years before the Christian era. And the companions of Alexander had learned their thoughts at the feet of the disciples of Socrates, who himself was not foreign to the teachings of Confucius and still more of the *Tao-Teh-King*.

But wherever you go in the East before the coming of the Christian era, you find books or stones enjoining on you either the desirability of following a virtuous and austere public life or complete retirement into hermitages. Those were the two great schools of Eastern thought, they too inextricably twining the one into the other over great regions of the earth. We have seen how Buddhism, a popular Indian religion, entered China and gave an added note of savagery and superstition to the popular religion of China. But you have also to think that the Buddha, who also was an almost exact contemporary of Confucius, was like him a reformer, with a philosophical system or religion that was without creed or rites. The inter-relationship between Chinese and Indian thought was at this period very close—if at times opposed. Thus, the Indian despising history as a record, to know anything at all of early Indian affairs it is necessary to consult the Chinese Imperial records.

And alongside that in India went the sterner, more rationalistic, infinitely stricter system of the Brahmins, whose three-in-one deities were Brahma the Creator, Siva the Destroyer, and Vishnu the Preserver; and they again were mental-poetic developments of the primeval religion of the ancient gods of India—the spirits of the hills, the rivers, the lakes, of the sky, of rain clouds—all under the presidency of Dyaushpitar, the Father of Heaven. . . . And if you consider how nearly that name resembles phonetically that of the father of the Greek gods, you will get one of those little philosophic shocks of suggestion that will affect you continually when you ·pursue the thoughts of the poets down through the ages—when, that is to say, you study the history of literature.

For tracing down to their sources literature and, more emphatically, the department of literature that is known as poetry, whether in prose or in verse, you traverse continually that double territory that is one part imagination, one part the search after truth, and yet another where the two mingle indistinguishably the one with the other. As if it were a riverine country divided into solid ground, marshy tracts and the great river itself! Nothing might be farther from your thought than any study of comparative or revealed religion; and no subject is more dangerous to peace or more apt to lead to confusion. But, if only because it has been the habit of those servants of the gods called priests continually to call to their aid those servants of mankind called poets, you have no chance of escape from that dangerous study once you embark on the search for poetic illumination. To avoid it, you would have to do without all the literature of the *Books of Stone*, of nearly all of Homer, of nearly all Greek drama, of all the Old Testament except perhaps the "Song of Solomon," of all the New Testament and an immense proportion of modern verse and prose.

The Hebrews themselves, being the most austere of all the believers with whom we shall have to do, limit what are called the poetical books of the Old Testament to three, those being the Book of Job, the Psalms and Proverbs—all three having been in the original Hebrew entirely written in alliterated, parallel and, very rarely, metrical, verse, with the exception of Job which has Prologue and Epilogue in prose. But the more liberal Catholic, and such of the Protestant Biblical critics as are inclined to be liberal, call "poetical" all the central books of Holy Writ—that is to say, in addition to the above three, the books called Ecclesiastes, Song of Solomon, Wisdom and Ecclesiasticus, the Protestants omitting Ecclesiasticus, and the Hebrews calling the other four the books of wisdom. The Latin Christian writers, in fact, like the Latin lay writers of today, considered that the books not called poetical by the Hebrews were nevertheless so inspired by passion and rendered so beautiful by the use of image and illustration that though written mostly in prose they could still be called poetry, whereas the Hebrews, like the Anglo-Saxons of today, insisted that whatever was not in verse was prose and so not poetical.

Settle that matter how you like, the fact remains that all priesthoods, stern like the Hebrews or relatively jovial like the priests of the Paphian Venus, have one and all called to their aid both verse poets and prosateurs in un-enumerable profusion and have accorded more or less reverence, according as they were liberal or austere, to the religions and philosophies that have preceded them. Thus, St. Augustine, as I have pointed out, being much nearer to the spirit of the more ancient religions, accords in the *City of God* considerable weight to holiness that had gone before and had differed in shades from his own. His example has been followed by most Roman Catholic commentators and missionaries since his day, Protestant writers and theologians being more exclusive and apt to believe that the pre-Christian religious were all heathens without light.

The difference comes out most fully in the relation of the various Christian Churches to the combined Confucius-Lao-Tsze system of conduct and belief. The eighteenth and nineteenth century Jesuit missionaries to China, basing themselves as it were on St. Augustine's declaration that the Church of Christ was not initiated by the Redeemer but had existed for generations in principle until Christ came to assemble all those preëxisting but scattered principles and creeds into one and to give that Church his name—the Jesuit missionaries, then, professed to see in Confucianism plus Tao-ism, as recorded in the *Tao-Teh-King* of Lao-Tsze, the whole of the pre-Christian religious system, filtering through the Hebrews and the Old Testament. They said those teachings had come to flower in the figure and teachings of Christ as recorded in the Gospels. They said:

The deity of this Chinese system is a triune deity: one god with three aspects, which we will loosely translate as Is-Was-and-Forever-Shall-Be-the-Eternal-God. According to the *Tao-Teh-King* he was mystically accompanied or even preceded by the mysterious and inexplicable principle called Ta-O . . . as who should say, the Word. So that the beginning of the *Tao-Teh-King* might almost be rendered in the very words of the Gospel according to St. John: "In the beginning was the Word, and the Word was with God and the Word was God." Again the triune eternal god was waited on by spirits to whom in moments of agony or peril even the common people might appeal, the worship of the eternal being otherwise reserved for the Emperor—thus foreshadowing the angels and archangels and saints of the Catholic rites. And still more remarkable and convincing, they said, was the fact that the name by which the Emperor addressed the eternal in his solstitial worship was I-Ah-Wei, in which, just as in the Dyaush-pitar of the Hindus we may trace the name of Zeus the Father, we may trace the name of the Yahweh of the Hebrews.

Even further: in the divided but not necessarily always conflicting figures of Confucius and Lao-Tsze—who himself was of miraculous birth—you would if you combined them see the earthly and the divine attributes of the Savior of Mankind himself.

Let us then consider—since we have no literary trace of I-Ah-Wei, the Chinese eternal one—the literary remains of the two great Chinese sages. To strike the strongest note at first let us say that it was Confucius who first amongst traceable men laid down the doctrine: "Do not as you would not be done by." But Lao-Tsze's whole doctrine was the enforcement of the Beatitude: "Blessed are the poor in spirit for theirs is the kingdom of Heaven." And it was Lao-Tsze who first amongst traceable men enunciated the doctrine—which was set into poetry by the Hebrews in the Book of Proverbs—"If thine Enemy hunger give him meat; if he be athirst, give him to drink." That became, in the words of Christ as recorded by St. Luke: "But love ye your enemies and do good and lend, hoping for nothing again."

To the Western mind the writings of Confucius are tortuous—an immense rag bag of eternal repetitions. Or rather of continuous attempts at the expression of thoughts in which each new attempt carries the thought sometimes only very little forward. As thus: in a dialogue between the Master and his disciples, quoted from *The Story of Confucius*, by Brian Brown:

> Yen Yuan asked, "What is love?"
> The Master said, "Love is to conquer self and turn to courtesy, for one day all mankind would turn to love."
> "Does love flow from within, or does it flow from others?"
> The Master said, "To be ever courteous of eye and ever courteous of ear; to be ever courteous in work and ever courteous in deed."
> Yen Yuan said: "Dull as I am, I hope to live by these words."
> Chung-kung asked, "What is love?"
> The Master said: "Without the door to behave as though a great guest were come; to treat the people as though we tendered the high sacrifice; not to do unto others what we would not have they should do unto us; to breed no wrongs in the State and breed no wrongs in the home."
> Chung-kung said: "Dull as I am, I hope to live by these words."
> Ssu-ma Niu said: "Love is slow to speak."
> "To be slow to speak! Can that be called love?"
> The Master said: "A gentleman knows neither sorrow nor fear."
> "No sorrow and no fear! Can that be called a gentleman?"
> The Master said: "He finds no sin in his heart, so why should he sorrow, what should he fear?"

Or again amongst the almost millionfold precepts by the following of which the superior man may mould himself into the perfect bureaucrat and in turn mould his province or his Empire into the perfect commonwealth:

"When one cultivates to the utmost the principles of his nature, and exercises them on the principle of reciprocity, he is not far from the path. What you do not like when done to yourself, do not do to others."

"In the way of the superior man there are four things, to not one of which have I as yet attained. To serve my father, as I would require my son to serve me, to this I have not attained; to serve my prince, as I would require my minister to serve me, to this I have not attained; to serve my elder brother, as I would require my younger brother to serve me, to this I have not attained; to set the example in behaving to a friend, as I would require him to behave to me, to this I have not attained. Earnest in practicing the ordinary virtues and careful in speaking about them, if, in his practice he has anything defective, the superior man dares not but exert himself; and if, in his words, he has any excess, he dares not allow himself such license. Thus his words have respect to his actions, and his actions have respect to his words; is it not just an entire sincerity which marks the superior man?"

The Master said, "In archery we have something like the way of the superior man. When the archer misses the center of the target, he turns round and seeks for the cause of his failure in himself."

"Some are born with the knowledge of those duties; some know them by study, and some acquire the knowledge after a painful feeling of their ignorance. But the knowledge being possessed, it comes to the same thing. Some practice them with a natural ease; some form a desire for their advantages, and some by strenuous effort. But the achievement being made, it comes to the same thing."

Lao-Tsze, on the other hand, wrote very little. Confucius moved about all over the Middle Kingdom followed by his pupils and trying to inculcate wisdom into feudal dukes and spreading his fame wherever he went. Lao-Tsze with a complete hatred for what today is called publicity, having been early made librarian to the Duke of Lu, remained, till his disappearance at a very advanced age, amongst his scrolls. If he promulgated his Quietist doctrines at all, he did so by word of mouth to such as visited his retreat. His fame, at least, was very widely spread—a fact that he continually deplored. He said, almost in the words of Keats, that he was one whose name should be written in water. Indeed, for him water was the most satisfactory of all natural symbols since it forever sought the lowest levels. And, said he, if all men imitated water and sought not the highest but the lowest places in the market place or in office, the world would automatically and at once return to its Golden Age.

In the end, the turbulence and disorder of the Empire having grown too great for him to support its contemplation, he betook himself to the solitudes of the outer deserts and was no more heard of. But as he went on his way the guardian of the gate of the valley that leads out of the Celestial Empire stopped him and begged that he would at least write one book so that his teachings might not be forever lost to the world. So Lao-Tsze stayed long enough to write "in 5,000 characters" the *Tao-Tseh-King*. It is a work, almost of poetry, alternating a deep mysticism when he talks of the Ta-o (the "Word," the First Principle) with parables and images of an extreme clarity. Thus, he will say: "Ta-o is an Emptiness;" and continue that "both in the processes of nature, known as the action of Heaven and Earth, both in the processes of T'ien* or Iah-Wei, and in the activities of man, what corresponds to that mystic Emptiness is a freedom from all selfish motive, or purpose centering in oneself." And then immediately he adds, according to James Legge in *The Religions of China*:

> It is said, "The sage deals with affairs (as if) he were doing nothing, and performs his teaching without words. (In the same way in nature) all things shoot up (in spring) without a word spoken, and grow (in summer) without a claim for their production. They go through their processes (in autumn) without any display of pride in them, and the results are realized (in winter) without any assumption of ownership."

* i.e., Heaven and earth united, and so the triple godhead I-Ah-Wei.

Those sentences curiously foreshadow the sayings of the altruist second century Roman Emperor. For, says Marcus Aurelius:

Whom then shall we call the virtuous man? Is it he who doeth good deeds in the expectation of a reward still greater? Not so. Is it then he who doeth good expecting the exact return of what he has given? No, it is not he. The truly virtuous man is he who putteth forth his good works as the vine lets fall its grapes and when they are gone hath no more any consciousness of them.

And that is not strange when we remember that the father of Commodus lived in the days of the Golden Age of the Chinese Empire and its literature, and that embassies frequently passed in those days between the shores of the Mediterranean and the rivers of Cathay.

Confucius, then, may be said to stand for the almost Divine Teacher of Statesmen; Lao-Tsze for the poet who was the more nearly Divine Educator of Mankind. And, indeed, during the few years when Confucius held office and directed the affairs of a state, he was so successful as to cause his own ruin. For, having brought the Dukedom of Lu to a high state of fiscal and military efficiency, it increased its territories and appeared likely to become a menace to all the surrounding duchies. So the crafty rulers of Chi decided to wean the affections of the Duke of Lu from his minister. They accordingly sent the duke a present of eight hundred concubines and eight hundred Celestial thoroughbred stallions. And the duke, corrupted by these joys, looked so coldly on K'ung-Fu-Tsze that the philosopher's dignity demanded that he draw his robes about him and depart forever from Lu. He found no other office and from thenceforth to the end of his days wandered mournfully, surrounded by his disciples, all over China. Indeed, rather than have no office at all he contemplated entering the service of a brigand chief who was laying waste whole dukedoms. He pointed out that, so long as his maxims were put into force and an ideal commonwealth was founded to serve as a model for restoring the Golden Age of Mankind, it mattered little what leader ruled the state.

The two great sages met once, Confucius calling on Lao-Tsze in his library. The interview seems to have resembled that between the young Heine and the aged Goethe—Confucius being aged about thirty and Lao-Tsze over eighty. Lao-Tsze, according to Brian Brown in *The Story of Confucius*, is reported to have said to his young visitor:

"Those whom you talk about are dead, and their bones are mouldered to dust; only their words remain. When the superior man dominates his time, he mounts aloft; but when the time is against him, he moves as if his feet were entangled. I have heard that a good merchant, though he has rich treasures deeply stored, appears as if he were poor, and that the superior man whose virtue is complete is yet to outward seeming stupid. Put away your proud air and many desires, your insinuating habit and wild will. These are of no advantage to you. This is all which I have to tell you."

And Confucius is said to have exclaimed on returning to his disciples:

"I know how birds can fly, how fishes can swim, and how animals can run. But the runner may be snared, the swimmer may be hooked, and the flyer may be shot by the arrow. But there is the dragon. I cannot tell how he mounts on the wind through the clouds and rises to heaven. Today, I have seen Lao-Tsze, and can only compare him to the dragon."

It is, however, to be remembered that those words are reported by Tsze-Ma Ch'ien, a disciple of Lao-Tsze, six hundred years after the interview.

So, from the literary point of view, we may agree with St. Augustine that the ideas of the church of Christ existed for millennia before the coming of Christ himself. . . . At any rate, it demonstrably did so in China. To sum up: we have there the single deity of three aspects, the ministrant spirits and the savior of mankind—divided, in this case, into the two sages. For if, to use a metaphor of Po-Chu-I from *The Ever-lasting Wrong*, we regard Confucius and Lao-Tsze as two birds each with only one wing, so that they may fly only together, we find almost exactly reproduced the figure of the Christian Savior. On the one hand, Confucius attended to the affairs of his earth, and kept his eyes on the past much as Christ did when He said "Render unto Caesar the things that are Caesar's;" or when He drove the money changers from the Temple; or again when He looked continually back for the examples and sayings of the prophets who had preceded Him. On the other hand, like Lao-Tsze, he looked continually forward to a Golden Age, that should be earned by meekness, by humility and by the extremes of frugality.

The influence of the Chinese sages on Jewish thought is not so easy to trace. If there were any, it came late and probably, as in the case of the Punjab, by way of the Greeks.

It is, of course, hopeless to attempt to date the actual writing of almost any of the books of the Old Testament. That is a task that has occupied men's minds for centuries. And we are hardly nearer the truth today than were the Christian fathers of the Church or the Jewish writers on the subject nearly two thousand years ago.

Those who believe that every word of any one version of the Bible in whatever language is in fact the word of God Himself, are perhaps today fewer than they were, say, half a century ago. But the moment any concession is made—the moment any imperfection is allowed to the text of Holy Writ—the matter becomes completely bewildering and no one but a master of Biblical exegesis could find any clue to that maze. It is one that has puzzled the minds of the wisest as of the most foolish for thousands of years, and one that as yet has found no solution.

So we may, not inappropriately, leave all that side of the matter to theologians and consider the Bible as if it were an anthology, in Hebrew, of the lore, the edicts, the religious discipline, the hygienic regulations, the legends, and above all, the poetry of an ancient and warlike people. They were at the height of their power a thousand years before the Christian era; subsequently they declined until in the early years of our era they were expelled from their own land, and have ever since been wanderers throughout the earth. Nor is it to be imagined that they left even their literary talents behind them. On the contrary, for many centuries after the Dispersal and more particularly in Spain, the Jews produced a plentiful, and always developing, literature particularly in verse. As was the case with the races who have produced the other living literatures of the world, the Jewish literary language and forms underwent considerable changes. Their verse like ours, or that of any other Western literature, gradually lost its Oriental characteristics of rhythm and adopted the metres and rhymes that were used by the people amongst whom they found themselves living. A part of the Bible was written in verse, and in all the rest of Holy Writ the prophets and chroniclers had the tendency, in moments of emotion, to burst uncontrollably into verse—but that very fact became obscured to the Jewish learned themselves, and it was actually an eighteenth century Protestant divine who first rediscovered the verse structures, alliterations and rhythms of the poetical books of the Old Testament, though two seventeenth century Jewish writers had before him called attention to the fact that alliteration played some part in the Hebrew biblical writings.

The moment one realizes the fact that a great part of the Hebrew Bible was written in verse and that that verse instead of being confined by the later devices of rhyme, scansions and the rest was of an extraordinary human quality, it becomes apparent that quite apart from its religious aspects, the Bible itself is an extremely profitable work to study from the merely literary side. And the moment that one approaches the Bible from that point of view, it assumes a completely different aspect.

Whilst you regard it solely as a record of the decrees of a jealous deity and of the acts of an isolated people, guided very imperfectly by those edicts, it remains something slightly minatory and aloof from the daily life of mere men. But, as soon as you regard it as a merely human compilation of legends, moralities, stage plays even, and fairy tales and folklore, you may arrive at a stage of mind at once of more wonder as of more equableness. If you have to consider the Bible as in very truth and in every word the inspiration of the Almighty, you are at once browbeaten by the authority and bewildered by the almost insane isolation and vindictiveness of your God and your fellow men.

To put it in another and less dangerous plane: The Greeks said that Apollo rendered his greatest poets mad so that they might the more nearly commune with him and render his thoughts for the perusal of mankind. But every poet having his passages of dullness, bathos and lengthiness, they considered that at such moments the poet was too rational—too insufficiently mad—to be in perfect communion with the godhead. For reasons of his own, the godhead had so willed it. So on occasion the Hebrew God refused His counsel to his anointed: "And when Saul enquired of the Lord, the Lord answered him not, neither by dreams, nor by Urim, nor by the prophets." Saul, that is to say, had for human reasons of his own, departed from following the counsels of Jehovah, and Jehovah withdrew his counsels from Saul. So did Apollo from his poets when he was displeased with them.

Thus, we may consider that, since poets and seers alike continued writing or prophesying whether or no they felt the divine inspiration, their poems or prophecies were more or less inspired according as, when they were doing any particular piece of writing, they were more or less *en rapport* with the deity. And, prophets and poets were often enough sufficiently wilful in face of the dictates of the godhead. Consider the case of Jonah. At first he would not go to Nineveh to announce that its wickedness had come up before the Lord. Then, being shown by Leviathan the error of his ways, he so vividly announced the displeasure of the Lord to that erring city that, not only did its inhabitants repent of their evil ways in sackcloth and ashes, but "God repented of the evil that he said that he would do unto them and he did it not."

That did not please Jonah, who betook himself out of the city and made himself a shelter, God subsequently providing him with a creeping plant that it might be-shadow the irate prophet. And then God made a worm that destroyed the gourd; and sent a vehement west wind; and the sun beat on the head of the prophet who was looking out to see whether Nineveh was going to be destroyed or not. So with sun and east wind the prophet fainted and said: "It *is* better for me to die than to live."

And God said to Jonah, Doest thou well to be angry for the gourd?

And he said: I do well to be angry even unto death.

Then said the Lord: Thou hast had pity on the gourd for the which thou has not laboured, neither madest it grow; which came up in a night, and perished in a night:

And should not I spare Nineveh, that great city, wherein are more than sixscore thousand persons that cannot discern between their right hand and their left hand; and *also* much cattle?

The moment you read that passage with the shadow of literal inspiration lifted from it—the moment, that is to say, that you read it as if it were a legend or a piece of folklore or part of a book of adventures —it becomes something touching and quaint, and above all humane with a humanity that one does not usually seem to find in the records of Yahweh. If, that is to say, you could regard the story as on a par with a tale of Apollo and one of his naughty old priests, you could take delight in the picture of the reasonable, reasoning, easily placated Godhead, dealing patiently with His rather insupportable prophet and showing kindness and consideration to a gentile nation. And, indeed, the moment you read the Bible freed from the shadow of unreasonable gloom and almost insane vindictiveness with which one is accustomed to invest the Sacred Writings, at once a great deal becomes plain that was not plain before. It is as if different and more humane highlights should spring up in a gloomy landscape.

We are accustomed to think of the Hebrews, portrayed in the Holy Writ, as a people of sadic gloom, ferocity, isolation and xenophobia. And of their God as equally sadic and vindictive. Actually, the note of benevolence and hospitality to the stranger within the gate, and of the Almighty's tolerance for mankind outside Jewry is sounded in the Commandments at the very beginning of the book and continues so to sound in it right to the very end. The God of the Old Testament so regarded is by no means implacable even to those who have not known His name. He is, indeed, not even insensible to human pleasures. He walks in His garden in the cool of the evening. He takes pleasure in the scent of cooked meats and hot showbreads, and in the shining gold decorations of temples. That His face was not implacably set against extra-Palestinian people, we have already seen in the case of Cyrus: "I have even called thee by thy name; I have surnamed thee though thou hast not known me." And we have seen it just now in the story of Jonah. And more markedly still you find it in the account of Solomon's dedication of the Temple, where the great King makes it abundantly clear that the Temple existed not merely for the salvation of the Tribes of Israel but also for "the stranger that comes out of a far country for Thy name's sake."

Moreover concerning a stranger, that *is* not of thy people Israel but cometh out of a far country for thy name's sake.

(For they shall hear of thy great name, and of thy strong hand, and of thy stretched arm;) when he shall come and pray toward this house;

Hear thou in heaven thy dwelling place, and do according to all that the stranger calleth to thee for: that all people of the earth may know thy name, to fear thee, as *do* thy people Israel; and that they may know that this house, I have builded, is called by thy name.

And, indeed, in later days, He appointed even His prophets to be not only His personal servants but also His messengers to the Gentiles. As it is written in Isaiah xlix, 6:

And he said, It is a light thing that thou shouldest be my servant to raise up the tribes of Jacob, and to restore the preserved of Israel: I will also give thee for a light to the Gentiles, that thou mayest be my salvation unto the end of the earth.

Before then, as in Exodus, according to the *Versio Recepta*, and in Deuteronomy according to the Septuagint, immediately after the Flood, the Lord shows His solicitude for the tribes of the Gentiles by appointing to each a special superhuman overlord and protector who shall act as His vice-regent for their affairs.

The trouble for the lay or literary reader of the Old Testament is that there exist so many versions in the original Hebrew and so many translations from one or other of the Hebrew versions, and so many of the Hebrew versions are in part written in Aramaic (the language of the Syrian-Mesopotamian descendants of Aram, the fifth son of Noah), that, though the general tone, tenor or impressions of the whole are singularly homogeneous, when it comes to ascertaining particulars on any given point of history or doctrine, you may try to ascertain the information that you need from any one of six or seven major versions and find them all differing in detail or *in toto*. The main versions that, if we went more deeply into the subject, we should have to consult would be the Hebrew versions in use amongst the orthodox Jews of today, of which, as far as is discoverable, only the Pentateuch, or first five books of the Old Testament, are considered to have been literally inspired by Jehovah; then the Septuagint, a version in Greek made by seventy Hebrew scribes for the use of the literary Pharaoh, Ptolemy Philadelphus, between 285 and 247 B.C.; then the *Versio Recepta*, an early Hebrew version accepted by the Church of Rome as being nearest to an inspired text. The Vulgate, the Latin version, in use by Roman Catholics to this day, was translated from the Septuagint before the day of St. Jerome and liberally retouched by that father of the Church. It was rejected by the sixteenth century leaders of the Reformation on account of alleged mistranslations and faulty readings —the most salient point of combat, to quote one solitary example, in which the translations of both the Old and the New Testaments are concerned, being the case of the heavenly host of the Nativity.

In the Vulgate those messengers of the Almighty announce *Pax hominibus bonae voluntatis* (Peace to such men as be of good will). In the Authorized and other Protestant translations, like those of Luther in German and of de Maistre de Saci in seventeenth century French, the passage of St. Luke runs: "And suddenly there was with the angel a multitude of the heavenly host praising God and saying: Glory to God in the Highest and *peace, good will towards men*:" the Reformers seeing in the "peace to men of good will" of the Catholic version an attempt to limit the peace of God to Papists alone.

If you should wish to follow the matter further you would consult Isaiah, ch. 57, v. 19, and you would find that prophet, whom St. Luke most frequently quotes, prophesying that the Jewish Messiah would bring: "Peace, peace, to (him that is) far off," which would imply 'to Gentiles;' "and to (him that is) near, saith the Lord. . . ." This would seem to support the Protestant version.

But if you read further on you will find in the next verse the Lord saying: "But the wicked are like the troubled sea when it cannot rest, whose waters cast up mire and dirt. . . . (There is) no peace to the wicked, saith my God." This would seem to imply that God limited his peace to those that are of good will.

Eventually, in 1546, the papal council of Trent decided, as far as the Church of Rome was concerned, that, though the original Hebrew, mainly in the version called the *Versio Recepta*, might be consulted by the faithful for historic or aesthetic data, the Vulgate must remain the authority in matters of belief. This decision is responsible for the relatively extreme latitude that Catholic commentators, writing with the full sanction of the Church, could allow themselves over matters like those of history, authorship, date of composition of the various biblical texts. So that whilst believers of other complexions were still shivering over the Assyrian discoveries of Delitsch in *Babel and Bible*, the Jesuit father Destrées, with the full *imprimatur* and *nihil obstat* of the Church, could cheerfully write that, far from being the product of a single inspired pen, the Book of Job must be regarded as a sort of morality play. The greater part of it, he says, being in verse by one or many hands, with a prose prologue of inferior literary quality and religious orthodoxy, written considerably later than the body of the work and in a period of great public disturbance and distress. The whole work, in fact, says he, is a collection of legend and verse from many periods and regions, swept together and edited by a masterful hand at a relatively late period of Jewish independent history.

So that, from a purely literary point of view, we may regard the Bible as being a composite work that underwent many editings—and that many of the editors, even before the *Diaspora*, made emendations to suit their doctrinal or political views. The great periods of these literary activities may be considered, roughly speaking, to have been, first, in the reign of Solomon, who was an enlightened sovereign of literary tastes and poetic and musical gifts. To his period we may assign the Pentateuch. That would be in the tenth century before the Christian era. At the date of the Babylonian captivity the priestly or so-called "Foundation" manuscript of the Pentateuch—which some sects of orthodox Jews still consider to have been literally inspired—was carried away from Jerusalem to Babylon. After the rebuilding of the Temple, which was not completed till about 515 (in the reign of Darius I, though the Jews had been permitted to return to Jerusalem a quarter of a century earlier), the sacred books were brought back to Jerusalem by Nehemiah. In the relative tranquillity of their subjection first to the Persians, then to the Greeks under Alexander, and then to the Ptolemies of Egypt—that is to say between 500 and 300 B.C.—Jewish editors made many additions to and rearrangements of the holy writings. This culminated in the collection of the Hebrew versions used by the seventy Hebrew scribes for the famous Greek translation called the Septuagint, which was made about 320 B.C. This contains many passages that will not be found in the accepted Hebrew versions and omits many that will.

A further period of great literary activity occurred after the Macchabean emancipation—between 167 and the subjection of the Jews by Pompey in 63 B.C. What is called, by purists amongst the reformers, the last of the canonical books of the Old Testament—the Book of Daniel—seems to have been edited in 165. And it is reasonable to consider that that may have seen the last of its editings, for from internal evidence of language and of fact it is obvious that the book, as we have it, is, like the Book of Job, a compilation of passages of prose and verse written at different dates and in varying places and dialects.

We may, therefore, perhaps consider that the Hebrew Bible as we have it today is a product of continual editings and reëditings beginning in the fifth century B.C., these being particularly active during the literature-loving era of the Ptolemies and in the hundred years of the Macchabeans. These reëditings did not stop even with the Dispersal when, mostly in Spain, the Jews compiled the work called the Talmud, which consists of an anthology of precepts, rabbinical traditions and comments on passages from the Old Testament. It has been accepted by a large section of orthodox Jewry as its final book of discipline;

but there are still dissenting Jewish sects that refuse to be guided by anything but the Old Testament.

It must be remembered that like all the great literary works that preceded the mechanical reproduction of books—like the *Iliad* and the *Odyssey*, the *Canons* of Confucius, the *Vedas*, the *Sagas*, *The Arabian Nights,* the *Mabinogion*, the *Morte d'Arthur* or the Border ballads, which may still be heard carried as it were from mouth to mouth during the centuries in the remoter districts of both Great Britain and the United States—like all those folk-products, the Bible as we have it must be considered as a mass compilation. Before Solomon, Hebrew lore would seem to have been merely traditional with very little of it even written.

Solomon may well, anticipating the practice of Confucius, have decided to gather these traditions into what became the "Foundation" manuscripts of the Pentateuch. And, according to tradition, that manuscript included some, at least, of the psalms. Obviously not all the Psalms of David are by that king, but some almost as certainly are. So during that Golden Age of Hebrew literature—for if the kings were poets, we may be certain that their subjects imitated them—a great many of the poetical and historical books found their first expression, whether they passed from tongue to tongue or were written down. And in one form or the other a certain mass of that literature returned from Babylon to be written down, edited, added to, pruned and rendered suitable to the morals of the day—and to have fresh poems and chronicles and Sapiential books grow up side by side with them . . . all through the days of Alexander, of the Ptolemies, and finally of the Macchabeans. And these last, coming last, certainly had the last word with them.

These final renderings were themselves usually coöperative labors executed by a sage and his pupils. And, indeed, there is a very old Jewish tradition according to which the major prophets themselves called in assistance for the transcription of their prophecies. Thus the tradition recorded in the Talmud as to Isaiah states succinctly: "Ezechias and his college wrote Isaiah," Cardinal Meignan making on those words the comment: "Thus orthodoxy is in no way at stake should the authorship of some of the prophecies of Isaiah be rejected"—

though he adds that the editor probably was "a holy personage other than Isaiah but fully in harmony with the feelings and general conceptions of that prophet."*

Nevertheless, though fashions in morals, doctrine and practical wisdom may have changed at various dates in the history of the Jews, a sufficiency of former tenets and views would remain after each recension to give to the whole work an aspect of inconsistency, a fact that may well be put down to the strong foreign influences to which during all of their history the Jews were subjected. . . . And this was particularly the case with their arts, their music and their literature and language. Throughout the Bible from the earliest books to the last one —that of Daniel—foreign words, particularly those expressing details of handicrafts and industries, are of continual occurrence. . . . Thus, to quote merely the first, the middle and last books of the Old Testament: in the story of Moses we read: "And when she could no longer hide him she took for him an ark of bulrushes and daubed it with slime and with pitch and put the child therein." The Egyptian word *teb*, meaning a coffer, is here employed by the Hebrew writer in the form *"tebbah,"* to mean what the translator in the Authorized Version has called an "ark." Towards the middle of the Old Testament again, in the relatively cosmopolitan days of Solomon, in addition to Egyptian verbal influences, a great many more western expressions for the products of handicrafts crept into the language; thus:

He *was* a widow's son of the tribe of Naphtali, and his father *was* a man of Tyre, a worker in brass: and he was filled with wisdom, and understanding, and cunning to work all works in brass. And he came to king Solomon and wrought all his work.

And he made the pillars, and two rows round about upon the one network, to cover the chapiters that *were* upon the top, with pomegranates: and so did he for the other chapiter.

And the chapiters that *were* upon the top of the pillars *were* of lily work in the porch, four cubits.

And the chapiters upon the two pillars *had pomegranates* also above, over against the belly which *was* by the network: and the

* Quoted in *A General Introduction to the Old Testament* by Father Francis Gigot, S.S.

pomegranates *were* two hundred in rows round about upon the other chapiter.

And, still more to our purpose, Hiram spoke a mixed language of an Aramaic-Palestinian type with a certain admixture of Greek. Thus, to disentangle the words used in the Hebrew *Versio Recepta* for the checker work and network and pillars and lily work and pomegranates becomes a feat of philological gymnastics that would be out of place in a work of this character. It is sufficient to say that every one of those words is of one of two foreign origins.

The process continued even into the days of the Macchabees. Thus in Daniel the names of the musical instruments are for the most part taken from the Greek—thus *Kitharis* becomes in Hebrew, *Githaris; Psalterion, Psanterin;* and *Symphony, Sumphonya.*

Today, having like the Hebrews the necessity to use Greek-derived words when it is a matter of the sciences or arts, we also say guitar, psaltery and, when we mean the accompaniment to the voice or other instruments, symphony—meaning something that is played simultaneously. This last instrument—the *Symphony* or *Sumphonya,* was used for accompanying chants or songs in the reign of Antiochus IV, King of Syria—one of the fiercest persecutors of the Jews. It was said to have been the favorite instrument of that monarch; and he died in 164 B.C., the final revision of the Book of Daniel having been made the year before.

CHAPTER FIVE

W E HAVE in the preceding chapter dealt, more elaborately than might at first sight seem to have been called for, with cosmopolitan influences on the philology, arts, handicrafts and points of view of the biblical Hebrew writers. But the point is of immense importance. It is one that affects all the thought and all the literature of the ages that have succeeded that of the Maccabees and the Dispersal. To see that, you have only to consider what we today should have been if the Old Testament had not colored our thought, or the New Testament, which is one stage further in the mingling of Hebrew thought into Greek-Chinese altruism, had not moulded our ethical conceptions. We might not, it is true, have remained naked savages, but certainly our faint simulacrum of a civilization would have had another—and an even more disagreeable—aspect.

And it is not merely that it would have been improbable to the point of incredibility that a literature so humane and so beautiful in its humanity should have proceeded from a limited tribe cabined deep among rough and sun-baked valleys, along the course of the only river in the world that finds no issue in the sea; it is that it is harmful for humanity to imagine that there should have proceeded from a tribe so circumstanced anything good· or beautiful or humane in the largest sense. The word "humane" means something that at once unites and belongs to all the races of mankind, and there is almost no manifestation other than the Old Testament that can so fully lay claim to that proud title.

It is, then, better and more credible and more true to consider that the Jews, owing to their geographical position between the true East and the far-stretching Occident, were peculiarly subject to foreign influences, either because conquering hordes passed over them on the way to further conquests' at a distance, or because, for short periods, they were themselves conquerors and found occasion to call in foreign technicians to add to their comforts or monuments of triumph. They were a race of great intelligence and vigor. They lived almost always in circumstances of considerable frugality, so the greatest expression of their aesthetic talents was in literature. For we may state roughly that no race yet has been able to express itself equally well in the three peacetime departments of life that are called Thought, the plastic arts and comfort (or luxury), and the poorer a race is, the less will be the number of its accomplishments. Thus the Egyptians, Babylonians, and particularly the Cretans, all attained to states of great material luxury and expressed themselves, above all, in statuary and domestic implements that in the case of the Cretans attained to an almost unbelievable beauty. Their literature, on the other hand, was relatively meager and utilitarian. Or the Chinese displayed great genius in Thought and the applied arts that minister to comfort without producing proportionately as much of great distinction in the fine arts. Or the Greeks produced at once the greatest of all Thought and literature and the finest of all the fine arts, whilst on the whole despising luxury or comfort. And the Romans, who carried non-imaginative writing and material comforts to the highest pitch attained to yet by any occidental race—so that, compared with a Roman patrician hedonist, the richest man of our day leads a life of relative squalor—the Romans then, much as it is today with us Anglo-Saxons, had so little of an aesthetic gift that all their *objets d'art*, their sculpture and their non-utilitarian or non-military architecture, were either literally stolen from the Greeks or executed by Greek slaves.

But, having neither great passion nor great opportunities either for displays of luxury or of the plastic arts, the Jews utilized their greatest talents on, and devoted the keenest of their thoughts to Humaner Letters. It is not, therefore, to be wondered at that they achieved not only to a marvelous vision, but also to a technique and verse form from which in later years we have done nothing but decline.

The great difference between the rhythmic verse of the Hebrews and the scanned or inflected verse of their Greek and Roman successors or again the accented or rhymed verse of the troubadours or ourselves, is that the unit of their versification is the thought, not the word imprisoned by letters. It is because of this that it seems as if you yourself were speaking from within your elemental self when you read:

As the hart panteth after the water brooks, so panteth my soul after thee, O God.

My soul thirsteth for God, for the living God: when shall I come and appear before God?

Yet the Lord will command his lovingkindness in the daytime, and in the night his song *shall be* with me, and my prayer unto the God of my life.

Deep calleth unto deep at the noise of thy waterspouts: all thy waves and thy billows are gone over me.

It is not a question of words; still less is it one of letters or metres; it is that, within your own mind, thought calls to thought, and the thought seems infinitely true.

As I have already suggested, the credit for making the beginnings of this discovery must go to an Anglican eighteenth century divine, Bishop Lowth, who died in 1787 and whose *De Sacra Poesia Hebraeorum* was published at Oxford in 1753. His definition of what he called "parallelism" reads a little vaguely at the present day, but that discovery has rendered a signal service to humanity and we may as well pay him the tribute of quoting his own words on the subject:

The correspondence of one verse or line with another, I call parallelism. When a proposition is delivered, and a second is sub-joined to it, or drawn under it, equivalent, or contrasted with it in sense, or similar to it in the form of grammatical construction, these I call parallel lines; and the words of phrases answering to one another in the corresponding lines, parallel terms.

And the Bishop's word "parallelism" has been generally accepted as defining not only Hebrew but also Egyptian and other Eastern verse. What it exactly means will be perfectly clear as soon as we realize that the Hebrew verse line consisted not of so many syllables with or without accents or rhymes. No, the Hebrew verse line consisted of one thought or statement. The Hebrew couplet was made up by the addition of yet another. The lines being incised or written parallel and one above the other, this was called parallelism.

O, come let us sing unto the Lord,
Let us heartily rejoice in the strength of our salvation

Let us come before his presence with thanksgiving
And show us glad in him with psalms.

For the Lord is a great God
And a great King above all gods,

In his hands are all the corners of the earth
And the strength of the hills is his also.

The sea is his and he made it
And his hands prepared the dry land

In those verses the second line always completes or adds to the thought or statement in the first one. But if we take other verses such as these from Proverbs X:

A wise son maketh a glad father:
but a foolish son is the heaviness of his mother.

Treasures of wickedness profit nothing:
but righteousness delivereth from death.

The Lord will not suffer the soul of the righteous to famish:
but he casteth away the substance of the wicked.

He becometh poor that dealeth *with* a slack hand:
but the hand of the diligent maketh rich.

He that gathereth in summer *is* a wise son:
but he that sleepeth in harvest is a son that causeth shame.

we find that the thought is completed not by a confirmation but by an antithesis. The first mode is called technically "synonymous parallelism," the second, "antithetic parallelism." There are other modes called, technically, the "synthetic," the "constructive" or the "climactic" which are too arbitrary for us here to follow them. They are a question of occasional plays on words or do not differ very essentially from the other two forms. Nor, indeed, are all the verses of the poetical books pedantically strict in form. This is poetry to give pleasure and to paint human life, and no arbitrary law is to interfere with it. Thus, you have in Proverbs IX, 16-18:

Whoso *is* simple, let him turn in hither:
and as for *him that wanteth understanding, she* (the strange woman) *saith to him,*

Stolen waters are sweet,
and bread eaten *in secret is pleasant.*

But he knoweth not that the dead *are* there;
and that *her guests* are *in the depths of hell.*

The first two-line verse is here neither synonymous nor antithetic; it is simply a continuation with unrelated matter as it might be in prose. But in the next two couplets the stricter mode is at once returned to.

Let us then consider a few examples from the six poetical books, from Job onwards. We have said that the Book of Job consisted of a prose prologue and epilogue, the body of the book being verse. There follow verses 11 and 13 of the second chapter in a sufficiently prosaic prose, and 1 and 2 of Chapter III, which are as it were the introduction to the verse form; then comes, like a river, the full strength of the magnificent verse.

Now when Job's three friends heard of all this evil that was come upon him, they came every one from his own place; Eliphaz the Temanite, and Bildad the Shuhite, and Zophar the Naamathite: for they had made an appointment together to come to mourn with him and to comfort him.

So they sat down with him upon the ground seven days and seven nights, and none spake a word unto him: for they saw that *his* grief was very great.

After this opened Job his mouth, and cursed his day.

And Job spake and said,

Let the day perish wherein I was born,
And the night in which *it was said*
There is a man child conceived.

Let that day be darkness;
let not God regard it from above,
neither let the light shine upon it.

Let darkness and the shadow of death stain it;
let a cloud dwell upon it;
let the blackness of the day terrify it.

As *for* that night, let darkness seize upon it;
let it not be joined unto the days of the year,
let it not come into the number of the months.

Lo, let that night be solitary,
let no joyful voice come therein.

Let them curse it that curse the day,
who are ready to raise up their mourning.

Let the stars of the twilight thereof be dark;
let it look for light but have *none*;
neither let it see the dawning of the day:

Because it shut not up the doors of my *mother's* womb
nor hid sorrow from mine eyes.

In the above, one may make the note, a certain number of three-
lined verses are introduced into the couplets—though I may as well
make the further note that a great many learned commentators do not
agree to regard a couplet or a triplet as a verse. And, indeed, the most
learned of all state that the Authorized Version in its verse arrangement of the Scriptures is indulging merely in a conventional form of
printing without relation to the verse form of the Hebrew. Neverthe-

less, sense groups of either two or three lines make up the entire body of the poetical books, call the arrangement what you will.

The sudden jump forward from verse back into prose as the book reaches the epilogue is almost more startling than the transition from the prose of the prologue. As thus:

He maketh the deep to boil like a pot; he maketh the sea like a pot of ointment.

He maketh a path to shine after him; *one* would think the deep *to be* hoary.

Upon earth there is not his like, who is made without fear.

He beholdeth all high things: he *is* a king over all the children of pride. . . .

Then Job answered the LORD, and said,

I know that thou canst do every *thing* and *that* no thought can be withholden from thee.

Who *is* he that hideth counsel without knowledge? therefore have I uttered that I understood not; things too wonderful for me, which I knew not.

Hear, I beseech thee, and I will not speak: I will demand of thee, and declare thou unto me.

I have heard of thee by the hearing of the ear: but now mine eye seeth thee.

Wherefore I abhor *myself*, and repent in dust and ashes.

And it was *so*, that after the Lord had spoken these words, unto Job, the Lord said to Eliphaz the Temanite, My wrath is kindled against thee, and against thy two friends: for ye have not spoken of me *the thing that is* right, as my servant. Job *hath*.

So it is perfectly obvious that at least two hands took a part in the writing of this book; and prose having come into use much the later we might regard the Book of Job as having been a compilation of verse of the Solomonic era, edited and provided with a prose framework at least after the time of Herodotus, probably under the Macchabees.

With the psalms we may leave these abstrusenesses nearly aside, and regard them almost as the libretto of an oratorio with the music faintly adumbrated. Musical directions, indeed, are just shown—the most usual of which is *"selah,"* a word frequently regarded as having mysterious significances. It means, actually, a pause between two chants, or integral parts of chants. So also we get a

"Shiggagion of David which he sang unto the Lord concerning the Words of Cush the Benjamite."

This is the 7th Psalm, which begins:

"O Lord, in thee do I put my trust;
Save me from all them that persecute me and destroy me."

which would appear to be a lyrical version of the words of David on Mount Olivet during his persecution by Saul. A *shiggagion* is usually described as being an "irregular dithyramb," but since nothing related to classical metres seems to characterize Hebrew verse structures, it is less confusing to regard the *shiggagion* as a musical form. Other recoverable headings for psalms, for instance *maschil* and *michtam,* would appear to be rather classifications of the literary significance or commendations of, particularly, psalms by the editor. A *maschil* is, apparently, "a particularly fine psalm" . . . Thus, Psalm 42 ("As panteth the hart") that we have already quoted bears in the Authorized Version the caption: "Maschil for the Sons of Korah." Or again forms singled out for particular attention as *michtams*—translated in the Authorized Version as "Golden Psalms"—appear to have oratorical or instructional purposes. Thus Psalms 56-59 are all *michtams*—or songs of deep import doctrinally. Consider for instance Psalm 58:

Do ye indeed speak righteousness, O congregation? do ye judge uprightly, O ye sons of men?

Yea, in heart ye work wickedness; ye weigh the violence of your hands in the earth.

The wicked are estranged from the womb: they go astray as soon as they be born, speaking lies.

Their poison *is* like the poison of a serpent: *they* are like the deaf adder that stoppeth her ear;

Which will not hearken to the voice of charmers, charming never so wisely.

Break their teeth, O God, in their mouth: break out the great teeth of the young lions, O Lord.

Let them melt away as waters *which* run continually: *when* he bendeth *his bow to shoot* his arrows, let them be cut in pieces.

As a snail *which* melteth, let *every one of them* pass away: *like* the untimely birth of a woman, *that* they may not see the sun.

What is for our purposes valuable in this connection of *michtams* is that being so placed together in the body of the psalms, we may consider them as proving that the remainder of the psalms were considered, at any rate by the final editors, as being, relatively speaking, lay poems—as if the *michtams* were gathered together and set apart for a special devotional reading or singing. The remainder of the psalms, then, in conjunction with the other poetical books, become rather a rendering of life than devotional pieces. They render, that is to say, moods, emotions, passions, adventures, domestic happenings, disasters—as if you should make an anthology of French or English verse from the earliest date to the present time and insert into them very properly a collection of devotional pieces. That the deity should be frequently invoked even in the less devotional poems is not unnatural. To simple and direct peoples, their deity plays an everyday part and is all-pervasive. The Jews, like the Pilgrim Fathers, had the name of God forever on their lips simply because in their usually desperate circumstances they felt the need for a continuous conviction of supernatural backing. The poetical books, in fact, are to be regarded as renderings of the normal life of a people in the relatively exalted frame of mind that will make a whole people find vent for itself in songs and music. And that product is group poetry.

That is not to say that poetry in the Bible is confined to the six poetical books. You will find songs or chants in the latest of the prophets as in the psalms, or the early fragments of books like Ruth. Indeed, occasionally in the latest books of Prophecy you find the evidence of music in every way as strong as it is in these psalms. Thus, in the Book of Amos you have a striking passage with a burden, "Yet have ye not returned to me, saith the Lord," which is as much evidence of chanting as you find in Psalm 136 with its burden of "For his mercy endureth forever." The psalmist no doubt sang, and his hearers chanted their monotonous refrain:

And slew famous kings: *for his mercy endureth for ever:*

Si-hon king of the Amorites: *for his mercy endureth for ever:*

And Og the king of Bashan: *for his mercy endureth for ever:*

And gave their land for an heritage: *for his mercy endureth for ever:*

So too intoned the prophet Amos, who would seem to have written in 750 B.C., whilst his hearers chanted their refrain:

So two *or* three cities wandered unto one city, to drink water; but they were not satisfied: *yet have ye not returned unto me, saith the Lord.*

I have smitten you with blastings and mildew: when your gardens and your vineyards and your fig trees and your olive trees increased, the palmerworm devoured them: *yet have ye not returned unto me, saith the Lord.*

I have sent among you the pestilence after the manner of Egypt: your young men have I slain with the sword, and have taken away your horses; and I have made the stink of your camps to come up into your nostrils; *yet have ye not returned unto me, saith the Lord.*

"I have overthrown *some* of you, as God overthrew Sodom and Gomorrah, and ye were as a firebrand plucked out of the burning: *yet have ye not returned unto me, saith the Lord.*

Amos was by far the most cultivated of the minor prophets. He would appear to have been, as it were, a rich country gentleman with herds of valuable sheep. He could afford to travel a great deal and must have had at his disposal all the literary tuition that was then available. Indeed, he seems to be the only one of the biblical writers who had a literary personality resembling those of modern authors. You could, indeed, regard his book as a poem, so near do some of his chapters come in literary method to that of the writers of the psalms themselves. So that for this writer, when he is letting himself be fanciful—and not in the least attempting to bind the reader to that conviction—Amos is the first discoverable author. Indeed, he helps us still further to see how the Bible is really constructed. The early Hebrews and at least one of the more modern Jewish rites regard the twelve books as being one book—the Book of the Minor Prophets. If you so regard it, it would appear, like the Book of Job, as a sweeping together of legends and of poems severely edited, perhaps by a college or perhaps by one or more editors. In that case, the Book of Amos may have been less interfered with than any of the others simply because of the superiority of his original style. He prophesied—and subsequently wrote down his prophecies—at a time when Israel was enjoying its richest, short spell of imperialism, luxury, and cosmopolitan contacts under the great ruler Jeroboam II. This king extended the kingdom until it filled again all the limits of the Kingdom of David. Indeed, the bursts of collecting and editing poems and prophecies would appear invariably to have gone on whilst Jewry prospered—under Solomon, Jeroboam II and the Macchabees. But most of the matter they swept up had been chanted in periods of anxiety and disaster.

We have not space to go very much more deeply even into the poetical books. I like, however, to imagine myself discovering internal evidence of one more literary figure. For didn't the pen that wrote for the psalms the *maschil* called A Song of Loves:

> My heart is inditing a good matter: I speak of the things which I have made touching the king: my tongue *is* the pen of a ready writer.

> Thou art fairer than the children of men: grace is poured into thy lips: therefore God hath blessed thee for ever. . . .

> All thy garments *smell* of myrrh, *and* aloes, and cassia, out of the ivory palaces, whereby they have made thee glad. . . .

> Kings' daughters *were* among thy honorable women: upon thy right hand did stand the queen in gold of Ophir.

> And the daughter of Tyre *shall be there* with a gift; *even* the rich among the people shall intreat thy favor.

> The king's daughter *is* all glorious within: her clothing *is* of wrought gold.

Didn't the pen that wrote that have a finger also in the play in which we read:

> Thy cheeks are comely with rows of jewels, thy neck with chains *of gold*.

> We will make thee borders of gold with studs of silver.

> While the king sitteth at his table, my spikenard sendeth forth the smell thereof. . . .

> The beams of our house are cedar, and our rafters of fir.

It would be a luxury to quote more of the Song of Solomon which is the blissful masterpiece of the greatest of all anthologies, but we must be getting on towards Herodotus. . . . Yet it is pleasant, and indeed juster, to think of Jewry of old having its feasts, its singings, its stage plays, its cedar beams, its cosmetics which were disapproved of and worse: "And she painted her face and tired her head and looked out at a window." Jewry had even, not only its alliterations but also its puns. Of those there are many in the Bible as in Jeremiah I.

> Moreover the word of the Lord came unto me, saying, Jeremiah, what seest thou? And I said, I see a rod of an almond tree.

> Then said the Lord unto me, Thou hast well seen: for I will hasten my word to perform it,

the Hebrew word "*shaked*" meaning both an "almond tree" and "I will hasten."

And it had its hospitalities:

> He asked for water and she gave him milk; she brought in butter in a lordly dish. . . .

which is this writer's unexplainedly favorite verse in all the Bible— if it isn't:

> It is vain for you to rise up early, to sit up late and eat the bread of sorrow: for so he giveth his beloved sleep.

And so, having come thus to the night, let us close with the words that always seem as if they must have been shouted amidst the re-sounding of brass:

> Praise ye the Lord. Praise God in his sanctuary: praise him in the firmament of his power.

> Praise him for his mighty acts: praise him according to his excellent greatness.

> Praise him with the sound of the trumpet: praise him with the psaltery and harp.

Praise him with the timbrel and dance: praise him with stringed instruments and organs.

Praise him upon the loud cymbals: praise him upon the high sounding cymbals.

Let every thing that hath breath praise the Lord. Praise ye the Lord.

And so we come to Herodotus and the art of prose, for it is about time that we attended to the handmaid of literature, and if we are to do that we may as well begin with the greatest exponent of that art immediately after attending to the greatest of all verse poems. Herodotus came about three hundred years after the poet-prophet-prosateur Amos, the date of Amos being about 750 and that of the historian of Cyrus being c 484 to c 425, B.C.—that two hundred and fifty years being about long enough for the full development of the art of prose in all its fineness. . . . And, in the end, we have to consider that the use of prose for records or for works of the imagination was really a matter of materials.

Until, say, 1,500 years before the Christian era, almost the only materials for rendering statements at all permanent were stone and bricks and tiles. These gave scope only for records that were quite literally as incisive as possible; a man who has to record his thoughts in stone will think a long time in order to make his expression as short as possible. For that purpose also most of the early eastern nations used hieroglyphs or, as in the case of the Chinese who still use them, idiographs—that is to say, highly conventionalized drawings of objects or ideas. Say, for instance, you make two parallel marks as thus ――――, you convey the idea of the horizon of the earth with, above it, the heavens. If you then join them together vertically as thus ――╱――, you set up the idea of some influence binding both the heavens and the earth. And so is conveyed the idea *"heaven-and-earth-in-one"* which we transliterate into *"ts'ien"* or "God." Or the Egyptians incised or portrayed in paint a male in a loincloth, the legs apart in profile with the two hands raised at the ends of half-

outstretched arms, and the idea conveyed was that of a man in the
act of worship. In between the two, the Assyrians and Medes and
Persians used a sort of writing called cuneiform—an arrangement of
wedge-shapes according to a convention that expressed ideas and
sounds. Say five hundred years later various convenient and easily
portable materials—the inner sides of hides, leather that grew finer
and finer, tablets of wood, metal sheets covered with wax, the inner
bark of the papyrus stem cut into sheets and toughened by various
processes—were used to hold thoughts expressed either, as in the case
of wax or wood, by incisions, or by paint brushes or reeds split to
make pens. Then—as it is generally agreed—the great seafaring and
trading race, the Phoenicians (who in themselves were illiterate in
the sense that they left no literature at all, being allied to the luxury-
loving, highly aesthetic Cretans) invented and in their journeys spread
through the earth, the idea of what we call the alphabet—the Greek
alphabet commencing with the letters "alpha," "beta" and the Hebrew with "aleph," "beth."

The letters of course expressed, not thoughts like the Egyptian
hieroglyphs or the Chinese idiographs, but simply sounds, the "t" representing the sound made by expelling the breath and setting the
tongue against the teeth, the "m" by doing the same thing and
checking the breath with the lips. So words, which today we regard
almost automatically as combinations of letters, became the units of
imaginative expression, and the practice of direct expression of thought
suffered a more or less gradual decline.

It is in many things a misfortune, for imagine how much more
convenient and educative it would be both for writer and reader if
a single sign could represent a complete idea—as, say, the stylized
picture of a man thumbing his nose (representing a common schoolboy gesture of insult) could be taken to imply: "We have the honor
to acknowledge the receipt of your letter but much regret that we
are unable to avail ourselves of your amiable offer. . . ." Humanity,
indeed, has ever since the discovery of the alphabet been engaged
in inventing symbols to take the place of words—a process which
you might symbolize as a progress from the Roman R.I.P. (*requiescat*

in pace) to the production of the Anglo-Saxon masterpieces "£," "$," "&," "%"—the "$" being an actual idiograph for "pieces of eight."

The matter is too technical—and too disputatious—to enter upon very fully here. But it would be a good thing to keep in mind various, as it were, mappings out of the territory of literature. Thus, we may as well surmise that Solomon ordered the getting together of the Pentateuch just as Ptolemy Philadelphus ordered the assembling and translation of the Septuagint. And the work of both Solomon and Confucius was very similar in nature. Both employed themselves with getting together oral traditions and roughly written or incised directions for rites, music, hygiene, habitations, so that the men of their day might find tabulated how their fathers had lived and regulated their lives, it being postulated that the men of their day had vastly degenerated from the habits of their sires.

Now supposing that, as some authorities state, the use of various early forms of the alphabet became fairly common in the countries bounded by the eastern shores of the Mediterranean about eleven hundred years before the Christian era; then that fact may well have occasioned and must certainly have facilitated the Solomonic collection and editing of the early legends and songs of the Hebrews. And, once that method of presenting literatures became widespread, it followed almost inevitably that the very spirit of that literature itself would change. Incised literature through necessity will be much more sparing in words or hieroglyphics than the literature expressed in paintings; words expressed by letters will, when put together, leave an entirely different impression on the mind from the record of thoughts expressed by hieroglyphics or conventional renderings of objects by means of paints. Man being intensely conservative, the change will come about with an extreme slowness. People used to expressing their meanings by symbols of thought will only very slowly change their habit. Probably they will begin by using words expressed by letters only for material purposes such as the keeping of accounts or the conveying of items of news. And even when the feat of converting ideas into words and then expressing them by letters may have been achieved, the tenacious mind of man will go on expressing itself to itself by wordless and unlettered processes.

But once the principle of keeping accounts or recording news by means of words transcribed by letters—once that utilitarian process becomes widely established, you will have two forms of literature running concomitantly. There will be the older form, that of verse poetry, which will come to serve more and more strictly for the expression of emotions. The modern invention will be more and more applied to material uses. Thus, prose of the prosaic order would be invented. I do not ask the reader to accept this as a dogmatic statement. But as a figurative image it may be taken to be fairly satisfactory.

As the new inventions gained force, the ambitions of their practitioners grew greater. The patient account keeper, inscribing columns of figures with a split reed pen on sheets of the prepared inner bark of the papyrus plant, would come to employ the new quick method of communication when desiring to let the Pharaoh know that his peach trees were in blossom or that a new and horrible disease had decimated the first born of numerous families in one province or another. He would ask himself why his form of the language might not be used for recording matters more sublime; for recording, that is to say, not merely the number of captives taken in a victory but the manoeuvres employed by the generals and the territories affected by such victories. So, gradually, the account-keeping scribe would, according to the light vouchsafed him, become a humdrum chronicler or a historian and even a great prose writer. In the specific case of Greece, these transitional prose scribes were known as logographers— writers of words. Their first function after the keeping of accounts was that of recording genealogies and family histories. Later they chronicled geographic and scientific discoveries and showed how historic events affected the boundaries of nations. But before the art of prose had reached even that rudimentary stage in Greece the various forms of verse poetry had developed themselves and reached perfection.

You had, to begin with, the heroic verse of Homer which dates back many centuries before even the discovery and practice of elegiac verse in the seventh century B.C.

It is unnecessary to debate here whether the *Iliad* and the *Odyssey* are to be considered as group poetry or as the product of the pen of one singular genius. Sometimes it is fashionable to consider that these great poems are, like the folksongs of other races, a collection of ballads recited over camp fires and corrected and recorrected to suit the taste of various reciters or audiences during periods of hundreds or even thousands of years. At other times it is the fashion to consider that they are the work of one great brain which gathered together folksongs and legends and, like Confucius in China or the editors of the Psalms of David or the Book of Job, made of them a work observing the unities of metrical poetry. Samuel Butler, the author of the *Way Of All Flesh* and *Erewhon*, even wrote a half-humorous volume to prove that the writer of the *Odyssey* was a woman.

We may, however, for the moment leave that side of the matter alone, contenting ourselves here with recording the fact that the two poems are two unities forming one magnificent whole. And we may add that the form of verse in which these poems are written, that of the dactylic hexameter, had been fully developed and perfected at a very early date and certainly before the seventh century B.C. Following them in that and the sixth century there came a great burst of exploration of various metrical forms. Chief among these were the elegiac, more or less graceful or occasionally mournful, pieces of verse, usually expressed, as was the case in the Hebrew poems, in couplets or groups of three lines. Thus Solon, the Lacedaemonian lawgiver—who is famous as having addressed to Croesus the solemn warning "Deem no man fortunate till he be dead"—used the elegiac form for addressing his legal precepts to the Athenians. Or Tyrtaeus, the Athenian poet, reanimated the failing spirits of the Spartans with his elegiac couplets during the second Messenian war. Or Mimnermus was fabled as being the inventor of the sentimental elegy, and Theognis the gnomic poems in elegiac form. All these poets adorned the early and middle seventh century. Archilochus of Paros, equally in the seventh century, invented iambic and other metres, and used them for addressing the fiercest of satires to anyone whom he disliked. Still later in the same century there were evolved the two forms of lyric verse for accompaniment by music, the Dorian which was severe and used for expressing only exalted sentiments, and the Lesbian which expressed romantic, sentimental or passionate emotions. The greatest proponents of this last form of art were Alcaeus and Sappho, and in the lighter vein, Anacreon. And finally in the same century there was evolved the choral lyric whose name speaks for itself. The earliest known writer in this mood was Alcman, who was born about 650. He was followed by the much greater Stesichorus who died c 620. Later in this mode there sprang up in the fifth century B.C. Simonides, who was the uncle of Bacchylides, who in turn was the uncle of Aeschylus; and Pindar, who for many centuries was considered the greatest of all lyric poets—though even in our eighteenth century, by poets like Pope, Bacchylides was considered almost his equal.

This of course is the merest catalogue of practitioners in the various forms of verse that were evolved in that really miraculous century. It is interesting to make the note that at the same time innumerable wars, revolutions, civil strifes and abdications were agitating the Greek world—interesting, because it will never be decided whether the arts flourish best in times of peace and prosperity or whether they achieve their highest forms when public attention, and no doubt that of the artist, is riveted on the disasters or developments of states in their forms of government.

Hitherto, as far as we have gone, we have seen that the art of writing seemed to flourish most when states were at their most imperialistically tranquil. That was certainly the case with the Egyptians, the Chinese and the Hebrews. That of the Greek poets would seem to cast a formidable vote on the other side.

Before returning to, and rather more minutely examining, the case of Greek prose, we must still give momentary attention to Greek drama. This other form of expression, like that of verse poetry, was extremely primitive in its origins. It began, that is to say, amongst the earliest mists of time in the dithyrambic dances and songs that accompanied the earliest Bacchic festivals. By the time of Aeschylus— who preceded Herodotus, the first great prose writer, by half a century—it had on its tragic side attained to a pitch of majesty and of technical perfection such as no other art of any other century ever reached. It lasted in this state of perfection, as far as we can judge by its remains, from the time of Aeschylus, who was born in 526 and died in 455 B.C., to that of Euripides, who was born in 480 and died in 406. His great rival, Sophocles, died the year after. The ferocious comic muse of Aristophanes flourished a little later; his dates went from c 456 to c 380, Herodotus being born about seventy years before his birth. What is called the "new comedy"—that of Aristophanes being known as the "old" and the "middle"—came considerably later; Menander, the greatest and most charming of its exponents, was born in 342 B.C. and died in 292. The new comedy, it is interesting to note, was a popular form of art almost exactly paralleling, at least in plot, the most conventional of sentimental dramas of the cinema of our day. The plot, that is to say, of nearly all of them showed a king's son or aristocrat of sorts, who falls in love with a supposed slave girl and after the usual searchings of heart and low-comedy passages, into which political allusions usually get introduced, the slave girl invariably turns out to be, herself, the daughter of a king. We thus observe the following facts as to the development of these relative forms of the literary art: First, heroic verse-forms develop themselves from prehistoric chants. These follow the developments of various metrical fancies and niceties and lyric perfections. Side by side with these went the primitive mimes which developed into the strictly formal tragic drama. At this point, prose steps in and gradually develops itself into an organ of the greatest fluidity or the utmost majesty. And so the major forms keep on their way until they lose themselves in conventional comedy, in technical tricks and agreeable frivolity, and until prose itself deteriorates into formalisms and degeneracy. And then the process must begin all over again.

It is, perhaps, fortunate for us that Herodotus seems to spring fully equipped and armed, from his background of unknown prose—like Pallas Athene from the forehead of Jove—straight into our consciousness. For, except for the drudgery of the logographers, Hecataeus and Hellanicus—and of them little enough has been preserved—almost no trace of pre-Herodotian Greek prose has come down to us. He stands, thus, alone, as he was the most perfect of prose writers and historians.

The great prose historians of Greece were three: Herodotus, Thucydides and Xenophon. Each was consummate in his way. But Thucydides was at once a great capitalist, a great public character, as well as a philosopher, so with his lucid prose there went a certain pomposity, a certain sense of importance. His history of the Peloponnesian War is distinguished at once by scrupulous accuracy and impartiality. These are the more remarkable in that the eight books of that work were written in exile, after as an admiral he had failed to save Amphipolis from the Spartans, he being at the time the Athenian naval commander. Thus, his history is a work of relative sophistication written by a man of importance in retirement much as histories of later wars are today written—but with so much less lucidity, temperateness and impartiality!—by unsuccessful generals and admirals retired. Of its class, his history, therefore, stands apart, as do those of Herodotus and Xenophon.

These historians succeeded each other in the following sequence: Herodotus B.C. c 484-424, Thucydides c 460-400 and Xenophon c 430-352. And their histories are characterized, respectively, by a sort of not unexpected sequence of developments. It is as if Herodotus, bursting into a new world, found everything so fresh and delightful that he had little desire to do more than chronicle the beautiful fairy tales, legends, and facts of which he was an eye-witness in that amazing corner of the Mediterranean world. Thucydides may have followed him by only fifteen to twenty years at birth, but he lived, if only a quarter of a century longer, into a world more tired, more self-conscious and more agitated. So that his work from its very striving after scholastic impartiality, has none of the delights and vivaciousness of the writings of Herodotus. He had traveled less. He had taken a greater part in public affairs. He was, in consequence, less spontaneous. The much later Xenophon, who was born some six years before the death of Herodotus and lived for some fifty years after the death of Thucydides, has all the geniality and composure of the rich country gentleman who becomes an admirable general, covering himself with the comfortable glory of one of the most successful military feats that time has ever known. To read his *Anabasis* at school is memorable, not merely as a coming into contact with one of the great literary mouthpieces of the world, but as if it were an adventure that you made yourself. You are one of ten thousand men retreating in good order from the defeat of the monarch who employed you. And, just as in the late war when you passed from under the command of any other general into that of Lord Plumer, you felt an extraordinary sense of safeness, so, after the defeat of Cyrus the Younger, who had employed you and your general, you passed under the sole command of General Xenophon, and you felt that you would be handled by a quiet, good-humored, absolutely competent leader. So if there were any human possibility of saving you and your comrades, he would bring you safe to the shores of the sea and the harbors that you had desired. And won't the little mannerisms of the beautiful writer remain with you until your dying day—the record that today we marched so many parasangs; that we went into a council of war; that someone suggested something optimistic and always *"Ho de Chlearchos eipe"* (Chlearchos suggested . . . courses more temperate.) And you were surrounded by semi-hostile tribes just as today would be the case in the hot sands of the desert; and you fought an outpost battle here and there. But always you had at the back of your mind the feeling of the comfortable, quiet brain of General Xenophon who was never unduly disturbed or despondent and who knew always what to do and how to do it. Until, at last, the leading files arrived at the top of a great dune and there went up a great cry: *"Thalasseh! . . . Thalasseh!"* (The sea! . . . The sea!).

This writer with a simple and gentle style is almost the first of authors to impress his personality through his writings upon the world. Homer remains a myth. King David of the psalms is visible to you only as a conception of Michelangelo, or any other painter. But Xenophon you can always see in khaki with gilt tabs—a man of quiet movements and of great wisdom as became one who had been the favorite pupil of Socrates and whose *Memorabilia* of the life and habits of that philosopher will stand for you beside Boswell's *Life of Johnson*, though all the writings of Plato may leave you cold.

But Herodotus is something finer than either the genialities of Xenophon or the relatively pompous philosophic analyses of Thucydides. Herodotus is so interested in the world that surrounded him that he hardly had time to leave any impress of himself on his writings. You don't ever see him. He is a being with a voice saying continually, "Look, look, how thrilling that is!" Like the prophet Amos he would seem to have been a man of a middling station of wealth— of a wealth sufficient to let him, with his insatiable curiosity, travel incessantly about the whole of the world that was known (or that was at least important) to the metropolitan and colonial Greeks of his day. He visited Asia Minor, Babylon, Phoenicia, Egypt, Thrace, the Ionian Islands, nearly the whole of Greece and very much of the greater Greece of the colonial system. And during all his travels he conversed unceasingly—with priests, with peasants, with satraps, with women carting wool, with packmen leading their mules down the rocky ways beneath the great pine trees of the Mediterranean basin. So that when, towards the age of forty, he was tired of travel or his funds gave out, he settled for a time in Athens with a head stuffed with the most delightful ana of the world. He knew what really happened to Helen after she was supposed to have eloped with Paris. He was acquainted with the most remarkable of all detective stories—how Rhampsinitus found out and rewarded with his sister's hand the thief who had stolen innumerable pieces of gold from the Imperial Treasury. He was at once credulous and cynical. He would recall marvels as if he believed every word that he was told, and in the end would slip in: "This is hardly to be believed." Or as in the case of the miraculous extinction of the fire that was to have burned Croesus, he would add: "Others tell this story differently." You see before your eyes the whole stretch of those singular climes from which have come all that is most bright and beautiful in our modern temperaments. You see spread out beneath you whilst you read him, the mountains between Thebes and Babylon, the seas from Asia Minor to Sicily, the Aegean Islands and the palms on the Nile bank. But, above all, you commune with a beautiful and humane spirit. For, after having spent some time in idleness or in the observation of the manners and customs of the citizens of Athens, Herodotus removed himself to one of the colonies that the Greeks were establishing in Italy. His removal is said to have taken place in the year 453—in which case he would have been forty-one years of age—and the colony was that of Thurium, otherwise Thurii in Lucania. Here he would seem to have been settled on a farm such as the Greeks provided for their colonists, the gift including a small income. The colony, as we know, suffered from inroads of the Italian barbarians and it never prospered very much. Nevertheless, in his office or in his home, Herodotus found time to write his matchless projection of the world of his day. His book purports to be the history of the struggle between the Greeks and the Persians which ended successfully for Greece when he was aged about four. But between the beginning and the end of that war he contrives to insert so many digressions as to the habits and customs of any of the tribes mentioned that, though the actual main subject of the war never goes completely by the board, his work presents the aspect of extreme and engrossing complexity. It is sufficient for any new character to be introduced into his pages to let Herodotus go off at once upon a new journey. Supposing a new character came, say, from Hyrcania: he would set forth either in person or imagination for that distant spot and would bring into his narrative descriptions of the religious rites, the agricultural customs and the vicissitudes of the inhabitants for generations back. That done, he would return to Babylon or Thebes or wherever he last left the seat of the war and after some digressions as to the habits and lore of the priests of Thebes with its hundred gates, he would record, as we have already seen, the Theban account of the wanderings of Helen of Troy and so carry Cyrus and his wars forward for a month or two until once more the opportunity for a digression permitted him to escape from his main stream.

The instructed reader will perceive that in thus handling his matter, Herodotus, 2,500 years ago, anticipated the technique most usual to the novelist and historian of the present day. His history of his own time, had it been written by, say, either the late Joseph Conrad or the living Aldous Huxley, could scarcely have differed in form, though obviously the recording temperament would be different. On the face of it, it might have seemed better to begin the story of the war at the beginning and to carry it straightforwardly onwards until. it arrived at the Grecian victory. Actually, as Herodotus knew, if you wish to present, say, Cyrus, as he lived, it is a good thing to get him in with oome vividness and then to abandon him for a time in favor of Rhampsinitus. Because, when you return to Cyrus, you will seem to be taking up an acquaintance again with an already known figure, and you will seem to deepen your knowledge of his habits or vicissitudes quite disproportionately. But whether you approve or disapprove of the literary methods of the great historian, you could never deny that the main astonishing note of this chronicle is that of humaneness. Croesus, the great and externally fortunate—but last—King of Lydia, drew from Solon, the Athenian lawgiver, as we have seen, the apophthegm "Deem no man fortunate till his death." And with his great and always increasing fortune in gold, with his splendid fleets and his noble alliances, Croesus received the saying at once with distaste and incredulity. But Nemesis attended on him, though what sin he had committed other than that of being too fortunate is not recorded. At any rate, it was his one misfortune that saved his life. He had, to his mortification, a deaf and dumb son. He conquered Asia Minor and the fame of his exploits and wealth became so great that they must needs attract the attention of Cyrus, the humane rebuilder of the Temple of Solomon. Cyrus, looking about for new worlds to conquer, led his legions against Croesus, and after a number of coincidental failures of his troops or the troops of his allies to arrive in time on the fields of battle, Croesus found himself shut up in the citadel of Sardis and surrounded by the troops of Cyrus. The citadel was supposed to be impregnable but, as happened in the Siege of Quebec by Wolfe, a certain number of Persian soldiers scaled its heights and, entering the chamber in which Croesus found himself, prepared to slaughter him. But at the sight, his deaf and dumb son suddenly recovered his voice and exclaimed, "Soldier, do not dare to slay Croesus, the King." So Croesus was temporarily spared and carried before Cyrus. Cyrus prepared to put him to death by burning. And just as Joan of Arc upon her pyre exclaimed three times "Jesus!", so on his, Croesus, remembering the Athenian lawgiver's dictum, cried out three times the name of Solon. And having not Anglo-Saxons but Persians to listen to him, and crying out not the name of his and their Redeemer but merely that of a revered lawgiver, Croesus was spared. For Cyrus, the humane and the pensive, remembered that of Cyrus, too, it might be said that he could not be deemed fortunate until he was dead, and decided to extinguish the brands beneath the body of the man who had brought that saying back to his memory. Nay, more, he made Croesus his counsellor in the conduct of his wars, and this proved admirably helpful not only to Cyrus, but to the subjects of Croesus himself. For Croesus, observing that the Persian soldiery were setting fire to the city of Sardis, disgorging its citizens and carrying off their wealth, exclaimed drily to his conqueror that it would be more profitable if he prevented his men from doing anything of the sort. For, said he, if Cyrus permitted his men to turn that opulent city into a desert and to slay its citizens, thus putting an end to their earning power, not only would Cyrus himself be impoverished to the extent that he would not be able to tax those citizens and otherwise enrich himself at their expense, but his troops being rendered fabulously wealthy would at least desire to desert his army, even if they were not rendered so proud-stomached as to attempt to mutiny against their owner with a view to assuming his royal dignities. So the inhabitants of Sardis were saved, and Cyrus, observing the humane rule of Croesus, not only prospered to the day of his death, but established one of the mightiest and most civilized empires that the world has ever known. For instead of attempting to establish, after the habit of most other conquerors to the present day, a homogeneous empire with all its subject citizens ruined and enslaved and bound down to the worship of the conqueror's god and the observance of his moral code, he permitted those he conquered to retain not only their creeds, habits and moral standards, but the greater part of their wealth, contenting himself by exacting in the form of normal taxes the tribute that enabled him to maintain his empire in peace or to go upon further wars. So that, although he perished gloriously in battle with the Masagetes, his son Cambyses succeeded to his wealth and power, and Cyrus himself, as we have seen, was blessed by Jehovah.

Thus saith Cyrus king of Persia, All the kingdoms of the earth hath the Lord God of heaven given me; and he hath charged me to build him an house in Jerusalem, which *is* in Judah. Who *is there* among you of all his people, the Lord his God *be* with him, and let him go up.

So that there in one story you perceive what must be so far the moral of this work, the doctrines of humaneness going, coiling as it were, from Sardis and Lydia to Babylon and again to Jerusalem and coming thus to us who sit here in times so infinitely more ferocious, to be to us at once a cause of shame and enlightenment.

CHAPTER SIX

T HE glory that was Greece comes down to us in fact not so much in great buildings or in memorials of an incredible splendor, like the "Winged Victory." It comes to us still more in the written rendering of spoken words. To see the Elgin marbles or the Nikeapteros or the Parthenon, the remains of temples and of palaces, you must journey to London, to Paris, or to Athens and the Isles of Greece. But you may never stir from the fireside by which you were born and yet all the songs of the Aegean Sea may visit you in your log hut in the Appalachian Mountains. Buildings must stay where they are set up, great memorials in marble are difficult to carry across the seas, but illuminated and enlightening thought will travel across waters as the messengers of the Gods could fly from the apex of Olympus to the pillars of Hercules and beyond. Everything in Athens was not merely Athenian. The mobs of the city, the markets, the rumors, the public back-bitings, the political intrigues were very much as they are in the cities of our day. If you will read the *Characters* of Theophrastus, you will see the Mr. Jones of the Athenian suburbs going to market for a dinner that he is giving that evening. After bargaining for a couple of lobsters he decides that the price is too high considering that his guests of that night are of no particular importance and unlikely to advance him in his public office. And so, he decides to feed them on tunny, the Mediterranean version of the tuna fish of the Gulf of Mexico. There will have been that morning an immense catch of those fish, so that they can be had for almost anything. And, he reflects, since his guests are coming from a distant village, they will not know how cheap that fish is that day. . . . No, the seething mobs of Athens did not differ much in preoccupations from those you will find now whether at Coney Island or on Hampstead Heath. They thought of the *sou* with all the avidity of the Paris housewife of today. And they had in matters of dress and cosmetics all the spirit of rivalry that you will find in a New Jersey or South England bathing place. But they expressed themselves more vividly. Their motions were more vivacious, and, above all—the world of knowledge being more circumscribed—they had infinitely more knowledge of the world than that possessed by either gentle or simple of the days that followed the evolution of the printed book or page. Thus, political and social knowledges were infinitely more realistic and interests more awakened. And the distillations from their street cries and rumors were, therefore, infinitely truer to the necessities and ideals of humanity than in our case they possibly could be. It is today, as it has been for many generations, a matter of extreme difficulty to draw morals from the lives of the men around us. We get our knowledge of life so seldom from the living fortunes or misfortunes of our fellow citizens and so almost universally from inaccurate and negligent printed matter. But Aeschylus or Sophocles, walking through the streets of Athens, had little but market rumors to distract them from the view of the humanity that surrounded them. And, in knowing what had happened in hundreds of lives, they could see and did not have merely to imagine how destiny works on humanity.

Let us now consider a little more carefully other forms of Greek Literature, which we dismissed with a word or two, before taking up the case of Greek prose.

It would seem to be unnecessary to say very much about the writing of Homer. We may presume that anyone who makes any pretense to any shade of appreciation of learning or literature must have at least some knowledge of the woes of Troy, the wrath of Achilles, the wanderings of Ulysses and the crowned labors of Penelope. Such a man must have read at least a little of the translations of Pope or Chapman or the remarkable translation by T. E. Lawrence or the very admirable vernacular rendering by W. H. D. Rouse, from which we shall later quote. In any case, to appreciate the beauty of Homer, all that is necessary is to read him. Nobody by his comments can enhance the pleasure that you will have from that reading. We shall nevertheless essay a more elaborate estimate when later we compare the *Aeneid* with the *Odyssey*.

But in pursuing our history of literature, which is in fact a history of human imaginative thought, certain exterior explanations cannot but be useful. It is necessary, then, again to remember that the *Iliad* and the *Odyssey* are undoubtedly a picking up, a recension of early legends, attaching to an immense Affair—an immense, almost chemical reaction between a higher, more luxurious and more aesthetic civilization from the East, attacking or attacked by a relatively lean, relatively puritanic, relatively, perhaps, better armed civilization coming from the West.

What the real cause of the struggle between Greeks and Trojans may have been we shall never know with certainty—whether it was a dynastic war, or whether it was a war in which the Greeks, exploiting the invention of a new material for armament, merely determined to enrich themselves at the expense of wealthier but less well armed neighbors. Or whether, in actual fact, since there is no end to human madness, the puritanic Greeks of that early day really did resent the carrying off of a woman by a too seductive and too beautiful Eastern prince—all these are things that we shall never know and may well, when occasion serves, debate until that day when the sun shall set in the East. And it is to be remembered—it should indeed be remembered with great vividness—that the Graeco-Trojan legend is by no means exhausted by the *Iliad*. Greek, Hellenic, Alexandrian, Asiatic and Latin commentaries and derivations must, were they today all discoverable, form a body of literature at least as great as the endless commentaries, expositions, interpretations and higher criticisms that have been devoted to our own Holy Writ since first the Hebrew tribes escaped across the Red Sea and those compilations began. Indeed, if you regard the *Iliad* and the *Odyssey* as the bible and the gospel of the entire Graeco-Roman Mediterranean civilization, with, attaching to it, innumerable apocryphal writings, you will at once gain a vivid insight into the whole matter. Let us say, then, that the Homeric writings were the holy writ of Lesser and Greater Greece, of the Romans and of all the civilizations that sprang directly from Greek or Roman influences on the world. For the work of Homer is at once a religion, a code of ethics, a map of chivalry, of health, domestic pursuits and of metaphysics. It embraced every subject that was necessary and desirable for primitive and undecadent Mediterranean mankind to know.

The parallels in the whole Affair would seem extraordinary were it not that from the days of Noah to Brigham Young the ethical and religious and ethico-religious necessities of mankind have always remained the same. Fabulous and glittering exploits have always been done in a half-forgotten day, long preceding all men's own. Confucius spent his life in the recovery of the half-forgotten records of a Golden Age before his time. Solomon did the like, gathering together the records of what transpired in Jewry after Moses and his fellow prophets had attempted, with the Ten Commandments and other hygienic, ethical and domestic enactments, to restore to Jewry a pristine virtue that presumably had been lost before the day of the Deluge. So—for that is the most reasonable way in which to look at it— Homer, the blind poet with seven birthplaces, was actually a sort of Moses-Confucius, who set himself the task of gathering together such records as, in his corrupt and degenerate day, remained of the virtues, heroisms, suffering and achievements of his ancestors in the purer, dim past. Our own day is always degenerate, and always we look back to the mighty men who preceded us. So let us say, and the dates are probably relatively accurate, that, perhaps 1,200 years before the Christian era, there was an Affair, large or small, between Greeks and Trojans. Four hundred years later, Homer, blind and, therefore, possessed of tenacious memory, was a slow traveler about Asia Minor and Greater Greece. Not hurrying as his dog or apprentice led him by string or hand from Tyre to Sidon, the Islands to the Peloponnesus, he could hold endless gossiping conversations with those who passed him on the roads or with librarians in their scroll-filled cells. . . . Homer gathered together such remembrances as in his day remained of the Greeks who went with their ships and the sons of Priam who withstood them. That gathering would be made, say, 800 years before Christ, and perhaps about the date when papyrus was first being used for recording human deeds and thought. We have no means of knowing exactly what records Homer made. So that in the succeeding 250 years in spite of, or perhaps because of, the fact that colleges, as it were, of monks and commentators—called generically *Homerides*—set themselves up, commented on the Homeric texts and even composed the celebrated post-Homeric hymns and chants, the state of Homeric learning and Homeric texts became gradually uncertain and confused. Then, 250 years later, it chanced that a mild, benevolent, and above all prosperous tyrant sat upon the throne of Athens. This was Pisistratus, who governed according to the rules of Solonian democracy for nearly forty years. On a given day he left his kingdom to his son Hippias; then disorders occurred and the state split in two. You make this parallel between Solomon and his successor complete when you add that Pisistratus instituted an order of inquiring editors called *Diascevastes*. The function of the sacred college they formed was nothing less than that of producing a final edition of the writings of Homer, so that the noble deeds of their forefathers might be shown to the degenerate Athenians of the seventh or early sixth century before Christ. And this text, more or less accurately copied, remained in the ascendency until it was re-edited by Aristarchus of the library of Alexandria about 150 years before the Christian era. As far as can be traced at present, the original text of Homer was written at times in an ancient Greek that was nearly forgotten by the day of Pisistratus, and at other times in passages in one dialect or another—dialects mostly of Asia Minor. The text of Pisistratus is very nearly in the classical Athenian of the age of Pericles. And the text of Aristarchus is slightly degenerated in the direction of the less masculine vocabularies of Apollonius or Callimachus.

But what is most necessary to get into one's head is the immense part that the Homeric text played in Greek life, whether metropolitan or colonial. As I have said, the embroidery that it has received and the additional legends and comments are innumerable. You have Herodotus quoting Asiatic speakers or commentators who said that the legend of Helen was altogether too absurd. Was it possible to think that the confederation of the Greeks could go to war for the sake of a single woman when eight hundred virgins could be bought every morning in the market place of Sidon for quite a small sum? Or again, you have the Theban legend that Paris never took Helen to Troy but cached her somewhere near Thebes so that Priam and his sons, however good their will might have been, could never have returned her to her husband. Thus, the war was fought for altogether false premises. Or, you have the legend of Helen in the tragedy of Euripides. This relates that according to the "Recantation of Stesichorus," not Helen herself, but a spirit or double got up to represent her, was carried off to Troy. Helen, meanwhile, remained perfectly true to Menelaus with whom, in the play, she was finally reunited "before the palace of the King of Egypt by the mouth of the Nile." But indeed most of the plays of Euripides that have come down to us, and perhaps a majority of those that have perished, were devoted to side subjects of the Homeric cycle.

And probably the most important influence that the work of Homer exercised on Greek life was that of forming, as it were, a central core for the East Mediterranean religion. For the Greek mythology must not be regarded as a thing apart. As time passed on, and, at first the empire of Alexander and then that of Rome extended themselves so as to give to the world known to the ancients a certain homogeneity, the religion of that entire world began to take on an aspect of Hellenic unity. Zeus, the father of Olympus, became not only the Jupiter of Rome, but the Dyuspiter of the eastern frontier tribes of the Empire; Aphrodite became not only known as the Venus of the Romans but assimilated her cult to that of the Astarte of the Syrians. Pallas Athene had Minerva for her Latin representative and was identified with the two Egyptian deities who accompanied the first of man's triple souls before the tribunal presided over by Osiris.

The Homeric deities thus acquired a sort of vested interest which, much as was the case subsequently with the Christian church, nearly all the elements of the state combined to support—and this all the more when actual belief in the Olympians had died out of all reasoning minds. It is impossible to think that the members of the tribunal that condemned Socrates to death and from whom Euripides fled for his life as an atheist suspect, could really believe that the Father of Heaven changed himself into a bull in order to have commerce with Europa or that he became a shower of coins in order to introduce himself to Danae. Nor could Pilate, who judged Christ, really have believed that Hercules was the Son of God.

But as actual belief in the legendary deities of Olympus paled, the greater grew the significance of and the necessity for their symbols in poetry and imaginative drama. They were necessary for the preservation of order and the maintenance of political hierarchy, and ably indeed the Greek dramatists and poets made their Simulacra seem to stalk before the eyes of the Greek world. It is perhaps impossible whilst looking on the streams of traffic in a New York avenue or Paris street today to believe that Prometheus actually first brought fire from heaven for the relief of mortal man. But it is almost equally impossible to read in solitude the *Prometheus Bound* of Aeschylus and not believe that that was the way it was.

Fire must originally have been first utilized by some man of unusual, of semi-godlike intelligence. And where could he have got fire but from the heavens—or from lava pouring from the mountain peaks on high? So you would have a demi-god giving knowledge to men who until then were naked beasts roaming the forests in ululating crowds in search of raw meat torn from bleeding beasts. Yes, when you open *Prometheus Bound* and have read for a very few pages, you have no doubt that from the fire of Prometheus, rather than from the apple of Eve, knowledge of good and evil came to mankind.

By the day of Aeschylus, the tragic drama was already an old art in the Eastern Mediterranean. It had for centuries been accustomed to carry the conviction that historic or tragic happenings were going on under the spectator's eyes, having on the stage merely one principal speaker with choruses to comment on or explain his actions or words. In this art, Aeschylus came as an innovator. He was the latest of the prehistoric dramatists and the earliest of the great triumvirate who gave to the world the greatest of all its art manifestations. When you have mentioned Aeschylus, Sophocles and Euripides, you have mentioned the only three practitioners of any art who ever produced works of art that were both immaculate and inevitable. You may look through the world when you will, before or since then, and you will find nothing in any art or in any human manifestation that will match them. The Bible approaches them in greatness of allure, in poetry and in projection of life. But it has neither the flawlessness of surface nor the sense of destiny that you will find in the Greek works that lie between the *Oresteia* of Aeschylus and the *Alcestis* of Euripides. The work of Homer has a flawlessness as great as that of Greek tragedy. But its necessity to use narrative form robs it of the sense of unity that Greek tragedy has. Nevertheless, the *Iliad* and perhaps, in a lesser degree, the *Odyssey* are projected with a technical skill that in itself must have had a great influence on the dramatic technique of the triumvirate. If you compare the long silence of Prometheus after his binding in the valley with the long silence of Achilles after the body of Patroclus is brought to his tent, you will see a very convincing instance of parallelism. And research in the text of the *Iliad* would give us many more instances that we have not here the time to follow out. It is as if—the writings of Homer being the bible of the Greeks—the great dramatists, producing works somewhat resembling oratorio, should have taken their subjects and some of their dramatic technique from those works. So you find the subject and the very cadences of the Old Testament and the Gospel underlying the dramatic effects and even the musical cadences of the *St. Matthew Passion* of Bach or the *Messiah* of Handel. The epic mode, in short, is necessary to one phase or another of all races. But once it has reached its highest point, it must give place to other forms of racial expression more necessary to the immediate needs of a nation. The epic, that is to say, recited at first by one voice and then by one voice with intermittent choruses, will suffice to a nation of few resources and enforced frugality of life. If you were pioneers going in wagons across the desert, you would have to content yourselves for your evening's entertainment with listening to single fellows with good voices who sang topical or anecdotal songs to the chorus of all the rest of you. But, once arrived at some destination, you at first draw your wagons in a square around the chosen extent of ground and afterwards set up your houses in the emplacement of your wagons. Thus, you will have achieved a town square on which almost inevitably you will demand seasonal entertainment though it be but morris-dancing or the pace-egging dramas that were the rudimentary beginnings of the literature that includes the plays of Shakespeare or of Sheridan. That, at any rate, was the process that took place on the eastern shores and islands of the Mediterranean from 1000 to about 500 years before the Christian era. You had the Homeric dactylic hexameters, at first recited no doubt *ore rotundo*, then sung by a single performer, then by a single performer with intermittent choruses.

At that stage you had a dramatic form that could be employed for the rendering of stories other than those told in the *Iliad* or for more elaborate projections of episodes in either the *Iliad* or the *Odyssey*. So, rudimentarily, with the addition of dance measures and more elaborate chorus arrangements, Greek tragedy gradually evolved itself. It became, even before Aeschylus, a sacrificial employment of time at the great religious feasts; it was employed from above by the governing class to instil into more or less turbulent proletariats the lessons of discipline and of obedience to rulers who had behind them the divine beings of Olympus.

In his own way Aeschylus was an inventor. Born in 525 or 526 B.C. in Eleusis, the home of the Mysteries, he fought at Marathon when he was thirty-five, at Salamis when he was forty-five and next year at Plataea, the final victory of the Greeks over the Persians. He was, thus, when he came to write his tragedies, a man with a profoundly religious background and a man of military action who had observed in the flesh the vicissitudes of thousands of his kind. His plays show you humanity under the crown, or the scourge of destiny in the hands of the high gods. Nay, more, he shows you the high gods themselves in the hands of destiny, developing as mankind develops under the blessings or the curse of fate. In this department of thought, the Prometheus trilogy shows you in *Prometheus Bound*, Zeus, peccant and roving, ready to abandon his duties in pursuit of any little terrestrial servant maid. But by gradual progression through *Prometheus*, through *Prometheus, The Fire Giver* and *Prometheus Unbound*, we arrived at a Zeus who has returned to his legitimate spouse and is prepared henceforth to remain the *bon père de famille* that is the ideal of French landlords.

A similar progression towards virtue is made by the fire giver. In *Prometheus* you have a hero whose equivalent today would be a gifted but insupportably arrogant and law-breaking militant Communist—or, as it might be, a John Brown determined within or without the

law to free the slaves of the South. But in *Prometheus Unbound* he
has become, as it were, the liberal leader of the deities' government.

It was against the law for Prometheus to give fire and, with fire,
knowledge to a humanity that was the chattel of the gods. But neither
Aeschylus nor the audience of his tragedies would have asserted that
the act of giving fire and knowledge to their ancestors had been in
itself an act of evil. Nevertheless, to act against the dictates of Zeus
or the Laws of Destiny was something deserving of almost unthinkable penalties. Thus, at the opening of the play, you have a desolate
mountain valley in which a nameless being, in expiation, is chained
to a weary rock having attendant upon him all sorts of commiserating
earth and sea spirits, some of whom applaud and others of whom
deprecate an unknown act of treachery to the high gods. This suspense of neither revealing his identity nor the crime for which he was
suffering is broken down eventually by a device of technique which
may be found in the other tragedies and may, indeed, be traced to
the *Iliad* itself.

Thus, before his identity is revealed, Prometheus is addressed in the
first place as "Common Felon;" then after an interval as "Betrayer
of the Gods;" and finally in the revelatory explanation: "Prometheus!"
Similarly in the *Electra*, on her entrance, Clytemnestra is addressed
as "Female;" then as "Royal Lady;" and then finally as "Clytemnestra!"

Prometheus, being thus identified, something like a slanging-match
takes place between Hermes, messenger of the god, who is of very
orthodox mentality, and Prometheus, who finally carries his outra-
geousness so far as to threaten Zeus with a disastrous secret of which he
is aware.

The remaining dramas of the trilogy have come down to us only
in so fragmentary a condition that it is impossible to follow their development with any detail. One is only aware that Prometheus finally
adopts a less recalcitrant attitude; the gods become more reasonable
and reconcile themselves at once to the liberalism of Prometheus and
to the fact that, though mankind may have both fire and wisdom,
neither possession is likely to encourage them to storm high Heaven
and throw the gods from their thrones.

The most considerable innovation of Aeschylus was no doubt the introduction of two principal characters at once upon the stage. In that way the famous art of dialogue of the Greek tragedy was invented. And the drama itself became a very different thing from the earlier dithyrambic embroideries upon the speech or song of a single central character. With the group of plays known as *Oresteia*, it reached at once to the highest level of its achievement. It was, no doubt, because of the disfavor with which the judges viewed his innovations that not until he was forty-one—after he had fought at Marathon, but before the victories of Salamis and Plataea—did he win the prize in the Tragic Contests, though later twelve of these were awarded to him, the complete number of his tragedies having been seventy.

The Tragic Contests were held in Athens and conducted by the state every year at the two Dionysian festivals—the lesser in January and the major in March. Of the three great tragic writers, Aeschylus, as we have seen, won the prize thirteen times, Sophocles, twenty, and Euripides, who was more unconventional than either of his predecessors, five times only. At such contests each writer presented a trilogy of tragedies together with a sort of after-piece called a "satyr," which parodied the tragic drama itself or referred to current events. This last was usually extemporized during the contest and the author himself, as a rule, took part in the performance.

There was a further, as if mystic, link in the destinies of these three great writers. For whereas Aeschylus fought at Salamis, Sophocles made his first public appearance—as a dancer—at the feasts celebrating that victory, and Euripides was born on the day of Salamis itself. And one may get yet a little more of the mystery of coincidence into the record of the mysterious affair that is the progress of human thought, for immediately after the birth of Euripides, Confucius died —as if the Spirit of Thought, seeing that a new thinker had come, could let the old one rest from his labors.

As against Aeschylus with his more terrifying doctrine of divine implacability and unreason, Sophocles passed in his day rather as a man of the world. He was of high birth and probably of great inherited wealth. Phrynichus, who wrote a funeral oration for him, says,

"Here came to happy end a life which passed without one single misfortune." His personal beauty would appear to have been great, since he was chosen to lead the choir of patrician boys who danced and sang paeans round the trophy to the victory of Salamis. At the age of twenty-eight he had already won the tragic prize with a trilogy that has disappeared. And at fifty-six his immortal *Antigone* so inflamed with admiration not only the judges but the populace of the city of Athens that he was appointed one of the ten generals (Strategoi) sent with Pericles himself against the aristocratic revolt in the city of Samos. And his subsequent life was full of public honors. He was for long president of the Imperial Treasury and after the disaster in Sicily, he was elected a member of the Committee of Public Safety. Still more, he was fortunate in the hour of his death, since he died a few days before the terrible defeat at Aegospotami in 405 B.C., which finally destroyed the powers and freedom of Athens. The walls of the Pyraeus and those between the city and the harbor were then torn down. The warships were surrendered to the enemy. Democracy was abolished and the oligarchy of the Thirty Tyrants in the pay of the Spartans was established. And the hegemony of the Spartans was set up, to last for thirty-three years. One of the earliest acts of the new régime was the condemnation of Socrates for atheism in 399, and a little later Euripides, the idol of the democracy, had to make his escape from Athens to the court of the King of Macedon. Here he was received with enormous honor but died within a very short period of his arrival. The career and destinies of Euripides were thus different, in nuances at least, from those of Sophocles. He came of an obviously very wealthy burgher family, his father, Mnesarchides, being stated by some authorities to have been a jeweler. His good birth is borne witness to by the fact that as a boy he took part in festivals of Phoebus Apollo that were closed to anybody not of high birth. And his great wealth is proved by the fact that once at least, he was called upon to provide a warship for the Athenian navy and that he was appointed consul for one of the Greek colonies, both duties being extremely costly.

His literary career was less easy. At the time of the production of his first drama, Aeschylus was dead, but Sophocles was at his most vigorous and there existed a very considerable body of playwrights whose names we do not know because their works have disappeared but whose tragedies were, at least by the judges, considered to be of sufficient merit to let them share the prizes with Sophocles and Euripides. That is to say, that, between the first bestowal of a prize on Sophocles in 455 and the bestowal of the last one to the body of Euripides, when it was brought back in 405 B.C. (a period of exactly fifty years), Sophocles and Euripides between them gained exactly twenty-five prizes.

We have already seen that the progress from Aeschylus to Sophocles was, as it were, a descent from implicit and severe belief in the powers of the gods over human destinies to a point of view in which your destinies were considered as being subjected to human action. In the *Prometheus* and the *Oresteia* of Aeschylus the main motif is the remorseless decrees of the divinities. That is to say, they decree such and such a thing and that thing and its consequences become the inescapable fate of the characters of the dramas.

But with Sophocles the supernatural action is diminished and man becomes subject to a remorseless destiny that may have been caused by man's own actions subjected to mere chance. There was nothing divinely predestined in the intolerably tragic fate of Oedipus Tyrannus. He was exposed as a child and adopted by a king whom he was taught to regard as his father. He actually slew his real father and became the husband of his mother who bore him four children, Antigone, Ismene and their two brothers. The result is the almost insupportable tragedy expressed in the trilogy, *Oedipus the King, Oedipus at Colonnus,* and finally, the *Antigone* with its forecasting of the end of *Romeo and Juliet*. In these dramas, the intervention of the divinities is relatively fortuitous. The end of Oedipus, become a blind tramp, is not death but mysterious disappearance presided over by the demi-god Theseus, acting presumably under the direction of Zeus. So that this ending is not tragic in our sense of the word, the Greek having a strong sense of the continuance of the individual soul after its severance of the body. Oedipus has undergone every tragic and predestined woe that fortune could inflict upon man. Nevertheless, having disappeared from earth and lying in an unknown tomb, his shade is blessed by the affection of his daughters. There are few passages in literature more beautiful than the last sixty or seventy lines of the *Oedipus at Colonnus*, where Antigone, declaring that her father's fate has befallen as he had planned, says:

"He has finally died in a foreign land but the one that he had desired, in a kindly earth where he shall pass in eternal sleep with his friends and children weeping above him. Let our tears show our sorrow. Thou hast had thy wish, Oh Father! Thou hast died amongst strangers when I was not there."

And at the less restrained sorrow of the younger sister, Ismene, the chorus comments severely that the end of Oedipus was blessed by the gods and that thereupon his daughter should cease from lamenting. And the demi-god Theseus bids the sisters go their way, back to their home at Thebes since, in order to gladden his dead friend Oedipus in his grave, he will take every care that their journey homeward shall be prosperous.

The note of Sophocles is in fact the note of humanity. His men stand on their own feet and, tragic though their destinies may be, they are never ignoble. They affront their sorrows as a skilled swimmer faces heavy seas, and they go to their ends without ever uttering ignoble lamentations.

This is the great real tragedy which is always stimulating to its audience. You may, as Jehovah did, pile woe upon woe on the head of Job, but in the spectacle of woes borne with sufficiency of fortitude, there is nothing harrowing and the enunciation of this great aspect of life is the great boon that the Greek tragic muse confers upon us men.

With Euripides the slope of tragedy makes a further descent in the direction of humanity. The awful and heavy Sophoclean note of divine interference in matters human had almost disappeared by the time Euripides was well under way. His stories are human stories such as you might hear at any market place and the interventions of the gods when they actually appear are relatively willful. This writer's prime favorites amongst the plays of this great author are the *Alcestis* and the *Bacchae* which he has re-read constantly ever since he was at school. After them, as reading for pleasure, he would place the *Iphigeneia at Aulis*, the *Medea*, the *Electra*, and *Andromache*, in about that order. Other critics will no doubt commend other plays and other sequences and, really to estimate the plays of Euripides, the reader must make his own valuation. The author of the *Alcestis* and the *Bacchae* seems instinct with a peculiar vitality, a lustiness and a polychromatic humor bordering at times on a sort of jovial frivolity. This last trait this writer, no doubt, derived from the fact that the *Bacchae* was the first Greek play he ever read at school. Then, the idea of Pentheus, the king with the psychology of a Pilgrim Father, being torn to pieces by Bacchantes, at the head of whom was his mother, under the auspices of a newly deified god of liquor, filled him with delight. It seemed to have a modern point of view that was exactly in tune with the ferocity of the proverbial fourth form schoolboy. In addition, this eminently moral drama was expressed with a beauty of language and a vividness of incident such as were undoubtedly part of one of the most exquisite experiences of a young literatus looking for the first time on a real world of letters. It is impossible to remember any emotion more excruciatingly exciting than that of the first reading of the last sentence of the great speech of Dionysus —the words running:

And he (the dead Pentheus) shall recognize Dionysus, the son of Zeus, who at last appears on earth as a God most terrible, yet most kindly unto men.

And then the triumphant first strophe of the answering chorus: "At last shall not my feet again gleam silverly in the night-long dance," and the images of the Bacchantes' heads thrown back in the humid, subtropical night and of the deer chased by huntsmen—as the Bacchantes had been by the puritan Pentheus—and escaping into the secret recesses of the dark forest. That is an image of romance that remains to one as vivid as ever it was nearly half a century ago.

It is obviously difficult in the space for quotation that is open to us here to give the accumulative sense of the great poetry that leads up to these inestimable passages. That is why we have hitherto been chary of quoting from these dramatists. And, indeed, to reproduce in another language the poetry of poets as great as Euripides, one must be a poet as great as Euripides—and one isn't. We may hazard the further biographical detail so as to make this attitude the clearer to the reader and thus let him more easily deduce what he needs for his private guidance. This writer's first literary work after being demobilized at the end of the last war was the translation of the *Alcestis* for production by Mr. Drinkwater at his Birmingham Repertory Theatre. Alas, what that translation was like there is no means of knowing. For, after the play was announced for rehearsal, Mr. Drinkwater found that he had lost the only copy of the manuscript. At any rate, let the anecdote prove that the writer's private life has been singularly dominated by Greek tragedy, and, what is more important, that the theatre manager of today considers Euripides suited for the modern stage.

Every man is by temperament either sentimentalist or cynic, or a mixture of the two. And that gives you the saturnine humor of the cockney, the Paragot and the New Yorker. This writer's favorite passages of Greek drama or Greek literature as a whole are those that could be stigmatized as sentimental. His favorite passage of all Greek drama is the famous one containing the lines which Euripides puts into the mouth of a serving maid,* and which we have tried to render as a serving maid might have spoken rather than as they would be translated by a university don in his study.

> Then she goes to their chamber and falls across their bed
> And her tears run down and she says as follows:
> "Fare you well, O bed, whereon I gave my maidenhead to this
>   man to save whom I must now die.
> I do not hold it against you, though it is for your sake that I must
>   go alone into solitude;
> I die that I may fail neither you nor my Lord.

* *Alcestis*, lines 166-7.

Another bride shall own you—one that shall not be truer to my
    Lord and you than I
But maybe more fortunate."
And so she falls again upon the bed, kissing it and the bed is wet
    with her tears.
And having cried her fill, she makes to go wavering from her bed.
And always as she is near her chamber door she turns back
And throws herself again upon her bed
The children clinging to her skirts and crying. . . .
And all her maids beneath the roof, crying. . . .
And not one so mean in state that she does not speak to her.

It is obvious that this does not exactly translate the words of Euripides because his lines are full of polysyllables and we use almost no
polysyllables in English. For, if we do employ them, they appear
pompous.

The Greek lines translated above contain the eleven longest words
of the Greek of this scene. But to give a simple and poignant expression of woe they have to be translated into English, monosylla-
bically.

On the other hand, Euripidean thought can be transferred into
English with fair exactitude because the sentiments expressed are
domestic sentiments common to every class in the world. Alcestis,
Admetus, Hercules and the handmaidens, though their words are
polysyllabic, express thoughts that today could be felt if not expressed,
say, by a coffee storekeeper, his wife who is ready to die for his sake,
their assistant with the store and the great jovial surgeon who shall
eventually save the wife's life. And it is this quality of Euripides
rather than any other overt expression of atheism—of non-implicit
belief in the legends of Zeus, Hera and Aphrodite—that made the
judges of the Tragic Contests so suspicious of his gifts that they
awarded him the prize only five times and made him so afraid for
his life that he fled to the welcoming Macedonian court. On the other
hand, the love of the Athenian populace for him was so uproarious and
the admiration of other Greek nations for him so great that twice
during his life victorious enemies forbore to push their victories over

the Athenians to the bitter end. And, when his body was brought home from Macedon, the Athenian crowd, in defiance of their masters, insisted that the tragic prize should, for the last time, be conferred upon him. . . . It was the last stand for freedom that the Athenians were ever to make.

CHAPTER SEVEN

THE fourth name of Greek drama is that of Aristophanes, the ferocious comic writer. An aristocrat *pur sang*, a religious reactionary, and a violent pacifist, he introduced—or at least perfected—the use of his art for the purposes of propaganda and, as was inevitable, hastened the decay of the Athenian arts, the Athenian military hegemony and the Athenian dominance of world thought. His attacks on Socrates for being a rationalist were responsible for the death of that philosopher and his attacks on Euripides caused the flight of that tragic poet to Macedon. His name has given the world the adjective "aristophanic," a word signifying a mood of cynicism and scorn expressed in gigantic laughter.

The humor of his plays is irresistible, sardonic, hugely coarse and always ferocious. In the effort to restore the true religion he will give you scenes of little naked girls running about on the stage with little naked pigs. And under cover of the laughter this scene creates, he will brew the juice of the hemlock that poisoned the master of Plato. His verse was of an extraordinary skill—of the sort of skill that goes consummately to the making of brilliant and moving tirades couched in terms of the most violent denunciation. And, Athenian political preoccupations and conditions being extraordinarily similar to those of our own day, the majority of his plays are easily adaptable to our stage. Almost every year the Greek play given at Westminster school —which is one of the great social functions of the London season— will be one of Aristophanes' dramas adapted to the denunciation or ridicule of prominent English politicians, members of the clergy or educationalists. And, though pacifism today has crossed from the right to the left in politics, his *Lysistrata*, a drama showing Athenian women taking steps to coerce their husbands and lovers into a peace with Sparta, is quite often nowadays revived in one country or another as a powerful argument in favor of world peace. Actually, if you considered Aristophanes as the precursor of M. Léon Daudet, you would have a very singular example of parallelism. Monsieur Daudet, as a critic, is probably of so great a genius as to be almost alone in the world. He is also a man of satirical gifts, aristophanic enough to make him the greatest single disruptive power in France and thus probably the greatest single threatener of the peace of the world. In the *Birds*, *Peace*, tho *Acharnians* and many other dramas, Aristophanes clamored virulently for peace and alliance with the Lacedaemonians because they were the age-long foes of democracy. So Monsieur Daudet today clamors for peace and alliance with German National Socialists, desiring to see, if not the actual installation of Mr. Hitler as the ruler of France, at least the organization of France on lines exactly similar to that of the National Socialists in Germany. Whether or no Monsieur Daudet will live to see his plans carried out, we do not at the moment know. But Aristophanes lived long enough to see the installation in Athens of the Thirty Tyrants who were the tools of Sparta. That happened in 404 B.C. when Aristophanes was fifty-two, Socrates being executed when he was fifty-nine and the Spartan Hegemony of Greece lasting until 371—nine years after the death of Aristophanes who could thus close his eyes in peace upon a humbled Athens and a nearly extinct Athenian art life. As we have seen, there was later another writer of comedies called Menander. But his works have come down to us only through their Latin adaptations, so we will leave considering them until we come to Terence. Menander wrote between 342 and 292 B.C.

The custody of the Greek Art of Letters passed to Alexandria, the city founded by Alexander the Great and endowed by the Ptolemies of Egypt with the museum and library that constituted one of the seven wonders of the world. And you may add a curious and familiar note to the description of this city if you say that Alexandria was the largest Greek, the largest Jewish, the largest Egyptian and eventually the third largest Roman city in the world. It was there that the Hebrew scriptures were translated into Greek by seventy Hebrew scholars in the version called the Septuagint, and it was there that, five hundred years or so after the death of Plato, Plotinus evolved the Neo-Platonism that became the basis of the philosophy of St. Augustine—St. Augustine being the only one of the Fathers of the Church whose teachings are equally implicitly accepted by the Orthodox, the Roman and the Reformed branches of the Church of Christ.

It would, in short, be impossible to exaggerate the part played by this city in the conservation and at the same time in the academicizing of the thought and the arts of that glorious world of which she became the *caput mortuum*. She was burnt by the Arabs when they destroyed that portion of the Roman Empire in 640. Nevertheless, so great was her hold upon academic life that if today you wish to read the work of Aristotle in the original, what, as like as not, you will read, will be the German text of a Greek renaissance rendering of a Latin text that is in turn a translation from the Arabic. And the Arabic text will be a translation of an Alexandrian Greek copy of Aristotle's writing, the whole having been brought together into a series of texts undertaken by one learned Hebrew of the nineteenth century and published by another.* I do not know any instance more extraordinary of the tenacity and vigor of human thought beneath every revolution or conflagration organized by human beings and in spite of the devouring tooth of time. Nor, indeed, can one find any more convincing proof of the fact that, if human thought is to persist or progress, it takes all the nations of the world to perfect the process. And this incredible cosmopolitanism becomes all the more impressive when you consider that Aristotle himself was the tutor of Alexander the Great, and that in the course of his conquests Alexander provided him with savants and observers of every imaginable Eastern nation in immense numbers. Thus was gathered for him the information as to the habits and health of monks, mice, cuckoos and gods that he needed for his encyclopaedic investigations. So that if today you read one of the volumes on physics of Aristotle, you may well be adding to your knowledge from the observation of a Persian, a Bactrian, or Punjabi, made two thousand years ago, and a hundred years later transcribed, arranged and edited in the library of Alexandria.

Aristotle is probably—but, indeed, he is certainly—the single lay thinker whose thoughts have had the greatest influence over mankind between his day and ours. But before we can give him the little atten-

* *The Loeb Classical Library.* Founded by James Loeb, LL.D. and published in London by William Heinemann Ltd.

tion for which we have space here, it is necessary to deal summarily
with another branch of the Greek literary art that we have hitherto
neglected—that of the Greek elegiac, iambic and lyric poets. To dismiss these in a few paragraphs may seem summary indeed, considering the immense pleasure that the poets from Sappho to Theocritus
have given to the world. It is, nevertheless, to scale. The Greek verse
poets, even allowing for the supreme beauty of the Greek language,
can be paralleled by the poets of several other tongues. For Homer,
the tragic poets, Herodotus and Aristotle, no other languages can
supply the equivalents.

The great Greek Lesbian, or purely aesthetic, poets were Sappho
and Alcaeus, who were contemporaries and rivals in the seventh century—hence the name Alcaics, given to the metres they used—and then
Anacreon, 560-478 B.C.

The poetry of these writers is of a wonderful, frequently excrutiat-
ing, beauty in the language in which they wrote. But it is almost
impossible to get over into another tongue the fullness of that beauty.
You may translate Alcestis' address to her bed and get the sense and,
consequently, some of the poetry over into your own language. And,
if you are a great poet, you will make poetry of it. So also, you will
with Sappho or Anacreon. But you will have transfused so much of
your own personality that the result will be merely a hybrid.

If you take the line usually regarded as the most memorable and
beautiful of all Sappho's writing, *Heeramen men ego sethen Athi palai
pota,* you see at once, if you have any Greek at all, that the literal
meaning is "I loved thee, Athis, long since, in ages past." But work
at your English version how you will, you will never—simply because
English vowel sounds are so indeterminate—get either the sonority
or the vowel coloring of the original Greek. Or you might possibly
get the vowel coloring at the expense of the limpidity of your language. My own favorite verses in English are:

> Less than a God, they said there could not dwell
> Within the hollow of that shell
> That spoke so sweetly
> And so well.

As in the line of Sappho, where the predominant vowel is the short "e," you will observe that in the English the main vowel coloring is the same: L*e*ss, sh*e*ll, dw*e*ll, w*e*ll—h*e*eram*e*n, m*e*n, *e*go, s*e*th*e*n. These short "e" sounds are relieved in the English by long "o" sounds: sp*o*ke, s*o*, s*o*. In Sappho's line the relief is afforded by the long "a" sounds—*A*thi, p*a*l*a*i, pot*a*. But in the case of both the English and Greek this vowel coloration is spontaneous at least as far as the poetic content is concerned. That is possible for anyone who has the industry. To take over a subject from another poet and to give the same or similar vowel effects is almost an impossibility. There are a million chances to one against your being able to do so. Yet the great pleasure of reading, and still more of hearing, verse lies precisely in this vowel-coloration which, technically, is known as "phonetic syzygy."

There are in fact too many obstacles. You could not at all nearly translate the Anacreontic poem beginning: *"Oh pai Parthenion . . ."* because literally rendered it contains words that to avoid the censor are normally translated for the use of the learned into Latin.

And although Mr. J. J. Edmonds of Jesus College, Cambridge, has attractively translated the hymn to Dionysus beginning: *"Onax, oh damalees Eerohs ḳai Numphi ḳuanohpides . . ."* with:

> O Lord with whom playeth Love, the subduer, and the dark-eyed Nymphs and rosy Aphrodite, as thou wanderest the tops of the lofty hills, to thee I kneel; do thou come unto me kind and lending ear unto a prayer that is acceptable and give Cleobulus good counsel, O Dionysus, to receive my love.*

The final effect is spiney as compared with the suave-passionate original. No man living can really render the more intricate Greek metres when reading aloud, so it is obvious that though the sense has been sufficiently well caught, the rhythm of the last three lines of the poem is not all conveyed by Mr. Edmonds' last eleven words, these words containing seven monosyllables as against the two monosyllables of Anacreon, who employs two four-syllabled, three three-syllabled and two two-syllabled words.

* *Lyra Graeca*, edited and translated by J. M. Edmonds. (Loeb Classics.)

Nevertheless, by continued reading even of relatively poor translations of these writers, you will gradually get a sense of a world so beautiful and of thoughts so exquisite that you will eventually attain to pleasure such as you will never find surpassed elsewhere in the realm of hearing.

With regard to the elegiac poets, I shall not do more here than re-catalogue the names of the most famous, so that the reader, if he wishes to pursue this form of pleasure, may look them up and read them for himself. He shall read for their melancholy or for their instruction in virtue: the poems of Tyrtaeus of the seventh century; those of Solon, the Athenian legislator who expressed many of his laws in verse and who lived from 640-558 B.C.; those of Theognis, a writer of the sixth century who wrote gnomic (highly condensed instructional) elegiacs; and finally Mimnermus of the seventh century, who gave to this famous verse-form a sentimental turn. Archilochus who "flourished"—who was, that is to say, aged about forty and at the height of his powers about 670 B.C.—invented several varieties of iambics, and was banished from Sparta on account of the licentiousness of his themes and the bitterness of his satire. The remaining great poets of the Greek Great Age were the choral lyric writers. They were Alcman, who flourished about 650 B.C.; Stesichorus, 620 B.C.; Simonides, 556-467; Bacchylides, of the sixth century; and Pindar, the most famous of them all, who lived from c 522 to c 433.

Pindar and most of his contemporaries made their living by celebrating the feats, the glories and the ancestries of winners at the Olympic and other games. This gives the great bulk of their work a certain monotony of subject. This effect they obviate by the music of their imaginations and their skill in the use to which they put the legends of the divinities and demi-gods of Olympus.

Pindar was regarded as one of the greatest poets and was read with enthusiasm even in Anglo-Saxondom until and during the eighteenth and a good part of the nineteenth centuries. The pleasure was doubtless of the referred kind. It came, that is to say, from the delight with which persons already learned in the classics recognized allusions to episodes in the life of Pallas Athene, Phoebus Apollo, Hermes Trismegistus and the rest. That knowledge having today almost died out, it seems unlikely that for the present the work of Pindar or Bacchylides, who was considered his great rival, could today convey any very widespread pleasure. But revolutions of taste, manners and wisdom are not uncommon in this world, and it is possible that our descendants, tiring of the polyphonics of the music producers of today, may once more taste and appreciate the simplicities of verses that were sung to the sound of the flute or the seven-stringed lyre. Then Pindar, Stesichorus and Alcman may well come into their own again.

In the French army of today, in the 115th Regiment on the eleventh of July, when the roll call takes place, the name of Henri de la Tour d'Auvergne is called. A sergeant of his company steps out from the line and exclaims: "Died on the field of honor." De la Tour d'Auvergne held back by himself an entire Austrian army in a narrow pass of the Alps in the year 1761. So, at the Olympic festivals for long after the death of Pindar, before the opening of the sacred Delphic banquet called the *Theoxenia*, the heralds who acted as masters of ceremonies called out: "Room for the poet Pindar."

And we may as well take a breathing space by recounting some of the honors paid to these poets and a little about how they lived or how they gained their bread. Perhaps greatest of all honors paid to any poet was that recorded by Marcellinus Ammianus, the Roman literary historian of the fourth century. Says he: When Socrates (*"destinatum poenae Socratem coniectumque"*) was thrown into prison and was awaiting the death penalty, it happened that a good musician outside the prison heard a man play and sing to the sound of a flute, a piece by the lyric poet, Stesichorus. The philosopher begged the musician to teach him that song so that he might be able to sing it before he could no more sing. The musician asked him what was the use of it to a dying man? Whereupon Socrates replied, *"ut aliquid sciens amplius e vita discedam"* (so that he might depart from life with a more amply beautified knowledge)—the word *"amplius"* meaning something more gracious and more cultivated than is implied by the English word *"ampler."*

Or Pliny the Younger, 700 years or so after the death of the poet, says in his *Natural History*, concerning the song of the nightingale (*"de lusciniae cantu"*) that Stesichorus' poetry was so sweet because at his birth the nightingale breathed upon his lips. Or again, in the Palatine anthology, Antipater says that according to Pythagoras, the soul of Homer had found a second lodgment in the breast of Stesichorus.

So poets were honored by their contemporaries and descendants. They lived well or ill according to their gifts or their private fortunes. Some of them amassed great wealth from the offerings of admirers or city governments. The writer remembers an anecdote of Stesichorus' parsimony which comes back to him from many years ago but which he cannot find again. . . . Stesichorus had two large money chests, one of them having a slit in its lid. If a neighbor or a stranger sought a loan or a favor from him, the poet would lead his suppliant to the two chests and would say: "These two boxes I have. The one holds the offerings made to me by this or that person, the other what I have to give in answer to requests." He would lift up one lid after the other. The chest that contained the offerings would be completely full and that devoted to favors would not contain so much as a maravedi. Those, however, were the great days when the Attic genius not only demanded and paid for, but could produce, exquisite poetry in great quantities. With the loss of her freedom, genius also seemed to desert not merely the Athenians but the entire Greek race.

Poets there were, but they were without genius and they found almost no patrons. In happy day for them, however, in 320 B.C., Ptolemy, the savior of the Egyptian fragment of Alexander's empire, became the savior also of these poor poets and of the third-rate philosophers and pedants who alone survived of the glory that was Greece. One of the most delightful idyls of Theocritus, the 14th, gives us a dramatic picture of the fortunes of such a poet.

> "*Aeschines.* All hail to the stout Thyonichus!
>
> *Thyonichus.* As much to you, Aeschines.
>
> *Aeschines.* How long it is since we met!
>
> *Thyonichus.* Is it so long? But why, pray, this melancholy?
>
> *Aeschines.* I am not in the best of luck, Thyonichus.

Thyonichus. 'Tis for that, then, you are so lean, and hence come this long moustache, and these love-locks all adust. Just such a figure was a Pythagorean that came here of late, barefoot and wan,—and said that he was an Athenian. Marry, he too was in love, methinks with a plate of pancakes.

Aeschines. Friend, you will always have your jest,—but beautiful Cynisca,—she flouts me! I shall go mad some day, when no man looks for it; I am but a hair's breadth on the hither side, even now."

Aeschines recounts how, the night before, he had given a supper to a rough rider, a bandit, and a friend from Argos. He had killed two chickens and a sucking pig and they had eaten truffles and oysters and opened four-year-old wine from Biblos. It became a drinking match and they got to drinking pure wine without water. They must name their toasts and they all did. But when Aeschines called out the name of Cynisca she said nothing. The guests began to jeer at him. Cynisca was suspected of having a lover, nicknamed "The Wolf," and all sorts of allusions to wolves went around the board. The four men were deep in their cups and suddenly the rough rider began to sing a popular song of the day in Thessaly, a song called "The Wolf." At this Cynisca burst out weeping.

. . . "Then I,—you know me, Thyonichus,—struck her on the cheek with clenched fist,—one, two! She caught up her robes, and forth she rushed, quicker than she came. 'Ah, my undoing' (cried I), 'I am not good enough for you, then—you have a dearer playfellow? Well, be off and cherish your other lover, 'tis for him your tears run big as apples!' "

So Aeschines determines to go into exile and the idyl ends thus:

Thyonichus. Would that things had gone to your mind, Aeschines. But if, in good earnest, you are thus set on going into exile, Ptolemy is the free man's best paymaster!

Aeschines. And in other respects, what kind of man?

Thyonichus. The free man's best paymaster! Indulgent too, the Muses' darling, a true lover, the top of good company, knows his friends, and still better knows his enemies. A great giver to many, refuses nothing that he is asked which to give may beseem a king, but, Aeschines, we should not always be asking. Thus, if you are minded to pin up the top corner of your cloak over the right shoulder, and if you have the heart to stand steady on both feet, and bide the brunt of a hardy targeteer, off instantly to Egypt! From the temples downward we all wax grey, and on to the chin creeps the rime of age; men must do somewhat while their knees are yet nimble."

The museum and library at Alexandria founded by Ptolemy, the friend of letters, had, then, long before the day of the bland Theocritus, become, as it were, the dried-meat storehouse of the works of the Great Age of Greece. It was also a sort of refuge and factory for all the pedants and uninspired scribes of a literature completely in its doldrums. It resembled the modern university whose province consists not in the production or aiding of new imaginative literature but in the support of great numbers of completely uninspired commentators on the texts of their inspired predecessors. So it was to remain until near the arrival of Christianity. From then onwards until its destruction by the Arabs, this city with its institutions—whilst Egypt herself was to become more and more the mere grain warehouse of the Roman Empire—Alexandria then, became less and less the home of inferior poets, philosophers and commentators, and more and more a center for the production of theological works of considerable violence, at first pagan and finally Christian. The language employed in these works continued to be Greek for a long period, but, since they were produced under the auspices of the Roman Empire, we will defer considering them until we arrive at the literature of the great, uninspiring Commonwealth. In the meantime, in the second or third —or second and third, for the dates are as usual confused—centuries before Christ, there was born in Sicily to the Doric Greek colony that had been established there, since the eighth century B.C., a short-lived, brilliant, literary form that was to have an enormous influence on all succeeding ages. This was the pastoral.

Exactly as, at the end of a great defeat, a last Véry light illumines the blackness of a field of battle, so the poems of the lovely Sicilian triad, Theocritus, Bion and Moschus, cast an extremely vivid light on the Graeco-Egyptian scene. This happened just before the final disappearance of the free beauty of Greece beneath the formidable claws of the grafters and scoundrels who bore the name or titles of Caesar.

That beautiful and serene world had, after the death of Alexander the Great, broken up into a sea of whirlpools, the struggles between all the successors to his empire the world over. Nevertheless, there remained here and there, as afterwards in the Dark Ages, some relatively sheltered nooks in which the arts could still carry on. One of these was the Doric settlement in Sicily. This Greek colony in an ideal climate, and partly because it was on an island, had retained the native simplicity of manners of the eighth century Greeks, along with a bucolic leisure and wealth in commodities such as had long been unknown elsewhere in Hellas.

It was for many centuries considered that the *Idyls* of Theocritus with the agreeable nymphs and cultivated, beautifully rhetorical shepherds were as artificial as were the dairy maids of Marie Antoinette's little Trianon. But Andrew Lang—to whom our entire world and day owe a debt of gratitude for his popularization of the *Idyls* of these three great poets—in his preface to his volume of translations that bears their names doughtily disposes of critics like Fontenelle. Fontenelle declared that he cannot believe in the delicacy of the Sicilian who wore "a skin stripped from the roughest of he-goats with the smell of the rennet clinging to it still." And he cries, "Can anyone suppose that there ever was a shepherd who could say 'Would I were the humming bird, Amaryllis, to flit to thy cave, and dip beneath the branches, and the ivy leaves that hide thee'?" But Mr. Lang disposes of that jibe by pointing out that the modern Greek shepherds who tend their flocks in the very pastures where once roamed Daphnis and Chloe, still sing songs which, if they were attributed to the ancient Greeks, would of a certainty be ascribed to one or other of the beautiful Sicilian triad. Thus he quotes a song from Epirus which was sung in 1896 by a shepherd:

"White art thou not, thou art not golden haired,
Thou art brown, and gracious, and meet for love."*

Or again

"Ah, light of mine eyes, what gift shall I send thee; what gift to the other world? The apple rots, and the quince decayeth, and one by one they perish; the petals of the rose fade! I send thee my tears bound in a napkin, and what though the napkin burns, if my tears reach thee at last!"

And, indeed, there exists a very charming, and almost ravishing, collection of modern Greek songs the words of which were discovered by Anton Rubenstein, the Russian composer, and by him set to music. Every one of them might have been written by Theocritus. The fact is that civilization, poetry and rhetoric and pretty speeches will be found eternally in climates fitted to produce them. The gift will appear, at intervals to go underground, but the songs will persist. The modern Greek lyric is a product of a second revival of poetry of which the beautiful triad's works were the first. Greek poetry before their day appeared to have gone underground and to have disappeared beneath the dust sown by the commentators. And then, suddenly, in them again it lived, and it brought a new and beautiful mood to bless humanity.

"To take a delight," says Mr. Lang, "in that genius so human, so kindly, so musical in expression, requires, it may be said, no long preparation." And much as this writer dislikes quoting the sentiments of other critics he could not possibly better that sentence. So we may take pleasure in once more mentioning the name of one who in his day was also famous as a man of letters and who was a very beautiful spirit. . . . Andrew Lang!

The genius of that triad, then, was infinitely human, infinitely

* *Theocritus and His Age,* by Andrew Lang.

kindly, infinitely musical in expression. It was in little a symptom of that return to simplicity of observation and method that we have seen to occur in several other cases. In Chinese poetry you had a period of great artificiality after which both poets and the public craved for simplicity and natural sentiment. And we have observed that similar revolutions have taken place in every literature that has a history of any length. So the poems of that triad filled the whole Greek world with admiration for its refound humaneness, kindliness and musical expression. And, no doubt, could the Greek empire and spirit have continued to dominate the world, a new great age of Greek Poetry might have been vouchsafed to us.

But Sicily, that had been for centuries one of the islands of the blessed, was, a little after the birth of Theocritus, ravaged at first by the Carthaginians and then by a tribe of robbers called "Mamertines." The natural courage of the Sicilians helped them to expel the invaders. But the leisure and the wealth of the islands seems to have passed from them. Thus we have the famous 16th Idyl of Theocritus, which runs:

> Ah, who of all them that dwell beneath grey morning will to-day open his door and gladly receive us poets within his house?

Formerly it had been the pleasure of the Sicilian rich, as of the earlier Athenians, to house sumptuously, and richly to reward such itinerant poets as would be prepared to entertain their hosts with their stories or to recompense them with praise in their verse. But the Sicilian rich were now either impoverished or spending all their money and all the money of the state—just as we do today—on armaments. So Theocritus continues:

> And these poets with looks askance, and naked feet come homewards, and sorely they upbraid me when they have gone on a vain journey, and listless again in the bottom of their empty coffer, they dwell with heads bowed over their chilly knees, where is their drear abode, when gainless they return.

Where is there such an one, among men today? Where is he that will befriend him that speaks his praises? I know not, for now no longer, as of old, are men eager to win the renown of noble deeds, nay, they are the slaves of gain! Each man clasps his hands below the purse-fold of his gown, and looks about to spy whence he may get him money: the very rust is too precious to be rubbed off for a gift. Nay, each has his ready saw; *The shin is further than the knee; First let me get my own! 'Tis the Gods' affair to honor minstrels! Homer is enough for every one, who wants to hear any other? He is the best of bards who takes nothing that is mine.*

And might not that lament have been written this morning in Chicago or Glasgow or New York or Paris . . . or London?

And, as a result, the triad seems to have starved at home and to have been driven to take refuge with Ptolemy Philopator in Alexandria. This Ptolemy reigned from 222-205 B.C.; Theocritus lived until 216, so we may imagine that he found six years of opulence and glory at the court of that monarch. Ptolemy would appear to have been of a kindly and generous disposition. He was guilty—which shocks Mr. Lang—of the indelicacy of marrying his sister, Arsinoë. But we may credit him with the good taste of being able to perceive that this completely new, revolutionary, and one would have thought, therefore, shocking, poetry was something to patronize and promote.

That it produced no great following may have had two causes: the forced emigration of the poets to the town and their consequent loss of touch with their native life; and, secondly, the town's inability to maintain, for so long, an interest in an alien and unknown form of life. That is the way of towns. You will find London for a couple of decades mad about Walter Scott and the Highlands; Paris for a little longer obsessed by the Provence of Daudet and Mistral; or New York, for less long, will be invaded by literatures of one American region or another, whose vogue, too, will fade soon. And nothing could have been more different from the lives of the flock-tenders in the blessed climate around Syracuse than the soul-deadening toil of the Egyptian *fellaheen*, growing grain in the parched desert of Egypt. And still more alien to the poets would be the life of the great, crowded, mercantile city.

In the absence of any dogmatic direction from the very learned—for nothing definite is known as to the dates of the triad and the details of their lives—we must get from their poems what we can, and we may plot out this affair much as we will. Theocritus went to Syracuse in 222 and lived there until 216 B.C., when he died—though there is some authority for saying that he returned to Syracuse on the accession to the throne of Sicily of the tyrant, Hieron II, who expelled the Carthaginians and the Mamertine brigands from that country. Bion would seem to have been the pupil, or merely the junior, of Theocritus. He appears to have been born in Smyrna—so that it is only as poet that he can be called Sicilian—and to have died in Alexandria in somewhere about the year 150 B.C., though some critics put his death after 100 B.C. His most famous poem is the *Lament for Adonis*, the first and part of the second stanzas of which Mr. Lang thus renders in *Theocritus, Bion, Moschus*:

> Woe, woe for Adonis, he hath perished, the beauteous Adonis, dead is the beauteous Adonis, the Loves join in the lament. No more in thy purple raiment, Cypris, do thou sleep; arise, thou wretched one, sable-stoled, and beat thy breasts, and say to all, "He hath perished, the lovely Adonis!"
> *Woe, woe for Adonis, the Loves join in the lament!*

> Low on the hills is lying the lovely Adonis, and his thigh with the boar's tusk, his white thigh with the boar's tusk is wounded, and sorrow on Cypris he brings, as softly he breathes his life away. . . .
> *Woe, woe for Adonis, the Loves join in the lament!*

His verse was more Alexandrian—as who should say marmoreal. It was made up of the legends of the more or less Egyptianized deities of the Greek mythology. He seems to have been succeeded by Moschus, who flourished in the year 150 B.C. His most known poem was his *Lament for Bion*, who according to him must have spread the fame of the Doric muse very far through the world.

Every famous city laments thee, Bion, and all the towns. Ascra laments thee far more than her Hesiod, and Pindar is less regretted by the forests of Boeotia. Nor so much did pleasant Lesbos mourn for Alcaeus, nor did the Teian town so greatly bewail her poet, while for thee more than for Archilochus doth Paros yearn, and not for Sappho, but still for thee doth Mytilene wail her musical lament;

[Here seven verses are lost.]

And in Syracuse Theocritus; but I sing thee the dirge of an Ausonian sorrow, I that am no stranger to the pastoral song, but heir of the Doric Muse which thou didst teach thy pupils. This was thy gift to me; to others didst thou leave thy wealth, to me thy minstrelsy.
Begin, ye Sicilian Muses, begin the dirge.

He was a Sicilian, having been born in Syracuse, and he seems to have retained a perpetual heartache when he remembered that he was not in Sicily.

. . . Nay, sing to the Maiden some strain of Sicily, sing some sweet pastoral lay.

And she too is Sicilian, and on the shores by Aetna she was wont to play, and she knew the Dorian strain. Not unrewarded will the singing be;

he chants in the same dirge. His last recorded poem runs:

Would that my father had taught me the craft of a keeper of sheep,
For so in the shade of the elm-tree, or under the rocks on the steep,
Piping on reeds I had sat, and had lulled my sorrow to sleep.

Darkness had settled down on the lands beloved of the Muses.

There remain two forms of verbal employment to which we must pay cursory attention. They are those of Rhetoric and Philosophy. Neither of them is necessarily literature. Both, at least in passages, may be. The greatest philosophers, like Socrates and Epictetus, conveyed their messages to humanity in conversations with disciples. Each usually found a disciple to reduce his teachings to letters. The reporter of Socrates was, of course, Plato; the Boswell of Epictetus remains unknown.

Similarly, many of the greatest rhetorical discourses were not written down before delivery, though in not infrequent cases they were actually written by what today we call "ghosts"—the Greeks calling them *logographers*. The art of rhetoric—if it be an art—embraced in its day persuasions as to every possible human function. In the book called *Aristotle's Rhetoric to Alexander*, the unknown author begins his exposition of the art with the words: "Speeches made before the city are three in kind: those made before a public assembly, those delivered at public assemblies, and pleadings in courts," and he goes on to divide up these three kinds each into seven species, the book being taken up with instances and explanations of various sorts of rhetorical practice. The book is by many people—and even by quite modern encyclopedists, supposed to have been written by Aristotle himself. But no one with any sort of literary ear or eye could possibly attribute its heavily written homespun sentences to the most brilliant of all philosophers. It is just possible to attribute it even to Anaximenes of Lampsacus. For he is said to have accompanied Aristotle in his voyages in Asia with Alexander the Great. And it is interesting to observe that he was himself both an orator and a logographer. And at any rate Quintilian attributes the book to him, so we may leave it at that!

It is, then, a capable and exhaustive guide to every manner of speaking and to every stratagem that can be employed by the orator. And still more, it affords an extraordinary picture of the Athenian psychology. There are directions as to grammatical constructions to be used:

XXV. First call everything you speak by its proper name, avoiding ambiguity. Beware of putting vowels in juxtaposition. Be careful to add the "articles" where necessary. Study the construction of the sentence, so as to avoid both confusion and transposition of words, since these cause them to be difficult to catch. After employing introductory connecting particles put in following particles. An example of putting in a following particle to correspond is: "I on the one hand turned up where I said I would, but you *on the other hand*, though you declared that you were going to be there, did not come."

As to the disingenuous handling of witnesses:

XV. It is also possible to get evidence by a trick, in such a way as this: "Callicles, bear me witness"—"No, by heaven, I will not, because the man did commit the crime in spite of my endeavor to prevent him." By these means in the form of a refusal to give evidence he will have given false evidence without being liable to prosecution for that offence. . . . If our opponents do something of the sort, we shall expose their malpractice, and call upon them to produce written depositions.

These suggestions inform us of the proper way in which to handle witnesses and evidence.

And perhaps, above all, as to the probable psychology of an audience and how it may be handled:

XXIX. Arising out of the present, the first thing that discredits speakers is their age: if a man who is quite young or quite old addresses the house, he causes resentment, because people think that the former ought not yet to have begun speaking and the latter ought to have left off. Next, a man encounters prejudice who makes a constant practice of speaking, as he is thought to be a busybody. Also if he has never spoken before, as in that case, he is supposed to have some special private reason for speaking contrary to his custom. These, then, may be said to be the ways in which prejudices in regard to a speaker will arise out of the present. The defence against them in the case of a comparatively young man must be based on the plea of lack of advisers, and on his special interest in the matter—I mean, for instance, in a case about the superintendence of a torch-race or about a gymnasium, or about armor or horses, or in regard to war, as those are for the most part a young man's concern.

The importance attached by the Greeks—and particularly by the Athenians—to oratory may seem merely evidence of an ineradicable loquaciousness attended by a desire to listen to orations. In the Acts of the Apostles (XVII.21) you may read of the Athenians of the Decline: "For all Athenians and strangers that were there spent their time in nothing else, but either to hear or to tell some new thing." Actually, however, we must remember that here for many centuries was a democracy of an extreme political curiosity and intelligence which was completely without any means of receiving official news or even diplomatic and international information. It was as if you should suddenly deprive an extremely animated city of today of all newspapers. Indeed, when a week after the French general election resulting in the Premiership of Mr. Blum, the newspapers, owing to the press strikes, stopped appearing in Paris, you found reproduced a condition that must have very much resembled the normal state of Athens. News—and, as a rule, news fairly authentic—ran from mouth to mouth. Self-constituted orators, more or less able, mounted on chairs in the café and the street corner, and every day immense meetings got together by word of mouth or by hand-written placards were addressed by one minister or prominent member of one opposition or another. That particular state of things came to an end in a day or two, but had it continued the logical consequence would have been the development of just such a school of rhetoric as existed in Athens from the earliest days until the final dissolution of Greek life under the dead hand of Rome.

In the earlier days, an intelligent people like the Athenians, could become sufficiently skillful in distinguishing between true news and false and between orators who were disinterested and others who were advocates in the pay of one faction or another or of a foreign interest. But by the day of Demosthenes, who was accounted the greatest of all Athenian orators and who lived from 384-322 B.C., the Athenian democracy seems completely to have deteriorated both in physique and intelligence. According to the laws of Solon, every citizen without regard to his wealth, must serve either in the infantry or on board the triremes. And the same with all the slaves. Similarly, a very wealthy man, as was the case with Sophocles, must not only bear the costs of the choruses of the tragedies but must provide at least one warship for the fleet. But by the beginning of the fourth century B.C., because of the wealth gathered in the age of Pericles, the Athenian citizen had become not only physically inactive but extremely unwilling to bear the expenses of the state. So that the climax, or the bitterest point of the Third Philippic of Demosthenes, he expressed in the contemptuous words: "In the second place, you must get yourselves ready, yourselves to embark upon the ships." In Philippic I, Demosthenes had demanded that a force of 2,000 infantry and 500 cavalry, of which at least one-fourth must be citizens, should be sent to blockade Philip of Macedon, off the small ports of his seacoasts. That relatively small expeditionary force was to be kept aboard ship and landed in places where military movements or embarkations should be observed to be taking place.* Indeed, the first Philippic that has come down to us is a document of relative composure. At the date of its delivery, the Macedonians, a hitherto small and despised tribe of Greek origin, had suddenly assumed the aspect of quite considerable invaders and conquerors of the Greek states to the north and northeast of Athens. Their monarch, Philip, was one of those phenomena that from time to time, with a special genius, overrun whole worlds. He inherited the throne of Macedonia in 359 B.C. and at once reorganized the finances of the kingdom and invented a new military formation called the "phalanx." This proved so irresistible that his son, Alexander, overran as we know, almost the whole of the then known world. But at the date of the first Philippic even Demosthenes was not unduly depressed at the thought of Philip. He points out to his fellow citizens that, though Philip by force or by breaking treaties had obtained possession of towns like Amphipolis,

---

* I take this to have been Demosthenes' meaning. Other commentators: Becker, Boekh, Reiske, Voemel, Ruediger of Berlin, Goettingen, etc., declare that the ships were intended solely for transporting the troops—which, considering their small number, seems absurd.

Pydna and Potidaea, in the Aegean Sea, "Nevertheless," says he, "you are not to suppose that Philip's present might is assured to him for good, as if he were a God; no, he is detested, feared and envied even by his allies who seem to be now most friendly to him." If, then, the Athenians took the efficient steps that he now asked of them, Philip's betrayal by one or more of his allies would appear to be certain. . . . And Demosthenes' demands completed themselves by his asking for, immediately, a very considerable fleet that should be held in readiness should Philip appear to be pushing them back. In that case, as we have seen, the fleet would have to be manned by the Athenian citizens themselves and not merely by the mercenaries, slaves and foreign residents, whom the Greeks had got used to employing in their wars.

The Athenians, however, remained almost unmoved by the words of the great orator. They regarded the Macedonians with the greatest contempt, placing them in the lowest class of barbarians, so that they hardly considered them to be, as you might say, Aryans—or even men. They contented themselves with sending Philip embassies. Philip bribed the ambassadors lavishly, so that he founded for himself in the city of Athens itself a very strong political party. The chief leader of this party—and the man who received most bribes—was Aeschines. This man was second only in oratory to Demosthenes himself and the feuds that he carried on in the interests of Philip against the great speaker were extraordinary for the brilliance that he used in advocating them. Demosthenes had at last succeeded in getting the Athenians to send a small force to blockade the mountain passages at Thermopylae against the phalanges of Philip. This expedition was successful. The Macedonians were thrown back and a private Athenian citizen called Ctesiphon demanded that the Assembly vote a laurel crown in gold to Demosthenes. This Aeschines opposed in the most brilliant of his orations, sometimes called "De Corona I" (Concerning the Crown). He alleged that Ctesiphon aimed at making Demosthenes dictator. But Demosthenes replied with a discourse so full of common sense and so forceful—it also is usually known as "De Corona"—that Ctesiphon was acquitted of any such intention and Aeschines had to flee from Athens. He went to Rhodes where he was said very much to have enriched himself by a school of rhetoric which he there set up. . . . Demosthenes continued his Philippics against the Macedonian invader and the Athenians continued only too languidly to follow his advice.

The population of the city consisted, as we have already adumbrated, of Athenian citizens, resident foreigners and slaves. And in their wars the citizens had for long taken no part. Thus, when they were at last aroused to the greatness of their danger and consented themselves to embark on their ships of war or to enlist in the cavalry or as foot soldiers, they formed troops of so little experience that at their first great battle, that of Cheironeia, in 338 B.C., they and their allies were completely defeated, and Athens became a mere fief of Philip's empire. After the death of Alexander, Antipater demanded as price of a nominal peace, that Demosthenes be surrendered to him. But Demosthenes, rather than be captured, betook himself to the temple of Neptune, and there swallowed poison.

The fate of Greek orators who were also true to Greece, was never enviable as compared to that of those who were ready to betray or to sell their republics. Thirty years before the day of Demosthenes and whilst the Persians still seemed menacing, his greatest predecessor, Isocrates, had incited all the Greek states to take arms against the Persians. He even included the Macedonians in his invitation. When he saw that this despised people were enabled by the wealth that they had acquired by the plunder of the Persians to become a serious menace to Athens, herself, he starved himself to death at about the date Demosthenes delivered his first Philippic. His orations, like those of Aeschines, were filled with every device and image that we should style rhetorical. Thus, they make rather monotonous and artificial reading. But delivered, as they must have been, with every kind of rhetorical grace and personal magnetism, they produced overwhelming emotions amongst their audiences. The most famous of Isocrates' orations in the Assembly was his magnificent "Panegyric of Athens." The most known of those of Aeschines were those called "Concerning the Embassy" and "Against Ctesiphon," which is frequently called, as we have seen, "De Corona." Any reader of these pages who intends to become an orator or wishes to improve his oratory, if he is already one, might do very much worse than to read these florid appeals to a credulous and excitable assembly.

The orations of Demosthenes, on the other hand, were written or conceived with no less skill and labor than those of either Isocrates or Aeschines. But his industry was given not to the evolution of flowers of rhetoric but to the amassing of fact upon fact until his arguments became overwhelming. Thus, if the reader wished not merely to acquire skill in the more sober and persuasive fields of oratory but also an extremely thorough knowledge of the personalities, conditions, and history of Athens, he had better read Demosthenes in preference to either of his illustrious rivals.

You might indeed, if you wished to, refuse him the name of rhetorician. He was by turns instructor to the Athenian public, their newsgiver, for it would appear that without him they would never have heard of the activities of Philip till he was within their walls. . . . And, like the great Marquis of Salisbury, he was the master of flouts and gibes. The purple patch he eschewed altogether, but got his effects, as it were, by the successive blows of bullets. He seems, nevertheless, to have produced an effect of unequalled enthusiasm in his hearers. Longinus, at any rate, in his *Treatise on the Sublime* (Section 12), praises Demosthenes especially for the force and brevity of his rhetorical questionings in Section 44 of Philippic I, saying that in them oratory is carried to its sublimest pitch.

The absence of any building up of effect or of making moving climaxes at the end of his orations is, nevertheless, very remarkable. The last sentences of the penultimate paragraph of Philippic I can be translated approximately—for there are many versions, this being that of the Paris manuscript: "If, disregarding all rumors, we fully realize that the man is our enemy . . . and that whatever we hoped he would do for us he has in truth turned against us, the rest depends on ourselves. For it is not needful to ask what is going to happen. It suffices to be sure that we shall taste adversity unless we understand how we should act. . . ."

And the whole closes on the quietest possible note. The great orator hopes that his sincerity will not have injured his cause. He had never been in the habit of saying, for the purpose of winning suffrages, anything that he was not sure would be for the common good. And he ends: "May what you vote (literally "may that measure win that shall") conduce to your general welfare."

A man of indomitable spirit, he subjected himself to unknown and ingenious disciplines to form himself for oratory. He put stones in his mouth and shouted against the raging sea to practice speaking in adverse surroundings. To insure simplicity in style he cut off half his hair so that he should appear ridiculous if he left his study; and then copied the works of Thucydides eight times on end—so that, since he wrote at night, his enemies declared that his orations smelled of the lamp. But he replied that his lamp lit other labors than theirs and continued his self-discipline. Finally he fought, body to body, as a common soldier, against the Macedonians at Cheironeia and essayed afterwards to gather together the scattered troops and to reform the alliance against first Philip, then Alexander.

A rugged and courageous man, his mind filled with human instances, Demosthenes was more akin to Aristotle, who voyaged with Demosthenes' enemy, Alexander, than to Plato who continuously discoursed in the green palaces of Academe.

But we cannot here devote much space to the philosophers; indeed, we can hardly spare enough to define what is philosophy itself. Literally, the word means "friendship for wisdom." And if we regard those words again as meaning a desire to gain, not to enjoy the fruits of, knowledge, we had better, I think, leave it at that. The Greeks, then, of nearly all the states whether of the Peloponnesus or Asia Minor were, beyond all men, avid in the pursuit of wisdom—and in its classification. And the results of their researches were so far-seeing and so brilliant that in many of the departments of that pursuit we today have by no means outdistanced them and in others, as a society, we are far enough behind.

Just as we have said that mankind divides itself into cynics and sentimentalists, so we may add the further aphorism that all men are born either idealists or realists, as who should say, either Platonists or Aristotelians. One of us will insist on seeing design or moral purpose in nature. Another man regarding merely the manifestations of nature will go on forever seeking knowledge in the hope of eventually seeing, before he dies, a plan in nature and the First Cause that devised that plan. He will always die before attaining to that vision. He is called an Empiricist.

The Greeks' search for knowledge would appear to have begun on any large scale about the date of the same nation's search for lyric metres—that is to say, early in the seventh century B.C. The first of the great, or at any rate the well-known, Greek philosophers was Thales of Miletus, who was born in 640 B.C. And the academy that he founded remained for so long famous, that it is interesting to remember it was on his road to study there that the Young Caius Julius Caesar, five hundred years after his death, was captured and held for ransom by pirates. To Thales an immense number of opinions are accredited by his successors until the present day, including a doctrine of chances that, by recurrences, explained human immortality. But what may here most interest us is that he took for his first principle—for that which is behind and both sustains and accounts for all occurrences—the element, water. That, *per se,* is of no interest, but when we consider that Lao-Tsze, who flourished about 600 B.C., and must, therefore, have been a contemporary of Thales, considered that water, if not itself the first principle, was nevertheless the best symbol for that *causa causans*—when we remember that, we have striking cause for thought. It would obviously be stretching the matter too far to say that Thales got his idea from Lao-Tsze, or Lao-Tsze his image from Thales. Nevertheless, even today, a bizarre rumor emanating, say, in Jaffa, will reach the ears of a Mohammedan tribe in India, crossing all Asia with a rapidity second only to that of the electric telegraph—so there would be nothing inherently impossible in the news of the birth of an idea being passed with extreme speed from the shores of the Aegean to the library of the Duke of Lu in the Middle Empire, for both Thales and his disciples and Lao-Tsze and the admirers whom he kept at a distance, were at least as greedy for the news of the birth of ideas as today are the Mufti of Jerusalem and the Mohammedan leaders of the Deccan states for news of religious bloodshed in Palestine. So we may as well permit ourselves the luxury of that fancy. What is, however, actually certain, is that the early years of the seventh century were a period of great intellectual excitement and research through the entire continent of Asia and its fringes. . . .

Mankind, then, divides itself into cynics and sentimentalists; into idealists and realists; above all, it divides itself into supporters of the Academics and supporters of the Empiricists—the Academicians being today vastly in the majority and having so been ever since the renaissance. The Empiricists enjoyed the earth during all the day of mediaevalism. From that we may deduce the further aphorism that mankind divides itself into a great many lovers of the renaissance and of few lovers of the mediaeval—or into a great many lovers of machine-made objects and a few who insist on the hand-made. The difference between Plato and Aristotle as philosophers is that the one tried to reduce the universe to a plan of his own, the other ran about over all the earth seeking instances, by the aid of which he hoped finally to see some Plan. In addition, you may say that the one was a poet nearly as great as, say, Euripides, and the other a prosateur nearly as great as Herodotus. It is obviously not our business here to write about philosophy as such. But it would be absurd, as we have at this point to write about philosophers, altogether to leave that Hamlet out of our play. As sentimentalists, realists and Empiricists, our hatred and suspicion of Plato the philosopher may be boundless. We may well see in him the root of all evil. His idealism through St. Paul, Plotinus and St. Augustine marmorealized the early Church and rendered possible that rending asunder of Christianity that is called the reformation. Having no basis at all, his philosophy abounds in completely self-destructive contradictions. He will banish poets from his ideal republic and yet he will say that his ideal republic begins to go to pieces when education consists of the dry study of law, rather than the consumption of the sweet fruits of the muses. At one moment he says, "In the brief space of human life, nothing great can be accomplished," or "it takes infinite time to make cities." And at the next, his ideal state is to be founded ready-made in all its parts in the course of a day. His *Apology of Socrates* is at least one third nonsense, one third local special pleading, one third wisdom such as is never likely to be transcended. In short, in the long arguments as to whether a creative artist can ever be a man of intelligence, those who oppose that theory may well acclaim Plato as their greatest instance. For, as in the case of the Bible when you leave out its religious aspect, so, as soon as you refuse to pay any attention to the claims of Plato to be a philosopher, you have, opened before you, an immense range of some of the most delicious, humane, beautiful and moving poetry that was ever written.

Judged by that standard the *Apology* becomes the magnificent presentation of a great and tranquil martyr before nearly imbecilic and malignant judges. Given that at bottom Plato was an academic marmorealist, the *Apology* need not fear being set side by side even with the trial of Joan of Arc. . . . And the apposition becomes the more striking when you consider that like the Saint of Domrémy, Socrates also had his Voices. And it is part of the dramatic genius of Plato that he uses the Voices as part of the hidden machinery of his dramas. . . .

This [says Socrates in the concluding paragraph of *Crito*] is the voice which I seem to hear murmuring in my ears like the sound of the flute in the ears of the mystic; that voice, say I, is humming in my ears and prevents me from hearing any other. . . .

Crito: I have nothing to say, Socrates.

Socrates: Then let me follow these intimations of the will of God.

or again:

O my judges—for you I may truly call judges—I should like to tell you of a wonderful circumstance. Hitherto the familiar oracle within me has constantly been in the habit of opposing me even about trifles, if I was going to make a slip or error about anything; and now as you see there has come upon me that which may be thought, and is generally believed to be, the last and worst evil. But the oracle made no sign of opposition, either as I was leaving my house and going out in the morning, or when I was going up into this court, or while I was speaking, at anything which I was going to say; and yet I have often been stopped in the middle of a speech, but now in nothing I either said or did touching this matter has the oracle opposed me.*

That, you see, at once absolves Plato, the poet and dramatist, for the fact that a great deal of Socrates' pleading makes nonsense, since we may well regard those passages as being sentiments considered by the supernatural being behind the voice to be adapted to the semi-imbecile beings who are trying him. Consider, for instance, the following passage showing Socrates' handling of the Chief Prosecutor Meletus:

Can a man believe in the spiritual and divine agencies and not in demi-gods? [asks Socrates. And Meletus answers] He cannot.

I am glad [Socrates then continues] that I have extracted that answer, by the assistance of the court; nevertheless you swear in the indictment that I teach and believe in divine or spiritual agencies (new or old, no matter for that); at any rate, I believe in spiritual agencies, as you say and swear in the affidavit; but if I believe in divine beings, I must believe in spirits or demi-gods—is not that true? Yes, that is true, for I may assume that your silence gives assent to that. Now what are spirits or demi-gods? Are they not either gods or the sons of gods? Is that true?

Yes, that is true.

But this is just the ingenious riddle of which I was speaking: the demi-gods or spirits are gods, and you say first that I don't believe in gods, and then that I do believe in gods; that is, if I believe in demi-gods. For if the demi-gods are the illegitimate sons of gods, whether by the nymphs or by any other mothers, as is thought, that, as all men will allow, necessarily implies the existence of their parents. You might as well affirm the existence of mules, and deny that of horses and asses. Such nonsense, Meletus,

* *The Works of Plato,* Jowett's translation. Vol. III, p. 131. (New York: The Dial Press.)

could only have been intended by you as a trial of me. You have put this into the indictment because you had nothing real of which to accuse me.*

On those lines, then, nothing is lacking to Plato. There are, of course, dialogues that are heavy reading because of the obscurity of the thought. But in a great majority of the pieces like the *Symposium* or *Phaedo* or again *Phaedrus*, the admixture of poetry, of observation of character and the drawing of characters, or the humor and the pawkiness of Socrates are so adjusted that the reading of a dramatic piece like the *Symposium* is, from beginning to end, not merely a matter of pure delight drawn from Socrates' depiction of the views concerning love of the most dissimilar characters, but a piece of observation so true to the essentials of all humanity that the banquet might have taken place yesterday or might as well take place five hundred years hence. We will illustrate from Professor Jowett's translation.

From its leisurely beginnings:

Apoll. Well, the tale of love was in this wise:—But perhaps I had better begin at the beginning, and endeavor to repeat to you the words as Aristodemus gave them.

He said that he met Socrates fresh from the bath and sandalled; and as the sight of the sandals was unusual, he asked him whither he was going that he was so fine.

To a banquet at Agathon's (Agathon was a young dramatist whose first tragedy had just won the first prize), he replied, whom I refused yesterday, fearing the crowd that there would be at his sacrifice, but promising that I would come today instead; and I have put on my finery because he is a fine creature. What say you to going with me unbidden?

Yes, I replied, I will go with you, if you like.

Follow then, he said, and let us demolish the proverb that "To the feasts of lesser men the good unbidden go;" instead of which our proverb will run that "To the feasts of the good unbidden go the good;" and this alteration may be supported by the authority

* *The Works of Plato*, Jowett's translation. Vol. III, pp. 115-116.

of Homer, who not only demolishes but literally outrages this proverb. For, after picturing Agamemnon as the most valiant of men, he makes Menelaus, who is but a soft-hearted warrior, come of his own accord to the sacrificial feast of Agamemnon, the worse to the better.

right through all the speeches of the various characters like that, say, of Phaedrus who said:

"Love ought not to be praised in this unqualified manner. If there were only one Love, then what he said would be well enough; but since there are more Loves than one, he should have begun by determining which of them was to be the theme of our praises. I will amend this defect, he said; and first of all I will tell you which Love is worthy of praise, and then try to hymn the praiseworthy one in a manner worthy of the god. For we all know that Love is inseparable from Aphrodite, and if there were only one Aphrodite there would be only one Love; but as there are two goddesses there must be two Loves. For am I not right in asserting that there are two goddesses? The elder one, having no mother, who is called the heavenly Aphrodite—she is the daughter of Uranus; the younger, who is the daughter of Zeus and Dione, whom we call common; and the other Love who is her fellow-worker may and must also have the name of common, as the other is called heavenly. All the gods ought to have praise given to them, but still I must discriminate the attributes of the two Loves."

right through to the very end with the intrusions of troops of revelers.

. . . there remained awake only Socrates, Aristophanes, and Agathon, who were drinking out of a large goblet which they passed round, and Socrates was discoursing to them. Aristodemus did not hear the beginning of the discourse, and he was only half awake, but the chief thing which he remembered, was Socrates insisting to the other two that the genius of comedy was the same as that of tragedy, and that the writer of tragedy ought to be a writer of comedy also. To this they were compelled to assent, being sleepy, and not quite understanding his meaning. And first of all Aristophanes dropped, and then, when the day was already dawning, Agathon. Socrates, when he had put them to sleep, rose to depart, Aristodemus, as his manner was, following him. At the Lyceum he took a bath and passed the day as usual; and when evening came he retired to rest at his own home.

there is hardly a break in the interest and we may add not a single departure from the extreme simplicity of language that was the great literary quality both of Socrates and of Plato. For we may regard Plato as once more an instance of a breaking away from complicated and conventional forms and speech to the extremes of simplicity. Indeed, it was one of the things urged against Socrates at his trial—that his language was so simple as to be an insult to the court.

And one has once more in excuse of Plato to point out that though he has done really great harm to the world by his recommending the exclusion of imaginative writers from the republic, and so giving excuse to every bourgeois scientist, priest, financier and politician to decry the muses, that was probably because the poets of his day were already decadent. And he was thinking of them rather than of Alcaeus, Sappho or Stesichorus. And, if he was hard on dramatists, Aristophanes with his bitter caricature of Socrates, in the *Clouds*, was undoubtedly really responsible for the trial and condemnation of the philosopher.

Platonic philosophers, then, sat around in gardens and beneath the Doric columns of porticos. Differing from the philosophers who had preceded them, they sought their cosmogonies amongst men, rather than in the way of their predecessors, amongst natural objects—the earth, the air, metals, humidities or droughts. They took, however, no part in life and their knowledge of humanity was drawn from the characters or the gossip of the relatively idle people who surrounded them. If your usual companions are Aristophanes, Alcibiades, Pausanias and Apollodorus, and if you, yourself, are Plato, reporting Socrates, your view of humanity, whether because of the licentiousness of Alcibiades, the venom of Aristophanes or the lofty nature of Socrates, will not be very close to the ground. So if from those characters you desire to draw your ideal of an anthropomorphic universe, your projection will be apt to be as marmoreal as the acanthus leaf of a Greek frieze.

But this process reversed itself when you came to Aristotle and the Peripatetics. The mere name shows you the difference. Except for short strolls from a clump of trees outside Athens to the city, the first Platonists sat eternally. The Peripatetics were continually running around like ants to every corner of the globe, to capture and bring back the detritus of minute facts that went to make up the immense aggregation formed by the writings of Aristotle himself and of his disciples and imitators.

It is not merely because we are advocates of the muses and, therefore, enemies of Philosopher Plato that we may dare to state a preference for Philosopher Aristotle. All professed philosophers are the mortal enemies of all poets. But those rare ones who make genuine and sustained attempts to ring the truth from the hard things that surround them—such rare philosophers are making the same attempts as the poets. And so they are, to some extent, kindred spirits. As if recognizing that, Aristotle, the wandering, gives in his *Politics* a sufficient space to the muses of verse and song—or would have done so if he hadn't forgotten or died too soon. He made, at any rate, the promise to do so.

But every proper man, be his label what it will, desires to see jobs well done. And no just one, even among his champions, can deny that, however it may have been with the poet Plato, Philosopher Plato retired too early from his researches and so broke the back of his job among the hot rocks of Athens. And, rising into the empyrean of otherworldliness and morals, he contented himself with dreaming a Utopia and calling it a philosophy. In that he resembled Cicero and St. Augustine and so many before him, and Sir Thomas Moore and so many others who came after him. For the harm that Plato did to the world was not merely that which he did himself. He encouraged too many who followed him and attained to rulership in this world to invent from insufficient premises and with the aid of faulty or unscrupulous imitations of logic, fallacious and too facile rules of conduct for the government of cities and men's lives. We may take the late Professor Jowett of Balliol as having been the doughtiest of Plato's champions. The famous Jowett is reported to have exclaimed:

> "Here I stand, my name is Jowett
> What there is to know I know it.
> I'm the master of this college
> What I know not is not knowledge."

Fortified, no doubt, with the maxims of Plato, Jowett turned out from Balliol College, Oxford, so many consuls, pro-consuls, governors-general and viceroys for the British dominion overseas that the British Empire has been called Jowett-land. Such a stamp did his disciples leave upon it, and so far may the influence of dreaming Plato be said to have penetrated! But indeed his influence has come down to us during innumerable centuries and from innumerable places. It is not merely that it came through St. Augustine from Alexandria or from Byzantium at the renaissance. The very Arabs who burned the library at Alexandria saved and carried away with them the works of Plato. So that, not only from Constantinople but from Carthage and from Spain itself under the Abencerages, did the middle ages, who learned so much of the Arabs, get their second-hand wisdom of Plato. And even the Persian poets of the thirteenth century like Jalal'U' Ddin Ru'Mi in the *Diwan-I-Shemes-I-Tabriz* and Fari'Da' Ddin' Attar are not chary of quotations from the *Dialogues,* so that when Europe went mad over the translations of those Orientals, we got the influence of Plato, once more, at second hand.

But even Jowett cannot but give the game away as between Philosophers Plato and Aristotle in innumerable places in his *Works of Plato.* Thus you have:

> . . . and whatever may be the obligations of this branch of inquiry to Plato, it is certain that his genius and zeal for natural science were far inferior to those of Aristotle, and that his achievements in this department bear no comparison with those of his

scholar, either in extent of knowledge, acuteness of observation, exactness of interpretation, or fruitfulness of result.

and:

The study of particulars seems to him scarcely more than an intellectual pastime, and if he has for a while occupied himself with it, he always returns, as if wearied out, to the contemplation of pure ideas.

or again:

What in the one was a matter of personal discipline, in the other becomes conscious method reduced to general rules; whereas the former aimed at educating individuals by true concepts, the latter seeks out the nature and connection of concepts, in themselves: it inquires not merely into moral problems and activities, but into the essential nature of the Real, proposing as its end a scientific representation of the universe. But Plato does not go so far in this direction as Aristotle; the technicalities of logic were not formed by him, as by his pupil, into an exact, minutely particularizing theory; neither for the deviation nor for the systematic application of concepts does he summon to his aid such a mass of experimental material. He cares far less for that equal spread of scientific knowledge into all departments which Aristotle desired, than for the contemplation of the idea as such. He regards the Empirical partly as a mere help to the attainment of the Idea—a ladder to be left behind if we would gain the heights of thought; partly as a type of the nature and inherent force of the ideas—a world of shadows, to which the Philosopher only temporarily descends, forthwith to return into the region of light and of pure beings.

It is not, of course, to be imagined that as philosophers, Plato and Aristotle sprang at once fully armed upon the earth. With very little scholarship, you can, as I have already said, trace the influences of Thales and Anaximenes on the mind of Plato. I imagine myself still more to find traces of Pythagorian ideals in Aristotle. The influence of Pythagoras and his numbers upon Plato, when he was writing his *Republic*, are sufficiently well known. But the very fact that Pythagoras was in fact, if not in name, a Peripatetic—that is to say, a wanderer— seems to have colored the mind of Aristotle, so that he left Athens and the teachings of Plato for the court of Alexander and his wide subsequent wanderings. Pythagoras from his travels in the East evolved a philosophy that had a striking resemblance to Buddhism. And the quasi-religious order which he founded in Crotona might almost have been a Buddhist monastery. Buddhism, however, was a phenomenon of the fifth century and Pythagoras founded what it is convenient to call his order about 520 B.C. He must, therefore, have found in the India that he visited, a set of doctrines or an atmosphere which were, as it were, getting ready for the appearance of Gauthama Buddha, much as the Christian world awaited the coming of Christ to found His Church. Similarly, Aristotle traveling through the East was to find in force two hundred years later, a vastly increased cult of that name which by his day had spread from India, as we have seen, to China and which today still finds nearly five hundred million worshippers. Unlike Pythagoras, Aristotle remained, on the whole, impervious to the temptation to be satisfied with any creed or cosmogony whether from the far or from the near East. He was a searcher after instances and to the day of his death had drawn very few conclusions.

The writings by Aristotle or those ascribed to him are extremely numerous. At least fifteen minor works remain on subjects ranging from "On Colors," "On Things Heard," "On Marvelous Things Heard," on "Indivisible Lines," "On the Names of Winds." Of larger collections, we have the thirty-eight books of *Problems*, to which we shall attend immediately, and the *Rhetoric to Alexander* to which we have already given some attention.

The question of which of the texts that have come down to us are the actual writings of Aristotle and which were written by disciples under his dictation and direction and which ones were more or less deliberate forgeries written after his death and in imitation of him— all these things form subjects that are eminently worthy of debate. They have been debated with violence for many hundreds of years.

In this matter we ourselves may well be exclusive and should regard a great number of books from the *Rhetoric to Alexander* to several of the pamphlets of the *Minor Works* as being certainly not by Aris totle himself That, however, Is the judgment of a critic of imaginative letters and may be disregarded should the reader be employed upon the career of a scholiast or decipherer of papyri.* It seems obvious, however, that the brilliant, whimsical and all-discerning mind that gave us the *Politics* can hardly have been the same as that which produced the *Rhetoric to Alexander* or, say, the *Eudemian Ethics*. But that again is a matter in which the reader must judge for himself. Let us then consider for a moment in the *Problems* the matters to which Aristotle devoted his attention. They are boundless. The first question is:

Why is it that the quantity of fruit needed to produce satiety is not proportionate to the amount consumed in the same persons, but varies according to whether they eat it after or before a meal? Is it because fruit is much heavier than the same volume of solid food? Figs prove this, if they are eaten last; for they are vomited last.

and the last

Why does the sun bleach oil but blacken flesh? Is it because it abstracts the earthy element from the oil? This is black like the earthy element in wine. But the sun blackens the flesh because it burns it; for the earthy element when burned always becomes black.

Or here we have the enormous canning trade predicted. He says:

Why is it that fruits and meats and all similar things which are

* The works of Aristotle are easily obtainable in the Loeb Classical Library, published in London by William Heinemann and in the United States by the Harvard University Press. Of these the general reader wishing to have sufficient knowledge of this greatest of philosophers might well read those entitled: *Politics, Poetics and Longinus, The Minor Works* and *The Athenian Constitution*. But, indeed, he might very well read every word written by or attributed to Aristotle and remain the better for it.

put in leather bottles remain without decaying, when the bottles are fully blown up, and that the same things happen in vessels whose lids are tightly sealed? Is it because movement is the cause of decay, and when the containers are full there is no movement? For movement is impossible without an empty space and these are full.

Or here are some further questions:

Why should one eat sweetmeats? Is it an efficient substitute for drinking? For one must drink, not merely because of the thirst which arises while eating solid food, but also after solid food.

Why is it that some men become ill, when, being accustomed to live an undisciplined life, they no longer live thus; for instance, Dionysius the tyrant, when in the siege he ceased drinking wine for a time, immediately became consumptive, until he reverted to his drinking?

And a question that might well be addressed to the administration of almost any modern state where robbery of the public is considered a venial offense:

Why is it that, if a man steals from a public bath or a wrestling ring or a market or any such place, he is punished by death, but if he steals from a private house his penalty is double the value of the thing stolen?

From all this it will appear—as, indeed, was the case—that the mind of Aristotle was primarily encyclopaedic and that what he and his fellow workers and disciples produced was the first *Encyclopaedia Graeca*. Nevertheless, it would be stretching the point too far to say that Aristotle never attempted any solutions of any of the problems that he stated. In the realm of what used to be called "natural philosophy," and today is usually styled "physics," this was relatively the case. But when it came to "politics" and what we still call "metaphysics,"

Aristotle was relatively ready to afford interpretations of these matters. (It is amusing to consider that Aristotle himself never heard the word "metaphysics." It exists because the first editor of the complete works of Aristotle had collected into one section the whole of the matter that concerned physics, and he then turned his attention to collecting Aristotle's writings on intellectual, moral and cultural questions—the word "metaphysics" meaning, in fact, simply "after physics.") In his *Politics* he gives you a complete system of government and one that is much more minutely documented and illustrated than is the *Republic* of Plato. Here he comes to the conclusion that since man is merely the physical matter of which states are compounded, individuals cannot make and change the state at will but it is the province of the state to form individuals. The family, property and slavery are natural institutions. The best form of government is a constitutional monarchy, but it becomes the worst when the monarch is despotic. Nevertheless, it is untrue to say that the same form of government is suitable to all nations and circumstances and the wellbeing of the state consists in a just proportionment of power between its various classes. (*Politics,* IV, 9.) His ethics, we may sum up by saying that for man the highest good is found in that happiness which is the result of equal and harmonious blending of the intellect and animal instincts. From that condition virtue is constituted—that intellectual virtue that in the mind is wisdom and in action is prudence or common sense. Plato held that virtue is the opposite of vice but Aristotle is the advocate of the Golden Mean. Thus, courage, one of the highest virtues, stands midway between cowardice and foolhardiness; and liberality lies between miserliness and prodigality. (*The Nicomachean Ethics of Aristotle,* II, 5.) It is impossible in a work of this scheme to quote much further from this great prose writer, but that the reader may have, as it were, a view of how Aristotle's mind works, let us here quote one of the passages that has always seemed to me most characteristic of his writing from the admirable translation by Dr. D. P. Chase in *The Nicomachean Ethics of Aristotle.*

Now, there is a state bearing the same relation to Greatness of Soul as we said just now Liberality does to Munificence, with the difference, that is, of being about a small amount of the same thing: this state having reference to small honor, as Greatness of Soul to great honor; a man may, of course, grasp at honor either more than he should or less; now, he that exceeds in his grasping at it is called ambitious, he that falls short unambitious, he that is just as he should be has no proper name: nor in fact have the states, except that the disposition of the ambitious man is called ambition. For this reason those who are in either extreme lay claim to the mean as a debatable land, and we call the virtuous character sometimes by the name ambitious, sometimes by that of unambitious, and we commend sometimes the one and sometimes the other. Why we do it shall be said in the subsequent part of the treatise; but now we will go on with the rest of the virtues after the plan we have laid down.

And so let us end this section of this book with what should most interest us students of art. The difference, says Aristotle, between nature and art is this: that her end or purpose is that alone which makes her act and exists beforehand in the beings or organic matter that she produces. The difference between nature and art is this: what the artist in action aims at exists before he takes action; it is already in his mind; in nature the aim is there only as an instinct. Thus the conception "bird" exists already in the egg and the conception "oak" in the acorn. Did the idea "ship" or "bed" exist in the acorn, the process of nature would be the same as that of the art of the naval constructor or the joiner. In the art, therefore, the mind of the artist exists between the egg and the bird, the acorn and the oak, the earth and the First Cause.

Part Two

CHAPTER ONE

A RISTOTLE,* then, may stand as the last of the Greeks. He was a symbol of the great division between the ancient and the modern world. For nothing could be more mistaken than in any way to unite the idea of the Greeks with the idea of the Romans. Into the completely materialistic world without art that was the Roman Republic and Empire, the few Greek manifestations that there penetrated were as alien and forlorn as would be a picture by one of the French Impressionists introduced into a mining town in Colorado or on the Murambigee River in Australia of the 80's of the last century. The few imitations "from the Greek" that made a short appearance in Roman life were so alien to the spirit of the Romans, whether patrician or proletarian, that they had the shortest possible lives and are for the most part hardly traceable. Thus, in 240 B.C. the Romans finally defeated the Carthaginian fleet under Hanno in the battle at the Aegadian Islands and the Carthaginians had sued for peace, given up all claims to Sicily and paid a war indemnity of four million dollars. Then Rome, which was at the time going through a constitutional struggle, decided to celebrate the end of a war which had lasted for twenty-two years by instituting athletic games and dramatic contests in imitation of the Olympic games and the Tragic Contests of the Greeks. The games were a success; the Tragic Contests never, as the saying is, caught on. The first drama, which has disappeared, was written by Livius Andronicus in 240 B.C. He was followed, amongst those whose works have survived, by Plautus who lived and died about thirty years after Livius Andronicus, and by Terence who died about thirty years after Plautus. Livius Andronicus was born in 284 B.C., Terence dying in 159 B.C. Tragedies never appeared at those Olympiads, but Plautus produced a number of gross comic plagiarisms from Philemon, Aristophanes, the *Alazon* and Terence; and not so many but less boisterous imitations of the relatively tender new comedy of Menander and

---

* The reader who considers philosophic speculations dull or who regards philosophy as having nothing to do with pure literature in which we are very inclined to agree with him, should here skip to p. 175 where we shall consider Catullus, Tibullus and Propertius and afterwards Roman imaginative literature in general.

163

other Greeks. During that century and a quarter there were other dramatists called Naevius, Ennius, Pacuvius, Accius, nearly all of whose works have disappeared. One knows of them only that those called *Togatae*, being acted in Roman dress and scenery, were more successful than those called *Palliatea*, which were Greek in costume and scenery. But even Plautus and the Roman-costumed dramas were not very successful. This was owing partly to the fact that the Romans did not approve of heroes and deities being represented by play actors—in which they resembled the Lord Chamberlain of today who censors the drama in England. And the drama in Rome gradually degenerated into pantomime and later became mere costume shows. They accompanied the hecatombs of men and wild beasts that, as we shall see, distinguished the later imperial festivities.

But still greater than the aesthetic schism between the Greek and the Roman eras was the metaphysical and religious one—this turning on the belief or disbelief in the immortality of the soul, and, more particularly, on retributions or rewards in the hereafter. Belief in immortality was always vague amongst the votaries of the deities of Olympus. Sophocles, as we have seen, portrayed an after-life for great men, and set apart for dead heroes and their female companions special subterranean paradises. But the belief in Charon and his wherry faded and disappeared from the minds of the intelligent Romans along with Zeus, Hera and Hermes shortly after, say, the death of Socrates. Aristotle set *finis* to the doctrine of immortality by affirming that the "eternal intelligence," which was the same as the Supreme Being, alone was eternal. This postulated the complete denial of individual immortality. After his death his Lyceum was taken over by distinguished philosophers like Theophrastus, Aristoxenus and Strato of Lampsacus. Aristoxenus denied the immortality of the eternal intelligence, Strato the very existence of God, so that either Aristotle's affirmation of belief in the eternal principle was merely a concession to the spirit of his time or his empire of thought was posthumously as divided as that of Alexander.

Since we ended our consideration of the Grecian era with philosophers, we may as well, a little to avoid breaking continuity, go on here to the philosophers of the Roman era. We will do this because the rival schools of philosophy identified themselves with the rival schools of politics and literature, and thus conduced very greatly to historical and literary happenings in post-republican Rome.

It is necessary, however, to pay some attention to history before going on with the metaphysicians. Aristotle, then, died in 322 B.C. Exactly fifty years after his death, Pyrrhus, King of Epirus, was killed by a tile thrown by an old woman. With his death came to an end the long triangular struggle that had been going on between his Greek coalition—such as it was—and the Romans and, finally, the Carthaginians. Pyrrhus died in 272 B.C. after his complete defeat by the new world power called Rome and the cession to it of Tarentum. Not very long afterwards the Romans were to begin their gradual swallowing up of Greek territory and of nearly all of the Empire of Alexander. But immediately they turned their attention to the Carthaginians and once more the name of the Mamertines and of Hiero II, the patron of Theocritus, must appear on the page. The Mamertines—a sect of sea-robbers—had invaded Sicily upon which Rome and Carthage had both begun to cast loving eyes. It was Hiero II, defending Syracuse, to whom—much as might any poet of today—Theocritus addressed the passionate appeal that that benevolent tyrant should spend his money not upon armaments but upon poets. The Mamertine robbers appealed both to Carthage and to Rome for assistance. But Hiero eventually formed an alliance with Rome, and in 263 B.C. a Roman force landed for the first time in Sicily. With the aid of Hiero it defeated the Mamertines and the Carthaginians. Then began the long Punic wars against Carthage. They lasted from 264 to 146 B.C. They ended in the latter year, after street fighting lasting six days and a conflagration lasting seventeen, in the capture and destruction of Carthage by the Romans. The Romans, thus, had complete control of the Mediterranean and even while the war against Carthage was proceeding, they were carrying on the fourth Macedonian War, which began in 148 and ended in 146 B.C. Macedonia became a Roman province and the whole of Greece passed into Roman power. By that latter year Rome possessed eight provinces: Sicily, Sardinia and Corsica, the two Spains, a large portion of Gaul, a great slice of Africa and finally Macedonia and Greece. And, gradually, all this immense stretch of the earth's territory containing the greater proportion of the world from which came the literatures of which we have hitherto treated, fell under the Roman yoke. They became, to varying extents, standardized as Roman provinces. For us it is chiefly necessary to remember that Athens continued to be for several centuries a home for schools of philosophy where it was deemed necessary for Romans of the upper classes to finish their educations. Horace, for instance, and the son of Cicero were both together there as pupils, meeting there also a great number of the sons of Roman politicians and officials. Athens, in fact, became a sort of pre-Christian Oxford where young men acquired ornamental learning and made useful acquaintances. A list of the subsequent friends of Horace reads exactly, *mutatis metandis,* like a list of friends that a promising young poet of Oxford or of Princeton might today accumulate.

With earlier Roman history we do not have much to occupy ourselves. During the seventh century, whilst the Greek lyric, elegiac and dramatic forms were the chief preoccupations of the Greeks, the Romans were a savage tribe subject, probably, to a much more highly civilized people called the Etruscans. Most of the Roman history of that period consists of legends invented long subsequently by Roman historians to give a respectable appearance to their ancestors. Towards the beginning of the sixth century B.C. Rome expelled her Etruscan kings and something like history, strongly mingled still with legends, began, with Lucius Junius Brutus and Lucius Tarquinius, the first Roman consuls about 510 B.C. The period between that date and the beginning of the first century B.C.—at, say, 106 B.C., the year of Cicero's birth—was occupied in the development of the two branches of genius that the Romans unexampledly possessed. They conquered, that is to say, the whole of Italy, made the Mediterranean safe for their keels. In the long and nobly contested struggle between plebeians and patricians they evolved a republic as nearly politically perfect as can be seen in the course of recorded history. And, indeed, if we wished to mitigate the

harshness with which we have spoken and shall continue to speak of
their aesthetic and literary gifts, we might postulate that the Romans
were the one people—with the possible exception of the British—to
show any democratic political intelligence in the course of history.
They had achieved a constitution of great elaboration which gave them
reasonable freedom, security of property and the right to express
themselves politically. But the one side of their genius which in the
end was purely materialist, inevitably and fatally destroyed the other.
If their political instinct was great, their military gifts were even more
astonishing. Their army conquered the entire world and then, as if it
were an immense snake, turned upon itself and devoured its own belly.
For, to whatever disparate causes the historians, from Gibbon to
Mommsen, may assign the downfall of Rome, one cause is unescapable to the eye that looks at this history without the preoccupations
of dislike for Christianity or the determination to bolster up the
throne of the Hohenzollerns. Some other historian has ascribed the
fall of the Empire to finance . . . and that is probably truer still. But
it was the financing of the Roman army with its continual murder
of its rulers and the continual, always heavier, donations of their
successors to that army that caused those financial exigencies. In addition, its choice of rulers fell exclusively on individuals whose virtues,
if they possessed any whatsoever, were virtues exclusively military
or strategical. And it was only on the rarest possible occasions that
they elected any emperor who was capable of paying any attention at
all to the arts or the necessities of peace.

To return, then, to our philosophers. The tutor of Posidonius of
Apamea was the Stoic philosopher, Panaetius of Rhodes. They died,
respectively, in 50 and 112 B.C. The Stoic philosopher Posidonius was
the tutor of both Cicero and Pompey the Great; thus the reason for
the influence of the Stoic philosophy upon Roman politics and arts
becomes at once blazingly apparent. The quality of Roman prose was,
before all, that of extraordinary verbal clarity and definiteness in the
exposition of the subjects. And Cicero probably carried those qualities

to their highest possible pitch and exercized an extraordinary influence upon everyone who thereafter has attempted to write plainly and with incisiveness. Posidonius and Panaetius in their turn were the spiritual descendants and heirs of Zeno who taught in the *Stoa Thoiliki* of Athens. From that building his philosophy took the name of Stoic.

The stoic philosophy had for supporters, the Left in politics and the religious in inclination. The most famous of all Stoics was the Emperor Marcus Aurelius. Thus, in his day, the whole power of Imperial Rome was at the disposal of Stoicism. Eventually—through Seneca and St. Paul, who may or may not have been a friend of Seneca's but who certainly was his fellow townsman—one branch of the Christian Church also supported them. The Stoic slogan was "Virtue for virtue's sake."

The other great school of philosophy was supported by the Right in politics; by the poet Lucretius; by Lucius Torquatus; by Pomponius Atticus, Caesar, Horace and Pliny the Younger. It was that of Epicurus. We are at some disadvantage in writing of this great philosopher who was born of Athenian parents in the colony of Gargettos in 341 and died in 270 B.C., being thus an almost exact contemporary within a few years of his rival the Stoic Zeno. His enemies triumphing and there remaining no one with any interest in preserving his works, they have almost entirely disappeared. So that if we want to know anything about what he actually wrote we have to find it in the quotations of various Greek writers, like the unknown author of that *Treatise About Physics* which was found in fragments at Herculaneum, or in Diogenes Laertius who, in the third century B.C., catalogued 300 of his writings. We may find his strong traces in the *De Rerum Natura* of the poet Lucretius, whose cosmogony was entirely founded on the Epicurean philosophy. But Epicurus being vanquished and his writings being either trampled on or misrepresented by his more pious imperial victors, it is not astonishing that Epicureanism should have been blackened at their hands until the name of his philosophy has come to mean nothing but a greed for the right kind of victuals. Actually, it is self-evident that that cannot be the case with a philosopher who was supported by some of the noblest of Roman spirits and poets. Someone—

I forget whom—has called Epicurus "Socrates doubled by Voltaire," and for an epigram, it is not a bad epigram.

Unlike Aristotle who loved science for knowledge's sake, Epicurus held that knowledge was the servant of human life. In that, just as Aristotle may be called the end of Greek thought, so Epicurus might be considered the beginning of Roman intelligence and action. Actually he was born perhaps nine, perhaps ten years after Zeno the Stoic. So that to be strictly accurate we should give Zeno the *pas* on the Roman philosophical literary scene.

Epicurus was a complete sceptic in religious matters; he loudly disbelieved in either the absolute creation or the absolute destruction of the world. If we desired to make him speak, since it is almost impossible to quote him, we might imagine his saying:

"How can we imagine that a world overflowing with evils is the creation of a deity? What surrounds us are scorched deserts, icy mountains, marshes filled with asphyxiating vapors, Hyrcanian snows, thorns and briars, hail storms, tornadoes, beasts of prey, sicknesses and too early deaths. Are these not all proof that no deity has any hand in governing things? Since all the nations of the world assert that deities exist, it would be superfluous to deny their existence. But to imagine that beings floating luxuriously in space, supremely happy, without the passions or the weaknesses of us men, could be moved by our wretchedness, by our crimes, by our sacrifices or by our prayers or praise . . . that, supposing we should postulate their existence, would be beyond reason.

"Neither should we think that they occupy themselves with our posthumous fate. They are completely indifferent to us. We should, therefore, cease either to fear the tortures of Tartarus or to anticipate immortal bliss. The soul is sensation and sensation is material. The soul, therefore, is material. It is influenced by the body and by the body exclusively, as is proved by faintings, deliriums, epileptic unconsciousnesses and being affected by injury and disease.

"In consequence, we should not be prevented by irrational fears from attaining what is the highest goal of our existence—happiness. But we should seek the pleasures of the mind in preference to any form of voluptuousness. For the pleasures of the mind endure whilst sensations vanish the moment after they have been produced. All excesses we must avoid, since all excesses engender pain which is the opposite of pleasure. On the other hand, you may confront certain pains such as those caused by medicines or operations, because they may procure health and consequent pleasure. Virtue is that sort of skill derived from knowledge by which the wise man guides himself towards pleasure, but it is also a permanent state—the state of profound and peaceful quiet and of that contentment in which we may feel safe from disaster or evil chances."

This philosophy was supported, of course, by infinite instances and encyclopaedic researches into the physical nature of things. In spite of that, it became of an immense popularity in the Roman politer world. It changed its aspect less than its rival, Stoicism, which in the course of Roman centuries became something that would have been unrecognizable by Zeno himself. The precise degree, for instance, of frugality that it was necessary to employ to attain at once to virtue and deep peace, contentment and immunity from disaster—that precise degree of frugality was infinitely discussed by innumerable minor writers between Lucretius and Horace. But that it contributed immensely to such amenities and reasonablenesses as the Romans displayed is obviously indubitable.

Disbelief in the immortality of the soul formed, then, the major item of the Greek philosophy that the Romans took over. On the other hand, the doctrine of the immortality of the soul plus posthumous retribution came from crowds of Eastern religions; from the ancient Egyptians; from the Indo-Chinese Buddhists of the fourth century, B.C.; from at least one powerful sect of the Jews and other Palestinian races. At the same time came monotheism. For we may safely say that all the great figures of late republican Rome despised the gods of Olympus and at least privately believed in a central Supreme Being.

In the mean time, as it were, on the side, Philo, a Jew of Alexandria, tried to reconcile Judaism with the Platonic philosophy. His central creed provided for a Word. In that he resembled Lao-Tsze. His Word, in effect, like the word of the Chinese philosopher, sanctified all things—the laws, the ideas, and the God of Moses, along with the laws, the ideas and Supreme Being of Plato. Philo was born in 20 B.C., so that he would be twenty-four at the birth of St. John who spiritedly adopted the doctrine of the logos, that, as we know, forms the first light of his Gospel.

From that date onwards to the third century of our era, Alexandria was to be the home principally of pagan and Christian philosophers and scientists. The chief continuer of the Graeco-Roman monotheist philosophy was Plotinus, an Egyptian, who founded a school that was half a religion, in Rome in 244 A.D. The chief doctrine of his philosophy was what was called emanatistic pantheism—the doctrine that all created matter, and thus the entire globe, emanated from the central being which was God. Much as if a bowl should have slopped over—or rather as if a molten drop of the spinning sun should have flown apart and become the human universe. As regards the immortality of the soul, he held that the individual soul was purified by philosophy here on earth, that it went through a further period of purification in space beyond the tomb. Then, purged of its last trace of individuality and earthliness, it was reunited once more to the eternal principle.

Plotinus' school became of such immense popularity among the Roman aristocracy and ruling powers that the Emperor Gallienus and the Empress Salonina both enrolled themselves amongst his pupils. He wrote nothing until he was fifty. Nevertheless, at his death he left 54 treatises which have come down to us in a fairly complete state. He died in 270 A.D. and was succeeded as head of the school by the very inferior disciple, Porphyry. There then began, as was inevitable, considering the birth of Christianity which was still hated by the Roman rulers, a reconstitution of a semi-mystic kind of the ancient Olympic deities.

The process was further continued by Plotinus' disciple Jamblichus, who completely reconstructed the pagan Pantheon. In deference to the natural leaning of the Roman mind towards monotheism, he established Jupiter as a central All-father or Supreme Being, surrounded by a triple halo formed out of the other gods and demi-gods. Jamblichus was of Syrian origin and gave to the Neo-Platonism of Porphyry a Syrian tinge of thought which was in no way shocking to the emperors. They, by that date, were mostly of African or Asiatic birth. With Proclus, we arrive at the last word not merely of Platonic or Neo-Platonic, but of all antique thought. He was the last successor of Plotinus. He practised even magic, and shortly after his death the school of Athens to which place Neo-Platonism had been expelled, was closed by the Emperor Justinian. For nearly two centuries, then, the empire had been in possession of Christians. Theorizing was finished and the dogma of the middle ages began its fearful reign.

Of pure literature these philosophic systems of themselves produced very little. It is proper to consider that literature consists of nothing but the highest forms of poetry and of imaginative prose. But rigidly to adhere to that rule would be to carry professional intolerance too far. In an effort after impartiality, we may, nevertheless, dwell upon these ideas rather than upon their literary expression. But, rightly to understand such really imaginative writers as Horace and Lucretius of the first century B.C., or St. Augustine of the fourth to fifth centuries of our era, it is necessary to have some idea of their background and of the religious thoughts that were at the back of their minds.

No doubt all the writings of all the philosophers from Plato to Proclus, and of all the theologians from the Apostolic Fathers, Tertullian and Lactantius who were savagely anti-philosophic, to St. Augustine who lived in the fourth and fifth centuries and was at once a great Christian and a great Neo-Platonist, are from one angle or another worth reading by those who find professional interest in them. Some selection we must, nevertheless, make.

But practically no philosophic works of the Roman Imperial period have any literary value at all except the writings of Seneca, those of Epictetus, as recorded by Arrian, and those of Marcus Aurelius. And amongst theologians there is little to satisfy one's literary desires except for St. Augustine's *City of God* and the *Confessions*. Tertullian is memorable for carrying his contempt for philosophy so far as to have written the famous phrase *Credo quia absurdum*. We may well find a certain pleasure in reading some of the works of the Apostolic Fathers —writers who had been in actual contact with the Apostles. Let us examine for a moment the first *Epistle of Clement to the Corinthians*. Clement, who has to reprove the Corinthian church for some piece of nepotism in the election of its priests, does so at enormous length. But he never once mentions the subject of his letter but exhausts almost the entire Old Testament in quotations which rebuke the sins of envy, pride and jealousy.

> Once [says Clement] you were all humble-minded and in no ways arrogant . . . with pious confidence you stretched out your hands to Almighty God in a passion of goodness. . . . Who has stayed with you without seeing the proof of the virtue and stead-fastness of your faith? . . . All sedition and all schism were abominable to you.

"But, alas," Clement goes on in his third section, quoting Deuteronomy, "my beloved ate and drank and he was enlarged and waxed fat and kicked." And he quotes biblical cases of jealousies, as thus: "It came to pass after certain days that Cain offered to God a sacrifice in the fruits of the earth. . . ." And when he is finished with the murder of Cain, he adds, "You see, Brethren, jealousy and envy wrought fratricide; through jealousy our father Jacob ran from the face of Isaiah, his brother. Jealousy made Joseph be persecuted to death and come into slavery." And this goes on for 65 chapters. So that it is amusing to consider the feelings of the Corinthians upon reading it.

St. Augustine, though accepted by both Roman and Reformed churches is, nevertheless, at times accused by the latter of heresy to a certain degree.* That is hardly our affair, though the association is

---

* The writer happened at the moment of writing these words to look at a *History of the Christian Church Including One of the Cumberland Presbyterian Church* published in 1835 by the Rev. James Smith in Nashville, Tennessee, and came upon the following words: "His works, which are more numerous than those of any other writer of this period, bear the marks of sincere piety, vivacity, and genius, but are chargeable with ambiguity and the impulse of a too warm imagination. *He was a zealous advocate for the doctrine of predestination!*"

probably justified because the saint's passion for Christianity was, in his writings, so mingled with the passion for Neo-Platonism—the emanatistic pantheism of Plotinus—that the two strains are at times indistinguishable. But after he became bishop of Hippo, his sermons and writings grew gradually more and more distinctively Christian. Nevertheless, from our point of view, he would seem to be eminently satisfactory because to Tertullian's *Credo quia absurdum* ("I believe because it is absurd"), Augustine answered *Credo ut intelligam* ("I believe in order to be able to understand"). And when Saints Jerome and Chrystostom—who were the favorite saints of St. Ignatius Loyola, the founder of the Jesuits—declared that it was permissible to lie in a good cause, Augustine answered from his episcopal chair, "Permit falsehood and you permit sin."

Of the great number of his writings, I should imagine that only *Confessions* and the *City of God* could much interest us or attract the reader of these pages. Those two works are, however, supremely worth reading on account of the beauty of their writing, the largeness of their tolerance and the humanity of their thought.

On the theological side the writings of St. Augustine put *finis* to the classical period in the history of the world's religion. Even one hundred years before the date of Augustine's death in 430 A.D., Constantine had issued the Edict of Milan making Christianity the official imperial faith. Its language became the Latin tongue and the Church took over the keys, at first of the spiritual, and then of the aesthetic and even the civil life of the Western world. But what is more important to remember from the point of view of the history of literature is that Constantine established the seat of his government in Byzantium, which was renamed Constantinople. From the tenth to the fifteenth centuries A.D., the Mohammedans more and more encroached along the shores of the Mediterranean and of Greece, so more and more Constantinople became a storehouse for the manuscripts of the Greek poets and writers of all the previous ages and the refuge of all the Greek scribes and commentators of the world that flew before the advancing pagans. Thus, when in 1453 Mohammed II took Constantinople, the Greek scribes once more fled before him, grasping their precious manuscripts, and the full flood of the renaissance burst upon the Western world. Incidentally, it is as well to remember that that Greek eruption was, as it were, the reintroduction of Platonic idealization to the Western world. The Empiricism of Aristotle had governed the thought of the middle ages from, as it were, the destruction of Rome to the discovery of America.

Having thus summarily disposed of the philosophers and theologians, we may turn our attention once more to pure literature and begin an examination of the Roman poets. Putting these in their order of merit, according to the tastes of this writer, we should name, first, Tibullus, Propertius and Catullus. Catullus was born in 87 and Propertius and Tibullus within two years of each other in 52 and 54 B.C. After them I should place Horace, Ovid, Virgil and Lucretius. Ovid was born in 43, Horace in 64, Virgil in 70 and Lucretius in 95 B.C.

Of these authors, according to this writer, Catullus, Tibullus and Propertius should be regarded as genuine poets who absorbed the very spirit of the Greek elegiac, iambic, lyric, or pastoral poets. They continued exploring and expressing the vicissitudes of humanity in exactly the same spirit as did before them Theocritus, Stesichorus or Sappho. Merely the language had changed.

And these three poets used Latin with such skill and softness that the harsh trace of the Roman tongue and mind completely disappears in their lines. The writer has always held that the most exquisite poetry in the world was contained in the following four lines of Tibullus.

> *Te spectem, suprema mihi cum venerit hora,*
> *et teneam moriens deficiente manu*
> *flebis et arsuro positum me, Delia, lecto,*
> *tristibus et lacrimis oscula mixta dabis*

They have at once a beauty and simplicity of words, a simplicity and truth of feeling such as are almost never found in the great range of the poets. But that is not to attempt to bind the reader to the same verdict. For criticism is not the warm expression of sentiment but the cool exposition of a man standing back and viewing with relatively cold eyes the object upon which he is to descant. Indeed, in its final depths, criticism is the explanation of the appeal made by a work of art to humanity. The critic—and the literary historian must be critical—must make a constatation, not primarily of the merits of the work but of the nature of its appeal. He must not say—at any rate, primarily—whether he likes a subject or not. Here is Dante; he has millions of readers. For hundreds of years his fame has endured and shows no trace of failing. The critic must analyze the causes for that appeal. It is only when he throws off his robes of office that he is at liberty to become a man and to state his preferences.

Of the three Latin poets, then, of whom we are about to treat, Catullus would appear to have had the greatest appeal to the Roman aristocratic public that made up the poets' audiences in the last days of the republic and the first ones of the empire. This is probably because there was about him more than a touch of the man of the world and more than a flavor of the conventional habit of backing up such of his verses as were natural with images drawn from the legends of the Greek gods and demi-gods. Putting that derived glory at its least and quoting a passage of Catullus which contains a good deal of observations of nature, there yet remains to the lines a touch of aristocratic condescension or aloofness. They are the observations of nature by the aristocrat, the man of the world, not the observations of either the naturalist or the peasant. Consider what follows:

Him when the damsel beheld with eager eye, the princess, whom her chaste couch breathing sweet odors still nursed in her mother's soft embrace, like myrtles which spring by the streams of Eurotas, or the flowers of varied hue which the breath of spring draws forth, she turned not her burning eyes away from him, till she had caught fire in all her heart deep within, and glowed all flame in her inmost marrow. Ah! thou that stirrest cruel madness with ruthless heart, divine boy, who minglest joys of men with cares, and thou, who reignest over Golgi and leafy

Idalium, on what billows did ye toss the burning heart of the maiden, often sighing for the golden-headed stranger!*

Catullus really does seem to have loved a Lesbia who was reputed to be the most beautiful, the most influential and the most licentious of Roman women. Her infidelities to her husband, and in consequence also to himself who aspired to be her lover-in-chief, were many and apparently ostentatious. But Catullus had for her a passion and in the end that passion would seem to have driven him to despair and death. The only other things that are known of him are small details that go to prove that he lived in the best—the most politically and intellectually active—society of the Rome of his day. His father, for instance, was an intimate friend of Julius Caesar. His friends and contemporaries were poets, wealthy landed proprietors and friends of Augustus. And although it is apparently certain that his passion for Clodia, the wife of Quintus Metellus Celer, really wrought his ruin, it is extremely difficult to disinter from his work any passages which express deep grief or real concern. . . . Indeed, one may say that the deepest grief he ever showed was over the death of a sparrow—the famous lines that begin:

> *Lugete, O Veneres Cupidinesque,*
> *et quantumst hominum venustiorum.*
> *passer mortuus est meae puellae,*
> *passer, deliciae meae puellae, . . .*

and which Mr. Cornish has translated thus:

Mourn, ye Graces and Loves, and all you whom the Graces love. My lady's sparrow is dead, the sparrow my lady's pet, whom she loved more than her very eyes; for honey-sweet he was, and knew his mistress as well as a girl knows her own mother. Nor would he stir from her lap, but hopping now here, now there, would still chirp to his mistress alone. Now he goes along the

* *The Poems of Gaius Valerius Catullus I*, translated by F. W. Cornish. (The Loeb Classical Library.)

dark road, thither whence they say no one returns. But curse
upon you, cursed shades of Orcus, which devour all pretty things!
My pretty sparrow, you have taken him away. Ah, cruel! Ah, poor
little bird! All because of you my lady's darling eyes are heavy
and red with weeping.

It is perhaps not difficult to explain the attraction of Catullus to
his contemporaries and to western Europeans during the eighteenth
and the early years of the nineteenth century. These last, it must be
remembered, were nearly as buried in Roman affairs as were the contemporaries of Catullus himself. You get from him innumerable
sidelights upon Roman and, above all, Roman suburban life. The
Roman suburb was vastly more rural than the suburbs of the great
cities of today—consisting, indeed, of real farms, the owners of which
made a great deal of money out of them with slave labor. Catullus'
approach to nature was, therefore, on the one hand and when he was
in the mood, purely realistic. He spoke of the nature of soils, of profits,
of the extent of estates:

Mentula has something like 30 acres of grazing land, 40 of
plow land; the rest is marsh. His estate has many fine things in
it; water-fowl of all sorts, fish, pasture, arable land and game. But
it is useless to him, he outruns the produce of it by his expense.

He is keen. He is hard. He is at times almost vitriolic. At times he
almost resembles Heine. Only when he is in the mood to be profes-
sionally poetic, as in his hymeneal odes, does he introduce his con-
ventionalizings of streams and woods and myrtle trees and fleeces and
bosoms. And these are to be found in the works of other imitators
of Theocritus and the Sicilian pastoral poets. He is, in fact, in himself two poets in one—or even three. As we have seen, something
like sentimental regret overwhelms his mood over the death of Lesbia's
sparrow. Had he been in his more professional mood he would have
remembered that doves and sparrows were the birds most devoted
to Aphrodite. He would have begun his poem with a great and sounding legendary exposition of Venus and her charms, alluding only in

the end to the fact that her feet were surrounded by a fluttering carpet of the birds affected to her. But in his mourning for the sparrow the pained lover observes the little things in the ambience of his mistress and so he approaches poetry.

He has, then, the quality of revealing to us the Roman world of his class and scale of wealth. That is in itself not a literary merit. But when things not of themselves literary are consummately done they become well worthy of the attention of the devotee of literature as an art. Let us take some quotations. Here is Ode XXXVII, a projection of what you might call Roman night club life, beginning:

> *Salax taberna vosque contubernales,*
> *a pilleatis nona fratribus pila,*
> *solis putatis esse mentulas vobis,*
> *solis licere, quidquid est puellarum,*
> *confutuere et putare ceteros hircos?*

and translated:

Gallant pot-house, and you brothers in the service, at the ninth pillar from the temple of the "Brothers in the hats" (Castor and Pollux); are you the only men, think you? the only ones who have leave to buss all the girls, while you think everyone else a goat? Or if you sit in a line, five score or ten maybe, witless all, think you that I cannot settle ten score while they sit? Yet you may think so: for I'll scribble scorpions all over the pot-house front. My girl, who has left my arms, though loved as none ever shall be loved, has taken up her abode there. She is dear to all you men of rank and fortune—indeed, to her shame, to all the petty lechers that haunt the byways; to you above all, paragon of long-haired dandies, Egnatius, son of rabbity Celtiberia, made a gentleman by a bushy beard and teeth brushed with your unsavory Spanish wash.

And here is an expression of dislike as caustic as it could well be, which, incidentally, gives information as to the care of its teeth by the Roman society. It begins:

Egnatius, quod candidos habet dentes, renidet usquequaque.

Egnatius, because he has white teeth, is everlastingly smiling. If people come to the prisoner's bench, when the counsel for the defence is making everyone cry, he smiles: if they are mourning at the funeral of a dear son, when the bereaved mother is weeping for her only boy, he smiles: whatever it is, wherever he is, whatever he is doing, he smiles: it is a malady he has, neither an elegant one as I think, nor in good taste. So I must give you a bit of advice, my good Egnatius. If you were a Roman or a Sabine or a Tiburtine or a pig of an Umbrian or a plump Etruscan, or a black and tusky Lanuvian, or a Transpadane (to touch on my own people too), or anybody else who washes his teeth with clean water, still I should not like you to be smiling everlastingly; for there is nothing more silly than a silly laugh. As it is, you are a Celtiberian; now in the Celtiberian country the natives rub their teeth and red gums, we know how; so that the cleaner your teeth are, the dirtier you.*

And this is what happened to you in those days after too much night life:

> *O Funde noster, seu Sabine seu Tiburs, . . .*
> *fui libenter in tua suburbana*
> *villa, malamque pectore expuli tussim, . . .*

My farm. . . . I was glad to be in your retreat, 'twixt country and town, and to clear my chest of the troublesome cough, which my greediness gave me (not undeservedly) whilst I was running after costly feasts. I wanted to go to dinner with Sestius, and so I read a speech of his against the candidate Antius, full of poison and plague. Thereupon, a shivering chill and a constant cough

* Ode XXXIX.

shook me to pieces, till at last I fled to your bosom, and set myself right again by a diet of laziness and nettle broth. So now, having recovered, I return you my best thanks because you did not punish my error. And henceforth, if I ever again take in hand the abominable writings of Sestius, I freely consent that the chill shall bring catarrh and cough, not upon me, but upon Sestius himself, for inviting me just when I have read a stupid book.*

And this is for this writer an amusing proof of the theory that he has for many years entertained, that the London cockney—that is to say, the real costermonger, with his dark eyes and head like Julius Caesar and his wife with flashing teeth, raven locks and love of bright colors —is actually a descendant of the Romans who built the Tower of London.

> *Chommoda dicebat, si quando commodu vellet*
> *dicere, et insidias Arrius hinsidias. . . .*

Arrius, if he wanted to say "honors" used to say "*h*onors," and for "intrigue" "*h*intrigue"; and thought he had spoken marvellous well, whenever he said "*h*ambush" with as much emphasis as possible. So, no doubt, his mother had said, so Liber his uncle, so his grandfather and grandmother on the mother's side. When he was sent into Syria, all our ears had a holiday; they heard the same syllables pronounced quietly and lightly, and had no fear of such words for the future: when on a sudden a dreadful message arrives, that the Ionian waves, ever since Arrius went there, are henceforth not "Ionian," but "*H*ionian."†

Three poets in one, then, and all three producing a singular prophecy of Heine. For though there are poets who have been as tender or as cruelly satirical or as much in the grand manner, I cannot think of anyone else save Heine who united all the three characteristics.

He was born some thirty years before either Propertius or Tibullus

* Ode XLIV.
† Ode LXXIV.

and, more than they, he came under the influence of the Greek
lyrical and pastoral schools in Alexandria, so that on the one hand he
was relatively derivative and on the other purely Latin.

But Propertius and to a still greater degree Tibullus were Latin
poets who had learned of the Greeks not so much of their manner as
the method of working of their minds—of their approach to life.

Propertius was once more of much the same social rank as Catullus
and had much such a history. He was born at Assisi in 52 B.C., his
father having been a landowner who was apparently much impoverished since Octavian and Anthony in 41 B.C. had seized his lands
and distributed a great part of them to their veteran legionaries. He
would appear to have been a hereditary knight and to have begun by
studying for the bar, abandoning that career in favor of writing
poetry. Like Catullus, his life was ruined by an unfortunate passion
for a relatively abandoned woman called Cynthia to whom, nevertheless, he seems to have been quite frequently unfaithful. Apparently,
according at least to Apuleius, Cynthia was a courtesan. That rendered it impossible that he should marry her. The Lex Papia Poppea
forbade the marriage of a man of free birth with a prostitute. We may
gather a great many particulars as to her person and tastes from Propertius' own poems. She was tall and blonde with black eyes. She sang
and danced well and wrote poetry.* She was also apparently a hit-
and-run charioteer of the most inveterate description. Consider Book
IV of Propertius' *Elegies* as translated by Mr. H. S. Butler:

Learn that this night struck panic through the watery Esqui-

---

* " 'Twas not her face, bright though it be, that won me. Lilies would not surpass
my mistress for whiteness; 'tis as though Maeotic snows were to strive with Spanish
vermilion, or rose-leaves floated amid stainless milk. 'Twas not her hair flowing trimly
o'er her smooth neck, 'twas not the twin torches of her eyes, my lodestars, nor a girl
shining in Arabian silks: not for such trifles as these am I a gallant lover! 'Tis rather
that at the revel's close she dances wondrously, even as Ariadne led the Maenad dance;
'tis rather that when she essays to sing to the Aeolian lyre she rivals the harp of
Aganippe in her skill to play, and challenges with her verse the writings of ancient
Corinna, and counts not Erinna's songs the equals of her own." (*The Elegies of
Propertius*. Book II. Translated by H. E. Butler.)

lene, when all the neighbors ran headlong through the New Fields. . . .

Hither was my Cynthia drawn by close-clipped ponies. She pleaded Juno's worship; more truly had she pleaded rites of Venus. Tell forth, prithee, thou Appian Way, what a triumphal journey she made before thine eyes, as her wheels whirled madly over thy paving stones. . . . She was a sight to see as she sat there bending over the pole's end and daring to drive amain through rough places.

Since so oft she had wronged our bed, I had resolved to change my couch and pitch my camp elsewhere. There is a certain Phyllis, that dwells nigh Diana on the Aventine. Sober she pleases me little; when she drinks all is charm. Another there is, one Teia, that dwells 'twixt the Tarpeian groves; fair is she, but when the wine is on her, one lover will be all too few. These two I resolved to summon to make night pass less sadly, and to renew my amorous adventures with loves still strange to me. . . . Lygdamus had charge of our cups; we had a service glass to suit the summer with Greek wine that smacked of Methymna. Thou Nile, didst provide us with a piper, while Phyllis played the castanets, and, fair in her artless beauty, was right content to be pelted with roses. Magnus himself, with short and shrunken limbs, clapped his deformed hands to the sound of the hollow boxwood flute. But, though their bowls were full, the lamp-flames flickered, and the table's top fell upside down on the feet that had supported it. And as for me, while I sought for sixes from the favoring dice, ever the ruinous aces leapt to light. They sang to me, but I was deaf. They bared their bosoms, but I was blind. . . .

And lo! of a sudden the door-posts groaned harsh with turning hinge, and a light sound was heard at the entrance of the house. Straightway Cynthia hurled back the folding portals, Cynthia with her hair disordered, yet lovely in her fury. My fingers loosed their grasp and dropped the cup, my lips turned pale though drunken with wine. Her eyes flashed fire; she raged with all a woman's fury. The sight was fearful as a city's sack. She dashed her angry nails in Phyllis' face: Teia calls out in terror on all the watery neighborhood. The brandished lights awakened the slumbering citizens, and all the street rang loud with the madness of the night. The girls fled with dishevelled raiment and tresses torn, and the first tavern in the street received them.

This obviously contains an echo of the idyl of Theocritus, which has been quoted here, in which the popular song "The Wolf" was sung to the discomfiture of the banquet giver. But actually it is much less an echo than are the Catullan renaissance paintings in his *Wedding Ode*. Indeed, it might be almost safe to say that Propertius is, as it were, mediaeval as opposed to the renaissance of Catullus. The Renaissance, as we shall amply see, was an imitation of Greek details. Propertius, on the other hand, with something of the Greek tradition still in his mind, was an exact, an almost empirical observer of the life surrounding him—and of his own life. But the life that surrounded him was in every detail brutal, besotted and agrarian. Propertius, too, drew his revenues, such as they were, from a farm.

But, though his companions were besotted brutes and the object of his adoration a very flashing courtesan, the innate poetry of the man was so great that at times he wrote lines as beautiful as have ever proceeded from mortal pen. From this writer's earliest childhood, amongst his collection of ten or fifteen of the most beautiful lines that were ever written, have stood the first four or five lines of the twenty-sixth elegy of Propertius' second book.

> *Vidi te in somnis fracta, mea vita, carina*
> *Ionio lassas ducere rore manus,*
> *et quaecumque in me fueras mentita fateri,*
> *nec iam umore graves tollere posse comas,*
> *qualem purpureis agitatam fluctibus Hellen,*
> *aurea quam molli tergore vexit ovis.*

No translation can give the poetic feeling or the equivalent of the extraordinary beauty of the Latinity of this poem. For whereas Catullus frequently indulged, as we have seen in the case of the poem about

Arrius, in verbal quips and plays upon words, and neglected frequently the sound of his words, using popular locutions and consonantal harshnesses, the Latin of Propertius is almost always of great beauty, smoothness and vowel music.

Let us for a moment glance at the difficulties that meet a translator faced by lines as liquid and as graceful as those of Propertius quoted above. The passage is a picture. In his dreams Propertius has seen his Cynthia, swimming in the Ionian Sea. She is weary, her hair is weighed down with brine and as she swims she confesses the wrong she has done her lover. At intervals, the tips of her palms hardly show any more above the waves and, her hour having come, she calls him by name. . . . And after some compliments addressed to his mistress the poet ends with the words: "I was thinking to cast myself from the rock on which I was when my terror at the sight broke up the dream. . . ."

It is a universal subject for a poem: there is hardly a man or woman who has never awakened in the night in the dread caused by some such vision and any merely respectable poet could put it, if he did it at all spontaneously, into agreeable verse. But, faced with the incomparable, ringing, marble bas-relief of the Latin, you will be overcome by paralysis. The English language with its harsh sounds and soft, gluey effects of meaning, as compared with the clear Latin, can hardly ever be marble or ringing. And carried out in English, the Latin hexameter-pentameter verse has an artificiality, if only because to use it you must employ polysyllables of which, in common speech, we have almost none. And Englished-Latin hexameters have a monotony that ends in a boredom almost without equal. Or if we attempt to render in the daintier English verse forms the grave Latin clarity, we shall feel as if we were setting dancing a flock of little ballet dancers—and crudities!

You could render Propertius, but not literally, in his own metre by something like what follows:

Vidi	t'in som	nis frac	ta mea	vi ta	ca	rinā
I have	seen you	in my	dreams, lady	swimming the	ocean

Cleaving I	onian	waves	wearily	drifting to	doom
Ioni	o las	sas	ducere	rore ma	nus

That is rather horrible!

Or, literally translated you would have:

> I have seen you in dreams, cleft, *oh my life, your keel*
> In the Ionian wave propel (lead) the weary hands.

But what makes these particular lines almost untranslatable into English are the words *fracta carina*. They mean, "thy keel having been broken" or "your vessel having sunk"—and, in effect, they are a solecism since they destroy the unity of the image. The image is of a woman swimming, the white arms against the ultramarine waves: the solecism is that of introducing the *reportage*—the journalism— of the broken ship. Propertius, no doubt, chanced the solecism for the sake of the extraordinarily beautiful words *"mea vita carina"* (which should be pronounced "mayah veetah kahreenah" and not "meyer vaïter keraïner"). . . . And the Romans had a great love for that beautiful word *"carina,"* bringing it in wherever they could (cf. *"male fidus carinis"* of the *Aeneid*, etc.), perhaps because they really loved the sea as the stamping ground for their unnumbered piracies and the road for their unceasing invasions. But for us Anglo-Saxons it is extraordinarily difficult in this particular case to get away with: "vessel," "craft," "keel," "ship," "bottom." "Trireme" might be better but we have no warrant for thinking that Cynthia's *carina* was anything of the sort.

Translation, in short, the real carrying over of image, sense beauty and music of a poem is impossible. If a reader—preferably with a little knowledge of the original language—can completely ignore the awkwardnesses of a literal translation, a perfectly literal translation like "I have seen you in dreams, cleft, oh my life, your keel" may be of use to him. Otherwise there is neither right nor reason in verbally approximating a translation to the original. What one should read should be adaptations: Fitzgerald's *Rubaïyat* in English, Baudelaire's *Poe* in French.

To obtain a really satisfactory translation of any great poet a nearly as great, or as great, or preferably greater, must steep himself in the spirit, the imagery, the rhythm of the first writer; but he must avoid memorizing the words. After having turned possible translations over in his mind for a long time so that the original has become only a memory, as if of color, sound, image, he may then sit down and work at his transference—remembering only that his wording must not be too glib or of the moment.*

To get however the normal, not too tender, not too harshly cynical temperament of Propertius and his picture of Rome we may as well make the following quotations:

Here is a homecoming:

> Like as the maid of Cnossus lay swooning on the desert strand
> . . . even so, meseemed, did Cynthia breathe the spirit of gentle rest, her head propped on faltering hands, when I came dragging home my reeling feet, drunken with deep draughts of wine, and the slaves were shaking their dying torches in the gloom of night far-spent.†

Here is Roman morality:

> What profits it for maids to found temples in honor of Chastity, if every bride is permitted to be whate'er she will? The hand that first painted lewd pictures, and set up objects foul to view in chaste homes, first corrupted the unsullied eyes of maids and refused to allow them to be ignorant of its own wantonness. *May he groan in torment who by his vile art first wakened strife 'twixt lovers, strife lurking secret under silent joy!* Not with such fig-

---

* After nearly half a century of carrying these quoted lines of Propertius in his head this writer has arrived at producing the following: . . . after Propertius:

My life, I see you in dreams, wearily cleaving the wide
Ionian; you, sinking fast with the weight of your hair in the tide,
Confess all the wrongs done my fame by your numberless lies great and small. . . .
You, spent, and your palms in the tide, hardly emerging, to call
Faint and more faintly, my name.

But that is about as many rhymed pentameters as, I imagine, the English ear will willingly support. And, comparing this rendering with the original, I see that, not only have I unrepentantly cut out Propertius' *carina* but I have actually introduced the adjective "wide" without its having any equivalent in the Latin.

† These and the following translations are again those of the Loeb Classics, by H. E. Butler.

ures did men of old adorn their houses; then their walls had no foul deeds painted on them. But deservedly have cobwebs gathered o'er the temples and rank herbage has overgrown the neglected gods

the ethical strength being however a little discounted by the underlying meaning of the lines underlined above: as who should say, "Curses on lubricities in image and word for they will send an otherwise chaste imagination a-roving and so infidelities are born." And here again is the modern note.

Even now, mad girl, dost ape the painted Briton and wanton with foreign dyes upon thy cheek? Beauty is ever best as nature made it; foul shows the Belgian rouge on Roman cheeks. May many an ill befall the maid in hell, that in her folly dyes her hair with lying hue. Away with these things! I at least shall find thee fair; fair enough art thou to me if only thou visit me often. If one stain her brows with azure dye, does that make azured beauty fair?

And here in the next is the eternal note of lovers:

Does my love think of sailing long leagues of sea, I will follow her. One breeze shall waft us on, a faithful pair, one shore shall give us rest when we sink in slumber, one tree overshadow us, and oft shall we drink from the selfsame spring. One plank shall yield a couch to lovers twain, whether my bed be strewn by prow or stern. I will endure all things, though the wild East Wind drive our bark and the South's chill blast sweep our sails, whither we know not; though all ye winds should blow that once tormented the hapless Ulysses and wrecked the thousand ships of Greece on Euboea's shore, and ye also that parted the two shores, when the dove was sent to Argus to guide his bark over an unknown sea. If only she be never absent from my sight, let Jove himself fire our ship! For surely our naked corpses will be cast together upon the same shore; let the wave sweep mine away, if only thou find burial in earth.

This indicates the greatest of self-sacrifices, since to be unburied after death—even if only with the ceremonial three handfuls of sand—was the greatest of all calamity in the Romans' eyes.
And finally:

. . . Not yet do drooping breasts forbid thee to make merry; that be her care that hath borne a child and counts it shame. While the Fates grant it, let us glut our eyes with love: the long night hasteneth on for thee that knows no dawning. And oh! that thou wouldst bind us in this embrace with such a chain that never the day might come to break its power!

Of Tibullus almost nothing, externally, was known. His father was of equestrian rank, which means that he possessed land worth at least 400,000 sesterces—which you might put at $500,000. At any rate, socially and politically, he was of the second rank in the Roman hierarchy. His son, Albius Tibullus, the poet, lost these lands at Pedum—about sixty miles from Rome—by confiscation. He seems later to have recovered the greater part of them. One gathers that he had as patron the distinguished soldier—M. Valerius Messalla, a friend of Augustus. One gathers also that he was not of robust constitution, since, having at the age of twenty-four accompanied Messalla on his campaign in Aquitaine, he was too much invalided to go with him on his later campaign to the East. So for the rest of his life he lived on his farm, loving—and writing poems to—a lady called Delia who caused him many heart searchings. One may or may not believe that Delia was married. In the second canto of his Book II he purports to send his mistress such a potion for her husband that not only will the husband refuse to believe any tales he may hear about them but: *"Non sibi, si in molli vident toro"* (he will not believe his eyes even if he catches them in the act of love).

But a poet of the realistic merit of Tibullus would hardly publish his secret directions to his mistress. On the other hand, the husband appears to have been frequently absent in the wars.

> For me [writes the poet] he may go on chasing the mobs of routed Alicians and may let his forces camp on captured ground. Covered from head to foot in armor of silver and armor of gold, let him set his swift charger under that gaze of crowds; so only, with you, my Delia, I may yoke as before my oxen, pasture my flock on their accustomed hill. And, if it is but opportune to hold you in my young embrace, my sleep shall be soft even upon the rough ground.*

Or, of course, Tibullus may not have intended his poems for publication until after his death.

And that may, indeed, have been what happened. Having been born in 54, he died in 19 B.C. at the age of only thirty-five—the thirties being usually considered to be the proper age at which poets should relieve the world of their presences. His poems would appear to have been published by the glorious M. Valerius Messalla himself in 19 or 18 B.C. After Tibullus' death the publication would seem to have taken the form of an anthology. Anthologies were not unusual in an age when any wealthy patron of the muses could get together and send to the publisher collections of poems addressed to him by his poet-clients. At any rate, it is fairly safe to consider that Tibullus had nothing to do with writing Books III and IV of the poems ascribed to him. They are relatively pedestrian and conventional performances; six of them are certainly by a poet called Lygdanus, five short pieces being addressed to a female relative of Messalla, six very short verses by the lady herself and a four-line threnody over the death of Tibullus by one Domitius Marsus.

So, not concerning ourselves with Books III and IV, let us address ourselves to the poem with which we opened the pages here devoted to the poetry of the Romans of the late republican and Augustan age. They mean exactly:

* Tibullus, I, ii. Author's translation.

May my eyes fall on thee when the last hour shall have come
    for me,
May I hold you with my weakening hands.
You shall weep, Delia, and when I have been placed on the bed
    that shall soon be set on fire
You shall give me kisses and sad tears intermingled.
You shall weep, your breast is not cased in hard iron
Nor in your soft heart is there any stone.
From that funeral rite neither youth nor virgin
Shall return with his eyes dry
You shall not humiliate my ghost by your absence, nevertheless,
Do no violence to your loosened hair nor to your soft cheek.*

And all Tibullus is of that sweet and gentle rusticity. He is the completely composed poet of the soul. The objects he limns are the natural objects of the hillsides; his attendant deities are the little gods and dryads of his fields and coppices; his lyre is tuned, like that of Ausonius, literally, to the note of water dropping into rock pools. His songs are as old as those of the first navigators and his mind as young as that of Colonel Lindbergh when he first flew the Atlantic. It goes as directly to his goal. He is Poet, as the moon is the moon; or Philomela, the nightingale.

Having said that, you will be facing a challenge when you quote him. Do not be afraid: *ab aestimatione non timebit.*

Here then are the first words of his to reach us. He had been wounded and permanently invalided in the Aquitaine campaign of Messalla and he says:

Let others gather together heaps of the ruddy gold
And others, many thousand-acred bonanza farms,
Let their preoccupations be with the enemy at the gate
Their sleep broken by the martial rumble of the drum
But for me, let my poverty lead me by quiet paths,
Whilst on my hearth burns an ever tender fire.
Let it be mine now to live contented with little
Nor ever again to follow the long road,

* Tibullus, I, ii. Author's translation.

And then the beautiful lines:

> sed Canis aestivos ortus vitate sub umbra
> arboris ad rivos praetereuntis aquae.
> nec tamen interdum pudeat tenuisse bidentem
> aut stimulo tardos increpuisse boves
> non agnamve sinu pigeat fetumve capellae
> desertum oblita matre referre domum.

which may be adapted thus:

> But in the days when the dog star rises above our horizon
> To live in the shade of trees on the banks of a swift stream.
> Nor shall it shame me from time to time to go hoeing
> Or to hasten the plodding oxen on with my goad,
> Nor yet shall it weary me to bear home in my arms
> Lamb or kid forgotten and left by its dam.*

And so he rejoices in that with his own hand he plants vines and orchard trees, sows his grain and half defies the fates to give him heaped bins and overflowing vats of wine. For, says he, where offerings of flowers are laid on a tree stump or a flat old stone at a ventways, there he genuflects and the first apples of the year he offers at such shrines to the countryman's god.

A little self-sufficing life; little half-forgotten shrines and gods. . . . Truly Tibullus was the first and best of those of us who are small producers, and certainly he most beautifully voiced our pleasures and cares. . . . With his contempt for the large commercial farms run by slaves! And his scarlet scarecrow, shaped like Priapus and holding a scarlet sickle to keep the birds away. And his Delia must be chaperoned for his sake, even in the house of her husband—who no doubt was the famous, martial Messalla in his armor "all of silver and all of gold."

"*At te, casta maneas,*" he prays her that she remain always chaste— always with her aged duenna at her side to guard her sacred innocence.

---

* Tibullus, I, iv. Author's translations and adaptations.

Then, when the lamps are lit, the old lady shall entertain his Delia
with her stories, drawing the thread from the full distaffs. . . .

And does not the *"haec orbi fabellas referat positaque lacerna"*
of Propertius prophesy the *"le soir a la chandelle assise au coin du
feu, devisant et filant"* written by Ronsard fifteen hundred years
later, with its maids nodding over the fire at their stitching and
starting at Ronsard's name? Just as *"puella paulatim somno fessa
remittat opus,"* Delia's maids nodding gradually into sleep let their
sewing slip from their fingers.

"And then suddenly," he cries, "I shall come in unannounced; and
may I seem as if I came from heaven to your side! Then, just as
you shall find yourself, your feet bare, your hair unsnooded flying
behind you, you shall run to meet me." . . . And so, fields and hinds
having been duly purified in the spring and the country god having
driven away at once all field pests—and, indeed, the smoke of their
spring purifying fires may well have kept the Roman orchard free
of grub!—the harvest has been good. . . . So, the autumn being
come, *"tunc nitidus plenis confisus rusticus agris."*

The countryman, with his shining face, having done well to trust
for fortune to his field, lets heap great tree trunks on his blazing
hearth. And a crowd of children—that sign of a lusty cultivator—
born to the hands of the estate shall play before the fire, building
themselves little huts out of the kindling sticks. And then indeed

Nunc mihi fumosos veteris proferte Falernos!

Now bring us, steaming, wine of old Falernum:
  Sever the rushes round the new Chianti:
Wines crown today! . . . And hard we sweat to earn 'em,
  Olive and pear, apple and fat-eared wheat.
Drink hearty, lads! For sure I should not want 'ee
  Hence to go home with steady-stepping feet.
And each that drinks shall cry: "All hail Messalla!"
  And name the fere he is most fain to meet.*

And in the distance swelters Rome.

* Author's translation.

Those three, Tibullus, Propertius and Catullus were Rome's Sicilian triad—and it is a mere matter of taste which of the two threes you estimate as the first in beauty of the elegiac lyric writers of the world And like the Greeks, those Romans left no successors. . . . You have to go probably three hundred years, to the days when already Rome began to founder, before you get the sudden shaft of sunlight of the *Pervigilium Veneris* with its lilting burden:

> He who has never loved, let him love tomorrow:
> The lusty lover, let him love again.

To that we shall come in due course.

CHAPTER TWO

I F YOU wish to retain in your mind an image—maps, as it were—
of Roman literature, it is a good thing mentally to divide even
the Age of Augustus into two. There were the orators, historians
and bepatroned poets of the town. And then the almost patronless
poets of the countryside and the provinces. . . . This writer at least
always has in his mind an image of a golden, as if subterraneous
cord. It stretches from the Roman triad who were all dead before
the birth of Our Lord to the little groups of African, South French
and other provincial poets who three hundred years later, seem to
give a little glow of life to the dark scene just before the establishment of the Christian church. You could not call Nemesianus of
Carthage, Tiberianus of the same place, Ausonius of Bordeaux, the
Christian Prudentius of Calagurris in Spain, the unknown author of
the *Pervigilium*, or Claudian of Alexandria, great poets. They all
however flourished in the fourth century A.D. and were all distinguished by a cheerful and contented love of natural objects. That
makes them, if they were not nightingales, at least something like
the low-voiced linnet of the hedgerows.

So that one's imagined map of Roman literature from the last
days of the republic till the end of the empire might take the form
of a string of islands in the Mediterranean Sea. You will have the
islet of Petronius, Catullus and Tibullus; the larger island of the true
Augustans, Lucretius, Horace, Virgil, Ovid; orators like Cicero;
historians like Livy; and then, stringing themselves out in gradually
diminishing groups from which poetry had almost disappeared, except for Lucan, went other islets out in a sea of unthinkable butchery
and crime. You had under Nero who reigned from 54-68 A.D. the
group that contained the very fustian philosopher, Seneca. He was
Nero's tutor and wrote extraordinarily commonplace Stoic philosophy
and still more commonplace heroic tragedies. There was also Lucan
himself, to whom we will return, and Petronius. With him the history of imaginative prose may, as far as we are concerned, be con-

sidered to begin, since he antedated by more than a century Longinus and the Greek *Tale of Chloe*. You get, then, a long blank until you arrive at another prose writer, Apuleius, whose history of the *Golden Ass* may be considered to be the first of novels, though earlier Greek prose tales went into its making. And then a very considerable gap. Then we arrive—under Hadrian, Diocletian, Constantine the Great and Constantius, when the empire was already divided into two and the end could be seen approaching—at the little group of African, Spanish, Southern French and other provincial poets at whom we have already glanced. And after that, nothing until the nun Hroswitha, who at the darkest period of the dark ages wrote for performance in her convent little plays imitated from those of Terence. So that if you consider that Terence, in his turn, in his plays imitated those of Menander, the fourth century B.C. Greek comic-writer, you see how extraordinarily the flame of civilization is carried from century to century, though imperial cities fall and the whole world crash in ruins. Menander, through Terence, inspired Hroswitha, whose work is the first flicker of light in the dark centuries. Apuleius, inspired by almost earlier Greeks, inspires in turn Cervantes; Tibullus, Ronsard.

So I find it difficult to believe that in the four hundred years or so that separated Tibullus from whoever the author was of the *Pervigilium Veneris*—that in those four hundred years there occurred no poets at all to hand the sacred fire, the one to the other. There must have been underground passages—a popular poetry unknown to those who sat in high seats, and, when its poets were not being butchered by imperial edict, heedless of their deeds. For, particularly in the South of France and Italy, the underground creeping of the fires of verse beneath storm-stricken lands has been continuous down the centuries. There has been hardly any interruption between the local poet Ausonius of Bordeaux in the fourth century and today's local poets of the lowest social orders—the plowmen, the bakers, the vine-tenders and gardeners that you see today anywhere in Provence. These descendants of the Romans still compose their rustic and simple *lais* and *virelais* in the hinterlands of the shore that runs from Spain to Italy. And still, as I have elsewhere pointed out, in the lost hills and difficultly found bays of the shores of Languedoc, the peasants play, modify, and add to dramas that were originally composed before the very foundation of Rome, and have been handed down hardly mutilated. For those are the very shores of poetry and there without any discontinuity little people below the cognizance of the historian have continued to sing as they sang in the mists that preceded all the histories of our era.

The major literature of the Romans that reaches us today may seem a little meager and very official in tone, but we probably do not known one hundredth of what was produced in those days.

The inhabitants of Rome, an immense city, had necessities very similar to those of the inhabitants of the great cities of today. And one of those necessities was a hunger for communications in the written or the spoken word. Their substitute for our newspapers were innumerable historians, rhetoricians, small philosophers, magicians and great crowds of people finding action in their pens or their tongues. That great master of gossip, Suetonius, when he has finished giving almost invariably veracious details of the lives of the Emperors from Augustus to Domitian, enumerates, and gives also the livelier spots, the details, of a whole horde of grammarians, of rhetoricians and of other professors. Then, in his *Lives of Illustrious Men*, he sets to work on the poets from Terence to Passienus Crispus. Nearly all these teachers were Greeks. So, from time to time with a foreigner-hating energy such as can be very exactly paralleled in our own day, the rulers of the republic or the empire would set energetically to work to expel these undesirable aliens. In the consulship of Gaius Fannius Strabo and Marcus Valerius Messalla, the ancestor of the Messalla of Tibullus, in the year 161 B.C., Praetor Marcus Pomponius persuaded the Senate to expel all the rhetoricians and grammarians and teachers of philosophy from the Roman dominion—on the plea that the Roman youth passed its days in idleness listening to those fellows. That attempt was in vain since Greek was the official and polite language of the empire, much as French was once in England. So any youth of any ambition must get his Greek grammar right.

And the art of rhetoric was really the Latin equivalent of the art of the journalist today; so it was necessary for any advancement in all public offices. Thus, the demand for instructors in these things was invincible and the teachers of grammar, rhetoric and the rest crept always back in yearly increasing swarms.

And, as is the case today, all these professors, instructors and speech writers left not only textbooks about their arts, but many of them, literary works of their own. . . . Thus, Lucius Voltaulius Plotus was a slave, then a chained doorkeeper. Then he was freed because he had helped his employer with literary work. He became a teacher of rhetoric and had Pompey the Great for his pupil. He finally wrote the history of Pompey and his father and was thus the first of all freed slaves to take up the writing of history—an occupation till then permitted only to those of the highest birth. But similar cases appear to have been innumerable, the Roman of position being as a rule not so much illiterate as afflicted with difficulties in self-expression.

The most famous of all these cases is, of course, that of Epictetus. A slave of Epaphroditus, the favorite of the Emperor Nero, his master sent him whilst still very young to attend the lectures of C. Musonius Rufus, the great Stoic philosopher. He is said to have been treated with the greatest ferocity by his master. Nevertheless, the philosopher seems to have attended on Epaphroditus when he aided the emperor to kill himself and helped his master to prepare his own defense. Domitian, Nero's successor, put Epaphroditus to death after Epaphroditus had been his own secretary for several years. Since he seized all the ex-favorite's property, it would appear to have been he who freed the philosopher. Epictetus began to teach philosophy at Rome; but the emperor having expelled all the philosophers from the city, he retired to Nicopolis in Epirus and taught till his death in extreme old age.

He did not, as we have already seen, write anything with his own hand but his recorded *dicta* make up one of the most important items of the major writings of the Roman day. . . .

That immense quantities of minor writings, whether those of yeomen farmers or the less important philosophers of the city, should have disappeared is only natural. But the *Discourses* of Epictetus was a work that became almost an official textbook as the empire drifted through

Stoicism to Christianity. So it had all the protection that officialdom could give it. A manuscript written on the finest and most permanent material and housed in the marble coffers of temples or of palaces will have a hundred chances to one of survival as compared with the poetry of peasants. These last may not have been written down at all or may, like the *Pervigilium*, have been put into letters by an editor searching for folklore a hundred years after it was first sung. Supposing that Tibullus should actually have founded a school of plebeian poets in the Sabine hills, their works would be the first to disappear because of the growing tooth of time and the barbarians' torches set in the thatches of their farms. But the odes that Horace addressed to Augustus or the Epic that Virgil wrote to provide that same ruler with respectable ancestry—those masterpieces official Rome would not willingly let die.

The later Christian emperors might well destroy the writings of the Epicureans because they advocated a pleasure-loving atheism beloved by the Augustans. But they would not destroy an *Aeneid* which purported to prove that Augustus was descended from the Trojans since they all claimed misty descents from Augustus, and, calling themselves by his name, could well wish to share his fabulous ancestry.

Let us begin, then, to attack the official major Augustan poets. Of these, Lucretius, who hymned in his *De Rerum Natura* the philosophy of Epicurus, preceded the Empire of Augustus by so long that it is only because of the enthusiasm with which his work was regarded in the Augustan court that he merits the name of Augustan at all. If one were inclined to be severely exclusive, one might permit oneself almost to refuse him the name of poet altogether. The subjects of the sections of his verse bear titles like (Section 147) "Nothing can Arise out of Nothing; but Like must Arise from Like;" (Section 148) "The Universe is made up of Atoms and the Void;" (Section 149) "Matter is Eternal;" (Section 150) "The Atoms of Matter divide into Parts but these Parts are absolute Minima—not able to exist Alone—abiding therefore in the Atom from all Eternity;" (Section 151) "The Motions of the original Atom may be illustrated by those of Motes in the Sunbeam;" (Section 155) "The Existing Universe is the result of a certain

Option of Movement in the original atoms from which they swerved from the Perpendicular while traveling down Space in parallel straight Lines; From this also arise the phenomena of voluntary Motion." It is obvious that from such subjects nothing which we should normally consider poetry could be evolved. This is not because poetry in itself is unable to confront serious subjects but because poetry consists in the projection of passions, moods or objects and not in their constatation. Nor are the subjects of Lucretius relieved by any particular beauty of language or sinuousness of rhythm. His *dicta* are nearly always enshrined in hexametrical couplets—thus:

> *Nam si de nilo fierent, ex omnibu' rebus*
> *Omne genus nasci posset, nil semine egeret.*

> *E mare primum homines, e terra posset oriri*
> *Squamigerum genus et volucres erumpere caelo;*

> *Armenta atque aliae pecudes, genus omne ferarum*
> *Incerto partu culta ac deserta tenerent.*

> *Nec fructus idem arboribus constare solerent,*
> *Sed mutarentur, ferre omnes omnia possent.*

There is here nothing of the overlapping of line into line that gives beauty at once to the hexameter-pentameter verse of Ovid, grandiloquence to the dactylic hexameters of Virgil or rhythm to the later blank verse of Shakespeare.* Nor is there any beauty of vowel coloring. I cannot imagine an uglier verse for instance than: "*Corporum officium quoniam premere omnia de orsum.*" Still, a great many ages since his death have regarded Lucretius as being of the sublime order of Dante, or at least of Milton. That is probably because he brings before the reader, without rendering them, numbers of sublime subjects such as "the formation of the Cosmos out of Chaos." The more naïve sort of reader, being obsessed by the mere names of the subjects, thus receives

---

* We ought here to make the note that one of our highly academically accredited predecessors in writing a history of Latin literature, purporting to be for use in American universities, utters this dictum: "His (Lucretius') poem is the most majestic verse that has come down to us." The writer of those words states that he does not himself read Latin. Nevertheless, students for honors in the Classics of American—and, indeed, in other—universities had far better be guided by his tastes in the matter.—F. M. F.

a sensation of sublimity. So he considers himself to have been in contact with an august genius. Indeed the aesthetic practice of making the reader do his poetizing for himself whilst supplying the mere names of objects or subjects—that practice is so frequent in the Augustan, renaissance and eighteenth and nineteenth century writers of all nations and is regarded as being legitimate by so many critics that we must, whatever our private tastes, acknowledge that aesthetic practice as being sufficient to constitute an accepted poet and one worthy of critical examination. And, indeed, many poets whom, whether we agree or not with that practice, we must consider to be really great poets will fill many pages with references which are no more than quotations from the works of imagination of their predecessors.

Thus the exquisite poet Horace will begin the for all time famous poem: *"Eheu, fugaces, Posthume, Posthume, labuntur anni . . ."* with a stanza that is simple and as direct as one could desire:

> Alas, like fugitives, Posthumus, oh Posthumus, the years slip by, nor shall all thy virtues obtain for thee any delaying of thy wrinkles, the oncoming of thy senility or thy inevitable death.

and, soothed by the lilting and agreeable alcaics and the great simplicity and vowel coloring of the Latin, we get so much propulsion from the first lines as to read a whole catalogue of names—Pluto, Geryon, Tityos, Cocytos, Sisyphus, Terra—with degrees of satisfaction varying from the Epicurean ecstasies of the eighteenth century to the more Stoic pleasure of such Latinists as exist today. The reader is supposed to know all about those deities and so the poet saves himself the trouble of expounding various difficult matters.

But Lucretius does not even give us those minor satisfactions. He just states not very new philosophical doctrines in a Latin almost as dry as that of Suetonius. Nevertheless, he has been regarded, as we have said, as a divine poet by so many millions of learned readers that it is not for us to say that he was not a divine poet . . . for learned readers. The reader should make the test for himself.

Let us then deal with the true Augustan poets, Virgil, Horace and

Ovid.* It would seem best to begin with Horace and with the last two of his odes because they will give you the measure of the Augustan period. They will tell you what the world expected of Augustus as saviour of mankind, and will show you why so many and so considerable poets prostrated themselves before him.

> . . . *nam sibi quo die*
> *portus Alexandrea supplex*
> *et vacuam patefecit aulam* . . .

For on the selfsame day that suppliant Alexandria opened her harbors and her empty palace to thee, propitious Fortune, three lustrums later, brought a happy issue to the war and bestowed fame and hoped-for glory upon the deeds wrought in fulfilment of thy commands.

> . . . *custode rerum Caesare non furor*
> *civilis aut vis exiget otium,*
> *non ira, quae procudit enses*
> *et miseras inimicat urbes.*

While Caesar guards the state, not civil rage, nor violence, nor wrath that forges swords, embroiling hapless towns, shall banish peace. . . .†

And, indeed, to the Romans harried by centuries of wars and civil strifes, Augustus with his slogans of peace, democracy and plenty may well have appeared almost in the guise of a messiah. Indeed, his deification must have seemed to his materialist devotees much more reasonable than that of a Jew who could promise his worshippers here on earth nothing but poverty and hardships whatever our fate might be on the other side of the Styx.

Horace—Quintus Horatius Flaccus—then, was born in the year

---

* It is usual among the scholastic to group Catullus, Tibullus, Ovid, Horace and Virgil, because of the *Eclogues,* as elegiac writers, leaving Propertius, because of the brilliancy of his writing and his famous avowed *pastiche* on the methods of the Greek Alexandrian school, all by himself as derivative. But we are concerned not with scholasticism but with literature.

† *Horace: Odes and Epodes,* Book IV, Odes xiv, xv. Loeb Classical Library. English translation by C. E. Bennett.

64 B.C. and died in 8 B.C., six years after the death of Augustus. His father, once a slave, had become a tax collector and had amassed a small fortune in the provinces. This fortune he expended coming to Rome, almost entirely for the education of the young Quintus. So you may read in *Song Satires*, I, 6, an expression of filial gratitude that few poets could parallel. He not only provided for the boy the best education that money could buy but he even conducted him, as Horace tells us, every day from and to school. And when the boy was nineteen he was sent to finish his education by the study of philosophy and the Greek poets in Athens. Here he met with not only the son of Cicero but with the famous Marcus Valerius Messalla of whom one hears so often in the poems of Tibullus. He made the *faux pas* of interrupting his studies to fight on the wrong side, with Brutus and for republicanism, at the Battle of Philippi in 42 B.C. He declares himself to have shown no great valor with his little shield which he cast away, but since those words were written in the days of Augustus against whom he had been fighting we may perhaps discount them. After the battle, Horace found himself reduced to complete penury. His father was dead and Octavian—afterwards Augustus—had confiscated the small patrimony that had been left him. He managed, however, to obtain a post as a quaestor's clerk, and during his spare moments he wrote a great deal of poetry. These verses attracted the attention of Virgil, who was also then beginning to be a poet, and through Virgil he made the acquaintance of Maecenas. This famous man was not only the intimate friend and adviser of Augustus but of such generosity and wealth that his name has ever since been the synonym for a man who lavishly patronizes the arts. When he was 32, Maecenas presented Horace with the famous Sabine farm. This enabled him for the rest of his life to live in plenty, to offer lavish hospitality and to pass his leisure hours in singing, usually, of the good things of this earth. He lived in the society of the most distinguished men of his day—with the general Agrippa, with the great Messalla, with Virgil, Pollio and a great many other patrician or literally celebrities, amongst whom the poorer Tibullus could himself be named. His first two works were called by himself *Satires*, of which the first book was published when he was 30, the second five years later. Actually they show a good-humored acceptance of the things of his

day, written in an everyday language. They poke a little fun at the habits of the great, recount a good number of autobiographical and amusing incidents and comment, always agreeably, upon the short-comings and the cranes of his day. At the age of 36 he published his *Epodes*, which are a cross between his so-called *Satires*, and the *Odes* which are the chief glory of his muse. The first three books of these were published in 23 B.C. They raised him at once to the most exalted rank amongst the poets of his day and of all time.

This is a statement of fact. No one could deny that, ever since his own day, Horace has stood along with the ten or the dozen greatest poets on the slopes of Olympus.

It is because he fulfills the need of one side of the human heart. We must have—or we die—some figure forever prosperous, forever sunny, forever frugally generous, and we must have, above all, the views of life and the poetry of such a figure to take about with us. The fortunate, however, seldom find the need to express themselves; so it is only by the rarest and most blessed of coincidences that the poet and the happy man are found to inhabit the same skin. It was not merely that Horace, like Browning, held that we fall to rise, are beaten to fight better. It was that Horace established the claim for humanity to live in unruffled felicity or at least in a felicity no more shadowed than by the casting away of one's little shield at one Battle of Philippi or another. This, Horace appeared to be able to claim as of right; and, if Horace, why not we or some millions or some tens of millions of our compatriots and fellow citizens? Still more, he seems to present us with a picture of a Utopia such as we might find just around the corner if human good will did not lack. Even to the old age concerning which, as we have seen, he warned his friend Posthumus, he was able to present a tranquil brow. In the last of his odes but four, he was able to write his famous Birthday Ode which begins:

Est mihi nonum superantis annum
plenus Albani cadus; est in horto,
Phylli, nectendis apium coronis;
* est hederae vis*
multa, qua crines religata fulges . . .

and which is translated by C. E. Bennett:

> I have a jar full of Alban wine over nine years old; in my garden, Phyllis, is parsley for weaving garlands; there is goodly store of ivy, which, binding back thy hair, sets off thy beauty. The house gleams with silver vessels; the altar wreathed with sacred leafage yearns to be sprinkled with the blood of an offered lamb. The household all is hurrying; hither and thither rushes the mingled throng of lads and maids; the flames are dancing as they roll the sooty smoke aloft in wreaths. . . .

It seems to us today curious not so much that Horace should consider that his verses had gained for him an immortality that would outlast Rome and pass on to the most distant of futures as that he should have had any conception of the pen or the stylus as producing work of sempiternal durability in the minds of men.

The pen and the stylus as we have seen cannot have been in existence at the longest for very much more than eight hundred years, whereas the infinitely more ancient monuments of the Egyptian Pharaohs must have been familiar to him, at least by report. Nevertheless, on his taking his farewell from literature with the Thirtieth Ode, at the end of his third book, he utters the most famous of all boasts. *"Exegi monumentum aere perennius."* And it was true that with his odes he had raised up to himself a monument more lasting than brass. He had really a sincere desire at that time to lay down his pen for good; but the very glory of the writings that thus constituted his monument was so great that he must once again take up his writing implements and add a fourth book to his other three.

One is apt to be suspicious of potentates who are too loudly hymned by their poets. But Augustus would seem really to have had for both Horace and Virgil—and indeed for Ovid until Ovid became too intimate with the emperor's vagrant sister—a genuine personal affection and to have felt such admiration for their work and to have taken such delight in their society that, as these poets stand alone in the estimation of humanity so he may well stand alone amongst the great lords of the earth. It is not merely that his rewards to the poets were enormous indeed, but his desire for their society and his trust in their judgments were unceasing. Thus, Augustus writes to Maecenas, according to Suetonius:

> . . . "Before this I was able to write my letters to my friends with my own hand; now overwhelmed with work and in poor health, I desire to take our friend Horace from you. He will come then from that parasitic table of yours to my imperial board, and help me write my letters." Even when Horace declined, Augustus showed no resentment at all, and did not cease his efforts to gain his friendship. We have letters from which I append a few extracts by way of proof: "Enjoy any privilege at my house, as if you were making your home there; for it will be quite right and proper for you to do so, inasmuch as that was the relation which I wished to have with you, if your health had permitted." And again: "How mindful I am of you our friend Septimius can also tell you; for it chanced that I spoke of you in his presence. Even if you were so proud as to scorn my friendship, I do not therefore return your disdain." Besides this, among other pleasantries, he often calls him "a most immaculate libertine" and "his charming little man," and he made him well-to-do by more than one act of generosity.

As for Virgil, after the poet had read to him the second, fourth and sixth books of the *Aeneid*, it was the common gossip of Rome that so great was the admiration and gratitude of Augustus for this deification of his supposed ancestors that Augustus actually proposed that Virgil should have shared the purple with him. But Virgil died of sunstroke whilst journeying through Greece with the emperor. As for Horace, Augustus insisted on the poet's writing after he considered that he had earned his retirement, *The Carmen Saeculaire,* the odes to Drusus and Tiberius and to himself. So that, with the Birthday Odes that we have already quoted, and the ode to Melpomene, the poet made out his fourth book of odes.

Horace suffers a little from the fact that every schoolboy who has to read him or every other person who reads him for pleasure carries around with him for the rest of his life almost more quotations of single lines than he carries lines of Shakespeare or the Bible. There can be almost no one who has read any Latin at all who has not somewhere in his mind at least the *Exegi monumentum* that we have just quoted or the *Eheu fugaces, Ille et nefasto te posuit die* or *O Saepe mecum tempus in ultimum* with its *relicta non bene parmula* or perhaps the most famous of all *Aeauam memento rebus in arduis servare mentem.* It is unfortunate because with the lovely words and the soothing rhythms always in the ear one takes them to be all that there is to Horace. So one is apt to think of him as primarily a writer of a certain *chic*, a certain indifference, a certain jocundity, of even a certain heartlessness. You carry initial lines about with you without ever much tormenting your memory as to the content of the poem begun by those lines. You pick up from time to time a Horace, say, in a friend's house; read a verse here and a verse there. But I fancy that hardly anyone ever reads the *Odes* right through, or even sufficiently to revise any judgment he may have formed years before. For the whole of his life he may never read the body of a poem or the tailpieces to the headlines held by his memory. So we go to our graves doing injustice to this poet.

Nay, one may even carry about with him lines of Horace merely for the sound. For years this writer has been visited just before dropping off to sleep by the words *"Vivet in extento Proculeius aevo,"* taking pleasure in the sound and hardly thinking whether they had any meaning at all. So it was only yesterday that he realized that one, Proculeius, would live in reputation to a remote antiquity because of benevolence to his brother—and that the ode is one that gravely extols fraternal devotion.

So, after that bland beginning of *Eheu fugaces, Posthume, Posthume* the ode soon takes a deeper note. Let us translate it right through:

> Alas, like fugitives, Posthumus, oh Posthumus, the years slip by.
>   Nor shall all thy virtue suffice to delay for thee thy wrinkles,
> thy oncoming senility or thy inevitable death. You may seek to
> propitiate Death; He remains implacable in his decrees; and be

we great kings or poor peasants, all we who have battened on the fruits of the Earth, we must presently traverse his gloomy stream.

It goes for nothing that we may escape the accursed wars, the breaking seas of the loud Adriatic. It shall go for nothing that, the autumn past, we may have escaped the dread effects of the enervating sirocco. At the last, we must confront the sluggish current of his river and be witness of the plight of the victims of his remorseless decrees.

We must pass from off the Earth; we must leave our familiar roof-trees and our kindly wives. Of the trees that today we plant none shall follow us save for the sad cypress that shall shade our burial places.

Our worthier heirs shall drink our Caecuban vintage from the cellar with a hundred locks and waste on the mosaics of the floor a wine such as is not drunk even at the feasts of the pontiffs.*

The accepted image of Quintus Horatius Flaccus will no doubt continue to be one of a sort of Omar Khayyam, reclining, becushioned on high, in the cerulean air, on the terrace of Augustus, above the ultramarine Mediterranean where the white teeth of its foam gnaw at the pink marble rocks. Emperor and consort, senators and knights, consuls and quaestors, freedmen and fellow poets will be all a-strain not to miss one word that falls from his semi-divine, slightly inhumanly smiling lips, and he with the conviction that all posterity is doing the

* *Odes* II, xiv. Author's free rendering. And here is a free version in rhymed English alcaics of the famous *Persicos odi, puer apparatus,* (I, xxxviii), showing the poet in a mood of revulsion from Oriental luxuries:

> Rich meats I hate, boy, from Iràn or Paris,
> I'll wear no garlands striped and stitched with cunning;
> Give over searching where the late-blown tea-rose
>   Droopingly tarries.

> Bring me but myrtle, fit for hinds or heroes,
> Simple, uncostly. You all keep on pruning!
> Whilst in the arbor where the wine leaves twine down
>   I put the wine down.

like in the shades behind them. Nevertheless, in the back of his brain must have remained the remembrance that he too was once the son of a slave, freed to become a tax collector and saving his every penny to give his son a good education. The froth of the blue wave is the surface of his poems; but he is not as unmindful as all that of their shadowed depths.

He is occasionally called no poet because he never hymned, like Catullus or Propertius, the pains and passions of unhappy loves. But fortunate love is not so unworth the hymning—and that hymning is the more difficult and, so, rarer in the extreme. The burden of such few songs of fortunate loves as exist is, even at that, almost invariably, "Ah me, the dawn, the dawn it comes too soon!"

But consider the most famous of all Horace's odes—but which is really the most famous of all his odes?—Book I, Ode xxii. It begins: *"Integer vitae, scelerisque purus,"* and ends with the most beautiful words ever written concerning fortunate love: *"Dulce ridentem Lalagen amabo, dulce loquentem."*

You cannot translate those verses. They mean: "I shall love the sweetly smiling Lalage!" But there is no word for *"loquentem."* It means "conversing," or more in French "devising." It certainly does not mean either "prattling" or "chattering." No, it renders the talk of a woman who loves and is beloved, talking quietly of nothings or of somethings as the lazy hour brings topics to the lips.

But between the *Integer vitae* and the *Dulce loquentem* what courages, endurances, toils are not rendered in this epitome of life! . . . Do not believe that the beautiful words end the jazz rendering of love for a little tart picked up on a week-end on a pleasure beach. Nor is it the expression—and that is what is material—of the calmly lascivious sexuality of a Roman noble owning an infinity of girl slaves. No, it is the moral drawn from life of a man who knows that, only after he has affronted the darts and poisoned arrows of the Moor, the sweltering paths of Syrtes, the frozen passes of the Caucasian Mountains, the attacks of monstrous wolves—only then can he know the calm ecstasies of love: the true Epicureanism of the passion. Nor is even that the end of the lesson: For he shows us that love enduring in dead, dusty regions; beneath heavy mists and lowering skies; or on parched, undwelt-in lands, where the blazing chariot of the sun almost touches the desert sands. . . . Lalage shall smile and discourse most sweetly even there. As who should say:

> Only the love-lives of the just
> Smell sweet and blossom in the Dust.

It is, of course, not this writer but Horace who discourses, the rendering being to be taken as a fairly close transference into English of the thought of the poet. . . . And we do not know that life, at its end, has any other moral to offer us. A sterner writer has phrased it: "In the sweat of thy brows shalt thou eat thy bread." But is sternness your only virtue?

And of this, one may be certain: It is not merely that if there had been no Horace we should have had to invent him; it is that without him we should have been thirty, forty, fifty—I don't care if you say a hundred per cent more savage brutes than we have made ourselves today. For the essence of civilization consists in its domination by a mood of frugal happiness: we are the best citizens who most have been tamed by the Horatian note. And, indeed, if at dawn one could not now and then as it were hum to oneself:

> *Musis amicus tristitiam et metus*
> *Tradam protervis . . .*

one would probably not much want to rise and affront the long day and its little thin oatmeal of recompense for sufficient labors.

We need not doubt, then, that, whether in the mediaeval or the renaissance sense, Horace was indeed a poet. And once a man is a poet his stature as such is of no importance. You cannot profitably weigh in the balance one against the other, Sappho, Walther von der Vogelweide, Petrarch or Christina Rossetti. To the level of the light vouchsafed, the poet must, truly, shine in his place and be content. Still more must the reader accept what Apollo vouchsafes to him in the way of poetry, since it is the only thing that differentiates between mankind and the beasts.

Horace, then, is poet: but one may remain for long in doubt concerning Virgil; or at any rate concerning the Publius Vergilius Maro who wrote the *Aeneid*. The *Bucolics* is another matter. They and the *Georgics* were written in the ten years during which he passed from boyhood to grown man's estate and are full of direct observations from nature and husbandry.

Publius Vergilius Maro of Mantua—more usually known as Virgil —was born in lowly circumstances, his father having been a hired man, who, owing to his sobriety, skill and industry, rose to marrying his employer's daughter. Subsequently, owing to a continuance of those qualities, he increased his store by the acquisition of woodlands and by the raising of bees. What more lovely occupations could be found for the father of a poet or upon what more lovely objects than woodlands and bee-skeps could the eyes of a poet open? It was considered a singular coincidence that Lucretius should have died on the day on which Virgil assumed the *toga virilis*—at the age of fifteen. In the same year he commenced to be a poet, writing his celebrated stanzas on the death of Ballista, the schoolmaster-racketeer and highwayman. Ballista was stoned to death in the neighborhood and Virgil wrote these lines for his tomb:

> *Monte sublapidum tegitur Ballista sepultus*
> *Nocte die tutum carpe, viator, iter. . . .*

as who should say:

> Under this mountain of stones, roofed in, Ballista lies buried:
> Traveler, fare on the way, scatheless by night as by day.

By way of Cremona and Mediolanum where, no doubt, he acquired some education, mostly in medicine, mathematics and rhetoric, he arrived at Rome where his beginnings would seem to have been mediocre. Melissus reports that at his first appearance in court, where he only pleaded one case, he spoke very slowly and like a scarcely educated man. Since he was subsequently nicknamed "Parthenias the Virgin," on account of his oncoooivo ohynooo, wo may imagino that ho was not at his best in the courts.

He tried his hand first at writing a history of Rome, but finding out that he knew almost nothing of Rome and very little of history he decided to write about rural subjects and in three years turned out the *Bucolics*.

They vary a great deal in interest and in writing but one or other of the earlier ones would seem to have attracted the attention of Maecenas. To him, at any rate, the collection is dedicated in the famous First Pastoral, the one that begins with the line *Tityre, tu recubans sub tegmine fagi* (Tityrus, reclining beneath thy roof of beech-leaves), which must I imagine have been the most quoted line of poetry ever since Virgil first wrote it. . . .

For the rest the *Pastorals* tell in easy verse a good deal of the history of the poet. As was the case with all the other poets, Augustus, on his return to Rome, rewarded his veterans—who were all hardened kitchen gardeners—with all the lands capable of intensive culture about Rome. Thus, Virgil too had had his patrimony, the coppices and beeskeps, confiscated and conferred on a centurion called Arion. But Maecenas, loving these Pastorals succeeded in making Augustus return his lands to the poet. This good fortune Virgil adumbrates in his First Pastoral. A problem that must have occurred to most of us—How did the dispossessed soldiers take their dispossession?—is solved in the Ninth Pastoral when the bailiff of Virgil, Moeris speaks. Moeris had gone to retake possession of his lands for Virgil. He was thus received by Arion:

> *M.* Then the grim captain in a surly tone
> Cried out: "Pack up ye rascals and begone!"
> Kicked out, we set the best face on't we could
> And these two kids to appease his angry mood
> We bear. . . .

upon which his shocked friend, Lycidas exclaims:

> L. Now Heaven defend, could barbarous rage induce
> The brutal son of Mars to insult the sacred Muse!
> Who then should sing the nymphs? or who rehearse
> The waters gliding in a smoother verse,
> Or Amaryllis' praise, that heavenly lay
> That shortened as we went our tedious way. . . .

They proceed incontinently to sing each to the other a number of songs, the implication being that, touched by the beauty of the songs, Augustus was induced to send soldiers to turn out the centurion who had already nearly killed the poet.

The *Georgics*, obviously written at the desire and for the agricultural instruction of Maecenas, form a remarkable manual of farming—of a type of farming that is still almost exactly followed in Provence by the incomparable wine and olive and first-fruit growers, the descendants of the veteran Roman legionaries who so loved kitchen gardening.

Interested as we are in the transference of ideas down the generations—and we shall later refer to the once most famous of all the Pastorals, Number IV in which Virgil making use of the sayings of one of the Sybils prophesies the coming of the Messiah—we cannot very well give space here to many passages of agricultural prescriptions. Let us give just one. The translator is Dryden:

> But various are the ways to change the state
> Of plants, to bud, to graff, to inoculate.
> For, where the tender rinds of trees disclose
> Their shooting gems, a swelling knot there grows.
> Just in that space a narrow slit we make
> Then other buds from bearing trees we take;
> Inserted thus, the wounded rind we close
> In whose moist womb the admitted infant grows.
> But when the smoother bole from knots is free
> We make a deep incision in the tree,
> And in the solid wood the slip inclose.

The battening bastard shoots again and grows.
And, in short space, the laden boughs arise
With happy fruit aspiring to the skies.
The mother plant admires the leaves unknown
Of alien trees and apples not her own.

And let us quote two passages more obviously "writ poetic:" Here is a spring song: *Ver adeo fronde nemorum, ver utile silvis** and Dryden very freely translates:

The Spring adorns the woods, renews the leaves;
The womb of Earth the genial seed receives.
For then Almighty Jove descends and pours
Into his buxom bride his fruitful showers;
And mixing his large limbs with hers, he feeds
Her births with kindly juice, and fosters teeming weeds.
Then joyous birds frequent the lonely grove
And beasts by nature stung, renew their love.

And for contrast a Scythian winter, for the *Georgics* embraces the agricultural practices—and particularly the agricultural practices which the wise Roman veterans adopted—of a large part of the globe known to the ancients.

At non, qua Scythiae gentes, Moeotiaque unda,
Turbidus et torquens flaventes Ister arenas

it begins,† and again Dryden, this time a little more closely, renders:

Not so the Scythian shepherd tends his fold,
Nor he who bears in Thrace the bitter cold,
Nor he who treads the bleak Moeotian strand
Or where proud Ister rolls his yellow sand
Early they stall their flocks and herds for there

---

* *Georgics,* ii, 323-8.
† *Georgics,* iii, 349-61.

No grass the fields, no leaves the forests wear.
The frozen earth lies buried there below
A hilly heap, seven cubits deep in snow. . . .
The brazen cauldrons with the frost are flawed,
The garments, stiff with ice at hearths are thawed;
With axes first they cleave the wine and thence,
By weight the solid portions they dispense.
From locks uncombed and from the frozen beard
Long icicles depend and crackling sounds are heard. . . .

With the *Aeneid* a totally different sphere of ideas is entered on. This is the Command Performance *par excellence.* Augustus being a demi-god, it became necessary that he should be provided with remote, divine parentage. And the Romans, if less pressingly, must be relieved of their commonly received ancestry—which was that of robbers and outlaws. Augustus being so physically beautiful, what must his divine ancestor have been? Naturally, Venus. And since Venus, as against Athene of Greece, stood for Troy, what more natural than that the Trojans should have been the ancestors of the Romans!

That being settled, the machinery of the epic becomes easy. All that had to be done was to translate the Trojans to Italy under the leadership of a semi-divine Trojan prince. The Old Anchises, then, of the highest Trojan family, must have an affair—when young and because he was surpassingly comely—with Venus. Its issue was the Pious Aeneas— a sort of Romanized, as it were, renaissance version of the crafty Odysseus, called Ulysses by the Romans. He too must be surpassingly comely and princely. . . . All the invented ancestry of Augustus must be that. And so he is!

> . . . *haud illo segnior ibat*
> *Aeneas* . . .*

which Dryden in his richest courtier's manner, and no doubt thinking of James II, renders:

* *Aeneid,* iv, 149-150.

But far above the rest in beauty shines
The great Aeneas when the troop he joins,
Like fair Apollo when he leaves the frost
Of wintry Xanthus and the Lycian coast . . .
A golden fillet binds his awful brows;
Green wreaths of bays his length of hair inclose;
His quiver sounds. Not less the prince is seen
In manly presence, or in lofty mien.

And so all that has to be done in the twelve books of the epic is to transport a remnant of the Trojan forces under the leadership of Aeneas somewhere to the shores of Latium. . . .

Now, it is not to be imagined that the *Aeneid* is the sort of pompous dedication piece such as starving authors of the English eighteenth century addressed to Lord Chesterfield or to the Duke of Marlborough in the hope of receiving a few guineas in return. It is more than anything a work astonishing in its naïveté, so written it is to please. At the date of its writing Virgil was already a man of monstrous wealth and influence over his sovereign.

"*Possedit prope centiens sestertium ex libertatibus amicorum . . .*" writes Seutonius. "He possessed nearly ten million sesterces of gold from the liberalities of his friends and he had a house at Rome on the Esquiline, near the gardens of Maecenas, although he usually lived in retirement in Campania or in Sicily."

He was in fact literally wealthy to weariness, and when Augustus further offered him the confiscated property of some rich exile, he could not bring himself to accept it—remembering perhaps the ferocious centurion of his Pastorals.

So that, when he wrote the *Aeneid*, he wrote it to give pleasure to a splendid friend . . . and perhaps also to provide himself with a prince of semi-divine origin of whom to be proud. And he was so shy, or he so disbelieved in the merit of his work, that for years he would not show it to the prince. Again and again, and at last with kindly threats, Augustus ordered Virgil to send him "either the *brouillon* of the poem or any *stances* that should please him." And it is interesting that when he was writing of literature Augustus had to use Greek phrases, the

Latin, even as is the case with our own English, having no technical literary terms.

But not for years—until the whole was roughly in shape—did Virgil consent to read to him the second, fourth and sixth books of the poem. It was his habit to write his epic book in prose and then to turn it without sequence into verse: *"Ac ne quid impetum moraretur"* ("And so that he might not check his *élan* in writing, he left parts temporarily incomplete and, as who should say, stanchioned up others with hardly suggested words which, he was accustomed to say in jest, served as wooden props until the marble pillars should be delivered.")

He was the competent journeyman workman, in fact, intent on a labor of love. And immense pleasure he gave, not merely to Augustus but to an infinity of others. The Empress Octavia, when he was reading his sixth book aloud, fainted and could only be revived with difficulty when he came to the words "Tu Marcellus eris!", referring to her son. And Sextus Propertius writing of the *Aeneid* before it had gone very far, exclaimed triumphantly:

> Yield Roman writers; cease ye Greeks!
> In greater lines than Homer's this man speaks.

Virgil, on the other hand, was so overwhelmed by the imperfections that he felt in his work and by the critics' accusations of plagiarism from Homer that he planned to leave Rome for three years and in Greece and Asia Minor set himself to polishing up his verses and to eliminating the traces of his blind predecessor. On his voyage, however, he met Augustus at Athens and, the prince, clamoring for his company, went with him as far as Megara. There he was stricken with sunstroke, dying of fever on reaching Brindisi, in his fifty-third year.

Virgil must have been personally one of the most attractive of poets . . . and now and then the personal attractiveness of poets gets through into their works. Though, more usually, their works, like those of Walter Savage Landor, who wrote "I strove with none for none were worth the strife" and passed his life outrageously quarreling with everyone from his landlady to his barber, his parson, his relatives, his trustees and the loafers at the corner of his Venice street—more usually, the works of a poet will represent rather what they would desire to be than what they are in person. But the timidity, the modesties, the ungrasping nature, the complete want of megalomania in the Duke of Mantua—all these things so round off his verse that he has had an irresistible attraction for at least half humanity for nearly a couple of thousand years after his death.

He was tall, stoutish and dark; he suffered much from indigestion, laryngitis and headaches. He was extremely frugal in his drink and diet, and was called, even by his friends, very rustic in his bearing. He entertained passions for various boys—a fact regarded as hardly even a peccadillo in his day. And he is said to have had an affair with a rich matron called Plotia Heria upon whom, it was rumored, he had modelled his Dido. But after his death the lady obstinately insisted that Virgil had as obstinately refused her favors. And *"Cetera sane vitae et ore et animum tam probum constat ut Neapoli Parthenias vulgo appellatus sit,"* as says Suetonius ("For the rest he was so modest in speech and soul that at Naples he was nicknamed the Virgin. Moreover, whenever he appeared in public in the city of Rome, whither he came very rarely, he was apt to be followed by crowds, pointing at him and cheering: then he would take refuge in the next house he came to.") For it is to be remembered that in addition to his fame in the circle of Augustus he enjoyed amongst the populace a popularity such as is today reserved for the stars of Hollywood. His *Bucolics*, as they appeared, were at once set to music and sung on the popular stages, and it was as one who had eclipsed Homer of the "little Greeks" that he was applauded by the Sicilian butchers and Greek-descended monument builders' slaves of the Appian Way. . . . You may find parallels in eras nearer our own for that!

But it was not merely for his patriotism, for his giving the Roman populace a remote and respectable ancestry whether they were true citizens or, as who should say, merely hyphenated, for his conferring on his ruler a divine origin—it was not merely for that that Virgil was then and for a millennium and a half subsequently so adored. It was that his poetry struck the note of delicate, imaginative artificiality that is craved by at least half mankind and by almost the entire totality of the city dwellers of the generations that have followed him. . . . It

is to be remembered that the Roman, gentle or simple, pretended for
nine months of the year ardently to desire rustic bliss, exclaiming
O rus quando te aspiciam! . . . For the other three he really desired
to disport himself in trimmed and statue-lined walks, well-swept parks
and suave landscapes. . . . And with that landscape, in at least the
Pastorals and the *Aeneid* as well as a considerable portion of the
Georgics, Virgil exactly supplied them. You had, indeed, an exact
parallel of that situation in London of the eighteenth and most of the
nineteenth centuries. . . . And in other towns enough.

Similarly the Augustan Romans who might never have seen a short
sword, except when some Caesar felt the need to decimate them by
cutting their throats—the Roman, then, full of the pride of his illustrious and martial antiquity, desired to have set before him pictures
of war that should be as near like war as the frescoes of a Boucher
resembled the campaigns of a Louis XIV or a Marlbrouck. That is a
settled desire of urban humanity. It was not merely an idle patriotism
that made the Romans cry that Virgil had surpassed both *Iliad* and
Odyssey. For them he really and authentically had. Their figure of a
hero was not the lean Odysseus with his brine-polished cheeks and
eyes full of the light of desperate stratagems. Their hero was the plump-
ish, garlanded Aeneas, with his long locks tied also in garlands, standing romantically on a prow, pointing to the new world with, in his eye,
still the traces of a tear for the fate of his abandoned Dido.

To parody Caesar, we might well write: *Tota humanitas in duas
partis divisa est.* There are those who like their wines neat and those
who like synthetic alcohol flavored with raspberry juice; there are those
who seek in their books to meet with *les émotions fortes* and those who
consider, along with the British Censor, that all art must be arranged
so that it shall not shock pregnant women. . . . It is, indeed, the difference between the mediaeval and the renaissance. And, essentially,
it is the difference between the ferocious rendering of life by those who
have lived or have at least speculated on life and the rendering of
stylized and expurgated manners by those who have studied the others
and know how to select passages for imitation and tempered verbiage
such as shall not be injurious to our mothers before childbirth.

The *Aeneid*, like the *Gierusalemme Liberata* and like how many epics for so many centuries after the taking of Constantinople, was the product of the impingement of Greek art on Rome. For you are not to imagine that the complete conquest of aesthetic Hellas over the Quirites was the walk-over of a day. For several centuries the introduction of Greek masterpieces into Rome was forbidden by a law precluding Roman governors from bringing back to Rome either foreign statues or foreign manuscripts. This was partly meant to protect the populations of acquired districts from spoliation. But it was still more ardently considered to be a means of protecting Roman youth and husbands from the demoralizing influences of non-Aryans. You get the patriotic sentiment good-naturedly expressed by Horace in the *Persicos Odi* poem. That, nevertheless, lets one see between its lines that the influences of soft *Irán* had already done some work in the shadow of the Capitoline and the Neapolitan beaches. But still more you get it in Cicero's prosecution of Verres—the Roman governor who was impeached because he had carried off half the Greek sculptural masterpieces of Sicily.

In this—which we may well call the most magnificent, simple and entertaining of all his orations—Cicero again and again expresses his noble Roman disdain for the arts of the Greeks. Verres is accused of stripping Sicily of all her Greek statuary. Cicero terms that a sort of madness; and repeatedly he affects to be ignorant of the names of the greatest of the Greek sculptors. He states categorically that such things are not of value to him. Nevertheless, they must be regarded when estimating the thefts of Verres at their regular auction prices— which he admits were enormous. But, says he of Verres, he was so covetous of the reputation of being the world's greatest connoisseur that lately—"and note this man's infatuation," Cicero interpolates— when he was as good as already condemned, being at a banquet given by the great connoisseur Lucius Sisenna, he examined every piece of plate belonging to Sisenna and commented on it loudly. "But," adds Cicero, "Sisenna's servants . . . never took their eyes off him and never departed out of reach of the plate. . . ."

Cicero, of course, in speaking with such contempt of the arts was indulging in a little patent hypocrisy whilst at the same time pretending to the older and harder Roman virtues. And, of course, the whole prosecution of Verres—richly as that infamous being deserved it—was a political manoeuvre in support of the triumvirate of Pompey, Caesar and M. Licinius Crassus. They being democrats against an oligarchy could well do with the name of stern upholders of the nation's ancient virtues against the Greek corrupters of a degenerate day. Cicero, indeed, hardly ever mentions the Greeks except in terms of "Graeculi"—much as the late Mr. Kipling, before the late war, never spoke of the French save as the *Bander-Log*—the chattering little people, thus monkeys. The parallel is, indeed, very striking and might without disadvantage be much further extended.

Nevertheless, even by the date of the comparative youth of Cicero and of the Triumvirate, that ancient xenophobic slogan was fairly obsolete. The Romans were going towards luxury with no uncertain steps, and luxury could mean nothing else than aesthetic Hellenization. As a vigorous American writer expressed it just a hundred years ago: "Greece, industrious, learned and polite, subdued, by the admiration which she extorted, the ignorant, unlettered and rude barbarians who had conquered her by force."* By Cicero's thirtieth year there may have been fifty millionaire connoisseurs in Rome. By, say, the year A.D. 7 when we may consider that Virgil commenced the *Aeneid* (a matter of seventy-five years, say), they were uncountable. Every imaginable type of masterpiece of the plastic and applied arts had poured into Rome from Athens and her dependencies, the rate of exportation being limited simply by the amount of transport available. Similarly, there had poured in whole nations of Greek sculptors, painters, draughtsmen, cooks, pastry cooks, philosophers, poets, prose tale writers, magicians, teachers of rhetoric, writers of orations for illiterate Roman parvenus, all slaves—whole nations of those whom Cicero could still pawkily style the lesser breeds without the Law.

If, arbitrarily, we take the year of the final sweeping away of all barriers between Rome and her province to have been the year of the birth of Our Lord, we may take the state of Rome to be aesthetically exactly the same as that of Rome, Florence and the great Italian prin-

* *Orations of Cicero.* Translated by C. D. Yonge. (Cincinnati, 1840.)

cipalities 1453 years later. In that latter year all the Greek scholars, gradually driven for protection into Constantinople, fled all over Italy, all carrying manuscripts or works of art. From then on the arts not only of Italy and the fifteenth century but of all the world and all the succeeding centuries took on, imitatively, a bastard-Greek aspect. And that was called the renaissance.

It could more justly be called the second renaissance. Ariosto who was born twenty-one years after the taking of Constantinople and wrote the *Orlando Furioso*, and Tasso who was born eighty years after the birth of Ariosto and wrote the *Gierusalemme Liberata* must have been visited by muses exactly the same in temper and imagination as those presiding at the birth of the Duke of Mantua who raised Venice, as we have seen, on a foundation of eggs. And further to complicate the matter we might almost say that Tasso bore to Dante—who was born in 1265—a relationship very similar to that that unites Virgil to Horace. Dante was a bitter man who had seen Hell; Tasso was a gentleman who had read about Jerusalem.

CHAPTER THREE

Let us now carefully examine a number of passages from the *Aeneid* and afterwards compare other passages with yet others from the epic of Homer. At first sight it may seem as if we were devoting too much space to Virgil and that if we were to give some to Homer, it would have been better so to do when we were treating of Greek antiquity.

It is true that, in order to finish this book within reasonable length, we shall be unable to treat any other author so lavishly. But no other author will merit so much from our point of view, since what we are about is a history not of authors but of comparative literature. There is no author, after Virgil, who merits so much attention, not for the divine character of his imagination and the majesty of his mighty lines, but for the fact of his standing at so singular a crossways in the history of imaginative writing. The problems he stirs in our imagination are almost infinite. Ronsard, Villon or Racine; Chaucer or Shakespeare; Dante or Tasso; Peire Vidal or Vogelweide; Goethe or Heine—all these are authentic poets, the greatest their races have produced, the most nearly unassailable. But they are just poets. Ronsard may have had some hand, like Chaucer—or, indeed, like Fréderic Mistral—in remoulding his native tongue, and Shakespeare, as the greatest translator of all time, may have had a great hand in civilizing his savage countrymen by familiarizing them with the French, Latin, Italian and a little of the Greek thought, of the days before his own. . . . But once we have given what thought we want to those sides of their activities, they do not have to abide our third-degreeing any more.

But supposing ·that, being an adorer of Villon, you have decided that Virgil was never a poet save in one or two of the *Pastorals*; or having been brought up to be an admirer of Goethe, you have decided that the author of the *Aeneid* was as sublime as he was divine and as divine as he was sublime: in either case, when you have decided that, the problem that he sets up will still remain insoluble.

Let us take up now the question of his poetic quality, at first from

the point of view of the practicing writer of today who will certainly
be of the Villon faction and prize *le moyen âge* far above *la renaissance.* By digging industriously—and, of course, mostly in Book II—
he will discover some lines of great beauty and some passages that,
even from his point of view, are poetry: *"Suadentque cadentia sidera
somnum"* ("And the stars, descending in their courses, persuade us to
sleep") is beautiful in the extreme in the Latin and poetic in content even in English. . . . And, indeed, the opening of the speech of
the pious Aeneas has a poetic tone that is not contemptible:

> *Quis talia fando*
> *Myrmidonum Dolopumve aut duri miles Ulixi*
> *Temperet a lacrimis.*

That you will not find ignoble, if you take the trouble to dramatize it
and to consider that here was a man mourning the eradication of his
great city and its peoples from the earth and saying: "Who of the
Myrmidons, who of the Dolopes (the most terrible of the Grecian
hosts), or what soldier of the cruel Ulysses could at that thought
withhold his tears." And the complete passage in the Latin is of a remarkable beauty of vowel coloring. For let us repeat once more that
the Latins took great delight in vowel colorings that dramatized the
action that the poem described. . . . And the long "o's" and the shorter
hissing sounds of the "i's" admirably represent lamentations and the
bitter saltiness of tears.

You will perhaps say that the great poet should be above the taste of
his day; that that sort of onomatopoeism is an artificiality . . . but
wait a bit. Had this particular book been written for the eye of the
reader, that might be a just criticism. But it is an obvious fact that will
be apparent to every practicing writer—though I have never before
heard it suggested—that at least Books Two, Four and Six of the
Aeneid and the *Georgics* in their entirety were written with a view to
being read aloud. It is not merely that they were so in fact. These
books of the *Aeneid* were the ones that, after years of entreaty mounting nearly to threats, the poet took to read to the emperor . . . and

read them with such effect that "Octavia fainted and could not for a long time be brought to." At the end of the sixth book the whole passage describing Aeneas' visit to the—as yet unborn—souls of Augustus' ancestry in Hell, is a masterpiece of not epic but dramatic writing. . . . Think of what a subject even today it would make for the moving pictures. . . .

There was Virgil, with his voice that is said to have been almost miraculously sweet and moving, reading of a trip that, thousands and thousands of years before, Aeneas took to Hell.* And there he saw— waiting to be born—all the ancestors of Augustus from the days of Aeneas to those of the early kings and to those of the Julian clan. And, the excitement growing every minute, to Augustus' immediate parents. . . . And then suddenly on the screen they see the glorious shade of Marcellus (Marcus Claudius) who slew with his own hand King Viridomarsus of Gaul. . . . And the pious Aeneas goes on talking. . . . Who, he says, is this unborn, yet faint and wavering shade of a boy who stumbles faintly beside the glorious figure of the king-slayer?

Now, you have to understand that Octavia, the sister of Augustus, had had a son called Marcellus who had married Julia, Augustus' daughter, and had been nominated Augustus' heir. He had been a youth of great promise of virtues but he had died at the age of eighteen.

So in the poem—which here is exactly like a scenario for Hollywood—the atrocious Aeneas goes up to the thinly wavering unborn spirit and says: "You shall be another Marcellus (Marcus Claudius)." (*"Tu Marcellus eris."*) That would seem to be a bit thick—so thick, really, as to be hardly credible. But there the words are in Book Six line 884. Virgil in the voice of Aeneas had really brought up her dead son thus to the eyes of his mourning mother. . . . And, of course, Aeneas burbles piously on: "Ah, youth, deserving indeed of pity. Your death is fated but if by any means you can elude your destiny what a Marcellus you will turn out to be. . . . Bring me lilies in handfuls. Permit me to strew the blooming flowers. . . ." And at that point *Octavia defecisse fertur atque aegre focilata est.* . . .

And, believe it or not, Virgil had so neatly arranged the matter that

* *Aeneid*, vi, 268-884.

there remained to him only a few lines of no importance, to finish his readings with. And what a curtain it gave him!

No! The accusation is frequently made by modernistic critics that Virgil did not know how to construct a story. And, indeed, of modern preparation, progress in effect, or architecture he had very little apparent knowledge. He dismisses momentous intrigues with a line or two. The whole building of the wooden horse is got rid of in eight lines, beginning:

> *Fracti bello, fatisque repulsi*
> *Ductores Danaum tot jam labentibus annis*
> *Instar montis equum, divina Palladis arte*
> *Aedificant, sectaque intexunt abiete costas . . .**

Englished, this intrigue would run:

> Broken by the war, frowned upon by the Fates,
> The Danaid leaders after so many years had elapsed
> Build, by the divine art of Pallas a horse as big as a mountain
> And cover its ribs with cut rushes.
> They pretend that it is a votive offering for their safe return to
> Greece.
> That rumor spreads itself abroad.
> Into this, on its blind side (as far as Troy is concerned),
> They introduce picked bodies of men, in secret, and the dark rib-
> spaces
> They fill with armed soldiery, and the immense belly.

I always sigh with relief when I come in my thoughts to this, the twentieth line of this book. . . . For incredible as it may seem, Virgil has got rid of his introductional lines, his apologies to Queen Dido, his two little spots of near poetry and this whole affair of the building of the horse in just a score of dactylic hexameters, no more! So that it makes heavy, bald reading.

---

* *Aeneid*, II, 13-20.

And then pleasure comes with the lines:

> *Est in conspectu Tenedos, notissima Fama,*
> *Insula dives opum Priami dum regna manebant,*
> *Nunc tantum sinus et statio male fidus carinis*
> *Huc se provecti deserto in litore condunt.**

(You perceive once more the beloved word *carinis*.)
The whole story then comes alive. The Greeks being hidden in the Isle of Tenedos, the inhabitants of Troy issue from the walls to inspect the abandoned camps and mooring stations of the Greeks. . . . It is done in a sort of fictional shorthand with the baldest— but not ill-selected—details.

> *Pars stupet innuptae donum exitiale Minervae,*
> *Et molem mirantur equi . . .†*

A part of the sightseers is struck with wonderment at that parting
  gift to Minerva
And wonder at the great bulk of the horse. Then first Thymoetes
Counsels that the horse be brought within the walls and placed in
  the fortress
Either because he was a traitor or because the destinies of Troy
  were nearing fulfilment.

But Capys and others urge that the horse should either be thrown into the sea or hacked to pieces and burnt, and the mind of the populace is divided. And then, really dramatically:

> *Primus ibi ante omnes magnâ comitante caterva*
> *Laocöon ardens summâ decurrit ab arce*
> *Et procul: O miseri quae tanta insania, cives?*
> *Creditis avectos hostes? . . . ‡*

---

* *Aeneid*, II, 21-4.
† *Aeneid*, II, 31-2.
‡ *Aeneid*, II, 40-4.

First, then, before all the peoples there, accompanied by an im-
mense crowd,
Burning with rage, Laocoön runs down from the heights of the
citadel
And begins whilst a great way off: Oh wretched citizens, what
madness is this?
Or does any gift from the Greeks lack guile?
Is not Ulysses sufficiently known to you?

And so, working himself up to the famous final line of his tirade:
Quicquid id est timeo Danaos et dona ferentes! ("However all that
may be, I fear the Greeks, especially when they bring offerings!")
Then with immense recklessness, considering he was a priest and this
apparently an offering to a major goddess—with all his great might he
hurled his massive spear at the juncture of the flanks and belly of the
monster. It remained quivering there and all that cavernous space let
forth a hollow groan. . . . "And," comments Aeneas, "had the gods
seen otherwise, or had our minds not been featherheaded, he had
coërced us into cleaving open the Grecian hiding place. And, Troy,
thou shouldst still stand and the lofty citadel of Priam."*

At that point you would imagine that Virgil would have in-

---

* The translations and condensations from Virgil, Cicero and Suetonius in this
chapter, and those in the preceding one, after the last quotation of *Aeneid*, IV, 149
et seq. are by the author. It seemed to him that at this juncture something more down to
the ground and less florid than Dryden was necessary since we were trying to get some
sort of critical exactness into our views. But they make much less pleasurable reading
than Dryden's verse, and approach much less nearly to Virgilian sonorities. But we may
as well now return to Dryden. Before that, however, it might be as well to give our
down-to-the-ground rendering of Homer's account of the wooden horse episode as
seen by the Greeks in *Odyssey*, VIII, 612.
Ulysses has requested his minstrel Demodocus to sing a short account of the episode
of the horse.
    Ulysses finished. The minstrel felt the inspiration of the godhead. He began
singing of where the Greeks threw firebrands into their tents and, betaking themselves to their brave keels, sailed off—to Tenedos . . . all save the troops that sat
beside the famous Ulysses in the belly of the horse, hidden from sight in the very
Trojan crowd. They meanwhile had drawn it to the citadel, and there it stood
surrounded by the Trojans who discussed it, sitting on the ground and knowing
not what to do with it. They were of three opinions in turn: one to hew up the
huge trunk of the horse; or to drag it to the top of the citadel and cast it from
there amongst the rocks; or, finally, to leave the enormous idol standing there
unharmed, as an offering to the gods. . . .

troduced his celebrated rendering of the remarkably renaissance fourth-period *Laocoön*. This Vatican marble, executed by three sculptors, is of no very great account as sculpture and, acquired in one way or another by the emperor Titus, was placed in his bath. . . . And in this passage in the *Aeneid* Virgil remarkably renders the white statue. . . .

But his account of that episode is not to come yet. You will have to read the immensely long episode of the treacherous Sinon. That may very well have had a political coloration. Greek-baiting—as it were a sort of Aryan anti-Semitism—was not yet by any means an extinct occupation amongst the bloods of the court of deified Augustus. For

> "*Accipe nunc Danaûm insidias, et crimine ab uno*
> *Disce omnes.*"*

exclaims the triumphant Aeneas, omitting in his fervor to finish his line, Dryden translating him:

> "Now hear how well the Greeks their wiles disguised:
> Behold a nation in a man comprised!"

which, indeed, is a very good specimen of how Dryden adapted his Virgil . . . for in any literal transference of thought rather than words the sense must be:

> "Perceive now how guileful are the Greeks and from this one crime be instructed as to all of them. . . ."

You hear the true Roman patriots cheering when Virgil read those words!

And so, after a digression lasting 150 very long lines in a poem that is as yet only 202 lines long, Virgil comes back to his serpents and Laocoön. Here Dryden is nearer his model. "*Horresco referens,*" sings Aeneas. "*Ecce autem a Tenedo tranquilla per alta . . . immensis orbibus angues.*"

* *Aeneid*, II, 65-6.

And sings Dryden:

"A greater omen and of worse portent
Did our unwary minds with fear torment,
Concurring to produce the dire event.
Laocoön, Neptune's priest by lot that year,
In solemn pomp then sacrificed a steer,
When, dreadful to behold, from sea we spied
Two serpents ranked abreast the seas divide
And smoothly sweep along the swelling tide.
Their flaming crests above the waves they shew,
Their bellies seem to burn the seas below; . . .
Their ardent eyes with bloody streaks were filled,
Their nimble tongues they brandished as they came
And licked their hissing jaws that sputtered flame.
We fled amazed; their destined way they take
And to Laocoön and his children make.
And first around the tender boys they wind,
Then with their sharpened fangs their limbs and bodies grind.
The wretched father, running to their aid
With pious haste but vain, they next invade. . . ."

This might seem exaggeratedly pompous and too fluidly facile. But it does not do more than represent Virgil's own grandiloquent facility. None of the adjectives of a writer who has never followed the sea or seen sea serpents or even men in agony are wanting in this Latin. It is a masterpiece of dramatic vowel coloring. No one has ever bettered: *"Fit SonituS Spumante Salo"* or *"ArdenteSque oculoS Suffecti Sanguine et igni Sibila,"* with all the "s's" to represent snakes' hissings, going strong. Not even the enSanguined SeaS are absent.

This may be taken as the bitter criticism of an ascetic *prosateur* of empirico-mediaeval leanings and one inclined in any case to be impatient of the tricks of verse writers. But it is not. It is a simple constatation of what is a masterpiece of phonetic syzygy. It is certainly something that in its way you could not, whilst retaining claims to be a poet, do better. No one has ever bettered it. And Luebke and Dante and Mommsen and Byron and Nipperdeyer and Goethe or Carl Schultze or Lamartine or Ariosto and ten thousand others will tell you that it is of all specimens of the divine-sublime, the sublimest and the most divine—that and the Vatican statue being taken together.

Suppose, then, that we compare that with a quite ordinary passage from Homer's treatment of the episode of the wooden horse. It has always seemed to me to be one of the most beautiful, natural, dramatic and tender set of verses that is anywhere to be found—though I have never come across any critic who particularly noticed it. Certainly it is not as famous as the Virgilian Laocoön lines. It occurs in the fourth book of the *Odyssey*. Menelaus is exchanging reminiscences of the great siege with Helen now restored to him. He is recounting how great a man was Odysseus:

> Consider [says he] what that hero suffered and achieved!
> We, the chosen of the Greeks
> Sat pent within the horse,
> Destined to bring to Ilium her downfall and death.
> You, Helen, came to that place,
> Moved, I must suppose, by some godhead that was avid of glory
>   for Troy.
> You walked three times about the hidden us, within that hollow
>   framework.
> Three times you tapped the sides and called us Argive chiefs by
>   name
> And imitated the voices of the wives of other Achaeans amongst us.
> Diomed and I,
> Crouching beside Ulysses in the darkness,
> Heard your calls and at once stood up
> To answer and go forth. But he
> Calmed our impatiences and made us stay. All the Achaeans
> Kept silent. Only Anticulus
> Let forth one cry and him Odysseus
> Constrained, his immense hands

Holding Anticulus' jaws together, until Pallas
Tricked you away from there and we were saved.*

We have made the translation as down to the ground as possible; but, even as it is, with none of the extravagant beauty of Homer's breath-taking verse, you can easily see how pathetic and consummate a situation Homer has there conceived. And, given the prodigy of the horse—for which, however, there are several historic parallels—how simple are the means employed! . . . Just imagine Helen creeping in the darkness round that wooden monstrosity, tapping on its sides and calling out names . . . and the men inside, after ten years of war and absence from their homes, trembling with eagerness. . . . That is a situation!

Homer, in fact, was a born story-teller who saw the scenes he set down; Virgil, who was no sort of narrator, followed the stories of others, saw his scenes in pictures and statuary and imparted to them, above all things, urbanity. He is in short the good, upper middle class townsman against a blind beggar who followed the roads and used his ears. . . . This is a constatation not a sneer. The world is made up of comfortable townsmen and blind beggars and, presumably, the one has as much right to have his literary wants attended to as the other. Above all, the townsman's heirs must not be handicapped by the perception by their mothers whilst they are still in the womb, of *les émotions fortes*. The conception of the actually adulterous Helen, still striving to ruin her husband and his friends, creeping and tapping on the rough planks: that is a strong emotion. It might well give ideas to women in parturition. Whereas, what could be more beneficent than that the eyes of such a woman going, let us say, to receive the benediction of the Holy Father, should fall on the elegantly washed and curled figures of the marble Laocoön and his sons? You can't believe that they actually suffer; the very snakes are obviously delicate creatures. It is, in fact, no more noxious than the publicity for someone's new soap. . . . A well-bred lady knows that such things must be. Fathers and sons must be devoured by snakes. It is not necessary to

* *Odyssey*, IV, 351 et seq.

think of that sort of fact very often just as it is not desirable too often to think about the poor. But if your attention is to be called to them it is in the Virgilian method that they should be presented to you.

Let us then consider one or two more Virgil-Homer parallels, calling on the famous translation of George Chapman for the Englishing of Homer. Let us consider, first, death pieces of which in both epics there is really such a plenty! Here is the death of Priam according to Virgil translated by Dryden:

> 'Then Pyrrhus thus: "Go thou from me to fate
> And to my father my foul deeds relate.
> Now die!" With that he dragged the trembling sire
> Sliding through clottered blood and holy mire.
> (The mingled paste his murdered son had made.)
> Hauled from beneath the violated shade
> And on the sacred pyre the royal victim laid.
> His right hand held his bloody falchion bare;
> His left he twisted in his hoary hair.
> Then with a bleeding thrust the heart he found.
> The lukewarm blood came rushing through the wound
> And sanguine streams distained the sacred ground.
> Thus Priam fell and shared one common fate
> With Troy in ashes and his ruined state.*

As against that, let us put the picture of Achilles at the death of Hector.

> Thus Death's hand closed his eyes;
> His soul flying his fair limbs to Hell; mourning his destinies,
> To part so with his youth and strength.
> Thus dead, thus Thetis' son.

Achilles to Hector.
> (His prophecie answered): "Die thou now; when my short thred
>   is spun
> I'll beare it as the will of *Jove!*" This said, his brazen spear

* *Aeneid*, II, 580 et seq.

He drew and struck by. Then all his arms (that embrewed were)
He spoiled his shoulders off. Then all the Greeks ran in to him,
To see his person and admir'd his terror-stirring limbo. . . .

"O friends," said stern Aeacides, "now that the Gods have brought
This man thus downe, I'll freely say he brought more bane to
    Greece
Than all his aiders. . . ."

Achilles to the Grecians.
"We have slain Hector, the period
Of all Troy's glorie; to whose worth all vow'd as to a God! . . ."
This said, a work not worthy of him he set to; of both feete
He bored the nerves through from the heele to th' ankle and then
    knit
Both to his chariot with a thong of whitleather; his head
Trailing the center. Up he got to chariot, where he laid
His arms repurchac't, and spurred on his horse that freely flew.
A whirlwind made of startl'd dust drave with them as they drew
With which were all his knotted curls knotted in heaps and filed
And there lay Troy's late Gracious. . . .*

Let us contrast that ferocity with the behavior of the respectable but
hesitant Aeneas over the body of Prince Turnus whom he has just
slain—and in slaying has concluded the *Aeneid*. Aeneas is standing
over the fallen but not yet deceased prince:

In deep suspense the Trojan seemed to stand
And, just prepared to strike, repressed his hand.
He rolled his eyes and every moment felt
His manly soul with more compassion melt.
When, casting down a casual glance, he spied
The golden belt that glittered on his side
The fatal spoil which haughty Turnus tore
From dying Pallas and in triumph wore.
Then, roused anew to wrath, he loudly cries:

---

* *Odyssey*, XXII, 313 et seq.

—Flames while he spoke came flashing from his eyes—
"Traitor, dost thou, dost thou to grace pretend,
Clad as thou art in trophies of my friend?
To his said soul a grateful offering go!
Tis Pallas, Pallas, gives this deadly blow!"
He raised his arm aloft and at the word,
Deep in his bosom drove the shining sword.
The steaming blood distained his arms around
And the disdainful soul came rushing through the wound.*

Or let us compare escapes from watery perils, setting two of Virgil's—
who rather shuns that element—against one of Homer's, who knew it.
Here is an escape by water of Turnus, hard-pressed by the Trojans:

The foe, now faint, the Trojans overwhelm,
And Mnestheus lays hard load upon his helm.
Sick Sweat succeeds; he drips at every pore;
With driving dust his cheeks are pasted o'er.
Shorter and shorter every gasp he takes
And vain efforts and hurtless blows he makes.
Armed as he was, at length he leaped from high,
Plunged in the flood and makes the waters fly.
The yellow God the welcome burden bore
And wiped the sweat and washed away the gore.
Then gently wafts him to the farther coast
And sends him safe to cheer his anxious host.†

And this is how Aeneas deals with storms at sea. Aeneas is leaving
the unfortunate Dido and, whilst sailing towards Italy, sees her funeral
pyre blaze on the cliffs behind him. A storm then approaches:

But soon the Heavens with shadows were o'erspread;
A swelling cloud hung hovering o'er their head.
Livid it looked, the threatening of a storm,

* *Aeneid*, XII, 900 to end.
† *Aeneid*, XII, 810 to end.

Then night and horror ocean's face deform.
The pilot, Palinurus, cried aloud:
"What gusts of terror from that gathering cloud
My thoughts presage! Ere yet the tempest roars,
Stand to your tackle, mates, and stretch your oars! . . ."
Then to his fearless chief, "Not heaven" (said he)
"Though Jove himself should promise Italy,
Can stem the torrent of this raging sea. . . .
'Tis Fate diverts our course and Fate we must obey! . . ."
Aeneas then replied: "Too sure I find
We strive in vain against the sea and wind.
So shift your sails: what place can please me more?
Than what you promise: the Sicilian shore . . ."
The course resolved, before the western wind
They scud amain and make the port assigned.*

Which shows you how easily life might run were you a child of Venus, an ancestor of Augustus and a character of Publius Virgilius Maro. Let us then take a storm of Homer's—a few sections only because Homer's storms are very long, sea-technical and tortuous:

> Whilst this discourse he held
> A curst surge, gainst a cutting rock impelled
> His naked body which it gasht and tore
> And had his bones broke if but one sea more
> Had cast him on it. But She prompted him
> That never failed; and bade him no more swim
> Still off and on; but boldly force the shore
> And hug the rock which him so rudely tore. . . .
> The worst succeeded, for the cruel friend
> To which he cling'd for succour, off did rend
> From his broad hands the soaken flesh so sore
> That off he fell and could sustain no more.
> Quite under water fell he, and past Fate
> Hapless Odysseus there had lost the state

---

* *Aeneid,* V, 11 et seq.

He held in life; if (still the grey ey'd Maid
His wisdom prompting) he had not essayed
Another course; and ceas't to attempt that shore,
Swimming, and casting round his eye t'explore
Some other shelter. Then the mouth he found
Of fair *Callicoe's* flood. . . .
Then forth he came, his both knees falt'ring, both
His strong hands hanging down; and all with froth
His cheeks and nostrils flowing. Voice and breath
Spent to all use; and down he sunk to Death.
The sea had soaked his heart through; all his vaines
His toils had racked, to a labouring woman's paines.*

(We omit calling your attention to the last half line.)
   But to get away from the *émotions fortes*, let us compare a Virgilian
and a Homeric feast. . . . Here is the banquet Dido gave Aeneas on
his arrival:

                                    The queen already sat
   Amidst the Trojan lords in shining state,
   High on a golden bed: her princely guest
   Was next her side; in order sat the rest.
   Then canisters with bread are heaped on high;
   The attendants water for their hands supply,
   And, having washed, with silken towels dry.
   Next fifty handmaids in long order bore
   The censers and with fumes the Gods adore;
   Then youths, and virgins twice as many, join
   To place the dishes and to serve the wine.
   The Tyrian train, admitted to the feast,
   Approach and on the painted couches rest. . . .
   The meat removed, and every guest was pleased
   The golden bowls with sparkling wine were crowned
   And through the palace cheerful cries resound,

* *Odyssey*, V, 560-613.

From gilded roofs depending lamps display
Nocturnal beams that emulate the day.*

It is curious to observe that Virgil apparently knew as little of cooking as of the sea. He suffered as we know from severe indigestion. Banquets and plate and scents for hand-washing waters he knew no doubt from observation in Augustus' halls. And his banquet is as airless as it is joyless . . . the feast of a heavy people, suffering no doubt, they too from indigestion and cares.

But consider the most celebrated feast of Nausicaä, the nymph who, like the so different Dido with her Trojan, received and made much of the battered Odysseus after his shipwreck:

The servants then (commanded) soon abaid
Fetcht coach and mules joyn'd in it. Then the Maid
Brought from the chamber her rich weeds and laid
All up in Coach in which her mother placed
A maund of vittles varied well in taste
And other junkets. Wine she likewise fill'd
Within a goatskin bottle and distill'd;
Sweet and moist oil into a golden cruse
Both for her daughter's and her handmaid's use
To soften their bright bodies when they rose
Cleans'd from their cold baths. Up to coach then goes
Th' observèd maid; takes both the scourge and reins;
And to her side her handmaid strait attains.
Nor these alone, for other Virgins grac't
The nuptial chariot. The whole Bevy plac't,
Nausicaä scourged to make the coach mules runne;
That neigh'd and paced their usual speed; and soone
Both maids and weeds brought to the riverside
Where Baths for all the year their use supplied.
Whose waters were so pure they would not staine;
But still ran fair forth; and did more remain
Apt to purge stains; for that purged stain within

* *Aeneid*, I, 697 et seq.

Which by the water's pure store was not seen . . .
. . . And then where
The waves the pibbles washt and ground was clear
They bathed themselves; and all with glittering oil
Smoothed their white skins, refreshing then their toil
With pleasant dinner by the river side.
Yet still watcht when the sun their clothes had dried.
Till which time (having dined) Nausicaä
With other virgins did at stool-ball play . . .
. . . But when they now made homewards and away'd
Ordering their weeds, disordered as they play'd,
Mules and coach ready; then Minerva thought
What means to wake Ulysses might be wrought
That he might see this lovely-sighted Maid
Whom she intended might become his aid,
Bring him to Town and his return advance;
Her meane was this (though thought a stool-ball chance).
The Queen now (for the upstroke) struck the Balle
Quite wide off the other maids and made it fall
Amidst the whirlpools. At which out shrieked all
And with the shriek did wise Ulysses wake.*

The reader may like to compare this version of Chapman with the admirable prose version of Mr. W. H. D. Rouse from his *The Story of Odysseus.*†

They got ready the mule-cart outside, and fitted it with a fine set of wheels, and brought up the mules and yoked them in; and a housemaid brought a handsome cloak from her chamber and laid it in the cart. Her mother packed a hamper full of eatables, everything the heart could desire and plenty of it, not forgetting the meat, and a goatskin full of wine. Then the young girl got into the cart, and her mother handed her a golden flask of olive oil to use after the bath with her attendant women. Then the girl picked

* *Odyssey,* VI, 101 et seq.
† *The Story of Odysseus,* by W. H. D. Rouse. (New York: Modern Age Books, Inc.)

up the whip and reins, shining with polish, and whipt up the team: the mules went rattling along and did not shirk the pull, so on went load and lady together—but not alone, for the maids were trotting by her side.

In due time they reached a noble river. The washing-tanks were there, never empty, for the water came bubbling up and running through them enough to cleanse the dirtiest stuff. There they took out the mules and let them go free, driving them down to the eddying stream to browse on sweet clover. Then the maids unloaded the wagon and carried the clothes into the deep water, where they trod them out into the pits, all racing for first done. And when the washing was over, and all was spotless, they flew in a long string to the seashore, choosing a place where the sea used to beat upon the beach and wash the pebbles clean. There they bathed, and rubbed themselves all over with olive oil. After that they took their meal on the river bank, while they waited for the clothes to dry in the sun.

When they had all had enough, both maids and mistress, they threw off their veils and began playing at ball, and Nausicaä led the singing, with her white arms flashing in the sunlight as she threw the ball. She looked like Artemis, when bow in hand she comes down from the mountains, over lofty Taÿgetos or Erymanthos, to hunt the boars and fleet-footed deer: round about her the nymphs make sport, those daughters of Zeus who frequent the countryside; and her mother is proud indeed, for she lifts head and brow above all the troop, and she is preëminent where all are beautiful. So shone the fresh young maiden among her girls.

But just as she was about to yoke the mules, and fold up all the fine clothes, and set out for home, Athena decided that Odysseus should awake and see the lovely girl, and let her take him to the city.

So then, the princess threw the ball to one of the maids; the ball missed the maid, and fell in the eddies, and they all shouted at that. The noise wakened Odysseus, and he sat up and began to think. . . .

So that there you have air and joy and light meats and good diges-
tions and carefree-ness . . . and the blind beggar washed up by the
sea. The difference between that and the banquet of Dido is then the
difference between Greek and Roman; between frugality and monstrous appetite. And, going a step further, by a queer reversal of parts,
the difference between mediaeval Latin and renaissance Greek. For
the mediaeval mind was oddly observant, empirical, cruel often, sometimes joyful and always what the French call *accidenté*—full of unexpected happenings and mental adventures. It supported Latin as an
official language for centuries, because it was the language of the
Church; for centuries it read and worshipped—literally—Duke Virgil
of Mantua, because that was nearly the only reading that came down
to them. Nevertheless, the underlying Romance language and literature, as they developed, largely skipped the influence of the official
Roman literature and Church language. So that, actually, the little
feasts of the *Decameron* of Boccaccio are near in spirit to the feast of
Nausicaä. And Dante himself took Duke Virgil as his guide through
Hell not because he was the student of Virgil's *Aeneid* but because of
the Pastoral addressed to Pollio.* In that Virgil seemed to prophesy the
coming of Christ. So the middle ages accorded him the reverence due,
if not to an apostle, then at least to a prophet. *The Divine Comedy*
may owe its inception to Aeneas' visit to Hell in Book VI of the
Aeneid, but the bitter spirit of Dante, who passed his life in exile eating
the salt bread of aliens, was far nearer to the spirit of the sea-ruined
man who was cast up at the feet of Nausicaä.

These are all matters to which we shall have later to return. They
will then seem easier. Let us for the moment consider where we stand.
We have examined the work and figure of Virgil with an apparently
disproportionately elaborate attention and have called up from the

---

* Dante's references to Virgil as a prophet are spread throughout the *Inferno*. His
weightiest single reference runs:

> Art thou that Virgil then, the mighty spring
> Who form'st of language that majestic stream?
> O light and glory of the race who sing!
> Let it avail me that with love extreme
> And zeal unwearied I have searched the book:
> Thou my choice author art and master, thou.
>
> (Cary: *Inferno*, I, 79-85.)

past the mightier shade of Homer just because, with the passing of Virgil, a whole set of circumstances came to an end—as it did with the birth of Christ who entered this world nineteen years after the death of Virgil and lived until fourteen years before Augustus died.

It was as if, then, divinity passed at once from the figures of emperors and poets to light up figures vastly different—to St. Simeon on his pillar, to St. Joan on her faggots and, say, to the late Mr. Spurgeon of the City Temple . . . which only yesterday was, as if divinely, saved from fire! . . . It may seem shocking to say that the last of the great Latin poets died with Virgil when after him Ovid and Lucan and others went on with the business of versifying, and Callimachus and the other Alexandrians went on composing the epitaphs and epigrams which make up the bulk of the exaggeratedly praised *Greek Anthology*. . . . The literary pot went on bubbling along the Mediterranean for another three centuries, but, except for Dante and of course Goethe, world poetry was at an end and world prose was to have its reign. (Shakespeare was so little of a figure and so much a slightly cynical smile that we have literally nothing to put for him beside the great marbles of Homer, Sophocles, Aeschylus, Plato even and Virgil.) And the Divinity of the Ruler went finally into the hands of the Pope, though African, Spanish and Asiatic emperors continued to be deified by the senate. But their divinities were mostly of a plaster fashion. And even the thunderbolts of the Napoleon legend are a little tawdry when considered beside those of the Great King, of Alexander of Macedon, of Augustus. The glance of ambition was no longer to embrace a whole world but to center itself on little duchies or republics—Urbino, the Republic of Florence, the Kingdoms of Naples, Sicily and Provence. Of that the birth of Christ was either the cause or the symbol—as you will. In any case, in the year O the water-clocks of humanity took on a different rhythm. . . . Let us then do a little sweeping up.

Publius Ovidius Naso was born 43 years before the birth of Christ and died in exile 16 years after that event as it is conventionally placed. He is the Man in the Iron Mask amongst poets. He was exiled to

Cimmeria for no reason that has ever been definitely discovered. A brilliant man about town, more sought after by the courtiers than even Virgil or Horace, he disappeared from under the cerulean skies of the Mediterranean at the age of 52 and passed the next seven years until his death in writing *Tristia*—sad things in which without avail he prayed for his recall. It seems fairly obvious that he was one amongst the innumerable lovers of the emperor's daughter—though some, whether emulous for, or detractors of his fame—declare that his exile was due to the fact that the eroticisms of his *Amores* shocked Augustus. One would have thought Augustus more a man of the world!

The fact of his exile robbed our poet of most of his divinity; the rest of it he got rid of with his querulousness. Had he been content with silence he might have gained dignity from mystery. As it is, even the humblest—but very useful—encyclopaedia of today describes him as *"Poète facile, gracieux et brillant, plutôt que réellement inspiré."*

Alas, he was always one of this writer's favorite poets, because of his imagination, his invention, his gay draughtsmanship—his almost mediaevalism! This writer at least puts· the flower-picking scene of the *Persephone Rapta* alongside the *Nausicaä* for its gaiety, alongside Chaucer for its color, and alongside the fresco of the *Unicorn* in the castle of Avignon for its picture. . . . And he has had few equals as a fairy-story teller. He was never very grave and he became querulous; he was never very naturalistic—about as much so as Tennyson of the "burnished dove." Indeed, you might call him the Tennyson of the Augustan court: he was less moral but infinitely less of a materialist than the Virgil of Victoria.* His constructive gifts as a story teller were not much more considerable than those of Virgil or any other poet of his day. The *Persephone* itself begins with four lines of Sicilian topography; two lines are given to the banquet of Arethusa, two to the pretty descriptive lines

> *Filia consuetis ut erat comitata puellis*
> *Errabat nudo per sua prata pede.*

* Tennyson, by the way, wrote of Virgil as "Wielder of the stateliest measure ever moulded by the lips of man. . . ." (But how do you wield a measure that you have moulded—as if it were a cast-iron marling-spike? But, obviously, Tennyson's admiration for Virgil was very great. He thought much less of poor Ovid.)

Then come two lines descriptive of the spring-moistened valley where Persephone walked . . . and then Ovid lets himself go. Not in the direction of introducing kidnapper Pluto with his cerulean horses. No, he says: *"Tot fuerant illic quot habet natura colores."* ("There were there as many colours as Nature can show.") and dashes off with the maids to gather chromatic blossoms. They pick into baskets quickly woven out of rush: marigolds, violets, poppies, hyacinths, amaranths, thyme, mezereon, meliliton; many pick roses and many flowers of which Ovid does not even know the name, and they pick the tender crocus and the white lilies. Never was there such flower-picking. But then Persephone was the daughter of Ceres, goddess of flowers and crops. So there are twenty-five lines. Then Ovid remembers that he is really writing about a kidnapping so he suddenly sets down:

This her paternal uncle sees and, having seen it,
With his funereal steeds to his own realm swiftly carries her off.*

Just like that!

It seems, however, to this writer to be very lovely and there is room in the world for that sort of fluidity and grace. Ovid wrote a very beautiful elegy on Tibullus which contains the lines:

Cui Nemesis, Quid ait, tibi, sunt mea damna dolori?
Me tenuit moriens deficiente manu.
Si tamen e nobis aliquid, nisi nomen et umbra,
Restat, in Elysia valle Tibullus erit.†

and the "Cave of Sleep" passage (Met. XI, 592-615), the "Phaeton Struck by Lightning" (Met. II, 304-328), the "Narcissus and Echo" and the "Palace of Fame" all come back to this writer as memorable pieces. But the verdict of the schoolmasters has gone out against Ovid as being light and frivolous—and this writer is in no mind to make a fight out of it. The reader should judge for himself. Ovid is very easy reading. It would be better if he were studied in schools before Virgil.

* *Fasti*, IV, 445 and 6.
† *Amor*, III, IX, 57-60.

He would be less likely to give young things, who instinctively dislike pompousness, a fatal distaste for the Latin language. But, indeed, it would be delightful to see our old and valued friend Suetonius—who verified his statements with the industry of any German and yet retained a sense of humor—substituted in schools for the grim Caesar and the insupportably dull Cornelius Nepos.

Of known official poets there remains Lucan. . . . Marcus Annaeus Lucanus was born in Cordova, Spain, in 39 A.D. His grandfather was Seneca (called the Rhetorician), his uncle, Seneca (called the Philosopher), the tutor of Nero, Polonius of that monster's court. Lucan received, therefore, instruction from the most reputed professors. Their lessons and no doubt the influence of Seneca the Philosopher turned him at an early age into a Stoic adept. But his fame as a rhetorician and poet flew with greater rapidity across Rome. He was, therefore, recalled from Greece before he had completed his studies; admitted to the intimacy of Nero; given a quaestorate before he was of legal age and made an augur before he was twenty. . . .

Unfortunately, his uncle—who had become a more than multi-millionaire—fell at that time into disrepute with Nero . . . ostensibly because he did not sufficiently admire the emperor's verses and singing. Actually, it is not difficult to discern, it was because he had business with plotters against the person of the emperor. Gibbon, indeed, suggests that he had also designs on the purple.

However that might be, his situation at court became extremely awkward for the boy Lucan. And he showed no tact. Even in the first book of his *Pharsalia* he poked veiled fun at the corpulence and defective sight of the emperor, and after the prudent Seneca had retired into exile, Lucan perpetrated lampoons and libels against Nero. His end was inevitable. Before he was twenty-five and—after having accused his mother of taking part in a conspiracy—in order to save his own arteries, he ate an immense meal and called in his doctor to open his veins. . . . As for his mother, Acilia, Tacitus reports that she was neither pardoned nor put to death.

His very numerous minor writings, ballets, *saturnalia,* eulogies of the emperor and libels against him, together with all his occasional pieces, were suppressed after his death. But his widow, Argentaria

Polla, who seems to have been tenderly attached to him and his memory, preserved intact the manuscript of his *Pharsalia* and, after the death of Nero, published it in full.

It is a long, dull, but by others much admired epic about the civil wars of Caesar, Pompey and the rest. It is—as it should be as the work of a boy of his age—very derivative. The poet takes whole phrases from Horace or Ovid and endless opinions from his uncle, commonplacedly and complacently lashing the wickedness and degeneracies of his age . . . attributing them naturally to foreigners.

His Latin is heavy and contorted:

> *fecunda uirorum*
> *paupertas fugitur, totoque accersitur orbe*
> *quo gens quaeque perit: tunc lorgos jungere fines*
> *agrorum et quondam duro sulcata Camilli*
> *uomere et antiquos Curiorum passa ligones*
> *Longa sub ignotis extendere rura colonis.**

As who should say:

> We had abandoned that simplicity of manners that had conduced to the bearing of so many heroes and had introduced from all over the world the things that conduce to the downfall of nations. In that day they joined field to vast field. The very ploughlands that had formerly been bitten into by the ploughshare of Camillus, which had been levelled by the primitive harrows of the Curii, have been joined up to make vast bonanza farms cultivated by the slave labor of alien immigrants.†

. . . the complaint that is almost the oldest of all and that yet falls fresh from the lips of every highschool boy—as Lucan was when he wrote those lines—everywhere and eternally.

Otherwise the *Pharsalia* seems to me to be an intolerably long, commonplace account of the civil war told, one does not exactly know why, in heavy dactylic hexameters. It is, in fact, the only verse of a

---

* Lucain: *La Guerre Civile,* Book I and II, 165 et seq. The text is that of the magnificent recension made by Dr. A. Bourgery in 1926.

† Author's translation.

highly reputed Latin poet that it is better to read in translation, though you could say the same of the prose of the lovely *Golden Ass* of Apuleius.

Lucan, then, would seem to be the last of the Latin poets to be—deservingly or not—credited with the name of great. There were, nevertheless, as we have already adumbrated, whole shoals of lesser lights of official standing. Many of their works—the majority—have disappeared. But some works and fragments of works of poets whom we have not mentioned still survive and are worth your running through for the light they throw on Roman history, economy or manners. Of the First or Republican period, usually taken to extend from B.C. 240-80, the following are just worth mention:

Pacuvius, Accius, Claudius Quadrigarius, Lutatius Catullus, Porcius Licinius, Valerius Aedituus. Of the last three Aulus Gellius quotes a not too bad epigram apiece. Of the Augustan period—B.C. 80-14 A.D.—there remain two unimportant poets of whom we have said nothing, Quintus Cicero and Caelius Bassus. Of the last, the Panegyric on *Calpurnius Piso* is just worth reading. His versification is agreeable.

The Silver Age is usually said to extend from A.D. 14 to 180. Its noticeable poets are Phaedrus (B.C. 30–A.D. 44) who wrote agreeable versions of Aesop's fables intended as satires against his age; Valerius Flaccus (his dates are not very certain but he certainly flourished under Augustus—he died about 90 A.D.) wrote a quite agreeable and quite readable pastiche of combined Homer-Virgilian sea adventures called the *Argonauts*. If neither of those others had written we should esteem him more. Silius Italicus, a poet again difficult to date, wrote almost avowedly in imitation of the *Aeneid* an epic called *Punica*. He was probably a Spaniard and occasionally turned out some fine lines. He died about 101 A.D. The passage in his fifteenth book, when Scipio chooses virtue in preference to vice, is usually much commended. Of Statius, the invitation to dine with the Emperor Domitian in his *Silvae* is agreeable, but both the *Thebaïs* and the *Achilleïs*—both dedicated to Domitian—are rather tiresome. He died about 96 A.D.

The reader must at this point very carefully not omit to remember one immense fact—or all will be lost! The poets with whom we have

been dealing were the Official Poets of the Roman Imperial Court—
and, of course, of the intelligentsia and the gentry like Pliny the
Younger. The stanzas of a Virgil might be sung on the populai stage,
but, as a rule, the infinitely hybrid, sweated, uproarious populace who
stank and pullulated in the latifondia beneath the Capitoline Hill
would not know anything of the hexameters and pentameters that
majestically rolled above their heads. . . . And in the mean time they
evolved a language and verse measures that suited their lazy tongues
and roaring mouths. In those subterraneous darknesses they were
evolving the language and the poetry of the Romance period—of
Chaucer, of Ronsard and the French, Italian, Provençal and Spanish
of today . . . and of all that is intelligent in our own language and
poetry. What they did in those centuries is the real heritage that Rome
gave to the world because, in effect, they gave us ourselves.

We cannot unfortunately trace the process in its early years. There
are rude verses scrawled on the walls of Pompeii and rude passages of
prose of a nature barbarous and horrescent to the ears of those used to
the clarities of the Classics. At any rate, all that we have here space to
point out—though the subject is one to which we shall have to return
—is that, even whilst poets like Lucan were writing and rhetoricians
like Seneca orating in classical phrases, the language of the populace,
as will happen when a relatively pure race is hybrid in its lower
strata, was disintegrating, growing easier to handle, losing its individuality.

Rome gradually became a great industrial city with thousands and
thousands of hands employed in each unit of the latifondia. . . . Some
of the vast blocks of apartments contained as many as forty thousand
workers apiece. The patron and owner had usually his residence in the
vast inner courtyard which would contain trees, gardens, running
water, aviaries, statues. The publisher of Horace, a freed Greek slave,
lived in such a vast mansion belonging to Maecenas. He employed
from four to seven thousand slaves, according to the pressure of work.
They were nearly all Greeks, Egyptians or Jews—all slaves; and he
hired them from patrician Romans. He could turn out from fifteen to
sixteen hundred illustrated copies of the *Odes* of Horace in a day. It was
in such hybrid overcrowdings that our languages evolved themselves.

CHAPTER FOUR

THE two chief glories of Latin imaginative prose which gradually superseded verse as the Grecian impetus died away, were Petronius and Apuleius. The one was one of the greatest artists in prose there has ever been, the other, one of the most delightful imaginers writing a language of the worst artificiality. But before we deal with them we had better attend to the masterpieces of not specifically imaginative writing, a branch in which the Romans excelled all other peoples. Gibbon is probably as great a prosateur as any of the Latins and so was, say, Chateaubriand, but the arbitrary and troublesome law of both the French and English languages—the compulsory and monotonous sequence of subject, verb, object which at any rate the modern forms of those languages exact—must always give to modern prose effects a certain monotony. A language which insists that we should say: "When Goliath was dead he slew thousands," as a sole norm of statement, must at least be less rich, precise and varied than one in which you can employ in addition the form: "Thousands, Goliath dead, he slew." And the brain of the reader who must be pap-fed by monotonies is apt to be less perceptive than that of one who can do a little quick thinking over the form of a statement. That of course is a matter of opinion, but it is an opinion worth considering for a moment.

But, however that may be, it must be conceded that in that borderland of literature where exist history, oratory, correspondence and the essay, Roman writings are serenely rich and unattainable. No one has ever used language with more clarity, utility and ferocity than Cicero in his *Orations*; no one has ever more skillfully used the letter form to convey information or to draw his own character; no one has more agreeably written essays with the head and tail pieces of letters than did Pliny the Younger. No one ever used prose so with the stroke of an iron chisel on stone as Caesar. No historian was ever as terse as Tacitus, as measuredly luxurious as Livy. . . . And it is in thinking of them, along with one or two Frenchmen—but far more of them than of the one or two Frenchmen—that we, each one of us for generations, have imagined to ourselves what might be good English . . . and come inevitably back to Gibbon.

Let us put any random passage of Gibbon's against one of Tully's just to remind ourselves how the human mentality goes backwards and forwards through thousands of years to find itself methods for the expression of itself to other minds. For, if we seek to exercise ourselves in prose, it is merely that we may make our meanings clearer to others.

Says Gibbon then:

> When the law was given in thunder from Mount Sinai, when the tides of the Ocean and the course of the Planets were suspended for the convenience of the Israelites and when temporal rewards and punishments were the immediate consequences of their piety or disobedience, they perpetually relapsed into rebellion against the visible majesty of their Divine King, placed the idols of the nations in the sanctuary of Jehovah, and imitated every fantastic ceremony that was practiced in the tents of the Arabs or in the cities of Phoenicia. As the protection of Heaven was deservedly withdrawn from the ungrateful race, their faith acquired a proportionable degree of vigor and purity. The contemporaries of Moses and Joshua had beheld with careless indifference the most amazing miracles. Under the pressure of every calamity, the belief in those miracles has preserved the Jews in a later period from the universal contagion of idolatry; and in contradiction to every known principle of the human mind that singular people seems to have yielded a stronger and more ready assent to the traditions of their remote ancestors than to the evidence of their own senses.

It seems to this writer—and there one may presume oneself to be in agreement with the majority of one's fellows—that in that prose we have an unequalled vehicle for the conveyance of facts in the category of affairs treated by this author. It is a vehicle capable of conveying states of mind at once of the extremest serenity, of indignation, of enthusiasm, all as one might say without so much as raising or lowering the voice. . . . And it is an English that for good or evil is the standard from which all other styles and usages take their departure. . . . Let us put against that a passage' from Cicero, chosen almost equally at random—for with both Gibbon and Cicero the level of style is so equally maintained throughout their works that one passage will almost always serve as well as another for the displaying of their qualities. This is a passage from the oration in favor of M. C. Marcellus. Marcus Claudius Marcellus, a man of the greatest strength of character, had been one of the chief and certainly the bitterest opponent of Caesar; but Caesar having pardoned him, Cicero is expressing the gratitude felt by the Senate: when later, we read Cicero's letter on the subject we may form an opinion of the sincerity of the speech:

All things, O Caius Caesar, which you now see lying stricken and prostrate—as it was inevitable that they should be—through the violence of war must now be raised up again by you alone. The courts of justice must be restored, licentiousness must be repressed, the increase of population encouraged, everything which has become lax and disordered must be braced up and strengthened by strict laws. In so vast a civil war, when there was such ardor of feeling and of warlike preparation on both sides, it was impossible but that—whatever the ultimate result of the war might be—the republic which had been violently shaken by it, should lose many ornaments of its dignity, many bulwarks of its security, and that each general should do many things while in arms which he would have forbidden to have done while clad in the garb of peace. And all those wounds of war thus inflicted now require your attention. And there is no one except you who is able to heal them. Therefore, I was concerned when I heard that celebrated and wise saying of yours, I have lived long enough to satisfy either nature, and I will add, if you like, or glory; but, which is of the greatest consequence of all, certainly not long enough for your country!

This translation from *Pro Marcello*, VIII, by C. D. Yonge seems to be a very good, standard translation, warped neither by too great effort after brilliance nor by the effort to express the translator's personality.

This writer is always a little uncertain what to do about the original
Latin text. He has hitherto taken it that the reader who did not know
Latin well could here dispense with it. The Latin-reading reader, on the
other hand, would probably also have his Latin texts, so that it should
be sufficient to indicate for him the first lines of passages. But where
the matter is intimately one of prose style, the exact wording of the
original becomes of primary importance, so that he hereby transcribes
the original of the above passage:

> *Omnia sunt excitanda tibi C. Caesar unit, quae iacere sentis belli
> ipsius impetuquod necesse fuit, perculsa atque prostrata: constitu-
> enda judicia revocanda fides, comprimandi libidines, propaganda
> suboles; omnia quae dilapsa iam defluxerunt, severis legibus,
> vincienda sunt. Non fuit recusandum in tanto civile bello, tanto
> animorum ardore et armorum quin quassata respublica, quicumque
> belli eventus fuisset, multa perderet et ornamenta dignitatis et
> praesidia stabilitatis suae; multaque uterque dux faceret armatus
> quae idem togatus fieri prohibuisset. Quae quidem tibi nunc omnia
> belli vulnera sananda sunt, quibus praeter te mederi nemo potest.
> Itaque illam tuam praeclarissimam et sapientissimam vocem
> invitus audivi: "Satis diu vel naturae vixi vel gloriae." Satis, si ita
> vis, fortasse naturae, addo etiam, si placet gloriae; at quod maxi-
> mum est, patriae certe parum.*

This prose, whether in the English or in the Latin, has not the fierce
life of the Gibbon who writes as if he were throwing at you pieces of
his own heart. But then Ciceronian oration almost never has anything
to do with Cicero's heart. Let us begin by saying that in them he was
not a poet; he was a special pleader: and his orations had every purpose
in the world save that of revealing the real Cicero. That is not hypocrisy; it is honesty on the part of the pleader. Thus, when you have read
his orations with care and made allowances for the special purposes
for which each one was written, you may arrive at some fairly precise
view of what sort of a man he was.

But in his much more simply written *Correspondence* he conceals
himself much more mysteriously. . . . It is customary to say that in

his letters Cicero shows the heart of the simple, benevolent being that he was. Consider the passages that follow:

To Atticus in Rome, 12 June B.C. 44
from Arpinum

Let me tell you, this place is charming; retired, to be sure, and, if one wishes to write, free from interruption. But somehow or other, "there is no place like home;" and so I shall hie me back to Tusculum. Besides, I should soon tire of the scenery here; it is so tame, so flat. I fear rainy weather, too, unless my studies in prognostications fail me, for the frogs are declaiming.

13 June

The Queen is a regular nuisance. The idea of her shedding around shady stories about some presents she promised me! Her agent Hammonius knows that the requests I made of her were quite consistent with my position in the State and amongst scholars and such as I should not be ashamed to cry abroad. When I call to my mind the insolence of the Queen herself during her stay in the gardens across the Tiber I can hardly contain myself. Therefore I will have nothing to do with her or her crew.*

The Queen was Cleopatra. Cicero had been exchanging rare books with her.

On the face of it, Cicero's letters are very simple. They are written in a carefully constructed idiom of Cicero's own contriving, full of rustic constructions and, above all, of diminutives. A coat has to be a coat-ikin, a jaguar a jaguarling, a book a booklet. And you can never tell whether the real meaning of any statement is not to be understood at its exact opposite. The letter about Cleopatra may be really about rare books. But it might very well be (a) private information to Atticus that he intended to oppose the cause of the Queen's lover of

---

* Letters CVI-CVII, translated by Arthur Patch McKinlay, 1926. This is a good rendering of the original into modern colloquialnesses but of course modern colloquialnesses always become a little shocking after they have been published a decade or two. In the case of Cicero's letters, there is, however, nothing else to do since as we shall have later occasion to point out they were written in a carefully originated "little language" almost of his own.

the moment, or (b) it might as well be that he desired to warn Caesar —who was the lover of the moment—that if he did not make some concession to Cicero, Cicero might put some spoke in his wheel. This writer, at any rate, has never been able to take Cicero's intimacy with Atticus at its face value. Atticus was the most odious type of money-lender and, if Cicero really liked him as much as he said, it was little to his credit. But if Atticus was also half agent, half stool-pigeon for Cicero, the matter grows at once more understandable.

Let us, however, not draw another red herring across our sufficiently complicated trail; it is sufficient to say that in both his magniloquent orations and in the managed simplicities of his letters Cicero was almost always playing a game. Not always, but nearly. . . . It seems feasible to think that Cicero felt real sympathy for the unfortunate Sicilians whom Verres stripped naked. He had occupied an official position in the island and had both liked, and been very much liked by, them. And it is impossible to doubt his expressions of grief for his daughter Tullia, who was the only creature with whom he had really human relationships. . . . Nevertheless, within a month of her death he was giving testimonials to her atrocious husband, Dolabella, who had been, by his brutalities, the cause of her death. . . . That was no doubt political.

For Cicero at once becomes clear when one understands that the one passion of his life from which he never wavered was that for constitutional fascism—the "optimate school" of political philosophy. But he had to express his devotion for that policy in a parliament of such a complicated deviousness as no other country has ever seen the like of. The Senate consisted, on the one hand, of a great group of "anonymous and irresponsible kings;" but on the seats allotted to the Roman order of knighthood, sat a body of merchants and financiers of great perspicacity when it came to be a matter of securing graft for their order. So that what happened to bills introduced into the Senate was something always complicated and frequently incomprehensible. You might consider Cicero inconsistent or even treacherous when, after having spoken with acrimony and voted against Rufio's homestead, or small-holdings' bill, in less than a year he voted and spoke enthusiastically in favor of a measure enacting exactly similar provisions for settling the

Roman poor on the land. But the Rufio Bill contained a clause making retrogressive penalties against great landowners who refused to part with their lands in parcels to small holders. This was to give Cicero's enemies in the Senate a chance to indict one of his political friends who, some years before, had refused to part with some land to a private individual.

In the same spirit very few of his orations were exactly what they seemed. The *Oration for Marcellus* that we have just quoted was far more a declaration of optimate policy and an offer of collaboration with Caesar than, in the main, a real expression of joy for the release of Marcellus who was a distinguished man mainly optimate in his views. The second oration against Clodius, which seems purposeless in view of the fact that Clodius had fled, is at once a reaffirmation of the policy of Cicero's party and a publication of the news that Clodius *had* fled. For it is necessary to reaffirm here that neither the Greeks nor the Romans had any news service. The Roman Senate had a journal which registered the doings of the Senate and any *very* memorable happenings in the city. . . . And indeed there would appear to have been a news-sheet in the city itself. But Petronius complains that the most startling items of its news consisted in announcements that such and such a citizen and his wife had been blessed with twins; that an unusual calf had been born in the First Suburban Region, and that such and such gladiators hired from the troop of Pomponius Atticus would fight at the entertainment given by Minnius on the Ides of March at his house.

Thus an Oration of Cicero's stood nearly always at once for the official news that his party desired to be spread and for a dozen leaders in the *Times* declaring the policy of the Right Centre on any given subject. In those circumstances it is obvious that the accusation of hypocrisy—and still more of tergivization—cannot reasonably be laid against Cicero. His party stood for only one thing; but the circumstances surrounding itself might change from day to day. So then must be the measures that they took to meet those circumstances. There was no more than that to their changes of policy. They—and Cicero with them—would support the Triumvirate whilst it seemed likely that the Triumvirate could attain to power and promote order in the city. They supported Pompey when it seemed as if Pompey might become their absolute ruler. They supported Caesar even though they disliked him. And Cicero might well have become the right-hand man of Augustus had not Augustus showed signs of playing dictator and had Cicero not one evening stuck his head out of a litter and had it cut off by a waiting assassin.

What, in fact, Cicero and his supporters wanted was a ruler—any ruler—who would have the strength to seize the supreme power and hold it . . . preferably with the support of the Senate and in conformity with the ancient constitution. The most odious of all commentators on Roman affairs, Mommsen, in his incredible search for details that would go to prove that his royal masters, the Hohenzollerns, were the Caesars returned to life, permitted himself to call Cicero the "parvenu political turncoat." That was because Cicero was not entirely devoted to Caesar and, indeed, permitted himself to shriek with joy on hearing the news of his death. . . . Nor, indeed, need anyone today consider that the word "fascist" is derogatory to Cicero, the special pleader.

To understand that, it is necessary to know something of the condition of chaos into which the city had fallen by the days of the end of the republic. It was then not in a state of civil war. It was in a state of twenty civil wars raging at once—no modern gangsterism has ever paralleled it, nor yet even the state of Italian principalities in the middle ages. Every citizen—not merely the Mr. Huey Long's of the day—on setting out for the Senate must surround himself with a bodyguard of hired bravos whose number varied according to the victim's purse, importance or information as to the movements of other gangs of bravi. Still more was this necessary in the case of Cicero. He had his regular army, staff and intelligence service. He knew when armed bands were marching on Rome from Milan or from Sardinia to offer themselves for hire. When certain Sardinians had been refused the citizenships which they had come to Rome to seek, Cicero said: "If they are not citizens, they are at least lusty fellows. Let us take them in among the number of our men."

That, obviously, was a condition of things that would be insupportable to any man that really had the good of the republic at heart. He must grasp at any straw. We have quoted the passage from the *Oration for Marcellus* above, in order to quote, nearly parallel with it, the passage from the letter below. . . . Cicero having been approached by Caesar had courageously declared his loyalty to Pompey and had even visited Pompey in his camp. But it had been impossible for him not to see that Pompey was the vainest weakling, without energy, without martial spirit, without even a political programme. Thus, on his return when he had met with no persecution at the hands of Caesar and, considering that Caesar was behaving with the greatest magnanimity and that he also showed some signs of restoring something of the ancient governing system to Rome, he writes in October B.C. 46 to Sulpicius, who was in Greece:

When—in the Senate—Marcellus' case was brought before him Caesar at first criticized his bitterness—that was the term he used—and in most honorable words praised your fairness and foresight: then suddenly, beyond all hope, he said that not even in the case of such a man as Marcellus would he deny the Senate's requests. For, when Caesar's father-in-law had brought up the question of Marcellus' pardon and Caius Marcellus had fallen at Caesar's feet, the Senate, by preconcerted action, rose in a body and approached him humbly.

In short that day seemed to me so beautiful that I had a vision as it were of the rebirth of the State; and so, when all the Senators, as the roll was called, thanked Caesar . . . I, being called upon, changed my mind. For, not from laziness, but from longing for the old constitution, I had determined to keep quiet forever. But Caesar's magnanimity and the Senate's loyalty broke down my resolution, therefore I made a long speech in praise of Caesar.

But, even at that, the personal reconciliation between himself and the virtual ruler of Rome never reached any sort of cordiality. The sources of Cicero's powers were rather mysterious; but by that date he had arrived at almost the position that he had always announced as being the height of his ambition. He had always wanted, that is to say, to hold the highest office in the state and then to retire taking up the position of an Elder Statesman who should act as a moderator, being listened to by all the parties in the state. As he now was, the strength and inviolability of his character, his courage and his feared eloquence, put him beyond anxiety as to persecution even by anyone as nearly omnipotent as was Caesar. . . . But, indeed, at that date the omnipotence of Caesar was much less than today it seems to be. He was the all-powerful leader of a party, but there remained an opposition too powerful to be ignored. Pompey, it was true, was dead but the number of people who still maintained the tradition of his ideals was sufficiently respectable to make it impossible to rid the state of them without having recourse to a massacre that was no part of Caesar's programme. So the two men remained on terms of, as it were, social politeness. Pompey being dead, it was no disloyalty on the part of his former henchman to invite the Caesar to spend a week-end with him. And so he did and the invitation was accepted, and Caesar came:

> To Atticus in Rome
> Puteoli. 19 Dec. B.C. 45

What a fearsome guest! And yet I do not regret his visit. For it was very delightful. On the second day of the winter holidays he put up at the villa, near here, of Octavius' stepfather, Philippus. The company so packed the establishment that there was hardly a place left for Caesar to dine in; two thousand men there were. You may be sure I was disturbed as to the morrow. But Barba Cassius came to my relief; he posted guards, made camps in the fields and protected my villa.

Caesar stayed with Philippus until noon of the next day; nobody was admitted to his presence; no doubt he was going over his accounts with Balbus. Then, on the way here, he took a walk on the seashore; at one o'clock a bath. Then word was brought him concerning Mamurra's conspiracy. He did not move a muscle of his face. He next took a rub down in oil, after which he dined. Since he was undergoing a course of emetics, he ate and drank without fear and with pleasure. The dinner was well got up and not only that but it was well-cooked and well-seasoned; the conversation was delightful and, take it all in all, everything went off agreeably.

Besides, in three rooms, Caesar's suite was entertained very bountifully. The ordinary attendants and the slaves had all they wanted. The more fashionable guests were served right elegantly. In fact, I showed off as a good provider.

As for my Guest, he is not one to whom one would say: "Pray, my good fellow, stop off again with me on your way back." Once is enough. The talk avoided politics but fell much on literary topics. In short, he was in a charming and agreeable mood. He was to spend one day at Puteoli and another at Baiae. There you have an account of his visit. Or shall I say, his billeting, which though it brought me some trouble, as I have said, occasioned me little annoyance.

We may regard this letter, if we like, as giving to Atticus his official position with regard to Caesar, and Atticus no doubt spread the news about Rome. . . . And, indeed, we may regard it as a real expression of his feeling for Caesar as man and companion.

Nevertheless, time passed and Caesar assumed more and more the aspect of a solitary tyrant and less and less that of the champion of the Senate and an artisto-arbitrary constitution. So the disillusionment of Cicero turned gradually to actual personal hatred and, as I have said, he shrieked with delight on hearing of Caesar's death.

In the confused period of interregna that followed the death of Caesar, finding that Marc Antony had the ambition of taking exactly the place of Caesar in the republic and even of taking to himself greater powers still, Cicero with extreme courage came out of his retirement and delivered the three famous orations against Antony that are usually called, in memory of Demosthenes, his Philippics. (The second in order of these, making up four in all, was never delivered as a speech but was written down in the form that we have it.)

Octavian—afterwards, of course, Augustus—welcomed these speeches as aiding his cause, and for a time Cicero would seem to have been content with his promises. But finding at last that he aimed at an imperial power more rigid and absolute than that of any of his predecessors, Cicero became as outspoken as he had ever been before in reprehension of the usurper. . . . His death, as he knew, must soon follow. Octavian made some faint attempts to have him guarded—but persons ready to assist monarchs to get rid of pestilent priests and others are never lacking. And the clock had run down. There remained no place for Cicero on this earth.

We have I think thus witnessed his consistency, his personal and political courage and his probity. This excursion into matters usually regarded as purely biographical was necessary if we are able to understand the sources of his prose, his prose being of such enormous importance to the world. For if, even today, you read the proceedings of any public assembly in the western world, it is always one voice that speaks. You may read the speeches of Jefferson Davis, of the late Mr. Baldwin, of Bismarck himself, of the late M. Delcassé, of the still extant Duce of Italy—and the cadences, the antitheses, the expressions of magnanimity, the reasonablenesses, even, of the perorations of any one of those speakers will all be exactly similar in form . . . and the form will be that of one or other of the Orations of Cicero. The national representatives of Oklahoma, or of the slum divisions of Glasgow or of Roubaix may imagine that in their assemblies they will make speeches running over with their native salt and interruptions cutting like whip-cracks. . . . So they will, through the fairway. But the moment they get ready to do things, to gather in their crop from the sown salt—at once they drop into the one only form that really moves assemblies. Because that is what assemblies will have.

It is no doubt, in the end, the personality of Cicero that thus dominates the orating world. *Le style c'est l'homme.* But, at once to disengage your personality and then to let it make its effect through the veil of conventionalized perorations, is a work calling for no mean industry and pertinacity. The discipline to which Cicero subjected himself was similar to that of Demosthenes, and was pursued eventually in the same city. In Rome as a boy he studied under the greatest Greek masters—Archias the poet, for whose citizenship he subsequently pleaded; the two Scaevolae, jurists; Antonius and Crassus, the orators; and actors, philosophers, Academic, Epicurean and Stoic, galore. Later he traveled and studied for two years in Greece, completing his studies under Appolonius of Rhodes, who had already taught him rhetoric in Rome.

With all these studies—and at the end of them, on his return to Rome—he wrote: "I returned home, not only a finished rhetorician but a changed man. The overstraining of my voice was ended, the trifling-ness of my illustrations was gone. Even my person had acquired a certain substantiality." With all these studies he became, as was necessary, daily more and more Greek in inspiration. There had been Roman orators before him—the fiery Appius Claudius, the implacable Cato with his *"Ceterum censeo, Carthaginem esse delendam,"* the Gracchi, Antonius and Crassus. But to them remained, even till the last, the heavy, formidable over-ornate and monotonous Roman style, fitted for conveying facts, bitternesses, threats—but adapted for little else. Cicero —and Cicero chief of all—began that process of alleviating the natural Roman stiff savagery by introducing Greek constructions into the language and Greek processes into the thought. It came down even to words, for so rigid was the aboriginal Latin that—as is the case with our own tongue—there were whole phases of life for which it had not even any vocabulary. Thus, if his orations are full of Greek thought processes, assemblages of arguments and perorations, in his letters he could hardly approach any theme without using Greek words for the mere expression of the merest nicety. . . . This is a tendency that we have already pointed out. But this writer cannot lay claim to having been the first to do so. For Professor Tyrrell, in his monumental two-volume edition of Cicero's correspondence, gives a complete list of Greek words used by Cicero for which there was no Latin equivalent —and no English one! *"Akeedia"* can only be translated by "ennui" and there was no Latin equivalent at all; *"adiaphoria"* was "non-chalance;" *"nenikohs,"* "en bloc;" *"dusopia,"* *"mauvaise honte."* There was no Latin or English, but there were Greek words for savant, grand seigneur, fracas, ingénu, faux pas, coup d'état . . . and so for innumerable other words for which we have no space here. . . . There is, however, one other point that is, for us, very worth making. In the course of time Latin itself developed terms for frames of mind which in Cicero's time could only be expressed in Greek, and they are Latin terms which we use almost daily. Thus, Cicero could only write *"ouch hosin phthimenoisin"* when he meant *"de mortuis nil nisi bonum;" "meede dikeen,"* for *"audi alteram partem;" "sohma"* for *"Corpus" (Poetarum)*. . . . That is a point that we must carefully remember when we come to consider the transition from the Latin to the Romance tongues.

But for the rest (as has happened to almost every English writer with any knowledge of French), Cicero must cudgel his brains until he found equivalents for the Greek. He did so invariably in his orations in which Greek words figure relatively rarely.

The clarity, balance and cadence of his Orations he learned, then, from the Greeks—and his tremendous range of manner, rather than mannerism. The earlier school of Roman orators whom he replaced had been noted for what was called Asiaticisms—huge gestures, dramatic changes of the voice, threatening intonations, rantings. I do not know any quotation qualifying Cicero's voice, but his manner has had many tributes to it. Thus, when Cicero was about in the Senate to deliver his *Pro Ligario*, which is the simplest of all his orations, Caesar exclaimed: "We will not listen any more to that pestilential fellow." And then differentiating the man from the artist, added: "But we must all listen to Cicero." Whilst he listened, though it is said that Cicero never so much as raised his voice from beginning to end of his speech, every change of thought was visible on the usually immovable face of Caesar. So that when Cicero said: "You pardoned Marcellus at the prayer of the Senate; grant this man to the prayer of the people," it was already known that Caesar had decided to grant that pardon before Cicero had so much as finished his speech.

The *Letters* stand a little further on the road towards conscious art. His unrivalled oratorical technique he evolved by studying the tastes of audiences—in the records of speeches that had pleased, in the instructions given by teachers of rhetoric, by observing the efforts of others to please their hearers, by his own experience. The rules of the art of rhetoric are as ascertainable as those of music. But, indeed, you might almost call it a science.

The art of letter-writing, though it had not as definite a technique, was one of great importance to the republic. It conveyed the news.

Cicero used it above all to convey to his contemporary compatriots, no doubt with a side glance at posterity, the sort of person that he desired to be taken to be—not certainly the sort of person that he was. . . .

His correspondence might at any time be taken by the spies of his rivals and read by undesirable eyes. Thus, in even his family letters, he tried to give a sense of himself as someone kindly, changeable and rather lazy. To this end he had to have a little short-phrased, almost syncopated Latin. And astounding as this may seem to the Anglo-Saxon who in the mass believes that any kind of technique is unnecessary, when it is not deleterious to the writer, Cicero actually took his language and his pretended frame of mind—the latter mostly from the gentle comic writer, Terence, and the former, very much from Plautus who, if his plots were coarse, had originated a Latin stage dialogue that was at once one of great lightness and great strength. So that for the writer of his letters Cicero conjured up one of those gentle seemingly desultory old men of Terence, beings all made of benevolence, of gentle humor in the outwitting of villains, of gentle determination that good shall triumph—and his language was a pastiche of those of the more virtuous characters of the *Miles Gloriosus*, sprinkled plentifully with the diminutives that Plautus so freely used.

We have no further space here to devote to these matters. The reader must take them in hand himself—with the assurance that the task will be accompanied with much pleasure and interest. And, indeed, we must very soon take our leave not only of Cicero but of the Latin language—at any rate for the moment. That we shall ever finally shake them off either in this book or in this world is extremely unlikely. . . . But to gild the pill of parting let us read one more passage of perhaps the most famous and beautiful of all Cicero's familiar letters. It will answer a question that the Anglo-Saxon reader must have often asked himself:

to M. Marius at Cumae
Rome, October, 55 B.C.

If it was ill health that kept you from the Games I congratulate you on your good fortune; but if it was your dislike for such diversions that detained you I rejoice doubly: that you are well and that you are sane enough in mind to scorn the silly entertainments of the populace. I say this, however, on the supposition that during the days of the Games you were putting in your time profitably. You would withdraw, no doubt, to that den of yours which looks out over the Bay of Naples and, in the seclusion of your charming retreat, you would spend the morning hours in light reading; whereas we who left you for the Show were going to sleep over that performance. The rest of the day you passed according to your fancy, whereas we had to put up with the plays that had passed the board of Censors.

The Shows were in honor of Pompey's dedication of his new theatre —the first permanent theatre in Rome. It accommodated 40,000 people. For his opening, according to Pliny, Pompey had got together twenty elephants and 500 lions. The slaughter of these unfortunate beasts was so revolting that even the Roman populace were moved to pity when the elephants, seeing their escape cut off, seemed to beg for mercy. . . . Dion Cassius declares that the audience called for the head of Pompey, Pliny that they rose *en masse* and hooted at him. Cicero seems to be more troubled by the stage shows—and mostly because the old stars of the stage insisted on coming out of their retirement to grace the new theatre. Their voices failed them and they forgot their parts.

The voice of Esop, your particular favorite, failed him in a particularly impressive passage. And why should I say more? Being familiar with such programmes you know what events came next. These did not have the charm even of ordinary shows for the elaborateness of the spectacle took away all delight. I am sure you missed the display, with perfect equanimity. How could one be pleased with 600 mules in the *Clytemnestra* or three thousand punch bowls in the *Trojan Horse*? Or varied paraphernalia of cavalry and infantry in battle scenes! . . .

Why should I suppose that you would have regretted missing

the athletic games when I know that you scorn gladiators? In these performances even Pompey acknowledges that he wasted his money and his pains. The final event consisted of hunting scenes, two of them continuing for five days. Magnificent, to be sure; but what pleasure can a gentleman take in seeing a puny man torn to pieces by a monstrous beast or a beautiful animal pierced by a spear? The last was the day of the elephant-baiting which brought the crowd much wonder but little pleasure. Nay rather, the beasts aroused a sense of pity as if there were some community of feeling between them and man—so that the crowd rose up and cursed Pompey.*

One may add the final subcynical comment that you need not be by any means certain that Cicero was as humanitarian as here appears. It will be observed that he had set himself the task of consoling his friend for his absence from the show . . . and the slight complacency of the closing words of the letter gives him the air of asking: "Well, my friend, have I not marvelously succeeded in what I set out to do?"

We shall have to devote only a few minutes each to the remaining authors of Latin renown with whom we propose here to deal. But it should be remembered that the authors of whom we must treat most fully are those who not merely produced masterpieces, but by the example and tone of their works more than others handed down the torch of literature and the civilizing influences of consummate thought consummately expressed. Cicero handed down so much of the moderate and clear-sighted influences of his Greek masters to the middle ages, the renaissance itself, the eighteenth century and our own day, that really his influence is subterraneously and unsuspectedly Greek, whilst to the unthinking he will pass for the most Roman of them all. But of that there is nothing in Tacitus, Livy, Caesar or Pliny the Younger, who was the very perfect Roman gentleman. On the other hand, the actual moral and disciplinary effect of Plutarch on

* Translation by A. P. McKinlay.

the governing classes of half a dozen centuries was all-powerful; but his point of view presents no interest, and literary problems with him were unimportant. He may very well be said to be responsible for Victorianism, but a person who showed the remotest curiosity as to what sort of a fellow Plutarch himself was is yet to seek.

Of them all Tacitus seems to be the greatest literary figure. His simple short-sentenced paragraphs are as cadenced and as clear as it is possible to be with words. He studied the Latin language with an intensified care, and he left it a tool more flexible than it ever was or has ever since been. His main motive was patriotic. He desired to present to the degenerate Romans of his day so clear a picture, in language so unescapable, and in an atmosphere so attractive, that his compatriots should find it impossible to ignore his lessons. Being a moralist it was permissible to him to blacken the character of men whom he disliked, and being a poet who wrote in prose he modeled his cadences and thought-lengths on those of Virgil, much as Cicero modeled his letters on the dialogue of Terence' plays. . . . The Romans were like that.

He was a voluminous writer, and he was one of those writers who have experience of life and action by which to set the tone of their writings. He was a fine soldier,* he was the son-in-law of Agricola, though his birth does not seem to have been noticeably noble. He was praetor in 88 and occupied the supreme office of consul in 97 B.C. He was reputed to be one of the most eloquent orators of his day. Of his orations none have come down to us and of his many works the most notable that have survived are the *Germany*, the *Life of Agricola*, the *Annals* and the *Histories*. Let us take a passage from the *Germania* in which Tacitus holds up to his countrymen a better way of life than their own, and a passage from the *Agricola* in which he admirably presents how decent men feel in days of horrors they can do nothing to prevent.

Here then are the pure Aryans of their day:

Quamquam severa illic matrimonia nec ullam morum partem

---

* It may be remembered that Gibbon frequently stated that his year in the militia was of more service to him than any of his other experiences.

magis laudaveris. Nam prope soli barbarum singulis uxoribus contenti sunt exceptis admodum paucisque non libidine sed ob nobilitatem plurimis nuptis ambiuntur. Dotem non uxor marito, sed uxori maritus affert. Intersunt parentes et propinqui, ac munera probant, munera non ad delicias muliebres quaesita, nec quibus nova nupta comatur, sed boves et frenatum equum et scutum cum framia gladioque . . .

The translation, by C. C. Yonge, slightly modified by this writer, follows:

The matrimonial bond is strict and severe among them, nor is there anything in their manners more commendable than this. Almost alone among barbarians they content themselves with one wife; a very few of them excepted who, not through incontinence but because their alliance is solicited on account of their rank, practice polygamy. The wife does not bring a dowry to her husband but receives one from him. The parents and relations assemble and pass their approbation on the presents—presents not adapted to please a female taste or decorate the bride, but oxen, caparisoned horses, shields, spears and swords. By virtue of these the wife is espoused and she, in her turn, makes a present of arms to her husband. This they consider as the firmest bond of union, these the sacred mysteries, the conjugal deities. That the woman may not think herself excused from the exertions of fortitude or exempt from the casualties of war, she is admonished by the very ceremonial of her marriage that she comes to her husband as a partner in toils and dangers; to suffer and to dare equally with him in peace and in war. . . . Thus she is to live, thus she is to die; she received what she is to hand down inviolate and honored to her children. . . .

And then, from the *Life of Agricola*—written in the relatively humane reign of Trajan, after the death of Domitian:

Filia atque uxore superstitibus potest videri etiam beatus; in-

columi dignitate florente fama salvis ad finitatibus et amicitiis futura effugisse. Nam secuti durare in hanc beatissimi saeculi lucem ac principem Trajanum videre, quod augurio votisque apud nostras auras ominibatur etc . . .

*Tu vero felix Agricolae, non vitae tantum claritate sed etiam opportunitate mortis . . .**

His (Agricola's) wife and daughter surviving him, his dignity unimpaired, his reputation flourishing and his kindred and friends yet in safety, it may even be thought added happiness that he was thus withdrawn from impending public evils. We have heard him express his wish to live till the dawn of this auspicious day and beholding Trajan as prince—in which wish he foresaw what has happened; so it is a great consolation that by his untimely end he escaped that latter period in which Domitian aimed at the destruction of the Commonwealth.

Agricola never saw the senate house besieged and the senators shut in by a barrage of arms, nor in one havoc the massacre of so many men of consular rank. . . . Soon after we as senators with our hands dragged Helvidius to prison; ourselves were tortured with the spectacle of Mauricius and Rusticus, and sprinkled with the innocent blood of Senecio. Even Nero withdrew his eyes from the cruelties he commanded. Under Domitian it was the principal part of our miseries to behold and to be beheld: when our sighs were registered and that stern countenance with its settled redness, its defence against shame, was employed in noting the pallid horror of so many spectators. . . . Thou indeed wast happy, O Agricola, not only in thy renowned life, but in the occasion of thy death. . . .

There flourished, in particular, in the reign of Domitian when almost no other form of literature can be said to have flourished, above all the satire—and the most famous of all satirists, Martial and Juvenal. They lashed Domitian unceasingly with their diabolic scorn—but we must delay our consideration of them till we arrive at the

* *Agricola*, XLV, 19.

other age when the satire, both Latin and English or French most flourished—the middle and latter eighteenth century. . . . And similarly both Petronius and Apuleius we must leave until we come to the specific consideration of the history of the novel—a form that they initiated. . . . In the mean time, should the reader wish to stall off his impatience with one of the most delightful pieces of irresistible gaiety which the world contains, he might read the *Apologia* of Apuleius, which reads like a parody by Lewis Carroll of the *Defence of Socrates* by Plato. He was accused of having induced a wealthy widow to marry him by various magical devices. One was the possession of a mirror, another that when they saw him in front of an altar little boys would falter and stumble—if they were epileptic. . . . Finally, he had been seen searching the nets of fishermen for unknown fishes with which to make magic brews! . . . One of the lost writings of Apuleius was a treatise on the natural history of fishes. This trial, of course, took place not in Rome but in Carthage, then a small provincial governorship.

We must, however, return our cursory inspection to the historians—not because they are more important in the literary scale than Martial or Juvenal or Petronius or Apuleius but because they have been so hammered into the heads and small clothes of generations that their names loom disproportionately in the world mind. Let it be a question then of the histories by Caesar, Sallust, Livy and our much loved Suetonius. We may be taken to have agreed that Tacitus of them all was the greatest both for his matter, his sort of afflatus and, above all, for the admirable clarity of his Latin and the impeccable manner with which he marshals his facts.

The prose of Caesar is the prose of a man of action who has made just sufficient study of rhetoric, grammar, philosophy and oratory to pass amongst men of intelligence and to avoid the Asiatic extravagances that still distinguished the writing of the majority of the Latin orators of his day. He had (as a military historian must have) an intellect that could grasp and keep going all together great numbers of unrelated matters—several widely severed campaigns, small tautical problems by the score, conspiracies of friends or amongst the enemy peoples, political intrigues at home—and at the same time he thought on various dissimilar topics such as languages, astronomy and divination. Of all his writings only his *Commentaries* on the Gallic and Civil wars have reached us at all intact. They are remarkable in that not only do they present us with the best military history that exists and that they act as justifying him in the course he took against the Senate—with hardly a shred of argument but just simply by his marshaling of facts.

Unlike nearly all the writers of whom we have hitherto treated, he was not of the equestrian middle class but of the highest blood-aristocracy that Rome could show. His awareness of this led him to indulge his contempt for most of his fellow men with a cool insolence and a contemptuous courage—whether to dictators or pirates. He came of course to a hastened end; but the outlines of his work endured for centuries. Let us make from him, too, a couple of citations.

One wonders how many readers of a certain age shall not feel a certain minute strain of horripilescence when they shall read the words: *"Gallia est omnis divisa in partis tres,"* and let their minds go ahead thinking of "the Belgians, the Aquitanians and the Celts, called by us the Gauls."

For the writer, the bleak winter morning feeling comes still more at the words *"Lucio Domitio Appio Claudia consulibus,"* for much as he disliked Caesar for putting him to those tortures at all, he could manage to construe his way fairly well through the first four books. But with the fifth something seemed to happen to his mind—there is no knowing why and we will not waste time on the enquiry. But the end of his assaults on quite small fragments of that text always came in the headmaster's direful words: "Boy, let down your small clothes!"

But let us make the quotation of the first words of the first book of the *Bello Gallico*, all the same:

Gallia est omnis divisa in partis tres—quaram unam incolunt Belgae; aliam Acquitani; tertiam qui ipsorum lingua Celtae, nostra Galli appellantur. Hi omnis lingua, intitutis, legibus inter se differunt, Gallos ab Acquitanis, Garumna flumen, a Belgis Matrona, et Sequana dividit. . . . It is obviously unnecessary to proceed, nor indeed to afford a translation. . . . If your breeches have tingled in your day, you will know it all; and even if you had no Latin the cadence of those chisel strokes of sentences, getting in a whole region of the earth, must spring to the eye.

The following passage of the *Commentaries on the Civil War* (Book III, Chap. xlvi) has always seemed agreeable to this writer—as one once interested in the handling of infantry.

Caesar, being uneasy about the retreat of his soldiers, ordered hurdles to be carried to the further side of the hill and to be placed opposite to the enemy, and behind them a trench of a moderate breadth to be sunk by his soldiers under shelter of the hurdles, and the ground to be made as difficult as possible. He himself disposed slingers in convenient places to cover our men in their retreat. These things being completed, he ordered his legions to file off. Pompey's men insultingly and boldly pursued and chased us, leveling the hurdles that were thrown up in the front of our works, in order to pass over the trench. Which as soon as Caesar perceived, being afraid that his men would appear not to retreat, but to be repulsed, and that greater loss might be sustained, when his men were almost halfway down the hill, he encouraged them by Antonius, who commanded that legion, ordered the signal of battle to be sounded, and a charge to be made on the enemy. The soldiers of the ninth legion suddenly closing their files, threw their javelins, and advancing impetuously from the low ground up the steep, drove Pompey's men precipitately before them, and obliged them to turn their backs; but their retreat was greatly impeded by the hurdles that lay in a long line before them, and the palisadoes which were in their way, and the trenches that were sunk. But our men being contented to retreat without injury, having killed several of the enemy, and lost but five of their own, very quietly retired, and having seized some other hills somewhat on this side of that place, completed their fortifications.

Of the other historians, Sallust was probably the most consummate stylist of the earlier Roman manner; he had a remarkable power over his pen and a sentence of his is like a pebble, so rounded, so flawless and complete. Unfortunately so little of him has come down to us that he ranks almost with Hesiod or Sappho. . . . And then the favorite of all Roman historians for the writer was Suetonius. There is about him and his writing something at once careless and scrupulous. So he is usually accounted a gossip of the type of Pepys. Actually, he was almost as careful with his documenting as any modern historian of Oxford or Bonn. Born in the short day of the detested Galba, he died in the reign of the saintly Marcus Aurelius; and it is characteristic of his scrupulousness that the farther away the emperor of whom he wrote the more remote and the longer were his chronicles. This was because the state documents of, say, Augustus, were open to him, whereas those of the later Hadrian or Antoninus Pius were locked away from the historian's gaze—for reasons of state. And he conscientiously refused to be responsible for any statement of which he had no documentary proof. He did not write extraordinarily well; his paragraphs are more in the nature of notes than careful structures in words. But he shared in neither the piety of Marcus Antoninus, the imperialism of Augustus, nor yet the ferocity of a Nero. He regarded the world with rather disillusioned eyes and gave us what he saw.

I regret to have almost no space to give to Pliny the Younger, since he was the very perfect Roman gentleman. His famous *Letters* are all very carefully constructed essays and have, therefore, the artificiality of the letter writer who is always conscious of his public. Otherwise he managed to keep his head on his shoulders from about A.D. 62-120. He passed through the reigns of Nero, Galba, Otho, Vitellius, Vespasian and Titus as a boy, survived Domitian and enjoyed office, esteem and riches during the peaceful empires of Trajan and Hadrian. He was an upright official and one astoundingly sedulous in the interests of his dependants—and more than astoundingly generous to everyone who approached him. His gifts to needy people of his own class were literally enormous; he gave away money by tens and scores of thousands of sesterces, and at times thus so impoverished himself that he would have to wait for the next harvest to pay his own way. And all that calmness, that good fortune, that infinite charity are reflected in the essays called his *Letters*. I can think of but one parallel to his figure in all the history of writing: it is that of the late Mr. Galsworthy. Here is a much too short specimen of his prose: Pliny has been describing for the benefit of a friend his "cheaper" villa. It was only seventeen miles from Rome, so that he could pass his evenings there after doing his day's official work in the city. . . . And so he goes on to describe dozens of rooms—those with views on the sea; rooms specially cooled for the summer; others specially central-heated for the winter; sound-proof rooms; sun parlors with views on the sea, the wooded hills, the neighboring villas. . . . And the following details may relieve the apprehensions of the modern believer in sanitation who imagines that there remain no more worlds for him to conquer:

> *Inde balinei cella frigidaria spatiosa et effusa, cuius in contrariis parietibus duo baptisteria velut eiecta sinuantur:: abunde capacia si mare in proximo cogites . . .**

This is thus rendered in Melmoth's famous translation as revised by Mr. W. M. L. Hutchinson, and a little further modified by the author:

> From thence you enter into the spacious and decorative cooling-room attached to my baths. From its opposite walls two basins curve outwards as though the wall were pressed into half hoops; these are large enough (for the cold plunge after the hot chamber) when you consider that (for more extended cold bathing) the sea is close at hand. Contiguous to this is my anointing-room, the furnace adjoining, and the water-heating chamber; then come two other little bathing-rooms which are fitted up in an elegant rather than opulent manner: annexed to this is a warm swimming bath of a singular invention in which one may swim and have at the same time a prospect of the sea. Not far from hence stands the tennis court, which lies open to the warmth of the afternoon sun. From thence you ascend a sort of turret, which contains two entire apartments below; there are the same number above, besides a dining-room which commands a very extensive prospect of the sea and coast, together with the beautiful villas that stand upon it. There is a second turret, containing a room which takes both the rising

---

* C. Plinii Caecilii Secundi: *Epistolarum*, Lib. II, xvii.

and setting sun. Behind this is a storeroom and larder, and underneath a spacious dining-room where the sea roaring in tempest is not felt, but only heard, and that faintly: it looks upon the garden and the allée, which surrounds the garden.

With Plutarch we arrive at a completely different problem—and one vastly more formidable. Let us shirk it, for it would lead one into politics. It is sufficient to say that having served as the mirror and mould of the governing classes for centuries, today he is damned by the Left for having taught the ruling classes how to rule. What is more interesting is the picturesque nature of his mind and style—which in their minuteness of observation and building up of a character by tiny points are really almost mediaeval in character. We are by our pastors and masters taught to believe him marmoreal and a generalizer. Nothing could be farther from the truth. Actually, as a gossip Suetonius is pale beside him. Consider the two following passages concerning subjects that Shakespeare has derived from him, probably through the translation into French of Amyot. The first is from the historian's *Life of Marcus Antonius*, the second from his *Life of Coriolanus*. And consider them in the marvelous English of Sir Thomas North:

> Now whilst she was at dinner there came a countryman and brought her a basket. The soldiers that warded at the gates asked him straight what he had in his basket. He opened the basket and took out the leaves that covered the figs and showed them that they were figs he brought. They all of them marveled to see so goodly figs. The countryman laughed to hear them and bade them take some if they would. They believed he told him truly and so bade him carry them in. After Cleopatra had dined she sent a certain table, written and sealed, to Casear and commanded them all to go out of the tomb where she was, but the two women; then she shut the doors to her. . . .
>
> Her death was very sudden. For those whom Caesar sent unto her ran thither in all haste possible and found the soldiers standing at the gate, mistrusting nothing, nor understanding of her

death. But when they had opened the doors they found Cleopatra stark dead, laid upon a bed of gold, attired and arrayed in her royal robes, and one of her two women which was called Iras, dead at her feet; and her other woman called Charmian half dead and trembling, trimming the diadem which Cleopatra wore upon her head. One of the soldiers, seeing her, angrily said unto her: "Is that well done, Charmian?" "Very well," said she again, "and meet for a princess descended from the race of so many noble kings." She said no more, but fell down dead, hard by the bed.

And here is Coriolanus in the house of Tullus Aufidius:

It was even twilight when he entered the city of Antium and many people met him in the streets but no man knew him. So he went directly to Tullus Aufidius his house and when he was thither he got him up straight to the chimney hearth and sat him down and spake not a word to any man, his face all muffled over. They of the house spying him wondered what he should be and yet they durst not bid him rise. For illfavoredly muffled and disguised as he was, yet there appeared a certain majesty in his countenance and in his silence; whereupon they went to Tullus who was at supper to tell him of the strange disguising of this man. Tullus arose presently from the board, and coming towards him, asked him what he was and wherefore he came. Then Martius unmuffled himself and after he had paused a while, making no answer he said unto him: "If thou knowest me not yet, Tullus, and seeing me, dost not perhaps believe me to be the man I am indeed, I must of necessity betray myself to be that I am. I am Caius Martius who hath done to thyself particularly and to all the Volscians generally great hurt and mischief which I cannot deny for my surname of Coriolanus that I bear. . . ."

And so the famous speech goes on. . . . No, if your schoolmaster and the Langhorne translation of the *Lives* have given you the impression that Plutarch was still and marmoreal, just read again in North's marvelous Elizabethan English, say, the account of Marc Antony's retreat before the Parthians. There is nothing more magnificent, rich or real in the pages of whom you will.

Thus we pass from the day of the Roman official great writers, the rest of Roman writing till the fall of the city being nothing but scholastic variations, anthology collectings and notations. It is, that age, the vastest blank in history.

Towards the fourth century there glimmered for a short period the African school of poets, the French and Spanish provincials, amongst them Ausonius of Bordeaux and the Moselle for whom the writer has a great affection principally because he writes gracefully of the fishes and wines of rivers and countrysides that he most likes. But where room for quotation is so scant it would not be reasonable to quote him. Let us then attack the *Pervigilium Veneris*.

Nothing is known of the history of this poem or of its author. It blazes solitary in the Southern skies, like the great planet called Soheil that is the omen of the coming of Mahomet and his men. And, indeed, the *Pervigilium* was that. Mahomet's own men were to come to Carthage soon enough.

For I think it is impossible not to believe that the *Pervigilium* is a fourth century African poem. You have in favor of that the slackening of the classical Latin syntax in the direction taken later by Provençal; and the slackening of the verse from the classical quantitative or stressed forms towards our accented forms of today. That was probably due to the influence of the Christian hymns which were then, in Africa, taking the place of all other forms of sung things.

For myself I should be inclined to ascribe the poem boldly to Tiberianus of Carthage, who flourished round 340 A.D. His language, accented verse and his love of birds and trees sound to me exactly like those of the *Pervigilium*. In that way you would have another poet of something of the value of Theocritus in *Tiberianus*. On the other hand, you would lose one of the agreeable mysteries of literature and the possibility that there actually was in the Roman province a folk-poetry group that not only produced this poem coöperatively but carried on its tradition in the hidden valleys of Maritime Alps until it emerged in the exquisite movement of the troubadours and the almost more valid string of peasant poets who have gone on till this day writing the beautiful poems of Provence. But, however you arrange that with yourself, here are some bits of the famous poem as arranged by Dr. J. Mackail—for there are almost as many ways of arranging the lines as' there are lines

> *Cras amet qui nunquam amavit, quique amavit, cras amet!*

> *Ver novum ver iam canorum, ver renatus orbis est;*
> *Vere concordant amores, vere nubunt alites,*
> *Et nemus coman resolvit; de maritis imbribus*
> *Cras amet qui nunquam amavit; quique amavit cras amet.*

> *Jussus est inermis ire, nudus ire jussus est,*
> *neu quid arcu neu sagitta neu quid igne laederet,*
> *Sed tamen cavete, nymphae, quod Cupido pulcher est,*
> *Totum est inermis idem quando nudus est Amor.*
> *Cras amet qui nunquam amavit; quique amavit cras amet.*

I provide the following free rendering of those two verses rather as an attempt at the spirit and movement and gaiety than as giving the metre—which is ecclesiastical—and the wording, which must convey to one's verse a certain traditional stiffness. You might, I mean, translate the first two lines:

> Spring is new and Spring is singing, Spring is reborn to the earth;

> In the Spring the loves agreeing, join the mating birds in mirth.

But it would not be very gay. Whereas what follows is so, at least a little:

> He that has never loved, let him love tomorrow; the lusty lover, let him love again.

> New Spring, singing Spring now comes ringing in the singing new Spring lands,

And new lovers love in concord and the maying birds in bands;
The fair forest frees her tresses to the showering nuptial rain.
He that has never loved, let him love tomorrow; the lusty lover,
   let him love again!

Cupid's naked, without harness, lacking arrow, bow and brand,
But advise ye, maids, advise ye, he's the subtlest in the land,
Love unclothed is then most armored; Love unarmed can wreak
   most pain.
He that has never loved, let him love tomorrow; the lusty lover,
   let him love again!

Part Three

CHAPTER ONE

W<small>E ARRIVE</small>, then, at the dark ages. . . .
When approaching these very faultily charted and tene-
brous seas, it is necessary that the student should regard all his teachers with scepticism—and, above all, himself. For whether he know
it or not every man is either a confirmed mediaevalist (or Aristotelian), or an obstinate renaissance-ite (or Platonist). So that no
man may write of this period with impartiality.

Relatively unprejudiced pedagogues and encyclopaedists of today
will tell you that the dark ages began with the sack of Rome in 476
A.D. and ended with the rediscovery of the pandects of Justinian at
Amalfi in 1127. This is fair enough in its way. An age having at
its disposal a great, and above all usable, code of laws can no longer
be called dark. But at least the Digests of Justinian were in use in
Paris fifty years before the rediscovery of the whole body of the
Laws of Justinian, so we may well set forward the date of the conclusion of the dark ages and the beginning of mediaevalism by at
least half a century. . . . It is, indeed, in many ways convenient to
say tentatively that the dark ages came to an end and the middle
ages began at the date of the Norman conquest of England in 1066.
At any rate, at that date the future confines and boundaries of settled
world states had begun to reappear from the welter caused by the
disappearance of the empire of the Caesars.

It is necessary here to strike strongly the note that the interests
of the student of literature and those of the student of pure history
are by no means identical. A whole literature may be produced in one
room provided it be surrounded by some of the conditions of peace;
to produce a civilization from an historian's point of view, whole
eons of time and whole hemispheres must be plunged into not merely
peace but internal accords of manners.

The historians may well date the beginning of the dark ages from the sack of Rome by Odovaker and his Prussian tribes. The student of literature may well set the date 400 years earlier—at the assassination of Nero by praetorian legionaries. For, from the moment when those legionaries learned the trick of assassinating the Caesar and holding out the purple for auction to any African, non-Aryan, Spanish or Teutonic highest bidder—from that moment, as we have seen, the central territories of the empire shuddered continuously beneath the feet of Roman army marching against Roman army, and, although at the confines of the empire in Alexandria, in Carthage, in Spain, or in southern France, slight flickers of literature may have continued to shine, the heart of the empire itself produced nothing in the way of the imaginative literature whose history it is here our task to trace.

The Roman world then, from the middle of the first century after Christ, found itself in the condition ascribed by the late President Hoover to the territories of the North American republic at the date of his holding the reins of power. That is to say that in no territory of the settled world were conditions of human life, labor, or property so insecure as in the heart of the empire. During these centuries you might at any moment be murdered at the behest of the Caesar, sold as a slave at the order of the tax-collector, or dispossessed of your land and goods by imperial rescript in order that the hunger of the legionaries might be assuaged by the consumption of human property.

And at any moment vast hordes of the most savage barbarians— the troops of one aspirant to the purple—would thunder across your lands to meet, just beyond your confines, hordes of barbarians still vaster in the employ of some semi-negroid competitor for the imperial authority.

Literature and the arts then retired to the confines of the empire, since there at least they found some traces of the fabulous *Pax Romana* and some remnants of a stable government.

For when the Romans determined to have stability they found and founded it. Thus, it is significant that when literatures again showed themselves in the world it should be in Provence, the province above all Roman that was the buffer between imperial Italy and the outer Gallic, Hun, Gothic and Teutonic barbarisms—in Provence then and the desolate regions of the furthest Thule that they showed themselves. For whatever date we as students of the unbroken chain of thought that is literature may assign for the beginning or the ending of the dark ages it is certain that their so-called darkness began first to be illuminated by the lights of imaginative literature at the hands of the troubadours of Provence on the one hand and those of the compilers of the Arthurian legends on the other. It was in fact in Provence and in Britain that the Roman system of government lasted its longest. The Romans departed from both places before the end of the fifth century. But their almost feudal frame of government persisted until much later—the system, that is to say, of having a whole network of nearly independent viscounts who, for purposes of war, united and took orders from an imperially nominated count. And so permanent were these governmental frames that traces of them still exist even to the present day. Thus, in England the Romans founded an east-coast protective system of viscounties and fortifications under the hegemony of a Comes Littoris Saxonici (or Count of the Shore) liable to attack from the Saxons, and the institution is today still extant in the vice-royalty of the Cinque-Ports with their parliaments and their lords warden who still in token of their former protective function on the eastern coasts hold the canopy over the British sovereign on the occasion of his coronation.

So we may well consider King Arthur to have been an historical, if difficultly identifiable, character—some holder of the Roman warlordship over the heads of innumerable British septs. And in token of the relative security of his dominions we have the *Morte d'Arthur* and the innumerable Brittanno-Celtic legends that make it up.

Similarly with Provence. The moment the clouds of complete darkness begin to roll up over that corner of the estuary of the Rhone, we perceive a governmental system of innumerable counts and viscounts, the counts all semi-independent imperial generals, and over them the kings of Provence who were nominally their warlords. And, relative security being thus established whether against the barbarians to the North or the paynims to the South of them—across the Mediterranean—at once we see the beginnings of the growth not only of the illustrious and shining lays and cantos of the aristocratic troubadours but the really more salient popular plays of the local *conte-*

fablistes, produced by the furriers, the gardeners, jewelers, blacksmiths, and burgesses of the little towns that were protected each by its count and governed solely by its viscount.

It is customary—and it is, perhaps, politically salutary—to consider that the dark ages were produced by the incursions into the South of barbarians coming from the deep forests of Russia and North Germany. In addition, the popular conception of these ages gives you, in hidden valleys or on inaccessible pinnacles of rock, numerous hidden monasteries whose inhabitants preserved and handed down to us the vestiges of Latin civilization and the arts that are the foundation of our own imperfect skeleton of civilization. You are given to imagine that in dimly lit cloisters or chambers, innumerable monks or nuns bent over writing pulpits turning out by the hundred illuminated *Books of Hours* and fair copies of the *Orations* of Cicero, the *Letters* of Pliny or the Virgilian account of the visit of the pious Aeneas to Hades.

As a popular conception that image may stand. Indeed, as far as civilization depends on religion we may go on considering that the inmates of those hidden convents and monasteries actually did play a major part in handing down to us most of what we know as our Mediterranean civilization. But when it came to either the aesthetic illumination of psalters or the providing of fair copies of Latin classic masterpieces, the founders and rulers of the great monastic bodies had their spiritual children much too closely in hand to allow for any such waste of time.

The monasteries existed ostensibly for prayer and in the second place for handwriting; and it was customary in those days to believe that you could get yourself into heaven more easily and there find a higher place, by writing than by prayer. The Church in those days had a prodigious—an almost unbounded—need for books of prayer, Bibles, psalters with the music indicated. For Christianity spread, and always new churches were built; so more and more guides to the ritual of the Church came to be needed. And it stood to reason that if you were a Cistercian monk with the task of providing copies of the psalms for a monastery lost in the German forests, you would be rewarded by your temporal superiors and the heavenly hosts only if your manuscript was extremely readable and your notes of music as clear as possible. They would have to be read by German choristers with no special knowledge of liturgical Latin or the theory of the Great Scale. And, indeed, it was strictly forbidden to the Cistercians to add any ornament whatever to their writings. Similarly any trifling with the Latin classical imaginative literature was deprecated. We know that the great monastery of Mont Saint Michel had in its library not only copies of the *Letters* of Pliny, but a Saracen treatise on mathematics; but we know it only because the librarian and the superior of the monastery were reproved from Citeaux for having let such doubtful works creep onto their shelves. So that it was only in their capacity as hostels or free inns for travelers that the monasteries became, when they were at all, centers of the Humaner Learning of the more decorative arts. In their lay refectories a gentleman who had just bought in Padua a manuscript of Cicero might meet a courtier of Charlemagne going from Aix-la-Chapelle to Rome, in order to receive delivery of a manuscript of the sainted Duke of Mantua that had been promised by the Holy Father to the Frankish Holy Roman Emperor. They might converse about the classics. But that would be about as far as it would go.

So that if we wish to have a down-to-the-ground view of European literary conditions from the eighth, to, say, the thirteenth century we must consider two main conditions of that age: In the first place, its humanity was consumed with a thirst for expression that, wherever conditions of sufficient peace subsisted, there his poems, his little dramas in prose, his chronicles, or his moralities, would spring up and brook no hindrances.

Thus, in the relatively secure tracts of country where the remains of Roman organizations secured some measure of peace for the inhabitants, there sprang up, on the one hand, the plentiful poems of the troubadours and the rarer prose dramas of the *contes-fablistes.* On the other hand, there grew up the innumerable prose or verse legends of the remote but eternally besieged Britons, Welsh or Bretons. And the moment some sort of secure government was established by the Carolingian rulers and the later Holy Roman Emperors you immediately had new centers for the upspringing of the works of the imagination. They sprang up, in fact, everywhere: in Bagdad under the Barmecides, in Spain under the Abbassids—and still more unexpectedly in Iceland itself. So into the main stream of European literature that is known to us there introduced themselves the strains of not merely popular tales such as are found in *The Thousand and One Nights* but the great note of great Persian Mohammedan poets like Firdousi. At the same time, in remote and, therefore, secure Iceland the Norsemen established a little specimen of a civilization. Under proud and inordinately wealthy bishops this eventuated in the *Eddas*, which were to have so powerful an influence on European and particularly Anglo-Saxon literary fashions in the late nineteenth century.

Nothing is, indeed, more parochial than to imagine that, whilst the European literary and aesthetic movements marked time, the rest of the world neglected to provide its normal quantum of literary and plastic masterpieces. You have, on the contrary, to imagine those dimnesses surrounded by a veritably flaming sea of such faiths and enthusiasms as are most conducive backgrounds of great achievements in the arts. This must go to the account of Mohammedanism—a religious practice which produced in its day an altruistic cosmogony as great as any other combination of the chivalric and ecclesiastical order. And it should not be forgotten that whilst Snorri Stureson compiled the mournful and ferocious records of northern life, the great Firdousi was making his compilation of earlier Iranian legends and customs, a record that for central Asia worthily takes the place of the Homeric writings in Greece, of the Holy Writ in Asia Minor, or of the Canons of Confucius in the confines of the Orient. This work, the *Shahnama*, was completed in the year 1011.

It is none the less a mere episode in a great literature abounding in range, in spirit, in passion . . . and in humanity. This writer, at least, does not know any passage in any literature more essentially humane in its teaching than the passage which follows from the life of the philosopher Bayazid of Bistami that was written in the year 1225 by the great poet Faridu'ddin Attar.

One day he was walking with a number of his disciples. The path was very narrow. He saw a dog coming along and stopped to let it pass. One of his disciples blamed him secretly and thought to himself, "How can Bayazid, who is king of the gnostics, make way for a dog?" Bayazid said, "This dog asked me with dumb eloquence, saying, 'In the eternal past what fault did I commit, and what act of grace didst thou perform, that I am clad in the skin of a dog, whilst the robe of spiritual royalty hath been conferred on thee?' This thought came into my head and I made way for the dog."

It is related that he said, "A man met me in the road and asked whither I was going. I said, 'To make a pilgrimage.' 'What money have you?' 'Two hundred dirhems.' 'Give them to me,' he said, 'for I have a wife and children and walk around me seven times: this will be your Pilgrimage.' I did so and returned home."

It should be remembered that the Crusades were preparing whilst Firdousi was compiling his matchless work and that, whilst Faridu'-ddin Attar was writing his life of Bayazid, the Siege of Béziers was taking place at which the disciple of St. Dominic uttered the immortal and atrocious words: "Slay them all; God will recognize His own."

It is not here but much later that we shall have to consider the influence of Oriental imaginative writing on our central European literary stream. We shall have, that is to say, to consider the influence of the Moorish tale tellers in Cordova when we have to turn our attention to the birth of the modern novel in sixteenth century Spain; and not until the beginning of the nineteenth century do we have to think of the influence of Persian poetry on our own Byron-Pushkin-Romantic movements.

A sort of contraband communion of souls between the Mahommedan and the Christian shores of the Mediterranean distinguished, nevertheless, the whole of the dark ages no matter where exactly you place those ages. The Moors under the Caliph Oman destroyed Alexandria and burned her library in the year 640—on which occasion the Caliph Omar who was directing the operations is said to have uttered a speech as celebrated as the other one that we have just seen was pronounced at Béziers. Said he when asked whether the library should or should not be burned, "Burn it all the same, for if the writings it contains run counter to the teachings of the Koran it is fit that they should be destroyed, whereas if they agree with the Koran they are superfluous and should equally be gotten rid of."

Nevertheless, it is not to be taken for granted that all the Greek texts whether classical works of imagination or mere records disappeared entirely in that conflagration. An immense number of them remained in the hands of flying Greek savants and sages. These as the Mahommedan power gradually spread up the shores of Asia Minor, retreated, still clutching their manuscripts, until they found shelter behind the walls of Constantinople. There the successors of Constantine the Great still wielded some sort of authority. And, though of this there is no historical trace, a considerable body of Greek texts probably remained in the hands of Arab and Moorish learned men, this of course being contrary to the orders or the wishes of the caliphs, those successors of Mahomet.

As we have already seen, during the pagan interregnum between the gradual disappearance in Arabia of the Olympian cult and the swift spread of the Islamic faith in those regions, the man who could merely write, and still more the poet, was accorded the sort of veneration that humanity has always devoted to its magicians. They were regarded as having special knowledges, whether of mathematics or prophecy, of astrology or alchemy. In the earlier days of the Hegira the prophet looked askance on these possible rivals to his power. But when it became a matter of the compilation of the Koran and the recording of his triumphs, like other priest-conquerors he must needs call to his assistance the poets and the learned men of his day. And this necessity was felt by his successors, the caliphs and their subordinate kings or army leaders. Their triumphs, too, must be recorded, to the greater glory of God. And their soldiers must be heartened by marching songs. Writers, therefore, whether mere recorders of spoils taken after victory, prognosticators of future extensions of Islamism or the singers of such idle days as were vouchsafed to the advancing hordes—all writers were then accorded, if unwillingly enough, certain laxities whether of faith or of morality. The Persian poets sang the glories of wine, the North African learned treasured the sayings of Plato, the astronomical doctrines of Ptolemy or the searchings after the encyclopaedic all-wisdom of Aristotle. To satisfy this desire for knowledge the whole of Aristotle's works had been translated into Arabic by the beginning of the tenth century. By the thirteenth practically all the writings of that Greek sage had, for the benefit of the European mediaeval mind, been translated from Arabic into the Latin that was the common language of the European Occident. You had thus on both sides of the Mediterranean a similar cultural condition. The ecclesiastical rulers, whether Mahommedan or Nazarene, had fierce, proselytizing faiths and practices. Nevertheless, nearly all the intelligentsia—whether of France, Spain, Provence or Italy; whether of Cordova, of Tunis, of Horassan or of the Sultanate of Ghazni in India—were relatively indifferent to the tenets either of the Prophet or of the crucified Son of Jehovah. They paid probably as much lip service and deference to their faiths as the upper class leaders of the Roman Senate attached, in the age of Cicero, to the cult of the Olympian deities. But, similarly, their intellects were given over to a passionate study of the Aristotelian views of matter and of life. Thus within two years of the translation of Aristotle from Arabic into Latin, the University of Padua was founded for the promulgation of those knowledges, and within the decade four other universities had been similarly founded within Northern Italy and in Provence. Thus, ironically—or, if you prefer it, symbolically—enough, the Aristotelian point of view which was so eminently sympathetic to all mediaeval manifestations came not direct from the hands of the Greeks themselves but by a round-about course from Egypt through the hands of the paynims, by way of the Sicilies, of the district of Salerno, of Provence or of Gibraltar. So that when, at the fall of Constantinople, Plato was ready with his renaissance legions to fall upon western Europe, the ground was to be already strongly holden by the metaphysical troops of his great rival in old Hellas.

For, whatever may be the disadvantages of wars, invasions and

the burning of libraries, it should not be imagined that either invaders or invaded altogether avoid the civilizing process that inevitably takes place whenever two differing races are brought intimately
into contact with each other. For you can never go into any new
land, however barren in comparison with your own, without finding
some herb to transplant into your own regions or some habit or merely
some superstition that you will take back with you when you return
home.

The art of cigarette-smoking was introduced into Western Europe
and lands even farther west by the French and British troops returning from their Balkan adventures in the Crimean War; the peach
tree and the whole modus operandi of our kitchen-gardening of today were brought back by Roman and Greek soldiers after innumerable campaigns in the direction of Teheran. Still more, as we have
seen, even today in the Punjab—the Hindoo district of the Seven
Rivers—you will find traces of the legal systems and habits of mind
of the invading Greek soldiers of Alexander the Great. The result
is an inevitable confusion, so that in half the manifestations of human
thought you will find it difficult or impossible to distinguish which
one preceded the other or which race first produced this ideal or
that habit of mind.

Believers in the Eddic myths, for instance, proceeded not merely
from Iceland to Normandy and Hastings but, fantastically, right between the Pillars of Hercules to the two Sicilies, to Naples and even
up the Rhone to Arles, Tarascon and Nîmes. It astonishes you to
see that the castle of the good King René of Tarascon is actually
a typical Norman bastide, foursquare and affronting the heavens for
all the world like a block of trans-atlantic skyscrapers. But your
astonishment will grow a little less when you find in Naples harbor
an exact reproduction of that Norman edifice and you remember
that the first kings of the two Sicilies, Naples and Provence were
the descendants of Roger deHauteville. With his long ships he took
the city of Messina in the Mediterranean six years before his relative,
Duke William of Normandy, slew Harold at the Battle of Senlac.
And, indeed, the good King René and the not so virtuous but infinitely beloved Queen Joan of Provence both boasted Norman and

North French titles and principalities that had come to them not by sea in the train of Roger deHauteville but, as it were, overland at the hands of the Angevin kings of England, France and Normandy.

These historic details will come creeping in. You may consider yourself as an exclusively literary historian but the production of the letters that you sing will have made the conditions in which they were produced and the human contacts that incited them to exist. And all these things are, as we have just said, irremediably confused. Thus, the earliest traces of the Arthurian legend to appear in middle-western European consciousness are to be found in the *Brut* of Layamon, a French writer of the thirteenth century; but he would appear to have copied a good deal from Wace, a twelfth century Jersey, Franco-Norman chronicler. And Wace, in turn, as far as he occupies himself with early British history, would seem to have borrowed extremely freely from the chronicle written in Latin by the Gallo-Celtic writer, Geoffrey of Monmouth.

So, at all to appreciate the origin and developments of Western European literature it is well to have, for one's private use, an image of the literary dark ages, as if it were a violently, centrifugally agitated teacup. Its center was eventually to define itself at the first ford from the sea of the River Seine. In Paris, that is to say.

At any rate, it is well to keep in one's mind a sort of map of the literary dark and middle ages. In it there shall be at least three points of light forming a geographical triangle. These were as we have seen the courts of the little princes of Provence; the uncharted hinterland behind the country of the Saxon shore in Britain; and the court, wherever it happened to be, of the Carolingian Emperor or the Holy Roman emperors that succeeded him. There were other points of less-pronounced—learned, rather than specifically imaginative—literary lights. These found themselves in the shadows of the great cathedrals—and all the more certainly when these cathedrals became places of pilgrimage. From the earliest days the shrine of Saint James of Compostella was a meeting place at once for doctors and for poets coming from almost every city in Christendom. Immediately after the murder of Saint Thomas, Canterbury became likewise such a center, not only for the religious and laymen of all the world, but for such literary colleagues of Chaucer as could scrape together the wherewithal to take them to that famous shrine.

In addition, the major historical contacts spread new fashions and letters from side to side everywhere in the pen-wielding world. The new Holy Roman emperors were at least nominally the overlords of the Provençal counts, and when there was any chance of making the imperial writ run, one or the other of the princes of the Langue d'Oc would appeal to the emperor to confer on him some little privilege at the expense of another prince. Thus, Bérenger des Baux, desiring confirmation of the title that he had assumed for himself of viceroy of Provence, traveled with the retinue of the troubadour knights to the Turin court of the Emperor Frederick I, who was king of Naples and the two Sicilies. And the literary and musical gifts of those troubadours afforded to the emperor such pleasure that he not only confirmed Bérenger in his assumed title but himself burst into the composition of lays and canzoni and enjoined on his Norman knights that they too, attended by a minstrel or so, should travel the world over, intent not so much on the rescue of distressed damsels, as on holding tournaments of song in honor of the always merciless lady who should at that moment be martyrizing their hearts. So the practice of the *trouvères*, the singing knights of the Northern Langue d'Oï and of the Teutonic *minnesingers* was, if not initiated, at least imperially recommended and furthered. Thus, early in the reign of Frederick II you had the full activity of the *minnesingers*, Walther von der Vogelweide, Gottfried von Strassbourg, and Wolfram von Eschenbach, as well as, a little earlier, those of the North French *chansonniers de gestes*. These last gave us not only the *Chanson de Roland* but also the poems of Marie de France and of Chrétien de Troyes, as well as the immense allegorical machine called the *Roman de la Rose*, and not to leave out a prose work almost as beautiful as the *Morte d'Arthur*, the *Chronicles* of Froissart.

A matter worth speculating on at this point is why to the north of the line drawn from east to west in France and separating the Langue d'Oc from the Langue d'Oï, poetry should almost always have taken a narrative, or at least a moralizing form, whereas in the South the listeners to poetry took their delight almost exclusively in technical tricks. The poetry of the troubadours divided itself sharply into two *genres*: there were the *canzones* which hymned to love and the *sirventes* which told narratives or expressed invective—which, in part, were poems written with a purpose. Regarded from the point of view of content the cantos of the troubadours, like the similar poems of the Chinese, give an effect of a certain monotony and, indeed, to northern eyes and ears a certain want of interest. Just as Chinese poetry limits itself when it is not expressing the laments of an exiled and degraded official, to lamenting the desertion of a lover by his mistress or a wife by her husband, so the topic of the troubadour, when he wasn't engaged with his *sirventes* in insupportably insulting his feudal superiors or the monarchs of the earth, was almost invariably that of the cruelties of his mistress who was quite invariably too highborn to give ear to the poet. The reasons for this are doubtless manifold—no doubt we of the North with our stronger jaws demand of our poets and prosateurs something to chew on, whereas the Southerners were content to be diverted with mere rhymes and skillful ticklings of the lute. But the reasons for that explanation itself lie obviously deeper—in the divergence of human life, of climates, of environments. This writer must have been carrying on this battle with Mr. Ezra Pound for going on thirty years, and those who are passionately interested in the subject might do worse than to study our joint writings about this matter. But, to sum the matter up, we may postulate that the mediaevalism of Northern France and of Northwestern Europe distinguished itself by a gloom, a sadic ferocity, a bitterness of merriment such as would lead one to believe that, during whole periods, whole races exhibited nothing less than madness even in their very architecture. How else will you account for the devils of Notre Dame or the grotesquely obscene carvings on the revers of the miserère stalls of all Northern cathedrals and abbey churches?

It must be remembered that more than half of the northern year was given over to an intensity of boredom such as can have distinguished no other times or places. The mediaeval Arab proverb said

of life that it was a matter of half an hour per day of the fantasia—
the sword-and-spear play to the gallop of horses—of two minutes of
love and all the rest, boredom. But the northern knight in his insupportably cold and dreary castles would not have even the daily
relief of the half hour's galloping. He could not adventure himself
on horseback on his winter roads or pastures simply because his
charger would sink in to its belly in deep mud. So he used to find
intensive fun when the roads opened themselves in the late spring
and early summer and he could ride a-murdering.

In the South, on the other hand, the roads were always open;
you could ride to the assault of your neighbor's castle as practicably
in December as through the orange blossoms in shining March.
Topics of victory, adultery, chastisement, treachery and the rout of
paynims were never to seek in your lofty sunlit halls. You did not
need poets to sing your deeds to you; you lived them yourself every
day and all the day long. You demanded of your poets, therefore,
something superior and tittivating both in verbiage and music.

The music of the North was a matter of ponderous psalms and
part songs, that of the South was precisely one of tickling stringed
instruments and little, thin trills of sound that only the skillful ear
could pick up. If you read today the only manuscript of *Aucassin
and Nicolette* that exists, you must—when deciphering the musical
notes that accompany the sung portions of the beautiful *conte-fable*—
you must hold your breath or you cannot even mentally appreciate
the tones.

But the one thing that you have to keep in mind when writing—
or even when thinking—of this unique literary movement is not to
dogmatize. You may find the *sirventes* and above all the *canzones*
of Macabrun and the rest uninteresting because of the sameness of
content; yet it is tempting to say that the music to which they were
set must have had a charm all its own. But exactly the same claim
is continually being advanced for German folksongs, English border
ballads, for the lyrics of Shakespeare and his contemporaries, for
Herrick and for Burns. Nothing, in fact, is easier than to escape on
side issues the difficult question of what constitutes charm. Whether
we like them today or no the poems of the troubadours exercised in

their day an immense charm that was felt not merely in the country of the Langue d'Oc but all the world over, and for many centuries. And you may write almost the same of the poems of the *minnesingers* and of the border ballads in the fifteenth and eighteenth centuries, respectively. But the charm of the border ballads was a charm relatively down to the ground and easily analyzable. If we read:

> O what care I for my goose-feather bed
> The sheets turned down so bravely O;
> Tonight I'll sleep on the cold open moor
> Along with the raggle-taggle gipsies O.

we are pleased in the first place with the quaint realism of the bed and then we are astonished that a rather savage people should have any poetry at all—much as today we are astonished at finding accidental and mechanical touches of authentic poetry and charm in the Negro spirituals. And ballads and Negro spirituals alike are, when they are genuine, folksongs that have been mended and remended by hundreds, nay, even by thousands of hands and voices.

The writer happens to have been present at what you might call a popular recension of folksong during several weeks in the fall of 1916. His regiment having spent a disproportionate time in the trenches during the First Battle of the Somme, it was given a long fatigue to do at a long distance from the trenches, so that they might at once rest their weary bones and get some exercise. So that His Majesty's 41st Regiment of the Line was, therefore, given the task of repairing a very long line of trenches behind Knocke on the Belgian coast. There being no hurry at all over the task, this officer permitted the fatigues to sing what army songs they liked whilst working. (If you want a fatigue to work very quickly you tell them to start "Ap Jenkyn," the regimental quickstep, but if there is no hurry at all you can let it be "Land of My Fathers," that slowest and most lugubrious of national anthems. The men would dig in time to the music.) The regiment then being given, say, twenty to twenty-five days of digging which, being all miners, they would dig from four to seven times as fast as any London or country English, German, or French regiment, this officer would give them from half to three quarters of an hour's spells during which they could sleep or reflect or "even pray" as I once heard a French officer say of his own troops in repose. Actually these heroes made themselves into an informal committee for the revising of all the regiment's private versions of the British army songs—which are folk ballads by no means fit to be spoonmeat for babes. It is, therefore, to be regretted that the author cannot record the proceedings of that committee over the ballad relating to the fabulous adventures of Colonel Plant at Quetta or even the world-army famous adventures of the eighteenth century lady known as the Harlot of Jerusalem. But very dear and tender, as if at an old bruise, to the hearts of the men of the 41st was their private and particular quickstep called the "Rhondda Boys." The regiment was called the "Welsh" and when it was not recruited in South Lancashire cotton towns drew almost all its men from the famous valley from which comes almost all the hard coal used all over the world. So, before 1914 came with all its troubles, and whilst there was still some slick smartness to British regiments, the 41st were accustomed to sing during route marches between the peaceful hedges:

> We are the Rhondda boys,
> We are the Rhondda boys;
> We know our manners
> We straff pianers
> (*or* We spend our tanners)
> We are respected wherever we go.

This indicated that the cheerful regiment contained numbers of first-class musicians of a certain urbanity of behavior—or, in the alternative, a certain liberality with their sixpences. But with the attrition of war lasting for several years and seeming about never to end, the old-timers—the really old soldiers of the regiment which was a regular one—had so impressed upon the younger soldiers that they were a lousy, ragtime collection of useless scavengers commanded by officers who might be all right because they belonged to the regiment but who were hopelessly handicapped by having to carry out orders of a gen-

eral staff whose proper function would have been serving teas to nurs-
ing mothers in the crèches of the Ratcliffe Highway—the young who
were by then the great bulk of the regiment were so impressed by the
sense of their own unworthiness that the last thing they wanted was
an at all cheerful quickstep. So by fifties or hundreds at a time they
got to work on the words of that lyric, changing them over and over.
They began with the statement that they were the Rhondda boys—
one that the oldest privates jeered at, saying that though they might
have been born in the Rhondda valley, the Rhondda boys were men.
So they changed it for the statement that they were the ragtime boys.
And when it came to a record of their accomplishments those veterans
persuaded these youths that they had no manners at all and if any
one of them got near a musical instrument he would be perfectly certain to ruin it—whilst as to having any claim to being known as generous with their money they had only to ask the girls of the town
to be told that they were the meanest collection of unlicked galloots,
not even excepting the Scottish regiments, that had ever marched
through Ponturdulais . . . to its sorrow. Besides which it was well
known that being Welsh they were the greatest thieves that Christendom had ever seen. . . . So that, as to "respected"—deprecatingly, the
blushing workers changed the word "respected" to "detested." But,
having collectively a sense of the *mot juste* they arrived finally at a
word that expressed more exactly their own attitude and the attitude
of chance civilians towards themselves—the word being "dejected."
Thus, by the time they had finished with it, the words of that once
pert quickstep ran:

> We are the ragtime boys
> We are the ragtime boys,
> We've got no manners
> We smash pianers
> We are dejected wherever we go.

This recension took nearly three weeks, for it must be remembered
that all the thousand and eighteen other ranks had to pronounce upon
it, but as it finally stood it pretty well expressed the attitude of that

regiment towards itself, just as the final versions of the "Ballad of Chevy Chase" probably expressed the sentiments of Scots or English irregular borderland troops towards themselves and that affair:

> The child may rue that is unborn
> The hunting of that day.

a sentiment that is obviously collective and not one of any one poet.

But to get back, there is nothing of the popular touch about the *canzos* and *sirventes* of the troubadours. Practically every one of them is as hard and as clearly individual as the differing pebbles on a seashore. If you have any acquaintance at all with these poems you would never, for instance, mistake one of the almost stickily sweet stanzas of Quillem de Cabestanh for one made up of the harsh enigmatic lines of Arnaut Daniel or for the relative gaieties of Marcabrun—he who, after Bertran de Born, must have been the most individual of all the troubadours. We may add a note that of the fifty-seven troubadours known at any rate to this writer, no less than twenty-three were reigning princes, fourteen tradesmen or working men and the rest wealthy nobles or members of reigning houses.

That being the case, it is astonishing that their poetry should have come always so true to type. And it is as dangerous to say that the first troubadour, William IX of Poitiers, must have been the product of any school or tradition of verse as to say (as my father and the pedagogic writers on the troubadours in the late nineteenth century Germany and France unhesitatingly declared) that the troubadours were men influenced by no tradition at all but sprang fully armed with all their metrical and rhyming devices, like the soldiers of Cadmus, from the earth.

Politics, it must be remembered, comes into these matters; and the desire of the scientific monographer to render his subject portentous! It is true that no trace of verse in the Langue d'Oc is to be found before the day of Quillem IX of Poitiers. Thus, if you are the romance-starved student of metres, you can make a mightily romantic figure of that certainly warlike William standing up suddenly after the legions of nordic barbarians have thundered past, and whilst tickling his lute with fingers just out of the knight's iron gauntlets, intoning perfectly correct *albas* and *serenas* and *canzos* and *sirventes*. So, if you make him invent these forms with no guidance from other poets—why, William of Poitiers will become the most dramatic figure that ever breathed. And there is nothing to stop your saying all that—there is no historic proof against your theory.

But looking at the matter a little more reasonably and seeking the romance in the whole unparalleled movement rather than in the fifty-seven individual figures who made it up, romantic as any one of them may have been, it becomes evident that if ever a region was subject to ancient musical and metrical devices that region would be precisely the Provence of the troubadours. You cannot prove that the immediate ancestors of William of Poitiers or of Bertran de Born of Alta Forte ever actually read Theocritus or Moschus or works of the earliest Greek elegiasts, writers of alcaics or lyricists. We shall be able to prove, nevertheless, that some, at least, of the troubadours possessed libraries fairly provided with Latin and Greek imaginative writings. But the chief proof of connection between the troubadours and the innumerable Greeks, survivors of the Greek and Phoenician colonies that for centuries studded the shores of Provence, are the numerous Greek words that you find in modern Provençal: *"arton"* for "bread," our friend the Ciceronian *"ardée"* for *"ennui,"* and so on. And it is perfectly historical to consider that the Greek colonies of those and the opposite African shores continued to carry on their commerce and their piracies, and went on expressing themselves in the classical languages of ancient Hellas—and singing the songs not only of Theocritus but the much later ones of Callimachus, the esteemed librarian of Alexandria, who so much later wrote the *Elegy for Heraclitus* that was in its day so popular and that began:

They told me, Heraclitus, they told me you were dead,
They brought me bitter news to hear and bitter tears to shed;
I wept when I remembered how often you and I
Had tired the sun with talking and sent him down the sky. . . .

And there is nothing to force us to believe that in their fastnesses of the Bouches du Rhône the haughty, wealthy, contemptuous survivors of the Roman aristocracy did not go on compiling each one his own Greek anthology—the compiling of Greek anthologies having been the chief occupation of the later Roman aristocracy before Odovaker struck like a thunderbolt their doomed city.

At any rate, legend—and even the chronicles of those days and regions—makes frequent mention of well-fortified Roman outposts that just went on passing their time and amusing themselves with rhymes, whilst easily beating back the assaults of the barbarians. Sidonius in his *Historia Nea*, a Greek sixth century (probably African) compilation, makes perfectly confident mention of such a proud and safe Roman organized community in northwestern France. This may have been the beginnings of the Arthurian legend or of that of the Breton half-nation that still speaks Welsh. And, indeed, if Sidonius and others did not mention such oases of civilization in the collapsing world we might very well invent them or deduce them ourselves. If, for instance, the British rule in India should suddenly collapse, the native inhabitants of remote provinces would probably find it not only convenient but necessary to maintain the existing divisions of territory, the magistracies, the laws and the military organizations possibly for many centuries. And then little black children would, no doubt, go on singing the Mother Goose ballads and their poets modeling their verses on those alien and primitive forms.

So that we may well imagine centuries of Latin-speaking and wealthy and severe aristocrats going on perpetuating and improving on the deviations from the classical dactylo-hexameters that we find in the *Pervigilium Veneris*. They would be there, isolated from the remains of the rest of the Latin empire. But they would be singularly open to contacts with the remaining Greeks of the seashores, and the elaborate and delicate music and verse of the Arabs on the opposite coasts of the Mediterranean. Then, too, the troubadours were religious dilettantes, feeling no natural horror or awe for the heresies of the Greeks and Moslems, but importing, in the natural corruption of their hearts all the way from Bulgaria, a Quietist latitudinarian religion. It was all their own, and was known to good churchmen as the heresy of the Albigenses.

There is, as I have said, no direct documentary evidence of the fact, but if you consider that the troubadours were undoubtedly, as was the case with nearly all the inhabitants of the South Mediterranean fifth to eighth century shores, singularly prone to the influences of a disappearing Greek and a rapidly elaborating Mahommedan civilization, and if in addition you consider that the verse of the troubadours became almost exactly what the writers of the *Pervigilium Veneris* would have become had they been subject to such influences— if you consider all these things you may be pardoned if you are not weakened but strengthened in the belief that here too the stream of human consciousness passing from East to West, remained unbroken. There was in fact, here, no sudden cleavage and no sudden resurrection of civilization. The Greek and Oriental leaven of music and verse passed through the country of Provence into the woods of Gaul and Allemaign, exactly as the waters of any other stream, that breaks through a dyke, will fertilize, to the measure of the liquid quantities and the swiftness of its attack, the low-lying terrain beyond that levee.

We come at once with that to another of those absurd political divisions of thought that forever arise to confuse the issues for us students of comparative literature.

Anxious as much as possible to enhance the antiquity of the civilization of their ancestors, the German learned—who between the Franco-Prussian War and the War of 1914 studied the questions of Provençal, Romance and early German literature—insist very strongly on the influence that the Provençal poets who visited the courts of the Holy Roman emperors exercised on the native German singer. They declare that if Vogelweide and Gottfried of Strassbourg had any rhyming or metrical skill they got it from the companions of Béranger des Baux when at Turin they charmed the ears of the Emperor Frederick I. French students of the period writing about the same date and having, like their Teutonic colleagues, a certain patriotic urge, declare that those Provençal emissaries of Latin had no influence at all on the Teutonic barbarism of their northern contemporaries. They point

out, truly enough, that the metrical skill of a Wolfram von Eschenbach is such as might have been evolved for himself by any listener
to the German Volkslieder of the day and that the content—the stuff—
of the German poets differs absolutely from that of the aristocratic
singers from the South. The reader must then make his own decision
according as his mixed ancestry may have given him Nordic or
Meridional sympathies.

Let us in the mean time compare some of the poems of the two
schools of singers. The generalization that comes first and most powerfully to the mind is that even in their most lyrical efforts the German poets tended to be narrational. The troubadours, on the other
hand, in everything but their *sirventes*, tended more and more to
confine their verse to what we should call variations on a given theme.
Just as the majority of the Italian primitive painters took for their
most frequent exercises the subject of a woman with a child and on
that built up their fantasies of color, their patterns and their movements; so the troubadour, as we have said, in his *canzos* took invariably the one subject of the woe caused in him by the coldness of a
lady who was nearly always his feudal superior . . . and embroidered
on it. His narratives, when he wished to tell them, were strictly confined to his *sirventes*—or to prose. The *sirventes* was what the French
of today call a vulgarizer. His more precious *canzos* the knight would
set to music himself and would himself intone them for fear that
the professional jonglar might spoil them by the omission of syllables
or of grace notes. But his *sirventes* the knight would desire—particularly when they were denunciations of his superiors or of a rival—
to see spread as widely as possible. He would, therefore, teach as
many as half a dozen jonglars the words of his attacks or his short
stories, and, letting those fellows set them to such music as they
found, he would turn them loose on the world. Moreover, in neither
branch of his work would he make any great mention of the tiresome thing that we Nordics call nature. His only bird was the *ros-
sinholet salvatge*—the wild nightingale—and if he mentions any flowers they are almost invariably white; and that is all we are expected
to ask about them! In exactly the same way today in Provence if you
ask the cultivated of your friends: "What is that bird?"—or "that

flower?" he will reply with the most complete indifference: "*C'est que'que moineau*"—or "*C'est que'que giroflée*," ("It is some sort of a sparrow"—or "It is some sort of a wall flower.")

The *minnesinger*, on the other hand, was never indifferent—how could he be, poor devil?—to the nature of the weather or his crops. In Provence you step over the sill of your door as you step into your poem, with never a glance at the sky and you know that your vegetations will be as punctual and unfailing as your mainland trains. We have, indeed, given ourselves some trouble to discover any verses of the troubadours in which save for a word or two of conventional lip service to the pleasures of spring there is any mention whatever of nature. I have for the moment only two. There is the *Can Chai la Fueilha* of Arnaut Daniel—who, by the by, was reputed inimitably to render the song of the birds in his verses. A few of the lines of this poem Mr. Pound renders:

> . . . Though all things freeze here,
> I can naught feel cold,
> For new love sees, here
> My heart's new leaf unfold. . . .*

So that it will be seen that the fiery Arnaut had heat enough within him to let him sustain the vigors of the winter with relative optimism. How different that is from Walter von der Vogelweide when he sings:

> *Uns had diu Winter geskaded uberall*
> *Heide und Walder syn alle nu kal.* . . .

> The winter has been our ruin everywhere
> Hedges and woodlands are all now bare. . . .

and so continues recounting all the ills of the flesh and the hedgesides that malign season inflicts on them and the earth. On the other hand, the troubadours of greater range and awareness would now and then cite nature to give point to their meaning. Thus Marcabrun,

* *Make it New*, by Ezra Pound. (Yale University Press.)

intending to express the dislike, the contempt even, that he and most of his contemporaries felt for the Crusades, begins one of his *sirventes* with:

> *A la fontana del vergier*
> *On l'erbées vertz jostal gravier,*
> *A l'ombra d'un fust domesgier.*
> *En aizement de blancas flors*
> *E de novel chant costumier,*
> *Trobei sola ses companhier*
> *Cela que no volc mon solatz.*

which the author's father renders literally:

> At the orchard fountain
> Where the grass is green near the gravel
> In the shade of a tree belonging to her home
> In the beauty of white flowers
> And of the song of the nightingale
> I found alone without companion
> One who had no taste for my company.

> It was a girl of beautiful body
> The daughter of a lord of a castle;
> And when I thought that the birds
> Gave her joy and the greenery,
> And that because of the young season
> She would listen to my address,
> Soon were her manners changed.

> Near the fountain she cried from her eyes,
> And from her heart she sighed deeply.
> "Jesus," she said, "King of the world,
> My great grief grows through you,
> For your disgrace injures me
> Since the best of all this world
> Go to serve you, but it pleases you.

My friend goes away with you,
The beautiful and the brave and the gentle and the worthy,
From which great grief remains to me here,
Longing and often tears.
Alas! may evil befall king Louis.
Who makes commands and preachings
Through which pain has entered my heart."

Which is as much as to say that the young lady resents the absence of her lover upon a military expedition for the useless conquest of the birthplace of the Savior—and that the poet is in full sympathy. This idyll, catching at once the attention of the Crusaders and of the Head of the Church, was to work much woe to Provence—when Crusaders and churchmen should have leisure to wreak their vengeances!

Another major difference between the content of even the love poems of the troubadours and the knightly *minnesingers* is the complete absence of class feeling in the latter.

Pretending to find race characteristics is one of the most dangerous and derogatory occupations of the evilly feeble-minded. Nevertheless, when you get a whole territorial literature exhibiting social characteristics that continually differ in one direction from the characteristics of another territorial literature it is permissible—and not in the least provocative—to say as far as those literatures go: this is Greek, this is Teuton, this is Latin or this, again, is Provence singing. So that if you find, as is the case, that the poetic loves of the highborn troubadours are invariably ladies of high birth, of stately degree and of disdainful manners whilst the loves of the knightly *minnesingers* are as often as not (or, indeed, more often than not) goose girls and peasant maidens: and when, in addition to that, the heroes of the great German saga epics, like the heroes of the *Iliad* and *Odyssey*, were not men of a class set apart, but, in truth, heroes swift of foot, of steel muscles, of keen eyes and of unsurpassable discipline in personal combat whereas the paladins of Romance *chansons de gestes* were invariably men of illustrious birth and shrinkings from the habits of the vulgar herd*—

* cf. The distress of Launcelot when, having been seriously wounded, he was carried into the Arthurian equivalent for a casualty dressing station, just like any common soldier, in an ordnance cart.

so it becomes possible and even expedient to point out that class feeling, which plays a strong part in the Romance *chansons,* is completely absent (and very markedly absent) from both the *canzos* and the lays of the *minnesingers* and even more markedly absent from the great books making up the Icelandic saga-anthology collected by Snorri Sturleson in thirteenth century Iceland.

> *Under der linden*
> *an der heide . . .*

sings Walther . . .

> Under the lime trees
> on the heather . . .

at the opening, perhaps, of the most famous and certainly the most beautiful of all the German lyrics of that school. And the poem, if tending to be narrative, is the analysis of the emotions of a peasant girl, not of any châtelaine of *Las Tours* who might be presumed to have no emotions at all.

> *Under der linden*
> *an der heide*
> *da unser sweier bette was,*
> *da muget ir vinden*
> *schone beide*
> *gebrochen bluomen unde gras,*
> *vor dem walde in einem tal,*
> *tandaredei*
> *schone sanc diu nahtegal.*
>
> *Ich kam gegangen*
> *zuo der ouwe*
> *do was min friedel komen e.*
> *da wart ich enpfangen*
> *here frouwe!*

das ich bin saelic immer me.
kust er mich? wol tusentstunt:
tandaredei!
sehet, wie rot mir ist der munt . . .

The author's translation, which he made certainly no later than when he was twelve and which attracted, nearly half a century ago, a certain amount of attention on its publication, has lately been reprinted, but for the sake of the convenience of the reader it may as well be printed once again here:

Under the lindens on the heather
There was our double resting place,
Side by side and close together
Garnered blossoms crushed and grass
Nigh a shaw in such a vale:
Tandaredei,
Sweetly sang the nightingale.

I came a-walking through the grasses;
Lo! my dear was come before.
Ah! what befell then—listen, lasses—
Makes me glad for evermore.
Kisses,—thousands in good sooth;
Tandaredei,
See how red they've left my mouth.

There had he made ready—featy, fairly—
All of flow'ring herbs a yielding bed,
And that place in secret still smiles rarely.
If by chance your foot that path should tread,
You might see the roses pressed,
Tandaredei,
Where e'enow my head did rest.

How he lay beside me, did a soul discover
(Now may God forfend such shame from me):

Not a soul shall know it save my lover;
Not a soul could see save I and he,
And a certain small brown bird
Tandaredei,
Trust him not to breathe a word.

Nevertheless, discover what differences you may between northern and east-Mediterranean epic and central European, Latin or Romance *chansons de gestes*, you may find—alike in the Icelandic Sagas, in the English contemporary near-epics, and the *sirventes* of fighting trouba-dours like Bertran de Born—a certain similar development of occu-pational generosities and properties. Enough to spread a certain aspect of kinship throughout the world! Thus, besieged in his castle of Alta Forte by all the kings of the earth—the kings of England, France and Aragon and half the counts and viscounts of Provence—Bertran is told that admirable as has been the strategy of his enemies so that they all have converged on him at a given point, nevertheless they have had no General Grant to look after their commissariats so they have arrived with all their troops nearly starving, faint from the march. "Damn it all," says Bertran with his forked red beard pointing at them contemptuously over his battlements, "with those fellows in that condition we shall have no sort of a scrap tomorrow." So he sends them out great stores of beef, wine and olive oil and on the morrow is soundly thrashed and his castle taken. So with the epic poem of *Mal-don*, the English, bent on repulsing the Danes at the sea, arrive at the shore so soon and in such numbers that the Danes will have no chance of landing and all chance of battle seems to be off. "Hang it all," say the English commanders, "we shall have no chance of a good scrap like this." So, considerately, they retire a mile or so and give the Danes a chance to land and rest from the labors of disem-barking. So on the morrow they are soundly thrashed and England is lost.

It is interesting in another direction to observe that the narrator of Bertran's battle—and a supremely beautiful narrative it is—tells us that Bertran appeals to the world conscience, "for, contrary to the laws and dictates of humanity, his enemies have employed the devilish new instruments that, hurling stone balls both with fire and flame against his castle walls, had brought them down." Moreover, it was whilst going to take over the victuals and drink Bertran had provided for his enemies that the English master of ordnance had observed the cracks and weak places against which he had directed his stone balls.

Bertran said all this with his hands tied behind his back, having behind him a gallows twice as high as ordinary in honor of his knighthood and valor, and pointing his scarlet beard at the King of England who sat in the shadow of his lifted tent flap. He also threatens to ride his good horse to Aragon, where, meeting the king of that place, he shall cleave him exactly in half from crown to chin, so that the body precisely dimidiated shall fall, one half on each side of his saddle-bow.

"No, Bertran," said the king, "you shall do none of these things, nor are your complaints of any avail; for within the hour, from a silken cord you shall be suspended from the fine gallows that rises behind you. And this is befitting for one who has disturbed the whole of Europe with his *sirventes* setting neighbor against neighbor, subject against king, mother against daughter, and son against father."

"Ah, King of England," replies Bertran, "it was not thus, to the greatest grief I ever had, dying in my arms, your son Henry spoke to me." Then the King of England bursting into tears commanded that Bertran's bonds should be stricken off; that his castle should be rebuilded stronger than it had ever been, and that Bertran should be given the fiefs of I don't know how many manors and castles in Poitou, Aquitaine, the Narbonnais and Aragon.

CHAPTER TWO

Thus almost inevitably, as if ready for the arrival of devilish engines casting stone balls, there creeps into our record of poetry the narrative poem. In the end it shall as inevitably lead to the dominance over poetry of the prose narrative such as we see it today.

A natural itch tempts, as we have seen, all good soldiers to their ruin by making them give the enemy sufficient advantage of numbers or of terrain to put up a good fight. So, in this matter of narrative broadening down from verse, into prose, certain characteristics seem to unite all the widely separated races with whom we shall have to deal. The aristocratic poets, the knights, the ruling princes, and the heroes all passed their leisure in making, in verse, their variations on one original theme. This theme, as with the Chinese, Catullus, or the *minnesingers*, and the troubadours was almost always the one of melancholy love. Then there came the invention of prose which divided society into classes: that of the aristocrat who had the leisure to sing and that of the *roturier*—the white-collared class. These latter employed their pens in making statistical records of victories, of captives, of plunder. Below them, hieratically, were the immense mobs of unskilled workers who build pyramids, catacombs and sewers. Whilst they worked they sang their ignoble ballads and, whilst they rested, told their innumerable tales in prose or in loose verse or in a mixture of the two. And this is as true of the day and the land of Rameses II as of the immense territories of the mediaeval Teutons with their varied populations all exhibiting certain similarities of language or of cult.

It is very regrettable that, in a consideration of the history of imaginative writing, we have to leave out any adequate account of whole literatures, many of them as vast and as important as our own literature and language.

It will become evident at this stage that our story is now going to take a definite line of pilgrimage. We must go from Provence of the troubadours through France of the *chansons* and *fabliaux* to the England of Chaucer, to the sixteenth century Spaniards and seventeenth century Elizabethans, and so through the works of the *Pléiade*, the dramas of Molière and Racine and the novels of Richardson and Flaubert to our own Russo-German-French-Anglo-Saxon empire of the imagination.

This gives us no room at all to deal with whole great literatures, like those of India, Wales, Japan, Persia or Arabia, and leaves us only the leisure to talk of the very great literature of Iceland as being the field from which the relatively small literature of mediaeval and modern Germany very considerably derived itself.

For the moment all we have time to say is that the Icelandic is a highly refined and thought-over literature of one of the few earthly near-paradises that the world has ever seen—the only other having had its place in the triangle of earth between the Alps and the Pyrenees called Provence and the Narbonnais; or for its very short period, the Sicily of Theocritus, Moschus and Bion till the Carthaginians and Romans, like the accursed troops commanded by St. Dominic, came and forever laid it waste.

The little, shining Icelandic commonalty was founded by such Teutons as could not bear the encroachments on their liberties of the kings and the tyrants brought to the surface by the gradual crystallization of the western European body politic. It is necessary that we call "Teutonic" the inhabitants of all the countries, for the most part denizens of immense forests and boundless heaths, lying between the course of the Rhine and the North Cape and Cape Finisterre—the westernmost point becoming eventually the Lands End. These peoples spoke kindred languages from Middle High and Low German to Anglo-Saxon and Norse. So the founders of the Icelandic civilization were Norwegians. They were of the class of, let us say, gentlefolk who furnished the not so much lawless as unrestrained heroes of the great Teutonic epics. They were not aristocrats; still less were they scions of royal houses. They were *baros*—free barons, like the barons of the court of King John—who, if they held their lands from anybody held them direct from the king. But those Norsemen disliked paying even the king rent, so they went away to Iceland and being wealthy, hardy, courageous and cunning, set up a well-fed, peaceful and highly decorated civilization of their own.

This literature of the Icelanders that has come down to us was quasi-aristocratic—the product of a well-fed, well-housed, leisured class. It consists neither of the ballads of soldiers nor the folksongs of peasants. It has the verse texture of an epic, and the quality of the more striking passages of epics; it is, in fact, the product of a late and refined age.

In nearly all literatures you have two or three strands running side by side—the courtly, the purely literary and the peasant, plus the burgher. Thus, whilst the troubadours were writing their canzos, simultaneously in the market places and in shaded courts of their towns there was proceeding a very beautiful and still extant popular art—that of the *conte-fabliste*, the *conte-fable* being a sort of simple dramatic production consisting half of recited prose, half of chanted verse. In addition, you had the third strain, that of the balladists, who, without organization or direction, produced songs that you may still hear sung in the fields of Provence or on the stoops of the sufficiency farmers of the mountains of Kentucky or North Carolina. These three divisions of literature are always, and of necessity, there. The princes and the generals must have their evening entertainments of elaborately jewelled literature of escape. The burghers and the soldiers must have the same thing, less elaborately jewelled and more open to modification by—or to please—the audience. The peasants, ostlers, and postilions must have their folksongs, the semi-professional utterances of their occupations and crafts. The epic, on the other hand, was the means of mental escape for all classes of the realm or race. Almost invariably it has been cast in a sort of homespun, chantable, non-intricate verse, and the subject has been taken from the simplest of human motives; the decorations are of the homeliest kitchen-utensil and spinning-wheel order. In the school of literature with which we are immediately concerned—that of the Nordic races—this tendency is extremely easy to trace. Even in the comparatively late and too much edited English epic *Beowulf*, suddenly and without mental preparation one is conscious of a feeling of deep disappointment. The other day this writer was asked what were the relative values of the *Beowulf* and the fragments of the Royal Edda. He answered unhesitatingly and without thought that the literary value of the Eddas was infinitely higher, and that the *Beowulf* had all the imperfections of clumsiness that has distinguished English workmanship from time immemorial—and that most likely will go on distinguishing it. In a sense, that judgment was true. The Icelandic poems are elaborately wrought, impassioned, short masterpieces. The *Beowulf*, hastily considered, is a rather clumsily constructed sackful of legendary wisdoms, human instances and *longueurs*. And when you come to consider the *Beowulf*, making all the allowances that a proper reader should make —not omitting consideration of the veniality, corruption and bat-blindness of editors, publishers, pedagogues and all the innumerable parasites that batten on and deflower the lucid masterpieces of great poets—you suddenly perceive that the *Beowulf* is actually two unrelated poems, possibly by different hands, stuck anyhow together by the rather financially swell editor who in the tenth century gave us the almost too elaborate and ornate Cotton manuscript. That is all we have for judging a not at all early version of *Beowulf*. Orthodox opinion today sets the composition of this epic in eighth century England. This writer is inclined to consider that it was an English compilation from much earlier Teuto-pagan continental fragments, unified and slightly Christianized by an eighth century editor who made modifications to suit his own taste. A reader who desires final elucidation might very well himself study the sources—which are the sources of the literature and civilization of our day and race.

Be that as it may, there remains the fact that *Beowulf*, as we have it, is two unrelated stories, arbitrarily stuck together, the one with a texture of epic and naturalistic simplicity, the other a tired and relatively commonplace, individual dragon-slaying romance. And the feeling of tedium and overlength begins to beset the reader at the exact point of the junction after Beowulf's recitation to King Hygelac of his adventures with the troll, with Grendel. The recitation to Hygelac is one of those noteworthy technical devices that will be found in all literature between the day of the epic and the work of the conscious modern novelist.

The adventures of Beowulf in ridding the king's house of his *pol-*

tergeists have been fully told in the body of the poem. It is the narrative of the labors of a modern Hercules. The author has said to himself perhaps: "Some of the atmosphere of the earlier passages of my poem has not got through to my reader; he may not have completely believed the story. If, then, I repeat the story very succinctly with atmospheric touches and little passages of corroboration, my whole work ought to leave an impression of great truth and greater unity."*

That having been done, the first two thirds of *Beowulf* has a singular unity of its own—a unity as worthy of note as that of the *Odyssey* itself. And then to that perfectly complete work of art the eighth century editor has tacked on a sequel telling how in his old age Beowulf, who started out as a mere member of the Scandinavian unemployed, becomes a king of the Gaults, rids his country of a dragon and dies of that fabulous monster's Mephitic breath.

The Northern Teutonic, like the Greek epic, consisted of the rendering and development of a central type—the hero. He performs unusual and apparently supernatural feats surrounded by normal furnishings (the evidence of usual occupations) and minor characters such as gave the backing up of reality to the acts of the hero. If, that is to say, a hero fought a troll in a shed amongst ploughshares, bees-keps, hens' nests and piled-up roots, the episode would seem more real than if it took place by moonlight in a Druidic grove. And if an old nurse washes the wounds on the hero's feet and recognizes him by an old scar, the listener says to himself: "That's it. That's true. It's all true."

That is the perhaps unconscious, or the perhaps worked out, technique of all epic as opposed to all romance narrative. The romance writer begins by providing his always solitary hero with an aristocratic, kingly or semi-divine origin, hoping that thus the supernatural deeds of that hero may seem, to employ a French term, "justified."

On the face of it the *poltergeists*—or trolls—whom Beowulf undertook to drive out of the house of King Hygelac would seem unworthy of the attention of the epic muse. But *poltergeist*—the malicious en-

---

* Conrad and the present author must have uttered similar sentences fifty or sixty times, whilst elaborating their plots during their decade of collaboration.

tity who disarranged, disordered and overhauled the household, rising even sufficiently far in his malignity to strangle the master of the house in his bed at night—this minor, supernatural being was familiar to and believed in by everybody . . . and was by everybody feared and deprecated. He is so feared and deprecated over immense stretches of rural territory to this day. Whole countrysides that during generations have abandoned the Baal (plus Druidic or Olympian) religions that in regions of the West existed side by side; that subsequently abandoned the Nordic religions of Wotan and Tor; and that finally have grown rather indifferent to the cult of the Christ himself: these whole regions, nevertheless, continue to believe in the obscure existence of the *poltergeists*—those almost microscopic deities whose province is the humiliation and ruin of the hosts on whom they choose to inflict themselves. And the mere existence of a single *poltergeist* in a wide region is sufficient to cast the shadow of worry over that whole district until some substitute for Beowulf shall succeed in expelling or enchaining forever the detested visitant. The contemporary equivalent of Beowulf is either thirteen Protestant clergymen, if they can be gotten together, or one Roman Catholic priest with holy water, which is said to cost very dear in the Protestant countries.

The author lived once near a county seat of Kent in England, in a village hidden deep in the weald of Kent. One morning the village wise-woman invited him very hurriedly to come to a certain cottage, inhabited by a widow—or to be more exact by a wife who had let her bedridden husband be taken off to the workhouse, a very serious offense against Wealdan Kentish public opinion. According to the wise-woman the first thing that had happened that morning was that while the widow was dressing, the *boo-boy* had come down the chimney and jumped on the widow's back. (The *boo-boy* is a sack filled with straw to prevent drafts from coming down the chimney.) The bed clothes at the same time rolled off the bed, tore themselves into hundreds of strips like tapes and then tied themselves into thousands of knots. At the same time the memory pot had come out from under the bed and had gone downstairs without spilling a drop—to the sound of all the kitchen crockery on the dresser, flying out and smashing together on the stone floor. The author saw with his own eyes the drift of stone crocks smashed across the kitchen floor, the great old dresser that by that time had fallen down on its face, the whole cottage in a state of unbelievable disorder and, most curious of all, the sheets which really had been torn into strips and then knotted inexorably into innumerable knots. For if the widow, for purposes of mystification, or any other fellow villager, had undertaken that work, it must have cost even the most skilled of rag-rug tiers from eighteen to twenty-four hours to do it. So the whole little village—and, indeed, villages for miles around—was thrown into a state of extreme anxiety. If the *poltergeist* had come as the ministrant of an offended deity to chastise the secret sins of individuals, where would his visitations end? Finally a priest who had been eminently successful in laying the ghost at Bilsington Priory, which had once belonged to Chaucer, was persuaded to come and exorcise that minor demon. It was heard no more of then, until it reappeared in a hamlet about fifty miles away.

These minor beliefs, like the echoes of the great old epic tales themselves, die very slowly in Western European rural solitudes. If you could persuade that wise-woman that you were not a member of the Quality (in which case, ten to one, you would have designs on her little squatter's cottage) or that you were not a member of the white-collar class (in which case you would probably be watching out to prosecute her for selling her cowslip wine without a license): if in short you could secure her confidence, she would tell you by the hour, in prose interspersed with harsh song, whole histories that would seem whilst she told them, vaguely familiar to you. There would be the story of how the women of Kent, when the Kentish men had been worsted in battle by an invading nation called the Denes or Danes, had dressed themselves in green boughs and had marched down to Medway Bridge. And the Danes, thinking that a forest was marching against them, had been struck with panic and had never been seen in that countryside again. But she had much more elaborated prose epics which she would recite to whole roomfuls, all the elder members of the company nodding their heads and saying: "Yon's right. Meary is in the right of it." There would be thus the long, long story of the king's daughter who refused to tell the greatness of her affection for her father. And the father in his rage took from her all salt and made her sleep in the great garret along the top of the castle where there was no light and where all sorts of supernatural visitants tormented and tempted her. Nevertheless, she had between her breasts a little bag of salt that she had reserved for just such an occasion. There came a great tempest, one of the greatest ever, that burst in all the windows of the great banqueting hall and flooded the whole great place. Then, in her darkness, the king's daughter heard universal wailings go through the castle below. All the salt in the great cellar and on the banqueting table had been drowned by the great rain of the tempest and the king must die. His daughter, however, crept down from her lair and, pulling out from between her breasts the little bag of salt, poured its contents between the lips of the dying king. So the king had his life again but the princess, having no salt, must die.

So there came along the road a singing tramp who was known through all the countryside for his songs and marlocks and feats of strength. He heard the wailing in the great castle and when he heard that the princess must die for lack of salt he said: "Say you so." And he adventured along the road past the bridge into the strange country beyond. And there he met a great black-visaged man wrapped in a great black cloak. So the singing tramp wrestled with the great man for an hour and a day until he had from him the great black cloak that muffled him, and there within the cloak was a sack of full two pounds' weight of salt . . . so the life of the princess was saved at the last moment. It is in that way great literatures are preserved through dark ages and subjects are found for our writers of epics.

Let us then consider the extraordinary confusion that must have filled the minds of men and their leaders during the centuries that saw the transition in Western Europe from the dark to the middle ages. Imagine yourself an elderly, tough, rather slow-thinking leader of sea pirates, a castle owner on the crags of Finisterre, your simple mind occupying itself with the past cutting of throats and plunder and in contemplating more throat-cuttings and plunder to come. Then your spies report some rich vessel that would be leaving Quimper or some neighboring port. You were a God-fearing man, you did your best to keep the bellies of your dependants and their offspring well-filled, their backs well-covered, their thatches well-healed against tempests from the Northwest. Every night when you stopped at home, you fuddled yourself full of hot mead and one of your clerks read you about Iphigenia in Aulis, the adventures of Jove with Danae or with Europa, the lay of Roland at Roncevaux or the 109th Psalm, all lately translated into Welsh, the manuscripts having been brought in the ships of the Phoenicians from Marseilles or from some other Mediterranean port. It was confusing because though these strange gods and heroes were no great concern of yours, the people who wrote about them seemed to write truly.

At the same time the Druidic priests of the neighboring sacred grove were making alterations, if not in the Druidic faith, then at least in their practices. Instead of killing their victims with the sickle-shaped sacrificial knife, they bound them up in rush baskets and suspended them over great fires, thus paying tribute to Moloch of the Africans and to Baal, the Fly-God of the Babylonians. Phoenician shipmasters had persuaded the Druids to make these changes in their mode of religion. In the spring you yourself had to pass all your flocks and herds between great fires called baal-fires and the mountain on which stood your castle was hereafter to be known as Beal-Tan.

That was all well as far as it went, but there were of course worrying aspects. In the foreign tract to your East reigned some sort of Frankish or Saxon king who every now and then sent ambassadors to your Druids, demanding that the priests and their subjects adopt the worship of Thor and Wotan and Freya and Loge and a great number of other not repugnant but exceedingly drunken deities. His skalds would come among your people and would sing you ballads from the North, like "O the King's sons of Denmark." Then, suddenly, without rhyme or reason, that foreign king knelt at a font and had water poured over him by an unknown stranger from the South, of the name of Paulinus.

This is of course an exaggerated picture. It is unlikely that any one knight or count or prince would be subjected to all these cross-currents, philosophies, and cults unless he lived in some very central position.

Nevertheless, it is well to consider what must have been the states of mind of cultivated rulers like King Alfred who, whilst being chased around England by the Danes, translated Boethius into the English of his day and with unnatural absence of mind permitted the cakes to burn. Or, consider Alphonso the Learned of Aragon, who if he was a relatively inefficient and even ferocious ruler nevertheless protected such of the troubadours as needed protection and yet stood—subject to every possible Moorish attack or polemic—in the very forefront of Christendom. The reader will find below a list of the books and tales that are mentioned in the early fourteenth century Provençal romance, *Flamenca,* as being in the library of the heroine's husband or read by the hero of that remarkable tale. That library contained such "matter" and tales—"matter of Rome," "matter of Britain," and "matter of Charlemagne"—as the ordinary knight, burgher, or handicraftsman of southern or central France would normally hear told or sung of in the course of a year or so's usual night's entertainments.*

Such a hearer or reader would have a head extraordinarily full of mixed Olympian, Druidic and, in a less degree, Oriental religious matter. In addition, a countless tide of bizarre stories such as the mediaeval mind thirstingly desired would beat on him, on the one hand folk fiction from Bagdad, and on the other the matchless imaginations of the *Mabinogion* from, say, Chester. The list given in the footnote is quoted in *The Epic and Romance* of Professor W. P. Ker, a delightful—and, what is more unusual, a subtly humorous—scholar as to whom the present writer would be ungrateful if he did not say that the major part of what he and most of his contemporary students

* The full list included the tales of:

1. (Matter of Rome): Priam, Pyramus, Helen, Ulysses, Hector, Achilles, Dido, Lavinia (how she sent her letter with the arrow in it over the sentinel's head), Polynices, Tydeus and Eteocles, Appollonius of Tyre, Alexander, Hero and Leander, Cadmus of Thebes, Jason and the sleepless Dragon, Hercules, Demophon and Phyllis (a hard passage), Narcissus, Pluto and the wife of Orpheus, David and Goliath, Samson and Delila, Judas Maccabeus, Julius Caesar.

2. (Matter of Britain): The Round Table, Gawain and Yvain, Perceval, Ugonet do Perida, Governail the comrade of Tristam, Fenece and the sleeping draught, Guinglain, the *Chevalier de la Charrette* of Chrestien Guiflet, Kay Calobrenan, Mordred, the 'luck of Herelin, and how the Count Duret was dispossessed by the Vandals.

3. (Matter of Charlemagne): The wars of Charlemagne, Clovis and Pepin of France, Gui de Nateuil, Oliver of Verdun.

knew or know of Nordic epic came from his conversation far more than from the ponderous and humorless labors and outcries of his scholastic contemporaries. In the same volume Professor Ker quotes a similar list of tales mentioned in the *Complaynt of Scotland.** This, the last of the alliterative epics, was written early in the sixteenth century—that is to say, before the effects of the renaissance could be felt in Scotland. Both of the lists in the footnotes may be taken, therefore, as representing the literature that was available for mediaeval, princely and burgher audiences. And, no great additions having been made to the available classical literatures between the sack of Rome by Odovaker and the taking of Constantinople by the Turks, the whole range of this literature would be as available for central European audiences of the ninth as of the sixteenth century. Aristotle, of course, was introduced as a whole body of philosophy into the mediaevalism of the thirteenth century, and probably no great inroads of Oriental knowledge were made in central or Western Europe before the Saracens sacked Rome in the ninth century. So that by the tenth century practically all the fictional and poetical roots of the middle ages were available to any man with any desire for culture.

The mind of the reader may well be confused by all this—and it is well that it should be—for no clear outlines are to be perceived in the immense Christmas pudding that was the mediaeval mind. And the professors differ so much and with such bellicosity that it is almost impossible to get any clear guidance from them. German scholarship, on the one hand, between 1840 and the opening of the Great War furiously and menacingly denied—one can't see why—that the Mahommedans of the African shores of the Mediterranean had any mental influence on the populations of the shores of Italy and France. French scholarship, on the other hand, with more equanimity asserted the contrary. It seems more reasonable to agree with the latter theory. Nay, should we not even see evidence that African-Oriental influences

* Ptholome, Averois, Aristotle, Galien, Ypocrites, Cicero—among the classical philosophers and scientists—and the following tales: Taylis of Cantiberrye, Robert the dyabil duc of Normandie, the tayl of the volfe of varldis end, Ferrand earl of Flandris, Perseus and Andromada, the Prophysie of Merlin, the tayl of the giantis that ate live men, the Bruce, Ypomedon, tayls of Hercules, Robin Hood and Little Iohn, the Merveillis of Maundeville, Bevis of Southampton, Opheus King of Portigal, the Golden Targe, etc.

reached not only the delta of the Rhone but the very shores of the Rhine itself. There is not only the legend of the *Feindliche Zwei Brueder of Bornhofen* and the Saracen maiden, but in his travels across Europe that mighty wanderer Walther von der Vogelweide, accompanied by his fiddler and lutist, sang his way not merely through Provence but actually as far as Salerno, south of Naples, and so back to the Drave. But Salerno was the seat of the most famous medical university in the world—a university founded in the ninth century and fostered by the Norman rulers of the Two Sicilies and Naples. Here the professors were at first all Arabs, and the textbooks that they used were the actual case-books of Galen and, no doubt, copies of those of Aesculapius. And it is impossible to imagine that a man like Vogelweide should have found himself in the very center of Arab learning without at least some trace of it rubbing off on him. It has to be remembered that the craving for learning of all kinds was as great between the fall of Rome and the Siege of Constantinople as was the craving for salt during the same ages. It was not merely as their proverb had it:

> When land is gone and money spent
> Then learning is most excellent.

It was that, in the world of so many conflicting intellectual doctrines and spiritual claims, mankind longed, above all things, first for knowledge of the fountain of youth and then for that of how to permute base metals into fine ones. Almost as eagerly did men long for the gift of prophecy. So that you would suck in eagerly any learning in any of the departments of life whatsoever because you might by accident come upon the secret of the touch of Croesus or the knowledge of the warning stars that Ptolemy and the Arabs—holding both the territory and the manuscripts of both Ptolemy and Croesus—might possess. And it was very unlikely that, storm the Church as she might, you would refuse any scrap of Arab lore that came your way. Similarly, in the department of chemical lore and poetry, man was extremely anxious for all news of the potions that came from the land of the Druids, the juice of whose mistletoe berries was supposed to be the most necessary ingredient of those glamorous fluids. So the story of Tristram, presumably Cornish, so impressed the mediaeval imagination that his legend is treated or quoted not merely by the first and least significant of the *minnesingers* but also by the great Gottfried of Strassbourg himself, and not only by the relatively rough Norman writers of romance but by Chrétien de Troyes and the famous Peire Vidal. It would be difficult to find a more exact instance of one of the legends covering the whole of Western Europe.

There came then the day when the apparently slumbering but always vigilant Church found it necessary to sweep away all these foreign influences. We have read Marcabrun's poem against the Crusades and we shall very soon be reading Aucassin's even more injurious speech against the very joys and denizens of Heaven itself. We may lack exact evidence that the verses and ideals of the Saracens penetrated into the Provence of the troubadours. But there is no historic lack of traces of peaceful and even cordial mercantile relationships between the port of Marseilles and the hinterland and the ports of the Arabs on the opposite shores. Both intercourse and commerce the Church set out resolutely to destroy—as soon as she was strong enough to do so. You saw the beginnings of the Holy Inquisition whose agents went from Catalonia to Carcassonne, Arles and Nîmes, making inquiries, now and then degrading a priest or two here and there. It was alleged against the commoner sort of Provence that they were infested with the heresy of the Albigenses, a sort of Quietest agnostic frame of mind that had traveled from Bulgaria into Provence itself. Eventually the sovereign counts of Provence and the Narbonnais, as well as the reigning princes of Catalonia and Aragon took up their swords against the intrusive churchmen, in defense of their subjects. Then the King of France, incited to it by the Pope, gave the reformer Simon de Montfort an army with which to sweep the south parts free of heresy. The war lasted many years, the French troops being given the style and dignity of Crusaders. Finally, at the Battle of Muret to the chant of thousands of priests led by the unspeakable St. Dominic himself, the northern French completely defeated the Provençaux and Aragonese and wiped out the best of all civilizations. So the joy went out of mediaevalism leaving only sadic grotesqueries. At any rate, as far as we are concerned, it was the end of a memorable bright literature. Nor were even the *minnesingers* to be spared. At various dates the Church insisted that they and their followers must cease to sing on profane subjects and limit themselves severely to religious themes. So by degrees the great order of *minnesingers* passed into the rather grotesque burgherly organizations of *meistersingers*, and gradually under the Hapsburgs the spirit of song deserted both High and Low German upper classes.

In the unceasing struggle that has gone on through the ages between the advocates of free inspiration and those of technical rules for the perfection of literature, the troubadours occupy a peculiar position. The great body of their poetry seems to send out a light that for centuries enlightened the whole world and that once more today seems to be approaching an apotheosis. Yet their actual baggage in the matter of content was of the slightest. As we have seen, the subject of their, as it were, first-class literary products—the canzos and, to some extent, the tenzos—was one single theme: that of unrequited love. Such a theme might very well have become wearisome were it not that it was treated in continually changing metres and with innumerable new inventions in the way of images and even of allegories. So their work came nearly into the category of that heart's desire of all true *literati*— absolute imaginative literature, using the word "absolute" in the sense that it is used by musicians. For if you could read the secrets of the hearts of writers, you would find that every one of them in the end, in the spirit either of weariness or of aversion, craves enormously to write versified or cadenced words that shall have beauty and be almost without significance. You get tired of having to tell stories or to treat of subjects; the thought of words set in due order and of unchanging meaning seems to you intolerably fatiguing. You long to express yourself by means of pure sound as the musician can impress you and as nothing else can impress you, by a fugue that consists of nothing but notes. The one follows and mingles with the other but the whole has no meaning whatever. It depends solely on those sounds to influence your moods of the moment or such of your deeper emotions as may permanently affect your disposition.

Most literatures have not lived long enough yet for the author to find such expression or any sympathetic hearers, but in our own day we have had the phenomenon of Mr. Joyce whose content is of rela tively little importance, the excitement in reading him coming almost entirely from his skill in juggling words as a juggler will play with many gilt balls at once.

What would have happened to the troubadours if St. Dominic had left them alone is one of the puzzles of comparative literature. They would seem, whilst they flourished, to have changed either their verse methods or their approach to subjects extraordinarily little, so that Giraud Riquier the last, and William IX of Poitiers the first of them could perfectly well have changed places without altering the ordered sequence of that great flow of song.

What actually happened was that the note of lyric and elegiac verse disappeared for the time from the world. The *minnesingers*, as we have seen, continued for a while singing their songs which occupied themselves almost exclusively with one theme—the coming of the month of May—as those of the troubadours had with that of un-requited love . . . and with an effect of greater monotony. But, with the nearing dominance of the Church in temporal matters the note of the world became more stern—either because the Church so insisted or because ruling princes had to resist the encroachments of the church-man. You could not expect Henry II of England after the murder of St. Thomas to have much heart for lyric verse, and though Canterbury became one of the centers of learning in the mediaeval world, its preoccupation lay with spiritual rather than with metrical problems. On the other hand, the passion that men had to hear stories grew in pace with their preoccupations. The more they were worried with day-time problems the more men insisted in the evening on having their minds distracted by narratives, whether in verse or in prose. And, gradually, the demand for prose became the greater and so verse lost the hegemony in literature that it had had since the beginning of time. Verse and prose ran, however, neck and neck for a century or more after the Battle of Muret. The two most perfect pieces of work in the romance period—*Aucassin and Nicolette* and *Flamenca*—were composed the one in mingled verse and prose, and the other in verse alone. Perhaps a score of thirteenth to early fourteenth century tales have come down to us in the familiar category of works that the ordinarily cultivated man may be expected to know or to know of—*The Tumbler of Our Lady, The Lay of Sir Anis and Sir Amela, The Lay of Grailent,* at once the most charming and the best related. But it is to *Aucassin and Nicolette* that one must go if one wishes to see a high narrative form approaching that of the best of the subsequent novelists. The story of *Aucassin and Nicolette* is related with an exacter use of what is called *progression d'effet* and with only such employment of digressions as the unknown writer may have found necessary in his or her naïve heart. For it is unlikely, possible as it may have been, that the writer could have studied the Icelandic Sagas and learned from them how much a slight passage about interior decoration, cookery or clothing will add to the authority and verisimilitude of a narrative.

Various writers have ascribed this brightest of all little masterpieces to the pen of one woman writer or another, but as this writer cannot agree to any one of these ascriptions he will refrain from reciting the names of these poetesses. He has for a long time had the conviction that *Aucassin and Nicolette* was a gradually evolved folk product. As we have said, whilst the knights and counts were declaiming their canzos and tenzos in the yards of high castles, the peasants and citizens of their small realms composed and performed the little dramatic entertainments called *contes-fables* in their town squares. And Peirc Vidal at least, if not other plebeian troubadours who came to high estate, gained as it were his literary spurs by improvising the songs that were sung between recited passages of prose of these plebeian nights' entertainments. And the writer has been confirmed in his suspicion that this little masterpiece is of folk origin by the fact of having been present at the recensions and rehearsals of the *contes-fables* called today *pastorales* that the peasants of Provence still perform and still add to. The most striking of these additions that this writer has actually witnessed occurred in the course of a rehearsal of a *pastorale*—what we should call a Passion Play—of the Nativity, performed by the fishermen, vine-tenders, the barbers, the hotel chefs and their wives.

of the seashore not far from Marseilles, some four years ago. This particular *pastorale*, which was of extreme antiquity, began, before the streets of Bethlehem were reached, with some very ancient verses concerning themselves with Hannibal, in a Provençal so old as to be scarcely recognizable. It continued with a recital of the sufferings of Our Lady before St. Joseph found Her manger. This is in a prose of relatively modern French and in verse of a French extremely mediaeval; it went on with the story of the miraculous conversion of a Jew at the sight of the Sacred manger just after the Virgin and Child had left it. Then came alternate accounts in prose and verse—the prose being always intoned and the verse being sung to music which began by being plain song and ended in melodies singularly suggestive of the Viennese waltzes of Johann Strauss. This Passion Play continued with a representation of Christ on the Mount of Olives and on the cross; with the arrival by night in their miraculous boat, after the Crucifixion, of the Holy Maries—St. Mary the Virgin, St. Mary the Magdelene and their servant Martha—at the village of Les Saintes Maries on the shores of the Camargue quite close at hand; with a short account of Saint Louis leaving the port of Aigues Mortes equally close at hand. And then songs or prose passages about various episodes of Provençal history narrated or sung in the Provençal of a district so unfamiliar to us that we did not completely catch the meaning of any of the burdens, except for a song denouncing the chicaneries of the parliament at Aix with the burden running:

Three are the flails of Provence.
The parliament, the *mistral* and the Durance.

The Durance is a river that almost each year with inundations from the sudden melting of snows in the high Alps caused in those days the loss of hundreds, even of thousands of lives, and even today will claim its quota of victims. And immediately after that comes a prose lament in northern French for the hundreds—even thousands—of royalist victims made by the Bonapartists at Nîmes after the second coming of Napoleon. The performers who were all royalists omitted to mention that, both before and after the second coming of the Emperor, the royalists at Nîmes had completely extirpated the Bonapartists of that part of the Narbonnais. So with a chorale also in North French, and possibly Parisian, about *Les Trois Glorieuses*—the three glorious days of the revolution against Louis Philippe—the *pastorale* would have come to an end. But the village barber, a very ancient man having much authority among the performers, now insisted that it was time that they added something to that work. And, with a shaking but still fine declamatory voice, he sang a sort of ballad that as far as I could tell—for again I am not very well acquainted with the local *moko* variety of the Provençal language which contains a good many corrupt Italianisms—consisted of a furious, fiery and at the same time mournfully fatalist denunciation of Bismarck and the Prussians of 1870. Whether it was his own composition or not did not appear, but it seemed to be familiar to the peasants and fishermen, and, after several alterations by the one or the other had either been accepted or negatived, the song was finally accepted into the *pastorale* and the old man was deputed to sing it on next Christmas night.

Thus the art of the *conte-fabliste*, part imaginative narrative, part continuing chronicle, continues to be collectively practiced in the regions that saw the birth of that beautiful work of genius, *Aucassin and Nicolette*. And it is not to be imagined that the *pastorale* of which we have been speaking does not contain passages of great beauty and pathos. Indeed, the prose passage recounting the arrival of Saints Joseph and Mary in Bethlehem and there going from door to door, knocking in the silent streets, must be one of the most beautiful versions of that narrative that exists.

Aucassin and Nicolette, then, is also part imaginative narrative and partly a section of the chronicling of one of the innumerable little wars that went on between city and city in the *Provincia Romana*.

CHAPTER THREE

THERE comes thus to an end one of the greatest, certainly the most sparkling, of all literary episodes that go to make up the history of our literature today. It is a literature without bitterness, without sadism, without suspicion; it reflects the light of a great sun-lit district; it has the sound of the voices of a people whose whole life is expressed in song. It is, in short, Greek—of the Greece of the days of Theocritus. The difference between the *trobars* (the findings or inventions of the South) and the art of the *trouvère* (the finder or inventor of the North) is that the one is Mediterranean in origin, the other merely Latin. The whole of Mediterranean civilization went into the making of Marcabrun and Arnaut of Merveil. The language and thought of the *trouvère* were cast in a Latin mould and influenced by Roman circumstances. No single ruler or set of rulers influenced the lives and psychologies of the southern triangle of sun-baked plains. The Frankish civilization, when in its forests it came to be one, was dictatedly Roman—a cosmogony willed on those regions by the Church and by such despots as destiny awarded them. Chilperic II erected and endowed for his people two arenas where wild beasts devoured non-Christian heretics and where gladiators fought with gladiators. Like Charlemagne, Chilperic would be Roman at all costs; he even wrote hymns in Latin that would not scan, and a treatise on the Laws of Justinian.

While, on the one hand, the first Christo-Frankish kings employed Christianity for the praying to death of all their kinsfolk, the southern peoples had at their disposal the religion of Olympus, that of the Druids who even in the days of Roman power still exercised their cult in the woods of remote mountain tops—and, whatever nationalistic literary commentators may say, they certainly had at their disposal the tenets of Islam. For when you come to examine the history as distinct from the letters of these regions you find indisputable proof that the official language of Provence, even before the fall of Rome,

328

was not Latin but Greek,* and that the knights of the South of France fought side by side with Arabs in resisting the Roman encroachments of Charlemagne. And it should not be forgotten that the Gauls in the South of France and the Roman Provence in particular were of undiluted Celtic blood, without any of the mixture of Teutonic origins that successive invasions of the Île-de-France gave to the inhabitants of Eastern Brittany and the country served by the River Seine.

This alone should be sufficient to differentiate between the South French and the North French muses. Let us concede, if you will, that the spiritual and aesthetic influences of the Saracens were almost nil. Of what they consisted and of their extent you may judge from the story of *Aucassin and Nicolette*. The two nations fought side by side or made war the one upon the other; they took, enslaved, or exchanged innumerable captives of both high and low degree. They did this to such an extent, and varying Mediterranean nations had done it for so many centuries, that the adventures of royal slaves and their eventual marriage to the sons of dukes or business men had become the stock subject not merely for the twelfth century Provençal novelist but for Terence and Plautus in Rome, and, long before then, for Menander. It is not necessary to think that the author or the people who composed *Aucassin and Nicolette* had actually seen plays of Menander in the great city of Marseilles—which remained Greek in blood, language and the habits of its populace, until even after the North French had sacked and taken possession of Provence and the Narbonnais. And, indeed, there were Greek theatres in Nîmes, Arles and even in Aquitaine whose inhabitants protested, like the Rhodian Greeks of Lyons and of the Rhone, that they were not Greek colonists but pieces of Greece herself that had been picked up and deposited in these distant barbarian territories, so that the Greek-descended clients of Pliny pleaded through him to be allowed the privileges not of Roman but of Athenian citizenship.

We have, therefore, to regard the literature of Provence and the civilization for which it stood as a Graeco-Celtic wedge pushing itself

* The funeral oration for Constantine the Younger, brother of Constantine the Great, who was suspected of his murder, was delivered at Nîmes, in Greek of a quite classical type and is still extant.

into northern forests and surviving even the occupation of its lands by the Burgundian, the Rhine-Lander and the Visi-Goth who were the most humane of these Teutonic invaders.

For it is to be remembered as a time-long characteristic of the hordes of Northerners who, during every fifty years of recorded history, have attempted to reach the Mediterranean that, by the time they have passed Lyons, their appetites or necessities for rapine and plunder have become very much modified. By then their ambitions limit themselves to settling amongst and ruling these southern peoples. Since the Visi-Goths no longer contemplated bringing vast wealth back into Germany they did not plunder the peasants, and since they desired to be supplied with pleasant foods by these same peasants they neither trampled down their growing corn nor burned their harvests—nor even cut down their fruit or olive trees. The northern parts of Roman Gaul, like Italy herself, had to suffer a great deal more; that and the much greater mixture of northern blood make their literature coarser in texture and their temperaments and even the very details of their architecture more sadic in character.

Nevertheless, it would be a mistake to forget that in their literature, too, the successors of the *trouvères* exhibited strong Celtic characteristics. It is customary for quite temperate scholars to declare that the Arthurian subjects of the North French mediaeval romanticists were of Welsh or purely British origin: *"Le roi Arthur,"* says Villmarqué, *"était un cadeau de la grande Bretagne à la France."** But it should not be forgotten that the whole of the Western world from Marseilles to the extreme north of Wales was originally peopled by one race and there is every probability that the Arthurian legends had their origins in the popular imaginations of almost every region of that Celtic world —and that long before there was any question of composing, chanting or writing down the stories of Launcelot or Gawain. The story that Merlin was the son of the devil by a Perigordian lady, was a Christian modification of an original Druidic story of the Toulousians, which had it that that enchanter was the son of a mortal woman by the Druidic equivalent of Balder the sun god. So that for one's private chart one

* Villmarqué: *Les Romans de la Table Ronde et les Contes des Anciens Bretons.*

may well say that the legend of Merlin was born near Toulouse before the Romans occupied Provence and so traveled by word of mouth
to Roman Britain. And there, when the Roman power had been withdrawn and the Roman organization was still remaining, a great war-
lord of Roman-British origin arose to combat the Saxon hordes and,
proving himself very strong, courageous, cunning and wise in warfare,
the popular worship of him of the day, and afterwards, accorded him
as counsellor one who was the son of a wise and cunning deity. And
when the successors of Arthur finally removed their court from Corn-
wall to Brittany, being thus swept away by the conquering Saxons
from South England, the song went with that court and became an
integral part of the scattered literature that Malory collected to make
up the *Morte d'Arthur*.

So all the Arthurian legends, no matter who were the rulers, went
backwards and forwards between Provence and Wales. And one story
or another, modified by the folk processes of various districts, would
finally be taken as the subject for a poem or a story by one French
writer of Romansh or another. Thus the *fabliau* of the *Chevalier de la
Charette* was written by Chrétien de Troyes, who flourished in
Champagne towards the beginning of the thirteenth century. It relates
naïvely and with a certain rustic charm, such as hardly distinguishes
the Welsh legends that we have today, a story of Sir Launcelot of the
Lake. Sir Launcelot rides to the rescue of Guenevere before her marriage to Arthur, Guenevere having been taken prisoner by a magician
who wishes to prevent her union with the king. The horse of Launcelot is killed and the knight has to travel in the cart of a peasant—to
his great shame. This, of course, is a pure interpolation of phantasy
of the famous district of Champagne. So the *Knight of the Wagon*
may be taken as typical of the change that was coming over the whole
spirit and practice of letters.

Before the thirteenth century the practice of letters—except for a
brief space during the Roman Empire—had been a matter of con-
tagions and singers who sang by impulse and because they had to.
The author as such hardly existed. He was part of an impulse or a
fashion carried away on a current of desire—the desire of himself to
express himself for the pure sake of expression and the desire of his

compatriots and contemporaries to hear the expression of the individuality of a favorite being. Already with the troubadours you had the postulation that literature might be waged for gain—for gain not in coin but in kind, in honors, even in emoluments attaching to a post. The troubadour according to the appreciation that he received was personally rewarded by a night's or a week's or even a year's board and lodging; he would receive from the lord of a castle gifts of old clothes which were very splendid and valuable affairs. Or he might receive an appointment—in the retinue of the *châtelaine*, or, if he happened to be able to write and cipher, one in the account-keeping department of the reigning sovereign. But the idea of direct payment for a piece of imaginative work was hardly yet known in the warm South.

The change which was to come was to be, as it were, a milestone between the literary practices and frames of mind of the old poetry and the modern narrative.

The output of Romansh* legends, whether in the form of *chansons* or *romans*, was between the twelfth and fourteenth centuries very great. The rewards for such a work, as we have said, took the form, even in late days, of old clothes, periods of maintenance, or clerkly jobs supposing the writer able to use pen and ink. But, gradually, the practice of payment at least for manuscripts came in. It came in, as it were, on the side. We have not been able to discover any traces of direct payment for a work of the imagination as such before the middle of the fifteenth century—or, indeed, until the art and industry of printing was well on its way. But a new literary side-wind began to blow towards the middle of the fourteenth century. Rulers began to find that metrical and rhymed records were less easy to understand than the same records in prose and in the language spoken by the common men in their realms. And the same idea invaded the minds of the commonalty itself. Thus, not only did the written Romansh speech

---

* The writer uses this term abitrarily to denote all North French literary products dating from before French hardened into a language. "Romance" is apt to cause confusion in a popular work of this sort if applied to anything but the "romantic movement" proper.

begin to tend to harden into the modern French of today but a class
of hackwriters arose whose job was to unrhyme the verse chronicles
of the *trouvère* and to render them in the common speech of the day.
These writers were paid, either in salaries or by the piece, by the lords
who commissioned their products. It is recorded of a clerk called
Birton that for one lord or another he thus as it were castrated upwards
of 90 romances and *chansons de gestes*, passing off several of them as
his own compositions. Amongst those that he treated were the songs
of *Roland*, of *Huon de Bordeaux*, of *Duolin de Mayence*, of the English *Ogier le Dane*, and of the highly sentimental semi-Teutonic romance of *Les Loherains* (the Lorrainers).

The activities of M. Birton obviously robbed the originals of some
of their interest and authenticity. That he much affected their literary
value this writer would not care to say. Neither the *chansons* nor the
romances of the North French school, with the exception of the
Chanson de Roland, ever caused him enthusiasm or even pleasure. The
Chanson de Roland is in places delightful merely because of the story,
the casting down of his gauntlet by Roland and the appearance of
the archangel to take up his challenge to the Almighty, and so on.
But even at that, this author is impressed more by wonder that the
naïve and unpracticed author of the song should have imagined anything so impressive and entertaining than with actual admiration for
the invention as such. The contrivance, that is to say, is impressive as
coming from the pen of a very early and unpracticed writer; it would
have been nothing very singular if it had been thought out by, on the
one hand, Sophocles, or, on the other, Mr. Henry James.

The fact is, if one wishes really to be sincere with oneself, the judgment of early naïvetés in the arts is one of extreme difficulty. One is—
this writer at least was—from his earliest days impressed with the idea
that every product of between the fifth and the beginning of the fourteenth century had about it a certain primitive glamour, a directness—
a quality of romance in fact, using that word in its most modern sense.

On the other hand, those whose fate it is to be brought up under
renaissance auspices are apt to be given the impression that everything
written after the fourth decade of the fifteenth century had a glow of
Parthenonic symmetry such as rendered every word, every chisel stroke

and every trace made by a paint brush semi-divine. Or, indeed, divine. It must be the Divine Leonardo, the Divine Michael Angelo, the Divine Pico de Mirandola, the Divine Goethe.

In either case, with approaching manhood we react, as is inevitable, against the tenets of our pastors, parents and professors. We feel, nevertheless, a little as if we are renegades if we go back on either the mediaeval or the renaissance masterpieces which overclouded our youth. So that it is with a sort of feeling that he *renie les dieux de sa jeunesse* that this writer sets down that he has found nearly all the literary productions of the *trouvères* and their successors dull and unreadable in the sense that reading should above all things be a pleasure. One is at times astonished by little bits of observation. There are tiny touches of domesticity in the romance of the *Loherains* as in the *Knight of the Wagon*, and expressions of beautiful sentiment in the *Ginglamour* of Marie de France. But Chrétien de Troyes and Marie de France are the bright lights that stand out of a period much as Swift stands out of the eighteenth and Chaucer of the fourteenth century. In neither case does it strike you as singular if you come upon a domestic passage in the midst of a fabulous romance, showing you a young girl seated under a tree in summer reading the *Roman de la Rose* to her father who to avoid rheumatism lies upon a silken rug, whilst behind him stands the mother commenting on the instances of love cited in that romance. But genius and passion at all times transcend the technical level of their day. And, instinctively or by means of study, these two writers had hit upon what is not so much a device as a truism founded on the human heart—that of the old epic idea that if you want to convince a reader of fabulous happenings—and still more if you wish to be readable and delightful—you must suddenly introduce passages of extreme naturalness into your full rapture of the supernatural. Consider how immensely the gloom and predestination of the story of Sisera and Jael is enhanced by the sudden introduction of the words:

> He asked for water and she gave him milk;
> She brought him butter in a lordly dish.

It is that technical knowledge or that instinct, if merely for the interest caused by contrasts, that differentiates between the authentic writer like Chrétien de Troyes and whoever else may have been the author of the *Roman des Loherains* or any other of the semi-commercial products of the *trouvères* and their successors. It is, nevertheless, the duty of the proper man to try reading not only the *Chanson de Roland* but *Duolin de Mayence* and a great many other of the romances and the *chansons de gestes* of the French and South German thirteenth and fourteenth centuries. He should, as far as possible, read them with a perfectly open mind, forgetting whether his grandfather told him that they were merely the muddy and repulsive excrescences of the putrifying centuries that preceded the renaissance or whether his maternal uncle has told him that all joy, all sweetness, all charity and delight came to an end when the Greek professors burst out of Constantinople—as this writer was quite literally and continuously told by his maternal uncles, Dante Gabriel and William Michael Rossetti.

In any case, the tract of time occupied by what it is convenient to call the literature of the *trouvères* lies across the path of the pilgrim who is pursuing the great highroad of humane literature and thought from, say, Lao-Tsze to, precisely, Mr. Henry James. It is not good to pass through a tract of country and know nothing of its features. Your rear will be unmapped. At any rate, with the passing of one great literature in Provence the Almighty saw fit to provide suffering mankind with yet another of the greatest modes of expression given by Him to us beings whose first necessity is that of self-expression.

Thus whilst the eyes of Giraud Riquier, the last of the troubadours, were closing in Aragon, the eyes of Villeharduoin were intent upon the vellum on which he was inscribing the first sentences of French prose. And after Villeharduoin with his dry, concise and admirably clear account of not merely the strategy but the tactics of the crusaders who took Constantinople, you had the almost supernatural character-drawing and much less dry prose of Joinville's projection of the person of St. Louis. Joinville wrote between 1224 and 1317, and St. Louis died on his crusade in Africa in 1270. And so with Froissart who lived from 1325 to 1400 the whole round table of French prose is complete and that wonderful gift to humanity is in the saddle for good.

Let us, then, before passing to other spheres, as we shall have to do immediately, compare the prose of Villeharduoin, Joinville and Froissart.

Joinville wrote a lighter French than Villeharduoin, the language having a little developed, and he had, as a writer, his wits much more about him. He could not only chronicle the ways of his time and nation—which was as much as the more austere Villeharduoin could do—but his character drawing of the saint whom he accompanied on his adventures is so vivid as to have a quality almost of weirdness. This writer at least cannot read *La Vie de St. Louis* without feeling that he actually sees the saintly king whose mother would not let him see his wife alone so that the young couple had to meet on the back staircase between their apartments. The saintly king moves and moves so ghostily in the corridors of his palace that this writer reading Joinville almost feels a certain discomfort as if he had intruded upon the private moments of one of the most singular of the saints. But, indeed, Joinville in his character drawing of kings and the great has somewhat of a Shakespearian character and, in addition, as we have said, he did not lose his head in the effort to set down the happenings of wars or the characters of noble personages but kept his eyes open, saw what there was about him and gives you charming descriptions of cities and the landscapes.

With Froissart, who was born twenty-one years after the death of Joinville, we come upon one of the really great writers of the world. His *Chronicle* is an immense fresco full of colors and lights and gilded and embossed corselets dented by the heavy strokes of war. And it is also to be remembered that he was a gracious and dainty poet of a great productiveness. His method of getting together his material was that of Herodotus. Having almost no written sources to quote, he must travel the world over to ask questions of the actors in political dramas and the leaders who had incited troops to battle. He became the Troubadour as Historian, voyaging from principality to principality, from stronghold to stronghold, from royal city to royal city, and gained his board and lodging, for himself and his single squire, not by telling tales but by asking for veridical stories from heroes or villains who should have taken part in the scenes that they related. And do not believe that either King Edward the Third of England or the black-smith of Pennebroth was backward in giving information, board and lodging or free horseshoes to a troubadour who, they were as per-fectly aware as you and I should have been, would make them front page news to all eternity. Something of Herodotus then but also some-thing of Malory for, if the *Chronicles of Froissart* have not the super-natural overtones of *Le Morte d'Arthur*, they have a quality of life that almost no other chronicle will be found to possess. Malory in fact painted for us exquisitely the dying world of a Celto-British civiliza-tion; Froissart shows us our modern world and language coming to life at a period almost as momentous for the one or the other as was the first century of the Christian era. And Froissart was not unaware that, differing from all chroniclers who preceded him, he was writing not only with clarity and vision, gayness and good humor, and with, except for a partiality for the King of England, a certain fairness—not only with those qualities, but with that other one of authority that raised him from the rank of chronicler to that of historian.

Leaving French prose at the moment, it is interesting to consider what we Anglo-Saxons were doing during those generations, and straightway we have the fact that Chaucer was born two years after Froissart, and died four years before he did. If we examine the prose rather than the verse of Chaucer, we find that in that pure branch of English literature he is relatively rough, and, as it were, nude, com-pared with his verse. In verse, in fact, Chaucer could do anything; he had a language of great subtlety and even of beauty which he could employ, and he employed it with the consummate ease of a ring master wielding his whip. Compare the very opening of the *Canterbury Tales* with the first paragraphs of the *Tale of Melibeus*:

> Whanne that April with his shoures sote
> The droughte of March hath perced to the rote,
> And bathed every veine in swiche licour,
> Of which vertue engendred is the flour;
> Whan Zephirus eke with his sote brethe

Enspired hath in every holt and hethe
The tendre croppes, and the yonge sonne
Hath in the Ram his halfe cours yronne,
And smale foules maken melodie,
That slepen alle night with open eye,
So priketh hem nature in hir corages;
Than longen folk to gon on pilgrimages . . .

with:

A young man called Melibeus, mighty and riche, begate upon his wif, that called Prudence, a doughter which that called was Sophie.

Upon a day befell, that he for his disport is went into the feldes him to playe. His wif and eke his doughter hath he laft within his hous, of which the dores weren fast yshette. Foure of his olde foo han it espied, and setten ladders to the walles of his hous, and by the windowes ben entred, and beten his wif, and wounded his doughter with five mortal woundes, in five soundry places; this is to say, in hire feet, in hire hondes, in hire eres, in hire nose, and in hire mouth; and leftem hire for dede, and wenten away.

Whan Melibeus retorned was into his hous, and sey al this meschef, he, like a mad man, rending his clothes gan to wepen and crie.

Prudence his wif, as fer forth as she dorste, besought him of his weping for to stint; but notforthy he gan to crie and wepen ever lenger the more . . .

Is not the one the fluid attempt of the consummate artist working with a quite good medium as against the same artist reduced to timidity by having to employ a form of language as to which you could say that neither he nor anyone else knew either its potentialities or its resources? For, as was the case with every other language, the populace laid early hands upon English as a medium for the songs and dances with which they could not dispense. The richer and more learned classes still used Latin or even Romansh for the expression of their personalities. French reached its perfection, for facility, in the *Institution* of Calvin who was born in 1509 and died in 1564; English prose reached its magniloquent apogee in the suppressed introduction to the Bible by Archbishop Warham, the last of the Roman Catholic Archbishops of England. He pre-deceased Calvin by 52 years. Or perhaps the real high-water mark of English prose, the sentences the most pregnant, the most suggestive ever written, not only in our own but in any other language will be found in the prose passages of Shakespeare. For what could you find to beat this passage:

Besides, there is no king, be his cause never so spotless, if it come to the arbitrement of swords, can try it out with all unspotted soldiers. Some peradventure have on them the guilt of premeditated and contrived murther; some, of beguiling virgins with the broken seals of perjury; some, making the wars their bulwark, that have before gored the gentle bosom of peace with pillage and robbery. Now, if these men have defeated the law and outrun native punishment, though they can outstrip men, they have no wings to fly from God: war is his beadle, war is his vengence; so that here men are here punished for before-breach of the king's laws in now the king's quarrel: where they feared the death, they have borne life away; and when they would be safe they perish: then if they die unprovided, no more is the king guilty of their damnation than he was before guilty of those impieties for the which they are now visited. Every subject's duty is the king's; but every subject's soul is his own. Therefore should every soldier in the wars do as every sick man in his bed, wash every mote out of his conscience: and dying so, death is to him an advantage; or not dying, the time was gained: and in him that escapes, it were not sin to think that, making God so free an offer, He let him outlive that day to see His greatness and to teach others how they should prepare.

That being said let us betake ourselves to the Italy of Guido Cavalcanti and of Dante.

CHAPTER FOUR

IN OUR more western branch of literature, in, let us say, our French-descended Anglo-Saxon branch of the art, we may consider ourselves to have reached 1340, the year perhaps of Chaucer's birth. From now on literature is to take to itself a different aspect. It will no longer be a spontaneous emanation of peoples or the courts of princes. It will much more self-consciously supply a demand. It will no longer be at all important in any branch of public activity; its functions in the state will appear more and more to narrow themselves. Chaucer was a necessary member of the court of the sovereign and wrote verses to satisfy himself and those princes who were his patrons when state business was not pressing. Shakespeare was an hostler's boy, holding the horses of the gentry when they came to the theatre in Southwark. Later he perceived that there was a profit in supplying mass-products to a populace whether they were tavern-hangers-on, citizens, or the gentry. And he supplied that to them, making a fortune and retiring, much as would anybody today who, being born in a log cabin, might invent a gadget whose income should carry him well on the way to political power.

Let us sum up for a little. We have seen the deathless literature of Provence shine like a flame in its limited triangle of territory; we have seen it physically and violently extinguished by Saint Dominic and his accomplices. Nevertheless, it remains there defined, bright, as many-faceted as a crown jewel—the product of a light-hearted and indefatigable technique.

For poets and the consumers of poetry divide themselves into two distinct classes. We might almost say that they so divide themselves geographically. You are acquainted with the rules of a technique; you write by these rules more or less spiritedly, and the more spiritedly you write according to these rules the more applauded by your hearers will you be. That takes place in all countries to the south and east of the English Channel. The Anglo-Saxon regards these things differently, between the North Foreland and the Golden Gate. If you find—which is eminently unlikely—anyone to talk, either with authority or merely as a consumer, about writing, the chances are that you will be told that everything lies in the content—the manner is of almost no importance. So you have Mr. Kipling writing:

> There are five and forty ways
> Of inditing tribal lays
> . . . And every single one of them is right.

That is merely the English soldier and gentleman putting literature in its place. Actually, there are five and forty thousand techniques, each one being right for at least one subject. And, what is even more important, for every subject there is only one best possible means of treatment. Arnaut Daniel or Bertran de Born making their canzos, their tenzos, or their *sirventes*, invented for each new one a new metric, a new vowel-coloring, a new frame of mind. So, though their subjects remained the same eternally, they achieved a new technical masterpiece with everything that they wrote, and these masterpieces it is impossible to resist. Even the most misty-brained of us northerners, once he has acquired a little knowledge of the Langue d'Oc, could not fail today to be rendered for the moment brighter, more musical, gayer, and therefore momentarily a better man, when he first read *La Franca Captenensa* of Arnaut de Merveil.

And the magic of this technique ran, as we have seen, like wildfire into the damp forests of Germany and France, and the Frankish kings. That Walther von der Vogelweide would never have written *Tandaradei*, or the *trouvères* or the jonglars their *gestes* or *fabliaux*, if Peire Vidal had never cured furs, ridden roads, or written hymns to La Louve of the two castles is more than the modest historian of letters would care to say. But that the *minnesingers* or northern French writers were preponderantly influenced by the exponents of the *gai sçaber* not even the most ferocious Teutophile would care to deny. And so you had the great mass of rhymed narrative of the *trouvères*, almost none of it of any great appeal to anyone not especially attuned to their works. And, gradually emerging from them the one or two long tales so admirably conceived, architected and beautified, *Aucassin and*

Nicolette and the *Flamenca* to which we shall return—or the *Palamon and Arcite* of Chaucer. So the western branch of literature proceeded on its way. But what of one of the homes of the muses, what had become of Italy?

For most of the world when you speak of the beginnings of Italian literature you speak of Guido Cavalcanti and Dante.

The history of Italy had been that of Provence and of the Narbonnais, only more cruel. On the face of it the existence of the great city of Rome should have kept Italy together. Italian territory is practically self-contained, guarded by perfectly distinct frontiers of rivers, mountains and sea. And the great tradition of the Romans which spread so far and remained so tenaciously beyond the bounds of Italy should have given to that country a spirit of unity and internal peace such as she was actually never to have until the nineteenth century had run two thirds of its course. Italy more disastrously than any other part of the Roman Empire had to pay for the fact that she lay round the ruins of Rome. A constant succession of plunderers, from Odovaker and Theodoric the Goth, to the Saracens, and, most cruel of all, the Lombards, harried and sacked all the territory between the Alps and the Tiber. And though the Saracens gave a certain culture to Sicily and towns to the south of Naples such as the famous Salerno, their culture was, on the whole, materialistic. They taught the Italian middle ages, as they taught the rest of the mediaeval world, astronomy, astrology, medicine, and the philosophy of Aristotle. Their influences were in no great sense either literary or imaginative. Italy was to wait for literarily imaginative influences until the days of the troubadours.

Apart from the sackings and plunderings, two major struggles went on side by side in that unfortunate territory. They were those between the Popes who were determined that there should be no Italian unity, and the German emperors or Frankish kings. These had the declared ambition to reëstablish the Roman Empire in its integrity under their rule. Underneath that, went on the struggle between the languages— between the classical Latin and that French of the Romansh which was to become Italian. This struggle was of course obscure and influenced by many singular side winds. Romansh and Italian were the products of a sort of continual attrition from the language of Cicero. You have to imagine, as if they were rats, the sharp tongues of the Romans or the Tuscans biting away continuously here a gender, there a case termination, and adding here and there an article or a preposition.

Instead of case terminations they used *"ad"* meaning "to" and *"de"* for "from" or "of." They cut in two the written word *"ille"* and made of it one pronoun and one article. *"Il"* and then *"le"*—and so, with *"il"* and *"le"* and *"de"* and *"à"* they had at least the French Romansh and the pure French tongue already started on their ways.

This process of disintegration had, of course, begun much earlier. It had already well begun by the days of Pliny the Younger, as inscriptions on the walls of Pompeii still testify. Where Cicero would have written:

> *Equum   bonum   habeo*
> A horse warranted sound in wind and   limb   I have

the Roman grooms, gladiators, barbers or fig-sellers said:

> *Ego habeo   bellum   caballum*
> I   have   a good-looking beast of burden

The language thus began to approach our own in structure whilst becoming tautological and vaguer. For it is obviously tautological to say *"ego habeo"* when *"habeo"* alone means the same thing.

In Italy which, as we have already said, surrounded Rome, there were, by the thirteenth century, many folk dialects, each one showing different variations from the original Latin. But the governing, official, learned, and wealthy classes throughout the Peninsula hung desperately on to classical Latin as if it had been a proud, personal heritage.

Thus, there existed in Italy between the fifth and the thirteenth centuries a whole body of non-literary writings on every subject under the sun from agriculture to astrology; but during all that period hardly a word of imaginative literature in Italian is discoverable. Indeed, the earliest authentic verse in Italian was a *sirvente* written partly in the Sicilian dialect by, of all people in the world, Raimbaut de Vaqueiras, a troubadour whose acquaintance we have already made. That is easily explicable.

Whilst early thirteenth century Italy was producing and glorying in an immense, it desiccated, body of middle class and priestly writing, the lower classes, contrary to the usual habits of populaces, were producing no discoverable regional music or folksongs. If they sang to their dancing, they made use of songs in a Latin derived from those of the period that saw the production of the *Pervigilium Veneris*. Thus, a sudden inrush of poets practicing complicated and gay metrical and lyrical effects, to the theme always of neglected love—such an eruption must of necessity prove immensely infectious. One saw something of the sort in the earlier decades of the present century when both England and the United States, having no very marked music or verse or song-and-dance of their own, were suddenly invaded by African jungle effects of both music and words, and fell before them as they might have fallen before a vast infection.

Similarly, the music and song of Provence fell upon mediaeval Italy. But, being essentially aristocratic, its influences extended only very faintly outside the innumerable Italian small courts and independent cities. Its vogue, nevertheless, was widespread enough. . . . You had in Italy the very country of all countries for song and love lyrics, but it was an Italy completely starved of those necessities of the proper life. Suddenly, a saint and his bullies exterminated a beautiful, musical civilization in the territory that marched immediately upon the north Italian borders. So the great majority of such Provençal poets went to Aragon; some to Germany; a few even to the English court. But the majority fled to Italy.

At just that date, without that eruption, the odds were that Italian lyric verse would have become a branch of the great literature of the Mahometan East. The successive Norman and Arab conquerors and re-conquerors of Sicily and of Italy south of Naples, found themselves, when they were not actually fighting, to be perfectly able to live peaceably side by side. And the Mahometan civilization being infinitely the more ordered, luxurious, enjoyable, and humane, it was that civilization that colored the lives of those regions. At this date—almost exactly that of St. Dominic's Battle of Muret that destroyed Provence—there had come to the throne of the German Holy Roman Empire one of the most extraordinary and epoch-making sovereigns that ever decorated the high places of this earth. This was Frederick II (the Hohenstaufen) who in addition to being emperor by quasi-election was also the hereditary king of the two Sicilies. He had, moreover, been actually born in Sicily of an Italian mother, and his youth had been passed in that full luxury of Saracenic civilization. It was a civilization of cushionings, fountains, rare viands, luscious fruits, perfumes, music, harems, eunuchs, and inner courtyards of a lacelike magic of architecture. And none of these delights were grudged to the young Sicilian prince. But it was also a civilization of an intensive erudition, of erotic tales and innumerable lyrics expressing the passions and despairs of love.

This civilization Frederick cherished in his personal dominions during his whole life. And its literature and its learning he spread passionately throughout the other dominions of which he was the temporal overlord. It was he who established Italian universities like Padua and Bologna whose function was to be the spreading of the doctrines of Aristotle, the beloved of the Saracens. To them he presented the works of that philosopher that the Arabs had translated in their entirety into their own language, and it had been at his behest that they had translated them further . . . from Arabic into Latin so that they should be comprehensible to the rest of the Western world. And the letters with which he accompanied his gifts of the manuscripts to universities and to princes breathe a real passion for learning and the arts and for their dissemination throughout the world. Today they read very touchingly.

For it is impossible not to waste, however tantalizingly, a minute or two in speculation as to where we should sit today could Frederick II have realized his civilizing and pacific ambitions. He would have then left behind him a dominion on a Roman *cadre*, a Latin-Oriental-Romanized Teutonic Roman Empire spreading from the Rhine by way of the Danube down through all the peninsula that ends in Sicily. It might have lasted; it might not have. Nevertheless, its great tradition would have remained—a tradition establishing a mode of peaceful penetration, an opening for the Northern hordes that unceasingly sigh for possession of the shores of the Mediterranean.

And that comity of nations would have had all the better chance of survival because blood was not the argument of that emperor. . . . He was not a conqueror, but a hereditary and elective ruler . . . with a passion for spreading culture and thought throughout the world.

His dreams were to be shattered by the Papacy, grasping at universal temporal power. That is an historical fact as to which it is useless to comment. It was, no doubt, the duty of the Popes to sigh for not merely the spiritual but also the material resources of the Heritage of Peter.

But what is important for us was that outpouring of the troubadours that succeeded the Papal bid for the hegemony of Provence in the early thirteenth century. In Germany and in Frederick's Italian dominions outside the Sicilies their aesthetic influences speedily eclipsed the Oriental strains that Frederick had sought to introduce. In Sicily itself they had to be content to adapt themselves to the rare meats, cushionings and be-fountained courts and to occupy their soft leisures with making poems in the Italian vulgar tongue or contending with tenzos and *sirventes* against the emperor himself and the numerous ruling marquises of his realm. The *sirventes* of the first Frederick receiving Bérenger des Baux had been spirited enough. But it can hardly be advanced that the stanzas by Frederick II beginning:

> *Valimente mi date, donna fina,*
> *Che lo mio core adesso a voi s'incline,*

(meaning that his heart turns always toward her), or, indeed, any other of his verses equal that poem of Frederick I beginning, as we well remember:

> *Plasz me cavaler frances . . .*

Nor, indeed, are any of them to be regarded as a real expression of his personality, his pride, or his passions. His poems run exactly along the lines, as far as subject went, of the most sickly-sweet canzos of Guillem de Cabestanh. And, since he maintained at the same time a well-filled and well-guarded harem and more than one queen escorted duly by eunuchs, it is impossible to attach much credence to his sighs over the cruelty of a disdainful fair one whose humble vassal, in due Provençal fashion, he declared himself to be. But the exiled troubadours spread themselves out all over Italy at one court and another, most frequently at that of the Marquises of Montferrat, and there, as at the court of the great family of the Estes in Ferrara, they found new patrons in the princes themselves against whom to write tenzos and to vie, side by side with them, in writing aubades to imaginary, disdainful, ladies. They spread in addition southward to Pisa, to Florence.

Peire Vidal got as far as Malta and stayed there, and Raimbaut de Vaqueiras remained to his death in Sicily. As a result, Provençal being an easy language for those of Latin minds, poetry in Provençal with the lyric forms of the troubadours went on being written by the later aristocracy and idle rich all over Italy for well over a century.

This, of course, only indirectly helped the development of the Italian vulgar tongue. But those who were concerned saw at least that a democratized and simplified form of Latin—the Romansh language —was admirably suited for the poetic needs of princes, nobility, gentry, and great municipal officials. And if one such vulgarized version of this Latin could be so used, why not another? Moreover, the emperor himself had expressed his conventional Provençal longings in poems written in the Italian vernacular.

The situation, then, in Italy during the first decades of the thirteenth century was this: the Church and those who supported her, the clergy, the learned, the essayists, the lawyers, the astronomers, went on turning out in Latin learned works on their different subjects until a very great body of writings had seen the light. And, as far as what is called learning is concerned, the Roman writers of Latin disseminated their type of civilization throughout the world. Writers like Bouncompagno made themselves ridiculous by vowing that their Latin was more correct and their styles more vigorous than those of Cicero. But really great scholars like Lanfranc or really great churchmen like St. Anselm, leaving their spiritual birthplace in Rome, established themselves the one in Normandy and the other in Canterbury, and there set up schools of philosophy, polemics, or theology. These schools became of such efficiency and such tradition that the pupils outstripped the very masters. It was no longer to Rome that you went either to lose your faith or to gain learning. The world center for medicine in the middle ages had long been in Salerno, and now to study law at its best you must go to Bologna, for theology to the Sorbonne in Paris, and for a real, just, appreciative sense of classical authors you must go to the University of Orleans.

Another poetic invasion of Italy—that of the *trouvères*—almost synchronized with, if it did not precede, that of the troubadours. But, since this was an invasion rather of subjects than of the poets themselves, it is more difficult exactly to date its beginnings. What it meant was that all the subjects, all the stories of the North French, Norman, the Welsh, and the German romantic writers spread with extreme rapidity and thoroughness through the whole at least of Northern Italy. And not only the romances and tales of Western Europe: all the magic and romantic stories of the East met them on their arrival, coming from the South. Innumerable collections of tales in prose began to be made all over Italy towards the middle of the thirteenth century. Thus, not only in these literary remains shall we find traces of all the stories of the *Arabian Nights*; but, even in the most popular of them all, the *Tales of the Five Sages*, we have the exact reproduction of a Hindoo variant—more complicated and more refined—of the *Arabian Nights*. This story is that of an Indian prince who has been educated by the five greatest sages of India. He finds himself, when grown up, rather in the position of Joseph in the house of Potiphar. His father's wife, his own stepmother, makes advances that he virtuously repulses. His stepmother then accuses him to his father of having made advances to her and he is immediately condemned to death. The five sages then come to his rescue. Each tells a tale which, continuing till the dawn, has to be interrupted and recommenced on the morrow. But, to give variety to the form, after each of the sages has spoken, the stepmother renews her accusation against the young man in the form of a tale which also continues to the dawn. The Indian story teller and his Italian imitator thus achieve a variety in form that is in itself extremely refreshing.

All the Italian stories, however, are told in prose dialects of the vernacular. They cover an enormous field. The most famous of all these compilations—the *Cente Novelle Anticche,* popularly better known as the *Novellino*—is an immense ragbag of every type of romantic story from every portion of the then known world. You have the story of *Tristan and Iseult,* of *Roland at Roncesvaux,* of *Sir Lancelot du Lak;* a whole set of tales about the taking of Troy; six or seven of the stories of Scheherazade; stories from the Old Testament and stories from the Provençal vaguely suggesting the beauties and cheerfulnesses of *Aucassin and Nicolette.*

These collections are written in every sort of Italian dialect mingled with words of classical and corrupt Latin, of Provençal, of the Langue d'Oï; nevertheless, one recognizes the first flowering of that magic gift called tale-telling that was to flourish in later years in the *Decameron* of Boccaccio, the *Heptameron,* the *Cent Nouvelles Nouvelles* and not a few of the tales of Chaucer himself.

The more heroic of the *chansons de gestes* were reproduced in verse, and, what is more singular, translators would translate the North French or Norman version not only into Provençal and Italian dialects, but also into variations of North and Norman French of their own.

You have to have, then, an image of an entire Italy struggling as it were in an agony for expression against the network of language that was her inheritance from the classical language of Rome herself. And the struggle took all the longer in that the cultural official language of the world was the Latin of the church services. Thus every man, whether he knew or used the vernacular, must of necessity be acquainted with the Latin of the Vulgate.

The effect left on the mind is that of an immense confusion—and it is just as well that that should be the effect, for unless one should have a special predilection for that sort of pursuit, no particular purpose would be served by the minute study of this philological maelstrom into whose turmoil there entered the languages, the imaginings and the political passions of half a world. There remain to us two singular facts.

On the face of it, you would not say that the greatest of all works in any tongue would come at the moment when that language first emerged, as it were, dripping from the whirlpool of its birth. But within the space of a century that was to happen not only in Italy but in England. You were to see then Guido Cavalcanti as the precursor of Dante and then Dante himself: but Langley, more often called Langland, the precursor—or, indeed, the almost exact contemporary—of Chaucer, and then Chaucer himself.

Let us make a little chronological table. The Emperor Frederick II died in 1250, Cavalcanti being at that date aged twenty-five; and Dante was not born until 1265 when Cavalcanti was already forty. Cavalcanti wrote his famous:

> *Donna mi priegha perch'i volglio dire*
> *D'un accidente che sovente efero*

in 1290 when Dante was twenty-five and he himself forty years older.

The writer has made a chronological table for his own purposes at this point. It may be useful to the reader:

France	*Italy*	*England*
Villeharduoin (1150–1212)		
	Frederick II (1212–1250)	
Joinville (1224–1317)	Guido Cavalcanti (1225–1300)	
	Dante (1265–1321)	
Thibaud III de Champaigne (fl.* 1301)		
	Petrarch (1304–1374)	Gower (1313–1408)
	Boccaccio (1313–1375)	Langland (1332–1400)
		Chaucer (1340–1400)
Froissart (1338–1404)		
Christine de Pisan (fl. 1367)		
Charles d'Orleans (fl. 1415)		
Villon (1431–c 1500)		
Comines (1445–1509)		
	Ariosto (1474–1533)	
Calvin (1509–1564)		
	Tasso (1544–1595)	
		Shakespeare (1564–1616)

These dates are interesting when we come to consider the rather

* This abbreviation signifies "flourished."

vexed question of the influence of Cavalcanti upon the author of the *Divine Comedy*.

For the moment, however, let us pay attention to the parallelism of the appearances of Dante and Chaucer on their respective scenes. In each case these two greatest of poets made their appearances in the very foam of a language struggling for birth. That is to say that both English and Italian were hardly definitely in existence when Chaucer wrote his earlier lyrics and tales and Dante his earlier minor works. The English of Chaucer existed as a compromise between the French of the Angevin courts and the variant Middle High German, colloquially called Anglo-Saxon, with very faint traces of the early occupation of the country by Cymbric and Norse tribes. In each case, they were preceded in their countries by no very remarkable precursors. As we have seen, there were practically no great English poets or writers of any kind before the birth of Chaucer. There had been, of course, British chroniclers like the author of *Annales Cambriae*, who wrote in Latin in the last decades of the tenth century, or the *Black Book* of Carmarthen, which was written in Welsh and continued at least till the death of Madog, Prince of Powys in 1159, or even Robert of Gloucester, who had preceded Chaucer by perhaps 100 years and whose chronicle contains so many passages of rare beauty—like the history of Lear upon which Shakespeare drew—as to force one to say that he was an historian rather than a chronicler. For it is convenient to consider, at any rate for one's private purposes, that the difference between the chronicle and the history is that the latter is the former conceived in a spirit of some humaneness. Thus, such chroniclers as Froissart with his story of Eustache St. Pierre, or Robert of Gloucester with his account of the death of Lear had so large a proportion of the rendering of human surroundings and vicissitudes that their works may well be considered achievements of no mean order in literary art. They did, however, nothing towards helping in the development of the English language as written by Chaucer.

Similarly with Dante. There had existed, as we have seen, for several centuries before his death a considerable body of writing in Latin in the way of chronicles and scientific works, but there existed also in the vulgar tongue a certain *corpus* of, particularly Florentine, written matter, municipal and domestic accounts and such ana. These are not without their interest. We may suppose no subject has been so continuously interesting to humanity as the cost of living is. And there has come down to us from the early thirteenth century a book in sheets called the *"Ricordi di una Familia Senese"*—the family accounts of one Matasala of the great family Di Spinello of Sienna. The prices there recorded would be sufficient to make a modern housewife weep, since it would appear that you could buy a brace of ducks for a cent. But that is scarcely literary, and the first traces of a literary prose of which we can be certain—for forged thirteenth century manuscripts are extremely common in Italy—the first instance, then, of prose of the imagination is that of the *Novellino* to which we have already referred. This would appear to have been compiled about 1260, Dante having been born in 1265. And the few poets who flourished roughly contemporarily with Dante were none of them, except Guido Cavalcanti, much his seniors. Thus, though we do not know with any certainty the dates of their birth, we know that the Cecco Angioleri died in 1312, that Cene dalla Chitarra still flourished in 1314, and Fulgore da Gemignano in 1315. Hardly any of these subsidiary poets is of any literary interest except for those who have a special love for the sort of verse that they produced. But nearly all the most minor poets using the vulgar tongue have a great deal of interest as casting light on the history of conditions of Florence of that date. That—next to Athens—most marvelous of all cities for its arts and civilization was already, as we start the century before the birth of Dante, in a position of great prosperity . . . and of some temporary quietude. Her marvelous buildings were beginning to go up and were some of them already in place; her commerce spread to the bounds of the then habitable globe and the fame of her painters even further and more enduringly. Her civilian life was of an extreme urbanity; she welcomed strangers of distinction with spectacles and gifts of unexampled magnificence. With church and profane feasts, her holidays lasted the year round. Even the stern grammarian Buoncompagno, whose contempt for Cicero we have already recorded, deigns to notice a festal habit that was peculiar to Italy.

Certain societies of young people [he says, in 1215] are being formed in many parts of Italy. They adopt names such as the society of Falcons, the Lions, the Round Table, and the like. And although this custom is spread over the whole of Italy yet it is specially prevalent in Tuscany, seeing that here it would be hard to find young people in any town who are not bound together by oath.

These societies of the young were called *"brigate"*—as you should say, "brigades." Thus, Villani in his chronicle writes in 1283—when Dante was eighteen—that a society of young people was formed under the auspices of the powerful de' Rossi family and under the leadership of Girolamo de' Rossi who had titled himself the Lord of Love. And this society dressed itself entirely in white silks and velvets and, says Villani:

> devoted itself to nothing but games and pleasures, dances of ladies and knights and burghers who joyfully and merrily marched through the town with trumpets and other instruments and came together at banquets.*

This Court of Love, as it was called after the more famous feasts of the troubadours, lasted for two months and during that time it was visited by noble strangers from all over the West.

The number of these societies in Florence was also legion, the most famous or the most egregious of all being the *Brigatta Spindericcia* —the brigade of spendthrifts. This body of young men got together a hardly computable sum—say, roughly speaking, fourteen times a quarter of a million dollars—and purchased with it a great house in a park on the banks of the Arno, and in ten months they had squandered all their money. And, their parents apparently refusing further supply, they were according to Fulgore reduced to indigence for the rest of their lives. The richness of their cooking was so abnormal that several of their dishes, notably the *Garofano*, were mentioned by Dante

---

* Villani, VII, 89. Oelsner's translation. Cf. also Boccaccio's account of these societies in his story of Guido Cavalcanti. *Decameron,* Third Day.

in his *Inferno*. The brigades were, however, by no means all so spend-thrift, and Fulgore himself chronicles none of their pleasures that would have been incompatible with a certain refinement. He represents those companions as passing their time living merrily, delighting in the goodly fruits of the earth each in her due season, hunting, fishing, jousting, and the gentle sports of love, dancing and games, wandering through fresh gardens and beside green springs. . . ."

The chief theme, indeed, of the minor poets who preceded all the contemporaries of Dante was, when they were not engaged in quarreling among themselves—or with Dante himself, for that matter— these scenes of pleasure and cultured magnificence. Nevertheless, from time to time, one or the other of them would be moved by the turbulences and the internecine strife that ran as an undercurrent of all those glories—the one or the other of them would be moved to verse of an extreme bitterness and some power. Thus, after the Battle of Monti Cattini when the Florentine Guelphs and Robert of Naples were completely destroyed by the Tuscan Ghibellines, Fulgore, who was an enthusiastic supporter of the Guelphs, wrote his three famous sonnets in which he deplores the incompetence and inferiority of his party leaders. In an almost more famous canto he renounces the praise and service of God because He had not supported the Guelphs with His right arm when their own abilities had betrayed them. . . .

> *Eo non ti lodo, Dio, e non ti adoro*
> *E non ti prego e non ti rengrazio*

These mediaeval civil wars in Italy had, nevertheless, not the ferocity nor yet the devastating effects of those that we stage today. The Guelphs or the Ghibellines, representing roughly on the one hand the German emperors, on the other the French kings, fought not to destroy the cities that they desired to inhabit and possess and not, indeed, to exterminate their neighbours or brothers, but principally to expel them—as Cavalcanti and Dante and how many more were expelled from Florence. The presence of ruling princes, the emissaries of king or emperor drew them into the open and they fought pitched battles. But the normal struggles of the two parties had rather the aspect of municipal elections at which both parties should bear personal arms without employing cannon or torches to destroy the churches or municipal buildings. . . . They had at least digested the lesson that, as we have seen, Croesus taught the great Cyrus—that if you let your troops and supporters ravage and burn the cities you capture there will remain precious little for you.

So these tumults were insufficient to make the writing of poetry as a pursuit impossible and, all in all, Florence presented that aspect of flourishing tranquillity that would seem to be most usually propitious to the muses.

We come, then, to one of those stupendous mornings of human thought that, appearing from time to time and at great intervals, restore to us, in the general drabness and imbecility of the world, some of the respect for humanity that otherwise we must surely and definitely lose. The *Divine Comedy* of Dante stands out above the welter of sadism and ferocity of its era as the Cathedral of Chartres stands out and watches over all the plains of France and as the more gay Cathedral of Amiens dominates those terrible witnesses of human ferocity and madness—the fields behind the Somme. . . .

Indeed, it is to the cathedrals of the middle ages that you must go to parallel the fruits of the imaginings of Dante Alighieri. You have in one as in the other the almost incomprehensible mixture of sublimity and the infinitely ferocious. You have the soaring spire and, just as beneath all the surfaces of those spires you have the grotesque and obscene representation of monks, apes, salamanders, fiends—so with the imaginations of the sublime in the *Paradiso* you have in the *Divine Comedy* the hideous ferocities of Malebolge and the following, deeper circles of Hell.

These great products of the human imagination are rare, indeed— the immensely great ones. The really fine cathedrals of the world do not number more than a dozen. The immense cathedral-like works of the literary imagination, not nearly so many. When you have said the names of the *Odyssey*, of the Bible, of *Oedipus Tyrannus*, of the *Divine Comedy* itself and the great and little testaments of Villon you have almost exhausted the catalogue of the great and omniscient works of humanity. . . . You might, if you liked, add Rabelais.

The dominating quality of these writings is precisely their omniscience. It is unnecessary for Boccaccio to tell you that Dante knew all knowledge. You feel that with every line that he writes. Only a man tranquilly and consummately sure that there was no department of human or spiritual life that he could not confront with equanimity and for which with an equal equanimity he could not find the solution—only such a man could have written any one of the lines of the canzone which begins: *"Io son venuto al punto della rota."* And it is not merely to that most consummate of all his works that one must go to get the conviction that this man is consummate in every word that he wrote. Nor is it a question merely of the content or meaning. It is the way in which the words sit, as a painter would say, on the page. There is nothing particularly unusual or surprising in the line from the first canzone of the *Vita Nuova: "Donne che avete intelleto d'amore"* or in the description of the daybreak that Dante sees on the banks of Lethe or the costume into which he puts Beatrice on her appearance in Heaven:

Sovra candido vel cinta d'oliva
Donna m'apparve sotto verdi manto
Vestita di color di fiamma viva

which is in Rossetti's translation:

Over her snow-white veil with olive cinct
Appeared a lady under a green mantle
Vested in color of the living flame

conveys no emotion at all and is almost barbarous in its harshness. Yet the beauty of the Italian, the exquisite nature of the Italian vulgar tongue and the definiteness of the language conduce to an excitement that makes that celestial meeting one of the great dramatic points of the world. So that the crucial words *"Guardami ben, ben son, ben son Bea-*

trice!"* ("Look at me closely, I am in truth, I am in truth Beatrice!")
have at once the triumphant quality of Piers Plowman's "There the
poor dare plead," and the extraordinary dramatic note of Webster's
"Cover her face; mine eyes dazzle; she died young. . ." which all
seem to the present writer to be the most dramatic words ever written
in the English language.

The *Divine Comedy*, then, occupies itself with the journey of a
bereaved lover through Hell and Purgatory to his meeting with the
beloved woman on the verge of Heaven. It becomes necessary to talk
of the quality that the mediaeval writers called love. This is a phenomenon so different from the modern Anglo-Saxon conception of the passions that it is only with difficulty that we today can begin to understand
the attitude of Dante or of his contemporaries. So that one is tempted
to say that the love of Dante for Beatrice like the love of Peire Vidal
for La Louve was purely allegorical or symbolic. That is dangerous
doctrine but let it stand for a moment in order to make the matter
plainer. Our curious Anglo-Saxon confusion of the sexual and spiritual
sides of the passion is apt to make it very difficult for us to believe that
whole races like the Chinese and whole periods like the middle ages
completely separated those two sides of what we consider to be a composite passion but that they considered to be two completely separated
attributes of humanity. Accustomed to think of a purely spiritual love
as being part of a quite familiar world, the mediaeval writers—and,
more particularly, the mediaeval Italian writers—could, with perfect
equanimity, write whole epics of love story that had in it no carnal side
at all. To put the matter exaggeratedly for the sake of clearness, the

* *Del Purgatorio,* Canto XXX:

> *"Guardami ben: ben son, ben son Beatrice:*
> *Come degnasti d'accedere al Monte?*
> *Non sapei tu che que è l'uom felice?"*

The Rev. Henry Cary's translation:

> "Observe me well. I am, in sooth, I am
> Beatrice. What! and hast thou deign'd at last
> Approach the mountain? Knewest not, O man!
> Thy happiness is here?" Down fell my eyes.

serious Italian writer considered that spiritual love alone could be dignified by the name of that passion, the sexual act having no more to do
with it than eating or drinking. Once that is firmly established in the
mind and the slightly absurd aspect of a poet who could see the lady
for once in the street and pass his whole subsequent life in lamenting
their separation—this slightly willful absurdity disappears altogether.
It is to be wished that we could say definitely and once for all that
Beatrice was purely an allegory—that she represented an idea or an
ideal such as that of the Christian church or, say, the philosophy of
Aristotle. The whole attitude of Dante, his confessions of infidelity to
his Beatrice, and still more his Beatrice's almost acid reproaches for
those infidelities on the occasion of their meeting in Heaven—all these
things would at once become plain and recognizable.

And whole schools of the learned have held that view. It was, indeed, only finally discredited and abandoned, about 1900, after a long
duel between Francesco d'Ovidio, Antonio Lubin, Fornacciari, Perez,
and of course a whole host of German commentators from Gaspary
downwards. This controversy was at its height in 1894 and died with
the defeat of the allegorists about 1900. It had, indeed, been of long
duration. Even Boccaccio, whilst establishing that Beatrice Portinari
was an actual, living and married lady, who died in childbirth at
the age of twenty-five—even Boccaccio was inclined to see in Dante's
rendering of her a figure that was nothing more or less than a Filosofia. And one is tempted to be hardened in that view when one considers that Dante himself talks of the other lady whom he met in
the street and with whom he confesses to have been unfaithful to
Beatrice—as precisely, a Madonna Filosofia.

Still, the learned are probably in the right of it and, in writing of
Beatrice, Dante was as it were embroidering in the air around a
real married lady who really died young. We have, in confirmation of
that, his poem on the death of Beatrice, one of his most felt achievements, so that it would seem that by the nature of his work itself we
are forbidden to consider that the *Divine Comedy* is a purely allegorical work.

Nevertheless, in our private minds and acknowledging that we are wrong, we may still regard Beatrice for the greater part of the work as an allegory. In that case, we should arrive at a frame of mind not unfamiliar to that of a great number of Anglo-Saxon poets. One of these will make it far more clear than did Dante in the poem that he is writing of a perfectly clear and tangible lady. He will then go on to attribute to her all sorts of fantastic, supernatural and unreal fiction.

So we may consider that Dante was presenting to his reader and postulating to himself the perfectly real lady, and went on to attribute to her—and it must be remembered that this happened after her death—purely arbitrary mystic functions. These, however, are to be taken as similitudes and not verities. And yet they may well be the higher verities.

It is to be remembered that when it was a matter of truth the mediaeval mind was no one-ply mind. Today one truth would exclude all other truths as to the subject with which it concerns itself. But the mediaeval mind could let all the gods of Olympus coincide with the personages of the Christian verities; nay, fantastic as it may seem, a Dante or a Chaucer can even compare the efficacities of Olympus as against those of Paradise. Thus, when Dante wishes to express the utmost brightness of the Paradisaical light he can find nothing better to do than to compare it with the legendary sun of Ovid's *Metamorphoso*. As this, in Canto IX:

> E'en the sun's (light) itself
> Were poor to this; that chariot of the sun,
> Erroneous, which in blazing ruin fell
> At Tellus' prayer devout, by the just doom
> Mysterious of all-seeing Jove.*

And thus Chaucer, in the *Merchant's Tale*, having devoted innumerable passages to Priapus and Pluto and Proserpine and Argus, as if they were all real beings, suddenly, in lines 10013-10017, paraphrases the "Song of Solomon:"

* Cary's translation.

The turtles vois is herd, myn owen swete;
The winter is gon, with all his raines wete.
Come forth now with thin eyen colombine.
Wel fairer ben thy brests than ony wine.
The garden is enclosed all about.

And Dante sees nothing incongruous in letting Virgil guide him through a Judaeo-Christian Inferno and Purgatory into the very presence of purely Aryan Christian angels, nay into that of Beatrice's soul—though it is true that, at that vision, the spirit of Virgil melts, as it were, away. So that we may regard—and still more we may consider Dante as regarding—the spirit of Beatrice as the very quintessence of the Christian faith. Thus, when she reproaches him with his infidelity and he himself acknowledges his unfaithfulness with the Madonna Filosofia whom he saw one day in a window, we might regard Beatrice, in that aspect, as being under the quintessence of Christian mysticism as set against some form or other of one of the Greek philosophies. As if Dante had for a time turned aside from the faith and had dallied with the metaphysical ideals of the Stoics or the Epicureans.

Nevertheless, we cannot regard Beatrice as being all through allegorical.

The mysterious passage about allegory in the *Vita Nuova*:

> It were a shameful thing if one should rhyme under the semblance of metaphor or rhetorical similitude, and afterwards, being questioned thereof, should be unable to rid his words of such semblance, unto their right understanding.

would appear to mean that if a poet once launches himself upon an allegory it would be shameful if he did not stick to it consistently throughout his work. But, indeed, the passage is susceptible of many other explanations and the distinguished commentator Perez interprets the passage as meaning: "Shame to him who does not speak always in allegory." Which, of course, is a probably willful misunderstanding.

Nevertheless, interpret the passage how you may, it will still have the air of implying that inconsistency in matters allegorical is a shameful thing.

That would seem to get rid altogether of the belief that the Beatrice of the *Divine Comedy* is a figure purely allegorical, symbolizing orthodox Christian faith as against the pagan musings of the great philosophers. For, had Beatrice been nothing but a form of faith, there could have been no separation between the poet and herself. Faith is a thing that you have always with you—except, of course, when you dally with other philosophies. But Dante toyed only for a short time with his Madonna Filosofia and, in consequence, his Madonna Beatrice could only have been expelled from his thoughts for a similarly short period.

It is perhaps a good thing that we know very little of Dante the man. It is, indeed, always a good thing when we know very little of the personal lives of poets. Their work then occupies the position that it should in the public mentality. How much has not the poetry of Shelley suffered because of unnumbered volumes of chatter about Harriet; and how much has the figure of the great writer of English that Dr. Johnson was, not suffered because of the innumerable, relatively comic anecdotes of Boswell.

Of Dante, then, we know very little. But we do know just enough to be aware that he was, personally, what you might call an ordinary man—*un homme moyen sensuel*. His detractors—and, of course, he had many since he was a vigorous politician—his detractors then, like Cene dalla Chitarra have tried to assure us that he was, at least, incompetent, gluttonous and too fond of money. But, since we have nothing but their adjectival accusations, we are left with nothing but the liberty to think that where there was a good deal of smoke some at least minor conflagration may have occurred. And, indeed, Dante when he occasionally talks about food—as in the case of the famous *Garofano* of the *Inferno* and from the fact that one of his most intimate friends was Succi, reputed to be one of the greatest gourmets of the day—may very well, like Confucius himself, have taken an interest in how his food was prepared. And does not he say: "How salt his bread who treads upon another's stair!" in reference to his exile at the court of Can Grande della Scala? And there are passages enough in his poems to let one see that he was not entirely unacquainted with carnal love. *"Così nel via parler voglio esser aspro"* is as human and energetic an expression of physical passion as will be found in the work of any other poet of a vigorous complexion. The very vocabulary is rough, unusual, and expresses, as it were, agitation of no mean degree. And, if more calm, the *sestina*—an unusual form that Dante borrowed from its inventor Arnaut Daniel—is human enough in the desire that it expresses. And the *canzone*, at least, is addressed to a quite identifiable lady called Pietra. And did he not eventually marry Gemma dei Donati and have children like anyone else? Indeed, he was in addition an ardent and embittered politician and capable of hatred of an almost unexampled virulence. He was also a good musician, he painted well, he was an accomplished theologian and a fine linguist. He fought with distinction at the Battle of Campo Dinno and in other skirmishes against the Ghibellines, and is said by his knowledge of tactics to have contributed greatly to those victories. His contemporaries considered him to possess all knowledge and women shivered when they saw his bronzed face in the street, for was he not reputed every night to visit Hell? We might add, parenthetically, that the women of Rye in England shivered when they met the late Mr. Henry James in narrow streets of that town, because they considered that he had all knowledge, that he could look you through to the backbone and that he went on journeys with the foul fiends. So little does humanity change in its attitude towards those reputed to be great writers or thinkers.

Dante, then, in the estimation of his age, was more than a proper man, for in the thirteenth century in Italy as in England they considered that a proper man was one who had built a house, planted trees, written a book and begotten a son. For the rest, says Boccaccio in his little biography of Dante:

Our poet was of middle height; his face was long, his nose

aquiline, his jaw large, and his under lip protruding somewhat beyond the upper. His eyes rather large than small; his hair and beard thick, crisp, and black, and his countenance sad and pensive. His gait was grave and gentlemanlike, and his bearing, in public or private, wonderfully composed and polished. In meat and drink he was most temperate. Seldom did he speak unless spoken to, though he was most eloquent. In his youth he delighted in music and singing, and was intimate with all the musicians and singers of the day. He was of marvelous capacity and the most tenacious memory; inclined to solitude and fond of study when he had time for it.

We may as well add here the sonnet in which Guido Cavalcanti "rebukes Dante for his way of life after the death of Beatrice." It should be remembered that Cavalcanti was forty years older than Dante, who at the time was only about twenty-five.

> I come to thee by daytime constantly,
>> But in thy thoughts too much of baseness find:
>> Greatly it grieves me for thy gentle mind,
> And for thy many virtues gone from thee.
> It was thy wont to shun much company,
>> Unto all sorry concourse ill inclined:
>> And still thy speech of me, heartfelt and kind,
> Had made me treasure up thy poetry.
> But now I dare not, for thine abject life,
>> Make manifest that I approve thy rhymes;
>> Nor come I in such sort that thou mayest know.
> Ah! prythee read this sonnet many times:
> So shall that evil one who bred this strife
>> Be thrust from thy dishonor'd soul and go.*

The fine, bitter virility of Dante and the fact that he was a man very essentially of his own age expresses itself in all his works, but

* D. G. Rossetti's translation.

most of all, probably, in the Malebolge of the *Inferno*. Here the queer, infernal, jocular, sadist ferocity of the gargoyles and devils of the Gothic cathedrals achieves such reality in words that when you think of them the stone horrors become by comparison dim. Reading that part of the work you realize that what Dante has given us is, indeed, the human rather than the divine comedy. It is in short the speculum and the history of the earth of that day.

In the *Paradiso* he attempts the impossible task of rendering supreme bliss and just as for one reader of *Paradise Regained* you will find a hundred for *Paradise Lost*, so it is, and in a vastly increased ratio with the *Inferno* and the *Paradiso*. It is as if, after the ferocious and grotesque joys of the Malebolge, the reader's mind accepts without enthusiastic anticipation but still resolutely the ascent of the heavier slopes of *Purgatory*. We must have our happy ending. But once we have come to the triumphant *"Guardami ben, ben son, ben son Beatrice,"* the human interest goes out of the comedy. All nature loves the toiling lover, but once his labors are rewarded with bliss he becomes a fainter figure. In addition, Dante here has to call the supreme supernatural to his aid—hitherto the *Inferno*, and even the *Purgatorio*, had been in lessening degree of the earth and human. What is supernatural about them is, or was in the middle ages, a rendering of normal, human happenings. Hell is everywhere around you, and of what was happening to the poor souls, your near kin, in Purgatory, your thoughts were unceasing. A large proportion of your labors and their fruits went to their redemption and you passed a very perceptible portion of your time in attendance at masses for their early translation into Paradisaical blisses. But the blisses of Paradise are completely outside at once of our comprehension and our experience. You cannot make them real even by rendering the minutenesses of domestic life and the queernesses of the human mind. The *Odyssey* has its intense reality and shines with an infinite and lucent sublimity simply because of the spun cloths of Penelope, the puddings and pies, the household washings, and the games of ball of Nausicaä. But you can get none of these touches of simple reality into your projection of Heaven, because there there are neither meat nor plates, nor cold spells and the necessity for clothes. Except when there are military archangels, *cap à pie* in steel and silver, the garments of the angels are apt to be of amorphous nightwear. The most you can do can be done only with rendering of landscapes and of the astral bodies. Thus, what there is to be achieved, Dante in the *Paradiso* does achieve with exquisite presentation of sunsets and the stars above seas of gold. Or, as we have seen, with his supreme and yet whimsical genius, he can make the celestial luminary bright by telling you that it outshone Jove's chariot of the sun. For the gods of Olympus being as real and familiar to you as fairy tales or dreams, the mention of Jove in the face of the dazzling effulgencies of Jehovah is like contrasting the not quite realizable likenings of the hero's soul with Penelope's twenty-year-old distaff and spinning wheel. So we may consider the *Inferno*, and even at a pinch the *Purgatorio*, as being made up of the broadnesses of epic; the *Paradiso* must always seem to be merely allegorical.

According to the mystic theory of mediaeval love, love itself does not begin until both parties to it have reached the non-physical stage of existence. And Beatrice herself was capable neither of conferring or receiving the true mystic love until she was dead and lived the changed life, in the mediaeval phrase. The love that Dante offered Beatrice was virtue and religion. Dante was a man of his day and in his day the Church had so enjoined chastity upon her communicants that those communicants could only believe that chastity was love, and love, chastity. What humanity will always consider to be the supreme point of the *Divine Comedy* and of literature is reached with the conception and rendering of Paolo and Francesca locked in each other's arms and drifting on the waves of a hollowly real wind, as rendered in Canto V of the *Inferno*. And of all phrases in the world, "That day we read no more" must be the most memorized and the most memorable. The passage begins:

> *Noi leggevamo un giorno per diletto*
> *Di Lancillotto, come amor lo strinse;*
> *Soli cravamo e senza alcun sospetto.*
> *Per più fiate gli occhi ci sospinse . . .*

and the Rev. Henry Cary renders it thus:

> "One day,
> For our delight we read of Lancelot,
> How him love thrall'd. Alone we were, and no
> Suspicion near us. Oft-times by that reading
> Our eyes were drawn together, and the hue
> Fled from our alter'd cheek. But at one point
> Alone we fell. When of that smile we read,
> The wished smile, so rapturously kiss'd
> By one so deep in love, then he, who ne'er
> From me shall separate, at once my lips
> All trembling kiss'd. The book and writer both
> Were love's purveyors. In its leaves that day
> We read no more."

And the whole gamut of human emotions is run in the *Inferno* between the above passage of extreme tenderness and the passage of tenderness in Canto XXXII which contrasts with the almost unmentionable scene of Count Ugulino de' Gherardeschi and the Archbishop Ruggieri, coming after the horrid scene of Bocca degli Abati, and making up the final climax of horror.* It begins thus:

> *Allor lo presi per la cuticagna,*
> *E dissi: E' converrà che tu ti nomi,*
> *O che capel qui su non ti rumagna,*
> *Ond' egli a me: Perchè tu mi dischiomi . . .*

and Cary translates it as:

> Then seizing on his hinder scalp I cried:
> "Name thee, or not a hair shall tarry here."

---

* In view of what follows in the text, the following anecdote may be illuminative. A member of the Rossetti family—whose adoration for the work of Dante is a matter of history—once recited with immense dramatic enthusiasm that passage to the writer. And then added: "You know, I don't think I should like to have been in the same room with the man whom I knew to have an imagination like that."

"Rend all away," he answer'd, "yet for that
I will not tell, nor show thee, who I am,
Though at my head thou pluck a thousand times."
Now I had grasp'd his tresses, and stripp'd off
More than one tuft, he barking, with his eyes
Drawn in and downward, when another cried,
"What ails thee, Bocca? Sound not loud enough
Thy chattering teeth, but thou must bark outright?
What devil wrings thee?" "Now," said I, "be dumb,
Accursed traitor."

This latter passage, almost next famous to the episode of Paolo and Francesca, appears to throw a sinister light on the character of Dante. But it is merely to say that Dante was a man of his time. The time spoke and acted with a ferocity that most educated people of today would consider insupportable, but it is to be remembered that Dante considered himself to have high retributive duties to the Church, to the unity of Italy. He had filled the most important magisterial post in Florence; he had been ejected from office by the treachery of the creature he chastised, and he considered himself to have still the magisterial duty of performing that chastisement. He was, in short, acting as an officer of the state, and the state knows no remorse.

It is, in the end, a matter of comparative coloring. Then there is the unendurably horrible passage that begins the episode of Ugulino de' Gherardeschi, which is at once the climax of the poem and the most remarkable witness to Dante's skill as a manager of narrative —a faculty which with Chaucer he shared to the highest degree.

As the Italian story of the *Seven Sages* goes the *Arabian Nights* one better by duplicating the machinery of the narrators, so in this climax of his great work Dante takes a step forward in technique by doubling the passions that lie behind the story. He relieves the hideousness of an incident dripping with blood and brains and horror by a passage of lamentable tenderness such as has been as rarely equalled in literature. Ugulino of the Gherardeschi, by command of the archbishop Ruggieri, has been shut up in the tower of Pisa with two sons and two grandchildren, and there they have been allowed all five to starve to death—a circumstance that must be the most horrible that a father can have to endure. The passage describing the starvation is of such harrowing vividness that we think better to omit a translation. It reaches its climax at the moment when the youngest of the grandchildren throws himself at Ugulino's feet crying out, "Hast thou no help for me, my father?", and so dies.

> Gaddo mi si gittò disteso a' piedi,
> Dicendo: Padre mie, che non m'aiuti?
> Quivi morì:

This passage of agonized domestic tenderness, set side by side with the hideous revenge that Ugulino takes and is to go on taking through all eternity upon Ruggieri indicates exactly the scope of the miseries of Hell, as between the scene of Francesca floating in her lover's arms through the Infernal tempest and the hideousness of the episode of Bocca degli Abati. This is a device singularly resembling the technique of the modern "impressionist" novelist who may be considered to have stretched technique almost as far as it could go. The novelist, to keep his work together, and, as it were, within one frame, repeats at the end the mood, and recalls the episodes of the beginning, of his book. This is exactly what Dante does with the episodes of which we have been speaking.

It is hardly necessary to point out that the whole of the *Inferno* and the greater part of the *Purgatorio* are, at least theologically, solecisms. Properly speaking, according to religious ideas, the souls of the dead are pale phantoms taking no interest in affairs passing in this world—whether they be in Hell or Heaven. But, disregarding that fact of which he must have been fully aware, Dante fills his Hell with the most human creatures—the most humanly passionate that the world had seen since the day of Greek tragedy. Cavalcanti was singularly right when he said that after many centuries—since, indeed, the days of Sophocles and Euripides—Dante had restored humanity to the world.

That was the measure of his great achievement. The drawing of supernatural pictures built upon a purely arbitrary background is relatively easy. Everything plays into the inventor's hands, so that at best the finished product is a *tour de force* and falls into a very secondary category in the realm of imaginative literary achievement. The innumerable commentators and expositors of Dante during the six centuries that have succeeded his birth have drawn attention almost exclusively to the allegorical and supernatural sections of his writings. In that he did not stand alone. We may consider that he was surpassed by Homer and equalled by Virgil as a mystic narrator of voyages into the Underworld. And, indeed, there are many other mediaeval instances of such narrations—the most impressive of them being the Irish *Voyage of St. Brandon* and, the also Irish, narrative of *Tun wuall*. With Homer, Dante was perforce unacquainted, but it is probable that he must have known at least the two poems that we have just named. Be that as it may, it is as the creator of living beings that Dante stands almost by himself. He was, then, a man drawing pictures of the vicissitudes of human life. He came at a period when human ideas were freeing themselves and were taking on broader aspects than had been the case for many generations. But, compared with, say, Guido Cavalcanti, he was of a disciplined, and almost reactionary frame of mind. He wrote his chronicle—for what, in the end, is the *Inferno* but a chronicle of a diabolical genius?—with all the prejudices of churchmen and the ruling classes of his day. For that reason he must place in Hell two such very dissimilar sovereigns as Frederick II the Hohenstaufen, whom we have already seen at work, and King John of England, as well as three widely differing Popes whom he personally hated. According to him, they were united by a common sin, in that they were all three simoniacs, so all three pass eternity head downwards in Hell with the soles of their shoes blazing over them in the fire-shot gloom. This, of course, is the grotesqueness of the mediaeval mind, but one should guard oneself well from imagining that they are comic. The very ferocity of the presentation forbids that as it does in the devils and the carved Miserère stalls of the Gothic cathedrals. They speak with the voice of retribution recording the inescapable effects of causes.

That, indeed, is Dante's message to the world, and it is a misfortune that his reputation has fallen into the hands of innumerable critics who find in mysticism a sort of escape from an always retributive destiny. He has been most usually represented to us as if he were a sort of prototype of the English aesthetic poets who were prepared to faint at the smell of a lily and to swoon at a glance from a pair of handsome eyes. Dante was a statesman, a soldier, a lute-player, a lover, a begetter of many children, an exile suffering, a man of hate glorying in the expression of his hatred.

That at least is the view of him most in harmony with the present age. Such readers as prefer to look at him from a more mystic and aesthetic standpoint will find an infinitude of support from the millions of commentators ranging from his sons, who wrote almost the first exposition of his mysticism, to Carducci, who was at least a fine poet and a critic of illuminative insight.

The influences of Dante upon the ages that have succeeded him have been innumerable and far-reaching. We shall refer to them under the dates when we find them at work.

As we have already seen, popular poetry, which as a rule provides one with folksongs, is singularly lacking in the Italy of pre-Dantean days. This is, probably, because the popular mind was given to producing or applauding religious songs in Latin of which no great trace remains. And there is almost as strange a lack of minor poets in Dante's day. We have mentioned three of Dante's contemporaries— Fulgore da Gemignano, Cene dalla Chitarra and Cecco Angioleri. But they were all three rather comic poets; Dino Fescolato, Cecco d'Ascoli, Giovanni Quirino were not as topical—but all six are what you might call regional. If you love their period and their Florence with an especial love, there is no reason why you should not delve into their ana, extol the beauties of their lines, and indignantly call philistine those who do not perceive all their beauties. That is very fitting.

For major or nearly major poets of that date one is limited really to Guido Cavalcanti and, just possibly, Cino da Pistoia, for whom this

present writer has a certain tenderness. He both wrote to, and received
sonnets from Dante and wrote a very memorable canzone in lament
for Selvaggia as translated by D. G. Rossetti:

> Ay me, alas! the beautiful bright hair
>   That shed reflected gold
>   O'er the green growths on either side the way:
> Ay me! the lovely look, open and fair,
>   Which my heart's core doth hold
>   With all else of that best remembered day;
>   Ay me! the face made gay
> With joy that Love confers;
> Ay me! that smile of hers
>   Where whiteness as of snow was visible
> Among the roses at all seasons red!
>   Ay me! and was this well,
> O Death, to let me live when she is dead?

And here is a note to Guido Cavalcanti:

He owes Nothing to Guido as a Poet

> What rhymes are thine which I have ta'en from thee,
>   Thou Guido that thou ever say'st I thieve?
>   'Tis true, fine fancies gladly I receive,
> But when was aught found beautiful in thee?
> Nay, I have searched my pages diligently,
>   And tell the truth, and lie not, by your leave.
> From whose rich store my web of songs I weave
> Love knoweth well, well knowing them and me.
> No artist I,—all men may gather it;
>   Nor do I work in ignorance of pride,
>   (Though the world reach alone the coarser sense;)
> But am a certain man of humble wit
>   Who journeys with his sorrow at his side,
>   For a heart's sake, alas! That is gone hence.

It should be noted that small as was the literary company in the Florence of Dante, it was distinguished by as much bitterness as will be found in larger circles. We have already read Cavalcanti's reproof of Dante and Cino da Pistoia's of Guido himself. And not one of the minor poets here mentioned but at one time or another attacked Dante himself. But it should be remembered that in disturbed Florence the motives for attack on distinguished people were nearly always political. That is to say that though the attack itself consists nearly always of reproof of the other poet's morals, the motive and reason for making the attack were, as is the case in excitable times today, invariably political.

Of them all, Guido Cavalcanti stands up nearly alone. If his writings have not either the bulk or the appeal of Dante's, his skill with the pen was very great and his personality nearly as striking. Or, in a different mood, you might put it that Cavalcanti is a poet of cosmopolitan proportions. In making a deep study of him you would still be studying a world period, whereas deeper study of the others would have to be justified along the lines of profound regional passions—as if one should make a profound study of the poets of the American South before the Civil War.

We have here space to make no such investigation. It will have to be sufficient if we make one more quotation and if we add that Cavalcanti as a poet stands up beside his greater contemporary as if he were a spirelike rock. If Dante were not there in the landscape, he would seem proportionately larger, but the authenticity of his work would in no way be added to.

As a mentality, Cavalcanti was a sceptic of the type of Fontenelle, with passages of winged fierceness, as in his attack on Pope Boniface VIII after that Pontiff's Interdict drove most of the great Guelph houses out of Florence. In that sense he was a figure more modern than Dante, Dante having been by temperament extremely orthodox and a defender of all that was orthodox.

But let us quote a poem that is pure poetry without any political or topical innuendos:

Concerning a Shepherd-maid

Within a copse I met a shepherd-maid,
More fair, I said, than any star to see.

She came with waving tresses pale and bright,
  With rosy cheer, and loving eyes of flame,
Guiding the lambs beneath her wand aright.
  Her naked feet still had the dews on them,
  As, singing like a lover, so she came;
Joyful, and fashioned for all ecstasy.

I greeted her at once, and question made
  What escort had she through the woods in spring?
But with soft accents she replied and said
  That she was all alone there, wandering;
  Moreover: "Do you know, when the birds sing,
My heart's desire is for a mate?" said she.*

The most world-famous of all his poems in his day and for some centuries afterwards is the canzone *"Donna mi priegha,"* which consists of an extended analysis, lightly sceptical in tone, of mediaeval love. It has no particular message for today, but in Italian its versification and language are of great beauty. It is, however, very obscure, the only texts available being either in bad condition or very corrupt. And no translation that I know, not even that of Mr. Ezra Pound, helps very much in the interpretation. Rossetti, the only other capable translator of Cavalcanti, does not include this poem in his collection. But Cavalcanti is well worth the reader's taking sufficient trouble to acquire his language and to study him, thus, on the spot.

---

* D. G. Rossetti's translation.

CHAPTER FIVE

I᛭ woᴜʟᴅ be as well now, by way of intermission, to give some account of the state of the drama in France and England towards the beginning of the fifteenth century.

The theatre—the play—of today has no relation to literature. It cannot be rendered by the written or the printed word; its technical rules are the exact reverse of those of the imaginative writer, and it offers no scope either for beauty of language or subtlety of imagination. It is, in fact, a thing apart—perfectly justifiable along its own lines, but apart.

It is the introduction of scenery and realistic devices that has done this. It is perfectly proper when your only indication of place is a placard hung on the back-cloth and explaining, "This is a garden in Venice."—it is perfectly proper, then, for the chief actor on the boards at the moment to describe the beauty of the moonlight, the luminosity of the golden globes of the lemon and the orange against the background of their dark foliages. That, indeed, is his function and that of the poet who is behind him. He must make the hearers see the landscape with the eye of the imagination. But the moment that housefronts, practicable moons and artificial lemon trees adorned with papier-maché lemons appear on the stage, the description of the landscape becomes purely tautological. In real life people do not describe the landscape to the people with whom they find themselves. Those people can see it for themselves. And the playwright must make his imagination square, at least to some extent, with the exigencies of the day.

But Shakespeare and his contemporaries and their predecessors had the fullest possible scope for poetic and imaginative writing. If you imagine their works as being really novels meant for recitation or even for ranting, the subject will become much clearer.

Let us then here consider how the Shakespearian drama gradually evolved itself.

It is customary to seek for the origins of the mediaeval Passion Play and its subordinate allies, the Mysteries, in Constantinople before the renaissance, and it is equally customary to give the Church the greatest part in the evolution of the very existence of mediaeval drama. It would certainly appear that in pre-renaissance Byzantium there prevailed in the churches a state of things with which we are today by no means unfamiliar. There were in that city a great many churches with more seating space than audiences to fill them. So there seems to have arisen in the incumbents of those churches a desire—nay, indeed, a financial necessity—for publicity. They, therefore, introduced stage plays as an attraction—and the plays seem to have continued whilst Masses were being sung, presumably at side altars. From the context we may judge that these theatrical pieces were actually Mystery plays. Nevertheless, the comic passages seem to have caused indignation amongst the more puritan of the Byzantians. Thus we find Cedrerne, the eleventh century Byzantine critic, writing:

> Theophylactes, of Constantinople, was the inventor of the still continuing practice of offending God in the memory of the saints on holy days, by indecent jokes, laughing and shouting in the midst of holy hymns which we ought to offer to God with contrition of heart for our salvation.

Theophylactes, it would appear, had collected what Cedrerne calls a company of disreputable characters and placed at their head a man called Euthymes, who appears also to have been the choir master. And, Cedrerne continues, he instructed them to mingle with the divine services Satanic dances, vulgar cries, and songs taken from the streets and the lowest haunts of vice. This is, of course, probably the nonsensical exaggeration of an irritable old gentleman. A Passion Play did contain what today we should call passages of low comedy, but these passages, representing, as they always did, punishment for ill deeds, were not intended to be taken as comic in our sense. They were not, for instance, parallel with the later Shakespearian introduction of clowns and clowning into tragedy. The Elizabethans needed passages of rest from training their attention on very serious matters; the apparently comic passages in the Byzantine plays were all an integral part of the psychology of the play. They represented devils in Hell being punished in various more or less grotesque fashions, and, the mediaeval audiences being accustomed to grotesque punishments as part of their daily lives, took these passages quite seriously as being tributes to the omnipotence of God who could punish the fiends and make them ridiculous and abashed in the recesses of Hell itself. Nevertheless, to an austere worshipper who wished to listen to a Mass for the repose of a relative's soul in a lady chapel, the noise made, the uproarious orgies of fiends on the stage set up in the chancel of the church, must, no doubt, have seemed repulsive, even though the orgy were followed by a scene showing the fiends being soundly whipped and hit over the head with bladders.

Thus, the first of the known Passion Plays, whether or not it was brought to Europe by returning pilgrims, has a scene showing the Savior being tempted by a horde of minor fiends and imps under the supervision of Satan. The attempt is a failure and Satan leads his cohorts back towards the gates of Hell. Watching them from there Lucifer says:

> *Lucifer.* Is it Satan that I see?
> And Berith coming in a passion?
> *Asteroth.* Master, let me lay my lash on.
> Here's the thing to do the deed.
> *Lucifer.* Please to moderate your speed
> Nor lash behind nor lash before thee
> Till you hear them tell their story.*

The story told, Asteroth and his forces fall upon that unfortunate collection of supernatural evildoers and flog them out of Hell, back into the desert, where they are told to begin all over again. Such a passage may well have been noisy, but it is quite wanting in any irreverence of purpose.

According to the learned, then, certain pilgrims of the fourteenth century, returning from Constantinople, had the idea of representing the Passion Play before Charles VI of France on the occasion of his marriage to Isabel of Bavaria. And the play was such a success that

* J. B. Angell's translation.

the players were given royal license to form a body called the Fraternity of Passion Players who should continue to produce that and kindred plays. They added, gradually, to their repertoire plays dealing with the Nativity, the flight into Egypt, the raising of Lazarus and even Old Testament pieces, all these passing, then as today, under the name of Passion Plays. They were given this license in 1386 and, shortly after, a company of lay citizens began to play similar plays in the streets of Paris itself. They were, however, suppressed by royal edict, and the *Clêrcs de la Bezoche*, a body constituting at once a board of censors and of supervisors of public revels, took up, in turn, the production of plays. The plays that the suppressed citizens' troop had produced were almost exactly identical in substance and treatment with those produced by the Fraternity of the Passions, but to save clashing with the Fraternity, the merchants called their plays Mysteries or Moralities. The clergy of La Bezoche called their productions Miracles, Moralities and Parables. These again were echoes of the first Passion Play. But, gradually, they began to introduce into their repertoire, plays of modern life showing the fate of imprisoned debtors, of blackguards, and other misdemeanants. These, in turn, gave way logically before representations of incidents in the lives of lawyers, until just before Francis I suppressed all stage plays whether sacred or profane, the Society of the Bezoche produced a play called *L'Avocat Pathelin*, which was so modern in conception and construction that it still holds the stage in France.

The actual stage upon which the Passion Plays and Moralities were performed was a three-decked structure. The top floor represented Heaven; the central one, the Earth; and the lowest, the Infernal Regions. So the angels, from trap doors, could direct, and the fiends from below interfere with, human affairs. A great use was made of decorations, furnishings, and what are called "machines." Fire always blazed or smouldered in the lowest compartment; many candles diffused light in the uppermost one. The stage for the plays of the Fraternity of Passions was erected in the body, the porch, or the precincts of a church—that of the merchants stood in the open air— or, when there were arcades, in the arcades of the market place. Later, more particularly in Belgium and in the neighborhood of Arras, the

Society of the Bezoche found it worth while to erect public theatres having pent roofs to shelter both audience and performers.

It is difficult to select salient passages from these plays. Even their printed versions form immense volumes, the plays themselves taking several days on end to perform. They resembled in that the plays of the Chinese, one disconnected, or nearly disconnected, episode following on the other. But the following passage is of interest as showing both the verse and the stage direction of the first Mystery of the Passions, which was first composed apparently at Byzantium in the thirteenth century and went on being performed in both France and England until the fifteenth.

> Here Jesus enters the waters of Jordan all naked, and St. John takes some of the water in his hand, and throws it on the head of Jesus:—

> *St. John.* Sir, you now baptizèd are,
> As it suits my simple skill,
> Not the lofty rank you fill;
> Unmeet for such great service I;
> Yet my God, so debonair,
> All that's wanting will supply.

> Here Jesus comes out of the river Jordan, and throws himself on his knees, all naked, before Paradise. Then God the Father speaks, and the Holy Ghost descends in the form of a white dove upon the head of Jesus, and then returns into Paradise; and note, that the words of God the Father be very audibly pronounced, and well-sounded, in three voices—that is to say, a treble, a counter-treble, and a counter-bass, all in tune; and in this way must the following lines be repeated:—

> *Hic est filius meus delectus,*
> *In quo mihi bene complacui.*
> *C'estui-ci est mon fils amé Jésus,*
> *Que bien me plaist, ma plaisance est en lui.**

---

* "This is my well-beloved son in whom I am pleased." Quoted in James B. Angell's *Mysteries and Moralities.*

The literary value, in short, of these productions is very small. The language used is harsh and obviously the work of almost illiterate collaborators who with extreme difficulty clothe an idea in the most homespun verbiage. They make, thus, monotonous and dull reading, illumined only occasionally by flashes of naïveté. They have their sociological value as casting light on the lives of the poorer middle classes of that day. But except for the student of sociology they have no great value.

That is the usual official account of the origin of modern drama, its outlines having been much the same in England as in France, except that in England the succession of plagues and the Wars of the Roses eliminated this, as all other, forms of art. In Germany, too, nearly all art forms were destroyed by the breaking up of the Hohenstaufen Empire, the removal of the seat of government to Prague, and the continual internecine struggle of princes, bishops, and the jealously free cities. Thus, for three hundred years after the production of the extremely beautiful *Parzival* of Hartman von Auc and the *Tristan* of Gottfried von Strassbourg practically no official literature of any note was produced in the whole of Germany—though of course the folksongs that subsequently asserted a tremendous influence on all subsequent German poetry, went on being evolved.

It is interesting to observe that this wiping out of German court literature synchronized very nearly with the disappearance of the troubadours. A similar process went on in Provence, the national literature and national arts going, as it were, underground and continuing, their existence hardly suspected, right until the middle of the last century. Then the Félibristes under that great poet Fréderic Mistral triumphantly reasserted their existence even in the market places of indifferent Paris herself. For the note of the Parisian, the Northern French and the German learned is, rather jealously, to ignore the arts of the Mediterranean shores. Thus, you will have a comparatively genial scholar, like the late M. Gaston Paris, quite casually and arbitrarily denying that the author, whoever he was, of *Aucassin and Nicolette* ever had any contact with the Moors of Africa or with Oriental literature in general. There is no particular reason why he should have; the Oriental note in that *conte-fable* is by no means strong, nor is it particularly necessary for the story. The visit of Nicolette to Carthage is described almost completely without either landscape-drawing or local color:

> . . . So the oarsmen rowed until the galley cast anchor beneath the city of Carthage, and when Nicolette gazed on the battlements and the country round about, she called to mind that there had she been cherished, and from thence borne away when but an unripe maid; yet she was not snatched away so young but that she could clearly remember that she was the daughter of the King of Carthage, and once was nourished in the city.
>
> Now is sung:
>
> > Nicolette, that maid demure,
> > Set her foot on alien shore;
> > Marked the city fenced with walls,
> > Gazed on palaces and halls.*

That is all of Carthaginian color that the little drama asks for.

Aucassin and Nicolette is an extremely short piece, occupying about twelve hundred lines—say, forty pages of an octavo book. Yet, because of its extreme beauty, modern commentators in great crowds have descended upon it and fought over it with all the acrimony that only the learned know how to put into the assertion of their convictions. Hardly one of them, as is usually the case in that sort of literary combat, agrees with any other one, except upon the two points: that the *conte-fable* cannot have been composed in Provence, and that the story has nothing Oriental in its origin. It very likely had not, if the works of Terence imitated from the plays of Menander the Greek comic-dramatist of the fourth century b.c. had no Oriental origin . . . which, however, they had. The motive of the story of those two lovers was a world motive for many centuries. You will find it again

* Mason's translation.

and again in the Oriental bazaar stories of the whole East. You will find it not only in Menander and Terence, but also in the *Metamorphoses*—and in the plays of the eleventh century Alsacian nun, Hroswitha. That situation must inevitably arise, if only in the imagination of poets, at whatever period of the world's history slavery is a normal condition of society and the sacking of cities or garrisons for the very purpose of carrying off slaves and booty, the normal daily occupation of humanity. Then the daughters of emperors and kings will be taken captive in early youth, and, their identity being forgotten, they will become almost nameless slaves. Haven't we, indeed, seen both Propertius and Catullus encouraging depressed lovers to continue in their love for slave girls because the slave girls may very well turn out to be the daughters of foreign and romantic emperors? So we may as well take it for granted that the subject of this little play was taken from one of those legends that were floating in the air along the Mediterranean shores and in the south, but not in the north, of Spain.

The intrusion of the learned into the fields of literature is almost always a disaster and the whole paraphernalia of universities, scholars, professors and dons, serves, as a rule, for little more than philological exercises having as much use for the world as, say, a collection of postage stamps. But in one department the learned have a chance to be useful, and sometimes they avail themselves of it. That is the department of providing us with the best texts of the classics. For most of the original manuscripts of the classics before the invention of printing are full of the errors of transcribers, of lacunae caused by rats, mice, and damp; and the patient scholar, patiently collating manuscript versions may succeed in evolving from a hideous confusion final texts of a startling limpidity. Unfortunately, in the case of *Aucassin and Nicolette* the scholars have devoted themselves almost exclusively to philological and topographical minutiae. Some hold that the little play was written by a Belgian for performance in the theatre at Arras in the early thirteenth century. Others insist that it was written by a Picard in fourteenth century Picardy. No one takes the fairly obvious line that it was originally one of those folk plays that were then, and still are, performed in the market places of Provence. This *conte-fable* is the only one of its kind traceable in the North French language. But *contes-fables* in Provence are frequent and numerous and are still in the process of being evolved.

And the thirteenth and fourteenth centuries were the very centuries of translation. M. Gaston Paris and most of the German commentators, following him, have decided that the frequent Provençal words, like *"viole"* and *"bailies"* that are found in the very corrupt Paris manuscript of the play—that these Provençal locutions were introduced by the Picard or Belgian author in order to give local color to the work. That seems to be carrying philological farfetchedness to the point of farcicality. Would it not be more reasonable to consider that actually the Paris version which is the only one now extant is a translation from Provençal and that the translator in the course of his task let several Provençal expressions remain in his text?

The matter is of no great importance. There the beautiful little work is. But the whole affair is a convenient example to prove what a breaking on the wheel of things of beauty scholarship really is. Upwards of fifty—I have noted the names of fifty-seven—really learned North French and German professors have paid attention to this tiny work. And what is really lamentable is that hardly one of them has paid attention to the state of the text. The Paris manuscript is carelessly written and it is in places almost impossible to tell the "c's" from the "o's," the "oi's" from the "a's" or, indeed, any vowel from any other vowel except possibly the "u's." So that many lines of the *conte-fable* are practically undecipherable and, indeed, in the very opening of the play, the first four lines, even as given by the last and the best scholastic editor, M. Mario Roques, are frankly incomprehensible. Its latest English translator, Eugene Mason, renders them:

> Who will deign to hear the song
> Solace of a captive's wrong,
> Telling how two children met,
> Aucassin and Nicolette. . .

But "solace of a captive's wrong" is no sort of translation of the second line of:

Qui vauroit bon vers oïr
del deport du viol antif
de deus biax enfans petis,
Nicholete et Aucassins,

because *"del deport du viol antif"* is, frankly, incomprehensible, no
one knowing, and few people having even made a guess as to what
the word *"antif"* means.

It is, fortunately, not very material. You gather that the *conte-fa-*
bliste invites you to listen to verses describing the adventures of two
fair young things, and with that one may read on with pleasure.

The play of Aucassin and his beloved is, roughly speaking, divided
into three acts, though the text as we have it runs uninterruptedly.
It is without stage direction, except the *"Or Se Cante"* when the
story is going to turn into song verse and the *"Or Dient et Content et*
Fabloient" when it is to be recited by the principal actor. The first
division of the story concerns itself with the love of Aucassin, the son
of Comte de Beaucaire, for Nicolette. Nicolette is a pagan slave girl
who has been purchased by an official of the court of the Comte and
has been baptized and brought up as a member of the family of the
official. The parents of Aucassin very much object to their son's passion and the lovers are separated. The Count of Valence makes war
against the Count of Beaucaire and besieges him in his castle with
a formidable force. Aucassin refuses to lead his father's troops unless
he is permitted to see his Nicolette. His father promises that if he
will lead the army he shall see the girl. Aucassin sallies forth at the
head of the troops and does marvels in the field, finally taking the
Comte de Valence prisoner and leading him to Beaucaire by the nose
of his helmet. This is the beginning of the scene of that capture:

Or Dient Et Content

Aucassins fu armés sor son ceval, si con vos avés oï entendu.
Dix! con li sist li escus au col et li hiaumes u cief et li renge de
s'espee sor se senestrehance! Et li vallés fu grans et fors et biax
et gens et bien fornis, et li cevaus sor quoi il sist rades et corans,
et li vallés l'ot bien adrecié par mi la porte. . . .

Mr. Eugene Mason renders the whole of this passage thus:

Now they say and tell and relate

Aucassin was armed and horsed, as you have heard. God! how bravely showed the shield about his neck, the helmet on his head, and the fringes of the baldric upon his left thigh. The lad was tall and strong, slender and comely to look upon, and the steed he bestrode was great and speedy, and fiercely had he charged clear of the gate. Now think not that he sought spoil of oxen and cattle, nor to smite others and himself escape. Nay, but of all this he took no heed. Another was with him, and he thought so dearly upon Nicolette, his fair friend, that the reins fell from his hand, and he struck never a blow. Then the charger, yet smarting from the spur, bore him into the battle, amidst the thickest of the foe, so that hands were laid upon him from every side, and he was made prisoner. Thus they spoiled him of shield and lance, and forthwith led him from the field a captive, questioning amongst themselves by what death he should be slain. When Aucassin marked their words,

"Ha, God," cried he, "sweet Creature, these are my mortal foes who lead me captive, and who soon will strike off my head; and when my head is smitten, never again may I have fair speech with Nicolette, my sweet friend, whom I hold so dear. Yet have I a good sword, and my horse is yet unblown. Now if I defend me not for her sake, may God keep her never, should she love me still."

The varlet was hardy and stout, and the charger he bestrode was right fierce. He plucked forth his sword, and smote suddenly on the right hand and on the left, cutting sheer through nasal and head-piece, gauntlet and arm, making such ruin around him as the wild boar deals when brought to bay by hounds in the wood; until he had struck down ten knights, and hurt seven more, and won clear of the *mêlée,* and rode back at utmost speed, sword in his hand.

The Count Bougars of Valence heard tell that his men were

about to hand Aucassin, his foe, in shameful wise, so he hastened to the sight, and Aucassin passed him not by. His sword was yet in hand, and he struck the Count so fiercely upon the helm, that the head-piece was cleft and shattered upon the head. So bewildered was he by the stroke that he tumbled to the ground, and Aucassin stretched forth his hand, and took him, and led him captive by the nasal of the helmet, and delivered him to his father.

"Father," said Aucassin, "behold the foe who wrought such war and mischief upon you! Twenty years hath this war endured, and none was there to bring it to an end."

So far the little play has a prototype in one of the many legends of the famous Moorish king, Alcessem of Cordova, in Spain. These are still told by mothers and nurses to children in the neighborhood of Avignon, more particularly at Maillanne, the home of the poet Mistral, who, a quarter of a century or so ago, narrated several of them to the author, calling attention to their parallelism with the story we have been considering. Similarly, the general frame and several incidents and phrases in what we may call the second act will be found in the story of *Unsel Ujud et el Ward fil Aumor* that is found in some of the editions of *The Thousand and One Nights.*

As regards that second act, the Comte de Beaucaire refusing to keep his promise and let Aucassin see his Nicolette, Aucassin sets free his prisoner, the Comte Bougars de Valence, and is once more in enmity with his father. Nicolette has already been confined by her master to please the Comte de Beaucaire and now Aucassin is thrown into another jail by his father. And the story says:

Now they say and tell and relate:

Aucassin was set in prison as you have heard tell, and Nicolette, for her part, was shut in the chamber. It was in the time of summer heat, in the month of May, when the days are warm, long and clear, and the nights coy and serene. Nicolette lay one night sleepless in her bed, and watched the moon shine brightly through the casement, and listened to the nightingale plain in the garden. Then she bethought her of Aucassin, her friend, whom she loved so well. She called also to mind the Count Garin of Beaucaire, her mortal foe, and feared greatly to remain lest her hiding-place should be told to him, and she be put to death in some shameful fashion. She made certain that the old woman who held her in ward was sound asleep. So she rose, and wrapped herself in a very fair silk mantle, the best she had, and taking the sheets from the bed and the towels of her bath, knotted them together to make so long a rope as she was able, tied it about a pillar of the window, and slipped down into the garden. Then she took her skirt in both hands, the one before, and the other behind, and kilted her lightly against the dew which lay thickly upon the grass, and so passed through the garden. Her hair was golden, with little love-locks; her eyes blue and laughing; her face most dainty to see, with lips more vermeil than ever was rose or cherry in the time of summer heat; her teeth white and small; her breasts so firm that they showed beneath her vesture like two rounded nuts; so frail was she about the girdle that your two hands could have spanned her, and the daisies that she brake with her feet in passing, showed altogether black against her instep and her flesh, so white was the fair young maiden.

She came to the postern, and unbarring the gate, issued forth upon the streets of Beaucaire, taking heed to keep within the shadows, for the moon shone very bright, and thus she fared until she chanced upon the tower where her lover was prisoned. The tower was buttressed with pieces of wood in many places, and Nicolette hid herself amongst the pillars, wrapped close in her mantle. She set her face to a crevice of the tower, which was old and ruinous, and there she heard Aucassin weeping within, making great sorrow for the sweet friend whom he held so dear; and when she had hearkened awhile she began to speak.

Both Aucassin and Nicolette escape from prison and, meeting romantically in a forest, they go off together upon many adventures until Saracen pirates capture them in the council of the King of Tore-lore, who had given them shelter. They are separated, Aucassin being carried off as a prisoner in a ship that is conveniently wrecked just by the castle Beaucaire. The third act shows us Nicolette a captive on a ship going to Carthage. In a passage that we have already quoted it has been related how in Carthage she recognized her birthplace and was in turn recognized by the sultan of that place as his daughter. But nothing will suit Nicolette but that she rejoin her Aucassin. So, dressing herself as a boy-minstrel, staining her face and taking her viol, she made a bargain with the ship's captain to take her to Provence as a recompense for the song she was singing. Then, as a jongleur, she journeyed, carrying her viol and playing through the country until she had come to the castle of Beaucaire where was Aucassin. So, still disguised as a minstrel, she sang to Aucassin and his friends in the courtyard of the white castle of Beaucaire whose high tower is still a landmark for all those lads of the road. The song that she sang began thus:

> "*Escoutés moi, franc baron*
> *cil d'aval et cil d'amount;*
> *plairoit vos oïr un son*
> *d'Aucassin, un franc baron,*
> *de Nicholete la prous* . . ."

Mr. Mason translates it as:

> "Lords and ladies, list to me,
> High and low, of what degree;
> Now I sing, for your delight,
> Aucassin, that loyal knight,
> And his fond friend, Nicolette.
> Such the love betwixt them set
> When his kinsfolk sought her head
> Fast he followed where she fled.
> From their refuge in the keep
> Paynims bore them o'er the deep.
> Nought of him I know to end.

But for Nicolette, his friend,
Dear she is, desirable,
For her father loves her well;
Famous Carthage owns him king,
Where she has sweet cherishing.
Now, as lord he seeks for her,
Sultan, Caliph, proud Emir.
But the maid of these will none,
For she loves a dansellon,
Aucassin, who plighted troth.
Sworn has she some pretty oath
Ne'er shall she be wife or bride,
Never lie at baron's side
Be he denied."

So Aucassin recognizes his Nicolette, and the singer sings that he must bring his tale to an end since he knows nothing more to say.

As for the exact way in which these little plays were produced we have no means of really knowing. They would seem to have been composed for two people, the reciter and the singer, and they were, no doubt, so performed by wandering players. But upon high occasions the singer was probably reinforced by a chorus, and additional play-ers recited dialogues with the chief performer. So, at least, it is with the *contes-fables* that they still play in the villages of Provence. The practice, however, is quite irregular. Sometimes the chief performer will recite alone for quite a long period, the other characters and the chorus sitting in a half circle on stools. But every now and then one or other of the characters will get up and carry on the dialogue; and no doubt so it was done in the thirteenth century, too. You have to understand that at least England, France and Germany were filled with as great avidity for leisure-time occupations, particularly during the winter nights, as we are at present. Thus, throughout all those lands and, no doubt, many others ran a passion for attending or playing in a theatrical representation as today the whole world has a passion for the movies. You have to imagine all those countries as if filled with a yearning for charades; even in the churches every kind of old garment was treasured up for making costumes. For, whether the first Passion Play did or did not come from Byzantium, they suddenly found countries that were admirable soil for the seed they sowed. As had been the case in Byzantium, the western European churches found the necessity for adding to the attractiveness of their Masses by some sort of rudimentary theatrical entertainment. On Good Friday a priest with his arms extended as if on a cross would be suspended above the high altar and would utter the words of the Savior at Calvary. Or three priests dressed as women, all in white, would pretend to be the Virgin going with her attendants to the sepulchre and, after appropriate dialogue, would go to the tabernacle of the Holy Sacrament and find the Host gone. This symbolized the disappearance of the body of Christ from the tomb. An angel with golden wings would comfort them and tell them where the master would be found walking. Animals also entered into these representations, which, as often as not, took the form—and still do so—of processions. You saw the ass that carried Jesus into Jerusalem, the cock that crowed to the shame of St. Peter, even the whale that swallowed Jonah . . . and, indeed, in Provence, where nothing dies, these or similar things are still done in the churches on saints' days and feasts. Thus, in Moustier on Good Friday a priest robed in white still stands on high, his arms extended and supported by a cross, during the canon of the Mass. In one of the churches at Hyères all the characters of the Crèche—the shepherds, the Virgin and Saint Joseph and the farmyard animals—go in procession round the church and stand in front of the very elaborate real Crèche during the celebration of the Mass; and in Tarascon during the festival of Saint Martha who is there, buried in the cathedral, the miraculous image of the Virgin—for which, according to the legend, Our Lady herself sat—is carried in procession from Saint Etienne des Grès through the fields, so that the Virgin may pay a six weeks' visit to her old handmaiden. And the miraculous image is met at the cathedral door by all the local matadors in bullfighting costume and all the sportsmen of the society of Saint Hubert in green velvet. They march around the cathedral firing off their fowling pieces, and the fanfare of the bullfighters playing the "Toreador March" from *Carmen*. That, possibly Byzantine but certainly almost universal, habit of mixing the drama with sacred ceremonies, thus, dies very hard in those old countries, so that it is unnecessary, really, to trace the origin of western drama to Constantinople. In almost all countries, at any rate in the middle ages, a sort of folk art corresponding to and underlying the princely or the priestly forms of art went on being practiced simultaneously. In Provence of the troubadours, as we have seen, whilst the knights and their ladies held the courts of love—in which, whatever Nostradamus may say, we may believe or not as we wish—the common people, the furriers, the cord wainers, the blacksmiths and whitesmiths and their wives and servants staged the *conte-fable* with the local songs and dances and jig-tunes. And, similarly, in great towns of the North, particularly in Arras, rich merchants would call into their large rooms companies of mummers to give grotesque imitations of the Passion Plays.

As time went on the plays grew more and more profane, until the practice grew so frequent that several merchants combined would set up a semi-public theatre of their own at which nothing but profane comedies were produced. It was, thus, that in the sixteenth century the play of *L'Avocat Pathelin* was produced and the foundations of the house of Molière laid. That play has given us at least one proverbial saying. It concerns itself with a lawyer who is defending a client accused of sheep stealing. The lawyer continually wanders from the subject of his brief and the judge as continually recalls him to his subject with the by now time-honored phrase: *"Revenons à nos moutons."* These plays, then, in France grew gradually more profane in the sense of not concerning themselves exclusively with religious topics. But that is not to say that they permitted themselves to be either irreligious or anti-religious. The twelfth century *trouvères* and dramatists—such as Ruteboeuf and Jean Bodel—wrote plays that were merely lusty. The *Miracle de Théophile* by Ruteboeuf occupies itself with the Vidame of Adans who sells himself to the devil at a price very similar to that paid by Mephistopholes to Faust. But he indulges in none of the delights offered by Satan and, finally, uttering to the Virgin the prayer which begins:

"Dame je n'ose
Flors d'aiglentier et lis et rose;
En qui li filz Diex se repose,
Que ferai-gié?",

he is pardoned by Our Lady and reinstated by the bishop in his official position and thus is beyond reach of the evil one. Or again, the *Jeu de Saint Nicolas* by Jean Bodel is based on an even more rudimentary tenth century play written by a man called Hilarius. It recounts how Tergevant, the god of a Mussulman king, failed to keep robbers out of the king's treasury. The pagan king transfers his allegiance to Saint Nicolas, who guards his treasure for him without the aid of bolts or bars, thus converting the pagan. There is nothing anti-religious in that, but the play abounds in tavern scenes with dice and drink and brawl. That was nothing incongruous with the good Christianity of those days, when so high a churchman as the English Walter Mapp, Bishop of Salisbury, one of the earliest classicists of the English among writers, could write, apparently with seriousness: *"Mihi propositum est in taberna mori."* ("My intention is to die in a tavern.") And it is to be remembered that the church in which the plays of Ruteboeuf and Bodel were performed was at once the social meeting place, the village market, and the crowd promenade of the inhabitants of the villages. The priests welcomed that because it let them have the superintendence of their flock in its hours of leisure. It is, thus, the more unlikely that *Aucassin and Nicolette* was performed in a church, since it is not only completely irreligious in tone, but contains Aucassin's celebrated tirade against the priesthood and the joys of Paradise. Aucassin is warned that if he marries a pagan maid he will forfeit the joys of Paradise. He answers:

"In Paradise what have I to do? I care not to enter, but only to have Nicolette, my very sweet friend, whom I love so dearly well. For into Paradise go none but such people as I will tell you of. There go those aged priests, and those old cripples, and the maimed, who all day long and all night cough before the altars, and in the crypts beneath the churches; those who go in worn old mantles and old tattered habits; who are naked, and barefoot, and full of sores; who are dying of hunger and of thirst, of cold and of wretchedness. Such as these enter in Paradise, and with them have I nought to do. But in Hell will I go. For to Hell go the fair clerks and the fair knights who are slain in the tourney and the great wars, and the stout archer and the loyal man. With them will I go. And there go the fair and courteous ladies, who have friends, two or three, together with their wedded lords. And there pass the gold and the silver, the ermine and all rich furs, harpers and minstrels, and the happy of the world. With these will I go, so only that I have Nicolette, my very sweet friend, by my side."*

It is unlikely that censorious priests walking about a church to listen for heresies in the plays that were there being performed would give their sanction to such a piece of scurrility. But if we consider that the play was written for performance in the market places of Arles or Tarascon or Béziers, such scurrility would have been absolutely in tone with the Quietism of the Albigenses, and there the priests would be kept at a distance, at any rate until the date of the Battle of Muret. That might seem to us decisive as to the Provençal origin of the little play. The Paris manuscript that still remains to us may very well be due to the pen of one of those translators for which thirteenth century Picardy was so famous. Was it not they who first translated parts of the Bible into Northern French—or for the matter of that into any modern vernacular? And having been so translated *Aucassin et Nicolette* may very well, some fifty years after its original composition, have been actually played in the house of one of the rich merchants of Arras. It was, at any rate, as far as we can discover, in 1261 that the first performance of Adam de la Halle's *Jeu de la Feuille* was performed in such a merchant's house. And that is nearly as scurrilous against lawyers, the rich laity, monks and priests, as were the writings of Rabelais.

But it is unnecessary to draw any close lines at all as to the develop-

* Eugene Mason's translation.

ment of the drama in any place or at any date. It is sufficient to remember that the world of the late middle ages and the early renaissance was drama-mad. Anyone, anywhere, in France, Spain, England,
Italy or Germany might set out alone on the road and in any corner
of the market place might, all solitarily, perform a pantomime—a play
which consisted entirely of miming, of gestures alone without words
or music. Or there might be two players, one of whom mimed, and
one who played the lute and sang words to it. Such might very well
have been the first condition in which our *contes-fables* were played—
by a single mummer, or several mummers supported by a chorusing
assistant. All would find audiences. Or whole countrysides, villages,
and the populations of cities might join together to form enormous
pageants in which from six to a score incidents of Holy Writ or profane history might unroll themselves, miming and with choruses as
the procession moved along the streets. They would be lined with foreigners, coming from all the four quarters of the world to witness the
famous feasts of the Passion. Even today you will find that happening
in Oberammergau, no doubt to the edification of the faithful of all
countries, but certainly to the extreme enrichment of the tourist
agencies.

Then we may consider the play as passing for its performances, as
we have seen, into the houses of rich merchants, the nobility and
princes. And since these performances were given in secret, behind
closed doors, their ribaldry could be as unbridled as you could please.
This again would bridle itself when it came to be a matter of the transference of these semi-secret plays into the market place or the roofed-in
public theatre.

The development of the religious play in Germany followed similar
lines to those of France or England, but its development took, as it
were, a larger curve. Until the death of the Emperor Frederick II in
1250, the German Passion Play very much resembled that of France
or England in the simplicity of the religious belief that it expressed and
the relative want of literary quality of its text. Its history was probably much that of the French Passion Play. Germany having already

ecclesiastical theatrical performances, and so being remarkably good soil, the returning Crusaders brought back, as they did in France, the seed of the Byzantine Passion Play. Before then the priests had been accustomed to act quite elaborate scenes from the Passion in the garden and the Nativity, between the choir stalls in front of the altar. Thus, the development into the elaborate, three-decked Passion Play was merely *sui generis*. But with the death of Frederick and the disposal of the courtly *minnesingers*, official art disappeared from the country and almost the entire communal aesthetic energy went into the production of Passion Plays of an altogether higher *genre*. It was as if priests and people united their talents to produce real works of art. Thus, you had plays acted for the most part, like the *conte-fable*, in the market place and instinct on the religious side, with an extremely high and fine mysticism. On the other hand, the people contributed, as it were, those touches of quaint realism that are so exceedingly far from the comic and that embody that essential spirit of Germanism such as is found in the wood engravings of Duerer and Holbein and the paintings of the Kranachs. There is a fifteenth century Hessian Nativity play that follows if not word for word, then certainly incident for incident, the *Pastorale* of Cassis of the Mediterranean, whose rehearsals we have already described. But whereas the Cassis play continues after the birth of the Child in a series of grandiloquent tableaux showing the adoration of the Magi and the conversion, before the manger, of Jews, criminals and fallen women, the Hessian Nativity scene ends on a much quieter domestic note. The Virgin has been too poor to make swaddling clothes for the child. But Saint Joseph, rummaging in the straw, finds a pair of old trousers, and out of these fabricates the necessary wrappings for the Child. The Child, thus swaddled, is rocked before the fire on the knees of the immensely pleased Saint Joseph. And the play ends with Saint Joseph crooning as he rocks, one or other of those beautiful German Christmas folksongs that may well be one of the chief prides of that imperial and much harassed people.

And, indeed, the German people giving itself during this period— from the middle of the thirteenth century to the days of the reformation—to the production of folksongs, that product during that period was most exquisite . . . and was innumerable. And they gave the note to the character of almost all subsequent, living German verse, from the lyrics of Goethe to those of the greatest of all lyricists, Heine, and of other hundreds of lesser known and more humble names.

Lamentably, just as it is impossible to translate Heine, so it is with these early folksongs; they have a quality of exquisiteness in their wording and of dramatic skill in expressing poignant positions in the fewest of words such as not even the Chinese poems of Rihaku have much excelled. What immense landscapes of romance of the generic type are not opened by verses beginning *"Dort oben auf dem Berge"* or merely: *"Zwischen Berg und tiefem Thale"*! But you carry over none of the romance when you translate such words by: "On high upon the mountain" or "Betwixt the mountain and the low prairie." The entire glamour vanishes with the change in words.

You can occasionally parallel, say, our own Border or the Kentucky mountaineers' ballads with one or another of these *Volkslieder*. For instance, against:

> Where have you been all the day,
> Ronald my son?
> Where have you been all the day,
> My pretty one?

you can set:

> *Kind, wo bist du hin gewesen?*
> *Kind, sage dus mir!*
> *"Nach meiner Mutter Schwester,*
> *Wie we ist mir!"*
>
> *Kind, was gaben sie dir zu essen?*
> *Kind, sage dus mir!*
> *"Eine brue mit pfeffer,*
> *Wie we ist mir!"*

(which means, literally: "Child, where have you been?"—"To my mother's sister . . . woe is me."—"Child, what did they give you to eat?"—"A broth with pepper . . . woe is me!"). Both these songs have that somewhat heavy monotonous mournfulness that comes in a folk-song when it is more under the influence of the musician than of the poet. But such a little real poem as the one beginning:

> *Ich hort ein sichellin rauschen,*
> *Wol rauschen durch das korn,*
> *Ich hort ein feine magt klagen:*
> *Sie het ir lieb verlorn . . .*

(which means nothing more than: "I heard a rustling . . . a rustling in the corn. I heard a fair maid complain that she had lost her love."), is at once its own lyric, its own music, its own drama. It is exquisite and altogether untranslatable.

One other form of real literature was that provided not by the people but by the preaching friars whose lives were passed among the people and along the hedgerows. These friars were exclusively preachers and, in contradistinction to the great parish or cathedral clergy, were sworn to and lived lives of poverty. Rome, feeling that under the ordinary clergy alone the Church was losing influence on the German populaces, gave licence to these friars to preach in all the parishes of the realm without permission from the incumbents of parishes, and the bishops saw to it that the parish clergy made much of them.

They had about them a beautiful mysticism, a deep cheerfulness; they were in no sort the haughty churchmen and kept no barriers between themselves and the poorest of their hearers. And you will find peculiar echoes in their sermons—passages that might have been written by the English clergy of the post-Shakespearean age, who were also mystical preachers and beautiful poets. Writes George Herbert of the humbler occupations of humanity:

> Each servant with this clause,
> Makes common things divine,
> Who sweeps a room as for Thy cause
> Makes that and the action fine.

So the great Benedictine preacher Tauler points out that the commonest crafts performed in the name of God and His Son confer on the artificer a fineness unknown to princes. "One can spin," says he, "another makes shoes and some have great aptness for all sorts of material arts, so that they can earn a great deal, while others are altogether without this quickness. Nevertheless, all these gifts proceed from the Spirit of God. If I were not a priest but were living as a layman I should take it as a great favor that I knew how to make shoes, and should try to make them better than anyone else."

And a similar universality of sympathy distinguishes the even more beautiful pronouncements of Friar Suzo. This is, for instance, how he represents himself as meditating whilst he sings the *Sursum Corda* which introduces the Low Mass:

> I set before my inner eyes myself in all my being, with body, soul, and all my faculties, and placed around myself all creatures which God ever created, in heaven, on earth, and in all the elements, the birds of the air, the beasts of the forests, the fishes of the water, the leaves and the grass of the land, and the countless sand of the sea, and thereto all the little dust-flakes which shine in the rays of the sun, and all the little water-drops which ever fell or fall from dew, snow, or rain—and wished that each of all these things had a sweetly swelling sound of harps, well-prepared from the innermost essence of my heart, so that there would rise up from them a new jubilant hymn of praise to the beloved, gentle God from evermore to evermore. And then the longing arms of my soul spread out toward the countless beings of all creation, exhorting and inciting them even as a zealous precentor incites his fellow-singers to sing joyfully and to offer up their hearts to God: *Sursum corda.*

I know of no passage of Christian mysticism more beautiful than that. And three preaching friars Maestar Eckhardt, Heinrich Suzo, and Johann Tauler, the first dying in 1327 and the last in 1367, carried for sixty or seventy years Germano-Christianity to as high a pitch as Christianity can anywhere have reached both before and after them.

From the death of Tauler to the middle of the reformation, German preaching, which in Germany must be given the rank of rhetorical literature, was distinguished by a much more florid appeal, and probably was of a greater popularity. Thus, Berthend Regensburg is said to have rivalled Bernard of Clairvaux in the size of the audiences that he drew and in the enthusiasm aroused by his fiery words. As one chronicler said: "Many thousands listened to him at Zurich before the gate;" another mentions audiences of tens of thousands. It is interesting as bringing out the holiness of this preacher as against the more reserved mysticism of the other three, to quote a somewhat similar passage from one of his sermons:

Of the glory of God we can speak only in images. For all that we could ever say about it, that is just as though the unborn babe in its mother's womb were to tell of all the beauty and glory of the world, of the shining sun, of the shining stars, of the power and manifold colors of precious metals, of the power and perfume of noble spices, of the beautiful things made of silk and gold, of all the sweet voices of the world, of the song of birds and the sound of harps, and of the variegated colors of the flowers. As little as the babe in the mother's womb, which never saw either good or bad and never felt a single joy, could talk of this—so little can we talk of the unspeakable delight which is in heaven, or of the beauteous face of the living God.

It would thus be wrong to imagine that the German aesthetic popular art was by any means a product of an uncultured populace. The preaching friars were obviously exceptional men who set thousands of minor preachers imitating them throughout Germany and Austria. And even the folksongs cannot be taken as being more than works, originally composed by local masters of song and subject, that popular audiences would change here and there after each repeating. Of that there is plenty of evidence in the songs themselves. Thus, Uhland quotes two thirteenth century stanzas, each pointing out that their author was exceptional either on account of his riches and position or because his faculties had been sharpened by travel. The first runs:

Wer ist der uns das liedlein sang
Auss freiem mut, ja mut?
Das tet eins reichen bauren son,
War gar ein junges blut.

This points out that the original author of the ballad that follows was a rich peasant's son, full of courage and a lusty young blood. On the other hand, we have:

Der uns diss neuwe liedlein sang
Er hats gar wol gesungen,
Er ist dreimal in Frankreich gewest
Und allzeit wider kommen.—

meaning that the author of the song that follows sang very well because he had been three times to France and each time had come safely back.

So that here once more we see traces in mediaeval Europe of the traveling of ideas from nation to nation as was the case in Asia itself before the coming of Christ. And we have one more instance, as in the case of the Provençal arts, of an art that, as it were, went on under the ground and continued itself whilst overhead the feudal lords galloped in battle, and wars were waged and cities fell in flames. The courtly and beautiful *Minnegesang* descended, as it were, into the homes of the rich burghers living securely behind the walls of their cities and deteriorated into the rather grotesque literary and the musical performances of the *meistersingers*, with their nonsensical and arbitrary rules and conventions. But all the other arts continued, shining and almost untrammeled amongst the peasants, between the acres and the rye!

And we must seek other pastures. As who should say:

Die muele ist zerbrochen,
Die liebe hat ein end;
So gesegen dich got mein feines lieb
Jezt far ich ins elend.

The miller's wheel is broken
And love's dead in our hearts,
So fare 'ee well my bonny, bonny belle,
I'm bound for foreign parts.

Part Four

CHAPTER ONE

B Y THE middle of the fourteenth century—say about 1350—the whole of the literary field was beginning to change its aspect. In a little more than a hundred years the change was to be completed.

In 1350 Chaucer was either ten or twenty, the date of his birth being disputed by the learned. Boccaccio was thirty-seven and had certainly begun the *Decameron* which was given to the world in 1353; Petrarch was forty-six and Froissart twelve. Langland, author or part author of the *Vision of Piers Plowman* was eighteen, Wycliffe was already contemplating the translation of the Scriptures. Let us then make the initial note that in England Chaucer was to be called the father of English poetry; in Italy Boccaccio, the father of Italian prose, and in France Froissart may certainly be regarded as the father of French prose. In Germany, as we have just seen, the three great preaching friars were writing and delivering their sermons that later were considered the beginnings of aesthetic prose in the Northlands.

Another note which it is important to make is that of the eminence of authors. Roughly speaking, from the death of Virgil until the birth of Dante the author was relatively of little national or social distinction. We may make an exception for the cases of the troubadours and the *minnesingers*; but in both cases it is the literature rather than the isolated figure that would appear to be of importance. This is a literary factor that will vary according to social conditions and the spirit of the age. But, as a general rule, when you have great literary figures, literature will be in abeyance, whereas where you have a very high level of literature a great figure will be absent. Bertran de Born the troubadour, was great in his day, but rather as a political and martial figure who fought with all the kings of the earth than as the author of *sirventes*, even though one of them should be as famous as the *Lament for the Son of Henry II*. And the other troubadours are merely part of a great literary movement. Or, to carry the idea one stage further forward, you had in Germany the very remarkable literature of the folksong and there, although we know that the regional poets must have achieved a certain output and local celebrity, we are unable to recapture the name of any one of them. Or, if we take the case of England, you will find a great work like the *Vision of Piers Plowman* which is popular in its inspiration and yet with a quite indefinite authorship. The poem is usually given to William Langland or Langley who was an almost exact contemporary of Chaucer. But we know next to nothing of this author. And his poem has curiously the air of having been written in a place of public assembly. As if, while he wrote, individuals came up and whispered into his hooded ear: "Don't forget the poor cooks," or: "Remember the hostlers," or: "Whatever you do, don't forget to expose the scandalous living of the lousy friars."

But Boccaccio was not only the father of Italian prose; he was the first man of letters to be regarded as a great figure because of his writings alone. He may thus be regarded as the first man of letters. Dante, Chaucer, Froissart were all men of action, Dante a prominent politician and aristocrat, Chaucer a prominent official and bureaucrat, Froissart also a politician and aristocrat. All three were fighting soldiers in their early years. Chaucer was taken prisoner at the Battle of Rethel near Reims, and it is said that in the leisure of his imprisonment he undertook the first of his literary works—the translation from the French of that rather tiresome allegory, the *Romaunt of the Rose*.

Boccaccio, on the contrary, did nothing but write . . . and no doubt enjoy his life of leisure. The illegitimate son of a rich man who, nevertheless, acknowledged and richly supported him, he passed, except for his writing, a life of idleness that appears to have been dominated by his amours with Maria, illegitimate daughter of King Robert of Provence and Naples, whom he names Fiammetta in his writings. The nearest that he came to public employment was when he wrote apologies for the "good Queen Joan," also of Provence and Naples. He also went for her on several diplomatic journeys. She murdered her husband and led a life of notorious irregularity, though in her own countries she is still regarded as a prime figure of past romance.

And there is about him little trace of popular contacts. Langland is exclusively of the people; Chaucer has his democratic aspects in that in the personages of his *Canterbury Tales* he permits the unprivileged and lower class Wife of Bath, Friar, Miller and the rest, to be admitted to the company of the Knight and the other aristocrats; and even to have a voice as to the selection of the tale tellers. . . . Boccaccio's body of narrators in the *Decameron*, on the other hand, are all perfumed aristocrats, as if he could not bring himself to let anyone undecorative approach his darling Fiammetta who presided at those feasts of hardy imaginative fiction. That he must have fallen under the influence of the popular literature of his day is obvious, because except for Dante and Petrarch, both of whom he was never tired of praising, there were few other influences under which he could have fallen. But it is difficult to find definite traces of such influences. According to the father of this writer, one of his early works was framed upon "that sweetest and purest blossom of French mediaeval literature," *Aucassin and Nicolette*, which is said to have been one of the favorite pieces of the Florentine tale teller. So it is pleasant to think that if Chaucer really met Boccaccio during one of his diplomatic visits to Florence, and if Boccaccio really gave Chaucer a copy of the *Decameron*—and all these things are alleged in the pleasant legends of literature and the middle ages!—then may not Boccaccio have slipped in among the pages of his own book a copy of the little *conte-fable* of which we have made such great case? So the history of the two fair children may very well have influenced Chaucer's conception of the gentle passion. Dr. Hueffer, however, gives no sources for his allegation that *Aucassin* was the favorite reading of Boccaccio. His poem *Amoreto* is, nevertheless, a love tale told alternately in prose and verse, in the manner of the *conte-fable*, and the mother of Boccaccio was a French woman and he himself, like Chaucer, spent much of his youth in Paris and the South of France.

The third characteristic of this transition period in literature is the marked emergence of the tale teller and the relative relegation into the background of formal and purely imaginative verse. This is no doubt due in part to the contemporary emergence of prose as a vehicle for tale-telling and in part to the eclipse of the popular arts in the hideous welter of pestilences and famines, added to the fabulously murderous wars that distinguished all that era. It is the shibboleth of one of the parties to the state today that literature, or any other art, cannot be great or even supportable unless it devote its attention to the public question of the time. The question is interesting and we may consider it for a moment, historically, here. We have seen that the period from the death of Frederick II to the beginnings of the reforma-tion in Germany was one of great popular aesthetic activity. There were the Passion Plays and one may even include the *meistersingers*; there were the preaching friars and there was, above all, produced spe-cifically by the people the extremely beautiful body of folksongs.

On the other hand, in England the corresponding period—say from the birth of Chaucer in 1330 or 1340 and still more, perhaps, from the birth of Langland, about 1332, to the day when, after the Wars of the Roses, the Tudors were firmly seated on the throne and the unparal-leledly glorious period of English literature opened—in all that period which was one at first of popular awakenings and then of almost unceasing pestilence, famine, local wars, civil wars, the murder of kings and dynastic revolutions, no traces of literature whether courtly and academic or popular, and almost no trace of any of the other arts, is discoverable. These seeming antitheses disappear when we examine into them. The German disturbances were matters in which the Ger-man people were relatively little concerned, except when they were being butchered or their houses destroyed. The internecine wars which ravaged that great territory were wars between princes or between prince-bishops and the municipal nobilities of great free cities or, at least, cities claiming freedom. The populace had no part—and, in-deed, no heart—in these transactions. It was all one whether they were the serfs of, or paid taxes to, the prince-bishop of Brunswick, the chief burghers of that city or any other hereditary or elective no-bility.

In England, on the other hand, at least a proportion of the popular mind was given to social matters. The *Vision of Piers Plowman*, whilst being in parts a poem of extreme beauty, is, in other parts—and those the majority—an attempt to assert human rights. Or, at any rate, an assertion that in heaven, which this earth should—if it didn't—resem-ble, the poor would have equal rights with their lords. The keynote of the poem is, as we have already said, sounded in the words: "There the poor dare plead."

It was thus—and the poem with its infinite number of readers is evidence of the fact if any evidence were needed—that the attention of the populace was not merely fixed on public affairs alone. And public affairs were disastrous enough. In 1349 came the first great pestilence, called the Black Death; in 1362 the second; in the same year an immense tempest wrought such great damage in England that it was said that half of the wealth of the country was destroyed in seven hours. (It was in this year also that the first draft of *Piers Plowman* was written.) In 1369 came the third invasion by the Black Death; in 1375-6 the last. In 1377 the second version of *Piers Plowman* was published. From 1361 onwards, England had had peace from foreign wars. Popular unrest grew. Promoted by the preachings of John Ball, it was occasioned by the loss of population and of wealth caused by the successive Deaths and by great frosts and tempests and the miserable condition and serfdom of the common people. Thus, while the author of the *Vision* and Chaucer wrote, you had the revolt of the peasants under Wat Tyler and John Ball, the preacher, their capture of London, and the burning of the Savoy Palace of John of Gaunt. You had also in the same year—1381—the denial of transubstantiation by Wycliffe and his followers. So Chaucer wrote his *Canterbury Tales* between 1386 and 1387; the *Confessio Amantis* of Gower, a relatively humdrum achievement, was completed in 1390, and the final text of *Piers Plowman* was written about 1392. And it is interesting to consider that in 1388 was fought the Battle of Otterburne or Chevy Chase, when the Scots under the Douglas defeated Lord Henry Percy. And presumably the first draft of the most famous of all Border ballads was written.

The House of Lancaster, under King Henry IV, who had murdered Richard II, came into power in 1399, and both Langland and Chaucer died in the following year.

So that the poetry produced in this age goes little towards deciding whether or no the best literature is produced by those who are what is called socially minded or no. The lives of Chaucer and Langland coincided almost to a day, and, although it would be bold to compare the genius of Langland with that of Chaucer, the *Vision of Piers Plowman* is a poem sufficiently inspired by genius not to give away the whole case of propagandist literature. It is true that when it becomes propagandist it becomes also tiresomely allegorical, but, nevertheless, in its passages of realism—and they are frequent enough—the genius of the poet shines without shadow. And the frame and detail of the *Vision* have a marked resemblance to those of the *Tales:*

I saw in that assembly, as ye shall hear hereafter,
 Bakers, butchers, and brewers many,
Woollen weavers, and weavers of linen,
Tailors, tanners, and fullers also,
Masons, miners, and many other crafts,
Ditchers and delvers, that do their work ill,
And drive forth the long day with *"Dieu vous sauve,* dame Emma."
 Cooks and their boys cry "Hot pies, hot!
Good geese and pigs, go dine, go dine!"
Taverners to them told the same tale
With good wine of Gascony and wine of Alsace,
Of Rhine and of Rochelle, the roast to digest.
All this I saw sleeping, and seven times more.

So runs a sort of program of the poem given in the prologue, and it has about it the real Chaucerian—or, perhaps, it would be more just to say the real late fourteenth century—touch. It has, moreover, nearly all Chaucer's genius of language.

That overtone of the written or printed page which conveys the genius of the great writer is one of those standing miracles which has its most striking exponents in such poets as Chaucer—if, indeed, there is any other poet like the author of *Palamon and Arcite.*

Why is it that when for the many hundredth time you read:

Whanne that April with his shoures sote
The droughte of March hath perced to the rote,
And bathed every veine in swiche licour,

you feel a sort of quickening of the veins, a sort of reöxygenation of the blood, as if from your usual dimnesses you had come out into a keener and purer air? Or, perhaps, to make the image more precise still, one should say: as if one were setting out on a journey to where the air should be pure and alive. . . . At any rate, it is an excitement.

Yet the content of the words is merely meteorological, and not strikingly exact at that. Nevertheless, the words live and, as it were, bubble in a little cauldron and, as if the friction evolved electricity, they exhale it. . . . And still the explanation is insufficient. You may add, say, that the contrast of the three "ou" sounds in "shoures" and "droughte" and "licour" contrasted with the "o's" of "sote" and "rote" give the effect—the "ou" being properly pronounced "oo"—of cuckoos calling in a spring shower. They probably do. And that gives pleasure.

Nevertheless, all that is insufficient to account for the standing-aloneness of Chaucer. Because, like Dante and, in his different degree, like Heine, he is completely solitary, deriving solely from the world that surrounded him and in which he delighted, without predecessor or school. It is, in short, probably the quality of having lived, and remaining self-contained. Dante took for his motto the proud words: *"Fidandomi di me piu che di un altro"* ("Trusting to myself better than to any other man"), and one may imagine that the great—perhaps the greatest—English poet was upheld by a similar self-trust. He was probably, however, insufficiently self-analytical to put that characteristic into the form of the Dantean boast. His work is in the highest sense as impersonal as that of most modern writers. Nay, as impersonal as that of Flaubert. When you read *Palamon and Arcite* you are so carried away by the story that you have no time to bother your head about what manner of man the author was. You are enveloped in an affair. That is the quality of great art. He was obviously a moralist —everyone in his day was—but his moralizings are so exactly those of everyone else of his day that they in no way distinguish him from anyone else. He was a moralist, as proper men today are clean. Then, you washed yourself in a certain quality of moralizing, as today you use soap. The celebrated characterization of Chaucer to be found in the *Canterbury Tales* is generally disputed by the learned for one of those reasons known only to the learned themselves. The host of the Tabard, catching sight of Chaucer amongst the other pilgrims, shouts at him thus:

What man are thou? quod he.
Thou lookest as thou wouldst find an hare,
For ever upon the ground I see thee stare.
Approache neai, and looke morrily.
Now ware you, sire, and let this man have space.
He in the waist is shapen as well as I;
This were a puppet in an arm, to embrace
For any woman, small, and fair of face.
He seemeth elvish by his countenance,
For unto no wight doth he dalliance.

This would seem, as a portrait, to be convincing enough. But since Chaucer in various places, but notably in the *House of Fame*, is accustomed to make fun of his own person and everywhere to depreciate his own talent, the too ingenious learned enjoin upon you that you must take him to have been the exact opposite of what he herein describes himself as being. But his portrait is so exactly brought in and so convincing that the artist, knowing better than a professor how a brother artist would get his effects, will almost certainly accept this portrait as the just one. In any case we have no real means of knowing since there exist no memoirs of Chaucer or of other people that, by the way, tell us how Chaucer looked or how he lived and talked. The host's portrait does at least tally with the little miniature in the margin of one of the Chaucerian manuscripts.

One perceives a specifically little, hooded man, with a small beard, and eyes obviously accustomed to gaze to the side—with eyes, that is to say, that will see what, to his right or left, you are doing, whilst, his face being not towards you, you are unaware that he is observing you. . . . But within that definite frame everyone must make his own portrait of the great, little poet.

One imagines him, then, with the quality of the unobserved observer that distinguishes the naturalist like the late W. H. Hudson, that incomparable writer of English prose. He was so unobtrusive that neither man nor bird took alarm at his presence, and so observant that without taking a note he could give you the exact fold of a hood, detail of an ornament, facial wrinkle or trick of speech. You get, indeed, from the host's address to him that he was considered as somewhat of a snooper; nevertheless, the characteristic was unresented. Some men have that attribute; when they write they become great writers.

And he had lived before he wrote. The son of a vintner of the city of London, he began life in a situation full of interests for a note-taker. How he became in boyhood a "valettour" of princes at the King's court, one has no means of knowing—but the relations of wine merchant and client are frequently intimate. Between one wrinkling of the nose over a titillating cup and another, Chaucer *père* may well have slipped in a plea to have his son given a gentleman's place about the court. Once there, he behaved with modest efficiency and captured the heart of Philippa, a lady of honor whose family name has not come down to us, but one of whom everyone in those treacherous circles spoke more than well—and who was beloved by her Lady Princess. You do not, then, need more explanation of Chaucer's honorable career at court. It is all the battle won to have behind you a lady universally beloved.

So he fought at the Battle of Rethel and was taken prisoner and in due course ransomed, having spent his forced leisure, as we have seen, in translating the *Romaunt of the Rose* and so having acquired a taste for the practice and glories of writing. Because with his little virelais and garlands he was soon known as a gentleman poet and well known at the French Court, when he subsequently went there as an envoy, as "the Translator." And so he became a diplomat and passed years in France and later in Italy, negotiating with princes and statesmen, devising with Froissart and perhaps with the young Christine de Pisan, and with Boccàccio, and perhaps with Petrarch himself and with the works of those exquisite creatures buzzing in the courts where he worked. . . . And so he was Francified and Italianized as were most English writers from his day to ours, only no doubt more thoroughly than most. He is alleged—by this writer's father and again without reference given—to have revelled in *Flamenca*, before even he studied the *Decameron*. He may well have, for *Flamenca* and his own *Palamon and Arcite*, the one in prose the other in verse, remain the model and highwater mark of pre-quite-modern tale-telling. The author of *Fla-*

menca is more the agreeably *blasé* man of the world. You might take him to be a Maupassant writing a short *roman à trois*.

As far as one can judge, *Flamenca* was written in the early part of the thirteenth century, probably in 1233 or 1234. As it is written in the Langue d'Oc—the Provençal of the troubadours—one may take its author to have been one of the nobles exiled from Provence after the extirpation by St. Dominic of the Albigenses. On the face of it, it would appear to be one of the many romances addressed to husbands by the troubadour romancers with the object of making them not jealous. But, though that may be the moral of the tale, its sardonic and urbane author shows no particular signs of having even ·that much morality in his composition. What he has is the nimble eye of Chaucer himself and almost more than Chaucer's great power of rendering atmosphere of decorative splendor and courtly amenities.

And still more essential is his gift of tale-telling.

The art of the *conte* was a very slow development and this little romance of the jealous husband, the beautiful wife and the exquisite, masculine young lover moves along, without faltering or digression, without having uncertain or superfluous verbiage, right through to the happy consummation when the husband is cured of his jealousy. As to the young couple, what happens to them is obscured by the fact that the last few pages of the early manuscript which is to be found in the library of Carcassonne, are missing. So that we are left not so much with the sense of a happy ending, though no doubt an author so easy must have arranged for that, as with the speculation as to what exactly in the middle ages husbands were for. Indeed, Chaucer himself, though much more official-minded and, at least in later years, more staid than the author of *Flamenca*, did not abstain from writing at least one work—*The Court of Love*—in dispraise of legitimate marriages. This work would, however, seem to have been written for the private ear of the fair maid of Kent, the widow of the Black Prince, a princess of broad and jovial taste, and, apparently, when not reading it to that lady, he kept it locked up in a chest.

Let us, then, try to place Chaucer exactly in his literary milieu as a poet. He marked the beginning of the day when the supremacy of poetry was first really challenged by the more pedestrian, and yet potentially more delicate, medium of prose. As we have said at the beginning of this chapter, he stands between Froissart (who may well be considered the father of French prose, though he was actually the writer of quite a quantity of charming verse) and Boccaccio (who was actually called the father of Italian prose).

To Froissart we have already given as much space as we can afford, but to distinguish him from Boccaccio we may say that his prose is the prose of a real prose writer. It is a medium that, like all great prose writers, he completely commands and uses as an artisan uses a tool with precision.

Boccaccio, on the other hand, is, in every line of his prose, a poet using an unfamiliar medium with the feebleness of approach of a man trying to use a stock-whip with too long a thong. The passages of delight in the *Decameron* are the descriptions of feasting and the short lyrics sung at the end of some of the *contes* by one or other of the narrators. All the rest of that famous work is of a tiresome and gross dullness without any literary quality at all. We may suppose that its emergence from the flood of works consigned to oblivion is due simply to the fact that a considerable proportion of humanity starves for want of essential information of a certain sort. It fulfills, therefore, a felt want, but the want is not a literary one. The ten days of the group of noble Florentine ladies and gentlemen who were taking refuge from the Black Death in a beautiful country domain were occupied by telling stories rather below the level of imagination that is to be found in any hedgerow inn, anywhere, at any time. There is about them no hint of humanity or even of humor, and it is astounding that things so essentially coarse and plebeian can have existed in a frame of the extreme beauty and aristocracy of the Italy of the *Trecente*. There is about the stories of sexual misdemeanor not a trace of Attic or Gallic salt, and the episodes narrated are the merest statements of physical action. The characters in the stories told might just as well be wooden marionettes. And all these episodes take place in an atmosphere of completely cynical theft, swindling and physical violences, such as could find home today only in the society of rather inferior gangsters. So that to re-read, as this writer has just lately done, this intolerably long work is a most iugubrious and tiresome occupation. Apart from certain passages in the setting and three little anecdotes, there is no relief.

Seven ladies, then, and three young men, meeting in the Church of Santa Maria Novella agree to betake themselves to a beautiful castle at a distance from Florence where the plague is slaying whole families. And Boccaccio's very long description of the plague is description and in no sense a rendering. You get a number of statistics of deaths and some details as to methods of irregular burial. But practically no horror. But as soon as these young friends, including the daughter of the King of Naples, get to their beautiful castle, the refrain of the story comes alive. In that Boccaccio in the *Decameron* is the exact opposite of Chaucer of the *Canterbury Tales*. One would have liked to hear more of the adventures of the pilgrims journeying from Southwark to the shrine of St. Thomas, but one hears practically nothing. Nevertheless, the characters told of in the tales of the pilgrims live in their habits as if they were beneath our eyes. They are as real and in cases more real than the pilgrims. A real poet, Chaucer lived amongst his creations with an intimacy greater than that he felt for the life around him. So Palamon and Arcite and their young woman and her relatives are for us more real than life, that being the quality of real art. Boccaccio, on the other hand, sees only his Fiammetta and her group of friends with real vividness, so that it is they and their landscape and their halls and silver and flowers that live and are vivid, whilst the characters in the stories they tell are non-existent. And, indeed, the only little anecdotes told by those characters that are real are the tiny story of the painter Giotto in the rain and that of Guido Cavalcanti successfully indulging amongst the tombs in back-chat with a company of toughs. Poets and painters had a quality of reality for the poet that Boccaccio was.

It is probably a question solely of medium. Whilst he was content to write verse, Boccaccio was a great artist; had Chaucer written the *Tales* in prose, they also might have been mediocre.

Certainly the prose *Melibeus* of the *Tales* is only mediocrely successful, and the *Persones Tale* is an exceedingly dull and long sermon made up of commonplace prose passages such as:

De Invidia

After Pride wol I speke of the foule sinne of Envie, which that is, after the word of the philosopher, sorwe of other mennes prosperitee; and after the word of Seint Augustine, it is sorwe of other mennes wele and joye of other mennes harme.

The fact, probably, is that to a man dancing in the apparent shackles of verse, prose seems so easy a matter that he imagines himself to be able to run about its fields like a hind let loose. But precisely because prose does not afford its devotees the props and corsets of metre, rhyme, assonances and parallelisms, it is extremely more difficult to write in it passages that hold and satisfy the ear. Nothing is really less true than the dictum of Molière to the effect that his bourgeois character spoke "prose." What he spoke was a sodden matter that was not verse.

This matter is extremely complicated. Prose existed more and earlier on the Continent than in England, perhaps simply because wealth was there more distributed. In England the writing and listening to verse was still the occupation of courts and princes. It was that, too, in France and Italy. But in those latter countries there was coming into existence a class of wealthy, luxurious and magistral burgesses who demanded entertainment of their dependants even as did the princes. And verse, having no special prestige for them, they found that in prose you can get over bawdy and other stories more clearly and effectively. So, writing the *Decameron* in prose, Boccaccio was merely supplying a demand. Chaucer had no such demand to meet. He, no doubt, obtained his place about the court by skill in rhymes and metres; or he may have gained his place in the heart of Philippa by writing to her:

> Your two eyee will sle me sodenly,
> I may the beaute of them not sostene.

And Philippa may have interceded with her royal mistress to give him a place about the court.

In that between-stage of literary circumstances the professional writer depended almost entirely on the patron. A patron had many uses for writing. He got his pleasure undoubtedly from it. On the face of it today it would seem singular that a royal court filled with careless aristocracy should take its delight—its principal entertainment—in listening to the works of the great poets and in making amateur verse for itself. Nevertheless, if one comes to consider the circumstances of courts in those days—without a press and hardly any means of communication, and, particularly in the winter when neither fighting nor field sports could occupy the long months—it will stand to reason that in those days the art of literature was more prized than has ever since been the case.

So, in courts full of active and intelligent young nobles and their women—like those of France or Naples in the day of Chaucer—you have the singular phenomenon of a quite light and frivolous literature being plentifully composed as if to throw a veil over the horrors of the time. In London the horrors of the time—except for the imperturbabilities of Chaucer who wrote his *Court of Love* to please a princess in private during the hideous time of the final visitation of the Black Death—the horrors and political stresses of the time all but extinguished the literature. But in France with the Hundred Years' War, the Black Death and the horrible war of the peasants known as the Jacquerie all raging together, whole butterfly flights of light verse, imbued with a certain grace and a certain skill, seemed to flutter above the horrors. It was one of those cases of which we have spoken in the beginning of this chapter when a literature flourished and the great literary figure hardly existed. Thus, during the time of Chaucer only two French writers are sufficiently memorable to form a part of our literary daily bread. A person of real culture ought to know the name of Froissart whose life was almost exactly coterminous with that of the author of *Troilus and Creseyde*, and of Christine de Pisan who flourished—or, rather, who didn't, poor thing, flourish—about 1367 when Chaucer was at the French court. For the patronage system, like every other system, promoted the work of one author whilst it depressed another's. Froissart found during all his prosperous life patrons to commission his writing the history of their glory. He rode comfortably from court to court . . .

Froissart d'Escosse revenoit
Sur son cheval qui gris estoit;
Un blanc levrier menoit en laisse . . .

. . . coming from Scotland on his grey palfrey with a white grey-hound in the leash at his side. He went from France to Scotland, Scotland to London, London to Burgundy and Allemaign. And in every court that he came to he was received with wines and warmth; great princes vaunted to him their prowess; archives were thrown open to him; knights, squires, arquebusiers, yeomen were sent for to come to him and give him their accounts of battle. Now and then he threw off an enchanting lyric. But poor Christine de Pisan . . . She had only her pen to support her; being a woman she was not eligible for diplomatic missions nor yet for places at court. So her really beautiful muse was employed by one unknown patron after another to write accounts of their usually quite imaginary and always highly decorated amatory exploits. It was a great pity, for in such real poetry as she had time to write, she left very beautiful and delicate things behind her.

For the rest, in France that day almost every young gallant and blood wrote his verses and almost every young court woman could answer with a virelai or a ballad. Deschamps was an original and vigorous poet at the court of the dukes of Burgundy. Gontier, Col, Eustache, Antoine de la Salle held on the first Sunday of every month a *fête de puy d'amour* where poems were read, music rendered, traveling expenses for poets provided, prizes given and poets crowned with laurels. The names of six hundred courtly and noble poets and poetesses are inscribed in the annals of this Burgundian society. The *maître d'école*—the accredited chief of the school—was Guillame de Machaut, a poet memorable in his day because he wrote over a thousand poems without leaving one single memorable or even readable line.

It was in such an atmosphere that Chaucer passed his days in France, being there more or less constantly on one mission or another, from 1360 or so until 1373. In 1373 he was sent to Florence and passed the next eleven years between Italy and London.

Various estimates are formed by patriots or cosmopolites as to the extent that foreign influences moulded the character of Chaucer the poet. You find excited Britons declaring that Chaucer never so much as looked at a foreign poem; you find persons of greater equanimity declaring that he was of the school of Guillaume de Lorris, the author of the first part of the *Rômaunt de la Rose*. That is, perhaps, going too far, though, since Chaucer actually translated that first part, Lorris may well be taken to have exercised a powerful influence upon his younger years. He became, nevertheless, too great to be spoken of as being of the school of anyone.

The example of Dante is said to have given him the idea of writing in the vulgar English rather than in the court French of the day. It may have, though we have no documentary evidence as to that point, and in any case these attributions of origin are merely beating the wind, considering how, in these pages, we have established the absolutely international nature of all literature. So that if it is necessary to talk about nationalities in the case of an author as hyper-great as Chaucer, it is better to consider that, if he were English, it was because he made England what she was and, having so made her, remains forever a part of his own creation.

Certainly you may look forever through the annals of his day in England before you will find such another Englishman as the author of the *Canterbury Tales* shows himself in his pages—such another kindly, shrewd, tolerant, traveled, sentimentalizing, gently cynical son of broad acres and shores where sing innumerable birds. And, indeed, in the characters of his journey he renders for you such another group of "Englishmen" as certainly you shall not find traces of anywhere else in his changing day. So that it is a question whether with his depiction of those pilgrimaging beings he did not fix the type of "Englishman" for good. And indeed, when we test a character to see whether he is a true Anglo-Saxon or not, we think rather whether he would have fitted in with those wayfarers who, when April with his showers sweet had pierced the drought of March, set out from the Tabard Yard to worship at the shrine of England's great martyr where he slept in the shadow of Bell Harry towering up into the Kentish skies. For whether it be because of Mediterranean provenance and culture or no, one thing is certain: Chaucer's England is our England.

It is expedient here to make the note that, his translucent character apart, what singles Chaucer out from all his contemporaries and most of his successors, is his wonderful gift of telling a story so as to suspend its interest until he has written the last word. His fellows all, with the solitary exception of the author of *Flamenca*, told their stories not with any skill at all as narrators but by either putting them down so that the great moral purpose of the author should be manifest or extolled—as was the case with *Piers Plowman*, to mention one extreme—or they told them, as did Boccaccio in the *Decameron*, as if they had verbally transcribed them from the lips of some rather dull boon companion in a hedgerow tavern or the equivalent of a fourteenth century Florentine night club or barroom.

So you had that most tiresome of all invented forms, the allegory, which exists mainly to please its author with the discovery of how easy it is to assimilate the most disparate characters or objects the one to the other. Suppose he chooses to liken his mistress to a pinetree, or chastity to a knight in armor. He will find his mistress to be soothingly silent like the tree or voiced by the gentle winds that run through the branches; he will find her as steadfast, as faithful to her home, as plentifully haired, with arms like the branches, in a green, sweeping kirtle, like the pinetrees. There is no end to it. Or similarly with Dame Chastity, the writer, like the author of Holy Writ, will find that she is terrible as an army set in array, is remorseless, is cold, is shining, communes with celestial beings, everyone of which may take a discursive canto for his description and history. . . . And all these things fit in with the elegant monotony of billiard balls running into pockets, and the reader who cannot get anything better will have to take it.

So you had the *Vision* itself. It sets out as a mystically romantic and spirited adventure piece, gets in a magnificent landscape and a stirring crowd, and almost immediately deteriorates into the long monotony of allegory, relieved here and there with touches of humor and humanity in which the great poet that was its author once again shines out. So that, unless you are inspired by the very afflatus of the collector of bric-a-brac, you just read the *Vision* as you read Wordsworth's *Peter Bell*—with almost infinitely prolonged skippings and very occasional butterfly-pauses, whilst you suck up the full beauty of the exquisite scattered passages of poetry.

But with Chaucer the story is the story and he plunges in at once and so continues hastening to the end with only here and there a pause for passages of description.

Nor need we ascribe his skill as narrator to his study of the art displayed in *Flamenca*—though nothing is more singular to consider than that with *Flamanca* and *Aucassin* written in the early thirteenth century, no divine afflatus of tale-telling should by the fifteenth have swept the world. That is because when it is a matter of fiction every man before he is a master must learn to be his own tale teller. He must ring true to himself and to his chosen audience. It is very well in your youth to study the technical tricks of Maupassant or Tchekov. Before you will have attained to mastery you will have to have discovered for yourself what audiences like and how you may prove attractive to them along the lines of not Maupassant's or Tchekov's personalities, but your own.

But once you have made the humiliating discovery that what your art stands for and consists in is the pleasure of your audience, you will make the gratifying simultaneous discovery that the prescription for this sort of proficiency is neither esoteric nor difficult. When thinking of your art or thinking out your story you will soon see that what would please you if you considered it from the outside will please a reader who is attuned to you. There will be no pleasing anyone else.

But it will have imperatively to be pleasure of the external type. You must call all your forces of discernment to your aid. You must learn to be all things to quite a number of men. But, indeed, to acquire the apparently forbidding thing called technique is not difficult. Technique is simply what lies below the art of pleasing. You must study a great many books that have pleased men to see how they have pleased. When you have learned that you will be fully equipped.

Chaucer, indeed, must have heard innumerable tales in his life, since tale-telling then was your only summer-and-winter night's entertainment all the world over. It was not merely that with his sideways-gazing eyes he can have seen how Petrarch pleased—Petrarch, the great type poet of the world who took in hand and modeled the accepted verse of all who followed; nor was it just that he can have seen Boccaccio pleasing—Boccaccio, the playboy of the tale-telling world; or Lorris, who tried to please by adding rare passages of dry humor to his allegories when even for him they grew too heavy. But Chaucer must have heard knights telling last tales during the long waits before going into battle; and priests waiting for the tolling bell to finish, telling edifying tales; and his father telling tales whilst the wine was a-syphoning from the great barriques of Bordeaux. . . . And, above all, he must have heard his customs' men telling interminable tales whilst he waited for the vessels to make the tides, coming up from Galleons' Reach to the Pool of London. . . . For, indeed, what could make you more patient, more wise, more cynical than to have been, as was the Father of English poetry for nearly a generation, one of the chief comtrollers of the Customs of the Port of London?

So he knew what tales pleased and how they were told. And when his day for retirement came he sat down and wrote his *Canterbury Tales*, and few tales have been better told. For this writer, as has perhaps sufficiently appeared, *Palamon and Arcite,* the plot of which he had from Boccaccio, remains, if you will read it for the story and forget that it is a world classic, one of the type problem stories of all time. It is ornamented as an Italian primitives' church, yet it is as breathless as Stockton's *Lady or the Tiger.*

And when you think of the man's wisdom, his pawkiness, his good-humor, his lovingkindness, his scorn now and then, his blues and scarlets and yellows and golden colors, and then discern, underlying all those gifts of God, the skill that he taught himself, you may be pardoned if, like this present writer, you think that he was the great narrative poet of all time.

He had, in short, some of that chief attribute of Petrarch himself. It is futile and useless to estimate the great authentic writers. Set against Dante who passionately limned the middle ages, Petrarch is a relatively temperate writer. But he was for all time, in a sense that Dante was not. So, set against Shakespeare, Chaucer lacked exquisiteness of verbiage; his language was not, indeed, yet "set." But just as Dante stands for the Italian middle ages, so does Shakespeare for the English Elizabethans. Shakespeare, indeed, was for all time—but to assimilate his thought you have to make a certain adjustment in yourself and to get into tune with the thought of the great day of James I. But the humanity of Chaucer is everyone's humanity, all the time. To appreciate it you have to make no more mental adjustment than you used to have to make when you listened to your grandmother telling the story of Red Riding Hood. . . . And, in addition to all his other qualities, there runs across all Chaucer's work the lovely, lambent flame of the spirit of chivalry.

It is, thus, pure tragedy that the fourteenth century language, smelling of new English, should lie like a bar between the English-speaking races and this most beautiful of all our poets. For a man cannot be a good Englishman or, indeed, a good American or colonial unless the leaven of Chaucer have worked in his mind. Nor, indeed, can anyone else appreciate without that what there is of the beautiful in the Anglo-Saxon tradition and arts.

CHAPTER TWO

So, just as the national vernaculars were settling themselves all over Europe and prose was gradually becoming the narrative-imaginative writer's vehicle, there burst upon the world the terrifically noisy bomb of the Italian renaissance. It was, indeed, all the noisier in that it did not come to an unprepared land, but fell rather upon a soil fully ready to accept it.

For, obviously, the new appreciation of Greek remains did not become a sudden fact with the taking of Constantinople, though it is convenient when forming one's mental map to say tentatively that it did. But the tendency to regard the knowledge of the middle ages as having crystallized only at that date disappears as soon as one considers at all minutely not merely the *quattrocento* which began with the death of Chaucer, but the age of Petrarch himself. Because the more you read him and think about him, the more you become convinced that he is the classic poet of poets. It is not merely that his poetry is the clear Italian evening, in which in the still air the black cypress stands up beside the low roof against the lucent sky with the one star shaking out its beams; it is not merely that it was his mind that functioned when Goethe wrote *"Kennst du das Land?"*, or George Herbert, "Sweet day, so cool, so calm, so bright," but he is behind Walter Savage Landor and Keats and Shakespeare of the sonnets. There is, in fact, no one who can be called poet but the shade of Petrarch stands behind him.

And you may be sure he did not attain to this classicism without pondering over the writings of his greatest compatriot-predecessors. He was the first great man to reach back to the imagination of that past with insatiability. He was never very wealthy, but he was a veritable Maecenas when it came to commissioning scribes to make clear copies of the decaying classics, and he it was who incited Boccaccio, scrabbling in the fuel huts of monasteries, to rescue fragments of parchments that the monks had destined for their ham-curings. . . . And in a sense he, more than anyone else, was thus responsible for the disappearance

423

underground of Italian poetry during the greater part of the fifteenth century.

For, for one reason or another, this century was a barren time in the imaginative literatures of all the nations of Europe. In England poetry stopped with Chaucer; in France poetry became the trifling occupation of court idlers; in Germany, as we have seen, only the peasant poets were active. Nothing more singular than these other phenomena really took place in Italy. But, one may suppose, because Italy has always been so much more the artistic cynosure than any other country, the learned have always been accustomed to speak not on the lack of quality but on the paucity of Italian great poets.

It is true that when you have said Dante, Guido Cavalcanti, Petrarch, Ariosto and Tasso, you have exhausted the Italian poets who are world figures—for many centuries. . . . And there are those who will cavil at the inclusion of Cavalcanti. And when you have added the names of a few lesser poets, like Cino da Pistoia, Politian (who was almost more classicist and philologer than poet), Boiardo (of the *Orlando Innamorato*), Pulci (of the *Morgante Maggiore*), or the beau- tiful imaginative *prosateur* Sannazaro who wrote *Arcadia* and exercised an extraordinary influence over the English Elizabethans—when you have paid your tribute to those relatively few satellites of the great luminaries, you have pretty well exhausted the Italian poets of that period to whom the stranger must imperatively pay attention.

But if the roll is short, the quality is extraordinarily high. There are not in the world many poets who could be said to surpass in individuality, tenderness, invention, beauty of language or rhythm Boiardo, say, or Pulci. Boiardo has not the might or the boisterous life of Ariosto. But he more resembles Chaucer in that the chivalry of his imaginations is fresher, more new, more ingenuous and sincere. You may read the *Orlando Furioso* today with enthusiasm for its story of adventure, but if you want to be touched and taken out of yourself, then read the *Orlando Innamorato*, of Boiardo, and a lovelier, smaller world of beings more real shall open for you.

The reasons given by the learned for this shortage of Italian poets are various—the Black Death, foreign invasion, internecine intrigues. But since all those causes operated also in all other European countries, the scholars have to allege a fourth cause that they state themselves to be unable to define—some defect in the earth, the land springs, or the seas. It is unnecessary to be so powerless before the problem. You could state it epigrammatically with the simple words that there were not men enough to go round. And then, also, in the immediate post-Petrarchan period the attention of the cultured, upper-class Italian was turned almost exclusively to writing in Latin.

It is curious to consider that the first reaction to the great Italian poems of Petrarch should—and by Petrarch's own encouragement and example—have been the declaration that Italian was a detestable and vulgar tongue. But so it was that before the so-called renaissance itself, there was actually a mostly Latin but also a slightly Greek movement that occupied nearly all cultured minds. The very circumstances of the world made that a necessity. There had to be a universally understood and practiced language simply because of the enormously increased tortuosities of diplomacy, the prevalence of international scientific correspondence and the world prevalence of a single faith. That language could only be Latin. And if you give a great deal of time to the cultivation of a language, the chances are that you will declare all other languages—and, particularly, such as might make a certain claim to rivalry—vulgar, deleterious and obscene. So you had the singular spectacle of schoolboys of the higher classes and freshmen of the universities being expelled because they had crept into corners and had secretly read the *Canzoniere* of Petrarch. . . . As if they should have been caught smoking.

That, of course, threw the balance too much on the side of Latin. . . . And it is not astonishing that a great quantity—an actual majority—of the official poetry of the day should have been written in Latin. In quality a great deal of it is by no means mediocre. The courts of the Italian princes filled themselves with gay beings who wrote more or less ephemeral pieces in good Latin. And the princes patronized, in addition, the great humanists who formed such a distinguishing feature of the Italian learned world of the day. These also all wrote in Latin, as did the historians like the great Villani.

It is obvious, however, that our concern is not with men like Poggio Bracciolini, a most elegant Latin writer and collector of manuscripts;

nor yet with Emanuel Chrysoloras, who "brought the Greek language
to Florence;" or again with his famous son-in-law who went to Constantinople to bring back a whole Greek library; any more than it is
with Aeneas Silvius Piccolomini who passed for the most elegant of
all men of letters writing Latin and, mostly in consequence, became
Pope Paul V. That Italian age demanded, above all things, scholars to
elucidate the manuscripts that had newly flooded in from Byzantium.
But this renaissance was by no means a thing of imaginative writing,
and in the end—and before very long—the reaction against not only
the scholarliness of the renaissance but also against the new, if rather
dusty, Latinity was to come about.

There remained, on the side, the extraordinarily vigorous growth of
popular verse and narrative which went on during all the period of the
eclipse of the bourgeois-princely forms of literature in the vernacular.
To examine into this at all closely would be the task of a specialist—
but if one were in want of a subject one might well find literary manifestations less worth specializing in. The Italian folksongs of this period
had, however, none of the roughnesses of the English border ballads
or the naïvetés of the German Volkslieder. By a long filtration from
Sicily, the birthplace of their kind, they had achieved by the time they
had reached Tuscany recognized forms, a sufficiently classical language
and a very marked singableness. Known usually as *rispetti* and *stornelli*
they were sung enthusiastically by the peasants, and the cultured classes
hearing them sung, laid hands upon them, turned them into madrigals
and sang them more staidly themselves. There existed also a whole
literature of prose romances and imaginative fiction which, in turn, is
much more refined, restrained and even tender than the folklore of
almost any other nation. There comes back to this writer such a fifteenth century folk story called *Ginefra*, which he heard several times
with emotion during his childhood but has not been able to recapture.
It is the story of a Florentine bride who, falling into a catalepsy in time
of plague, is taken for dead and buried with great haste in her family
vault. But the mason has been so hurried that when she comes to herself she is able to see moonlight through the cracks in the monument.
She extricates herself and in her white grave clothes runs to the doors
of her new husband, her mother, her uncle, her brothers—but all these

people, taking her to be a ghost, bid her to return with God to her grave. Then she bethinks her of the lover who was rejected by her parents. She falls starving and frozen on his doorstep and he, caring nothing whether she is spirit or mortal, takes her into his warm home and tends her till she is recovered. And one is glad to think that, according to the story, the Holy Father awards her to her lover whom in truth she had loved during all the time of the tale.

It comes back, then, after years, as having been simply and beautifully written . . . with the immensely tender, almost aching pathos of the Spanish plays of the type of the exquisite *Celestina*. The writer was under the impression that he had read the story in—or had had it read to him from—either Rubria's compilation of Tuscan folklore or John Addington Symonds' *Italian Studies*, but he has not been able to find it in either book. It is, in any case, or was until comparatively lately, one of the most popular and famous of Italian stories for the simple in heart.

In due course, with the approach of the sixteenth century and under the auspices of the splendid tyrant Lorenzo de' Medici, the Italian vernacular emerged from its eclipse. The Florentine Platonic Academy, under the presidency of Lorenzo, solemnly decided that "the Italian language was, indeed, of equal value with the Latin, and that men of wit and learning need not fear contumely if they wrote in it." And so, with the two great fixed stars, Ariosto and Tasso, shining in their places, and with huge masses of humanist, scientific, epistolary, artful, and a little imaginative prose thundering below the horizon, the milky way of the minor Petrarchan poets swept on its course, to be checked and disappear only under the disastrous sway of Spain, and that of Austria, which was even more antipathetic to poets.

The comparative merits of Ariosto, who was born in 1494 and wrote the *Orlando Furioso*, and Tasso of the *Gierusalemme Liberata* have been acrimoniously discussed by the learned for some three centuries or so. The discussion is entirely pointless, since the difference between them is essentially one of temperament. As versifier, Tasso was the more discreet; Ariosto the more abundant. The one was destined for madness and was careful to the point of meticulousness. The other had the frame of mind of the good banker with a large zest in life and occasional carelessnesses that had astonishing results. For nothing is really much more astonishing than in the midst of that jolly adventurous writing of the good Catholic and *bon père de famille*—which means something more staid than a mere father of a family—to come, then, upon the passages of sheer lubricity that Ariosto drags in *à propos* of nothing at all. They are inexplicable. No one has ever accounted for them. The writer once heard the late M. Taine—who was staid enough! —declare that when he found himself in the Oxford drawing-room of the Mark Pattisons—where donnishness was carried to its most sterilizing extreme—he felt an irresistible desire to shout at the top of his lungs *le mot de Cambronne*. He never, however, did so. Perhaps, it was really what Ariosto did.

In any case, as poet Ariosto was boundless in invention and, therefore, prone to imperfections; was extravagant; was perhaps unheroic. But as man he was tender, good-humored, patient. And so a great deal of his tenderness seeps through into his poem and makes it really more epic than that of the formally epic-heroic Tasso. He should, if possible, be read in the Italian, for what we may call the inevitable Rossetti tradition of translation of the nineteenth century, which today is plastered all over the English world, is peculiarly unsuited to his constant variation of note. That tradition, with its unchanging superfluity of adjective, its metrical suavity, reduces everything which it translates to a common and eventually very disagreeable smoothness of surface. So that whether you read Dante or Petrarch or Tasso or Ariosto or Guido Cavalcanti, the meat is always an insipidly prepared if tender sort of veal. The simile, alas, is rather coarse, but it is difficult otherwise to render the effect.

The difference, in fact, for this writer, between the *Gierusalemme* and the *Orlando* is that when you have read the one once, that is enough. It is a perfectly competent Italianate epic about an imagined historic event. It is expressed flawlessly in the language of Petrarch, and those whose tastes lie in its ordered direction will from it attain ecstasy. But it will never, as is the case with the great, liberal, international masterpieces, step as it were out of its frame and seize the indifferent beholder. You must be, I think, Italianately attuned to return to *Gierusalemme* to find new beauties.

But that quality of attracting the return of the mind very much distinguishes the *Orlando*. The profusion and endless variety of Ariosto's genius were such that his masterpiece is one of those works that few readers can sound to the bottom at a single reading. And it is one of those unconstrained pieces that the almost unlettered mind can appreciate and digest without any previous literary preparation. It is adventure, it is romance and it is, above all, tender passion such as distinguishes very little Italian work of that day or of all time.

And—but this will remain forever a vexed question—it is possible that Ariosto, differing from all the other imaginative writers of his Italian day, reflects a little of the frame of mind of the renaissance. The main body of his work is so nearly Petrarchan that it is just possible to classify him altogether as a Petrarchan. But the redundancy of his ornamental passages, his digressions and, above all, the astonishing passages of lasciviousness to which we have just referred were extremely distinct from the serene purity of the Petrarchan muse. And liberality rather than lasciviousness is the characteristic of the better work of the renaissance type; it was, nevertheless, a liberality that might include Ariosto's peccant passages.

Let us, before approaching the never-decided suit of the Renaissance vs. Petrarch, Boccaccio and Company, consider one or two of the external circumstances that influenced the shape and nature of the *Orlando*. Ariosto, as we have already said, was personally rather the type of mind of the happy banker than of the romantic poet. He was, nevertheless, of the type of those who are born to be cheerful in creditable rather than in luxurious circumstances. His whole life long he was engaged in creditable or glorious and usually successful diplomatic commissions for one cardinal, duke or potentate or another. And, perhaps because of his sunny and patient disposition, these magnificences were uniformly and basely ungrateful to him. They would, for instance, give him chains or ornaments of great value which he must wear for the greater adornment of their courts and so could never turn into ready cash. Cash, indeed, they almost never provided, so that he would appear to have maintained his status of courtier on one minute pension that some member of the Este family of Urbino would seem to have accorded him in a moment of absent-mindedness. He was, nevertheless, able to boast on his death bed that the house in which he died and the small plot of land on which it stood had been bought out of his own savings.

But even that small fortune was gained only at the cost of a courtliness that was destined at once to account for and to determine the nature of the *Orlando*. *Orlando Furioso* is, in fact, in motive an exact parallel to the *Aeneid*. Just as Virgil wrote his epic in order to provide Augustus with a heroic, legendary and respectable set of ancestors, so with the *Orlando*. Ariosto wrote it to provide the Este family with a heroic past. They were just respectable amongst the princes; Ariosto was set the task of providing them with an ancestor among the paladins. It is true that, in the boisterousness of his profusion, this purpose appears to lose itself in the intricacy of his plot and ornamentation. But a really careful analysis of the work reveals that, intricate as the plot is, Ariosto never lost from sight the main purpose of his intrigue.

And, by a singular coincidence, there existed for his *Aeneid* an *Odyssey* and a Homer . . . in the unfinished *Orlando Innamorato* of Boiardo, for which the Este family had commissioned Ariosto to provide the sequel and conclusion. You will find the haughty and puffed-up renaissance commentators actually stating that Ariosto evolved *his Orlando* from contemplation and improvement on Boiardo's unfinished poem. And they will add that compared with the rounded skill of Ariosto, the naïvetés of Boiardo exactly resemble "the timidities, the want of skill and the occasional barbarisms of Homer."

It is a curious line for the renaissancists to take. On the face of it, these pundits stand for Greece as against Rome, so that it is not Virgil but Homer that they should seemingly champion. But true to their own type and tastes when it was a matter of individual works, they could not but applaud the gentlemanly adiposities of the pious Aeneas as against the hardbitten feverish-eyed spectre of the cunning Odysseus. Their migration from Constantinople was the invasion of Western Europe by the bourgeoisie. Nothing could be less bourgeois than the middle ages with their Gothic comfortlessnesses, their grim gargoyles, their starvation-wrinkled faces, and nothing could be more bourgeois than the renaissance's overcushionings, the roundings-off of corners, the superfluous and meaningless application of acanthus leaves, dolphins and lyres to every smooth surface that a more severe taste would certainly leave unornamented. Their women, one could be certain, when about to reward their lords and masters with cherubic offspring, would never be permitted suddenly to come upon any shocking works of art. And yet nothing can be more shocking than to come across, say, the naturalistic drawings of crucifixions by Holbein, surrounded by frames drawn in pencil and portraying endless satires, cherubs, cornucopiae and waxen fruits . . . in the taste of the Swiss renaissance.

Actually this enormously publicized collectors' movement left Italian imaginative literature almost entirely unscathed. It, as you might say, let the legions thunder past and went unemotionally on its way. You will find, perhaps, in the *Arcadia* of Sannazaro, some traces of his having read and having even assimilated certain passages of Theocritus. He can only have done this with the aid of a manuscript brought from Constantinople and we may add, not so much by way of digression but in anticipation of what is to come, that since Sannazaro's poem had an enormous influence on Sidney and a quite sufficient one on Wyatt, Surrey, Shakespeare and Milton, his *Arcadia* was one of the channels by which the beautiful spirit of the lovely Sicilian genius was made to bathe our Anglo-Saxon shores.

The rage, then, of the renaissancists against Petrarch and Boccaccio is something to be seen before it can be believed in. To read John Addington Symonds, perhaps the doughtiest of all champions of that neo-Greek movement, when he comes to contemplate the two great fourteenth century champions of the Italian vulgar tongue, is like hearing some shrewish upholder of one form of faith berating a grandmother for teaching her grandchildren some deleterious form of heresy. It is really like that. Symonds points out almost with despair that if Petrarch and his accomplices had not existed, the whole course of Italian poetry would have set in another direction. That is, indeed, true enough, but it is true only because Petrarch and his accomplices had done the job that the renaissance accomplished in the other arts a hundred years before any Byzantine Greek came with manuscripts to Tuscany. Those two had, as we have seen, ferreted and paid for ferretings in the woodsheds of monasteries until they had unearthed as many Greek manuscript remains as the literature of Italy with its strong individuality could have been prepared to assimilate.

Mr. Symonds writes in his *Renaissance in Italy* (Vol. II, pp. 248-250):

That Petrarch and Boccaccio should have been chosen as models of Classical Italian style was not only natural but inevitable. Writers trained in the methods of the humanists required the guidance of authoritative masters. Just as they used Cicero and Virgil for the correction of mediaeval Latin, so Petrarch and Boccaccio were needed for the castigation of homespun intellects . . . yet the choice was in either case unfortunate, though for somewhat different reasons.

It was impossible for poets of the 16th century to follow Petrarch to the very letter of his diction without borrowing his tone. Consequently these versifiers affected to languish and adore woe, conceits and complained of cruelty; in the fashionable plea their facile mistresses became Lauras; or else they draped the lay figure and wrote sonnets to its painted eyebrows. . . .

We have further reason for resenting this devotion to (Petrarch) a poet with whose habitual mood men of that age could not sympathize. We know that they had much to say which remained buried beneath their fourteenth century disguises. . . . But their emotion found no natural channel of expression. It is not without irritation that we deplore the intellectual conditions of an age which forced these artists to give forth what they felt in one of two equally artificial forms. Between transcription from the Latin elegists and reproduction of Petrarch, there lay for them no choice. Consequently, the Renaissance lacked its full development upon the side of lyric poetry.

It is in this last sentence that we see where the shoe pinches . . . and in the sentence of the preceding paragraph that we have italicized. But, in fact, for the example of Petrarch and Boccaccio we might have had in sixteenth century Italy a whole robustious school of poets who would have transferred into the lyric the alluring opulences of a Titian, the voluminous bosoms and thighs of Rubens and eventually all the repellent gildings and sham lapis-lazuli of the Jesuit school of architecture and decoration. We are fortunately spared that, and indeed the world has enough of that spirit in the plastic arts, for it should not be forgotten that this age was that of the great flourishing of the Venetian school of painting and of the great renaissance buildings. The Italian genius was so immense, so vital and, above all, so occupied that even had Petrarch or Boccaccio not influenced both the moods and modes of the sixteenth-century Petrarchans, it is probable that the lyrical output of the day would have been small and of little importance. For wealth, excitement and glory were all more easily to be found in other careers.

And the sixteenth-century Petrarchans with the lovely, unwavering evening light of their beautiful and restrained language had another and far more important mission to fulfill than the rounding up of the tribute that western civilization must pay to the arrogant exiles from Constantinople. They gave us England—the England that reached an unsurpassed beauty with the Elizabethans . . . and has ever since declined.

Let us, then, sum up the matter of verse in Italy. In the fourteenth century you had great figures—Dante, Cavalcanti, Petrarch, Boccaccio —but no level of literature. In the fifteenth there was a real and abundant popular literature and no middle-class or aristocratic writings at all, all those latter activities being taken up with Latin. At the turn of the fifteenth into the sixteenth century you had the two great figures of Ariosto and Tasso and a whole, level, poorly inspired literature provided, in the triumphing vernacular, by a positive herring-shoal of disciples of Petrarch. If you crave for soothing drafts, there is no reason why you should not read Poliziano who died in the same year—1492— as his master the magnificent Lorenzo—or Girolamo Benivieni, who is really chiefly interesting as being the intimate friend of Pico della Mirandola, and of the formidably fierce enemy of the renaissance called

Savonarola. Poliziano wrote innumerable verses like this, his vision of perpetual Spring:

A fair hill doth the Cyprian breezes woo,
And sevenfold stream of mighty Nilus' sea,
When the horizon reddeneth anew;
But mortal foot may not there planted be.
A green knoll on its slope doth rise to view,
A sunny meadow sheltering in its lea,
Where, wantoning mid flowers, each gale that passes
Sets lightly quivering the verdant grasses.

A wall of gold its furthest edge doth screen
Where lies a vale with shady trees set fair
Upon whose branches mid leaves newly green
The choiring birds . . .

This going on for very long, with all its invertebrate syntax and redundant and utterly commonplace adjectives, reading it one is unable to avoid the rude conjecture that this must have been the verse that Mr. Bunthorne used to read to his bride.

The famous Dantesque sonnet of the friend of Savonarola runs, a little more actively excruciatingly, thus:

In utmost height of heaven I saw the choir
Of happy stars in their infinity,
Attending on the Sun obediently,
And he was pasturing them with his own fire.
And, wealthy with my spoil, I saw Desire
Unstring his bow and lay his arrows by
And proffer Heaven with all humility,
My heart which golden drapery did attire.
And, of this disarray'd, not half so fair
Smiles Earth to Sun when, by his crescent light
The ivory horn of vernal Bull is smit . . .*

* Cary's translation.

The reader should, in short, remember these verses for use when we shall arrive at the consideration of the English pre-Raphaelite poets. The verse of Lorenzo himself is more sprightly and individual, instinct with a faint, princely and not unpleasing lewdness. It is too good to be profaned by a pre-Raphaelite translator; the writer is unable, in spite of some effort, to afford a creditable translation of his own and he is unacquainted with any others. . . . This gallant member of the Medici family may at least have the credit of having introduced for the first time a strain of gallantry, as opposed to arbitrarily restrained passion, into his amorous verses.

Besides these efforts of the Petrarchan lyricists, innumerable other turbulent and haughty cultural activities must be taken as going on in an Italy that bubbled like an immense pot of internecine eagernesses before her final extinction for so many centuries. You had, thus, the romantic-epicists like Cassiodoro Narni, Francesco de' Lodovici, Vincenzo Brusantini, Giambattista Pescatore. . . . All imitators of the great Ariosto of the *Orlando*, they are at least readable for those who like the *genre* or desire to enlarge their intimacies with Italy of the *cinque cento*. . . . And a more important figure of heroic conceits was Giovanni Giorgio Trissino, who was born in 1478 and died in 1549—fifteen years before the birth of Shakespeare. His heroic tragedy *Sophonisba* was illustrious in its day and is still more interesting as being a milestone in the long road of the development of the drama . . . which so soon must again occupy our attention.

Beside these again went on the furious activities of the collectors, comparers and emendators of classical texts; the almost more profuse production of letters intended for publication; the numerous regional histories, hardly any of which rise to the level of literature . . . and then the considerable works in prose, which in many cases do approach the dignity and accomplishment of real literature.

You might, thus, with profit, read the criticisms and letters of the fortunate and magnificent Bembo, a cardinal who was adored in every courtly circle, who was born in 1470, died in 1547, and amongst his innumerable activities in Italian is famous as having been said to have "restored ciceronian Latinity to the world." Or you might try the letters of Aretino—and only those of all his profuse writings are worth skimming through . . . more particularly when his purpose was open blackmail. His unnumbered written indecencies are perfectly unreadable . . . unless by a hobbledehoy who has suffered under the yoke of too virtuous parents.

But three or four prose works have sufficient mass, elevation, temperament and readability to make them indispensable ingredients of the reading of anyone aspiring· to reasonable culture. The immense importance of fifteenth century Italy lies in its tremendous cultural influence over Anglo-Saxondom—over England, in particular—until the beginning of the eighteenth century, and over, at any rate, the Southern states of North America until considerably later. We are peoples of a civilization, such as it is, of an extreme complexity of origins—but no other single influence bulks anywhere near so largely upon our culture at its most critical and its greatest moments. So, if only for knowledge of Italian *cinque cento* modes of life and thought, it is imperative that one should familiarize oneself with the *Cortegiano* of Balthasar de Castiglione (1478-1529), the *Autobiography* of Benvenuto Cellini (1500-1571), the slightly earlier *Il Principe* of Niccolo Machiavelli (1469-1529). In addition, it is very advisable not to miss the *Lives of the Painters* by Vasari. So you will know the suave, eloquent, reasonable—but, indeed, entirely reasonable—lives of princes and courtiers in late fifteenth and early sixteenth century Tuscany. Castiglione, of course, omits the comment that that tranquil and beautiful life was supported on the dagger of the assassin and the culverins and morgensterns of mercenaries. But a sufficient view of the undersides of the courts of popes, princes and cardinals is afforded by Cellini whose autobiography is so consistently boastful and mendacious that it always comes true to scale. Similarly with Machiavelli: he was so consistently, by turns, cynical, amoral, ironic and in earnest, that the final picture is one of the consistent psychology of a princely publicist of that age. And all this prose is so direct, flexible· and illuminative that all these books are preëminently works of art, instinct with the personalities of their writers and rendering admirably, rather than just reporting, the vicissitudes of the lives of the men of their day.

Vasari's *Lives of the Painters* is actually slightly more repertorial. But when, for moments, it climbs into the plane of the work of art it is supremely picturesque and so may pass with the supreme works of the era.

To write, thus, is to dispose of masterpieces in the wholesale manner of the fishmonger selling sprats. But with the sixteenth century the art of letters had become essentially a matter of movements rather than one of solitary great figures. The world was never again to see lonely beings of the cathedral-bulk of Dante or of Petrarch. Beside them even Shakespeare shows almost frivolously pococurante—the gentleman, perhaps, but scarcely the scholar after the fashion of a Dante who knew all knowledge and walked bent beneath that burden. There was, perhaps, Goethe, but I can think of no one else.

The position of the writer was, indeed, changing. Very shortly he was to depend on the sales of his writings. Courts no longer contended for the presence of poets and, since they were no longer employed as diplomats, they lost the added prestige that office lent to their writings.

And as writing became more and more a business for promotion by entrepreneurs, so prose became of more and more importance. Of half a score of writers to whom we must pay all-too-scanty attention before arriving at the age of Shakespeare, seven will prove to be great prosateurs and only three, Villon, Ronsard—and as makeweight to complete the ten—Clément Marot, poets.

Here once more dates become amusing. Villon, whom we may well consider the last of the supreme writers of the middle ages, was born in 1431 and, rather astonishingly, Erasmus was thirty-two and Luther six in the year of his death. What is still more astonishing is that the then—and for long to remain—supreme prose writer of France, Calvin, who was thirty-seven in 1546, the year of the death of Luther, died in 1564 . . . which was the year of Shakespeare's birth. What more singular replacement of one great man by another can ever have taken place? Rabelais, on the other hand, died eleven years before Shakespeare's birth, and Clément Marot, twenty. But when Ronsard died in 1585, Shakespeare had just attained years of sufficient discretion to mourn the loss of the sweetest voice of his day.

Of the great English prose writers, Mallory is suposed to have flourished round 1470, and Warham, the last English Catholic Archbishop of Canterbury and author of that magnificent piece of prose, his Preface to the Bible, having been born in 1470, died in 1532. Three years later was executed Sir Thomas Moore, the beloved author of *Utopia*, and today the most beloved of the English saints.

Of all these thirteen men, ten French and three English, the first of them all was also incontestably the greatest as imaginative writer, for in his own person as poet Villon exemplifies the greatest truth that we can divine from the study of the art of poetry: it is from male suffering supported with dignity that the great poets draw the greatest of their notes—that sort of note of the iron voice of the tocsin calling to arms in the night that forms, as it were, the overtone of their charged words. In the fewest lines of the most frequently quoted but never hackneyed of his ballads you will hear that note as it were rustling. Consider merely:

> *La Reyne blanche comme un lys,*
> *Qui chantoit à voix de seraine,*
> *Berthe au grand pied, Bietrix, Alis,*
> *Haremberge qui tint le Maine. . . .*
> *Où sont-ils, Vierge souveraine?*
> *Mais où sont les neiges d'antan!*

> (That Queen as white as roses be
> Whose voice was like the linnet's lay,
> Large-footed Bertha, Marjorie,
> Alix and Joan and Desirée,
> Ah, Lady Virgin, where be they?
> But where are the snows of yesterday?)

There is the calm beauty of the words and then the thought of the melted snows, the refrain coming at first like a slight catching at the heart but glowing as the poem goes on till it has exactly the effect of the note of a church bell beating out the inevitable decree of destiny. This is not to say that the note of Villon was one of unceasing melancholy, nor yet one of obscenity, blasphemy, crime, squalor or disenchantment. You had, of course, *Repeues franches,* just as you had at moments the little perkinesses such as you find in the envoy of the ballade whose refrain is *"Il n'est bon bec que de Paris."* ("No mouth's worth kissing save in Paris.")

> *Prince, aux dames Parisiennes,*
> *Du beau parler donnez le prix:*
> *En dépit des Italiennes,*
> *Il n'est bon bec que de Paris.*

Certainly the ballades are very often quoted, but one could scarcely read too often in a day of disappearing faith the supreme outcry of agonizing Christianity—"The Ballade of Hanged Men":

> *Frere humains, qui aprés nous vivez,*
> *N'ayez les cueurs contre nous endurcis,*
> *Car, se pitié de nour povres avez,*
> *Dieu en aura plus tost de vous merciz.*
> *Vous nous voyez cy at achez cinq, six.*
> *Quant de la chair, que trop avon nourrie,*
> *Elle est pieça devorée et pourrie,*
> *Et nous, les os, devenons cendre et pouldre.*
> *De nostre mal personne ne s'en rie,*
> *Mais priez Dieu que tous nous vueille absoudre.*

Ye brother men who after us shall live,
Let not your hearts 'gainst us hardened be.
If of your pity to our shades ye give
God shall reward you with His charity.
We five or six that hanging here you see
Were once stark lowsels, stalwarts, overnourished.
Shredded away the flesh that once thus flourished,

Now we are bones and they too shall dissolve.
Mock not at us but, of your courtesy,
Give prayer to Him who can us all absolve!

There may have been more affrighting words than this epitaph to
the *codicille* of the *Great Testament*, but the note is the authentic
one of the *Inferno* itself, and it was written by a man on what he considered to be the night before his execution. But consider, nevertheless,
the sort of equanimity with which it is written, the deliberation of the
choice of words, the absence of lamentation, the erectness, as it were,
of the man's spine, the lack of any note of despair. And that brings us
to the second note of the supreme tragic masterpiece. It will never be
harrowing; it will always stimulate. When you read this epitaph you
feel none of the sensation of depression and of diminished vitality such
as you feel in reading works of an overcharged piled-up and arbitrary
gloom like Tolstoy's *Resurrection*. On the contrary, your heart beats
faster and more strongly the moment you have the conception of this
ragamuffin and thief—(And what Christian man of his day could have
been anything but a thief, since comfort was only attainable by means
of the assassin's dagger and the hangman's cord? . . . So that to be a
really decent man you must be destitute.)—the conception, then, of this
ragamuffin and thief, cast for death because of an assault on a priest,
and yet, as it were, swinging his ragged cloak arrogantly in the face
of destiny and calmly jotting down words which will never die.

There is, indeed, nothing but stimulation in the thought and, at it,
you may well quote in their literal sense Maubougon's immortally
ironic words, "*Cela vous donne une fière idée de l'homme.*" The
spectacle of this man's fortitude makes you proud to be a man since
one of your species has been capable of it. So arrogant in the face of
august but unreasonable destiny, touching his beret and uttering his
prayer for humanity to Christ, Villon, pardoned as one of the first acts
of the infamously reputed Charles VII, issues from the narrow postern
gate of the prison at Meung into the slime and the blackness of the
little vennel that still conducts the water of rains and sinks down from
the door. And so he is exiled from France, goes to England and

makes his famous retort to King Edward V*; is pardoned as one of the first acts of the reign of the infamously reputed Louis XI . . . and so vanishes amongst the snows of yesterday. Legend declares that he passed the last years of his life under a powerful and benevolent clerical patron in directing the state's production of Passion Plays in his native village. But the thought seems almost too pretty. In any case, the date and place of his death are unknown. . . .

Almost a hundred years after Villon came Ronsard who wrote the famous sonnet *"Quand vous serez bien vieille, au soir à la chandelle,"* which almost every subsequent author from Shakespeare to Thackeray and Mr. W. B. Yeats has paraphrased, and which this writer thus rendered in his youth:

When you are old and dim the candles burn,
Seated beside the fire, with distaffs, gossiping,
You shall read out this verse and say: "Why here's a thing!
Ronsard m'a célébrée du temps que j'etais jeune!"
There shall be no old spinster shall not turn,
Though half asleep above the brands that sing
And, hearing of my name cry: "Here's a thing!
Ronsard extols our dame from out his urn!"

My soul shall wander through the myrtle dust
Of fields Elysian; thou, as thou must,
Shalt bend, all bent, above the dying brands.
Ah, lady, seize the hour, the minute flies,
Resort thee hither where thy true love lies
Nor wait till winter's hail torture thy tender hands!

* Edward V showed Villon the arms of France emblazoned in a necessary apartment not usually mentioned in polite circles: *"Vous estes tres-sage,"* luy dit Villon, *"et tres-curieux de vostre santé et de sa conservation, d'en agir de la sorte, puisque cet objet formidable, ayant la proprieteé de faire transir de peur tous ceux qui le regardent, il vous esmeut, luy seul, de telle façon, qu'il fait sur vous, en ce lieu, ce que cinquante purgations ne sçauroient faire."* (The translation would not be suited to polite ears.)

The attentive reader of these pages will remember that the thought of the sewing maid falling asleep by the side of her mistress who is waiting for her lover comes from Catullus, for whom Ronsard had the greatest affection. But as Ronsard and Montaigne lived well into the time of the Elizabethans—Ronsard dying three years before and Montaigne four years after the defeat of the Spanish Armada, and thus, respectively, twenty-one and twenty-eight years after the birth of Shakespeare—we may defer considering them until the next chapter when we shall arrive at Eliza's spacious days.

BOOK II

Part One

CHAPTER ONE

THE period between the consecration of Archbishop Warham in 1504 and the death of Thomas Vaughan, the Silurist, in 1695 is the Augustan Age of Anglo-Saxon literature. It is the works that were written between those years that give our art its incontestable right to stand amongst the great literatures of the world. It was preceded by the limbo that stretched between the death of Chaucer and the birth of Warham. The eighteenth century, coming after it, may well glory in the name of a Silver Age—one of delightful imitations, pastiches, and conventions, for the most part. But that Tudor-Stuart period stands alone amongst the literatures of the world—along with the Ages of Homer, of Pericles, of Augustus, of Louis XIV, or, in a different degree, of Flaubert.

During that period, literature—coming on like a great wave from the Cathay with which we began our speculations, sweeping right up over Italy and the West of Europe—had not so much crossed the Channel as sprung from the country and climes of Petrarch and Boccaccio to land in our lost islands of the Atlantic. Our literature of that epoch may be said to have consisted of *Romeo and Juliet* and the *Duchess of Malfi* and their accompaniments and followers.

It was the beginning of the modern era. It is symbolical that a considerable writer like Raleigh should in those days have foreseen the triumphs of steam; it is still more symbolical that a great writer of the Elizabethan-Jacobean era should have made a considerable fortune by the application of mass-productive methods to the written and spoken word. Only two writers, Virgil and Shakespeare, in a millennium and a half, can be noted as having made large fortunes. Virgil acquired his by way of gifts. Shakespeare, by exploiting his own gifts as a theatrical producer, stands before us not merely as the greatest of poet-playwrights but as the first Anglo-Saxon big business man.

This rather startling conclusion is worth bearing in mind: not merely because it is literally true but, being literally true, it is almost blazingly symbolical. Shakespeare, fortunately, does not much abide our ques-

445

tion. As a personality he is most of all the face that with a good-natured scepticism seems to look up at us from the pages of his books. He might have been Iago; he might have been Hamlet. He was per-haps not Othello—or he may have been. He, probably, considered him-self to resemble his melancholy Jacques—and that, probably, because he considered himself *poète manqué*, a poet who had not, as poet, been able to make a success of things.

Let us, however, for the moment forget Shakespeare. He must of necessity bulk very largely in the consideration of English Elizabethan literature. But in the shadow of his bulk too many great poets are apt to be unduly beshadowed. Without any Shakespeare at all, Elizabethan-Jacobean England would still have a great literature; nevertheless, when you include him in your consideration of the period the whole of that literature is dwarfed. That is at once reasonable and not very reasonable.

It is reasonable because it is a human tendency almost to deify the supremely great writers. Then, beside them, the writers not so great are merely human. Homer is a god; Theocritus a delightful pastoral singer. Dante is a god; Guido Cavalcanti an entertaining atheist; Shakespeare is a god, George Herbert, a gentle hymnalist. . . . Yet without the three gods the three men would be very great poets.

This period began with the polyphonic prose of Warham, the arch-bishop, to end with the muted note of Vaughan, the Silurist poet. Warham was a great and gentle man, too gentle, perhaps, to be very great, but great enough to be a conciliatory factor in times of violence and mental confusion. A great lawyer, he was at once Henry VIII's chancellor and the Pope's Archbishop of Canterbury. So he had to be conciliatory. . . . And he was, finally resigning the chancellorship to Cardinal Wolsey and continuing without murmurs to be Archbishop of Canterbury. He was indeed one of the signatories of the King's peti-tion for divorce to Rome. But what is immediately most important for us to consider is that in his joint position as chancellor and archbishop he was a very wealthy man and that he devoted almost the whole of his wealth to the promotion of the cause and to the support of the bodies, of the humanists of his day. He subsidized impartially both Calvin and Erasmus. On Erasmus he conferred the archiepiscopal rectorate of the village of Aldington in Kent . . . and it is amusing to remember that in that village there is a building that Erasmus is still supposed to haunt, though there is no evidence that Erasmus ever went there. But the great tythe was regularly paid him as long as Warham lived.

This writer has always considered the great age of English prose as beginning with Warham's afterwards suppressed preface to the earlier edition of the translation of the Bible that Henry VIII at first sanctioned. It is true that that piece of writing has to stand up against the prose of Tyndale's translation from the Greek and Hebrew, and Coverdale's from the German. And if anyone is going to take up the cudgels for either Tyndale or Coverdale as against Warham, this writer will not enter the lists against any such champion. It is sufficient to say that Tyndale's prose has always the sub-coloring of the Hebrew quasi-verse, whilst Warham, as lawyer almost more than churchman, conveys into his prose, somewhat more resonance and considerably more directness.

It was not merely a verse-writer's and churchman's age. The pens of the lay prosateurs also became busy in the early years of Elizabeth. That was because of the activities of the humanists and because those writers appropriated prose for the purpose of what it is the custom to call "serious" literature. From their activities arose the modern languages: under the pens of Calvin, Luther and Warham—or one of his contemporaries—modern French, German and English first lived. To say that the language of the modern English or American newspaper exactly reproduces the language of Warham's Preface would be to exaggerate. But the backbone and structure of both languages are identical. It is by a continuous return to the Elizabethan of the prayerbook and the drama that the language is preserved as a relatively efficient medium for the communication of Anglo-Saxon thought. After Dr. Johnson, English was in danger of becoming an almost effete pastiche of Latin phrases; then the essayists like Lamb and Hazlitt and the new poets like Keats and, in a lesser degree, Shelley so bathed themselves in the phraseology of the Elizabethans that their writings gave a new turn to the language In addition, since then, the artificial Shakespearean studies of the schools and the more spontaneous reading of the Authorized Version and the Book of Common Prayer have made the language of the Elizabethan-Jacobean centuries the second tongue of almost every Anglo-Saxon individual . . . and of how many subject races? Indeed, you might put it that the lettered Hindoo of to-day could hardly set up for a properly educated man if he could not read *Gammer Gurton's Needle* at least as fluently as a headline in the *Manchester Guardian* or, in the alternative, the *Detroit Free Press*. And if that is true of the Hindu, how much more is it not true of the inhabitant of Lancashire in England or of the State of Michigan in the United States. Hodge, speaking as follows, is certainly more difficult to follow than the leaders of either periodical mentioned above:

Gammer Gurton's Needle: The fyrst Acte. The Second Sceane.

Hodge: Diccon

Hodge: See! so cham arayed with dablynge in the durt!
She that set me to ditchinge, ich wold she had the sqrt!
Was neuer poore soule that such a life had!
Gogs bones this filthy glaye hase drest me to bad!
Gods soule, see how this stuffe teares!

(He examines the rents in his breeches.)
Ich were better to be a bearward and set to keepe beares!
By the masse, here is a gasshe, a shameful hole indeed!
And one styltch furder a man may thrust in his heade!

But apart from the spelling whose mysteries any person of any lingual pretensions at all may perfectly easily pierce, and for which the printer is mostly responsible, there is nothing unfamiliar in the thought, the phraseology or the construction of the above sentences. "Cham" looks an unfamiliar word; actually it means nothing more unusual than "I (ich) am." At that stage of the language, just emerging from the welter of Anglo-Saxon and mediaeval Anglo-French, a good many words retained certainly their primeval pronunciation and not infrequently their spelling.

The having of this Elizabethan well of lingual purity and picturesqueness to which to return has of course its disadvantages. Without Shakespeare and the Bible behind them it is probable that the
headlines of the *Manchester Guardian* and the *Detroit Free Press*
would today be written in languages as different as is English from
Dutch. But the constant recurrence of the Elizabethan rhythms and
verbiages in the English of the succeeding centuries gives to the prose
of both sides of the Atlantic a certain monotony of cadence and a certain derivativeness of phrase which prevent its being as clear and
concise a vehicle for thought as it well might be. The writer of "serious" English books or articles, as long as he is merely rendering information, will be content to confine himself to a sort of pruned
Johnsonian. But as soon as he tries to enforce his moral or to urge his
fellows to better courses, he will be apt to introduce into his prose the
rhythms or verbiage of the Bacon of "On Gardens;" or, if he inclines
to be very exhortatory indeed, he will imitate both the rhythms and
the vocabulary of the Cranmer of the *Book of Common Prayer* or of
the Lancelot Andrewes of the *Authorised Version*. Imaginative writers
will even go as far as to introduce echoes of Lyly's *Euphues*.

Lyly is indeed a nice case in point. Consider the following:

Campaspe. The Prologue at Court.

We are ashamed that our bird, which fluttereth by twilight
seeming a swan, should be proued a bat, set against the sun. But,
as Jupiter placed Silenus' asse among the starres, and Alcibiades
couered his pictures, being owles and apes, with a curtaine imbroid-
ered with lions and eagles: so are we forced upon a rough discourse to draw upon a smooth excuse, resembling lapidaries who
thinke to hide the crack in a stone by setting it deepe in gold. The
Gods supped once with poore Baucis; the Persian kings sometimes
shaued sticks: our hope is your Highness wil at this time lend an
eare to an idle pastime. Appion, raising Homer from Hell, demanded only who was his father; we, calling Alexander from his
grave, seek only who was his love. . . .

Lyly was about twenty years older than Shakespeare and Marlowe —who were both born in 1564—and the younger men were fifteen when he published his *Euphues*, which was followed, in 1580, by *Euphues His England*.

It must have been the first "best seller"—the first novel to find enormous popularity. This was rather on account of the elaborate, ornate and perpetually antithetical nature of its prose than on account of its story, which is monotonous and cannot, one would have imagined, have had much interest even for the Elizabethans except for the exciting nature of its setting. *Euphues,* indeed, played little part in the evolution of the English novel; for that we have to go to the Spaniards. But it is quite possible to give Lyly much too little credit for his share in the maturing of English prose. His immense vogue lasted for thirty years after which, by natural process of reaction, he passed into the shadows of near-oblivion, only to reëmerge as rather a figure of fun. The word "euphuism" today stands for a white lie couched in too elaborate politenesses. That is mostly because of the instinctive Anglo-Saxon disbelief that conscious art plays any part—or, at least, ought to play any part—in the production of works of literature. What Lyly really did was to prove that English was a language that could be juggled with, the process giving delight to its practitioners and to such readers as could take pleasure in watching feats upon the tight-rope. And that is as much as to say that with him the English language came of age. Till his day it had in its written forms a certain stiffness: it was better for conveying menace or reproach or exhortation than for the promotion of delight. After *Euphues* it had command, as you might say, of all its faculties. It was the layman's contribution, as far as prose was concerned, to a form of communication that had hitherto been the almost exclusive purview of the churchman and the lawyer.

Nor is the style of Lyly fantastic, as the prevailing critics, who are contemners of all care about style, would have you believe. The passage from his *Alexander & Campaspe* quoted above was selected by this writer simply because he happened to have had it in his head since very tender years so that he could put it down without having to turn up a reference. That may be taken as evidence that upon at least one reader Lyly's style made a lasting impression. And, indeed, when this writer was aged twelve *Campaspe* bulked almost more largely in the shelf of his favorite literature than almost any other place of writing except perhaps *Lazarillo De Tormes*. He must have reread it more often than any other book. And even today, rereading it for probably the last time, he seems to recapture a good many of his childhood's pleasurable emotions.

Have that fact what critical value it may, it is none the less true that that quoted passage would seem to be pretty good English— simple enough, direct enough and quite convincing. I do not know any writer who could do much better than: "Appion, raising Homer from Hell, demanded only who was his father; we, calling Alexander from his grave, seek only who was his love," for agreeableness of cadence, simplicity of statement and ingenuity of poetic invention. It is, of course, a "made" antithesis of a professional prosateur rather than the artless and spontaneous babbling of the gentlemanly or scholarly writer. That may be decried. But it remains a fact that without the occasional labors of the rare professional prosateur, a national prose may very easily run off the road. Where for instance would our prose stand today without the straightening process that it went through at the hands of Cardinal Newman, George Moore, W. H. Hudson, to name only simplifiers, or Walter Pater and Joseph Conrad to include also those who added ornament and cadence.

That is why it seems appropriate—and, indeed, expedient—to begin our consideration of the Elizabethan-Jacobean period with Lyly rather than with one of the larger fixed stars of literature. Blank-verse drama and versified narrative would, on the face of it, appear to bulk more largely in the literary consciousness than does the prose of that era —even though the Bible and the Book of Common Prayer come to the aid of that prose. Of major prose writers of the earlier part of those two centuries, between the sixteenth and the eighteenth, hardly more than Saint (Sir) Thomas Moore of the *Utopia*—though to be sure that was written originally in Latin—; than Lyly himself; than Bacon of the *Essaies*; or than Sir Thomas Browne of *Urn Burial* leap immediately to the mind. Later, from Defoe to perhaps the greatest of all our prose writers, Clarendon, there were to be enough prose writers, whilst verse, in the hands of Donne, Crashaw, Milton, Herbert and the rest, was beginning to crystallize itself more and more into the aspect of a sweetmeat.

But when one thinks of the earlier years of that period one thinks of the dramatists, the writers of verse-narrative, like the *Fairy Queen* and the translators of the Bible and the compilers of Cranmer's Prayer Book of 1522. Beside them such prose works as Green's *Groat's Worth of Wit*, Coryat's *Crudities* or Culpepper's *Herbal* sink merely to the level of antique dealers' local curiosities . . . as which, indeed, it is a good thing to consider them.

By the turn of the century, that early part of the era was finally equipped with one perfected organ in the shape of its more bejewelled language of the boards. And yet a third was its carefully evolved and eminently practicable dramatic form. And then again the most precious endowment of the age was its unsurpassed mental activities; its unconquerable curiosities.

Men of Action are accustomed to think of Eliza's spacious age as one characterized by great deeds, colonizations, victories, explorings. Actually, as the Man of Thought soon comes to perceive, those lusty deeds occupied an infinitesimal portion of the population. The major glories of both exploring and settlement went to the Spaniards and when, a hundred and fifty years later than they, England really began to send out settlers to the New World, so averse were the population from trusting themselves to oversea adventure that the colonial contingents had to be made up largely of criminals and to be completed by the sweepings of the French gaols.*

* This sentence may perhaps startle. But Aubrey, in a passage that I have never seen quoted, states that Sir William Davenant—whom in his cheerful way he asserts to have been an illegitimate son of Shakespeare, Shakespeare staying with his parents regularly on his way to and from Stratford-on-Avon—Davenant then, seeking cutlers for Virginia, made an arrangement with the French king to buy all his cutlers who happened to be in gaol. . . . So going into the common gaol at Bordeaux and having only one word germane to the purpose he called out: "*Couteau!*" Whereupon every prisoner there, taking Sir William to mean that the mere possession of a knife would warrant their being set at liberty and being allowed to travel overseas. . . every prisoner there raised his hand, and many of them were taken . . . for the F.F.V.

The physical glories of the Spacious Age were thus relatively rare. With the very considerable aid of God—*afflavit Deus et dissipati sunt* —and of very superior armament, we almost bloodlessly defeated the Armada and plundered a number of helpless treasure ships. Raleigh also sent out some perfectly inefficient expeditions. If we like to be proud of that, we may. But our real glory of those days was in our arts. The country was so enriched by plunder of the Spaniards and trade with the Italians and others that great and comfortable houses began to dot all the English countrysides. Thus, there was born that sort of bastard domestic renaissance architecture which, being so much more satisfactory than the products of the real Italian renaissance, to this day constitutes the greatest treasure of the English countryside. In addition, the mental explorations, journeyings and plunderings of our scholars and poets were almost incomparable in any clime in any age since that of Pericles. A new translation of a classic thrown into that clamorous flood of writers would in an instant be torn into pieces, devoured or carried off to be inserted in the plunderer's fabric, much as, under the jaws of the bonito of South African waters, in five minutes the last thread of flesh will be stripped from a mule that strays into that stream. So our private—allegorical—image of the world of the English intelligentsia of that day may well be that of a small, dreadfully overcrowded mud-flat on which, on their tip-toes, teeter a packed mob of truculent, bearded, short-cloaked, bereted, literary thieves . . . on tip-toe, jostling, with their hands stretched over their heads, clutching desperately at the straws, feathers, dead leaves and other light, flying detritus of lore or culture blown over their heads, coming from the Mediterranean.

It might be going much too far to say—as has, indeed, been said— that Shakespeare never had a thought of his own but got it all from translations; it was, nevertheless, true that the immense tide of Mediterranean civilization burst, like a tidal wave, against the bulwarks of the last outpost of Europe. A continual stream of traffic went on between the English ports and Venice, Genoa,* Leghorn and the rest

---

* It is interesting to think that on a voyage on a Genoese merchant galleon bound for London, Columbus, escaping from Algerian pirates who had sacked his vessel, swam

of the Mediterranean. Far more gentlemen adventurers went from England to Italy with their cargoes—of hops, wool, cannon, kettles, chimneybacks—than ever ventured beyond the remote Cassiterides. It was, indeed, almost the Grand Tour that every gentleman must make . . . Cadiz, Marseilles, Leghorn, much more than the Westward Ho of which we have heard so much more fully. And since the means of locomotion were so much slower then than today, such gentlemen as went towards the Levant stayed much longer and became much more imbued with the local civilization. The Italian proverb —which you may still hear in Italy today—*Ingles' Italianato, Diavol' incarnato* ("the Italianate Englishman is a devil incarnate")—was formulated in the Spacious Days. It is a token at once of how many English the coastwise Italians must have seen and of how easily they lapped up the juice of the pomegranate.

Shakespeare himself would seem to have inclined rather to French than to Italian sources. It is, thus, plain from the scene showing Coriolanus in the house of Aufidius, in *Coriolanus*, that Shakespeare, rather astonishingly, read the French version by Amyot of Plutarch's *Lives* rather than the admirable translation of Sir Thomas North or the current Italian version. But that fact and the scenes in fluid French between Henry V and Katherine of France in *Henry V* become less astonishing when one learns that, whilst he was writing them, Shakespeare was lodging with a family of French silk-weavers in Spitalfields. At any rate, almost the only formal, legal record of his existence is to be found in the official transcript—still in the Rolls Office—of the evidence of the trial of a breach-of-promise case. In this the poet gives testimony in favor of the daughter of a French weaver with whom he was lodging. She was being sued for refusing to marry, not Shakespeare of course, but some compatriot amongst the silk-weavers. And there is nothing to prevent one's imagining that the charm of the poet's mind may have been the occasion for

---

ashore and was saved on the coast of Portugal . . . and so came to the Court of Spain. But for that missed venture it would have been to Elizabeth that he made his proposal for his voyage westward.

her not wishing to consummate the other union. Or, if you are that sort of person, you may draw for yourself the poet in his dim chamber, poring with the French young woman beside him, over a paper on which they are concocting the speeches of *Henry V* and *his* French young woman.

For it is not to be imagined that Shakespeare any more than any of his other contemporaries was above taking any help anywhere that he could find it. He certainly larded his lines with translations and, not merely that, he liberally accepted presents of lines or even scenes from Marlowe, Green, Fletcher and the rest. And probably he gave help as liberally. These things are difficult to determine. In a play ascribed to Marlowe and several assistants and called: *"The True Tragedie of Richard Duke of Yorke & the Death of Good King Henrie the Sixt"* the mind goes rather drowsily through rather humdrum verse and not very inspiring images or incidents, with classicisms dragged in, as in this passage from the account of the death of Henry VI:

> *Gloucester:* Why, what a foole was that of Crete
> That taught his sonne the office
> Of a birde and yet for all that the poore
> Fowle was drownde.

Henry VI replying:

> I, *Dedalus*, my poore son Icarus,
> Thy father Minos that denide our course,
> Thy brother Edward the sunne that fearde his wings . . .

the last line making nonsense until you explain it by saying that the barbarous printer has substituted an "f" for a long "s," so that the phrase should run: "The sunne that seared his wings," and as you read, your mind runs rather on such matters as printer's errors than on the poetry or pathos of the scene. You notice that the blank verse has completely broken down in the speech of Gloucester. . . .

Well, it was Marlowe's habit, apparently for the sake of relief, to introduce speeches in prose into the middle of his blank verse. So Marlowe or any other of his two or three collaborators may well have
written Crookback's speech in prose and the unspeakable printer—
for the printer of those days was really unspeakable when it came
to printing blank verse—may simply have broken the lines up. It is
all at any rate rather dull and amateurish and appears to echo better
matter. And so when you come suddenly upon:

> *Glo.* What? will the aspiring bloud of Lancaster
>   Sinke into the ground. I had thought it would have
>   mounted!,

your pulse gives a quick leap. Because, certainly, that is the voice
of Shakespeare, unmistakable and singularly moving in its human-
ness. Shakespeare, of course, was there collaborating!

The writer is supposing you to be not one of the fully equipped
textual commentators of Elizabethan verse, such as the universities
ceaselessly turn out by a process of mass production. No, you are someone that loves poetry and humannesses, and choose to form your estimates for yourself. You may be a poet. Then you will be hopelessly
bewildered.

The cloud of textual witnesses as to the Elizabethan minor texts
is infinite and all-obscuring. A great portion of the *True Tragedy* is
incorporated into Shakespeare's *Henry VI*, the earliest of his plays
to be attributed exclusively to him. Hundred percent Shakespeare-
worshippers amongst the critics explain this by saying that Marlowe,
Shakespeare, Green, the author of the *Groat's Worth*, and Peele,
author of the plays *David & Bethsabe* and the *Old Wives' Tale* . . .
all these four collaborated to write the *True Tragedie*. . . . And Shakespeare, very scrupulously, only took out his own lines and, aided by
Marlowe, from them put together his second and third parts of
Henry VI. Other sterner critics declare that Marlowe and Green
wrote the *True Tragedie* between them and that Shakespeare then
unscrupulously—or merely amorally—stole their work and incorporated
it into his own. They base the theory on the sole fact that the ill-

natured Green—who was to die before the *True Tragedy* was printed
—in the *Groat's Worth* calls Shakespeare an "upstart crowe." But you
can add a great deal of confusion to the affair by juggling a little
with the dates and pointing out that Green probably died, and at
any rate the *Groat's Worth* was printed, before the second and third
parts of Shakespeare's *Henry VI* appeared. In that case, Green's sneer
must be put down to simple jealousy . . . as it well may have been.

   This sort of delving into dates of the Elizabethan drama is as agreeable as any other form of stamp-collecting and not much more difficult. The more dignified and literary form of the pursuit is that of
examining the plays and judging, by the inspiration, the forms and
the rhythms of the passages, to whom to ascribe them. That the
reader may well do for himself with the assurance of mental profit
and dignity. The identification of the greater voices—Shakespeare,
Marlowe, the later Jonson or Webster—is not difficult. But the lesser
writers fell more into patterns and are more easily confused. That
was because in the earlier stages Marlowe, and, in the later, Ben
Jonson, exercised such an influence on their days that the days themselves were colored by them. A young writer had to be influenced
by one or the other, and unless he had, or developed, an individual
strength he was apt to remain so colored. The differences between
the greater writers were temperamental and as it were matters of
length of breath. In images Marlowe was as beautiful as Shakespeare
and kin enough to him.

> Was this the face that launched a thousand ships
> And burned the topless towers of Ilium.

is obviously as beautiful and as imagined as anything ever written
by Shakespeare or anyone else. Or so again is

> Cut is the branch that might have grown full straight
> And bruisëd is Apollo's laurel bough
> That sometime grew within this learnëd man.

But in each case, immediately afterwards, the rhythm and the imagination break down into the merest prosaicisms. In the first case, you go on for eleven commonplace and rather halting classicisms before coming again on poetry in:

> O thou art fairer than the evening air,
> Clad in the beauty of a thousand stars.

And then the rather inappropriate classicism closes in again with:

> Brighter art thou than flaming Jupiter
> When he appear'd to hapless Semele . . .

which, in itself, would appear to be a singular compliment to address to a beautiful lady, especially since the poet emphasizes the note by going on to compare Helen to blazing Jove in Arethusa's arms. But Marlowe, at any rate in the character of Faustus, had to have classical instances and, if he ran out of good ones, must use the next best.

Shakespeare, having perhaps less Latin, had more human and natural instances at his disposal and perhaps a greater sense of . . . humor. He could compare his lady to a summer's day and go on for fourteen lines at always the same level, bringing in for comparison the darling buds of May rather than Jove "in wanton Arethusa's azur'd arms." And he had the quality of the longer breath. Even in his least satisfactory earlier plays, before he ventures on an image he has the ground, as it were, prepared behind it, so that it shall not fall into anticlimax.

Take, say, this from *King John*:

> If that the midnight bell
> Did with its iron tongue and brazen throat
> Sound on into the drowsy ear of night:
> If this same were a churchyard where we stand
> And thou possessed with a thousand wrongs:
> Or if that surly spirit, melancholy,
> Had baked thy blood and made it heavy, thick . . .

and so on and on to:

> Or if that thou couldst hear me without ears,
> See me without thine eyes and make reply
> Without a tongue, using conceit alone . . .
> Without eyes, ears and harmful sound of words
> . . . I then could tell thee . . .

It is from the scene in which John is suborning Hubert to kill Arthur. And, given the dramatic circumstance, the piling of image on image, which otherwise would be plethoric, becomes here the real *progression d'effet* of the French. So that with each image, appropriate enough and sufficiently magically worded to hold the mind, you find yourself saying: "Why doesn't the man get on? What is he going to ask for?" So the actual beginning of the temptation of Hubert comes like an explosion.

One discovers usually that writing that has the aspect of extreme ease and fluency is written with the greatest difficulty and preparation. But that can hardly have been the case with Shakespeare. One is told that he never blotted a line—and, that apart, *King John* came in that middle period of his productivity, between 1594 and 1601, when he was writing at his fastest the comedies and the tragedies of the falls of kings. What with his acting and his preoccupation with the management of his theatres, he would hardly have had the time to do much halting or reflection over his play-writing. He must have written each play in one spurt and no doubt with assistants filling in passages whilst he was on the stage or in the box-office.

Then, by the constant practice of his art, he must have attained to a skill that at no moment failed him. He must have been consummate.

To that greater eminence, the perhaps more generous, careless and adventurous Marlowe never attained. He was the far more romantic and untidy figure: He was under a charge of atheism when he died whilst attempting to kill a man called Ingram Frizer. The coroner's verdict was that Marlowe was the assailant. He would seem also to have been employed in the contemporary equivalent of the Secret

Service. He was, too, adored and, dying aged less than thirty, had already his legend. Just as Lyly had the renown of his antithetic prose, so the renown of his mighty line made Marlowe the model for his generation's verse. He was, in short, the Steerforth to Shakespeare's Copperfield.

That Shakespeare, and no doubt Jonson and even Webster, profited by his precocity cannot be much questioned . . . Shakespeare in particular. He had been born in the same year as Marlowe; yet the precocious Marlowe has all the air of having been his preceptor, Jonson being the younger by nine and Webster, born in 1580, by sixteen, years. At any rate, it seems to be reasonably certain that Marlowe helped Shakespeare at least with the second and third parts of *Henry VI*. (Miss Elizabeth Lee who is the soundest and most human of commentators of the Elizabethan drama fairly well proves that, and thinks besides that Marlowe and perhaps Green and Peele collaborated in the *True Tragedy*.)

If you think of the Mermaid Tavern as a Hollywood director's ante-room; the bills of the plays, if there had been bills of the plays, as containing almost as many names of writers, musicians, lyricists, directors and collaborators of every sort as do the programmes of films today; and if you think of the names of those directors and participators as being not only Burbage, Henslowe and the later Shakespeare but the great stars Jonson, Kyd, Dekker, Webster, Heywood, Ford and the rest, you will not fall very far from the mark of the truth. For the great truth about the Elizabethan-Jacobean drama is that like all the art of great periods it was the result of a movement that was a revolt against tradition.

The almost sudden discovery that because of its possibilities of mass consumption the drama could be as money-making as the exploiting of the mines and unfortunate inhabitants of Golconda . . . that sudden new prospect, added to the coming into the field of the first pupils of the new grammar schools of Edward VI, caused a sudden rush to London of a completely new class of mental adventurers— the classically educated sons of the considerable merchants of the countryside. It was not just accidentally that Shakespeare, the son of a rich glovemaker, Marlowe the son of a shoemaker probably still better off, the one educated at the admirable grammar school of Stratford-on-Avon and the other at the still famous King's School at Canterbury, should simultaneously have gone to London and both have ended as playwrights . . . one at least as a gentleman with coat armor. These young men were the advance flight of a class that was later to take over the control of the realm. Their coming to the metropolis and founding a complete new industry was the forerunner of the unrest that was to make Charles I lose his head on the scaffold. Their generation wrote plays about the fall of kings; their sons made kings fall.

That perhaps goes a little beyond the limits of our immediate speculations. But it is worth while to make the note that the education given at the grammar schools founded by the little king was of as admirable and sound a kind as it was possible to have. The eminent Englishmen who since Shakespeare and Marlowe have had their first education at these institutions have been uncountable up to the days of Mr. H. G. Wells who must have had almost the same education, at a Kentish Grammar School, as had Shakespeare, Marlowe, Jonson and Webster. The consideration should be enough to dispose of those doubters of the Shakespearean origins of the plays who base their rather ignorant speculations on the question of where Shakespeare got his knowledge. Had there been no grammar schools, there might well have been no *Coriolanus*; but, since grammar schools there were and Shakespeare had his boundless curiosity as to the nature of men and waves and all things, there is nothing remarkable at all about the case. Shakespeare profited above the others, no doubt, in the fact that he did not go to a university. He passed the part of his life that Marlowe and Jonson spent at Cambridge apparently in running, like de Quincey, the cruel streets of London. That meant, if you like, that Marlowe could liken Helen to Jove in the arms of Arethusa, and Jonson, having read Theophrastus, acquired the trick of doing his characters all in one piece, each one with only one passion. But in the cold arms of his cruel stepmother Shakespeare learned at once how fortunes go up and down and how men bear the vicissitudes that beset all our lives. According to legend—and it is expedient to pay attention to legends, for though they will frequently be inaccurate as to exact fact, they will usually be pretty deadly in the portrayal of the sort of thing a man may have done or been Shakespeare passed eight years or so alternately as lawyer's clerk and ostler. He is said even to have traded in wool. He married at eighteen and within two years was on the London streets. That is authentic. And legend says that his first occupation was that of holding, outside the Globe Theatre, the horses of the gallants who came to display their many-colored cloaks on the very stage of the theatre. It adds, a little more luridly, that part of his duties was to bite off the heads of chickens that his patrons tossed him to prepare for their after-theatre suppers. . . . And so we can imagine Burbage coming breathlessly out of the Globe, a super having failed him, and engaging Shakespeare for the hind legs of one of Marlowe's jades of Asia . . . And so to being the ghost of Hamlet's father . . . and the father of Hamlet.

Marlowe preceded him by three years in being represented on the stage, his *Tamburlaine* having been produced in 1587 as against the 1590 of Shakespeare's *Henry VI*. As against that, the *Every Man in His Humour* of Jonson—who was nine years younger than the other two—was not produced until 1598. As regards Webster, his first play, written in collaboration with Dekker, was first produced in 1602, his immortal *Duchess of Malfi* not appearing until 1616. Of the other most notable dramatists of the day, the date of the birth of Heywood, author of the almost equally immortal *Woman Killed with Kindness*, is not known, though his death date is given as 1650. And John Ford, writer of *'Tis Pity She's a Whore*, was born in 1586 and died in 1639. . . . So from the birth of Kyd in 1558 to the death of Heywood in 1650 was nearly a century. The era of great drama lasted, thus, long enough—longer than that of most great literary movements.

Of these figures—and one may take them as forming the prominent group in the movement—one may imagine Marlowe and Jonson, supporting, as it were between them, the on-the-surface more diffident author of *Lear*. Marlowe, the generous, golden, untidy genius died young and found no one to say a word against him. Jonson, on the other hand, lived to be of considerable age for those years, surviving Shakespeare by two decades, and being the almost unquestioned dictator of the literary scene during the latter years of his life. He was accounted not only the best actor, but one of the most classically learned men—at any rate among the dramatists—of his day, and, since he was by no means conciliatory or patient with fools, he had his enemies. Thus, Dekker in his *Gull's Horn Book*, a sort of semi-satirical guide to the young man about the town of the day, conse-crates a good deal of his space to rather heavy abuse of the author of the *Alchemist*. Jonson replied by devoting a whole play, the *Poetaster*, to Dekker. That may have been in part professional manoeuvring.

For we may regard the gods of that firmament as tranquilly sup-porting Mr. Burbage, the doyen of the stage managers of the day. But his rival, Mr. Henslowe, managed to get together, with Drayton, Middleton, Munday, Dekker and, above all, Webster, a sufficiently vocal cry of hounds. He succeeded, also, in producing in the year of Shakespeare's death, in the *Duchess of Malfi*, one of the supreme trage-dies of all time.

But it remains one of the pleasantest of thoughts, in the usually rather vinegarish welter of literary affairs and rivalries, that the most intimate friend of Shakespeare's younger days was Marlowe and the most attached at his ending, Jonson. It relieves one, indeed, to think that Jonson frequently visited the gentleman-playwright at Stratford after his retirement. For one has at times the uneasy feeling that that complete retirement, the neglect of his proofs and the suing out of coat armor by the Swan of Avon, as well as the possession by him of a second-best bed to leave to his wife might have implied in that Swan a certain snobbish determination to cut himself off from his old friends of the Mermaid Tavern and from all memory of the fact that he ever wrote plays.

So that one might, if one liked to, think that the Bard *as* Bard was a disappointed man. He would, perhaps, have liked to have written quite other things than plays and quite other plays than the popular stuff that he wrote for money. . . . One is threateningly warned by the professors against believing that any of the utterances of Shake-speare's characters is to be taken as voicing Shakespeare's intimate opinions. It is quite wrong, they say, to imagine from Hamlet's soliloquy that Shakespeare was anything but a sort of imperialist-optimist-anti-defeatist. Nevertheless, one is human, and, once out of the classroom, it is almost impossible not to believe that Shakespeare himself—he caught it probably from Marlowe whilst Marlowe was writing his *Edward II* or collaborating in the *True Tragedy*—Shakespeare himself had a real belief in the divinity of kings, more especially whilst they were engaged in falling . . . or that the speeches of Menenius in *Coriolanus* did not represent Shakespeare's real views of the social question for all time. Still more impossible is it not to believe that in Hamlet's address to the players Shakespeare was voicing his own intimate views of literature and the drama in general and of his own performances in particular. It is impossible not to believe that, if he had not had to make a living he would have—or at least he thought he would have, for he would have probably done nothing of the sort—he would, then, have written tragedies enormously clotted in phrase and construction, full of violently overwritten similes, couched in a language made up of Lylian euphemisms. Or, perhaps, he would not have written plays at all. The nobility and gentry did not write plays. They wrote overburdened verse narratives like *The Faery Queen* and *Arcadia*, sitting in the sun-filled park of Penshurst with rapt lackeys to hold the noble poet's pen and sanderach . . . not panting in a scrabbling trio over sheets of paper on an inn table to get the last act written in time for the evening's curtain to go up.

So Shakespeare probably really was a discontented poet, a little ashamed—as what author of great popularity and some critical sense isn't?—of the way he·had made his money. . . . But, indeed, who amongst us that has merely made a few pennies by his pen but, if he is a proper man, regrets the way they were made and wishes, bitterly unavailing, that he could do it all over again? So we may acquit Shakespeare of literary snobbishness since even in the address to the players he only shows himself nearer to common writing humanity.

And with regard to the second-best bed, we may as well make two points. The leaving of it, and not his best bed to Ann Hathaway did not imply any disrespect or neglect to that lady. On the contrary, it was a sentimentalism: he was leaving her the bed in which they had slept together for thirty-four—interrupted—years, though Aubrey's story of the origins of Sir Henry Davenant would seem to prove that even during his London years his visits to that swan's nest were not infrequent. And then, the possession of a second-best bed implying that of a best one and a chamber to hold it, we have to consider that a high sign of the Shakespearean sense of hospitality.

We have thus, it would appear, been forced into giving more space to the character of Shakespeare than we may be taken as having at first sight intended to. Actually it is so much more to the character than to the work of the man that we have given attention that we may be regarded as having sufficiently adhered to our first intentions. As playwright, as the greatest of all masters of words, as pellucid observer of humanity, he stands so far above any of his contemporaries as to dwarf by comparison the greatest of them. But as man, in his peculiar Hollywoodish ambience, he was not more than third or fourth amongst his peers. For loudness, for picturesque character, for distinguishing traits he must have been far behind Marlowe, Jonson, possibly behind even Webster, Dekker or Ford. And, no doubt, as theatre owner and manager he had less "character" than either Burbage or any of Burbage's rivals. We have to imagine him as moving, as if circumspectly, in those virulent crowds, not roaring like Jonson or Dekker, not manipulating the sword like Marlowe—but snooping, as we have already described Chaucer as doing, with perhaps less sense of the comic but with certainly more sense of the values of a life that had suddenly become modern. He must have been aware that in everything that pertained to the theatre he could put, in the twinkling of an eye, anything right that his colleagues had muddled and must have smiled a perpetual inward smile. They roared and bickered and threatened in dimly lit rooms that had the great oak beams showing through their plaster. He sat waiting to put them right; thinking perhaps of Madame Davenant or the mademoiselle who helped him with his French. Or retiring to an inner chamber to write without blotting a line, containing himself, during that distasteful enterprise, with the thought that every line brought him so much nearer his

Stratford place, his grant of arms, his second-best bed and his seat amongst the town worthies.

At any rate, it is to do the state more service if you treat the Bard of Avon as the novelist would treat him, than if you treat him as does the professor or the professed moralist. No teacher can teach Shakespeare. You might perhaps point out hidden beauties in Villon, because of the difficulties of his language; or a very few annotations of Chaucer might help the reader, because of the complete differentnesses of the habits and frame of mind of his day. But Shakespeare is just ourselves at no excruciatingly esoteric mental level. The English or American adult male is said to remain all his life at about the intellectual high water mark of the fourteen-year-old schoolboy and there is nothing in the thought of Shakespeare's plays that an intelligent fourth-form schoolboy could not enthusiastically applaud and corroborate. You have Menenius as the solver of social problems and the *Taming of the Shrew* as the answer to the woman question. The most the "teacher"—and, alas, *quis docebit ipsos doctores?*—can do for a pupil is to perform the functions of an easier dictionary, telling the meaning of a tassel gentle, a hernshaw, a fardel, a bourne. But no one can explain why Shakespeare's words, set one beside the other, vibrate and live and charm the senses. You read

> Full fathom five thy father lies,
> Of his bones are corals made,
> Those are pearls that were his eyes.
> Nothing of him that doth fade
> But doth suffer a sea change
> Into something rich and strange . . .

and if you are anything like a proper fourth-form schoolboy, you feel all the emotions of first love, of spring freshets, of the call of the cuckoo, of moonlight on the Lido. There is nothing remarkable in the turn of thought; no unusual words are brought from a distance to add peacock's feathers to a fowl's tail. But the supreme verbal secret of Shakespeare appears in the sentence: "Those are pearls that were his eyes."—for that is the Shakespearean mind working.

You or I would think that by some queer process of accretions of lime the eyes would have become pearls, like the round white dead objects that you may see in a boiled fish. But Shakespeare wrote, supremely, "those *are* pearls," because for him those were what they were. Marlowe could write a beautiful image and could not continue in the vein because the image was just a literary device. With Shakespeare an image was an actual thing, as real as the east wind, and part of a frame of mind. He got up of a bright morning and seeing an absurd row of chimney pots leaning back or askew, posturing vaingloriously against a cerulean sky—not, you observe, seeming to do it, but doing it, since it was Shakespeare's mind that was taking them in—seeing, then, that absurd row posturing, irresistible hilarity had filled him. He had imagined Falstaff and his soldiers and knew the feel of the spring. And the sensation did not abandon him when in a dark inner room he took up his distasteful pen. He still smiled inwardly as he created Falstaff with the spring sky reflected in his harness. Falstaff for him was there as were the pearls that *were* eyes. That was his more real world. And that was the smile that seems to look up at you through the pages of his books.

That would be writing very fanciful for a professor of literature. It is the merest commonplace of history for the writer or the real reader who knows how the writer's mind works. Shakespeare had another world to which he could retire; because of that he was a greater poet than either Jonson or Marlowe whose minds were limited by their university-training to finding illustrations, *telles quelles,* from illustrations already used in the Greek or Latin classics. It was the difference between founding a drawing on a lay figure and drawing or painting from a keen and delighting memory.

Another department of the many knowledges indispensable at once to Shakespeare and all his competitors for public favor was that of stagecraft. In that Shakespeare made himself superior to Marlowe by the study of Marlowe at close quarters. But I am personally inclined to doubt whether in the actual atmosphere of the stage he was so immensely superior to his other contemporaries. We are accustomed in our pride to think that our modern stage with its elaborations of painted scene cloths and lightings and the rest is something superior to the bare stage of the Elizabethans. Actually, as a vehicle for conveying emotion, it is incomparably the more feeble. It is, at any rate, a vehicle for a quite other art.

The art of the stage of the Elizabethans differed from today's stagecraft in that it was infinitely more hypnotic. The Elizabethan dramatist had to hypnotize his audience not merely into sympathizing with the flesh-and-blood creatures on the stage but into seeing moonlight, laurel hedges, palaces, cracks in walls or forest glades. He had to write passages descriptive of all these natural objects. His scope for writing was, therefore, vastly larger. The modern stage writer is at his most effective when his text is the merest skeleton decked out with a few epigrams. The actors, lighting mechanics, scene painters and machinists will clothe that skeleton with flesh and give the epigrams gentle voices.

The Elizabethan wrote to be ranted. He needed overaction and vast, harsh voices to cow and affright his audiences. And his audiences were cowed and overwhelmed. The actor who announced the death of Lady Macbeth had a voice with the volume of that of a town bull and a hollow resonance like that of Greek destiny. The audience really shook when they heard him.

This may seem carrying an enquiry into the nature of drama into regions beyond those to which the historian of literature should extend his investigations. But the matter is one of such enormous importance to literature that the reader may well bear with this writer. For the fact is that these Elizabethan plays were not new dramatic experiments but new literary developments. *Hamlet, Othello* and the *Duchess of Malfi* were novels written for ranted recitation; *As You Like It* and still more *The Tempest*, were pieces of pure literature meant to be recited or read aloud by characters who overacted.

Let us give a few examples. We asked, for instance, Mr. Gordon Craig the other day which of all the innumerable plays in which he had acted or which he had witnessed was the best-constructed modern stage play. He said that undoubtedly *The Bells* was. The way in which the whole play worked up to the last passage in which the sledge bells were heard "off" was incomparable. Yet in its written text *The Bells* is a bare farrago of stilted exclamations. And, for what it is worth,

I am prepared to confirm Mr. Craig. That is to say that, of the thousands of modern plays that I have attended, the passage of the sleigh bells which finally sent the murderer mad is the dramatic episode that most remains in my memory and one of the very few that remains in my memory at all—the others being mostly scenes of Ibsen's. . . . And, regarded as literature, the plays of Ibsen are almost unreadable, and read indeed like stilted farces. On the other hand, the most tremendous, the most almost insupportable experience of drama—and I am tempted to say of real life, too—was a performance by actors well-trained to rant of Kyd's *Spanish Tragedy*, and another by the same performers of the *Duchess of Malfi*. Shouted and screamed by men and women in ordinary and very slightly stylized clothes in a studio rather dimly lit with candles as must have been the Elizabethan boards and provided with galleries at differing levels, the dreadful words of Webster and the unceasing assassinations of Kyd became something of such horror in gloom as to be, as I have said, barely supportable. Yet Kyd's tragedy at least, makes pretty poor reading: it seems almost incredible that the intolerably long narrative soliloquies of the Spanish general could ever have "got over." Yet, delivered as I have described, they filled you with an impatience that was of the greatest importance to the play itself. Just as I have described the effect of the midnight bell speech of King John in Shakespeare's play of that name—the effect of that makes you say to yourself: "Why *can't* the man get on?"—so Kyd's immensely long speeches hasten your impatience to know what is coming. And it has to be remembered that you can lay a book down, but to leave in the middle of a play is something repugnant to most audiences. So you have to hear the general.

The Elizabethan recited novel, then, is on its technical side much more a matter of prolonged psychological screwings up than one of snappy short situations backed by practicable property tables or real pumps. I remember discussing *Macbeth* with one of those vastly publicized and be-knighted actor-managers who used, a couple of decades or so ago, to render the London stage the laughingstock of the world. He was playing that part at the time and he horrified me by proposing to cut out altogether Macbeth's "Tomorrow and tomorrow and tomorrow" soliloquy. He said, in all seriousness, that although the monologue gave him a chance to show himself off, he was prepared to sacrifice that opportunity in order to get rid of what he considered an intolerable delaying of the action of the play. People, he said, when their wives die do not go off into tirades of philosophic speculations. The speech produced an almost comic effect of anti-climax. And I daresay that with his archaeologically correct but singular costume and the singular collection of bronze-age antiques with which his stage was strewn—with that continually to distract their attention—his audience might have welcomed the omission.

But given an audience lost in shadows and driven almost mad by the horror of the drama, the effect of the announcement of the death of an almost incredibly human and living type-being was such that they *must* have a breathing space. The speculative and quiet monologue fell upon their ears like dew upon intolerably parched and aching eyeballs. That is the high water mark of literary-declamatory technique. . . . And if you take the other high water mark of the same art and have Ariel's songs in the *Tempest* sung by a perfect-voiced Ariel to the music of Purcell, you have a perfection of that beauty which is happiness such as is only equalled in skill by the expressed horror of the *Macbeth* scene, supplemented by music such as is fit for the hearing of angels and archangels.

When, in fact, the music of Purcell was married to the verse of Shakespeare and the Tudor manor houses were going up all over her broad acres, you had an England of a beauty of aspect such as not only has she never recaptured, but such as placed her for the time on the level of the beautiful civilizations of the past—with Athens and with Arles of the troubadours. For to those you have now to add another exquisiteness—that of the verse of the Jacobeans . . . Laudian highchurchmen, mostly.

CHAPTER TWO

WITH the closing down of the theatres by the Cromwellians that new note became dominant like the soliloquy of an oboe, meditative, in a still evening. That happened in 1642. The lesson has been here missed if we have not given or gotten the image that the sound of the Elizabethan era was that of an immense orchestra of coöperative mental effort working at the fortissimo. And here once more one must make the note that the profuse Elizabethan output was coöperative. One man helped another with his play—or helped himself liberally to the lines of other poets of home or Mediterranean production. Except for Shakespeare, the poets of that age formed a congruous lump, singularly allied in color and frame of mind. There were one or two exceptions. Heywood's *Woman Killed with Kindness,* Ford's *'Tis Pity She's a Whore* or the anonymous *Tragedie of Arden of Feversham* sound an almost sentimental note of domestic happenings with, mostly, unhappy endings . . . a note suggestive even of the plays of Ibsen himself. But these exceptions were insufficient to dilute the major effect. The major effect was that of Hispano-Italianate red visions, prehistoric romance like that of *Macbeth* or *Cymbeline* or *Lear*—the Elizabethans being much preoccupied by imaginations as to the earliest predecessors of King William I—or Plautan comedies of mistaken identities in distant Mediterranean ports. And you seem to see them being written by fierce, cloaked, stiff-bearded, youngish men, in a crowded huddle like that of the American football game— breathing deep and fast in their haste to get their work done, looking over each other's shoulders, as often to make a suggestion for an improvement in a line as to crib a line or so of translation from the Italian—to the perpetual squeaking of the good goose quills, in a dim light that you would think would have runied their eyes . . . but that apparently didn't.

This is a rather impressionistic and hastened way of disposing of a great period. But it is the only way, considering the space at our disposal and the nature of our task, which is rather that of arousing than satisfying a curiosity. And, if the—hitherto—uninstructed reader will give himself the trouble to take a good read in each of the plays that have here been mentioned—a good enough read to ascertain whether he wants to go on reading or not he will have a sufficient nodding acquaintance with Elizabethan drama to let him know if he wants to *approfondir* his knowledge of the work of that period. And he might as well add a good read in one or other of the plays of Beaumont and Fletcher—say *Philaster* and *The Knight of the Burning Pestle*. There is about the one a peculiar beauty of a sort of wistfulness and as it were *défaitisme* that is a note too seldom sounded in the literature of Anglo-Saxondom. . . .

> What is't to die?
> 'Tis less than to be born, a lasting sleep,
> A quiet resting from all jealousy,
> A thing we all pursue. I do know besides
> It is but giving over of a gane
> That must be lost.

And the *Knight of the Burning Pestle* is delightful, light farce—to the manner English—a slight but not repellent vulgarization of *Don Quichote*. I have frequently wondered why the spirited actor-manager who gave us with such success the revival of the *Beggars Opera* did not extend his benefactions by adding those of the Beaumont and Fletcher farce, with *Gammer Gurton's Needle* to fill up the evening. This is a quite well-constructed rough-humorous affair calculated to keep a good-humored audience laughing for as long as it lasts.

There are, of course, other farces and roughly constructed plays like *Gorboduc*, also known as *Ferrex & Porrex*, or the *Ralph Roister Doister* of the Magister Udal who was the Latin teacher of the Tudor princesses. But these productions have rather—as showing the development of the play from the older Mysteries and Miracles—a historic than a literary interest . . . or there are plays of George Chapman, who is better and more appropriately known as the author of the glorious translation of Homer at which we have already glanced. . . .

For some account of these—for which we have obviously no time—
the uninstructed reader might well before reading the plays go to
John Addington Symonds' *Shakespeare's Predecessors in the Elizabethan Drama*, one of the most delightful books ever written. This
writer, at least, was never tired of reading in it when a boy.

We come then to the point when the shutting down of the dramatic orchestra lets the oboe notes of the Jacobean poets—from Donne
to Dryden, taking in Herrick, Herbert, Crashaw, Waller, Marvell
and Henry Vaughan—when their oboe notes sound out like the song
of the robin in the winter dusks.

It would, perhaps, be as well here to construct a time-chart of
Western European writers of the later sixteenth and the whole seventeenth centuries. The advantages of such charts is that they let us
realize the small and suggestive coincidences that otherwise will lie
rather dimly in the back of our minds. This writer, for instance, was
vaguely aware that Rabelais lived till just the middle of the sixteenth
century. But it is rather startling to visualize that he died when Spenser
and Raleigh were each aged one year . . . or that Spenser and Raleigh
were born within the same twelvemonth, Sidney being born the
year after Rabelais' death. And Bacon was born eight, and Marlowe
and Shakespeare eleven, years after the passing of the creator of
Pantagruel. Or, again, it is curious to observe how the stars come
coupled—Spenser and Raleigh in 1552, Marlowe and Shakespeare
in 1564, and Ronsard and his almost more beautiful pupil, Du Bellay,
forty years before them, in 1524. . . . Or, again, that the *Duchess of
Malfi* was written in the year of Shakespeare's death. Or that Isaac
Walton and George Herbert were born in the same year, and La
Fontaine and Marvell both in 1621 or, for the matter of that, Steele
and Addison both in 1672. Or that Boileau wrote *L'Art Poétique* in
the year of the death of Fuller of the *Worthies.*

It would be wrong to dismiss these synchronizations as mere coincidence. It would be overfantastic, too, to declare that destiny or a
muse presided over these births and deaths with the aim of keeping
the world continually supplied with these sweets. It is, nevertheless,

not entirely without significance that, the last touch of mediaevalism dying with Rabelais, Spenser being then already alive and Sidney coming the year after, the Petrarchan spirit—which was the still, fine flower of the Italian middle ages—should have been introduced into England, there to become as it were at once the test and the tradition of what is considered to be—or not to be—English poetry. Or, indeed, of world poetry. On the opposite page, then, is the chart.

Consider, too, how in this chart, these practitioners of the art of letters string themselves out in close bunches, one branch taking the place of the other, even if it had to cross the Channel to do it. Thus, Corneille and the strung-out bunch that ended in Racine arrived just in time to fill in the gap caused by the disappearance of the recited drama in England. He and Molière were both able by 1642 to keep the boards supplied, at least somewhere in the world, with drama that for its full perfection needs the hypnosis of the word spoken *ore rotundo* and going on for far longer periods than would be supportable in ordinary conversation. And as we progress further in this history we shall observe more and more markedly this tendency of a branch of this art flourishing in the one country, to fail a little, and then to cross a branch of the sea or ocean, to reflourish with an even greater luxuriance.

Thus with the novel which at about the date of which we are treating began more and more formidably to make its voice heard in the literary chorus. This form had a flourishing in Spain with the novels of the great Spanish period from Cervantes to the authors of *Lazarillo de Tormes* and *Guzman D'Alfarache*, both rogues and moralists. And these works had such vogue in Elizabethan-Jacobean England that their flourishing more than anything else may be said to have extinguished the popularity of Lyly and his *Euphues*. To supply a native article Defoe was born in 1661, his *Captain Singleton*, *Moll Flanders* and the rest almost exactly duplicating the roguish adventures and sanctimonious moralizing of his Spanish predecessors. So with less of roguery, as much sententiousness and with the admixture of the new English element of sentimentality, the loose novel made its appearance in the *Spectator* of Steele and Addison; to continue again, slightly more compressed, still more sentimentalized

TABLE OF ENGLISH AND FRENCH 16TH AND 17TH CENTURY
CREATIVE WRITERS

ENGLISH			FRENCH
DRAMA	OTHER VERSE	PROSE	
	Spenser (1552–99) Faer. Queen (1592– 06)	Raleigh (1552–18)	Rabelais (d. 1553) Urquhart Transln. (1653)
Kyd (1558–94)	Sidney (1554–86) Arc. (pubd. 1590)		Ronsard (1524–85) Du Bellay (1524–60)
		Bacon (1561–26)	(Pleïades,Belleau,
Marlowe (1564–93)			Jodel Dorat, Baif,
Tamb. (1587)			Thiard)
Faust (1588)			
Shakespeare (1564–18)			Montaigne (1533–92)
Henry VI (1590–3)			
Dekker (1570–41)			Essays 71–98
Wd. Hoe (1602)	Donne (1572–1631)		Florio (1603)
Jonson (1573–37)			
Every Man in his			
Humour (1598)		Burton (1577–26)	
Webster (1580–25)		Anatomy (1621)	
White Devil (1612)			
Duchess of A. (1616)			
Ford (1586–39)	Herrick (1591–1674)		
Heywood (?–1650)	Herbert, G. (1593– 63)	Walton (1593–83) Angler (1653)	Corneille (1606–84)
	Milton (1608–74)	Fuller (1608–61)	Le Cid (1636)
		Taylor, Jy (1613–67)	La Fontaine 1621
		Holy L. & D.	Fables(1658 &c.-95)
	Crashaw (1613–49)	(1650–1)	Molière (1622–73)
			Mal. Imag. (1673)
	Marvell (1621–78)		Boileau (1636–1711)
	Vaughan, Henry		L'Art p'que (1661)
	(1622–95)		Racine (1639–99)
	Dryden (1631–1700)		Phedre (1677)
			AND THE FOLLOWING
			DEVOTIONAL WRITERS:
			Dutch living in
			France:
			Jansen (1585–38)
			Augustinus (1642)
			Bossuet (1627–04)
			Pascal (1623–62)
			Fénélon (1651–15)

and almost infinitely more acceptable to both the English and French publics, in the pages of Richardson. And Richardson, as you might say, begat, as we shall later see, Diderot; and Diderot, Stendhal and Flaubert; and Flaubert—the novel again crossing the Channel, and then the Ocean—was the spiritual father of both Joseph Conrad and Henry James, with whom we arrive almost at our own times.

Those particular crossings of the waters are, I think, incontestable. The resemblances between the novels of Defoe and those of the Spanish picaresque writers are too exact to be merely fortuitous, and Diderot himself acknowledges his Richardsonian discipleship. But other water-crossing influences have been as violently denied by the patriotic as they have been asserted by the internationalists. Whole books have been and are being written to prove or disprove the influence of Rabelais, Montaigne and Ronsard on Shakespeare and the other Elizabethans and Jacobeans. As to that, again a reference to our time-chart will be useful. Rabelais, as we have said, lived just until the first Elizabethans were born—but the Urquhart translation was not published until the days of the Commonwealth, in 1653, when the stage had been closed to dramatists. Montaigne, on the other hand, was born well before the earliest of the Elizabethans, but died in the year of the production of the second part of Shakespeare's *Henry VI.* And Florio's translation of the *Essays* was published in 1603—well before the deaths of Shakespeare, Bacon, Burton of the *Anatomy of Melancholy*—and before the death of Herbert and the birth of Milton.

As far as this writer is concerned, the reader may make his own choice, seeing—or refusing to see—in Falstaff and his companions reflections of Pantagruel, or in the melancholy Jaques—whom some writers insist on calling a Shakespearean self-portrait—in the melancholy Jaques, then, an exact reflection of the pensive Montaigne himself. . . . Or he may consider the "influences" of Ronsard and Du Bellay and the rest of the Pleïadists as being wafted across the English skies as pollen is showered on the winds by the opening buds of May. Or he may completely refuse to believe anything of the sort.

But these speculations are well worth weighing privately in the mind, though we have no space here to indulge them further: they enlarge, nevertheless, the mind and point to the fact that our beloved art is the product of all humanity from the beginning of time. It is unnecessary to insist minutely on the derivations of Richardson from K'ung-Fu-Tsze or Po-Chu-I with whom we began these histories, though we have already chased out influences of the Sage of the Middle Kingdom to Voltaire. But it is as well from time to time to take the eye from the printed page and to consider that it is, our art, an immense stream, coming from the dawn and spreading its eddies for thousands of years and half the globe over, as an immense, an overwhelming, proof of the fact of the unity of humanity and of the products of the human mind.

To come then, specifically, to the most English of all writers— the Donne, Herbert, Crashaw, Marvell, Vaughan, Dryden constellation which shone from 1572, the year of the birth of Donne, to 1700, that of the death of Dryden. . . . We may, I think, without incurring suspicion of jingoism, call them specifically English, because the fare they provided was such as no other country or time has produced and because if there is any sustained beauty in the Anglo-Saxon soul it was they who proved its existence. There have been at other times flashes, but the light of those writers' muse is that of a steady, slow, long-burning candle, in a summer dusk.

It was the Golden Age of England as a country of the arts, those of domestic architecture, music and lyric poetry penetrated into the very fibres of the race as no art has ever done since first Dutch William came to the English throne. You may still see the great manor houses, listen to a song of Purcell's, learn from the pen of his wife that Colonel Hutchinson—the Regicide—was an incomparable fingerer of the lute.

You may read

> Sweet spring, full of sweete dayes and roses,
> A box where sweets compacted lie;
> My music shows ye have your closes
> And all must die

Or the great Donne's:

> For Godsake hold your tongue and let me love,
> Or chide my palsie or my gout,
> My five grey hairs or ruin'd fortune flout,
> With wealthe your state, your mind with arts improve,
> Take you a course, get you a place,
> Observe his honour, or his grace,
> Or the King's real or his stampëd face,
> Contemplate, what you will approve,
> So you will let me love

Or the less great but still always jocund Herrick's address to the Willow:

> Thou art to all lost loves the best,
> The onelie true plant found
> Wherewith young men and maids distrest
> And reft of love are crown'd.
>
> And underneath thy cooling shade
> When weary of the light
> The love-lorn youth and love-sick maid
> Come to weep out the night.

or Crashaw's

> As if the bargain had been driven
> So hardly betwixt Earth and Heaven;
> Our God would thrive too fast and be
> Too much a gainer by't, should we
> Our purchased selves too soon bestow
> On Him, who has not loved us so
>
> When love of us called Him to see
> If we'd vouchsafe His company
> He left His father's court, *and came*

Lightly as a lambent flame
Leaping upon the hills to be
The humble King of you and me.

. . . which last three italicized lines seem to me the most exquisite
of all passages of English-devotional—but, indeed, of all devotional
verse. . . .

Or the supremely beautiful poem to his dead wife by the almost
unknown Henry King—verses which are usually ascribed to Milton:

> Meantime thou hast her, Earth: much good
> May my harm do thee. Since it stood
> With Heaven's will I might not call
> Her longer mine, I give thee all . . .
> Be kind to her, and prithee look
> Thou write into thy Dooms-day book
> Each parcel of her Rarity
> Which in thy casket shrined doth lie.
> See that thou make thy reckoning right
> And yield her back again by weight;
> For thou must audit on thy trust
> Each graine and atome of this dust
> As thou wilt answer *Him* that lent
> Not gave thee my dear Monument.

Or Marvell's relatively unknown "Coronet":

> When for the thorns with which I long, too long,
> With many a piercing wound
> My Saviour's head have crowned,
> I seek with garlands to redress that Wrong:
> Through every garden, every mead
> I gather flow'rs (my fruits are only flow'rs) . . .
> That they, whilst Thou on their sweet spoils dost tread,
> May crown Thy feet, that could not crown Thy head.

Or Henry Vaughan's projection of life beyond the grave:

> Where no rude shade or night
> Shall there approach us; we shall there no more
>   Watch stars or pore
> Through melancholy clouds and say:
> "Would it were day!"
> One everlasting Sabbath there shall run
> Without succession and without a Sun.

Or, indeed, the quite different Milton who, whilst not believing in the divine birth could yet write *On the Morning of Christ's Nativity*.

> And Kings sat still with awful eye
> As if they surely knew their sovran Lord was by.
>   But peaceful was the night
>   Wherein the Prince of Light
> His reign of peace upon the Earth began
>   The Winds with wonder whist
>   Smoothly the waters kist . . .

and so on to:

> But see, the Virgin blest
> Hath laid her Babe to rest.
> Time is our tedious song should here have ending.
>   Heaven's youngest teemed star
>   Hath fixt her polisht car
> Her sleeping Lord with handmaid lamp attending
>   And all about the Courtly stable
> Bright-harnest Angels sit in order serviceable.

. . . which might very well have been written by a Roman Catholic nun or, perhaps, a Sister of Little Giddings.

But having, then, in a Tudor manor's room, in a cool, calm, light, listened to the incomparable fingering of Colonel Hutchinson's lute, giving you Purcell, and turned over at random *The Delights of the Muses* and anthologies and seeing such verses as those above, you become aware of an England—of an Anglo-Saxondom—that we may never see again . . . a country Christist, almost more than Christian, into which the intrusion of Milton's "Virgin blest" was almost a solecism, but, nevertheless, one in which, when you went into a barber's shop you found four instruments lying ready tuned. And whilst one of you was shaved, another played a ground, and three more played over it an air, and one sang, "Come unto these yellow sands and there take hands." For it is, perhaps, almost above all, the all-pervasion of music into those cool, bright, Laudian days that, together with the fervent, as if domestic love of the Redeemer who came, lightly as a lambent flame leaping upon the hills, that gave the note of those matchless years that have never returned.

And it is curious to think that it was a Laudian converted to Catholicism who gave us that strange, new and most beautiful note to the coming of Christ . . . whilst the incomparable Donne was a Catholic never converted to Laudianism but occupying, none the less, an Anglican pulpit, who wrote, with always a note of bitterness, doubt and some fear:

> O more than Moone
> Draw not up seas to drowne me in thy spheare,
> Weep me not dead in thine arms, but forbeare
> To teach the sea what it may doe too soone.

. . . and Milton, who believed perhaps nothing, evolving with something at once of the Elizabethan's drama and much, prophetically, of the rhetoric of the French seventeenth century playwright's quasi-pomposity, a Divine Comedy in which the shining figure of Satan is almost prophetic of Corneille's Cid. . . . Or, finally, George Herbert, serenely believing, after a youth of a proper young gentleman about town—but, indeed, all of them, including Donne, had that sort of youth—George Herbert, then, marrying most happily a young woman whom he had never seen but who received a double dowry because her father was so ravished that she should marry Mr. Herbert . . . George Herbert, I say, writing from the tranquillity of an unshakenly believing heart:

> Love made me welcome; yet my soul drew back,
>   Guilty of dust and sin
> But quick-eyed Love, observing me grow slack
>   From my first entrance in
> Drew nearer to me, sweetly questioning
>   If I lacked anything.

> "A guest," I answered, "worthy to be here"
>   Love said: "You shall be he!"
> "I, the unkind, th' ungrateful? Ah, my dear,
>   I cannot look on Thee."
> Love took my hand and, smiling, did reply:
>   "Who made thine eyes but I?"

> "Truth, Lord, but I have marred them; let my shame
>   Go where it doth deserve."
> "And know you not," says Love, "who bore the blame?"
>   "My dear, then I will serve."
> "You must sit down," says Love, "and taste my meat."
>   So I did sit and eat.

The last two lines enshrine the very essence, the essential oil, of that so-called metaphysical poetic age. And it is only in Christina Rossetti who, like Herbert in his day, was the only real super-master of Victorian English, that that Petrarchan-Christist note reëchoes—in the Bloomsbury shades, next door to an Anglican Convent for all the world like that of the sisterhood of Little Giddings itself.

It is impossible to keep the note of creeds out of the consideration of the literature of this age, since, at any rate in these manifestations, Christianity reached its last, finest and most rarefied, apogee . . . before sinking, predestinedly enough, into the Dutch-Germano brandy-sodden Established Atheism of Sterne's peripatetic parson. But if, difficultly enough, you ignore the weight of that elephant and seek to estimate those men as littérateurs alone, you arrive at singular uncertainties. It is not a case of saying, as it was when we considered Shakespeare and the Elizabethans, that if you leave out Donne you have still an appreciable literature. As writer pure and simple, Donne, though he bulks enormous as metaphysician, was merely one amongst the peers. He had certainly nothing like the metrical skill of a mere Herrick, nor had he the clear, still apprehension of English that were Herbert's or Crashaw's. He was clouded beside Marvell, even. But the great bulk of his work establishes for him a personality that is more in touch with today than is the case with any of the others.

His note is, indeed, singularly that of modernity. The eighteenth century certainly could not be expected to appreciate him, nor could the greater part of Victoria's spacious times. So much so was that the case that all that this writer knew of Donne until he (this writer) was well come to man's estate was that, as Dean of St. Paul's, he had his statue made for his tomb—in his shroud, his face peering out of marble folds.

That used to strike me as a boy as being in bad taste. And I don't know that as a grown man one is not inclined to say that the supreme attraction that Donne exercises over the minds of today is not due to manifestations of bad taste, like small explosions, that are supremely suited to a day when bad taste is, perhaps, our chiefest characteristic. But Donne's manifestations of bad taste are usually the impatiences of the supreme man of the world that he was, with his enormous memory, his vast reading, his hugely varied experiences . . . impatiences at the women, the love, the very faith of his day.

The vast gamut of his verse ranges between

> I can love both faire and brown,
> Her whom abundance melts and her whom want betraies,
> Her who loves loneness best and her who maskes and plaies,
> Her whom the country formed and whom the town,

Her who believes and her who tries,
Her who still weeps and spungie eyes,
And her who is dry cork and never cries:
And her and her and you and you and you,
I can love any, so she be not true.

and:

So, so, break off this last, lamenting kiss,
Which sucks two souls and vapours both away,
Turn, thou ghost, that way and let me turn this,
And let our selves benight our happiest day.
We asked none leave to love; nor will we owe
Any so cheap a death as saying: Goe!
Goe! . . . And if that word have not quite kill'd thee,
Ease me with death, by bidding me goe too!

with perhaps, as a final note:

Thou has made me. And shall Thy work decay?
Repair me now, for now mine end doth haste.
I run to death and death meets me as fast
And all my pleasures are like yesterday.
I dare not move my dim eyes any way,
Despair behind and death before doth call
By sinne in it, which it t'wards hell doth weigh;
Onely Thou art above, and when towards Thee
By Thy leave I can looke, I rise again.
But our old, subtle Foe so tempteth me
That not one hour my self I can sustain.
Thy grace may wing me to prevent his art
And Thou like adamant draw mine iron heart.

There is about that not much hope—and not so very much faith.
Donne's muse ranged through almost every mood save Herbert's and
Crashaw's serene belief in the Savior who saves . . . or Marvell's

serene, almost cavalier indifference. Donne, no doubt, had the thought, but could never have written:

> The Grave's a fine and private place,
> Yet none I think do there embrace.

nor yet:

> But at my back I alwaies hear
> Time's winged chariot hurrying near
> And yonder all before us lye
> Desarts of vast Eternity.
> Thy beauty shall no more be found
> Nor, in thy marble vault, shall sound
> My echoing song; then worms shall try
> Thy long preserved Virginity . . .

nor, indeed, had Donne Marvell's metrical agility. It was as if, impatient as he was of women, love, fools and God, he was impatient too of the close steps of metre. Had he achieved the last step of modernity and lived today he might well have written *vers libres*.

Equally he could never have written, confidently:

> Throw away Thy rod,
> Throw away Thy wrath,
>   O my God!
> Take the gentle path.

> For my heart's desire
> Unto thine is bent;
>   I aspire
> To a full consent. . . .

> Love is swift of foot,
> Love's a man of warre,
>   And can shoot,
> And can hit from farre.

Who can 'scape his bow?
That which wrought on Thee,
And brought Thee low,
Needs must work on me.

Throw away thy rod,
Though man frailties hath
Thou art God:
Throw away thy wrath.

And still less:

You must sit down, says Love, and taste my meat.
So I did sit and eat.

It would seem here to become necessary to form some more extended estimate of the English literature of that day, we having
already made the claim that the England of that era may stand beside
the Greece of the Great Age, Rome of the Augustans, Arles of the
troubadours, China of the second century, Italy of Dante, Petrarch
and Boccaccio, France of Villon and the Pleïad—and we may add
Spain of the period that began about 1460 with the writing of the
incomparable *Celestina* and ended with the death of Quevedo y Villegas in 1645. We have not yet arrived at the consideration of that
period. We have, indeed, delayed that consideration until we shall
come to that of that most formidable of all literary forms, the novel,
because that form was born with *Celestina* herself and attained its
majority with Mendoza, Alémán and the author of the *Sueños*.

The main feature of these other great literatures and literary periods is that each is distinguished by one almost superhuman figure
around which stand the other great grouped towers of cathedrals. So
for China you would have Lao-Tsze; for the Hebrews, Isaiah; for
the Greeks, Homer; for the Augustans, Horace; for the troubadours,
Peire Vidal; for the French, Villon; for the Spaniards, Cervantes . . .
and you can add as in the case of towns that boast more than one

central spire, Confucius, Theocritus, Aeschylus, the psalmist Augustine, Ronsard. . . . A great company.

And the greatest of all these great ones have invariably about them a note of otherworldliness: they have seen Hell, they have wrestled with God, they have sounded horrors superhuman and inconceivable. If you have seen what Villon has seen, or Dante in his *Inferno* or Isaiah, or St. Augustine, you have come out on the other side of humanity: you have about your work an overtone that can only be reached by those whose nature has been purged by the contemplation of supreme horror. It is a quality that makes you live not only for all time but for every variety of time, for the cataclysmic as for the serene. Thus, in the dreadful days in which we live when there is no spot in all the girdle of the earth that can be sure of security, the "sweet day, so cool, so calm, so bright" of Herbert has almost no message at all and even the quiet bare bodkin of Hamlet's soliloquy hardly makes its mark. That otherworldly note in earthly happenings is, indeed, singularly wanting in all English work. One runs one's mind backwards and forwards from Chaucer to Browning without coming in memory on any instance . . . perhaps in a few passages of *Timon of Athens* (in which Shakespeare is said to have collaborated with someone more obscure) there is a note of super-tragic destiny— of Destiny squeezing the last drop of blood from the victim's throat. Otherwise there is a certain vacancy until one thinks of:

> Thou hast made me. And shall thy work decay?
> Repair me now, for now mine end doth haste
> I run to death and Death meets me as fast!
> And all my pleasures are like yesterday.
> I dare not move my dim eyes any way,
> Despair behind and death before doth call
> By sinne in it which it t'wards Hell doth weigh. . . .

or again the more than affrighting:

> O more than Moone,
> Draw not up seas to drown me in thy spheare. . . .

We have in Donne, in short, a man who has seen into Hell and conceived of Heaven otherwise than on the smooth paths about the country vicarage's hedge—Heaven forbid that one should seem to despise Bemerton and its parsonage. Herbert's vision of a perfected High Church Earth, near Salisbury Plain with its high elms and smooth pastures, and Love's table set is of a beauty and confidence that we could ill, indeed, do without.

"You must sit down," says Love, "and taste my meat."
So I did sit and eat.

may well mark the final height to which devotional poetry may attain. But one has, if one lets oneself be fanciful, the image that round the vicarage hedge, mumbling a mildewed crust, stands hunched a great, hobo figure, the fruit of whose despairing meditations strike in English poetry a note that, lacking which, English poetry would have been something narrower, something merely regional with a tang at once of lavender and of the unimportant provincial.

Donne, in short, might well, in the eyes of the critical cosmopolitan foreigner—who must, after all, be regarded as the final appraiser of universal literatures, for we can't, alas, let that final judge be an Oxford or a Princeton professor—Donne, then, might be regarded as the supremely great figure who completes the gamut of English literature. And if we add to him the authors of *Piers Plowman*, of the *City of Dreadful Night,* of passages in the *Pilgrim's Progress* and of *Gulliver,* of the *Duchess of Malfi* and of some scenes in *Macbeth,* he will not stand as the single raven that is insufficient to make a winter's midnight.

His fame grows daily as our insupportable times grow more tremulous. Had this writer written as he has above in the days when he was a boy, a warrant in lunacy would have been sworn out against him and he would have been confined in Colney Hatch for the rest of his natural days. And even today in cloisters where the mortar-boarded and gowned, or in salons where the indifferent self-sufficient do congregate, this praise of a poet who lived, indeed, in his shroud may well be regarded as disproportionate. But Donne's fame today is still on the uptake and he would be a bold man who would undertake to set the limits to which it well may soar.

Donne's work is, perhaps, differentiated from that of his contemporaries—and, indeed, from that of most of his compatriots—by the unreasonably harsh nature of his contacts with individuals and with events. His contemporaries, Herbert, Crashaw, Vaughan and the rest were nearly all sheltered in their lives and materially saved from anxieties by the fact that, with zest and conscience, they filled cures, usually in the Anglican High Church. But it was, perhaps, not the smallest of Donne's many crosses that he was forced against his will, and possibly against his conscience, to become a churchman in order to obtain bread for the mouths of his dependants. Few poets can have been almost physically coerced by a slightly maniacal and incredibly obstinate king into taking orders in a church which they regarded as heretical. Yet that was actually the case with the future Dean of St. Paul's; James I having an almost inordinate belief in Donne's argumentative gifts insisted on securing the poet for the Church, in order that the poet should be forced by his occupation into championing the cause of the king as temporal head of that Church. And this royal coercion came at a time when Donne's mental distress over material poverty must have been almost maddening. For, once more, few poets can have had fathers-in-law so maniacally determined on the ruin not merely of the poet-son-in-law but of his own daughter and grandchildren. The father-in-law of Donne, not content with merely refusing to make his daughter any allowance, used all his considerable court influence to get Donne expelled from the job that he held and in preventing his obtaining any other. So that for many years Donne had to live the most hideous of all martyrdoms—that not merely of suffering himself from the direst poverty but of seeing dependants to whom he was passionately attached, passing days on end in a condition of starvation that could only be relieved by accepting charity.

Thus, the poetry of Donne, differing from that of all his fellow poets, was the work of a man into whose soul there had entered at once the iron and the irony of a destiny more than ordinarily wanting in reason or moderation. So that at times one is apt to regard him as scarcely English at all, so much does he resemble a metaphysically embittered Villon. He suffered, perhaps, physically less than the author of the *Testaments*, but spiritually he had only a sort of martyrized impatience as against a loud-mouthed and mordant humor with which to support himself and life.

CHAPTER THREE

W E COME, then, to the contemplation of the novel—a literary
form which in modern days has assumed if not an importance
then at least a portentousness such as has been attained to by scarcely
any other department of our art. For it is at least three chances to
one that if one talks of the literature of today of France, Spain,
Russia or any other of the main literary countries it will be of their
novels that one thinks. And, of the woefully small amount of time
that the world today devotes to reading, one may safely assert that
nine tenths of the time—when it is not given to textbooks—is devoted
to "fiction."

This is a phenomenon like another—like the increase of cold as the
days grow shorter or the fact that fruits ripen in the fall of the year.
One may deplore it, one may applaud it, but since one cannot change
it, one may as well investigate it with equanimity.

Story-telling of sorts has distinguished humanity since the very
earliest of civilizations and, as we have had occasion to observe, such
type-stories as those of "Sinbad the Sailor" and "Ali Baba and the
Forty Thieves" have persisted since the Egyptian legendary days, but
the novel as an extended form having at least the unity of a single
central character is something in the West as modern as the middle
of the fifteenth century. This writer is accustomed, as a mental convenience, to consider that the beginnings of novel-writing as an adult
occupation or fairly widespread trade must be put at about 1460 when
were written in Spain the first words of the play-novel *Celestina*, one
of the noblest and most affecting products of the human imagination—
which was some thirty years in the writing and was almost certainly
the work of at least two hands.

Obviously, there were novels and play-novels before *Celestina*. It
is hardly necessary to recall to you the *conte-fable Aucassin and Nicolette* or the short novel *Flamenca* of the French middle ages or the
classical, extended stories *The Golden Ass* of Apuleius or the *Satyrikon*
of Petronius Arbiter . . . or even, what is still more to our purpose,

491

the *Arabian Nights Entertainment* of the Oriental bazaars. The practice, indeed, of telling long stories, centered round one individual hero and the narration occupying several days or nights is one singularly widespread, enduring and ancient. Still in the bazaars of the whole East the practice continues, little crowds sitting round a narrator who continues to tell for day after day the adventures of some prince and a peri, or some sheikh and a genie. . . . And, indeed, the earliest adventure into sustained fiction of this writer must have been a tale of adventure, mostly amongst redskins, of a hero much resembling Harkaway Jack, which lasted for exactly thirty-two nights and first saw the darkness in the dormitory of Stratford School. But that piece of fiction, like innumerable others told down the ages, was never written down so that all traces of it are lost.

And so it has been with most of the long prose fiction that was imagined between *Flamenca* and the Spanish novel-play—as who should say *conte-fable—Celestina*. It was for centuries an art merely popular and despised. The teller would see no particular reason for recording or the hearers for memorizing its products. With popularly produced verse it was different. Verse memorizes itself easily, if with inaccuracy, and in one form or another verse masterpieces long or short got themselves at first written down either by poet or hearer—and then printed.

And it was, no doubt, the printing press—after the stage had done its work—that rendered possible the play-novel and that very soon made the form become more and more novel and less and less play.

The history of the composition of *Celestina* has always been obscure and must have been singular. In the introduction to the first edition of the work that I ever saw and that was given to me by my uncle, William Michael Rossetti when I was aged twelve, the writer stated succinctly that the first one-sixth of the writing was done by an author called Cotiz y Strega, of whom I have been able to find no other trace, and all the rest by a Spanish Jew called Fernando Rojas. To him the entire authorship is ascribed in the prefaces of several of the earliest editions, though later editors and commentators from Alonso Villegas in 1554 to George Ticknor in 1872 ascribe the first part of the work to Rodrigo Cota. On the other hand, Rojas himself says in a prefatory letter to the sixth edition that the first part was written by Juan de Mena—but all other commentators calling that ascription absurd, the whole question of the ascription of the authorship and the period of composition remains thus exceedingly obscure and it seems, lamentably, as if no credible solution would ever be found since nearly all the rare copies of the earliest editions would appear to have been, on one hand, destroyed in Toledo during the present Spanish Civil War, or to be liable to be burned as the work of a Jew in Vienna where the few documents relating to Fernando Rojas were to be found. From almost his earliest years, this writer has always considered and still considers the *Celestina* to be one of the greatest works of literature of all times and to be absolutely the greatest piece of prose fiction—both on account of its singularly skillful construction, its remarkably drawn characters, and the extraordinary clarity, beauty, and classic tradition of the beautiful Castilian in which it is written. And, because of this admiration, he has read such innumerable prefaces, commentaries, and criticisms written about it, that the over-stuffed brain almost reels when it is a matter of giving a coherent and reconcilable account of these matters. They are, fortunately, no real affair of ours since we are more concerned with the nature than the provenance of this great work. It is, nevertheless, a pardonable human weakness to desire to have some knowledge of the history of the works that one admires. So, as far as this writer is concerned, the, as it were, private history of the writing of this book that he keeps at the back of his mind is somewhat as follows: According to Rojas himself there must have existed before he came upon the scene a possibly rough and predominently lecherous, sketched-out plan of the earliest stages of the book. He says himself that, he being a licentiate of the law in Toledo, some of his friends drew his attention to this rough draft and pressed him to finish it. He eventually took up the project and in the course of many years not only rewrote the original sketch but added from twenty-five to thirty-five new scenes. He styles the original draft a comedy and the whole work, with his additions, a tragi-comedy—this being, as far as we have ever been able to discover, the first time that such a term was attached to a work of art. The confusion that obscures the whole matter we may well attribute to his shyness as to letting his authorship be known. It is probable that he himself regarded the original draft as being intended merely as a comedy of bawdiness. And, no doubt, for some time he continued his additions in the same spirit, so that he would have the feeling that his employment of his time in such an occupation would not enhance his fame as a lawyer of considerable gravity and reputation. But it is evident that as he went on with the work it became plain to him that he could make it not so much a piece of sententious morality as a guide for youth—or, indeed, for old age, against the perils and seductions of the world and women. The work would seem to have been in progress for some thirty years, its first presentation as a spectacle taking place between 1490—which this writer has always considered to be the probable date— and 1498 which is the date assigned to it by Ticknor and the more learned amongst later authorities. In any case, we may say with certainty that it was between those years that this work began to achieve its tremendous fame. Mr. Ticknor and other writers following him assert that during the century of its birth, *Celestina* sold more than thirty printed editions in Spanish alone, and translations into French, English, Italian, and even German were very numerous. But Mr. Ticknor's statement is rather vague because the words "the century of its birth" may mean either during the period between 1490 and 1500—i.e. in the fifteenth century—or may mean during the hundred years that ensued after 1490. This writer is not acquainted with more than five fifteenth-century editions. In any case, the dates 1490-1498 are very significant if we consider that Rojas was at once Jewish and inspired with some qualms as to a possible licentiousness in aspect of his great work. Granada was taken in 1492. The power of the Moors in Spain was then definitely broken and what was still more to the purpose, a strong Spanish government, with the necessary concomitant of the Holy and disastrous Inquisition, was established in almost the whole of Spain, with the full backing of Ferdinand and Isabella. During the long struggle that had resulted in the expulsion of the Moors, the Jews of Spain had played a part sufficiently important to have let them attain to high honors in the provisional governments and to contract alliances with the most powerful and proud of Spanish families. But with the ascent to power of the Most Catholic sovereigns and the establishment of the Inquisition as a national institution, the first breaths of anti-semitism were beginning to make themselves heard in that kingdom. And between 1490 and 1498, Rojas as a Jew may well have felt some reawakening of his fears as to the reception, not merely by the public but by that brilliant organization, of his *conte-fable*, on the score of morality. And I think we may be warranted in ascribing to that tendency on his part the fact that though several of the earliest editions of the work contain prefaces definitely ascribing the authorship to Rojas—some, indeed, actually containing prefatory letters in which Rojas himself as we have seen, definitely states that he was the author of six sevenths and the revisor of the earlier portions of the work—nevertheless, the prefaces of a number of the earliest editions give no author's name at all. But that again is a matter rather for the researches of a scholar designing to obtain honor in a German university than for our continued investigation in this place.

Let us then consider the work itself. Its story, although that is its least important feature, is well-projected, sustained, and developed and runs as follows: A gallant Spanish youth of good reputation and family is hawking. His hawk strikes down a bird in the garden of a noble Castilian young lady whose virtue and birth far exceed that of the young man. He is immediately struck with the most ardent love for her and proceeds to express his passion. This proceeding was contrary to the traditions of high-bred Spanish love-making which, from the earliest times, had taken the form, invariably at night, of serenades of hired musicians before the heavy iron grills of windows giving on to streets. Shocked, then, at the impetuous modernity of this daylight courtship, the young woman treats the young man with the coldness that might be expected of her. He, on the other hand, is possessed by a passion so ardent that nothing would suit him but that he must go to a noted procuress who shall procure for him the favor of the young woman by the foulest possible means if fair ones will not suffice. This procuress is the famous Celestina. She is an old woman, part wise-woman, part bawd, part local politician, part money-lender and in one capacity or another her powers of temporal intrigue in the city of the play reveal themselves as almost unbounded. She is, in fact, a figure that, in the days between fifteenth-century Spain and the twentieth-century United States must have seemed almost impossibly formidable. Today, however, she would be more easily understood in various of the more unreformed municipalities of the western continent. Earlier audiences must have taken her as a figure of almost supernatural dimensions, like Apollyon or Mephistopheles in Marlowe's *Faustus*, a figure whose kind would be familiar to, and accepted by them. She controls all duennas, domestics, grooms, valets, porters, alguazils, alcaldes, night watchmen, municipal officers, and all the other forces of obscure evil that can be found in a great city. Her powers of brow-beating, blackmail and coërcion by the use of hired bravos are only equalled by her almost supernatural eloquence and powers of persuasion. Such a catalogue of her attributes in cold English may seem neither very moving nor highly probable. But, projected as she is by the genius of the author of her being in a Castilian that can range between the hottest passion and the extreme cold of ironic etiquette, she becomes a figure almost too horrible to contemplate, and one not even remotely paralleled in any other of the literary masterpieces of the world. And it is to be remembered that, in contra-distinction to the other works of fiction of its day, the *Celestina* is handled with a technical skill of the most singular and distinguished genius. In the fact that Celestina is herself a rogue, the story might be classed as picaresque, but it differs from all the other picaresque works, whether Spanish or English, in that they consist merely of a series of episodes strung loosely and without sequence or relation round one central and exceptional figure; but the *Celestina* is essentially first a story—the history of an affair which needs a strong central character for its central figure. The very idea of destiny is absent from the pages of most picaresque novels. But in *Celestina* the sense of fate is almost as central a figure as it is in Aeschylus, and the construction of the book advances with remorseless and always hastening footsteps from beginning to end. In any event, Celestina's machinations are successful, the heroine succumbs; the hero, visiting her in the classical mode by means of a ladder, is cast down and killed in the street; Celestina herself is murdered by her own brothers, and the heroine casts herself from a high tower, the play finishing to the note of the grief of the heroine's father.

The usual picaresque novel from the date of Mendoza to that of Quevedo y Villegas was, as far as form is concerned, just exactly that of a long narration told in successive nights in a school dormitory by a boy of some talent. The three works to which I should recommend the modern reader to turn his attention are *Lázarillo de Tormes*, which is ascribed to the very great poet Diego Hurtado de Mendoza (1503-1575)—and *Guzman d'Alfarache* by Mateo Aléman (c 1547-1610). This was translated in 1631 by James Mabbe, who was the translator also of *Celestina*, the two works standing well level for sonority and beauty of English with any of the great translations that so distinguish that country and age. And, thirdly, *El Gran Tacaño*, by the greatest of all the picaresque writers, Quevedo y Villegas.

The relative formlessness of these picaresque masterpieces compared with the relative shapeliness of both Spanish and English plays of the same age both denote and mark the gradual divergence of the acted drama from the recited novel. With the wider dissemination rendered possible by the spread of printing, the novel as such ceased to be recited. It had been formless because it consisted of a number of episodes each with a beginning, a working up, and a culmination— such episodes constituting a day's or a night's entertainment. Such entertainments demand such workings up and developments, the audience being able to keep the whole story in mind for at least the space of a night's entertainment. That human factor regulated the form of the stage play with greater and greater insistence until, as we have seen (and as, alas, we see every day) the stage play divorced itself altogether from literature and became a thing of mere mechanical invention. The printed novel, on the other hand, could afford to remain a matter of episodes strung together. The reader of those days did not read very fast, and an episode in the life of a rogue sufficed him amply for a night's leisure. Thus, all the literary skill of a great writer like Quevedo was given to the ingenuity of his invention and the brilliance with which he depicted his scenes—these scenes being divided by intervals of moral reflection which were frequently very, and at times insupportably, prolonged. Thus, you have at once the extremely trying harangues that interrupt the story of Aléman's *Guzman d'Alfarache*, which, as far as this writer can at present recall, are only paralleled in nauseous prurience and hypocrisy by the introductions to chapters of Fielding's *Tom Jones*. Fielding, indeed, would appear to have been almost more than Defoe, Alémán's direct successor, though he did not flourish until a hundred and fifty years after Alémán's death This gives the real measure of the world prevalence of the picaresque form. From the birth of Mendoza in 1503 till the death of Smollett in 1771 was a matter of two and a half centuries, and although Richardson, who attempted to give some form and verisimilitude to his novels, was a child of the seventeenth century, nevertheless it was not until nearly a hundred years after the death of Fielding that with *Madame Bovary* the novel really appeared as a complete work of art, having at once *progression d'effet, charpente, façade, cadences, mots justes*—and all the other accoutrements and attributes of a work of art in its glory, for which the English language has no name. Till then the novel had to be content to be the patient Cinderella of all the seven arts.

A few lines of quotation are worth pages of exordium when it comes to making plain the nature of literary works. Let us, then, here make a little anthology of passages from the great picaresque romances, arranging them so as to give some idea of the career of the seventeenth-century Spanish rogue. It will be observed that all these narrations are set down in the spirit of complete and remorseless observation of effects and cause. The rogue is neither sentimentalized over as in the case of *Tom Jones*—which has always seemed to the writer to be one of the most immoral books ever written—or glorified as is the case with the toughs and gangsters of today's Anglo-Saxon novel. No, the picaro is a poor creature gifted with certain mean shortnesses and a metropolitan courage in facing adversities brought about by scoundrel-ism. He is the son of a man born to be hanged and he himself is predestined to the same fate. So that you have in these works en-joined upon you the great truth today too much obscured that the fox may run but he's caught at last.

Here then, in Thomas Roscoe's translation, are the beginnings of *Lázarillo de Tormes*, whose author was not merely a very great poet, but in the tradition of the mediaeval writers a very great gentleman, statesman and diplomatist. *Lázarillo* is regarded as being the first example of the *novella picaresca*.

You must know, then, in the first place, that my name is Lázaro de Tormes, and that I am the son of Thomas Gonzalez and Antonia Perez, natives of Tejares, a village of Salamanca. My surname was acquired by the singular circumstance of my birth, which happened in the river Tormes, and in the following manner. My father (to whom God be merciful) was employed to superintend the operations of a water-mill which was worked by the course of the above river (a situation that he held above fifteen years), and my mother at that time being *enceinte* with me, while staying one night at the mill was suddenly seized with the pains of labor, which terminating happily, it may with truth be said, that my surname, borrowed from the river, was not inaptly bestowed.

I had only reached my ninth year, when my unfortunate father was charged with administering certain copious but injudicious bleedings to the sacks of customers to the mill; a lowering system which was voted by them to be neither salutary nor profitable. He was forthwith taken into custody; when, not being able to deny the indiscreet application of his professional ability, he experienced the usual penalty of the law. It is, however, to be hoped that he is now reaping the reward which has been faithfully promised by the Evangelist to all those who have suffered persecution for justice's sake; for they are declared to be in the highest degree fortunate in such their tribulations. By this disaster, my poor father being thrown out of employment, joined an armament then preparing against the Moors, in the quality of mule-driver to a gentleman; and in that expedition, like a loyal servant, he, along with his master, finished his life and services together.

At a very early age, then, Lázaro is sold by his mother to a blind man who, in spite of his affliction, is of extraordinary strength, agility, cunning, miserliness, and skill in begging. Begging was, indeed, his chief occupation, it being Lázarillo's function to lead him from place to place. But he had a great variety of other sources of income. Thus:

Besides this, he had thousand other ways of making money. He could repeat prayers which were available for all occasions; for women who had no children; for those who had expectancy; for those likewise who were unhappily married, and sought to increase the affection of their husbands. He could also prognosticate truly to ladies whether the result of their *travail* would be a boy or a girl; and with respect to the medicinal art, he would tell you that Galen himself was an ignoramus compared with himself. Indeed, he acted as though he really thought so; for no one ever came to consult him, that he did not say without the slightest hesitation, "Take this, do that;" and in such a manner, that he had all the world after him, especially the women, who had the utmost confidence in everything he told them. By these means his profits were very considerable. He gained more in one month than a hundred other blind men would in a year.

With all this, however, I am sorry to say that I never met with so avaricious and so wicked an old curmudgeon; he allowed me almost to die daily of hunger, without troubling himself about my necessities; and, to say the truth, if I had not helped myself by means of a ready wit and nimble fingers, I should have closed my account from sheer starvation.

Under this master the unfortunate little rogue suffers innumerable and insupportable brutalities and hardships. For food he is almost dependent on what he can steal from the blind man, and when the blind man discovers the peculations he beats Lázarillo each time to within an inch of death. Here, then, being detected in one means of stealing wine he devises another.

Being thus deprived of my customary allowance from the jar, I was ready to die with longing; and finding my plan of the straw no longer available, I took an opportunity of boring a very small hole in the bottom of the jar, which I closed very delicately with wax. At dinnertime, when the poor old man sat over the fire, with the jar between his knees, the heat, slight as it was, melted the little piece of wax with which I closed the hole, and I, feigning to be cold, drew close to the fire, and placed my mouth under the little fountain in such a manner, that the whole contents of the jar came to my share. When the old boy had finished his meal, and thought to regale himself with his draught of wine, the deuce a drop did he find, which so enraged and surprised him, that he thought the devil himself had been at work; nor could he conceive how it could be. "Now, uncle," said I, "don't say that I drank your wine, seeing that you have had your hand on it the whole time." But he was not satisfied with my declaration of innocence, so turning and twisting the jar about in every direction, he at last discovered the hole, which at once let him into the secret of my ingenious contrivance. He concealed his discovery so well, that I had not the slightest suspicion that my *ruse* was detected; so the next day, having prepared my jar as before, little foreseeing the consequences, nor dreaming of the wicked thoughts which were passing in the old man's mind, I placed myself under the jar, which presently began to distil its delicious contents, my face turned towards heaven, and my eyes partly closed, the better to enjoy the delightful draught. The evil-minded old man, judging this to be the time to take his vengeance, raised with both hands the sweet, though alas, to me, bitter, jar, and let it fall directly on my mouth, adding to its weight by giving all the impetus in his power. The poor unhappy Lázaro, who little reckoned on such a disaster, but had quietly resigned himself to the delicious enjoyment of the moment, verily believed in the crash which succeeded, that the heavens with all they contained had fallen upon him. The blow was so tremendous that my senses fairly left me, and the jar breaking, cut my face in many places, several pieces remaining in the wounds, besides breaking nearly all my teeth, the loss of which I feel to this very day.

Eventually, Lázarillo, as is to be expected, decides to take leave of his master. And this is the stratagem that for that purpose he adopts:

Considering the injuries I had sustained, in addition to the ridicule to which I was continually exposed, I determined at all hazards to leave the old tyrant to his fate, and chose the following opportunity of doing so. The next day we went about the town to ask alms; but as the weather turned out very wet, we did not stir from beneath the arcades, with which this place is provided As the night approached, and the rain had not ceased, the old man said, "Lázaro, this wet weather is very unwholesome, and as night comes on it will be still more so, let us therefore get home in good time."

On our return we had to pass a small stream of water, which with the day's rain had considerably increased. I therefore said, "Uncle, the brook is very much swollen; but I see a place a little higher, where, by giving a little jump, we may pass almost dry shod." "Thou art a good lad," said the old man; "I like you for your carefulness. Take me to the narrowest part, for at this time of the year to get one's feet wet would be dangerous." Delighted that my plot seemed to succeed so well, I led him from beneath the arcades, and took him directly opposite to a pillar, or rather a large stone post, which I observed in the square. "Now, uncle," said I, "this is the place where the brook is the narrowest." The rain was pouring down, and the old man was getting very wet; and whether it was by haste he made to avoid it, or, what was more probable, Providence had at that moment beguiled him of his usual cunning, that he might the more readily fall into the snare, and give me my revenge; so it was, that for once he believed me, and said, "Now place me directly opposite the spot, and then jump yourself." I placed him exactly opposite the pillar, so that he could not miss it, and leaping myself, I took my position immediately behind it, crying out, "Now, master, jump with all your force, and you will clear the water." I had hardly said the words, when the poor old rogue jumped up as nimbly as a goat, giving all his strength to the leap, and taking a step or two backwards by way of impetus, which lent him such force, that instead of alighting on soft ground, as he supposed, he gave his poor bald pate such a smash against the pillar, that he fell on the pavement without sense or motion.

"Take that, you unhappy old thief," said I, "and remember the sausage;" then leaving him to the care of the people who began to gather around, I took to my heels as swiftly as possible through the town gates, and before night reached Torrijos. What became of the old man afterwards I don't know, and neither did I ever give myself any pains to enquire.

Let us then switch over to another of these romances and take up the career of Matéo Aléman's *Guzman* when he is attained to an age slightly more advanced than that of Lázarillo when we leave him. This is the rogue installed as a full member of a company of mendicants:

> On every festival we went early in the morning to church, where plenary indulgence was always granted us. We placed ourselves in the most convenient stations; we continued there the whole morning; and towards evening we issued forth into the neighboring villages, calling at the country seats and farmhouses on our road. From these we usually brought away some slices of bacon, bread and cheese, eggs, and sometimes old clothes and other articles; so successfully did we work upon the charity of the good people. Did a person above the common rank happen to make his appearance, we instantly united in setting up a loud lamentation, even at a distance, giving him time to put his hand into his pocket, and vociferating louder and louder the nearer he came, so as to compel him in a manner to be charitable.
>
> If we met a number of good citizens together, and had leisure to prepare to accost them in due form, each played his own part,— one the *blind*, another the *halt*, a third the *dumb*, a fourth the *paralytic*, a fifth the *idiotic*, and some with crutches, making altogether a complication of human misery and distortion, which, with the most able at our head, was sure to penetrate into the pockets even of the callous. Could you but have heard the concord of sweet sounds we made at the crisis that decided the balance in our favour. We beseeched the Lord to bless them with lovely children, —to return their bounty a hundred fold,—and long to preserve their precious health. Not a party of pleasure could be got up, not

a single festival pass but we had some share in it; so that however much others expended we gained by them; and so acute was our scent that we could smell the preparation for them at an enormous distance.

In the same way, the mansions of the cardinals, the bishops, and ambassadors, with all kind of open houses, were successfully besieged and occupied by us. Thus we might truly be said to possess all, levying as we did a tax upon all, though really having nothing.

There follows a long passage of philosophic writing as to the position in society of the beggar. And, indeed, Guzman as befits the obviously Teutonic origin of his author is more prone to indulge in fits of philosophy than are either Lázarillo or Quevedo's Paul, whose acquaintance we shall soon make. I do not wish to interrupt the impression of following the vicissitudes of a sharper by quoting such passages, so let us continue and see how Guzman, rising temporarily in life, became the servant of a cardinal. By this time Guzman had become an adept at feigning illnesses:

Having roused myself early one fine morning, according to custom, I went and seated myself at the door of a cardinal, concerning whom I had heard an excellent character, being one of the most charitably disposed in Rome. I had taken the trouble of getting one of my legs swelled, on which, notwithstanding what had passed, was to be seen a new ulcer, one that might set at defiance the most penetrating eye or probe of a surgeon. I had not this time omitted to have my face as pale as death; and thus, filling the air with horrible lamentations while I was asking alms, I moved the souls of the different domestics; but I was yet only beating up for game—it was their master I wanted. He at length made his appearance—I redoubled my cries and groans,—I writhed in anguish;—and I then accosted him in these terms:—"Oh! most noble Christian; thou friend of Christ and his afflicted ones! have pity upon me, a poor wretched sinner. Behold me cut down in the flower of my days;—may your excellency be touched with my extreme misery, for the sake of the sufferings of our dear Redeemer." The cardinal, who was really a pious man, stopped; and, after looking at me earnestly, turned to his attendants. "In the name of Christ, take this unhappy being, and bear him into my own apartments! let the rags that cover him be exchanged for fine linen; put him into a good bed—nay into my own—and I will go into another room. I will tend on him; for in him do I verily see what must have been the sufferings of our Saviour." He was obeyed; and, oh charity! how didst thou shame those lordly prelates who think Heaven in debt to them, if they do but look down on some poor wretch: while my good cardinal, not content with what he had done, ordered two surgeons to attend, recommending them to do all in their power to ease my agony, and to examine and cure my leg; after which they should be well recompensed.

The surgeons whom the cardinal employs to cure the young rogue, in spite of their crass ignorance, cannot but observe that the ulcer is a sham and they prepare to denounce their patient to the cardinal. But Guzman offering them all the bribes that he had at his disposal and pointing out that, if they pretended to cure him at the expense of a long illness they would gain great fees, they consent to become his accomplices. And Guzman is kept in bed for such an unconscionable time that he himself finds the captivity insupportable. However, in the meantime, the good cardinal visiting his invalid every day, conceives such an opinion of the young man's learning, extreme morality and agreeable turn of wit that he gave that rogue the position of one of his confidential pages. So, says Guzman:

Observe me at once in the character assigned to me of favorite page to his Eminence, an enormous step in life for me; though from that of rogue to private domestic, with the exception of the livery, there is not so great a distance as might be supposed. But to turn me from habits of idleness, and living by my wits, was something like trying to make a fish live out of water, for such was my element. The tavern was my province,—the primum mobile,—the centre on which I moved. But here everything seemed to go by clock-work; order and sobriety were general rules; and

I was either employed in showing people up and down stairs, or placed sentinel in an ante-room, standing like a hang-necked heron in a fish-pond, upon one melancholy leg. In short, I was at everybody's beck and call; sometimes behind my master's chair, at others behind his carriage; and always expected to be in twenty different places at once, without any respite from the first of January to the last day of December. "Wretched slave that I am," I exclaimed, "what boots it to put up with this unhappy life from week to week, and year to year. Alas! it will kill me, I must fly for it; once I was lacquey to all the world, and now my genius pines under a single master. I wear his livery; and what are my perquisites but candles' ends! Here, too, I run risk; unhappy Guzman! should I be detected, assuredly I should not escape under fifty lashes!" And in this way, I went on bemoaning my unfortunate condition. Besides the candles' ends, we used occasionally to help ourselves to any of the delicacies of the season; but this required more address than many of my companions could lay claim to; and one day I remember there occurred a disagreeable affair in consequence. A fool of a waiter, happening to be fond of sweets, laid hands upon some fine honeycomb, which he thought he had cunningly hidden in his pocket handkerchief. The weather was excessively hot; and the honey was soon running down the white stockings of the thief. As his fate would have it, the cardinal's eye came in contact with the phenomenon, and, suspecting what was the case, he burst into a violent fit of laughing. "See, my good fellow," he cried, "the blood is running down your leg, you have wounded yourself, what is it?" At this inquiry the attention of the whole company was directed the same way; his fellow-servants stared; and the wretched culprit stood before them with all the evidence of detected guilt glowing in his face. Yet too happy had he got rid of the affair with this exposure, for he paid far more dear for his whistle, so as to make it the bitterest honey he ever tasted.

The greater part of his companions were as little experienced in the light-fingered art as himself, while I, agreeably to my old custom, undertook to instruct them, by laying my hands on everything belonging to them, that came in my way. His eminence, in an adjoining cabinet, kept a large box of dried sweets, confectionery, and fruit of all kinds, to which he was extremely partial. Among other articles he had a choice store of Bergamot pears, Genoese plums, Granada melons, Seville lemons, oranges from Placentia, lemons from Murcia, cucumbers from Valencia, love-apples from Toledo, peaches from Aragon, and raisins from Malaga; indeed, everything most exquisite and alluring was to be found in this fragrant chest. My mouth watered every time I went near it.

Guzman, in short, employs his talents at once as thief and entertaining rogue to such purpose that the poor prince of the church is put in a singular dilemma. He feels that he ought not to keep Guzman in his employment not merely because of his thieving but because of the corruption that he spreads through the prelatic household and entourage. On the other hand, to dismiss him would prove his certain ruin. He, therefore, retained the boy near his person "in order that, thus well situated, he might have no motive for committing any great or serious crimes." So that in the end Guzman has to take French leave. He falls naturally into worse states than any he has hitherto experienced. Let us leave him, then, and take up the career of a rogue at a still more advanced age.

Paul, the hero of the best known of all the novels of the greatest and latest of the picaresque novelists, was the son of a barber and . . . a competitor of Celestina herself. His career is at first moderately successful. He receives some education at school, where he attracts the affection of the son of a rich merchant of the city of Segovia, Don Alonzo Coronel de Zunniga. During all his school days he acts as the sedulous courtier and servant of this young man and the young man is sent to boarding school and then to the University of Alcala, Paul all the while accompanying him as part his servant and part his instructor in every kind of villainous and amusing trick. All these adventures—and they are innumerable and fantastically disastrous—are recounted with a gravity and an ironic indignation that much surpass in quality and texture the work of all other writers of the sort. Smollett alone can compare with Quevedo in the quality of a sort of terrifying seriousness and, having a less fantastic world to project, even Smollett's projection of nightmare horrors and hardships are somewhat hodden and unvarying compared with the riotous night-scenes of Quevedo. Paul, then, is the attendant on the rich young Don Diego when he receives the following letter from his uncle, who is the public executioner of the city of Segovia:

My dear Paul,

The responsible office, and pressing affairs, in which it has pleased his Majesty to place me, have been the occasion of my not writing to you before; for if there be anything to find fault with in the King's service, it is the great trouble and attendance it requires; which, however, is in measure requited by the honour of being his servant. It troubles me to be forced to send you disagreeable news; but your father died eight days ago, with as much bravery and resolution as ever man did; I speak of my own knowledge as having trussed him up myself. The cart became him as well as it had been a chariot, and all that saw the rope round his neck, concluded he was as clever a fellow as ever was hanged. He looked up all the way he went at the windows very much unconcerned, bowing to all the tradesmen who had left their shops, and turning up his whiskers several times. He desired the priest, that went to prepare him for death, not to be too eager; but to rest and take a breathing, extolling any fine expressions that he used. Being come to the triple tree, he presently set his foot on the ladder, and went up it nimbly, not creeping on all fours as others do; and perceiving that one of the rounds of it was cracked through, he turned to the officers attending, and bade them get it mended for the next that came, because all men had not his spirit. I cannot express how much his person and carriage was applauded. . . .

He charged me to put on his cap a little to one side; and then he swung, without shrinking up his legs, or making ugly faces, but preserved such a gravity that it was a pleasure to behold him. I next quartered him, and fixed the several parts on the highways. God knows what a trouble it is to me, to see him there daily treating the crows and ravens; but I suppose the pastry cooks hereabouts will soon ease us of that sad spectacle, burying him in their minced pies. I cannot give you a much better account of your mother, for though still living, she is a prisoner in the Inquisition at Toledo, because she would not let the dead rest in their graves. In her house were found as many arms, legs, and skulls, as would have stocked a charnel-house; they say she would fly up a chimney, and ride faster upon a broom-staff than another can upon the best Andalusian horse. I am sorry she disgraces us all, and me more particularly as being the King's officer, which kindred does not become my post.

Probably because of these events—though it is not expressly so stated—Don Diego is commanded by his father, Don Alonzo, to dismiss the unfortunate Paul, who is thus thrown on the streets. He goes through a great many and very various roguish ups and downs until at last, on the road to Toledo, he falls in with a company of strolling players and, having enough money to pay his footing, he is accepted amongst them and becomes actor-author-playwright—for all the world as was Shakespeare at about the same epoch. . . . Because of that I quote rather in extenso from this portion of Quevedo's work so that we may see what might have been any author's progress in those rigorous days:

> We were all higgledy-piggledy, men and women together; and I was mightily taken with one of the crew who was the chief dancer and acted the queens and other great parts in plays, for she was a notable jilt. She asked me whither I was going, and some questions concerning my life and circumstances; and in conclusion, after much talk, deferred it to Toledo to act there.
>
> We diverted ourselves by the way the best we could; and I happened to act a piece of a play that I had borne a part in when I was a boy; which I did so well, that they took a liking to me; and being informed by my friend who was in the company, of all my misfortunes and hard circumstances, which I had made him acquainted with, she asked me whether I would make one among them? They so highly extolled their strolling course of life, and

I was then in such want of some support, and so fond of the wench, that I agreed with the head of them for two years. Writings were signed between us, to oblige me to stay with them; so they gave me my allowance and allotted my parts, and thus we came to Toledo. They gave me two or three prologues to get by heart, and some other grave parts, which suited well with my voice. I applied myself to it, and spoke the first prologue in the town, where we had a simile of a ship in distress, and wanting provisions, which put into that port: I called them noble audience, begging their attention, pardon for all faults, and so went off. There was a great clapping of hands, and I was liked on the stage. We acted a play, written by one of our actors, and I admired how they should come to be poets, for I thought it belonged only to very learned and ingenious men, and not to persons so extremely ignorant. But it is now come to such a pass, that every head of them writes plays, and every actor makes drolls and farces; though formerly I remember no plays would go down, but what were written by the greatest wits in Spain. . . .

By that time we had been a month at Toledo, acting several new plays, and endeavouring to retrieve our first fault; I was grown famous, and had given out that my name was Alonzo, to which the generality added the title of the Cruel, because I had acted a part of that nature, to the great liking of the mob and upper galleries. I had now got several new suits of clothes, and some heads of other strollers endeavoured to enveigle me away from my company: but I pretended to criticize upon plays, and railed at the most celebrated actors; finding fault with one man's gestures, censuring another's gravity, and allowing another to be a tolerable actor. My advice was always taken in contriving the scenes, and adorning the stage; and if any play came to be offered, it was left to me to examine. Being encouraged by this applause, I launched out as a poet in a song, and then wrote a small farce, which was well approved of. Next I ventured at a play; and that it might gain respect, made it all of devotion, and full of the blessed Virgin. It began with music, had fine shows of souls departed, and devils appearing, as was the fashion then, with old gibberish when they appeared, and strange shrieks when they vanished. The mob was mightily pleased with my rhyming to Satan, and my long discourses about his falling or not falling from heaven. In short, the play was acted, and well liked. I had more business than I could turn my hands to, for all sorts of lovers flocked to me; some would have songs on their mistresses' eyes; others on their foreheads; others on their white hands; others on their golden locks. There were set rates of all sorts; but I sold cheap to draw the more custom, because there were other shops besides mine. As for godly ballads, I supplied all the country clerks, and runners of monasteries; and the blind men were my best friends, for they never allowed less than eighty royals; and I always took care that they should be bombastic, and stuffed with cramp words, which neither they nor I understood. I brought up many new fashions in verse, as tailors do in clothes, and was the first that concluded my songs like sermons, praying for grace in this world and glory in the next.

CHAPTER FOUR

B EFORE going on to deal with English novelists and the novel in
general it would be as well here to make some investigation into
the medium in which novels are couched. The modern English language has never—or, at any rate, until the beginning of the present
century—been a very good vehicle for prose. To put it roughly, we
might say that the great periods and cadences of the seventeenth
century had, by the eighteenth, deteriorated into a sort of mechanical
rhythm and that by the nineteenth century, in the avoidance of the
sort of pomposity and the dry rhythm of the eighteenth century,
the language became so timid and indefinite that it was impossible to
use it for making any definite statement. So that it was not until the
nineties that English prose came alive again at the hands of W. E.
Henley and his group; and later, of Conrad, Henry James, Stephen
Crane, W. H. Hudson and other writers rather specifically American
than English. In the short period between the composition of the
Prayer Book and of Clarendon's *History of the Rebellion*, great English prose writers seem relatively innumerable. Between the death of
Swift in 1745—the year which, it should be remembered, saw the last
attempt of Jacobitism to raise itself from the dust—between, then, the
'45 and, say, the day of writers like Cardinal Newman and the Oxford
movement, almost no imaginative prose masterpieces saw the light
and English prose exhibited almost none of that sort of super-delight
that marks the writing of Sir Thomas Browne, of Walton, of Clarendon, or even of Pepys.

It is to be remembered that a passage of good prose is a work of art
absolute in itself and with no more dependence on its contents than is
a fugue of Bach, a minuet of Mozart, or the writings for the piano of
Debussy. Such a paragraph as that which follows from Sir Thomas
Browne's *Pseudodoxia* will be read by the prose lover with almost
breathless delight, though the habits of the stork mean no more to
him than he to the stork.

That Storks are to be found, and will only live in Republikes or free States, is a petty conceit to advance the opinion of popular policies, and from Antipathies in nature, to disparage Monarchical government. But how far agreeable unto truth, let them consider who read in PLINY, that among the THESALIANS who were governed by Kings, and much abounded with Serpents, it was no less than capital to kill a Stork. That the Ancient EGYPTIANS honoured them, whose government was from all thimes Monarchical. That BELLONIUS affirmeth, men make them nests in FRANCE. That relations make them common in PERSIA, and the dominions of the great TURK. And lastly, how JEREMY the Prophet delivered himself unto his countryemen, whose government was at that time Monarchical. The Stork in the heaven knowing her appointed time, the Turtle, Crane and Swallow observe the time of their coming, but my people know not the judgment of the Lord. Wherein to exprobate their stupidity, he induceth the providence of Storks. Now if the bird had been unknown, the illustration had been obscure, and the exprobation not so proper.

The above passage—though chosen purely at random according to a habit of this writer, of turning to page ninety of any edition of an author (in this case the 1927 Edinburgh edition of Browne edited by Charles Sayle) and then quoting the first paragraph of reasonable length that he comes upon—the above passage, then, has almost no interest of content, yet for the lulling nature of its cadences, the surprise and vivacity of its illustrations, and the composure of its writer, it will stand beside any passage of prose the greatest in the world. And I am prepared to leave it to the taste of my readers who may decide each for himself whether a passage of flawless prose gains or loses when the subject treated is one of universal interest. To ascertain that let us quote perhaps the most famous of all passages of Browne:

What Song the SYRENS sang, or what name ACHILLES assumed when he hid himself among women, though puzling questions are not beyond all conjecture. What time the persons of these

Ossuaries entered the famous Nations of the dead, and slept with Princes and Counsellors, might admit a wide solution. But who were the proprietaries of these bones, or what bodies these ashes made up, were a question above Antiquarism. Not to be resolved by man, nor easily perhaps by spirits, except we consult the Provincial Guardians, or tutelary Observators. Had they made as good provision for their names, as they have done for their Reliques, they had not so grossly erred in the art of perpetuation. But to subsist in bones, and be but Pyramidally extant, is a fallacy in duration.

It may be urged against such prose that it has about it a certain, as it were, decorative air inherited from the Psalms or the poetic books of the Bible. Its vivacity may seem to come, that is to say, from a certain antithesis or quaint instance set against quaint instance, much as we have observed the fascination of the Bible to come from the antitheses of contradictory thoughts set one against another. Actually that is a point of almost universal technique deeply founded in the mentality of all human beings. Someone has said that the prime quality of art, at any rate in literature, is the quality of surprise. That is to say that had Browne written: "What Song the SYRENS sang and what is the significance of the symphony in the Dido of the divine PERCELL" the carrying on of the kind of illustration would have rendered it possibly more clear to the understanding but certainly less delightful to the imagination than the speculation as to the name that Achilles bore among the women. And the reader, if he will take the trouble to make sufficiently minute investigations, will find that similar qualities distinguish nearly all great prose, whether it be that of Swift, of Chateaubriand, of Stendhal, or Joseph Conrad. This comes about partly because the device is enjoined by a definite technical rule, some writers at least knowing that such a quality of surprise is calculated to delight the reader and partly also because, perfectly spontaneously, a real prose writer likes to delight himself by the astonishment of juxtaposing instances that he takes from his own consciousness.

For me the great monument of English prose, the *Book of Common Prayer* of 1535 being set apart, is Clarendon's *History of the Rebellion*.

This writer has heard it said by critics whose views he much respects that Maine's *Ancient Law* runs Clarendon very close, but he is sufficiently a schoolboy to confess that if the quality of the writing be equal he would rather read a romance of adventure such as is Clarendon's *History* than the clearest of expressions of abstract truth. To contrast, then, a passage from a masterpiece of modern prose with the numerous examples from the seventeenth century which we shall here be citing, let us take a short passage from Maine's *Ancient Law* from the New York edition of 1867:

> The peculiar Roman idea that natural law co-existed with civil law and gradually absorbed it, had evidently been lost sight of, or had become unintelligible, and the words which had at most conveyed a theory concerning the origin, composition and development of human institutions, were beginning to express the sense of a great standing wrong suffered by mankind. As early as the beginning of the fourteenth century, the current language concerning the birth-state of men, though visibly intended to be identical with that of Ulpian and his contemporaries, has assumed an altogether different form and meaning. The preamble to the celebrated ordinance of King Louis Hutin, enfranchising the serfs of the royal domains, would have sounded strangely to Roman ears. "Whereas, according to natural law, everybody ought to be born free;"

The writer may be taxed with inconsistency when he states, at the one moment, that the English of the nineteenth century was a language ill-suited to the production of masterpieces in prose and then quotes as master-writing a passage of a work written by a member of the Supreme Council of India and Regius Professor of Civil Law in the University of Cambridge about 1860. But actually we are considering imaginative prose and the quotation from Maine is, as it were, on the side, since it is taken from a technical work. And technical writing, more particularly that of lawyers, abstract scientists, and, above all, field naturalists, is apt to be now and then extremely fine, simply because of the writer's necessity to express himself, not merely to the reader, but to himself, with extreme clarity and scrupulousness. Where, in fact, would English prose be without Walton's *Compleat Angler*, White's *Natural History of Selborne*, or W. H. Hudson's *Nature in Downland*? And, indeed, if you want to listen to admirable and lucid English, you could not do better than to go to the law courts and hear the Lord Chief Justice deliver a judgment about patent rights in boots.

The dividing line for us between what is to be regarded as imaginative and what technical prose would seem to draw itself along the line of to what extent the writer has expressed his personality. For, not infrequently, in spite of himself, the technical writer will let his personality so shine through even the dryest passages of the dryest possible subject matter that the reader may take as much delight in him as in Browne or Clarendon himself. Thus, for this writer, the most beautiful of all prose will be found in the letters of Thomas Edwards, an obscure Banffshire cobbler who watched birds with passion all his life and was unable either to read or to write until the latest years of his life, though he died actually a member of the Linnaean Society. He owed this honor to treatises that he had written about the habits of certain small fish.

Or how, indeed, are we to deal with Clarendon himself? Let us begin with quoting the famous "Conclusion of the whole history"—a relatively abstract passage relating to, and relating the history of, the Restoration of Charles II:

> The concourse was so great, that the King rode in a crowd from the bridge to Whitehall; all the companies of the city standing in order on both sides, and giving loud thanks to God for his Majesty's presence. He no sooner came to Whitehall, but the two Houses of Parliament solemnly cast themselves at his feet, with all vows of affection and fidelity to the world's end. In a word, the joy was so unexpressible, and so universal, that his Majesty said smilingly to some about him, "he doubted it had been his own fault he had been absent so long; for he saw nobody that did not protest he had ever wished for his return."
>
> In this wonderful manner, and with this incredible expedition, did God put an end to a rebellion that had raged near twenty

years, and been carried on with all the horrid circumstances of murder, devastation, and parricide, that fire and sword, in the hands of the most wicked men in the world, could be instruments, almost to the desolation, of two kingdoms, and the exceeding defacing and deforming the third.

It was but five months, since Lambert's fanatical army was scattered and confounded, and General Monk's marched into England: it was but three months, since the secluded members were restored: and, shortly after, the monstrous long Parliament finally dissolved, and rooted up: it was but a month, since the King's letters and Declaration were delivered to the new Parliament, afterwards called the Convention: on the first of May they were delivered, and his Majesty was at Whitehall on the 29th of the same month.

By these remarkable steps, among others, did the merciful hand of God, in this short space of time, not only bind up and heal all those wounds, but even make the scars as undiscernible, as, in respect of the deepness, was possible; which was a glorious addition to the deliverance. And, after this miraculous restoration of the Crown, and the Church, and the just rights of Parliaments, no nation under heaven can ever be more happy, if God shall be pleased to add establishment and perpetuity to the blessings he then restored.

Yet Clarendon and his *History* are hardly read at all, except by historical students if even by them, on the plea that he is the dryest of historians.*

Let us then take another passage of a more adventurous nature. The reader will probably be acquainted with the narration of the assassination by John Felton of the Duke of Buckingham as it is related by Alexandre Dumas—a writer *qui écrivait comme un cocher de fiacre,* if, indeed, a Paris cabman could be found to write so badly. Let us look at Clarendon's account of the same event. He describes John

---

* This is by no means the first time that this writer has written in praise of Clarendon, and each time that he has done so he has been taken to task on the plea that it is monstrous to call Clarendon a great prosateur because he was actually "the dryest of historians."

Felton as "an obscure man in his own person . . . whose captain had been killed upon the retreat at the Isle of Rhé upon which he conceived that the company of right ought to have been conferred upon him." It was refused to him by the Duke of Buckingham Felton, therefore, resigned from the army, retired into the solitude of the country, and came to the conclusion that he should do God a good service if he killed the Duke. "He chose no other instrument to do it with than an ordinary knife which he bought of a common cutler for a shilling." He arrived at Portsmouth, where the Duke was getting ready his forces for the relief of La Rochelle, on the Eve of St. Bartholomew. In the morning he hid himself behind the arras in the passageway between the Duke's bedroom and his antechamber. So, says Clarendon:

This morning of St. Bartholomew the Duke had received letters, in which he was advertised that Rochelle had relieved itself; upon which he directed that his breakfast might speedily be made ready, and he would made haste to acquaint the King with the good news, the Court being then at Southwick, the house of Sir Daniel Norton, five miles from Portsmouth. The chamber wherein he was dressing himself was full of company, of persons of quality, and officers of the fleet and army.

There was Monsieur de Soubize, brother to the Duke of Rohan, and other French Gentlemen, who were very solicitous for the embarkation of the army, and for the departure of the fleet for the relief of Rochelle; and they were at that time in much trouble and perplexity, out of apprehension that the news the Duke had received that morning might slacken the preparations for the voyage, which their impatience and interest persuaded them were not advanced with expedition; and so they had then held much discourse with the Duke of the impossibility that his intelligence could be true, and that it was contrived by the artifice and dexterity of their enemies, in order to abate the warmth and zeal that was used for their relief, the arrival of which relief those enemies had so much reason to apprehend; and a little longer delay in sending it would ease them of that terrible apprehension, their forts and works toward the sea and in the harbour being almost finished.

This discourse, according to the natural custom of that nation, and by the usual dialect of that language, was held with that passion and vehemence, that the standers by, who understood not French, did believe that they were angry, and that they used the Duke rudely. He being ready, drew towards the door, where the hangings were held up; and, in that very passage, turning himself to speak with Sir Thomas Fryer, a Colonel of the army, who was then speaking near his ear, he was on the sudden struck over his shoulder upon the breast with a knife; upon which, without using any other words but, "The villain hath killed me," and in the same moment pulling out the knife himself, he fell down dead, the knife having pierced his heart.

No man had seen the blow, or the man who gave it; but in the confusion they were in, every man made his own conjecture, and declared it as a thing known; most agreeing that it was done by the French, from the angry discourse they thought they had heard from them. And it was a kind of a miracle, that they were not all killed in that instant; the sober sort, that preserved them from it, having the same opinion of their guilt, and only reserving them for a more judicial examination and proceeding.

In the crowd near the door there was found upon the ground a hat, in the inside whereof there was sewed upon the crown a paper, in which were writ four or five lines of that declaration made by the House of Commons, in which they had styled the Duke an enemy to the kingdom, and under it a short ejaculation or two towards a prayer. It was easily enough concluded that the hat belonged to the person who had committed the murder: but the difficulty remained still as great, who that person should be; for the writing discovered nothing of the name; and whosoever it was, it was very natural to believe that he was gone far enough not to be found without a hat.

In this hurry, one running one way, another another way, a man was seen walking before the door very composedly without a hat; whereupon one crying out, "Here is the fellow that killed the Duke;" upon which others run thither, every body asking, "Which is he? Which is he?" To which the man without the hat very composedly answered, "I am he."

We do not imagine that for anyone who has once read this passage, Dumas's account of the event will remain in his mind. And that brings us once again to the question: "What makes imaginative prose?", which is once more the same question as: "What differentiates between literature and *biblia a-biblia?*" And we can't really find a better answer than the one we have already found—that imaginative prose or literature is that writing which most reveals the personality of its author. It is, in short, its humaneness that makes the humaner letters.

English, as we have said, is rather short in the item of great novels. It would, then, be almost a minor literature were it not for the prose writers whom we have been citing. They, it will be observed, are none of them novelists. And, indeed, it was not until comparatively lately that the English novelist paid any attention whatever to his prose. Perhaps the only one of them who could be styled, for fugitive passages, a really great prose writer was Dickens. There are passages in Dickens that will stand up against some of the finest of Flaubert, Turgenev, or Prosper Mérimée. But, great prosateur as he was, Dickens seems to have been it almost unconsciously and, as it were, with deprecation. For it is odd that until very lately it was regarded by English critics as a blot and presumption that the novelist should think about his "style" at all . . . or, indeed, about anything connected with the technique of the art. And this writer can well remember the time when the late Robert Louis Stevenson was roundly styled un-English because he announced himself as playing the sedulous ape to Sir Thomas Browne. That was because the English critic, disliking all the arts, was filled with disgust at the idea that another form of art should be forced upon his attention.

Be that as it may, the moment one becomes an impassioned student of letters—an old man or young man mad about literature—one perceives that English literature has one very great glory, a glory that of itself would suffice to let it be classed as a literature major, indeed . . . and that is the great series of works of which we have here been treating. They recount incidents, habits of mind, or of insects or of birds, theories, memories. And the passion with which these records are made, revealing the great, liberal personalities of the writers, makes them become under the almost unconscious pen great works of art. Such books as the late Robert Bontine Cunninghame Graham's *Mogreb el-Acksa*, Charles Doughty's *Arabia Deserta*, W. H. Hudson's *The Purple Land that England Lost*, Borrow's *Bible in Spain*, Beckford's *Letters from Portugal*, Thoreau's *Walden* or White's *Selborne*, Walton's *Compleat Angler* or Browne's *Urne-Burial* are none of them novels. Yet none of them is today a work of instruction about Morocco or about urn burial, as Cunninghame Graham and Sir Thomas Browne intended, and they have long ago been superseded. Nevertheless, they are deathless.

That is because in the end, mercifully, instruction in the natures of the men that were *el insignissimo scrittore inglesi*, the father of Ann Hyde, or the chronicler of the old tortoise is the purest form of entertainment. Humanity has one insatiable curiosity—that as to the inner natures of men. So, having, compared with most other nations, relatively few novelists with the conscience to give that information, the Anglo-Saxon has, in this department of human activity, most produced and delighted in these beautiful, beautifully set down, human documents. You would not go to Borrow for true information about Spain any more than you would go to Clarendon for an impartial account of the proceedings of the Duke of Argyll in the early days of the restoration of Charles II. You go to them for illumination as to their utterly partial, completely unscrupulous and gloriously virile personalities. Neither would you go to Browne for information as to the habits of storks. You go to him because he was of the type of mind to write "What Songs the Syrens sang, or what name Achilles assumed when he hid himself amongst women . . ."

Before taking up the English novel with Defoe and continuing the history of that form in its international aspects until nearly the present day—which will see us at the end of this our history—let us now consider the writers of other European countries until the eighteenth century was well under way. But before then, just to sweeten the cup, let us take leave of our Jacobean writers with a passage from Walton and add as a further *bonne bouche* the most famous passage, about the old tortoise, from the most beloved of all English naturalist-prosateurs. He, though he lived in the full be-wigged seventeenth century, went nevertheless so consummately native that he has left us a little monument that shall outlive and with its oaken stop outsound an infinity of other memorials all in the loudest sounding brass.

Here then is Walton* of the *Compleat Angler*:

Look, under that broad beech-tree, I sat down when I was last this way fishing, and the birds in the adjoining grove seemed to have a friendly contention with an echo, whose dead voice seemed to live in a hollow tree, near to the brow of that primrose-hill: there I sat viewing the silver streams glide silently towards their centre, the tempestuous sea; yet sometimes opposed by rugged roots and pebble stones, which broke their waves, and turned them into foam: and sometimes I beguiled time by viewing harmless lambs, some leaping securely in the cool shade, whilst others sported themselves in the cheerful sun; and saw others craving comfort from the swollen udders of their bleating dams. As I thus sat, these and other sights had so fully possessed my soul with content, that I thought, as the poet has happily expressed it,

I was for that time lifted above earth,
And possess'd joys not promis'd in my birth.

As I left this place, and entered into the next field, a second pleasure entertained me; it was a handsome milk-maid that had not yet attained so much age and wisdom as to load her mind with any fears of many things that will never be, as too many men too often do: but she cast away all care, and sung like a nightingale: her voice was good, and the ditty fitted for it: it was that

---

* Izaak Walton, 1593-1683. The *Compleat Angler* was first published in 1653; the *Life of George Herbert* in 1670.

smooth song which was made by Kit Marlow, now at least fifty years ago: and the milk-maid's mother sung an answer to it, which was made by Sir Walter Raleigh in his younger days.

And here, just for remembrance, is the author of the *Temple* as Walton knew him.

It was not many days before he [George Herbert] returned back to Bemerton, to view the Church, and repair the Chancel: and indeed to rebuild almost three parts of his house, which was fallen down, or decayed by reason of his predecessor's living at a better Parsonage-house; namely, at Minal, sixteen or twenty miles from this place. At which time of Mr. Herbert's coming alone to Bemerton, there came to him a poor old woman, with an intent to acquaint him with her necessitous condition, as also with some troubles of her mind: but after she had spoke some few words to him, she was suprised with a fear, and that begot a shortness of breath, so that her spirits and speech failed her; which he perceiving, did so compassionate her, and was so humble, that he took her by the hand, and said, "Speak, good mother; be not afraid to speak to me; for I am a man that will hear you with patience; and will relieve your necessities too, if I be able: and this I will do willingly; and therefore, mother, be not afraid to acquaint me with what you desire." After which comfortable speech, he again took her by the hand, made her sit down by him, and understanding she was of his parish, he told her "He would be acquainted with her, and take her into his care." And having with patience heard and understood her wants,—and it is some relief for a poor body to be but heard with patience,—he, like a Christian Clergyman, comforted her by his meek behavior and counsel; but because that cost him nothing, he relieved her with money too, and so sent her home with a cheerful heart, praising God, and praying for him. Thus worthy, and—like David's blessed man—thus lowly, was Mr. George Herbert in his own eyes, and thus lovely in the eyes of others.

Here finally is White's old tortoise:*

The old Sussex tortoise that I have mentioned to you so often is become my property. I dug it out of its winter dormitory in March last, when it was enough awakened to express its resentments by hissing; and packing it in a box with earth, carried it eighty miles in post-chaises. The rattle and hurry of the journey so perfectly roused it, that when I turned it out on a border, it walked twice down to the bottom of my garden; however, in the evening, the weather being cold, it buried itself in the loose mold, and continues still concealed.

As it will be under my eye, I shall now have an opportunity of enlarging my observations on its mode of life and propensities: and perceive already that towards the time of coming forth, it opens a breathing-place in the ground near its head; requiring, I conclude, a freer respiration as it becomes more alive. This creature not only goes under the earth from the middle of November to the middle of April, but sleeps great part of the summer; for it goes to bed in the longest days at four in the afternoon, and often does not stir in the morning till late. Besides, it retires to rest for every shower, and does not move at all on wet days. When one reflects on the state of this strange being, it is a matter of wonder to find that Providence should bestow such a profusion of days, such a seeming waste of longevity, on a reptile that appears to relish it so little as to squander more than two-thirds of its existence in a joyless stupor, and to be lost to all sensation for months together in the profoundest slumbers.

When I was writing this letter, a moist and warm afternoon, with the thermometer at fifty, brought forth troops of shell-snails, and at the same juncture the tortoise heaved up the mold and put out his head: and the next morning came forth, as if raised from the dead; and walked about until four in the afternoon. This was a curious coincidence—a very amusing occurrence!—to see such a

---

* Gilbert White, 1720-1793; from 1751 curate of Selborne, in Hampshire, the village of his birth. *The Natural History and Antiquities of Selborne* was first published in 1789.

similarity of feelings between the two *pherekeoi*: for so the Greeks call both the shell-snail and the tortoise. . . .

Pitiable seems the condition of this poor embarrassed reptile: to be cased in a suit of ponderous armor which he cannot lay aside,—to be imprisoned, as it were, within his own shell,—must preclude, we should suppose, all activity and disposition for enterprise. Yet there is a season of the year (usually the beginning of June) when his exertions are remarkable. He then walks on tiptoe, and is stirring by five in the morning, and traversing the garden, examines every wicket and interstice in the fence through which he will escape if possible; and often has eluded the care of the gardener, and wandered to some distant field.

The difficulties of our task—in space—become here enormously apparent. We have to get rid in a page or two of whole bustling worlds of writers, each one worthy of mention because of one characteristic or another, but hardly any of them meriting the name of "great." Both Spain and Italy, supine under economic and political pressures, seem after the Italian renaissance with which we have dealt as fully as we can, and Cervantes and Quevedo y Villega, to have become imaginatively quiescent. That is not to say that a man with a taste for all things Mediterranean might not get real profit from studying the Spanish or Italian literatures during those periods. A really brilliant history of the *Commedia dell'Arte* during the sixteenth, seventeenth, and eighteenth centuries would form one of the most interesting books ever written, but the subject is, perhaps, not the concern of the historian of literature proper, since for the most part these were comedies in which the author—or it might be more proper to call him the inventor—did as a rule little more than write the mere outline of the play and its various scenes and situations, the actors doing what is called "gagging" speeches and modifying the action to suit themselves. Yet obviously the *Commedia* must have had some influence on such considerable literary dramatists as, say, Monteverde (1568-1643), the composer, librettist, and inventor of the opera, whose *Orfeo* is still a thing very delightful to listen to; or Metastasio (1698-1782), the author of a number of suave tragedies in verse; or the able writer of really mondiall significance, Goldoni, who lived from 1707 to 1793. Of Goldoni, for instance, we know that he ran away from Rimini and, like the Paul of Quevedo, joined a company of strolling players and so got as far as Venice, where he settled down ostensibly to study law, but actually to pass his time reading over and over again the Greek and Latin comic dramatists. One risks exciting the wrath of patriotic subjects of Mussolini if one should say that Metastasio or Monteverde were figures less important than Shakespeare or Ben Jonson. But to anyone neither Italian nor extravagantly Italianate it is obvious that, judged by our particular standard of comparative literature, which implies that authors are rated according not merely to their home but to their international influence, any comparison at all between the two pairs of poets would be absurd. In fact, between the renaissance and the beginning of the nineteenth century the only Italian authors to have any wide international significance were Goldoni himself and Alfieri, who died in 1803, having been born in 1749. Goldoni lived into a period when Italy was beginning to feel the inflatives of desire for patriotic unity. Until that date we may put down the relative lack of great or inspired Italian literary figures as being due to the political supineness of a country hopelessly divided into small unities and crushed beneath the heels of Austria and Spain. The influence of Goldoni as comic dramatist on the Europe of his day was enormous. Indeed, polite comedy as we know it and as it has been ever since the early eighteenth century is all the world over a child of his fathering. You might say that the difference between pre- and post-Goldoni drama was the difference between the shapeless bawdiness of Wycherly's *Country Wife* and Sheridan's *School for Scandal*. Goldoni, in fact, relieved comedy of the intolerable burden of having no comic topic save those of rapes, seductions and illicit sexual contact, and gave to it lightness, form, and, on occasion, even beauty. The greatness of his influence over his day is showed by the fact that towards the end of his life he was called to Paris where he spent the last twenty-three years of his life as a pensioner of Louis XVI. It was for the wedding of that king and Marie Antoinette that he wrote in French one of the most charming of all his comedies, *Le Bourru Bien Faisant*. And we may take it as a rather wry-faced testimony to the esteem in which he was held in

France that though the Republic cut off his pension, thus leaving him to end his days by starvation, at the instance of André Chénier the Convention restored his pension to his widow. Of Alfieri, certainly Italy's greatest lyric tragedian, we shall have to treat more fully when we come to the romantic movement or other eighteenth century Italian figures. The only ones who would seem to be at all universal are those of Casanova, of Leopardi, and Silvio Pellico—the last two having been just born in that century, Leopardi, two years, and Pellico, eleven, before its close.

The journal of Giovanni Giacomo Casanova de Seingalt (1725-98), if we regard it as the most monstrous and egregious of picaresque novels, may well pass for a piece of writing of international importance, though not of international literary importance. The writer cannot call to mind any large crops of works that can be alleged to imitate the *Journals*. During our own middle years it was generally taken for fact that the *Journals* were in great part a forgery of that singular figure, the bibliophile Jacob. But today the balance of belief would seem to tend towards agreeing that they are almost altogether the writing of Casanova himself, the published form of the book being the result of a compilation of manuscripts left by Casanova in the library of Dax in Bohemia. Casanova passed the last years of his life as librarian in that castle. The vast majority of his readers today probably read him for the records of his innumerable seductions, which give to the book a certain monotony so that if an *édition du Dauphin* could be prepared leaving out the majority of passages of that kidney we should probably have something much more readable and inspiring, whilst the man of the world and the adolescent seeking useful knowledge would be advantaged by having all the salacious episodes grouped together at the end of the book. The *Memoirs* were actually published in French, so it is perhaps a solecism to call them an Italian masterpiece, though masterpiece they are. As an extended picture of the conditions of an era and a portion of the world's surface in a state of cultural decay and political horrors they have no equal and certainly no parallel save the diary of Pepys. And, as a work of art, the book probably merely gains in attractiveness because a large proportion of the work—as is conceded even by the staunchest believers in the Casanovian authorship—was magnificent lying, particularly in its non-amorous aspects. Casanova was by his own showing rogue, thief, pimp, spy, secret agent, suspect diplomat, gambler, sham magician, purveyor of obscenities, gaol-bird, rake and optimist throughout half a Latin world that was staggering through political grafts, felonies, betrayals, candle-lit festivals, debauches lit by burning towns, delicate music, elegances, wantonnesses—towards bankruptcies, revolutions and heroic struggles for national freedom from international oppressions. You might, indeed, read it as a book of prophecies whose results are not exhausted even in our own day. But, however you read it, you will become acquainted with a personality extraordinarily marked and defined, so that according to our late definition, it may well pass as a work of art. . . . Casanova was perhaps surpassed as a liar by Benvenuto Cellini, but he would certainly have made a more agreeable housemate for anyone of a disposition at all leaning towards the contemplative.

Ruinous wars, economic disasters, the stifling influence of the Inquisition, mental preoccupations with colonial and conquered territories, family struggles for power and the oppressive nature of power once secured—all these things extinguished literature in Spain of the eighteenth century almost more than the art was strangled in Italy by Spanish oppressions during the same period. Italians might, as we have seen, claim world eminence for Monteverde and Metastasio, but hardly any Spanish patriot could demand as much for the poet Ignazio di Luzan, whose verse shows hardly any poetic quality at all, though in his treatise on poetry he proves himself a critic of power and discrimination. As such, he exercised a certain influence on the French writers of his time. He lived from 1702 to 1754.

In the declining days of the Roman Empire small schools of poetry established themselves, as we have seen, in Southern France and Spain; so in this period of national darkness the Spanish people expressed themselves and satisfied their lyric desires with folksongs and dances, and various poetic centers grew up in the larger provincial cities like Seville or in university centers. The products of the school of Salamanca are curious and worth the attention of the literary-leisured, but otherwise the eighteenth century was completely barren of literary fruits. The great quasi-romantic poet Manuel José de Quintana was, it is true, born in 1772, but did not, as if by coincidence, publish the first of his thirty celebrated odes till the year 1800. He afterwards led the heroic literary war of incitement against the French occupation of the Peninsula, his "Ode to the Battle of Trafalgar" gaining him immediate fame. And with that struggle, literary Spain reawakened, playing a distinguished part in the romantic movement which, shortly after Waterloo, spread throughout the world.

Indeed, when we approach the literature of Germany, at any rate from the early eighteenth century onwards, we seem to see almost nothing but romantic literature. I propose to deal here merely with Friedrich Gottlieb Klopstock (1724-1803), Gotthold Ephriam Lessing (1729-1781), and Heinrich von Kleist (1777-1811), leaving the poets of the *Sturm und Drang* period—Herder, Wieland, Goethe, Schiller and the rest—until we deal with the romantic movement proper. The three writers first named fall well within our category as being international influences. I do not myself propose seriously to attempt to estimate their literary values. The patriotic subjects of Mr. Hitler would tell you that they surpass in value Milton, Victor Hugo, Lamartine, Lope de Vega and Shakespeare himself, except as translated by Schlegel and Tieck. Indeed, a German professor under whom for his sins the writer sat as a boy, reading *Nathan der Weise*, Klopstock's *Messias*, Kleist's *Michael Koolhas* and, indeed, the second and third parts of *Faust, Wilhelm Meister, Goetz von Berlichingen* and *Die Raeuber*—that German professor, bearded and spectacled and minatory-voiced, made the assertion as to the values of the German eighteenth to early nineteenth century writers so frequently and so threateningly that all that literature has been as completely ruined for me as were Shakespeare and Jesus Christ in English schools for Arthur Marwood. He, it will be remembered, said that both those figures had for him the faces of schoolmasters. The writer will not go so far as to say that either

Goethe or Schiller or Lessing seem, or ever seemed, to have the face of that German, but certainly when he thinks of them he thinks of something in white marble, like the *Laocoön*—or of a black marble clock on which has been placed a white marble recumbent lion, supported by nymphs.

He makes the confession not so much out of exhibitionism as to call the attention of parents to that aspect of literary gesticulation. If he had a child to send to school he would give the strictest possible orders that he was to be taken through none of the great classics by any teacher. He might read in class any of the innumerable second-rate bores and poetasters with whom literary historians make weighty their pages. He might read Marini, but not Dante; Southey but not Wordsworth; Ponson du Terrail but not Stendhal; Herder but not Goethe. The martyrdom of a young boy taken through the *Messias*, or Kleist's *Penthesilea* may possibly harden his character but it must give him such a distaste for all literature, and for German literature in particular, that such an educational practice can be nothing but disastrous. That educationalists will ever be induced to change their practices seems unlikely, but individual parents might do something to protect their offspring.

We make no apologies, then—or, indeed, we do make apologies but we can't help it—for the fact that our appreciation for what are generally known as German masterpieces until modern times and excepting the lyric poets is lukewarm. If it were left strictly to ourselves, we might say that German literature was not a major literature at all—or it might be more exact to say that if left to ourselves we should not reread ever, any German writings except those of Walther von der Vogelweide and the *minnesingers*, and Heinrich Heine, with *Wilhelm Meister*, the first part of *Faust*, the *Parerga und Paralipomena* of Schopenhauer, and several of the novelists who have written between, say, 1890, and our own day . . . between, say, Sudermann, Gerhart Hauptmann and Mr. Thomas Mann.

It should be remembered that in so far as this writer and the reader are united in taste we do what the French call *faire école*. We stand for Homer and the Greek lyricists as against Virgil and the Augustan Romans; for the middle ages as against the renaissance; for the seventeenth as against the eighteenth century; for the realists as against the romantics; and, above all, for the conscious literary artist as against the inspired person who, having looked upon the wine when it was red sets vine leaves in his hair and, seizing a pen, upon paper royal inscribes such stuff as it pleases—or perhaps does not please—God to send him.

That is, perhaps, as much as to say that we stand for the Mediterranean as against the Nordic tradition. Nearly all Mediterranean writers and critics acknowledge that if you want to write you should have some—nay, as much as possible—knowledge of the technique of your art. Nearly all Nordic writers and critics contemn the idea. It was, indeed, Ibsen who most regularly championed the vine-leaves-in-the-hair tradition and it is today—or so yesterday the writer was informed by a German professor of distinction—the accepted German university dogma that all works of art written according to technical rules must of necessity be dull and tasteless.

We take, then—the sympathetic reader and this writer—very definitely sides. But that, as already stated, should not prevent us from investigating works of other schools, nor should it let us say that works which have been acknowledged as masterpieces by hundreds of thousands of men for many generations are worthless or contemptible. Nor should the fact that we find the second and third parts of Goethe's *Faust* not much to our tastes blind us to the fact that many of his lyrics are exquisite, and the first part of *Faust, Werther,* and *Wilhelm Meister* in every sense of the word masterpieces spirited in invention, and tremendously alive. Let us see what we can see in Kleist, Klopstock and Lessing.

In seventeenth century Germany, then, literature was as much steamrolled out by the Thirty Years' War and other political crimes, oppressions and horrors as was the case in eighteenth century Spain and Italy. But by the third decade or so of the eighteenth century, on account of the political tranquillity and on account perhaps still more of the fact that the human soul insists in the end on self-expression, writing began again to be one of the occupations of the German people. And these three writers, but more particularly the first two, had certain international aspects. Thus, *Laocoön* and other critical writings of Lessing certainly exerted considerable influence on England and, in a lesser degree, on France, and *Nathan der Weise* had an international vogue that could almost remind one of the success of *Guzman d'Alfarache* itself.

Klopstock was also enormously widely read and must have been one of the most famous literary figures of his day and fifty or sixty years after. What illumination or satisfaction the good Christian can have got out of a book 618 pages long and made up almost exclusively of such a sort of pastiche of the Christ legend as the following passage, it is difficult to say.

> Here Philo, with wrathful countenance, returned to his place. Nicodemus stood with downcast eyes, like one who, patient under oppression, experiences in his own breast all that dignity and elevation of sentiment which arises from conscious virtue and purity of heart. Gravity sat on his face, and in his soul was heaven. The godlike man was filled with awful thoughts, and revolved in his mind the solemn night when he discoursed with the Messiah on mysteries sublime. While the Saviour spake, enraptured, he beheld his heavenly smile, his look of grace, the more than human lustre of his eyes: he saw the display of paradisaical innocence, the lofty, the resplendent traces of the Son of God. This now filled him with silent ecstasy; he was too highly blessed to be afraid of man. Elevated by a flaming ardour, a heavenly awe, to himself he seemed as if standing in the presence of God, before the assembled race of man at the general judgment. On him were fixed the looks of the whole assembly. His eye serene, filled with the irresistible fire of awful virtue, terrified the sinner, who beheld him enraged. His air commanded attention, and he thus began:

But there it is. Klopstock was enormously popular in his day and is still, or was until the present régime, a great deal read in the country of his birth. His later short pieces were almost as popular as his longer work. It is interesting to notice from the international point of view that they were nearly all derived from the work of Ossian, and thus laid the foundation for that sort of pre-romantic romanticism and sentimentality that were the strongest notes in German literature for a century to come.

But the real revival from the seventeenth century darkness came with Lessing, who was born five years after Klopstock—in 1729. He, again, is a figure of a double international significance. The influence of his *Laocoön* on the critical world of his day was very great, and, indeed, taking into account the difference of its author's tastes and critical dicta, it may still be said to be regarded as a standard critical work. And, on the other hand, Lessing himself was strongly under English influence. Not only in the *Laocoön* does he speak in terms of relative contempt of Molière and Racine as opposed to Shakespeare, but his first play, *Miss Sara Samson,* a tragedy of common life, was an avowed imitation of the English plays of his date. As a specimen of his critical writing we may well take the following famous passage.

Observe her chin of softness, her neck of marble—let all the Graces hover round them, he (Anacreon) bids the artist. And how? In the exact and literal sense? That is not capable of any pictorial realization. The painter could give the chin the most exquisite curve, the prettiest dimple, *Amoris digitulo impressum* [for the *eso* appears to me to signify a dimple]; he could give the neck the most beautiful carnation; but he can do no more. The turning of this fair neck, the play of the muscles, by which that dimple is now more visible, now less, the peculiar charm, all are beyond his powers. The poet said the utmost by which his art could make beauty real to us, so that the painter also might strive for the utmost expression in his art. A fresh example of the principle already affirmed—that the poet even when he speaks of works of art is not bound in his descriptions to confine himself within the limits of art.

And here is the character of Nathan the Wise:

Al Hafi The folk call him the Wise, call him the Rich.
Sittah. Yea, more than ever now he's called the Rich.
And the whole city hums of rarities,
The stuffs and jewels in his caravan.
Al-Hafi. So then it is the Rich has come again;
And with him comes, who knows? the Wise as well.
Sittah. What think you, Hafi? Could not you approach him?
Al-Hafi. For what, suppose you? Not to borrow, surely?
Ah, there you touch him! Nathan lend? His wisdom
Lies just in this: that he will lend to no man.
Sittah. That's not the picture once you drew of him.
Al-Hafi. To men in utmost need he lendeth goods—
But money? money never! Tho' for the rest
He's such a Jew as there be seldom found.
Has brains, knows how to live, can play good chess;
But marks him out in bad points as in good
From other Jews. I warn you, reckon not
On him. 'Tis to the poor he gives; to them
Even with open hand like Saladin,
If not so largely, with as good a will;
Without respect of persons. Christian and Jew,
And Mussulman and Parsee, all is one
To him.

Lessing's literary output was enormous and of his nine plays, three can be said still to hold the German stage, *Minna von Barnhelm, Emilia Galeotti* and *Nathan der Weise*, though the last is almost more a dramatic poem for recitation than a stage play and *Emilia Galeotti* is almost too terribly harrowing to be supportable by a modern audience. It was, indeed, only twice translated into English as against the eight translations of *Nathan*, and the seven of *Minna von Barnhelm*, the last having been made by Mr. W. A. Steel for the Everyman's Library as late as 1930. It was last performed in England, as far as we have been able to discover, in 1899.

The great quality of his plays—even such early and little known ones as *Der Junge Gelehrter*—is their really wonderful stage technique, which he is said to have derived from his study of the English drama of common life, though I am inclined to believe that Shakespeare had on him a greater influence than, say, either Congreve who died five years after, or Wycherley who died nine years before, Lessing's birth.

He was, however, hardly in any sense a poet and his blank verse is excruciating. Indeed, the writer is inclined to believe that his disinclination from Lessing and from German writing in general must have come from the really physical pain inflicted on a boy of fourteen, at the time really mad for the blank verse of Shakespeare or Marlowe or Beaumont and Fletcher, by being forced to read aloud and over and over again passages from *Nathan*. There is a dreadful didactic story of a ring introduced into the body of that "poetic drama" that still comes back to me in half-waking nightmares. Imagine an ear attuned to and longing for "Was this the face that launched a thousand ships?" forced to listen to its own lips reading aloud:

> *Sal.*   *Die Ringe! Spiele nicht mit mir! Ich daechte*
>   *Dass die Religionen die ich dir*
>   *Genannt, doch wohl zu unterscheiden waeren*
>   *Bis auf die Kleidung, bis auf Speis und Trank.*
> *Nath.* *Und nur von Seiten ihre Gruende nicht—*
>   *Denn gruenden alle sich nicht auf Geschichte?*
>   *Geschrieben oder ueberliefert!—Und . . .*

which the writer translates as:

> *Sal.*   The ring! Do not trifle with me; I thought
>   That the religions I named to you could be
>   Differentiated by their dress, their victuals
>   And their drinks.
> *Nath.* Only not on the side of their foundations.
>   For are they not all founded on history,
>   Written or handed down?—And . . .

and so on, for the shuddering memory refuses to go any further. And that boy—this writer—had to reread that passage every time that he faltered in reproducing a highly Prussian accent—every time that he read *Schpiele* and *Schpeis* instead of *Sspiele* and *Sspeis*—and it was his first introduction to the literature of a language that also contained *Tandaradei* . . . or, indeed, for the matter of that, Wieland's beautiful *Oberon*.

Nevertheless, Lessing the man stands out as a splendid character—as iconoclastic thinker, literary revolutionist and as a proto-martyr tortured through his whole career by the yelps of pedants, bigots and mental dwarfs. He bore, nevertheless, that clamor on top of near-starvation, the tragic loss in fruitless childbirth of a wife whom he had long loved—after a year of marriage. He was accused of atheism because his conscience and inclination would not let him become a parson; of treachery to the fatherland, because the king Frederick the Great and his court were under French influence in all things philosophic and Lessing, considering the French lecherous, preached the discipleship of Shakespeare, Steele and Addison; he was accused of being a gambler, although on a microscopic income he supported his destitute family and collected a great library. Finally, on the appearance of *Nathan der Weise*, he was ostracized and howled down by crowds of minor writers as a Judaeophil. He was universally accused of having received a gift of a thousand ducats from the Jews of Amsterdam as the price of writing the play. The Nazi is not merely a growth of our own day. He supported all the attacks with calmness; he gave always better than he got in controversy, but the attacks that he received over *Nathan* and a final charge of atheism which he triumphantly rebutted by proving that all his religious beliefs were supported in the writings of the early Fathers of the Church overtired him in the last two years of his life and he died worn out. Two years later died Frederick the Great and with him disappeared the last traces of French influence and the teachings of Diderot and Rousseau from the German cultural heavens.

This struggle for ascendancy of the partisans of rival civilizations has a peculiar interest. Germany, as far as she was civilized by the middle of the eighteenth century—Prussia was not wholly converted to Christianity until after 1762—was civilized largely under the influence of French elegances acting through the German courts. It was the aspiration of every German monarch, however small his domains, to have his own Versailles, his own Parc aux Cerfs, his own French plays, his own French wardrobe and court etiquette. An air of Gallic elegance, possibly meretricious enough, thus spread through all German wealthier life. And by such leaders of cultural and abstract thought as had been left by the long wars—say, until 1724, the year of Lessing's birth—a sort of French dictatorship of taste was almost irresistibly riveted on the German literary neck. At the time of Lessing's first activities as a writer, the literary dictator of the empire was a critic called Gottsched. He was an overwhelming friend to young writers and since the young writer of those days had no chance of publication except on the recommendation of a royal or princely patron and since Gottsched had the ear of practically all the courts in Germany, he established rather a stranglehold on the literary taste and activities of his day. Him, almost as soon as he could lisp, Lessing went for baldheaded, as the saying is. And in spite of the fact that all the critical organs and media of the country were on the side of Gottsched and fulminated against Lessing as if he had been an anti-Christ, it was Lessing in the end who gloriously triumphed, introducing into the country as strong a note of Anglophilism as that of the Francophilism that had before distinguished it.

The process by which this state of things come about is thus metaphorically indicated by Bayard Taylor, a distinguished traveler between the twenties and eighties of the last century, who became one of the most enthusiastic admirers of all things Prussian after the Franco-Prussian War and was in 1878 appointed United States minister to the German Court. He has the distinction of having made by far the best translation of Goethe's *Faust* into English and his knowledge of German literature of the period of which we are here treating was at once deep, wide and adoring. Says he:*

Although the influence of Rousseau and Voltaire, felt in Germany only less powerfully than in France, helped to break up the

* *Studies in German Literature*, by Bayard Taylor, New York, 1901. P. 230.

old order of things, there was not the least connection between their action and that of Lessing. He made Voltaire's acquaintance only to become involved in a personal quarrel with him, and his works show no trace of Rousseau's ideas concerning education and society. . . . When he died, the period of struggle was really over, although the fact was not yet manifest. Goethe had published *Goetz von Berlichingen* and *Werther*, and Schiller had just written *Die Raeuber*. Herder had given to the world his *Poetry of the People*, and Richter, a student of nineteen, had just awakened to a knowledge of his own genius. One by one, the pedants and the mechanical organ-grinders of literature were passing off the stage. French taste died two years later, in the person of its last representative, Frederick the Great, and the close air of Germany was at last vitalized by the fresh oxygen of original thought. Lessing's career, indeed, might be compared to a pure keen blast of mountain wind, let loose upon a company of enervated persons, dozing in an atmosphere of exhausted ingredients and stale perfumes. It was a breath of life, but it made them shriek and shudder. When they tried to close the window upon him, he smashed the panes; and then, with the irreverence of all free, natural forces, he began to blow the powder from their wigs and the wigs from their heads.

And yet, oddly enough, Mr. Taylor, to clinch Lessing's fame as an Anglophil innovator, writes:

In one of his early letters to his father (Lessing) says: "If I could become the German Molière, I should gain an immortal name."

As to which sentence Mr. Bayard Taylor writes a comment almost singular, "He did more than this: he became the German Lessing. . . ." As much as to say that Lessing was greater than Molière. The force of partisanship could not go much farther.

The question cannot be so easily settled. It is a matter of taste whether you prefer, like Mr. Taylor, presumably, *Minna von Barnhelm* to *Le Malade Imaginaire*. Lessing had not Molière's ineffable sense of the comic, his knowledge of humanity nor yet his command of language; nevertheless, his stage-sense was almost incomparable and *Minna von Barnhelm* is one of the world's best constructed comedies. It is not for nothing that even today in Germany Lessing's comedies are more often played than any of the dramas of Goethe—and that obviously because of a legitimate public demand having nothing to do with patriotism.

And when we add that in his *Emilia Galeotti* he shows such traces of study of Shakespeare and the Elizabethans that in performance the play is more insupportably harrowing than either the *Duchess of Malfi* or *The Woman Killed with Kindness* we come at once on what must irresistibly be our main topic as students of comparative literature, that of the spread of the tide of Mediterranean humaner culture throughout the world.

And when we consider that Shakespeare was strongly under French influences, Spenser and the sonnetteers almost parasitically imitative of Petrarch, and that the rest of the Elizabethans and Defoe himself were immensely colored—even when only thematically—by the Italians and Spaniards and through the Spaniards of the North African Mediterraneans . . . and when we consider that for the greater part of his life Smollett was almost the sedulous ape of Lesage; and Sterne, Fielding and Richardson only less strongly under French influences . . . and if, pursuing the Mediterranean stream even farther back, we consider the immense influence exercised on Lessing himself by Graeco-Roman statuary and verse, probably through Winckelmann, for oddly enough when at last Lessing was able to make a tour in Italy his letters contain not a single word of mention of either Greek or Roman statuary or architecture . . . when we consider all these things—and they are not even a hundredth part of all the influences that we might cite—we cannot get away from the conviction with which we started these investigations: Literature, the humaner letters, has been an immense river that, starting from Cathay and Nile sources, spread through Palestine, Greece, Rome and then, broadening out as the West mentally broadened, went lapping away in an immense, slow, boundless tide, not merely towards Ultima Thule but into the inmost recesses of the Teutoburger Wald.

That particular tide in a vigorous freshet entered Germany by means of the courts of princelings only to be dyked out by the efforts of Lessing, Wieland, Herder, Goethe, Schiller and the rest. It had, therefore, to flow round by way of London, a little adulterated by what was already Teutonic in the characteristics of Anglo-Saxondom—sentimentalism, want of directness of attack and the rest. That dyking-out was no doubt economically necessary. The Frenchified princelings were ruining Germany as Louis XIV and his successors ruined France. But whether the exclusion of the influences not merely of Racine, Molière and Corneille, but of Diderot, Rousseau, Montesquieu, Voltaire or the Encyclopaedists was an unmixed blessing either to Germany or to the world in whose fate Germany shares must surely be open to question.

CHAPTER FIVE

To proceed further along the road of that speculation would bring us perilously near politics. At any rate, we have arrived at the beginnings of the romantic movement. This may be said to have begun with Jean Jacques Rousseau, who lived from 1712 to 1778 and wrote his *Nouvelle Héloïse, Contrat Social* and *Émile* in 1761 and 1762. In England the movement is usually stated to have begun with the publication in 1798 of the *Lyrical Ballads* of Coleridge and Wordsworth. In Germany it is officially usual to say that it began with Herder, Goethe, Wieland and Schiller. Mr. Bayard Taylor, whom we may for convenience regard as the Anglo-Saxon official mouthpiece of pre-Nazi German literature, states, as we have seen, quite succinctly that the German movement began on the death of Lessing, with those writers in full production, in 1781.

The writer, if he had to dogmatize about the matter, would refine away very considerably from those hard and fast dates. Romanticism was a tendency of very complicated origins. Its most obvious aspect is that of a general revolt against the stifling conventions of the classicism of the eighteenth century. As such, you may regard it as a Nordic revolt against Mediterranean civilization—though to do that you have to call Rousseau a Nordic . . . and perhaps, since he was Swiss and a Huguenot, we may, though he wrote in French, so regard him.

But very much more went to the make-up of this chameleon afflatus that, once started, ran across the world with a speed equal to that of Christianity itself in the early centuries of that faith. It was compounded then of sentimentality, of the townsman's passionate desire to return to country conditions, of the profligate's desire to idealize natural purity, of the idealist's necessity to see in all pasts sufficiently remote, a golden age. It was as if the Periclean Greek who prayed: "The dear Gods make me chaste—but not soon!" should, whilst waiting, bury himself in the traces and thoughts of Homeric days. So the German romanticist went back to the days of the *Wehmgericht* or the Teutonic knights, Dumas to the days of the cape and sword, Scott and the subsequent pre-Raphaelite poets to the middle ages. But the sentimental motive was born, in England at least, in the seventeenth century. It is impossible, for instance, to regard the great Richardson—who was born in 1689—as anything other than a sentimentalist. And Law, the great non-juring divine, who was born three years earlier and died in the same year (1761) as Richardson—Law then, the author of the *Serious Call to a Devout Life*, shows both in his devotional works and in his letters traces not merely of sentimentalism but very decidedly those of a desire for a return to the fields. Thus, you have the celebrated passage about the starling which, since it was written in the year 1721—which year also saw the birth of Smollett—may well be called, both in its sentimental and return-to-nature aspects, the real forerunner of romanticism. It is, however, convenient when making one's mental map of the movements of the late eighteenth and early nineteenth centuries to consider, along with more official writers, that German romanticism began in France with Rousseau about 1762, in Germany with Goethe, Herder, Schiller and Wieland about 1781, and in England with the publication of the *Lyrical Ballads* in 1798. The chronology becomes otherwise almost too complicated to keep in the head. Nevertheless, one should subconsciously, as it were, make one's mental reservations as to Law, Richardson and the rest. A special reservation should also be made for the *Princesse de Clèves* of Mme. de Lafayette.

It will, perhaps, make things easier if here we deal with the *Sturm und Drang* period of German literature as fully as we have space for that operation. That will mean our having to return to the English seventeenth century, to Defoe, so as to trace the course of the English novel through Smollett and Richardson to Diderot. But when, as here we must, we are dealing with movements rather than supreme and solitary figures, there is nothing for it but backing and filling since one movement will overlap another. To the *Sturm und Drang* period then. . . .

The writers of the *Sturm und Drang*—Storm and Stress—period are usually given as Herder, Goethe, Schiller and Wieland. Nowadays the tendency is rather to turn the cold shoulder to this last, though for this writer he is the German poet of this period who can be read with the greatest active pleasure, his *Oberon* seeming one of the greatest, most charming pieces of poetic tale-telling. Goethe, talking to Eckerman, says that this work belongs to the naïve order of literature, a product of the "free, graceful play of the imagination"—and as he applies the same term to the *Tempest*, the supreme specimen of poem of that order, we may well concur with the great Weimarian. Certainly, Wieland is of all the great German writers the least "intellectual" and the least self-introspective. That is, perhaps, why apparently for the German of today he is the least great and the least German of their eminent figures. Yet I do not know of any German poetry more charming than the opening lines of the *Oberon*, which seem to be the prelude to everything that is whispering and lovely in the works of his great lyric successors!

> *Noch einmal sattelt mir den Hippogryphen, ihr Musen,*
> *Zum Ritt ins alte romantische Land!*
> *Wie lieblich um meinen entfesselten Busen*
> *Der holde Wahnsinn spielt! Wer schlang das magische Band*
> *Um meine Stirne? Wer treibt von meinen Augen den Nebel,*
> *Der auf der Vorwelt Wundern liegt?*
> *Ich seh', in buntem Gewühl, bald siegend, bald besiegt,*
> *Des Ritters gutes Schwert, der Heiden blinkende Säbel.*

which the writer translates thus:

Saddle once more the Hippogriff, ye Muses, that I may ride into the old land of faërie. How lovely, about my fettered heart, plays the sacred madness! Who kindled about my brow the magic fillet? Who drives from my eyes the mist that envelops the wonders of the past? I see in a gay tumult, now winning, now again beaten, the good sword of the Knight, the shining scimitar of the Paynim.

The non-German appreciator of what makes poetry a thing of extreme delicacies and motions need not ask for anything better. And the whole poem is of that quality.

And what distinguishes most the literature of the great German figures—as apart from the lyricists and writers of Volkslieder—is precisely the preponderance of the quality of intellectuality and the practice of public self-introspection. From these particular qualities Wieland was almost quite free. He translated Shakespeare, and from necessary deep study of the English poet he imbibed the lesson that the first quality of the literary art is delight. Goethe, on the other hand, making a less, but sufficient, study of the English dramatists came to the queer conclusion that the function of the literary art was a return to nature and complete license in the matters of form and convention. He arrived at this conclusion in Strassbourg where he studied law and had, at the age of twenty-six, Herder for his companion. Herder, who was really almost negligible as a writer, was, as an influence, of gigantic stature. More than anyone he was responsible for the Germanizing and avoidance of form of his contemporaries, and Goethe—the young Goethe—was particularly open to influences.

As a writer I think he is to be most favorably judged in his lyrics. Such a poem as *"Schäfers Klagelied"* seems to me to be as exquisite— and, indeed, as German—as one could need. And if I quote here Mignon's song in spite of its being so immensely well known it is rather to keep in the reader's mind the fact that in spite of the Germanizing influence of Herder the mature Goethe was as appreciative of the call of the Mediterranean as any other writer anywhere.

Mignon
Kennst du das Land, wo die citronen blühn,
Im dunkeln Laub die Gold-Orangen glühn,
Ein sanfter Wind vom blauen Himmel weht,
Die Myrte still und hoch der Lorbeer steht,
Kennst du es wohl?
Dahin! Dahin
Möcht' ich mit dir, o mein Geliebter, ziehn!

Kennst du das Haus? auf Säulen ruht sein Dach
Es glänzt der Saal, es schimmert das Gemach,
Und Marmorbilder stehn und sehn mich an:

Was hat man dir, du armes Kind, getan?
Kennst du es wohl?
          Dahin! Dahin
*Möcht' ich mit dir, o mein Beschützer, ziehn.**

But Goethe of all the supreme writers of the world is the only one whose personality is so immense, fortunate in opportunities and impressive, that, apart from his lyrics, it is almost impossible to form a purely literary judgment of his works. You cannot out of reverence for his lustrous personality and his tremendous activities in other fields say anything against his writing. You can't, indeed, even think anything against them. If you find the second parts of *Wilhelm Meister* or of *Faust* tedious, some spirit whispers to you whilst you read: "But this is *Goethe!*" And you feel that if anything is wrong it is with yourself rather than the author. The extraordinary good fortune that was his during all his illustrious and tranquil career thus attends on him down the years. His fame instantly pervaded continents and drifts undiminished down the future towards eternity. With *Die Leiden des jungen Werthers* he limited his autobiographic self-introspection sufficiently to fall into the proper German model. Every really German writer must analyze not so much his characters as himself, before the public. The Russian writers are great analyzers, but of their characters, not of themselves; and a certain shame which is, perhaps, a false shame, keeps English writers of any national tradition at all from putting the inner side of their personalities before the public. In America the practice of public self-analysis, particularly in novels, has of late years become relatively common. But that mostly with the Middle Western school of novelists who are more strongly under Teutonic and Nordic influence than those of other regions of the United States.

But quite early in life Goethe decided that his business as a writer was to give to the world confessions. *Werther* is that, *Wilhelm Meister*

* No one has ever made an even passably good translation of this lyric, which, like all German lyrics, is untranslatable; and for our part we refuse to render it banal by a literal rendering. The moral is that the reader who wishes to consider himself an at all cultivated being should learn at least enough German to read Heine and the other German lyricists in the original. As they all write with extreme simplicity, this should not be a difficult task.

is that; and in the early stages of *Faust*—for it went through many stages between 1790, the year when he published *Faust, a Fragment* till the summer of 1831 when he wrote the last word of the second part—in the early stages, then, he certainly read himself into the figure of the doctor and thus came very early to the conclusion that Faust could not be a wicked man—or, at any rate, one of essentially bad character. Therefore, the devil cannot have his soul, and he must be saved. It is, perhaps, only in the completely charming *Hermann und Dorothea* that he is in no sense at all self-introspective.

The passion for glorifying the German past which was his and his countrymen's from his day through all time, foreshadowed itself in his first published work, *Goetz von Berlichingen*. This work he began in 1771 at Strassburg. There he fell in love with the Alsatian maiden Fredericke Brion, who was largely responsible for "Germanizing" him. In *Goetz*, Goethe takes the career of one of the worst robber barons of the fifteenth century—a man who made the slow awakenings of a sense of order that were beginning to show themselves in the rest of Germany utterly impossible in his own neighborhood and for many hundreds of miles round. Goethe makes of him a splendid disciple of liberty, dying with the halo of a martyr to the cause of the poor and humble—as it were, a sort of Cisalpine Rienzi.

It is usual, officially, to call *Wilhelm Meister* the first German novel. I do not know why this title should not be given to *Werther*, which is actually a piece of fiction showing a considerably greater sense of form and a progressing effect. And, indeed, I should like to make a reservation in favor of a work which, whilst *Werther*, *Wilhelm Meister* and *Faust* were adding to the tortures of my youth, inspired me with a delight that I felt yesterday again on rereading it. This is Kleist's *Michael Koolhas*. This, of course, would fall rather under the category of a long short story, but it is told with a conviction, a sense of reality and progressional effect that makes it one of the most remarkable pieces of historic fiction that I know. Nothing, indeed, could be more modern than this almost passionless rendering of the career of another outlaw who really fought for a queer sort of freedom with the passion and determination of any Puritan martyr. The story is set in the days of Luther, and Luther himself figures in it, but Kleist in no way idealizes his singular hero who raised almost as if by magic a band of rebels. They set all Saxony on fire, yet he died by imperial prescript at the hands of an Elector, who executed him very unwillingly, almost handing him on the scaffold a martyr's crown and ennobling and enriching his two surviving sons. Kleist, in fact, had no exterior aim in writing this story—you might almost say that far from desiring to idealize old German times and figures he was as bewildered at the actions of his characters as is the modern reader.

Almost alone among the works of the supremely great writers of the world, nearly all Goethe's works are written not so much out of passion for his subjects as with one or other public purpose, or out of the passion to produce works of the intellect. Our friend Mr. Bayard Taylor succinctly states that Goethe was greater than Shakespeare because he could not only catch in his verse the beauty and fragrance of the rose, but he "could analyze the earth in which the rose was planted, prepare the mathematical table of its ingredients, . . . dissect the rose as a botanist, and show you a metamorphosis by which the stem becomes the leaf and the leaf the blossom." I doubt, however, whether Goethe would have made the claim for himself because over and over again, dissatisfied with his portrayal of the human heart, he made efforts, as in the case of *Egmont,* to introduce more drama, more passion, and more human feeling than in the *Iphigenie auf Tauris* which preceded it.

Humanity divides itself into two classes when it comes to viewing the arts. You have, precisely, those who consider that the essential qualities of a work of art are the imagination that gives it life and the skill in finding living words in which to embody that imagination. The other school insists that, the purpose of a work of art being to ennoble humanity, the essential ingredients of a work of art are intellect, solution of moral problems and the statement of truths such as are only to be discovered by the methods of the scientists. The two schools will never be reconciled. Roughly speaking, the Mediterranean

civilization has always insisted and insists that the province of art is
to delight and thus to ennoble humanity by permitting it to perceive truths for itself in the enlightenment given to it by that delight,
And, roughly speaking again, the Nordic races insist that the writer
—if he is to be called great or sublime—must be a director of the
public conscience, telling humanity what it must think and leaving
the quality of joy to take care of itself. That Goethe himself took this
latter view it is difficult to believe. He had a lawyer's degree; as a
young man he practiced white magic and the research of the philosopher's stone; later he progressed so far in the realm of science as
even today to be rated one of the first protagonists of the theory of
evolution. He was a German statesman who could yet reconcile himself with Napoleon and distrusted the Prussians as much as the
Russians, in his later years paying tribute to the clarity of French
thought and expression, which as a youth he distrusted. Nevertheless,
so great has been his influence on his compatriots that German
imaginative literature until quite lately—and always excepting its lyric
poets—is distinguished rather by the quality of intellect than by that
of joy or imagination. Goethe himself in his youth saw Shakespeare
as above all the iconoclast giving liberty to the drama that was bound
and chained by Racine, Molière and Corneille, and in his earlier efforts
sought once more to restore formlessness to literature. But later, more
particularly after his stay in Italy in 1786, he became as awake as
anybody else to the desirability of form. Thus, the *Iphigenie auf Tauris*,
which he wrote in Italy, itself is relatively formless, though of great
majesty of thought, whereas the *Egmont*, which he wrote when the
Mediterranean influence had had time to soak in, is much more down
to the ground, but much more technically accomplished. This fact is,
however, generally disregarded by those who adore in him the statesman, philosopher and scientist. Thus, the chief glories of Germany
are her philosophers who deal solely with the intellect, and the
musicians who cannot by any means get the expression of intellectual
truths into their works. In the latest official list, the most prominent
partakers in the romantic movement in Germany are given as Goethe,
Herder, Schiller, Tieck, Schilling, Kleist, Klopstock, the brothers
Grimm, Schopenhauer, Heine and Wagner. It is difficult to see how

the last three names can be ascribed to the same category that contains Klopstock, Herder and even Schiller, and still more difficult to account for the omission of Schlegel and, above all, Novalis. And why, if you include the last three, should you leave out Sudermann and Haupt-man, thus bringing the romantic movement right up to our own day? But such as it is, the list is a good one for the information of those who wish to make a sufficient study of German literature of the imagination. The only other supreme figure as a poet that it contains is that of Heinrich Heine. But since Germany—or, perhaps, one should say Prussia—never sufficiently honored, and has now expelled even the memory of the author of the *Lorelei* from its soil, we might as well leave our consideration of his work until we arrive at the French romantic poets, to whom, except for the language in which he wrote, he was really spiritually more akin.

To bring our France up to date we must go back to Corneille, Molière and Racine, Corneille being born in 1606 and dying in 1684, Molière in 1622-1673, and Racine in 1639-1699. They are the great glories of the French stage, or, if you need a more succinct estimate, Voltaire called the *Athalie* of Racine *Le chef d'oeuvre de l'esprit humain* and rated all the other plays of Racine and his two rivals only a shade lower than *Athalie*.

Few foreigners would rate them so high—certainly none who were not intimately acquainted with the sound of French. We have noticed how in the case of the Elizabethan dramatists the effect of the actual sound of blank verse was to exercise on their audiences a sort of hypnosis below which the actions and the very localities of the drama achieved an extraordinary air of reality. The hypnotic power of the verse of the three great French dramatists when recited—the tre-mendous long roll of the dodecasyllabic lines—is such as to render real not only the dramatic situations of character but to make the hearer's mind accept conventions, not only of the unfamiliar manners, but of all the classical formulae. I have, indeed, seen English and American young ladies at the Odéon shaking their sides with laughter over the predicament of the heroine of the *Cid* who was forced by fate and mankind to marry the murderer of her father—so far has Anglo-Saxondom gone on the road away from an older sense of the fitness of things. And, indeed, it is possible to view with fairly cold sympathy the somewhat similar predicament of the Sabine of Corneille's *Horace*:

> *Sire, voyez l'excès de mes tristes ennuis,*
> *Et l'effroyable état où mes jours sont réduits.*
> *Quelle horreur d'embrasser un homme dont l'épée*
> *De toute ma famille a la trame coupée!*
> *Et quelle impiété de haïr un époux*
> *Pour avoir bien servi les siens, l'État, et vous!*
> *Aimer un bras souillé du sang de tous mes frères!* *
> *N'aimer pas un mari qui finit nos misères!*
> *Sire, délivrez-moi, par un heureux trépas,*
> *Des crimes de l'aimer et de ne l'aimer pas;*
> *J'en nommerai l'arrêt une faveur bien grande.*
> *Ma main peut me donner ce que je vous demande;*
> *Mais ce trépas enfin me sera bien plus doux,*
> *Si je puis de sa honte affranchir mon époux;*
> *Si je puis par mon sang apaiser la colère*
> *Des dieux qu'a pu fâcher sa vertu trop sévère,*
> *Satisfaire, en mourant, aux mânes de sa soeur,*
> *Et conserver à Rome un si bon défenseur.*

But once the French language has come alive in your ears the lines become the most despairing ever written. Poetry divides itself into that which is meant to be sung, that which is meant to be recited without action; that which is meant to be acted and that which is meant to be read. And we may say that as the poet took to himself the external aid of action and the printed page, so the hold of poetry upon humanity decreased. It was not for nothing that the first novelist in England

* This passage is not easily translatable so as to show anything but rhetoric. It voices the woes of a Sabine lady married to a Roman hero. The line indicated and the one that follows it:

> To love an arm soiled with the blood of all my brothers;
> Not to love a husband who has put an end to all our wretchedness!

are the main note of the speech. The lady is torn between the two horns of the dilemma. In the French this is pathetic; in English it becomes rather ridiculous.—F. M. F.

appeared after the decline of the Elizabethan drama, or that the first Frenchman to make a living by the pen was a prose writer and came at the time of the decline of the great school of French tragic poets.

Le Sage, that is to say, was born twenty-nine years after Racine and published the first installment of *Gil Blas* in 1715—sixteen years after Racine's death. It is true that Voltaire came a quarter of a century after Le Sage and survived him by some thirty-odd years, and his tragedies, *Zaire, Alzire, Mahomet, Mérope* rank him as the third of the great classic tragedians. But already the decay of the classical tragedy was on the way and Lamotte Houdart had proclaimed that prose was the proper medium for the drama and that all the classical conventions should be swept away.

The classical conventions themselves must be regarded as part of the properties that recited verse had called to its aid in establishing in the audience that hypnotic condition that took the place of the realities of life. The classical tragedians made no call whatever on natural objects or scenery to give factitious illusion to the scene. All the scenic directions and properties of a play of Corneille's would be: "A palace as grandiose as you wish; in the third act, an armchair." So the verse, having to bear all the burden of the play, called to its aid the actor to give what touches of realism seem desirable.

It may well be said that the Elizabethans across the Channel called also on the actor, yet their verse is infinitely more free—and, in spite of its decasyllabic character, it managed to convey an impression of an infinite variety. Blank verse was, that is to say, another hypnotic, but its roll was tempered by broken and interspersing lines, and it called to its aid an infinity of invention and action.

These were almost completely wanting in the great French tragedy. If not so cabined by the unity of time as the Chinese, and occasionally rebelling as it did against the bonds of the other two Greek unities, those of space and action, the French taste of the day visited severely any marked breach of any one of them.

The unity of time meant that all the play must be represented as taking place on the same day; that of space insisted that the locality must be unchanging; that of action enjoined not only that there must be no sub-plot but that visible action itself must be banished from the scene, action being reported solely by minor messengers or by the major characters themselves. In particular, blood must never flow. Thus, in the edition of *Horace* that we have quoted, the murder of Camille takes place just off the stage; but on its first performance she was killed in front of the audience. And that crime against the unities was so reprobated by audiences, critics, Corneille's brother authors and the nobility and gentry in general that rugged and obstinate as Corneille was, he had to change that stage direction in his subsequent performances and edition.

In addition, the dramatic muse fettered the very feet of its verses. They must be rhymed and each quatrain must consist of two male endings followed by two dissyllabic ones, the double rhyme being formed usually by the sounded but muted "e," though occasionally that was replaced by the "strong" or "difficult" rhyme in which as many letters as possible must be identical in both rhymes. Thus:

> *Ce. discours me surprend, vu que, depuis le temps,*
> *Qu'on a contre son peuple armé nos combattants,*
> *Je vous ai vu pour elle autant d'indifférencë*
> *Que si d'un sang romain vous aviez pris naissancë.*

Or in the alternative:

> *Quoique le mien s'étonne à ces rudes* alarmës
> *Le trouble de mon coeur ne peut rien sur mes* larmës

These are pretty severe shackles and it is not to be wondered that most foreigners, including Herder, Lessing, Klopstock and Goethe can see very little of beauty or of poetry itself. The great writer of rhymed Alexandrines can now and then make his lines attain to a high pitch of rhetoric or even of passionate beauty, as witness the famous denunciation of Rome by Camille before her murder by her brother in the scene we have just mentioned.

And this passage from the *Horace* of Corneille marks more even than anything to be found in the *Cid* the differences between the drama that does not observe the unities and that which does—as it were the difference between the rhymed Alexandrine and blank verse. Camille addresses her brother Horace:

Camille
> *Rome, l'unique objet de mon ressentiment!*
> *Rome, à qui vient ton bras d'immoler mon amant!*
> *Rome, qui t'a vu naître, et que ton coeur adore!*
> *Rome, enfin que je haïs parcequ' elle t'honore!*
> *Puissent tous ses voisins ensemble conjurés*
> *Saper ses fondements encore mal assurés!*
> *Et, si ce n'est assez de toute l'Italie,*
> *Que l'orient contr'elle à l'occident s'allie:*
> *Que cent peuples unis des bouts de l'Univers*
> *Passent pour la détruire et les monts et les mers!*
> *Qu'elle même sur soi renverse ses murailles,*
> *Et de ses propres mains déhirent ses entrailles;*
> *Que le courroux du ciel allumé par mes voeux*
> *Fasse pleuvoir sur elle un déluge de feu!*
> *Puisse-je de mes yeux y voir tomber ce foudre,*
> *Voir ses maisons en cendre, et tes lauriers en poudre,*
> *Voir le dernier Romain à son dernier soupir,*
> *Moi seule en être cause et mourir de plaisir!*

Horace *(Mettant la main à l'épée et poursuivant sa soeur, qui s'enfuit)*
> *C'est trop, ma patience à la raison fait place;*
> *Va dedans les enfers plaindre ton Curiace!*

Cam. *(Blessée derrière le théâtre)*
> *Ah, traître!*

Hor. *(Revenant sur le théâtre)*
> *Ainsi reçoive un châtiment soudain*
> *Quiconque ose pleurer un ennemi Romaine.*

It would be absurd not to attempt to give the non-French-reading reader some attempt to render the sense of this crucial passage. It is, nevertheless with extreme diffidence that we offer our transference of the rhymed Alexandrines of the original into English rhymed heroics which, do what one may, must almost inevitably have the note of the somewhat ridiculously stilted diction of our eighteenth century bards. However, here is our translation:

Cam. (to Horatius)
> Rome, the sole object of my burning hate!
> Rome to whom thou didst immolate my mate!
> Thy birthplace, Rome, she whom thou dost adore!
> Rome that doth pay thee honors more and more!
> May all her foes, combining in one hate,
> Tear down her stones, from citadel to gate.
> And, if sufficeth not all Italy,
> May all the East with all the West ally . . .
> A hundred nations from Earth's utmost bounds
> Join in the chase and tear her flanks like hounds.
> Mountains and seas shake down her trembling walls
> And blood and entrails glut her shuddering halls.
> May Heaven's wrath enkindled by my cries
> Consume her towers beneath the flaming skies;
> May these two eyes but see that lightning fall,
> Her homes aflame, her vaunted laurels, all . . .
> And the last Roman send up his last sigh,
> So I, the cause, may in my triumph die.

Hor. (Setting his hand to his sword and pursuing his sister who flees)
> This is too much, my calm to sense give place!
> Down, down to Hell, to plain thy Curiace!

Cam. (Wounded, off)
> Traitor!

Hor. (Re-enters)
> May all receive such chastisement,
> That, daring thus, shall Rome's fell foes lament.

This is, of course, the passage whose stage directions in the first edition made Camille die on the stage, Corneille subsequently changing it, in deference to universal clamors until it stands as above.

Merely read to oneself those lines have a throbbing movement— almost a lilt—extraordinarily expressive of a passion that is still more enhanced by the relatively calm mechanics of the verse. So, when you have them recited by an even only mediocre representative of the House of Molière, the gradual mounting up of denunciation has an effect so almost terrible that, when you come to *"Moi seule en être cause et mourir de plaisir!"* you can understand why the nobility and critics of Louis Quatorze did not contemplate with equanimity seeing the blood of Camille flowing on the stage. They did not, like Homais, desire *les émotions fortes* either for themselves or their children yet to come and they, almost more than the Greeks, insisted on the observance of the canon that great art is never harrowing. That, indeed, with its implications, is the chief aesthetic message of this book.

A great many writers have said that Corneille played Schiller to the Goethe of Racine. Nothing could be more misleading. Racine appears the larger figure because of a sort of greater equanimity of aspect and he was perhaps more essentially poetic in his attitude. Someone—I think it was Sainte-Beuve, but I have not been able to verify the quotation—has said that whereas the characters of Corneille died for ideas, those of Racine died for passions and the dictum is more true than most. But that does not mean that Corneille was not by far the more passionate, active and busy figure of the two. Racine was at first destined for the priesthood and the fact colored his whole life, so that, his later dramas meeting with disfavor, he took to writing religious plays in retirement and died of a broken heart at a slight from Louis XIV directed not at *Athalie* but at a pamphlet that Racine had written for his benefit. It contained a scheme for reforming the finances of France in the direction of benefiting the poorer classes of the country.* *Athalie,* on the other hand, had been

---

* Louis XIV said: *"Parce qu'il sait faire parfaitement des vers, croit il tout savoir: et parce qu'il est grand poète veut il être ministre?"* ("Does he believe he knows everything because he can write perfect verse? And because he is a great poet does he wish to be a minister?")

withdrawn from performance by Madame de Maintenon for whose Demoiselles de Saint Cyr Racine had written the sacred drama. His enemies, however, had persuaded that almost too virtuous lady that Racine was unorthodox, a view that, not to go too closely into seventeenth century French Catholicism, has been refuted by the judgment of pious posterity as well as that of Madame de Sévigné, who says of *Esther*, its sacred predecessor: *"Ce poète s'est surpassé: il aime Dieu comme il aimait ses maîtresses."* ("This poet has surpassed himself: he loves God as he used to love his mistresses.")

But I do not propose to institute a parallel between him and the author of the *Cid*, nor do I propose to make any quotations at length from his poems. Those who have sufficient French to appreciate him must have read him or seen his plays in his own language; it is impossible for an English translation of him or, indeed, of any French verse of the period, to have any significance at all, since his significance lies not in any action, incident or theatrical device but simply in the harmony and correctitude of his verse. It seems curious to find oneself writing "correctitude" as a term of commendation; but the French stage convention of that day was so absolutely suited to the effect that it desired to give that the more correct the poet is, the more he approaches beauty. So let us content ourselves with what Voltaire said. . . . Voltaire had been asked why he had never written a profound study of Racine as he had done for Corneille. He answered that there was nothing to do about Racine: "He said himself all that could be said. All that was left for the critic was to write at the foot of his every page: *'Beau, pathétique, harmonieux, sublime.'* "

On the other hand, the redoubtable Professor Saintsbury said of *Le Cid* that it was the most epoch-making play that was ever written. And, if we mention as in the same category the *Cromwell* of Victor Hugo that really set romanticism flaming across France, we may accept the dictum. And with Voltaire's on Racine, the two pronouncements sufficiently confront the differing achievements of the two great men. Corneille was more rugged as a man, harsher, more impatient of criticisms or persuasions. If anyone criticized him to his face he would say: "But, it's Corneille you are talking of." He was a revolutionary in two spheres. He set both the new form of the tragedy with his *Cid*—which appeared outrageous in its day—and the new form of the French language such as we know it now . . . he and Descartes between them. Under his pen both the over-Latinization of the classicists and the didactic harshnesses of the Calvinists disappeared. French as we know it was there.

The innumerable enemies who broke the back of Racine were creatures merely of intrigues and jealousies; those who could never bend the tough head of Corneille—though to be sure for a time after the production of the *Cid* he had to disappear to Rouen, his birthplace—were those really shocked by his innovations or really injured by his scorn. . . . You might, indeed, say that he was, as a writer, Marlowe to Racine's Shakespeare, as long as you do not push the parallel too far. Like Marlowe, now and then, and, when the mood was on him, very often, he wrote couplets that are like streaks of electricity for their vividness and fire—and then whole passages would flag: Racine was much more level. Innumerable couplets of his have passed into the French mind permanently, like the quotations from Shakespeare that make up so much of the Anglo-Saxon mentality. But there is no falling away from these quotations; the next lines or the fifth and sixth after them would do just as well.

No, the real yokefellow of Corneille was Molière. There was a man! If a romantic of genius could write his life, what a book that could be! As far as I am concerned no other genius save Jefferson ever lived so completely. It is not our function to play the biographer. Like Shakespeare, he was an actor-manager, though I do not think that he ever engaged in the wool or any other trade. . . . Well, biography will come creeping in. Consider merely the circumstances of his death. His whole body racked with the pain of mortal disease, he wrote defiantly the play about a man who imagined himself racked with mortal diseases, partly, no doubt, to indulge himself in a dream of health. On the day of its fourth performance he found himself more tortured than usual. His friends begged him not to appear in the piece. It was *Le Malade Imaginaire* and he had the rôle of Argan. "No," said he, "how could I do that? There are fifty poor stage-hands who have only their day's pay to live on. I should reproach myself forever if I neglected to provide them with their daily bread whilst being able to do so."

He played his part. They carried him home. He broke a blood vessel, and, as he was unable to confess himself because of the blood in his throat, the Archbishop of Paris, Harlay de Chanvon, a man of notoriously evil life, refused him burial in sacred ground. But, yielding to public clamor and the request of Louis XIV, Chanvon permitted him to be buried with maimed rites in the portion of the cemetery reserved for suicides.

But what glories had gone before that—and what sorrows! Like Shakespeare, he was the son of a rich merchant—an upholsterer. But from an early age he was determined to manage a theatre. The time came when Louis XIV released the ban on acting as a profession and Molière enlisted a band of young men of quality to play comedies— at his expense in a theatre called *L'Illustre*. The venture was protracted but very unsuccessful, and Molière was several times imprisoned for debt.

He joined forces with a band of real actors and traveled the country. At Lyons his first great success, *L'Étourdi* was produced; at Montpellier, before the Prince de Conti and the States General of Provence, *Le Dépit Amoureux*. After ten years on the road he played at Rouen before the Duke of Orleans, brother of the king. The duke authorized him to take his troupe to Paris. Then he played before the king.

He was at that date thirty-six and, as they say, his life had been shared in equal parts between his art and love. He was the greatest of all instances of the picaresque-romantic hero and if we have to think of him as, in Provence, very scantily clad, leaping from a window to escape from an enraged husband, and if his loves between Madeleine Bejart, his partner in his strolling company, and Catherine Leclerc, whose beauty was so great and so well preserved that at sixty-five she could still play the rôle of *Agnes*, were notorious, do not be afraid. As was the case with all picaresque-romantic heroes, Nemesis awaited him.

His success with the king was instant and amazing. For the rest of his life he had the resources of the kingdom at his disposition and only the bigot Louis XIV stood between him and his chief enemy, the Church, with the Pope at its head. Imagine for yourself that bitter, frozenly proud monarch lunching alone day after day during years with his *valet de chambre*—for Molière by right of his father was "hereditary valet-upholsterer *du roi*" and yet sat down daily to table with the king. The sympathy between the two men was something, given the age, fabulous and unprecedented. . . . But imagine being privileged to sit every day at table with a wit like the author of *Tartuffe!*

And if that was fabulous, was it not a fabulous destiny too that united him, with an undying passion and fidelity, to a woman none too beautiful who betrayed him, and that semi-publicly, with every prince of the blood and duke of the French peerage? Imagine him with that cancer at the heart, during innumerable takings back and re-betrayals, lunching daily with the king and all the morning and afternoon writing his comedies over which a nation rocked and has ever since rocked with laughter. And his comedies have about them a bitter philosophic significance and seriousness such as distinguish the comedy of no other writer save perhaps Gogol. The humor of other nations has about it a cruelty. . . . Think what a hideous affair *Don Quichote* really is. We make fun of the poor, the weak, the old, the half-witted. . . . I was once at the Empire in London with Joseph Conrad. Mr. George Robey was representing to the life the woes of a wretched charwoman who had been got with child and deserted by the lodger. The house rocked with laughter till you would have thought it would have fallen down, and Conrad said violently: "Doesn't one feel a stranger in this beastly country!" . . . Something like that.

But underlying the comedies of Molière is always the idea; the sub-ject calling forth laughter is always the folly of those who have had the chance to know better; the smile of the muse is the grimly ironic smile of destiny herself. From his writings you could disinter a whole sardonic philosophy. Well, his wife was always renewing her unfaith-fulness to him and she was never out of his mind. She was not even specially good-looking but her charm was to him a flail of scorpions. The idea of it never deserted him. Read the *Bourgeois Gentilhomme.*

Covielle. Her eyes are small.

Cléonte. That is true, she has small eyes, but they are full of fire. They are the most penetrating in the world, the most brilliant and the most touching that you will find.

Covielle. Her mouth is large.

Cléonte. Yes, but one sees in it charms that are around no other mouth. That mouth fills you with desire; it is the most amorous mouth in the world.

Covielle. As for her figure—she is too small.

Cléonte. But she carries herself well and is well-proportioned.

Covielle. As for her wit . . .

Cléonte. She has the finest, the most subtle . . .

Covielle. She is always serious.

Cléonte. Would you have her give way to artificial fits of laughter, to always obvious repartées? Do you know anything more insupportable than women who are forever laughing?

Covielle. To sum up: she is the most capricious being in the world.

Cléonte. Yes, she is capricious, I grant you. But what better consorts with beauty than caprice? One must suffer everything at the hands of beauty.

That was La Béjart, *femme Molière,* as Molière saw her! When Molière married her she was seventeen, he forty.

I have permitted myself, contrary to rule, to descant on this biography because the very story itself is a Molière comedy. He was known—just as in their day were Chaucer and Shakespeare—as *Le Contemplateur,* the Snooper, as who should say. When he was silent they would whisper: "Look at the Snooper, watching life and habits." And it was his own life into which more than anything he snooped.

He arrived betimes in the world of French comedy. We left that art at the time, in the fifteenth century, when with plays like the *Avocat Pathelin* which still holds the stage, the French theatre was beginning to escape from the trammels of the Church, and plays were being performed in private houses. The actual public theatre was to come at the end of the century. Comedy—the comedy of writers like Grévin, Amboise, Jean de la Taille, Lebreton, Perrin, which the reader may very well sample for himself if the subject of comedy engrosses him—such comedies aped the classic forms and conventions of Plautus and Terence. Their ingredients, according to Suard, were:

> Imbecile old men, young libertines, women of every kind save the virtuous, three or four surprises, and as many recognitions behind disguises. . . . There was so little of the comic in the comedies and of elevation in the tragedies that the writers might have devoted themselves to either *genre* indifferently; therefore, nearly all the writers of tragedy of that day wrote comedies.

There came finally the classical Pleïades, who constructed both comedy and tragedy on more strictly classical models—Ronsard, du Bellay, particularly Jodelle. They essayed to turn the first night of one of Ronsard's tragedies into a Dionysiac revel and, on the way to the suburban spot where the tragedy was to be played, captured a stray goat, the image of the God Pan, and, garlanding it, according to some, with flowers, sacrificed it on the boards of their extemporized stage. . . . This caused great scandal in a Paris much in the hands of the devotees, as being a heathen rite, and the pendulum fell on the side of comedy which assumed more and more the aspect of farce. Farce writers like Turlupin, Grosguillaume, Bruscambille, Garguille "*obtenaient à Paris devant la foule un succès de fou rire. . . .*" In 1650 Paris had five theatres. In 1680 Louis XIV reduced the number to three troupes of actors, and from then dates the creation of the Comédie Française—the House of Molière where still they play with properties that Molière used and according to the traditions that he evolved. Let us look at him for a moment as actor and stage manager—and it was not for nothing that the greatest of all English dramatists and the greatest French comic writer were both actors and stage managers:

"Molière," says Perrault in his *Éloges des Hommes Illustres,* "had in his one self all the requisites of the comedian. Although mediocre in tragedy he was so excellent a comic actor that he has been only faintly copied by those who succeeded to his rôles. He also understood to perfection the individualities of his troupe, distributing to each the rôle that exactly suited him; and he then directed them so admirably that they seemed less actors in a comedy than real persons leading their ordinary lives."

Gueret, another contemporary, adds to this:

Even if his actors had physical defects he could actually profit by that, turning into real originals those whom you would have thought would spoil his effects. . . . In addition he was a man who had the gift of knowing his century as well as he knew his actors.

Finally one of his actresses, Mademoiselle Poisson, writes thus of *Le Grand Contemplateur:*

"He was neither stout nor thin, rather large than small, had a very proud carriage, a neatly turned leg. He walked gravely with a very serious air, had a large nose and mouth, thick lips, a brown complexion, black, strong eyebrows, and the differing expressions that he could give his features rendered his face extraordinarily comic."

More than any great writer he exemplifies the motto that he who would write should first have lived. He was one of few great writers who never served in a war. Even Goethe went with the Army of the Princes that the French Republican troops threw back into Germany. But, perhaps, what he kept from Mars he gave to Venus.

The period in literature was one of the most brilliant the world has ever seen. You have to think of innumerable names of bitter jocular writers, innumerable coat-skirts whisking round corners whilst the wearers ran to carry the latest *on-dit* to the salons or from group to group in Versailles. Do not imagine that the whole court did not whisper bitterly whilst Le Grand Monarque lunched solitarily with the author of *Les Précieuses Ridicules*. It is obvious that we must hasten through those brilliancies: it is equally obvious that you must read the letters of Mme. de Sévigné, the *Maxims* of La Rochefoucauld, at least the *Princesse de Clèves* of Mme. Marie-Madeleine Pioche de la Vergne, Comtesse de Lafayette (because it was the first French novel—published in 1677), or the *Caractères* of La Bruyère, which went into nineteen editions in eight years, being published in 1688, and because a whole world-school of caricaturing literature was founded on it. The eighteenth century was in the beginning relatively quiet in literature, if disturbed by incessant and purposeless wars, and it is not until we come to the *Encyclopaedia* of the group headed by Diderot that we need imperatively pause and consider. As a purveyor of imaginative work, Diderot is notable as the author of two works of fiction of an extreme bourgeois realism which he considered to have been inspired by the *Clarissa* of the great Richardson. So one should read him, Voltaire, Montesquieu and Grimm to see classicism gradually disappear from the literary—but, certainly, not from the political—scene, and so one comes to Chateaubriand, Béranger, Lamartine and the beginnings of the romantic movement. The last figures we shall have to reconsider. It becomes incumbent that we should begin the homeward run with the story of the novel—in England and finally throughout the world. For that till then—and till so lately—despised form was more and more to assume the aspect of the sole galleon on a sea otherwise only sparsely peopled by poetic dinghies and the pinnaces of essayists.

CHAPTER SIX

W E HAVE attended somewhat carefully to the novel as practiced by the Spanish seventeenth. century writers. They were, I think it can hardly be doubted, the direct ancestors of the English novel of the school of Defoe, Fielding and Smollett, though many commentators and authorities, swayed perhaps by patriotism, make of that English commodity a purely native product, basing the claim on a genealogy that would carry the tradition down through the *Heptameron* of Margaret of Navarre, Sidney's *Arcadia*, Lyly's *Euphues* and the prose writings of Peele and Nash.

That seems to this writer to be rather far-fetched . . . or, indeed, very arbitrary. It is difficult to see how it could be doubted that the novel as a form apart in England began with the works of Defoe— and it is impossible to trace the remotest iota of the fanciful, romantic influences of Margaret of Navarre, Sidney or Lyly on an utterly humdrum writer like Defoe. That there has been down the ages a certain desire both to write and to consume works of the imagination longer than the lyric or the *conte* is not to be doubted. But the first of the peoples to make of the novel what we have just called it—a commodity, a part of daily consumption and life—were the Spaniards; these Spanish novels had, as we have seen, an enormous popularity in England and when, coming on their heels, we find a commercial-minded writer turning out great quantities of prose matter exactly identical in form, conduct of the story, length, and above all point of view—with those first examples of sustained fiction, it would be unreasonable not to consider that Defoe, looking for new avenues by which to make a living by his pen, saw that there would undoubtedly be a market for English picaresque fiction—and supplied it. He did not, that is to say, turn his attention to novel-writing until every other approach to fortune from tile-making to editing periodicals, composing political pamphlets and seeking the patronage of the great had been closed to him. Born probably in 1661 and dying in 1731, he did not begin writing novels until nine years before his death. Then, in 1722, he wrote *Moll Flanders*.

It is difficult to write at all dogmatically about Defoe, in part because his historical position and his untiring personal activities in public fields obscure a little the critical vision. As in the case of Goethe, one hesitates to write down that in ninety per cent of his writings outside *Moll Flanders* Defoe is an unsufferable bore. Nothing is more dreary than the continual repetition of his accounts of piratical adventures and sneak-thieving in the lives of dull villains like Captain Singleton, Captain Avery, "the King of the pirates," John Sheppard, Jonathan Gow or the Six Notorious Street Robbers—and Jonathan Wild, the thief-taker, whom Fielding, later, more fictitiously illuminated. For a rambling collection of adventures, the characters depicted must come alive. Even Sherlock Holmes had his morphia. But with the one exception of his Moll all Defoe's characters are completely invisible and utterly, not so much dead, as unalive in the sense that tailors' dummies are unalive. Even *Guzman d'Alfarache* was lively, vivid and amusing compared to *Colonel Jack*.

But *Moll Flanders* is a book as engaging and attractive as Moll Flanders was herself. There is a sort of greatness of good nature, of homespun philosophy, about that humane cutpurse; her few hypocrisies —and it is difficult to believe that they really were hypocrisies—were such as her nature needed, to keep her going at her arduous and persecuted trade. And what a vividness there was about her adventures. One is inclined to say that the episode when, disguised in widow's clothes, she is arrested for the misdeeds of another sham widow who has been robbing a tradesman—and is triumphantly and very profitably acquitted—is the crown of all picaresque writing—of all writing about rogues. One may, indeed, account for the difference in quality in *Moll* by saying that—as one knows if one knows anything about male novelists at all—Defoe was at his best when writing about women. Emma Bovary and Becky Sharp are the vivid creatures that they are because Flaubert and Thackeray were, respectively, in love with their creations. . . . But in the Madame Arnoux of *Education Senti-mentale* Flaubert gives us a woman very nearly as alive as his Emma, whereas the *Roxana* that Defoe wrote two years after *Moll Flanders* is as dull as it is obscene, and as obscene as it is dull.

It would seem, therefore, that Defoe, delighting at once in a new art and in a new way of earning a living, started in with the enthusiasm of a new worker and, long as the book is, found, with his prodigious ease in turning out words, no difficulty in finishing the work with spirit. It was, perhaps, made the easier because in beginning the book he saw also the end. He had invented—or fate had given him, for the story of Moll Flanders is in part founded on truth—a new device in literature: the happy ending which was to become the final, in-variable concomitant of English fiction. . . . Here is how *Moll Flan-ders* ends:

> Thus, all these difficulties were made easy and we lived together with the greatest kindness and comfort imaginable. We are now grown old; I am come back to England, being almost 70 years of age, my husband 68, having performed much more than the limited terms of my transportation; and now, notwithstanding all the fatigues and all the miseries we have both gone through, we are both of us in good heart and health.

This is not to say that this is the first of the heroine's marriages, for she made five in all, one with her own unknown brother, a fact which produced nothing like an Oedipus complex in her. Neverthe-less, the former unions produced no sense of permanence for her, Defoe not having reached the happy Victorian conviction of the permanence of wedding bells, settled estates and children and New-foundlands tumbling together on the lawn. No, indeed, the earlier ways of that transgressor were made hard enough. As thus:

> On the other hand, though I was not without secret reproaches of my own conscience for the life I led, and that even in the greatest height of the satisfaction I ever took, yet I had the ter-

rible prospect of poverty and starving, which lay on me as a frightful spectre, so that there was no looking behind me. But as poverty brought me into it, so fear of poverty kept me in it, and I frequently resolved to leave it quite off, if I could but come to lay up money enough to maintain me. But these were thoughts of no weight, and whenever he came to me they vanished; for his company was so delightful, that there was no being melancholy when he was there; the reflections were all the subject of those hours when I was alone.

It will be observed that the writing, if not very trig or distinguished, is yet worthy of respect for a certain quality of balance and rhythm calculated to show off very skilfully the sense of the content. It is as if Defoe in beginning a paragraph saw at once its end, its convolutions, and its whole shape. And that is very high praise which could be accorded to few enough of his later successors.

But as he went on his career of outpourings of words, the life, very naturally, faded from his prose—the last traces of the seventeenth century prose tradition died out of it and the form of the paragraph went. Consider this from *Captain John Gow:*

The Frenchman, not fearing them, came on large to the wind, being a ship of much greater force than Gow's ship, and carrying thirty-two guns and eighty men, besides a great many passengers. However, Gow at first made as if he would lie by for them; but seeing plainly what a ship it was, and that they should have their hands full of her, he began to consider, and calling his men all together upon the deck, told them his mind—viz., that the Frenchman was apparently superior in force every way, that they were but ill-manned, and had a great many prisoners on board, and that some of their own people were not very well to be trusted; that six of their best hands were on board the prize, and that all they had left were not sufficient to ply their guns and stand by the sails; and that therefore, as they were under no necessity to engage, so he thought it would be next to madness to think of it, the French ship being so very much superior to them in force.

Sheer backbonelessness could not go much further.

It has to be remembered that by then Defoe must have been well into his sixties and, though a man in those years may still write good prose, the odds are that he will not be able to do it incessantly, untiringly and to earn a scanty living. Or he may pray to be defended from such a fate.

If we agree that he was born in 1661, then he was fifty-eight when he wrote *Robinson Crusoe*, which may pass for a masterpiece almost marmoreal and universally esteemed, though since we have all of us read it in our first childhoods, hardly any of us could form any exact estimation of its technical, literary value. Yet it may pass for the work of a man very alive to what he was doing.

But in 1722, being aged sixty-one, he wrote not only *Moll Flanders* but the magnificently realizing—rather than realistic—*History of the Plague,* which surely no one who has ever read it can ever forget; and the tiresome *Colonel Jack.* The achievement is almost fabulous. For it should not be forgotten that if mere prose-writing is a fatiguing occupation, the occupation of inventing, not merely plausible, but blindingly convincing details for page after page is more arduous than almost any other. So gradually to the tired brain, losing sense of both value and proportion in selection or appropriate invention of incident, the books become, each, one long piling on of similar adventure to similar adventure, without one least attempt to give the characters verisimilitude and thus to hold the sympathy and attention of the reader.

It becomes the merest hack-writing. . . . Nevertheless, *Moll Flanders* and the *History of the Plague*—not to mention the story of the master of Man Friday—are such unforgettable pieces of verisimilitude and pass as pieces of vicarious experience so integrally into the spirit of the reader—and, indeed, of the race—and Defoe, whether in truth he did or didn't ever stand on high, fearless and unabashed—Defoe, then, occupies a position of such literary-historical distinction in our annals that we shall have to produce yet many masterpieces, indeed, before his figure shall pass from the consciousness of posterity. He may have died a mere Grub Street hack but he shall be a hard, angular pebble indeed for oblivion to swallow.

It will be necessary to travel a little out of strict historical sequence if we are to trace the end of the picaresque influence on our literature and that of our neighbors, the French—if that influence can be said ever to have died. We have, that is to say, to deal with Alain René Le Sage, who lived from 1668 to 1747 and published *Gil Blas* in its first state in 1715, taking another twenty years in which to polish and repolish it; with Fielding, b. 1707, d. 1754; and Smollett, b. 1721, d. 1771, thus temporarily passing over Richardson, Swift, Addison, Steele, in England; and, in France, a host of writers between, say, Honoré d'Urfé, born in 1568, and François-Marie Arouet (de Voltaire), who died in 1778, seven years after Smollett.

On the French side, only Le Sage represents the Spanish school, the picaresque novel and frame of mind finding relatively little popularity and meeting with only sufficient sales to keep meagrely alive Le Sage who spent the greater part of his life incessantly translating from the Spanish. To such an extent was this the case that his immortal *Gil Blas* was for long—and with all the noise of heated controversy—accused of having been a translation. In revenge even today his translation of *Guzman d'Alfarache* is by most commentators and encyclopaedias attributed to Le Sage as an original work. That *Gil Blas* undoubtedly is; yet so strong is the Spanish influence on that work that such a passage as the following, where Gil Blas becomes the Archbishop's favorite, will at once be recognized by the reader as a very exact echo from a passage from *Guzman* that we have already read in these pages

> I had been after dinner to get together my luggage and take my horse from the inn where I had put up; and afterwards returned to supper at the archbishop's palace, where a neatly furnished room was got ready for me, and such a bed as was more likely to pamper than to mortify the flesh. The day following,

his Grace sent for me quite as soon as I was ready to go to him. It was to give me a homily to transcribe. He made a point of having it copied with all possible accuracy. It was done to please him; for I omitted neither accent, nor comma, nor the minutest tittle of all he had marked down. His satisfaction at observing this was heightened by its being unexpected. "Eternal Father!" exclaimed he in a holy rapture, when he had glanced his eye over all the folios of my copy, "was ever anything so correct? You are too good a transcriber not to have some little smattering of the grammarian. Now tell me with the freedom of a friend: in writing it over, have you been struck with nothing that grated upon your feelings? Some little careless idiom, or some word used in an improper sense?" "Oh, may it please your Grace," answered I with a modest air, "it is not for me, with my confined education and coarse taste, to aim at making critical remarks. And though ever so well qualified, I am satisfied that your Grace's works would come out pure from the essay." The successor of the Apostles smiled at my answer. He made no observation on it; but it was easy to see through all his piety that he was an arrant author at the bottom; there is something in that dye that not heaven itself can wash out.

That is so obvious an imitation from *Guzman* that it is scarcely necessary to labor the fact. It is none the less characteristic of the difference between the lightsome Le Sage and the rather insupportable Matéo Aléman—as, indeed, of the difference between the France and Spain of the period—that whereas Guzman fell into disgrace from stealing food Gil Blas was the victim of an author's vanity.

It is customary to say that this period in French literature was a great one for the novel—from the middle of the sixteenth to the middle of the eighteenth century. But one must be Francophil, indeed, if one would assert that the French novel of that period was remarkable either on account of its profusion or its quality. The *Astrée* of Urfé (1568-1625) has a certain *Midsummer Night's Dream* quality which makes it excessively agreeable reading, but this writer imagines himself to be the only man alive who can make the claim to have—in his hotter youth—read right through the voluminous and insufferable *Artaxerxes* of Mme. de Scudéry (1607-1701) or the even heavier and longer *Grand Cyrus* which needed the additional labors of the lady's brother Georges for its completion. They were much savored by the blue-stockings and *précieuses* of the age, but they are the dreariest possible quasi-tapestries in which stage swords and javelins forever wave over imitation brass helmets, prodigiously embossed and decorated with imitation horse-hair plumes. Had they come a century later they might have been styled the precursors of the romantics; as it is they are completely negligible.

I wish I had more space to devote to Madame de Lafayette's *Princesse de Clèves*. The reader should read it for himself. But one may say that in all those two hundred years only that book, *Gil Blas* and the *Manon Lescaut* of the Abbé Prevost (1697-1763) are worthy of notice. The last two are particularly so from the international literary point of view. *Gil Blas* exercised a major influence over both Fielding and Smollett, the first of whom was the major influence in his turn over all his successors, at least until, say, the death of Thackeray. *Manon Lescaut*, on the other hand, published in 1750, was the first notable French piece of fiction to be written after the publication—and the translation by its author—of the works of the great, the illustrious, Samuel Richardson. That author who was the major influence on the great French novels of the succeeding century may well be termed illustrious.

We must first, however, dispose of Fielding and Smollett before dealing with the author of *Clarissa*. That this writer should immensely prefer the coarser *Roderick Random* to the perfumed, colored and heartless paragraphs of Fielding's *magnum opus*, the reader will probably by this time be in a position to anticipate. We are—this writer and the reader—presumably serious persons, or the one of us would not have undertaken to write and the other to read this work. We may—and, indeed, do—appreciate the products of the comic muse from Aristophanes to Rabelais and from the Beaumont and Fletcher of the *Knight of the Burning Pestle* to—not to outrun our present period—either Pope on the one hand or Swift on the other. But all these are works inspired by a deeper seriousness. From them, differ as may their techniques and personalities, you may learn as much of life and the values of life as from Dante, Villon or the author of *Madame Bovary* himself. But for readers so minded it is impossible that the gorge should not rise at the mere wrongness of the vital outlooks of a Fielding or a Sterne. Who, indeed, would not be concerned if he thought the views of the values of life of the young person of today and tomorrow or the morals of any spiritual pastor of a flock should anywhere or at any time be guided by that police magistrate or that dissolute, brandified and atheistic parson? It is obviously not our province here to be moralists. But the high mission of the novelist and the high function of the novel in the republic is so to draw life that from their pages the public may learn at least that life is first of all governed by cause and effect—that if you are lousy, and I use the word on purpose, you will live like a louse and, if there is a hell, go to hell. And what other word could describe Tom Jones—the miserable parasite who was forever wreathed, whining about his benefactor's knees, whose one idea of supporting himself was to borrow money simultaneously from his heart's adored and two mistresses, and who was such a miserable hero of romance that in a dueling age he could not even handle a rapier? Or what thinking reader could read the episode of the porcinely alcoholized opulent Anglican parson and the starving Dominican friar in the *Sentimental Journey* and not consider that the worst words against the Christian religion that were ever written are there written? . . . For—and this is what is so lamentably puzzling—if you will read the best and most benevolent of the orthodox critics on the subject of those lamentable productions, you will find them bursting into paeans of lachrymose praise. This is a queer instance of obscured moralizing that follows. Some years ago this writer wrote a little history of the English novel in which in the course of a much milder scarification of Fielding than what is above written he had occasion to quote a late librarian of the House of Lords and great official Anglo-Saxon accepted critic as saying that *Tom*

Jones came into the stuffy scene of ordinary life like the pure breath of a May morning! And for this, if you please, this writer was stigmatized as "vitriolic"—nothing less!—by (and that is what is extraordinary!) the chief Roman Catholic organ of the United States. . . . So hard will *l'homme moyen sensuel* fight for his right to his *menus plaisirs.* . . . And what a queer echo is that dictum of the Peers' librarian of that of the American Ambassador to Germany writing of Lessing!

But so that we may not exhaust all the notes of exclamation in the printer's fonts let us turn to the consideration of the aesthetic values of Fielding and Smollett . . . merely premising that if ever writer grimly and seriously corroborated the scientific constatation that the wages of sin is death, that writer was Tobias Smollett. Consider this from *Roderick Random:*

"I have often seen," said she, "while I strolled about the streets at midnight, a number of naked wretches reduced to rags and filth, huddled together like swine in a corner of a dark alley; some of whom, but eighteen months before, I had known the favourites of the town, rolling in affluence, and glittering in all the pomp of equipage and dress. And, indeed, the gradation is easily conceived. The most fashionable woman of the town is as liable to contagion as one in a much humbler sphere; she infects her admirers, her situation is public; she is avoided, neglected, unable to support her usual appearance, which, however, she strives to maintain as long as possible; her credit fails; she is obliged to retrench, and become a night-walker; her malady gains ground; she tampers with her constitution and ruins it; her complexion fades; she grows nauseous to everybody; finds herself reduced to a starving condition; is tempted to pick pockets; is detected; committed to Newgate . . ."

Let us refrain from pursuing the passage further. Tobias Smollett was amongst many other things a doctor of medicine, and the details of the progress of the disease and the decay of the sufferer given in the ensuing lines, though they might prevent the reader from putting himself in the position to incur those disasters, are probably too repulsive for the queasy stomachs of today.*

Nothing is more curious than the revolution of tastes in these matters. In 1750 deans of the Anglican church used to read *Roderick Random* aloud to their wives before retiring for the night—or, at any rate, Dean Delaney so read that book to Mrs. Delaney who was everywhere known as the "pure and spiritually minded Mary Granville." But by the early nineteenth century Smollett was considered to be too coarse reading for the most experienced men of the world. On the other hand, the clergyman who edits the 1873 Edinborough edition of the works of Smollett says succinctly: "Nobody coming within any reasonable reach of Smollett's public will ever suffer moral taint from *Roderick Random*. If anyone does or says he does he tells about more than the book. Winifred Jenkins would not go near a lion after she was told that it roared tremendously at maidens who might have been misbehaving themselves. . . ." Thus does Dr. Herbert ingeniously restate, in the middle years of Victoria, the truism that to the pure all things are pure. Now, I fancy, we have reverted to a deeper state of unease at the idea of contemplating things susceptible of causing *les émotions fortes*. So much the worse for us.

It is usual to say that, through Le Sage, the Spanish picaresque novel had a great effect on Smollett, Richardson and Fielding. How that may be about Richardson I do not know, but with regard to Smollett the statement is demonstrably true. Have we not the celebrated passage from the preface to *Roderick Random* to prove it?

The same method has been practised by other Spanish and French authors, and by none more successfully than by Monsieur Le Sage, who, in his Adventures of Gil Blas, has described the knavery and foibles of life with infinite humour and sagacity.

---

* Glancing aside at the moment of writing these words the writer's eye falls upon a caption in the New York *Times* for this day. It states that one form of venereal disease is so on the increase in New York state that neither the medical nor the financial resources of the state are any longer able to cope with it. Had the victims read the "coarsenesses" of Smollett, rather than *Tom Jones*, they might have avoided that fate.

The following sheets I have modelled on his plan, taking the liberty, however, to differ from him in the execution, where I thought his particular situations were uncommon, extravagant, or peculiar to the country in which the scene is laid. The disgraces of Gil Blas are, for the most part, such as rather excite mirth than compassion: he himself laughs at them; and his transitions from distress to happiness, or at least ease, are so sudden, that neither the reader has time to pity him, nor himself to be acquainted with affliction. This conduct, in my opinion, not only deviates from probability, but prevents that generous indignation which ought to animate the reader against the sordid and vicious disposition of the world.

But what is much more curious is that Smollett should have imitated Racine in writing in blank verse *The Regicide: A Tragedy.* This lamentable affair deals with the murder of James I, the poet-king of Scotland, and is cast in the most severe form of the French classic drama, the unities of time, space and action all being carefully observed. It is true that the hero and heroine of the sub-plot die on the stage as did the Camille of Corneille's *Horace,* but since the reader has no medium of knowing of what they die the unity of action, if infringed, is infringed very little. And the curious thing is that poor Smollett knowing that people in the throes of death cannot complete passages in sonorous blank verse makes the curious concession to realism of letting the last two lines of the dying tirades of the lovers end thus:

Eleonora: Alas! that dismal groan
Is eloquent distress!—Celestial powers
Protect my father, show'r upon his—Oh! (*Dies*)
Duncan: O Eleonora! as my flowing blood
Is mix'd with thine—so may our mingling souls
To bliss supernal wing our happy—Oh! (*Dies*)

The play is a curious instance of the Gallic muse's refusing to find lodgement across the Channel.

And, indeed, nothing is much more interesting than tracing the mutations that take place in national arts once they transplant themselves. Thus, the serenely sardonic note of the Spaniard contemplating the changing fortunes of the vicious and the criminal becomes in France the sprightly and agreeable adventures of *Gil Blas* and later, in England, a sort of unwinking stare with which Smollett contemplates the hideousnesses and aloofnesses of his fellow men. For, if the faces that seem to look up at you from the pages of a Turgenev or a Shakespeare seem to bear tolerant smiles, the face of Smollett emerging through the serried ranks of print on his pages seems to be of a complete immobility, of a complete unwinkingness. More vivid in his renderings than Quevedo, Smollett is completely lacking in either the sardonic or the lambent humor of Le Sage. His jocularities have all the cruelty that attends on the Anglo-Saxon sense of humor, and have almost no sense of the comic at all. Indeed, if we regard the comic passages of even a work so "humane" as *Humphry Clinker*—if we regard them as anything other than mere pictures and manners—we must consider Smollett as being almost the most insensitive of this world's greatest writers. The chapter in which, in *Humphry Clinker*, the bibulous and gouty squire, by raising a false alarm of fire, makes Lieutenant Lishmahago descend almost nude in a December night from his window, Lieutenant Lishmahago revenging himself by rushing through the room where the squire lies completely incapacitated by gout and screaming that he is pursued by a mad dog . . . such scenes, to anybody of any sensibility at all—supposing him to have been hypnotized by Smollett into believing that his characters are really human beings—must seem of a cruelty only less than that displayed by Sterne in his passages about the Dominican friar. We are not particularly out to dilate upon the moral senses of these early writers, but there is this to be said of Smollett, that in confronting us with these instances of brutal horseplay, he was really depicting manners and customs of his day, whilst Sterne, by rendering for us the mental callousness of the parson hero of the *Sentimental Journey*, was rendering a cruelty peculiar to himself.

The great service that Smollett probably did the commercial English novelist lay in his vivid and even gloating descriptions of the happy endings of his characters. The happy ending of *Moll Flanders* we have already quoted. It is as dry as a descriptive passage from a catalogue; the union of Tom Jones with his Sophia is scarcely more glowing. But when it comes to *Roderick Random* the marital raptures are such that one almost hesitates to transcribe them.

> I shall not pretend to describe my own feelings at this juncture; let it suffice to say that, after having supped and entertained ourselves till ten o'clock, I cautioned my Narcissa against exposing her health by sitting up too late, and she was prevailed upon to withdraw with her maid to an apartment destined for us. When she left the room, her face was overspread with a blush that set all my blood in a state of fermentation, and made every pulse beat with tenfold vigour! She was so cruel as to let me remain in this condition a full half-hour; when no longer able to restrain my impatience, I broke from the company, burst into her chamber, pushed out her confidante, locked the door, and found her—O heaven and earth!—a feast a thousand times more delicious than my most sanguine hope presaged!—But let me not profane the chaste mysteries of Hymen, I was the happiest of men!
>
> In the morning I was waked by three or four drums, which Banter had placed under the window; upon which I withdrew the curtain, and enjoyed the unspeakable satisfaction of contemplating those angelic charms which were now in my possession! . . .

You might say that that passage alone taught the English public to demand happy endings from its novelists. But even that would not have been quite sufficient. What really tells, what really made it indispensable, is the description of the "settlements." Married bliss was insufficient. Really to round life off you must have two other ingredients—Family and Fortune. In *Roderick Random* this side of the matter is disposed of in comparatively short space. The last words of the book, which still contains several pages after the account of the wedding night and morning, run:

> Fortune seems determined to make ample amends for her former cruelty; for my proctor writes that, notwithstanding the clause in my father-in-law's will, on which the squire founds his claim, I shall certainly recover my wife's fortune, in consequence of a codicil annexed, which explains that clause, and limits her restriction to the age of nineteen, after which she was at her own disposal. I would have set out for London immediately after receiving this piece of intelligence, but my dear angel has been qualmish of late, and begins to grow remarkably round in the waist; so that I cannot leave her in such an interesting situation, which I hope will produce something to crown my felicity.

And, as an inducement to making the public demand always more and happier endings—that is again as nothing to the tale of bequests, settlements, estates, loans to redeem mortgages, and the rest of propertied details which, the triple marriage night being almost dryly recorded, decorate the closing pages of Smollett's last novel *Humphry Clinker*.

Opinions differ widely as to the relative merits of Smollett's works. The three most distinguished are usually given as *Roderick Random*, *Peregrine Pickle,* and *Humphry Clinker*, with, as a rule, a general chorus of praise for the last of the three, the product of Smollett's declining years. That is only to be expected. Compared with any other work of Smollett's, *Humphry Clinker* reads like one perpetual peal of bells and happy endings. The characters are all already in extremely comfortable circumstances; they have everything that wealth in that day could have bought; poverty and vice are completely excluded from the scene as from a fire-lit room the last rays of a December twilight are shut out by heavy curtains. And, as we have just adumbrated, in the end, by the careful rearrangement of all the estates of all the characters, their fortunes are all enormously enhanced and the story closes with the note that they will go on being so enhanced and that their domestics will go on being more and more respectful until the closing down of time. The last words of the book, written by a former servant who has married the squire's bastard son, to one of her former fellow servants are: "But as I trust you'll behave respectful and keep a proper distance you may always depend upon the good will and purtection of yours, W. Lloyd."

And, indeed, in the great task of keeping the servants of the rich, whether new or old, in subjection and the poor in a state of curtseying and cap-touching reverence, the English novel throughout the first Georgian and the Victorian eras, did yeoman service.

But the greatest benefit of all that the happy ending bestowed on the English novel was that it coerced the writer into observing some faint sort of form. The best image of the form of the novel as practiced by the mid-nineteenth and twentieth French and the late-nineteenth and twentieth century English and American schools of artists in fiction would be a space confined by two parallel lines running in perspective to the horizon. At the broad base and for a while the novelist may be a little leisurely. But, as the lines converge, his technique must become always tighter and more breathless, every word— but every slightest word—carrying the affair that the novelist is rendering always further and more and more swiftly to the inevitable logic of the end. And, indeed, it may be reserved for the last two or three words, like a tiny coda in a musical form, to cast light back on the whole affair and, thus, to give it its final significance.

The best instance of that form of ending that immediately comes back to this writer is that of Maupassant's wonderful, very long, short story or short novel, *Le Champs d'Oliviers*. Here, toward the end, neighbors and the police finding in the house of the Abbé Muret a helplessly drunken tramp and the Abbé himself dead on the floor, those spectators are convinced that the hobo has murdered the priest. There seems no possible doubt of that. But when the narrator adds: *"Personne ne crut que l'Abbé s'était donné la mort"* ("No one imagined that the Abbé had taken his own life") then, as it were, a lightning flash is thrown back over the whole story and all its parts fall into place in the mind. It is marvelously skillful.

This *charpente*, this *progression d'effet* and certainly that kind of *coup de canon* are lamentably absent from the novels of Defoe, Fielding and Smollett. But Richardson, having always at the back of his mind the happy ending of *Pamela* and the tragedy of *Clarissa*—and having as novelist a genius and common sense all his own—certainly got into his work at least such a cumulation of effect that as—in serial form—Clarissa neared her end he set all Europe screaming with apprehension. But his genius was very special. He stands, as it were, apart with Jane Austen and Trollope; and the influence of the happy ending on the novel form showed itself only very gradually. Exactly how great was the influence of Smollett on Dickens it is difficult to estimate. It is usual to say that the *Pickwick Papers* is almost an imitation of *Humphry Clinker*. That may be the case; but it would be almost as reasonable to consider that the fact that both books record a great deal of travel and the other fact that the *Pickwick Papers* being published in parts was of necessity entirely episodic—that these two facts gave to Dickens' first book an aspect of resemblance to Smollett's last that was merely accidental. There is, obviously, a certain kinship between Smollett's benefactors like Matthew Bramble, and Dickens' Cheeryble Brothers or the Mr. Jarndyce of *Bleak House*. And there is a slight kinship too between the writer's mood in *Copperfield* and the general mood of Smollett—and a great deal more still in the case of *Great Expectations*, which is Dickens' last and by far most serious novel. Indeed, except that Dickens was by far the greater prose writer, whole passages of that book might very well have been written by Smollett at his most grim.

Mr. Austin Dobson in one of his unbuttoned moments commits himself to the dictum that *Tom Jones* has been the model of all *manly* British fiction since his day. But it is difficult to think of any writers later than Thackeray who can have been much under the influence of Fielding. And it is at once the glory and the bane of Thackeray that for a considerable portion of his career he played the sedulous ape to the author of *Amelia*. But it is pretty safe to advance that during the lives and after the deaths of those two writers—during, that is to say, the whole of the first half century of the reign of Victoria—the British novel took to itself a sort of stereotyped but loose form in which, on its way to the wedding bells, the novelist dropped his moralizing and his digressions occasionally, and gave some attention to shoving his story forward. To that we must return.

The actual prose-writing of Smollett's novels, retaining some of the air and cadence still of the seventeenth century prose, is sober and good enough. One imagines, indeed, that he would have grunted despitefully if you had suggested to him that he might have lightened his sentences or given some grace to his periods. He would probably have said—to translate him into *modernese*—that he was none of your damn artists. He was a moralist. And it is remarkable how one-voiced all these novelists are in taking that line about their productions. Defoe roundly states that he wrote his novels so that they might be read in gaols and thus conduce to a sort of prison reform from within. Smollett declares himself equally zealous at once to reform the morals of his day and to effect the reformation of the navy in which he served—at a date when it was said that the officers were gentlemen but no seamen, and the ratings, seamen but no gentlemen. And Fielding in perhaps the most sober paragraph that he ever wrote—the beginning of the Dedication of *Amelia*—states succinctly that:

> The following book is sincerely designed to promote the cause of virtue and to expose some of the most glaring evils, as well public as private, which at present infect the country . . .

Tom Jones, on the other hand, makes in its Preface no claim at all to moralizing aims. On the contrary, the author announces that all his skill has been devoted in this book to delighting the reader —as if he had been at a banquet. As thus, in a paragraph that gives much more the quality of Fielding's prose than the one quoted above:

The excellence of the entertainment consists less in the subject than in the author's skill in well dressing it up. How pleased, therefore, will the reader be to find that we have, in the following work, adhered closely to one of the highest principles of the best cook which the present age, or perhaps that of Heliogabalus, hath produced. This great man, as is well known to all polite lovers of eating, begins at first by setting plain things before his hungry guests, rising afterwards by degrees as their stomachs may be supposed to decrease, to the very quintessence of sauce and spices. In like manner, we shall represent human nature at first to the keen appetite of our reader, in that more plain and simple manner in which it is found in the country, and shall hereafter hash and ragout it with all the high French and Italian seasoning of affectation and vice which courts and cities afford. By these means, we doubt not but our reader may be rendered desirous to read on forever, as the great person just mentioned is supposed to have made some persons eat.

From that one might deduce that Fielding not only paid attention to his technique but actually had the ambition to produce in his work a cumulative effect. That is true enough, but the technique to which he paid attention was that of eighteenth century wit and the cumulative effect he sought after was that of introducing his shapely person, with whisking skirts and whirling, clouded cane, more and more prominently on to the stage of his novel. Until there should be no soul in the audience that should not cry: "A damned clever fellow, this author," with all the ladies inscribing as fast as they may his *bons mots* on their tablets.

From the earliest days, as we have remarked in one of our earlier chapters, two schools of writers in successive periods have flourished and given way, the one before the other. There are those who seek by every hypnotizing device known to them to snatch their readers from earth into the ambience of their rendering of stories or affairs . . . and then those who by every trick of verbal juggling and mental smart-Aleckery seek to delight their readers, not caring at all whether their tales or poems convince or carry away. At times they will interrupt their tale-telling for, as it were, weeks, and wander off into hundreds of miles of digression and into not so much sub-plot but a perfectly different story from the one on which they begin and end. Each school finds for a period its public, the public of the jugglers being, as a rule aristocratic, that of the engrossed tale tellers being more plebeian or more all-embracing. As witness the age of the troubadours when the knights and ladies took delight in metrical felicities, the groundlings finding hypnotic escape from their surroundings in the illusions of the primitive *conte-fable* of the market place. . . . Or the matter may be more comprehensibly put by a speech addressed to the present writer early in this century by a young lion then expecting to supersede him in the public favor. Said he:

"Old fogeys like you and Conrad and Henry James go to unending troubles to kid the public into the idea that you provide them with vicarious experience. You efface yourselves like ostriches, never let yourselves appear through a whole long, blessed story, go to enormous trouble to get in atmospheres, to invent plausible narrators—old colonels, ships' captains, priests, surgeons—what do I know all . . . oh, yes, 'above all to make you *see*.' . . . But that sort of stuff will never succeed. It isn't what the public wants. What the public wants is to see monstrous clever fellows"—and here he slapped himself on the cheek—"monstrous clever fellows like *me*. . . . Handsome, elegant figures, striding, posturing, pirouetting, moustache-twisting, cane-twirling, gold-ball juggling, tight-rope dancing trapezists. . . . You're all done with, I tell you. To me the far-flung future. . . ." Well, Fielding might have said as much to Defoe and Richardson . . . even to Smollett.

But, to certain minds, writing like that of *Tom Jones* is teasing and worrying in the extreme. Even in the relatively sober *Amelia*, over which Fielding must have taken much more pains, the note of fussing over the narrative as a hen fusses over her chicks is almost insupportable. It is a good story. Critics of the older fashion would have called it "spirited;" but we may seem to trace in it a certain anxiousness . . . perhaps a certain fatigue caused by his duties or a magistrate and the earlier stages of the long illness that three years after was to finish his career. Or we may well imagine that his duties as a police magistrate may have added to his views of the values of life a certain ballast of seriousness. It was not for nothing that *Tom Jones* was published and its author appointed a justice of the peace for Westminster in the same year—1748.

At any rate, *Amelia* contains a good story. One is anxious to know what will become of Captain Booth, who is a poor sort of a hero, and still more anxious about Amelia, who is almost the perfect wife for a hero who was rather a poor sort of man. In fact, compared with the rather tinny note of heartlessness of *Tom Jones*, the note of *Amelia* is one of compassion and concern for poor humanity . . . and we know that as a magistrate in a horrible epoch Fielding showed himself very conscientious, a quality that in a magistrate calls most of all for compassion and concern. But even at that, *Amelia* is—not so much ruined—as turned into a sort of unceasing obstacle race by the continual intrusions of Mr. Fielding. Reading it for the story, one is perpetually forced to run round or jump over interminable pages of digressions—digressions for the interminable biographies of newly introduced characters, for the display of Fielding's knowledge of the criminal heart, of law, of divinity, of classical scholarship. And what is more trying still, be you the most skilled skipper in the world, Mr. Fielding will foil you—and that more in *Amelia* than in any of his other works. For *Amelia*, being a good story, one is anxious not to miss any detail of the unwinding of the tale. But Fielding will sandwich three lines indispensable to the comprehension of that story between two passages, each ten pages long, of theological discussions between the book's chief benefactor and a young Anglican seminarist. And that is a serious defect. You are, for instance, for quite a long time left under the impression that the matchless Amelia is a shade insensitive, so little emotion does she show at the revelation of her Mr. Booth's infidelity with Miss Matthews. And then, casting back a hundred and twenty pages, you discover, between two tirades of classical erudition by Mrs. ꞏAtkinson, that she has already had the news of that infidelity in a blackmailing letter from Miss Matthews some weeks before, so that she has had time to get used to the fact. . . . A serious defect.

Fielding, indeed, tries that trick at the very beginning of the book. After his first chapter called "Exordium," in which Fielding displays himself as something less man-of-the-worldish and more serious than the author of *Tom Jones*, he sets, with spirit, out upon his story. As, thus, in the first paragraph of chapter two:

> On the first of April in the year —— the watchmen of a certain parish (I know not particularly which) within the liberty of Westminster brought several persons whom they had apprehended the preceding night before Jonathan Thrasher Esq., one of the justices of the peace for that liberty.

And you will observe that Fielding has not gone fifteen words of his journey before the necessity to introduce himself into it becomes overwhelming. He *has* to inform the reader that, as author, Mr. Fielding does not "particularly" know in what parish his Mr. Booth was arrested. That is a kind of insouciance that may show the reader that Mr. Fielding was too much of a great gentleman to bother about details. An author ought to be omniscient as far as his tale is concerned or he has no right to write his tale. And it is an untruth too because Fielding *must* have known in what parish his Mr. Booth was arrested . . . or he cannot have read his own book. For the reader will observe that Mr. Booth, as an insolvent debtor, had taken lodgings in the "verges"—the sanctuary of Westminster Abbey, which was then included in the parish of St. Margaret's Westminster. And Mr. Fielding is careful afterwards to inform us that Mr. Booth had not ventured outside the verges for fear of arrest for debt. . . . Nor is that sufficient.

Having got in his five lines of the tale you would think that Fielding would have gone on with it for a page or two. Not a bit of it. In the very next paragraph after the words "of the peace for that liberty" he has to begin:

But here, reader, before we proceed to the trials of these of-
fenders, we shall, after our usual manner, premise some things
which it may be necessary for thee to know.

It hath been observed, I think, by many, as well as the cele
brated writer of three letters, that no human institution is capable
of consummate perfection. An observation which perhaps that
writer at least gathered from discovering some defects in the
polity even of this well-regulated nation. And indeed if there
should be any such defect in a constitution which my Lord Coke
long ago told us "the wisdom of all the wise men in the world, if
they had all met together at one time, could not have equalled . . ."
[And so on interminably.]

These are serious mismanagements in a story teller and we will
reconsider them in a minute or two because they are all the more
serious in that in *Amelia* Fielding shows that he really was a story
teller of some skill and more genius. In the case of *Tom Jones*,
the story is so negligible and the incidents are invented with such
listlessness that we have to regard the tale as a mere string on which
are threaded the pearls of Mr. Fielding's—cousin to the Right Honorable the Earl of Denbigh—Mr. Fielding, the man about town's, wit.
As such, for people who like the sort of thing, *Tom Jones* may well
pass as a masterpiece—perhaps only of the second rank, this being
an order of criticism of which we have little the habit. It is then less
ebullient than Rabelais, less obscenely divergent than *Tristram Shandy*,
less lewd in cruelty than the *Sentimental Journey*, less humane than
Don Quichote, less ferociously realist than the *Satyrikon*, which in
its determination to "make you see" gives you a night in the streets
of Rome that once read can never fade from the memory . . . and it
is less profuse in moralizations than Fielding's own *Amelia*.

It is in its own form, a neatly performed job. It begins with a
Chapter One which, being headed "The Introduction to the Work or a
Bill of Fare to the Feast," warns the reader at once that the story as
such is not to hypnotize him with its reality. For no author with a
real passion for his coming projection will begin his novel with an

exordium calling attention to the artificiality of his convention any more than any author with any passion for what he has projected will end up his novel with snufflingly calling attention to the fact that the tale is only a tale. Consider, in this respect, Thackeray; how, directly imitating Fielding, he ruins whole books of his by their introductions or their last paragraphs—those last paragraphs in which the real novelist strains every nerve to add reality to his closing so that the reader, rising from the book in the actual atmosphere of a West Chester library, goes about for an hour or so still beneath the palms of Malaysia or the lower reaches of the Thames. But what must Mr. Thackeray do but begin or end up his books with paragraphs running: "Reader, the puppet play is ended; let down the curtain; put the puppets back into their boxes, sweep up the programmes and orange peels from the sawdust." . . . and the whole effect of the long book is dispelled. . . . But the truth is that both Thackeray all his life and Fielding in *Tom Jones* were intent first of all on impressing on their readers that they were not real novelists . . . but gentlemen.

It is curious to consider how the mind when thinking on *Tom Jones* considers it as a wilderness of interpolations. Yet actually it is a matter of a hundred and six closely printed pages before Fielding interrupts his story for the first time. And when he does so he indicates plainly enough that it is only through sheer incapacity to carry on his story as a story . . . or out of a fear that the moral of that story has not made itself plain. He commits himself, therefore, suddenly to a number of platitudinous statements to the effect that: "Prudence and circumspection are necessary to the best of men," and the like, and then makes the avowal of want of skill thus:

I ask pardon for this short appearance, by way of chorus, on the stage. It is in reality for my own sake, that, while I am discovering the rocks on which innocence and goodness often split, I may not be misunderstood to recommend the very means to my worthy readers, by which I intend to show them they will be undone. And thus, as I could not prevail on any of my actors to speak, I was obliged to declare myself.

Fielding, in fact, had intended to make his *Joseph Andrews* a mere parody of Richardson's *Pamela* and then afterwards, finding that the story was going very well, turned the rest of the book into a straight and spirited narration. In the same way he had intended to make of *Tom Jones* a straight and spirited narration until he found that he could not swing it and, against his will, introduced himself into his own pages. A man of common sense and of great reading from Cicero to Le Sage, he probably felt that the introduction of himself spoiled, to some extent, the reader's illusion. Or, perhaps, it was merely that he knew that moralizing was not to the taste of *l'homme moyen sensuel* to whom principally he addressed himself. But having tried it in the passage we have just read, he must have found that he could compound a brand of moralizing such that neither the man of the world, of the town, nor yet of the street would by it be incommoded to the extent of cutting down his *menus plaisirs*—his lecheries, bibulousnesses, amorous deceits, borrowing from mistresses and all the manly exercises that rendered tolerable the lives of gentry of his kidney. And having satisfied himself that his self-introduction would give no offence, from that moment onwards Fielding gave himself *carte blanche* and pirouetted and winked across his pages whenever—and that was often enough—the mood occurred to him.

Nor is it to be said that these digressions in themselves make disagreeable reading. Such a passage as what follows is sprightly and pleasant and well-calculated to prove that Fielding as writer was a monstrous clever prestidigitator. And one would be curmudgeonly, indeed, if one grudged as much to the clever and full-blooded. It is merely that—as Mr. Stalin lately remarked of Mr. Trotsky—his practices were not in themselves wrong save in that they were untimely. In any other form but that of the novel this passage would make agreeable reading, but coming as it does at the very crisis of one of the only two at all excitingly rendered passages in the book it is *per se* simply disastrous.

As in the season of *rutting*, an uncouth phrase by which *the vulgar denote* that *gentle dalliance*, which in the well-wooded forest of Hampshire, passes between lovers of the *ferine kind*, if, while *the lofty-crested stag* meditates the *amorous sport*, a couple of puppies, or any other beasts of hostile note, should wander so near the temple of Venus Ferina that the *fair hind* should shrink from the place, touched with that somewhat, either of fear or frolic, of nicety or skittishness, with which *nature hath bedecked all females*, or hath at least instructed them how to put it on; lest, through the *indelicacy of males*, the *Samean mysteries* should be pryed into by *unhallowed eyes*: for, at the *celebration of these rites*, the female priestess cries out with her in Virgil (who was then, probably, hard at work on such a celebration),

> —*Procul, o procul este, profani,*
> *Proclamat vates, totoque absistite loco.*

—Far hence be souls profane,
The sibyl cry'd, and from the grove abstain.—Dryden.

(The words italicized above are not so italicized in the original.)
This sort of thing continues for some time more and then Mr. Fielding remembers his story and, thus, continues it:

> Thus, and more terrible, when he perceived the enemy's approach, leaped forth our hero. Many a step advanced he forwards, in order to conceal the *trembling hind*, and, if possible, to *secure her retreat*. And now Thwackum, having first *darted some livid lightning* from his *fiery eyes*, began to thunder forth, "Fie upon it! Fie upon it! Mr. Jones. Is it possible you should be the person?"—"You see," answered Jones, "it is possible I should be here."

It must, in short, be apparent to the most unpracticed reader that this adventure of Mr. Jones made a lively scene and that, by cutting it up in the middle, Fielding effectually scotched it.
Let us then quote the end of the book.

> *To conclude*, as there are not to be found a worthier man and woman, than this *fond couple*, so neither can any be imagined

more happy. They preserve the *purest and tenderest affection* for each other, an affection daily increased and confirmed by *mutual endearments* and *mutual esteem*. Nor is their conduct towards their relations and friends less amiable than towards one another. And such is their condescension, their indulgence, and their beneficence to those below them, that there is not a neighbor, a tenant, or a servant, who doth not most gratefully bless the day when Mr. Jones was married to his Sophia.

It is a mere statement of facts and as such carries relatively little or no conviction. Had Mr. Fielding done, as many of his successors had the skill to do—namely, put in a little picture of children and Newfoundland dogs tumbling together on a lawn he would have done much more to assure us that his Sophia really did achieve a measure of wedded bliss. Or had he done as Smollett did in ending his *Roderick Random*—pictured the wedding night lusciously and then almost as lusciously the nature of the "settlements;" or had he, as he himself subsequently did in *Amelia*—a book that grows and grows on one the more one reads *Tom Jones*—had he rendered the desperate, bitter straits to which poverty can reduce even heroines . . . had he, that is to say, showed us Sophia forced to such expedients as poor Amelia in whom mortification was added to the disaster of the theft when she found that the underclothing that had cost her thirty shillings was sold by the thief for a mere five . . . why, then, we might believe that the subsequent settlements might have brought her not merely contentment but a measure of soft bliss . . . in a really happy ending.

But that paragraph carries neither picture nor conviction. We gather from it no belief at all that merely by listening to the pious conversation of Mr. Allworthy—of which in his unredeemed condition he must already have had enough and to spare—that merely by that listening he would be converted from a rather crawling rake to a finely erect specimen of *homo sapiens Europaeus* . . . and "the best of husbands." We *know* that Jones, driven to desperation by the conventional periods of his uncle and benefactor, must one day seize his hat, rush out of the house, and so betake himself to the house of some Miss Matthews or other. Indeed, if we imagine that in writing the adventures of Mr. Booth of *Amelia* Fielding was merely continuing the post-marital career of Tom Jones we need not be too cynically in the wrong. Obviously, marital bliss is possible to the wives of the worst of rakes and to the rakes themselves. But to convince us that that is the lot of one or other of his characters the writer must take much more trouble . . . and write much better.

CHAPTER SEVEN

O N TOP of the complete materialism and sentimentality that over-whelmed Anglo-Saxondom with the coming of the Hanoverian kings, two other changes contributed to giving both English prose and verse a very altered character. In the first place the Georges imported professional musicians from Germany so that native music died. Secondly, the unit of English prose and thought became not the word but the phrase. This has had a very serious and very disastrous effect upon English prose. It operated in the first place towards loose expression of thought and in the second place towards the almost necessitated use of the cliché phrase. It is necessitated because if a man's vocabulary is small and he employs his words in groups of three or four, the number of expressions at his disposal will be proportionately limited and in consequence he will have to use—and all his fellows around him will have to use—the same phrase so often that it will finally become nauseating or ridiculous. The tendency began at the beginning of the Elizabethan period with poets like Spenser and the numerous sonnetteers. Their inspiration was exclusively from books. Their language had no connection with the Franco-Teutonic common speech but was founded on a non-comprehension of the spirit of the robust tongue of the Romans. Their habitations were ivory towers. They were the first men of letters and turned their backs on life. Their line ran from Spenser through Milton and Dryden to culminate in Pope and to continue in the crowd of hack verse writers of the eighteenth century. The Elizabethan dramatists, the metaphysical poets and the great prose writers lived full lives and wrote much as they spoke. The change as far as prose was concerned came with Fielding's catering to the taste of the wits of his day.

If you will give yourself the trouble to examine the passages from Fielding that we have lately quoted you will notice, being helped by the italicized phrases, the great number of ready-made groups of words that he uses. Yet the prose of *Tom Jones* is rather good prose for the eighteenth century. But only compare it with the passage from the *Compleat Angler* quoted previously in which microscopic scrutiny will not discover one single cliché phrase unless it be "tempestuous seas." And Walton may well have been the first to use that conjunction of words. You will then well see how one passage of prose may be artificial, pompous, unduly grandiose and ordinary. That will be because of its writer's use of linked words that have already over again been linked. But another passage of prose will have, indeed, the sparkle of dewdrops on a May morning, simply because its author sought for the simplest words and the most frugally exact adjectives and similes, having the exact eye and the passion above all to make you see. When, in short, you read Fielding—as when you read Virgil—it is as if you looked at an admirable but conventionalized tapestry. But when you read Walton you are sitting beside that author in the shade of a tree and all the landscape is plain before you. That is the difference between great artistry and even the most consummate virtuosity.

The case of Richardson is somewhat different. Intent on giving to his pages a polite surface, he seldom uses words that are either very vivid or very startling. From time to time, with deliberation he will insert a cliché phrase—but very rarely. The advantage of writing a novel in the form of letters is that the author obtains verisimilitude; he has neither temptation, nor indeed the possibility, to introduce his own person or comments into the narrative. But one defect of the form is that the prose he employs must be consonant with the character, upbringing, hereditary and social station of the characters he is thus presenting. Thus, practically all the letters in *Clarissa* were written by persons of a certain station, fortune and suavity of manners; so the prose of *Clarissa* very seldom has either vitality or distinction. Consider this random passage:

> I walked backward and forward. I threw down with disdain the patterns. Now to my closet retired I; then quitting it, threw myself upon the settee; then upon this chair; then upon that; then into one window, then into another—I knew not what to do!

And while I was in this suspense, having again taken up the letter to re-peruse it, Betty came in, reminding me, by order, that my papa and mamma waited for me in my father's study.

Tell my mamma, said I, that I beg the favour of seeing her here for one moment; or to permit me to attend her anywhere by herself.

I listened at the stairs-head— You see, my dear, how it is, cried my father, very angrily: all your condescension (as your indulgence heretofore) is thrown away. *You blame your son's violence* as you call it (*I had some pleasure in hearing this*); but nothing else will do with her. You shall *not* see her alone. Is *my* presence an exception to the bold creature?

Tell her, said my mother to Betty, she knows upon what terms she may come down to us. Nor will see her upon any other.

The maid brought me this answer. I had recourse to my pen and ink; but I trembled so that I could not write, nor knew I what to say, had I had steadier fingers. At last Betty brought me these lines from my father.

This, it will be observed, is perfectly good prose and the minutest scrutiny will hardly reveal any cliché phrases at all and only two words ("retired" and "re-perused") that one could possibly call stilted . . . or not in the ordinary conversational vernacular of Richardson's day.

Of course, just because these letters are letters, the question of prose style as displayed in them is hardly very valid. We don't know how Richardson would have written *Clarissa* had he chosen to write in his own person. He has told us that he began his literary labors at the age of thirteen by writing letters that young ladies might send to their beaux. His practice in this sort of composition would seem to have been enormous. And his first projected book was to have been a letter writer's guide, consisting of specimens of letters from young ladies in every possible tender situation or dilemma. He found it, however, advantageous, as being less monotonous and calling for less continuous invention of new situations, to hang the letters around one definite affair, obtaining variety from the varied incidents of a tale.

But no more than the personality of Shakespeare need the prose of this great writer await our question. He and Jane Austen alone, until nearly the end of the nineteenth century, relieve the British novel of the stigma cast on it when Prof. E. M. Foster declared that there never had been a first-class novel written in English. This writer, as will have appeared, is sufficiently exclusive but even he is not inclined completely to concur. Reservation must be made for those two. . . . What a match they would have made of it! . . . And there are also *Framley Parsonage* and *Mary Barton*.

When you think of the first class in novels, or in anything else, you have at once to become international-minded. It is insufficient to advance a very good English, German, Polish or what you will, writer. He must be one able to mix on equal terms with all the giants of all time—and he must be acknowledged as so doing by all the world. This—as is the case with Constable and Whistler amongst painters—has been the fortune only of Richardson and Henry James amongst Anglo-Saxon writers, Jane Austen being hardly yet sufficiently well known in either of the two Western continents. For there are, of course, very great authors whose fame by some irony of fate never crosses either Channel or Ocean.

You have to think of an intelligent, sophisticated and, perhaps, somewhat cynical foreigner and consider which of your national novels you would with confidence present to him. For, however little of a jingo one may be, it must be disagreeable to one to see the rictus of sardonic derision spread over a foreigner's face as he peruses one of one's treasured home-baked products. Of this one need have no fear in the case of Richardson and James, and, indeed, of Jane Austen, Smollett, Trollope and the book of Mrs. Gaskell. . . . And possibly also of Fielding. . . . Possibly also of Joseph Conrad. At any rate, they all wrote of topics fit for the attention of grown-up men with a skill sufficient not to disgust the reasonably lettered adult. That is as much as one can ask.

Really to account for how Jane Austen and Richardson achieved their masterpieces one has to resort to the very dangerous expedient of saying that they must have been natural geniuses. That is dangerous because once you make the concession the whole cry of hounds of the professorio-academic pack will be on your back, shouting: "You see, when it comes to real works of art this fellow has to admit that they can only be produced autochthonously—by writers and others who follow no traditions and know no aesthetic law." With the corollary that artists who do follow traditions and aesthetic rules are dull fellows whom nobody loves.

Your first answer to that is that neither Richardson nor Jane Austen are included in *their* list of geniuses. And your second would be that, according to their contention, neither of their two chief heroes, Shakespeare and Fielding—one of whom, at least, is assuredly one of *our* chiefest heroes—could come within their definition of the immortals. Both Shakespeare and Fielding wrote in the traditions of the group who founded themselves on Virgil, Tully, Livy, Petrarch, Boccaccio, the Pleïads and a thousand other Latin- and Greek-descended writers. And Shakespeare certainly had, and wrote with, an immense knowledge of the aesthetic laws that were the common sense of the Elizabethan stage. Fielding, perhaps, fell less under the Petrarchan-Italian influence than Shakespeare. But Fielding's day lay immensely open—too much, perhaps, open—to classical Latin influences. He himself lays claim also to a relatively profound acquaintanceship with Italian, Greek and French literary productions. And he had at least a nodding acquaintance with some common-sense technical rules; the passage as to the undesirability of the author's introducing himself into his own pages sufficiently proves that.*

As is the case with all French intellectual and aesthetic major movements, the exaggerated classicism which had distinguished the French court and upper classes crossed the English Channel relatively late and was relatively coarsened by the transplantation. The personal government of Louis XIV, freed from the tutelage of Cardinal Mazarin, lasted from 1661-1715. During that half century and more the court maintained standards of manners, honor, statuary and theatricals

---

* He makes as to himself the following assertion:

> Tuscan (i.e. the tongue of Petrarch) and French are in my head
> Latin I write and Greek—I read

and such learning as is needed in courts, all rather grotesquely supposed to be influenced by classical canons. The similarity of *le roi soleil* backed by the façade of the palace of Versailles and fronted by its fountains to Alexander the Great or to Jupiter does not very much leap to the eye. It was, nevertheless, insisted on in every form of statuette or monumental group, and in every fresco, easel piece, sonnet, ode, or prose address. All the seven arts were pressed into that service.

The tendency, as we have said, did not reach England until later and then by way of Germany. The reigns of Anne, William III and George I were, as far as the Court was concerned, merely numb and material. The Stuarts had kept England English, musical, lyric, witty and to some extent spiritual. Neither of the two first foreign sovereigns under whom the country was to lie supine meddled with English taste, so a sort of vague commerce of ideas and the arts still went on between the two countries. It culminated in the complete sweeping of France by the genius of Richardson.

There had been before then a sort of Frenchifying of English literary standards in the direction rather of Latin than of Greek classicism. Fielding wrote Latin and read Greek. But with the coming of George II in 1727 the Court began to exercise on the taste of the town as much influence as courts can exercise. George II hated "bainting and boetry." On the other hand he was passionate for music. English music being a dainty thing, he introduced Haendel and a host of foreign professional musicians. So both the art and the practice of music died in England. The harpsichords and zithers of the contredanse called "Sir Roger de Coverly" could not stand up against the brass of "The Trumpet Shall Sound." The great fighting leaders of the Roundheads could be incomparable ticklers of the lute, but the heroes of the Hanoverian Court considered it sissy for a man to play the clavecin. And, music dying, the lyric impulse that had given all its charm to English poetry died too. A blank verse line of Marlowe would not today very readily set itself to music, but it was near enough to the music of its own day and had a lilt of its own. But what could be further from music than:

Now hear what blessings temperance can bring.
(Thus said our friend, and what he said I sing),
First health: The stomach (crammed from every dish,
A tomb of boiled and roast, and flesh and fish,
Where bile, and wind, and phlegm and acid jar,
And all the man is one intestine war)
Remembers oft the schoolboy's simple fare.
The temperate sleeps, and spirits light as air.

That was Pope's lambent irony brutalized and coarsened by the
heavier classicism of the Hanoverian Court. It has been well said of
Pope that his work divides it into three periods which correspond to
the three reigns under which he wrote. Under Queen Anne he was
a personal pastoral English poet; under George I he was a translator
and "made much money by satisfying the French-classical taste of his
day with versions of the *Iliad* and the *Odyssey** and with bitter-
sweet poems of the bag-wig and sword-knot type." *The Rape of the
Lock* was actually published in its final version in the year of the
accession of George I—1714. But you could no more sing a verse of the
Rape than you could sing:

Achilles' wrath to Greece the direful spring
Of woes unnumbered Heavenly Goddess sing!

The heavy materialism and gross agnostic alcoholism settled on the
country that had driven out the Stuarts and forgotten the piety and
music of Herbert and Donne; so Pope turned his mind to the problems of his age. And in a series of poems that were "serious" and
censorious enough he made his muse sing his day. So by means of
Walpole's National Debt and other devices, that age riveted on the
country—apparently forever—the gross materialism that the Hanover-
ians brought to Anglo-Saxondom. It was great pity.

We have not, however, yet left Richardson. Our excursion about

* Henry Morley: *Introduction to An Essay on Man.*

Pope serves merely to "get in" the varying atmospheres of the days in which he lived. And to Jane Austen we shall return.

Richardson then was a genius: we do not know whence he got his gifts or derived his "technique." The supreme of art is the supreme of common sense . . . and surely the world cannot ever have produced two human beings more common-sensible than Richardson and Jane, nor two less capable of setting vine leaves in their hair and writing whatever came on paper-royal. The supreme of art is the supreme of common sense because the supreme artist, with no desire at all for aërian flights of fancy, coldly and consummately thinks out whatever in matter and manner will please the reasonably lettered of all time. In that light he sets to work with his pen. The result *must* then be masterly. It is merely common sense to see that personal incursions of the author will break the magic of a story; it is merely common sense to know that the ready-made phrase will retard the swiftness of a style and that by frequent repetition it becomes at first comic and then distasteful. The first man who wrote "blushing swain" or even "compliments of the season" made a momentarily new and felicitous contribution to current spoken phrases. The idea of a young hero —not the bride—blushing during the "celebration of the nuptial rite" was once new, delicate and amusing; the first substitution of the "season's compliments" for a longer phrase covering two major feasts of obligation would at least be welcome. But at the one hundred and sixty-seventh repetition in print or copper plate of each phrase the one becomes grotesque and the other completely unconvincing. You could use it for your grocer and he would know that you had not the least intention of paying him more punctually.

That Richardson knew any such rules before he sat down to write is to be doubted. No one before his day had formulated them, most eighteenth century literary rules being merely arbitrary. But that in his *for intérieur*—his subconsciousness—he knew them is apparent in all his works. He never intrudes. The cliché is at a minimum in his work. In that he shows that he was born and remained very much a child of the seventeenth century. In that day England was still

England and English, English. He knew French and well; that we know. Does he not correct the French translation of *Pamela* by the Abbé Prevost, the greatest French stylist of his day? But we may well doubt that he was at all really influenced either by French artistic rules or the Latino-French phrases that played the devil with Fielding, Pope and fashionable English.

The language used by the eighteenth century—and Samuel Johnson —was a translation. Pope's *Essay On Man* is a vast procession of phrases and always-adjectived nouns that were either cliché in his day or have since so become—*forbidden fruit, giddy heights, mother earth, vast immensity, gradations just, presumptuous man, words unnumbered, woods unnumbered, unnumbered men, eternal blessings on his shade attend.* In these phrases he and all the eighteenth century prosateurs were really translating. They thought in simple English, rethought their thoughts in schoolman's Latin and retranslated them into English. That English was as full of schoolman's Latin-derived resounding words as possible. They had to have adjectives, if possible Latin-derived, for *every* substantive. So that when he was on his higher horse Pope's verse must look like this:

> The *strong connections, nice dependencies*
> *Gradations just* has thy *pervading soul*
> Looked through?

It is quite possible that Pope used some of those connected words for the first time. But they immediately pervaded the common speech. They became part of the wearisome stock in trade of the man of letters. He, though he had little Latin and less French, was just beginning to see that he might make a living by writing. The livings were usually incomparably meager and sordid. But Pope made £8,-000 by his translations of the *Iliad* and the *Odyssey*. That made the writer's career an *ignis fatuus* for thousands who should have wielded any other implement than the pen.

Swift wrote an English as direct as that of Richardson. Nevertheless, he was at least as good a classical scholar and student of the French and Italians—nay, much better, than either Fielding or certainly Pope. Pope was next to no scholar at all, and resorted to rather discreditable stratagems to persuade the town that he had translated the *Odyssey*. The rough translation was really the work of two Grub Street hacks.

Swift is particularly difficult to quote. The content of his paragraphs is always so pungent, bitter and characteristic that the thought almost invariably hides the consideration of the verbiage from your eyes. This writer has spent the greater part of a day in finding the relatively unmoving paragraph that follows:

> In another apartment I was highly pleased with a projector, who had found a device of ploughing the ground with hogs, to save the charges of ploughs, cattle, and labour. The method is this: in an acre of ground you bury, at six inches distance and eight deep, a quantity of acorns, dates, chestnuts, and other mast or vegetables whereof these animals are fondest; then you drive six hundred or more of them into the field, where in a few days they will root up the *whole* ground in search of their food, and make it fit for sowing, at the same time manuring it with their dung. It is true, upon experiment they found the charge and trouble very great, and they had little or no crop. However, it is not doubted that this invention may be *capable of great improvement*.

In that passage there are only a few adjectives; only one phrase either was—or was capable of becoming—a cliché—"capable of great improvement." Yet Swift was intensely a man of his day and, more intensely than almost any other, of the Court. . . . And it will be observed the passage almost makes you see a landscape. The force of "technique" could not much further go.

Both Swift and Richardson have powers of inspiring, the one horror and the other disgust, which are rather unparalleled. This writer blenching not in the least before the "grossest" passages of Smollett or the most agonizing of Villon or Dante has found it almost impossible to read a great number of passages—not merely in the story of the Houynhms but all through the work of Swift. And he has found it perfectly impossible to face the whole last volume of *Clarissa.*

Both Swift and Richardson have a most unusual power of conveying scenes vividly . . . scenes rather of the sensibilities than of material objects and landscape. In that direction the gift of Richardson—and isn't "gift" here the exact *mot juste?*—was little short of miraculous. You feel the worries of Pamela with the same order of mental nerves, as that that you apply to your own financial troubles or the injustices from which you suffer. Did you not know that her ending was to be a happy one, your feelings would be still deeper. But with Clarissa, knowing as you do the atrocious catastrophe that always awaits her—for Richardson must have known at his inception of the story what the end was to be—with Clarissa the agony of mind of the reader becomes one of the great major agonies of the world. It is an agony of mind similar to those that attend on the awaited news of the destruction of defenceless towns, of unrescued liners at sea or the death of one's children. Colley Cibber, a man about town if ever there was one, said he would rather kill Richardson than let him let Clarissa come to the grief to which she did come. One naïve commentator on the story puts it, that the tragedy of Clarissa shows the triumph of virtue to such an extent that "when we get to Heaven we may feel certain of seeing her with one arm of the Blessed Virgin about her waist." But, even then, the consolation is not either very immediate or insistent.

For us, the writer and the reader, who desire to know how books should be written, there is one great aesthetic lesson to be learnt from this almost greatest of novelists. It is that the story of Clarissa is never in the least harrowing. In its most atrocious moments it is conducted with exactly the same composure as attends on the most untroubled and longest conversations in the cedar parlor of *Sir Charles Grandison.* The anxieties of Pamela, after her marriage with her "master," are sufficient to make you feel movements of personal uneasiness. But by the time Richardson had approached the end of Clarissa he had learned! Thus, far from being a depressant, that ending—and the whole work—are sufficiently stimulating to make the naïve reader believe that he will see Clarissa in the arms of Our Lady. The more sophisticated know that, if in the hereafter there shall be rewards for heroic virtue, Clarissa shall stand among the high ones there.

In Clarissa, Richardson has created a character—and English literature is honored by a figure!—moulded on the great lines of the tragedy of the Greeks. . . . She is moulded on the lines of Andromache, Iphigenia or Niobe herself. . . . Unnumbered palms depend above his brow!

The secret of the clarity of the English of Swift or Richardson may be that, though the main of their work was done in the eighteenth, they were actually born in the seventeenth, century. Swift was thirty-three, and Richardson eleven before the century turned. And even Pope was twelve. Yet Dryden died in 1700, which at first sight seems astonishing, when we consider the innumerable cliché phrases and overused Latinisms that distinguish the passages of his translation of the *Aeneid*. On the other hand, Smollett, who seems to have written in as seventeenth century a style as anyone else, was born actually fourteen years after Fielding in 1721.

This seems astonishing until we inquire more carefully into the circumstances of these writers. Writers are sometimes born before their age, sometimes they lag behind it; sometimes they are its very breath and essence. Sometimes their precocity is extravagant and for the time being they will reflect the colors of their youth. That was the case with Pope. In his earliest poems he is seventeenth century, rather imitative and poet enough. Of his first poem *Spring: The First Pastoral: or Damon*, Walsh, of whom Dryden in his postscript to his Virgil says that he was by far the greatest critic of his age, writes: "It is not flattery at all to say that Virgil had written nothing so good at his age." Pope's pastorals were written, however, in 1704, when all that Pope had of literature or education was still of a seventeenth century tinge. The echoes that one hears in the following lines which are the first Pope ever published are not the echoes of Latin writers; Pope had extremely little classical reading. Owing to the sickliness of his youth, he had merely the rather incompetent educa-

tion that a Roman Catholic priest—Pope was a Catholic—could give
him. The echoes of these lines then:

> First in these fields I try the sylvan strains;
> Nor blush to sport on Windsor's blissful plains:
> Fair Thames, flow gently from thy sacred spring,
> While on thy bank Sicilian muses sing;
> Let vernal airs through trembling osiers play,
> And Albion's cliffs resound the rural lay.

come from Dryden who was at once his constant cynosure and irritant.
His preface to the volume which contained this poem is a mere
pastiche of concealed quotations from the critical opinions of Dryden,
Fontenelle's *Discourse on Pastorals*, Heinsius's *On Theocritus*, Rapin's
Réflexion sur l'Art Poétique, and the works of a score of other French
writers!

It is really to Dryden, writing wholly in the seventeenth century,
that the eighteenth owes the peculiar fadedness of all its adjectived
nouns and Latinized cliché phrases. He translated not merely the
Aeneid but a tremendous number of other Latin poems—Theocritus,
Lucretius, Ovid's *Metamorphoses, Epistles,* and his *Art of Love*,
Juvenal, Persius, the first book and several passages of the *Iliad*. And
even three of the poems of Boccaccio. So he evolved a peculiar and
unfortunate jargon. Would you not say that the following passage
might have been written by Gay or Gray or Phillips or any poet of
the deep eighteenth century?

> Then thus Umbritius (with an angry frown,
> And looking back on this degen'rate town),
> "Since noble arts in Rome have no support,
> And ragged virtue not a friend at court,
> No profit rises from th' ungrateful stage,
> My poverty increasing with my age,
> Tis time to give my just disdain a vent,
> And, cursing, leave so base a government."

This characteristic is obviously due to the intensity of his pastoral studies. He was pushed into them in the illustrious school of Westminster under that great wielder of the birch rod, Dr. Busby. Later, at the University of Cambridge he completed the process! At Westminster School he made, at the age of sixteen and at the command of that Tartar of a pedagogue, his translation of the third satire of Persius. Thus, to Busby must go at least the credit of having discerned Dryden's great gift. But it would be a great injustice to Dryden to consider him merely from the translator's angle. He was one of the greatest of English poets. For the present writer the following passage from *A Song to St. Cecilia's Day*, written in 1687, is the most pleasurable verse in all English poetry. It further confirms our argument that English poetry depends upon music and died when music died in England. This poem was written in praise of music's patron saint.

> What passion cannot Music raise and quell?
> When Jubal struck the corded shell,
> His listening brethren stood around,
> And, wondering, on their faces fell
> To worship that celestial sound.
> Less than a God they thought there could not dwell
> Within the hollow of that shell,
> That spoke so sweetly and so well.
> What passion cannot Music raise and quell?

Dryden was what we should today call the county. He inherited from his father a sufficient landed estate to let him pass the first seven years after his father's death in post-graduate study at the University of Cambridge. The rest of his years he spent, without the impulsion of the spur of penury, in London itself. Dryden's early circumstances remain, however, rather obscure. Neither the year nor the place of his birth are exactly known. But from the internal evidence of several passages of his writing, it seems safe to say that he was born in 1631. It is certain that he was a zealous upholder of the commonwealth, and Malone alleges that he favored the sects of the Anabaptists and Independents—today the Congregationalists.

That is not astonishing. His father is alleged to have been an enemy of the Royal cause and was certainly a supporter of the extreme Left of Protestantism, It is uncertain whether Dryden was or was not a Committeeman—one of the members of Cromwell's higher executive organization. But on the death of Cromwell he expressed his grief with considerable emphasis. His "Stanzas on the Death of Oliver Cromwell Written After his Funeral" is no more a poem than is his "Astraea Redux: A Poem on the Happy Restoration and Return of his Sacred Majesty, Charles II." But it has a certain agreeable suavity and, perhaps, more real feeling than is usual in such productions. Its last two verses run as follows:

> No civil broils have since his death arose,
> But faction now by habit does obey;
> And wars have that respect for his repose,
> As winds for halcyons, when they breed at sea.

> His ashes in a peaceful urn shall rest,
> His name a great example stands, to show
> How strangely high endeavours may be blest,
> Where piety and valour jointly go.

The last stanzas of the poem to Charles II are more stereotyped:

> At home the hateful names of parties cease,
> And factious souls are wearied into peace.
> The discontented now are only they,
> Whose crimes before did your just cause betray:
> Of those your edicts some reclaim from sins,
> But most your life and blest example wins.
> Oh happy prince, whom heaven hath taught the way
> By paying vows to have more vows to pay!
> Oh happy age! Oh times like those alone,
> By fate reserv'd for great Augustus' throne!
> When the joint growth of arms and art foreshow
> The world a monarch, and that monarch you.

Dryden's transference of his allegiance has been both laughed at and condemned, but it is difficult to see what other course a man writing on public matters could have taken if he set the peace of a sufficiently tormented country above all other matters. His conversion to the Church of Rome was, perhaps, more sincere. It was more in tune with his real personality, as it is undoubtedly the cause of the eclipse of popularity that has ever since been his fate. His poem of "The Hind and the Panther" did not have the effectiveness of Swift's *Tale of a Tub*. Swift shows the injuries inflicted on the Church of England by papists and non-conformists alike. Dryden's poem, on the other hand, extols the sufferings of that innocent hind, the Church of Rome, at the hands of that blood-stained panther, the Church of England. Thus, it was not unnatural that a nation whose higher education has ever since been in the hands almost exclusively of Anglican divines should make of the *Tale of a Tub* a national classic. They relegate Dryden, as poet, to a place very much, indeed, in the shade. Pope's Catholicism did him little or no harm; he did not regard the poet as having any public function. But Dryden took the other view, and has to suffer the necessary penalty of upholding the older faith. Dryden's popularity, as opposed to the position that he might properly occupy in what it is convenient to call the Republic of Taste, is also affected—as is that of almost all the eighteenth century writers after him—by the immense percentage of his lines that occupy themselves with political questions or personal feuds. The reader who reads for pleasure or for aesthetic comprehension cannot expect to get any pleasure from "The Hind and the Panther" or "Mac Flecknoe." In such work Dryden sacrifices his aesthetic gifts to his determination to drag in one political or personal grudge or another. Such poems become almost incomprehensible unless either the edition is buried under explanatory notes or the reader is an expert in literary snarls and quibbles. They embrace the names of literally hundreds of otherwise perfectly obscure and rather crawling individuals. "Mac Flecknoe," it is true, enshrines the immortal lines:

> The rest to some faint reason make pretence
> But Shadwell never deviates into sense

Shadwell having been the bard who succeeded Dryden when, as a papist convert, he was ejected from the poet-laureateship and lost a very useful £300 a year, with a butt of sherry. Dryden, of course, does not introduce into his polemics the almost epileptic fury of a Milton—but Milton is, perhaps on that account, as a polemist the more readable of the two.

Actually, as we have said, the roots of the combative fury and the faded classical phraseology of the eighteenth century went far deeper than the beginning of that century itself. We have to seek the one in the fact that writers towards the beginning of the seventeenth century began to make money—and so pitifully little money!—by their pens. Before that date the writer was a man of inherited wealth won by his ancestors by the sword; or he supported himself on a place or pension gotten from a patron, royal or noble, who desired the pleasure of reading more of his work.   But the founding of grammar schools and the growing ease of access to the universities had spawned whole shoals of men disinclined for the labors of either the plough, the pen or the yardstick. Printers began to buy manuscripts; so the struggle for the few plums that fell into the literary pool resembled that of numerous fish in hungry waters—except that the fish content themselves with biting the plums, leaving their fellows unassailed.

The evolution of the classicism that was later to render the eighteenth century writer ineffectual and rather comic in his grander moments had, however, begun considerably earlier. It was not for nothing that the great Doctor made Phillips in his poem on cider turn his line: "Now, Muse, let's talk of mice," into "Now, Muse, let's talk of rats," alleging that the rat as the more majestic animal was more fitted to the Muses' lyre. . . . The wonder is that he did not substitute "rodent tribe" for "rats."

But, as we have said, with the coming in the sixteenth century of the immense flood of Mediterranean literature, there came also the evolution of the always minor strain of "literary" literature. These were the writings of those who drew their observation and selected their instances from Mediterranean books rather than from English life.* Consider even the delightful passage from the *Faerie Queen*, quoted by Mr. Renwick as an illustration of the influence of music on English verse form. (His opinion on that point confirmed comfortingly this writer's theories on the subject:)

> The *joyous birdes*, shrouded in *chearefull shade*
> Their notes unto the voice attempred sweet;
> *Th' Angelicall soft trembling voices* made
> To th' *instruments divine respondence sweet*
> The silver sounding instruments did meet
> With the base murmure of the waters fall;
> The waters fall with difference discreet,
> Now soft, now loud, unto the wind did call;
> The gentle warbling wind low answered to all.

Or consider the other verses, quoted as a contrast, by Mr. Renwick:

> He cryde as *raging seas* are wont to rore
> When *wintry storme* his *wrathful wrecke* does threat;
> The *rolling billows* beat the *ragged shore.* . . .

Here you get an effect that Shakespeare in the Scene of the Players in *Hamlet* gently, and as if regretfully, ridiculed. . . . And, indeed, we may well hazard the guess that his regret was that Fate and the necessities of the purse had not permitted him to continue such essays in the Spenserian school as his two failures, the *Rape of Lucrece* and *Venus and Adonis*, or his greater glories, the *Sonnets*. But the number of Spenserian-Petrarchan sonnetteers that that age produced was as enormous as their sonnets were insupportable.

Shakespeare escaped that tragic fate—by virtue, probably, of being, as well as poet, somewhat of a man of action. Spenser dallied with life under the shadow of a patron-bestowed office and never got

---

* The reader who wishes to *approfondir* his knowledge of Elizabethan literary aesthetics and practices should add to Symonds' *Shakespeare's Predecessors* which has already here been recommended to him, the extremely delightful and entirely readable *Edmund Spenser* of Professor W. L. Renwick, one of those rare books of scholastic criticism to be also a work of art.

rid of the Theocrito-Petrarchan-Ronsardian "aestheticism" that passed from Shakespeare and his greater competitors as if it had been a youthful greensickness.

It is always dangerous too much to systematize but, viewed in the light of the above paragraph, the whole literary affair of the sixteenth to eighteenth centuries becomes easily comprehensible: The place-men—or would-be place-men writers—became literary littérateurs partly because they were near courts, partly because they had a sufficiency of leisure really to gorge to repletion on Ovid's *Metamorphoses;* on Livy, Tully, Virgil, Theocritus, Petrarch, Ronsard, du Bellay, on *l'Art Poètique,* and later on French criticism of the formal type; on Racine, and in a far greater degree on Corneille. Thus, a whole section of Dryden's quite unreadable plays are so founded on Corneille that they might well be taken to be translations from him.*

There were, thus, two strings of pearls. The one connected Spenser with Pope and his successors; the other, Shakespeare with the Johnson Boswell caricatured, not the Johnson who wrote *The Lives of the Poets.* You had the marmoreal Latinisms, plus the Petrarchan sonnet mode, of Spenser and, in prose, Sidney; and, perhaps more potently, you had the immense impulsion towards Latinisms of the university-educated Ben Jonson. That impulsion carried the poetic wave well past Milton. On a social scale usually lower, you had the string that connected Shakespeare with Johnson. These men were usually men of action or parsons. They were men who had fought or been in the army like Gibbon, Smollett, Steele; they had been craftsmen like Richardson, or visited the sick like Herbert, or had known bitter poverty like Donne. These men were too busily occupied, at least in their youths, to have much dalliance with Latinity. They had seen life at close quarters, if only in the hearts of young ladies who wanted love letters written whilst their printing presses waited. Thus, Smollett was a ship's surgeon in a naval siege whilst Fielding and Addison twirled clouded

* A passion for formal drama *à la française* struck London town like a whirlwind in 1672 and remained in full boom for fourteen or fifteen years. Then it incontinently died. At the same time came a positive passion for French criticism of the official type. And Dryden made great hay while that sun shone. His plays of that type, except for one that had the honor of being set to music by Purcell are, one imagines, completely forgotten.

canes in Childs' coffee house, talked about Ovid's *Art of Love*, and mingled with the wits. Thrown down, the two strings would look like this—with one name, perhaps the most fertile of all, to play the father:

CHAUCER

WRITERS WHO HAD READ

> SPENSER, Sidney, Sonnetteers (a long string), JONSON, Milton, Shadwell, Otway (and a great many), Dryden, Pope, Fielding, Addison, Cowley, Gray (and the whole eighteenth century muse) to Johnson, author of *Rasselas* (and an infinity of critics).

WRITERS WHO HAD LIVED

> SHAKESPEARE (and many dramatists), DONNE, Cowley, Herbert (and others), Browne, Walton, SWIFT, RICHARDSON, GIBBON, SMOLLETT, Steele, Otway, Congreve, Gilbert White. And Johnson, author of *London*, and possibly Goldsmith.

It is Virgil against Homer; a field marshal who has risen from the ranks against any cabinet minister. Or, to put it another way, it is this Steele of the *Spectator*:

Mr. Thomas Inkle of London, aged twenty years, embarked in the Downs in the good ship called the Achilles, bound for the West Indies, on the 16th of June, 1647, in order to improve his fortune by trade and merchandise. Our adventurer was the third son of an eminent citizen who had taken particular care to instil into his mind an early love of gain, by making him a perfect master of numbers, and consequently giving him a quick view of loss and advantage, and preventing the natural impulses of his passions, by prepossession towards his interests. With a mind thus turned, young Inkle had a person every way agreeable, a ruddy vigor in his countenance, strength in his limbs, with ringlets of fair hair loosely flowing on his shoulders. It happened, in the course of the voyage, that the Achilles, in some distress, put into a creek on the main of America, in search of provisions.*

against this Addison, also of the *Spectator:*

I could not but look upon these registers of existence (tombstones) whether of brass or of marble, as a kind of satire upon the departed persons; who had left no other memorial of them, but that they were born, and that they died. They put me in mind of several persons mentioned in the battles of heroic poems, who have sounding names given them, for no other reason but that they may be killed, and are celebrated for nothing but being knocked on the head.

Γλαυαον τε Μεδοντα τε Θεσιλοχον τε.   HOM.
Claucumque, Medontaque, Thersilochumque.   VIRG.
Glaucus, and Medon, and Thersilochus.†

This is not to say that Steele was a better prose-writer than Addison. There are passages in the *Spectator* where Steele shows himself as indomitable a Latinist as Addison. And Addison now and then shows that he can use English more directly than Steele, as in his passage in Number V of the *Spectator* where he describes the sparrows that were let loose in the Opera to represent nightingales. The nightingales' voices were meanwhile represented by a "concert of flagelets and bird-calls which were planted behind the scenes." But the two passages do represent the difference between a Steele who had had contact sufficient with actual life to have risen from trooper to a commission in the horse-guards by discipline and smartness and an Addison who, whilst promenading in the cloisters of Westminster Abbey must—with an extraordinary justness as representing his age —turn "tombstones" into "registers of existence." So he cannot even meditate a moment amongst the homes of the dead without showing that he was acquainted with Greek and Latin. That passage is all the more apt since it reminds us that Virgil, who had never seen

---

* *Spectator,* 50-51.
† *Spectator,* 115.

battle or sea, had read Homer who had bathed deep, indeed, in both. Otherwise Virgil would not have quoted those three names in just that order. So those two Mediterranean authors foreshadowed in their literary relationships Steele who had sat his charge and formed squad, and Addison who had passed a large part of his placeman's life reading Homer and Virgil and could not let you forget it. . . . Did he not live to become a secretary of state and to marry the Countess Dowager of Warwick! (It will be remembered that Augustus proposed to make Virgil his private secretary.)

And it is well to remember what, philologically, the transmutation of good English "tombstones" into two overused Latinisms really signifies. It is the usual practice of the English language to employ for all raw materials Nordic-derived words: "sheep"=*"Schaf"*; "ox"= *"Ochs"*; "swine"=*"Schwein."* For the same words when the raw material has been transmuted by the culinary art we go to the Mediterranean languages. Thus "mutton"=*"mouton"*; "beef"=*"boeuf"*; "pork"=*"porc."* This shows that the Normans and Angevins knew how to cook. The Anglo-Saxons did not . . . a state of things that till this day subsists to such an extent that as soon as what appears on your table is something above roughage you have to write your menus in French. Or the merely mechanically converted raw material may remain Nordic. But as soon as an art is applied to it it becomes French. Thus: "wool"=*"Woll"*; "cloth"=*"Kleid"*; but "drapery" =*"drap."* In "tombstone" (as you might say, in death) the opposing forces in our hybrid tongue are united. They lie together, raw material *"Stein"* being united to the product of the "necrologist's art"—*"Tombe,"* *"Tombeau."* . . . And, indeed, what better instance could you have to show that the tendency still continues than that Helleno-American "necrologist," the substitution for the good Anglo-Saxon "undertaker." We go, indeed, almost further today. Thus, two Latin-derived words become Greek at the hands of practitioners wishing to make their art seem more dignified, "moving pictures" becoming "cinema" (Greek, *"Kinêin"*). But once more, at the hands of a populace who prefer Latin to Greek derivations, the Greek word becomes "the pictures," *tout court* . . . or still more often in good American "the movies." Similarly, in our more refined and sanitary age, old grave- and church-yards remove themselves from contact with life and become "cemeteries"="*cimétières.*" So Addison, standing amongst the products of the lapidary art, merely anticipates our own age, exhibiting the refinement that was material in procuring him the positions of secretary of state and the rest. He translates his Anglo-French joint words into something more remote and composed. A "tombstone" is a disagreeable reminder; a "register of existence" could not unpleasantly stir the bosom of a Sophia, a Narcissa or an Olivia.

These discourses on language may appear too technical for a work of this light timber (*timbre*), but they are necessary for the comprehension of what has happened to our own literary language as well today as two centuries ago. The eighteenth century retired from life that was coarse into a remoter region where individuals always became types and language more and more rarefied itself.

Thus, Milton, when he condescended to walk in an English meadow, must write

> To where the cock with lively din
> Scatters the rear of darkness thin
> And to the stack or the barn door . . .

His cock must be *the* cock and so dignify itself so as to be no common rooster; and a haystack must also become a type—as if they both were Jove's. Any farmer of his or our day would write "to where *a* cock with lively din" and "to *a* stack" or "to the nearest stack in the yard." (Any Frenchman: "Un coq chanta!") Similarly, our great-grandfathers, being more eighteenth century, falling ill at an inn would say: "Fetch *the* physician." But our gentle, but a little more modern, mothers would ask you to send for a doctor. Rats (*Rats*) are more majestic than mice (*Maeuse*). But "rodent tribe," as being less specific, is more refined still.

We arrive, then, at Johnson, the most tragic of all our major literary figures, a great writer whose still living writings are always ignored, a great honest man who will remain forever a figure of half fun because of the leechlike adoration of the greatest and most ridiculous of all biographers. For it is impossible not to believe that, without Boswell, Johnson for us today would shine like a sun in the heavens whilst Addison sat forgotten in coffee houses.

This was a man who loved truth and the expression of the truth with a passion that when he spoke resembled epilepsy and when he meditated was an agony. It does not need Boswell to tell us that; the fact shines in every word he wrote, coming up through his Latinisms as swans emerge, slightly draped with weeds, from beneath the surface of a duck pond. His very intolerances are merely rougher truths; they render him the more human—and the more humane. Think of an impassioned Tory who could write thus of a regicide:

"We are told that the benefit exchanged" [Davenant is alleged to have saved Milton's life at the Restoration in exchange for Milton's having got him pardoned by Cromwell] "was life for life. But it seems not certain that Milton's life was ever in danger. Goodwin, who had committed the same crime, escaped with incapacitation" [permanent exclusion from any public office] "and as exclusion from public trust is a punishment which the power of government can commonly inflict without the help of a particular law, it required no great interest to exempt Milton from a censure little more than verbal. Something may be reasonably ascribed to veneration and compassion; to veneration of his abilities, and compassion for his distresses, which made it fit to forgive his malice for his learning. He was now poor and blind; and who would pursue with violence an illustrious enemy, depressed by fortune, and disarmed by nature?"

Those would seem to be words very touching to write of a man whom, taking life and truth as seriously as Johnson took them, one hates with a personal hatred as deep as personal hatreds can go.

But for Boswell, there is little doubt that some of the monuments that Johnson left behind him might well today seem enduring. His *Lives of the Poets* is, indeed, a mountain of good reading; his vast common sense outweighs with its pronouncements any harm his more prejudicial moods and wrong-headednesses may in their day have caused. His *Life of Drake* is a compilation of the greatest picturesqueness and lingual vigor; his *Preface to Shakespeare*, an invaluable corrective to most writings about that poet.

His mode of writing was, till towards the end of his life, fantastic and wrong-headed. A really good style, in whatever language, must be founded on the vernacular; the nearer it can come to the common speech of the day without having a shocking, comic or gross effect, the better the style will be. Grossness, indeed, is preferable to overdelicacy for the writer who wishes his work to go down to posterity. For tomorrow very often accepts words and phrases that the writer's own day will shudder over as being vulgar neologisms. (In writing more-or-less technical matter like this present book, a certain number of technical foreign-derived words are necessary for the sake of clearness. "Neologisms" is in itself a not very attractive word, but technical words applying to the arts are, so to speak, in the English language so that one must use what one can find . . . and neither "new words" nor "new phrases" will give quite the effect.)

Occasionally, in fact, in English, actual foreign words must be used because they apply to nuances of method that are absolutely foreign to the Nordic spirit and no autochthonous word or combination of words will supply their sense. Thus, the practice of making a dispassionate exposé (which is not the same thing as an "exposure") of any subject or combination of circumstances is so antipathetic to the Nordic—the Anglo-Saxon plus German—frame of mind. Consequently, outside the law courts, no word or combination of words can be found to express that idea. The only word that one can use for it is the French expression *"constatation."* A "constatation" is an absolutely impartial, passionless and all-inclusive summing up. It is what a judge's charge to the jury should be.

Some such word is urgently needed in our language. That is proved by the number of times the attempt to supply it has been made in American. People really so often need constatations to guide them in their lives that "lay out," "low down" and "show down" have occurred as of necessity. None of them is likely to be permanent, for none of them is very expressive.

The practice of Johnson according to his own showing was to set down a rough draft of what he was writing—or merely to think it out for a sentence or two. Then he turned over in his mind all the Latin words into which the sentence could be formed. Finally, he made up Latin-derived English words to convey his sense. This practice of thinking in one's own language, translating into a foreign language, and then re-translating into one's own vernacular is not without its advantages and has been followed by a number of writers, notably, as we shall see, Gibbon, with great success. Joseph Conrad—as, indeed, is the case with the present writer—habitually thought in French and translated his French into English. This helped him enormously—as it has done the present writer. We, thus, acquired a larger vocabulary than is common to the Anglo-Saxon. In making a translation from any French word, phrase, or idiom, the mind must cast about through a number of words before it will find one exactly expressing the meaning that one desires to express and exactly suited to the mood or mode of the passage to be written. Supposing that you wish to express the idea that a certain person is exclusive. You think: *"M. UnTel n'admettait guère tout le monde dans son chez soi."* Literally rendered, this would mean "Mr. So-and-So did not admit easily (or scarcely admitted) just anyone to his home." But *"chez soi,"* though it means "at home," means also something like "inner thoughts." And the French, being a café-haunting people, so rarely invite people to their homes that the chances are that that idiom will most usually signify "inner thoughts." But "inner thoughts" has another French idiom for its expression in *"for intérieur."* The problem then begins. There are all sorts of nuances—fine shades—that can go to making this translation; so you may be a long time trying and rejecting words or phrases before settling upon one that is exactly right. When the statement is general, as in this case, you might very well render the sense by saying that M. UnTel "was exclusive." But supposing you wish to express

the particular: *"M. UnTel n'admettait pas X dans son chez soi"?*
This is more difficult. You might say that UnTel "did not tolerate the
society of X." That, however, is too strong, because it would mean
that he avoided M. X altogether. In that case one would have thought
in French: *"évitait."* Nor does our French text mean that M. UnTel
gave X the cold shoulder. Literally rendered, it might mean that he
did not "allow X to be one of his closest friends"—or again "did not
admit him to his close friendship." Or to use slang you might say that
he "did not tell him his middle name!" So one might go on for hours.
Indeed, Conrad and this writer did so go on for hours when wishing
to indicate, in the book called *Romance*, that one of the characters in
Havana gaol did not admit another of the characters "to his intimacy."
And the phrase "admit to his intimacy" being slightly stilted, exactly
expressed the attitude of one proud Spanish scoundrel covered with
rags and lice towards another. Had they been English characters we
should probably have used "close friendship." The word "intimacy"
implies "inner" or even "secret" thoughts and English characters in
the opinion of Conrad, and, indeed, of this present writer, hardly ever
exchange thoughts except those of the greatest simplicity. . . . And,
since we spent ten years in this pursuit—*à la récherche du mot juste*—
it is obvious that we must have gone through an enormous number
of words with, as has been said, the greatest possible advantage at
once to our vocabularies and to our moods and modes of expression.
The real greatness of the prose style of the seventeenth century was
due to the fact that all writers, and, indeed, all at-all-learned men from
the day of Archbishop Warham till that of the death of Dryden, knew
a prodigious number of languages. Almost every one of them knew
Hebrew and Greek so as to read the Bible in the original; a great
many, Spanish, so as to read the picaresque novels in Spanish; every
one, without exception, knew, wrote and in many instances thought,
in Latin. Italian was in common use, even in commercial circles, because the chief trade of London was with the Italian ports. French was
part of the necessary equipment of every wit. Such an array of languages, if properly used, can only be of advantage to the writer. The
introduction of foreign words or turns of phrase can hardly but be
of advantage. The difficulties of the exact expression of thought between

man and man are extremely great even when it is a matter of the simplest affairs; so the more tools one has at one's disposal, the easier the task becomes. Say one of your friends has an excellent—a really excellent—male cook. How much more convenient it is to say that your friend has a chef, or, if the cook is female, a *cordonbleu*. Or where should we be in the summer if someone had not Anglicized the French words "excursion" and "tour"?

The snag comes when, wishing to express the simplest matters or the commonest domestic scenes, a Spenser, a Dryden or a Johnson elevates into a mannerism the employment of pompous Roman substantives and links them invariably with resonant Latin adjectives. These they either manufacture from Latin or borrow from one another and over-use. *The Lives of the Poets,* however, is expressed in a language for Johnson of remarkable terseness and one relatively easy, clear, and explicit . . . and remarkable for common sense! What passage could be clearer, more terse, and more exactly to our purpose when we are wondering how Pope found such success in the reign of William III, than Johnson's comment regarding Addison:

> Soon after [in 1695] he wrote a poem to King William, with a rhyming introduction addressed to Lord Somers. King William had no regard to elegance or literature; his study was only war; yet by a choice of ministers, whose disposition was very different from his own, he procured, without intention, a very liberal patronage to poetry. Addison was caressed both by Somers and Montague.

Or how could you more expeditiously dispose of a misfortune that much affected the career of Thomson than in the following words:

> "Spring" was published next year [June 1728] with a dedication to the Countess of Hertford, whose practice it was to invite every summer some poet into the country, to hear her verses and assist her studies. This honour was one summer conferred on Thomson, who took more delight in carousing with Lord Hert-

ford and his friends than in assisting her Ladyship's poetical operations, and therefore never received another summons.

What a singular change there is here from the style of the younger Johnson who wrote *Rasselas*. Consider:

> I have been for some time unsettled and distracted: my mind is disturbed with a thousand perplexities of doubt, and vanities of imagination, which hourly prevail upon me, because I have no opportunities of relaxation or diversion. I am sometimes ashamed to think that I could not secure myself from vice, but by retiring from the exercise of virtue, and begin to suspect that I was rather impelled by resentment, than led by devotion, into solitude. My fancy riots in scenes of folly, and I lament that I have lost so much and have gained so little.

The secret of this great change is a simple one. For ten years after receiving his pension Johnson led a life of complete literary idleness and passed his time almost solely in conversation. He made of conversation a fine art for its vigor, its terseness, its clarity, the brilliance of its similes, its humanity, its intolerance, its knowledge of the fates of man, its humaneness. So, when refreshed and strengthened, he was approached, in 1777, by the London booksellers and others to write short prefaces to a complete collection of the English poets from Cowley onwards, he had perfected a style in the best of all schools. The province and duty of all writers of the imagination is the expression of facts or thoughts with all the exactitude open to them. For them the proper study of the language they shall employ will be found only secondarily in books and first and last in the vernacular of their day. This will be the language and the vocabulary of a society made up of reasonably communicative and, if possible, reasonably thoughtful individuals.

For such a writer there is nothing objectionable in the use of slang words that are not too ugly or merely foolish. But, if that writer's works are to remain alive merely even for the term of his days, he must be careful only to employ slang words that will also endure. The choice of them is difficult, but it is almost imperative, for as words grow old and prove distasteful their place must be filled with neologisms; otherwise the language will decay. Thus, Johnson declared that a villain who would employ the then new word "commence" would cut a throat. He would have done better to use it himself for since he was too majestic to "employ" willingly the word "begin" he had to fall back much too often on the worn-out Latinism "initiate."

But ten years' rest and the getting into his head of a conversational rhythm and a vocabulary comprehensible to most of the cultivated men of his day had on Johnson the effect of evolving a style that was at once sufficiently learned to save his face and sufficiently actual to let us read his *Lives of the Poets* with pleasure even in these anti-Latinistic days. It is a work that, had there been no Boswell, must have been a resounding monument to this great man. As it is, it stands almost forgotten like an Aztec temple lost in South American undergrowths. It is a great pity.

CHAPTER EIGHT

THERE remain to us two writers with whom we must deal before quitting the shades of the eighteenth century in England for the full glare of the world movement called "romantic." These are Gibbon and Goldsmith, the first having been born in 1727 and dying in 1794, and the second in 1728 and 1774, respectively.

This is, of course, to dismiss rather summarily a century in which small writers and poetasters were as plentiful as trout spawn in a hatchery. But we have arrived at a stage when both by reason of the necessities of space and consideration of the reader's brain we can only afford to deal with writers sufficient to characterize the shifting ages of international literature. And if the reader desires to deepen his knowledge of eighteenth century literature, to find the poets and poetasters he has only to read Johnson's *Lives of the Poets* and then as much of their verse as his taste and appetite will permit. This is not to say that there are not agreeable passages in Thomson, Gray, Pryor, Cowper and the rest, but merely that in a work in which we are forced to omit so many really considerable writers of all countries, to consider them here with any attention would surely be otiose. They were of that time, they wrote in the conventional language of their time; some of them had once lived in green fields, some had merely known the dripping arches of the Savoy and the garrets of Grub Street. Some had patrons and lived in comfort; some had no patrons and died in the gaol; some had patrons and died nevertheless in those same spunging houses. And so we may leave them.

But Goldsmith and Gibbon illustrate two phases of English literature and the English mind whose consideration it would be impossible for us to omit. Gibbon shows the English mind at its most incisive and most intolerant of confused thought and half truths, and English classic diction at its most illustrious and most shining. Goldsmith exhibits in his literary personality all those characteristics that for a century or so were to render English literature and the English mind almost incomparably trifling, materialistic and confused. It is, indeed, true that he wrote like an eighteenth century cherub, and no doubt he really talked like a Queen Anne parrot. He was, unconscionably, a literary hack. His best work probably was his *Natural History* though equally probably he never saw a bird in freedom to notice it. When he had a little money he bought a scarlet velvet coat trimmed with gold lace; when he had none he starved naked and wigless in a garret. *The Vicar of Wakefield* is a masterpiece, always with a tear of benevolence in one corner of its eye that would disgrace any other nation or any other time. In spite of the fact that he covered half Europe, supporting himself by playing on the flute, *The Vicar of Wakefield* is as far from displaying any knowledge of near-modern life as is, more warrantably, *Robinson Crusoe*. In place of displaying any sense whatever of invention, its plot is a rehash of the plots of every novelist who had preceded him, and the Vicar himself, the narrator of the story, is an impossible monster. He displays at once an eminently deleterious reliance on the material efficacy of prayer and a sheer materialism that is really horrifying. Is there *anywhere* to be found a more horrifying passage in the mouth of a minister of the Christian religion than this that follows?

> During this anxious interval I had full time to look round me. Everything was grand and of happy contrivance; the paintings, the furniture, the gildings, petrified me with awe, and raised my idea of the owner. Ah, thought I to myself, how very great must the possessor of all these things be, who carries in his head the business of the state, and whose house displays half the wealth of a kingdom; *sure his genius must be unfathomable!* During these awful reflections, I heard a step come heavily forward. Ah, this is the great man himself! No, it was only a chambermaid. Another foot was heard soon after. This must be he! No, it was only the great man's valet de chambre. At last his lordship actually made his appearance . . .

It is unnecessary to say that his lordship becomes the god out of the machine of this story, rescues the vicar and all his sobbing family from the debtor's prison, confounds, Apollo-like, the unspeakable villain who is no less a person than his nephew, marries one of the daughters of the vicar and showers "settlements" on everyone in sight.

This may be called breaking an innocent and personally vain butterfly on a wheel, but the passage so extraordinarily prophesies everything that has since stultified the Anglo-Saxon cosmogony that not to pillory it would be to fail in one's duty. You have here everything that rendered odious Victorianism and our own age—the implicit and unshakable belief that gilding, furnishing and material resources are the reward of the Christian virtues; that troops of servants are the hallmark of genius, and that though when you see God you die, if you can fall at the feet of a Lord—or a hero of industry—you will, if he raises you to your feet, find yourself an inmate of the home of the Christian saints here on earth. It is a point of view that must make the angels weep. . . .

It is distasteful to the present writer to belabor any of his fellow writers, living or dead, and, except Boccaccio, who also stood for a detestable human trait, he has here avoided doing so. But, indeed, it is much more the detestability of certain sides of humanity than the writers themselves that is here belabored. Goldsmith in apotheosizing material good fortune and Boccaccio in recording grossnesses of a hedge alehouse kind were merely supplying the demands of their readers and it is rather their readers that should be damned than they —for you can hardly much condemn a poor fellow who commits crime in order to put a bit of bread in his belly or a scarlet velvet coat on his back. That was the case of Goldsmith. Otherwise he was an agreeable-enough vain fellow, but there must have been something more to him than mere agreeableness and vanity or he never would have been allowed to be a member of the awful club whose other ornaments were Johnson, Gibbon, and Burke, not to mention Garrick. You had there the late eighteenth century in its quintessence.

His *She Stoops to Conquer* still forms an agreeable night's entertainment for the simple and the childlike who are rather below a man's estate. But our history here takes leave of the drama which with

Congreve and Wycherly and the rest finally abandoned the literary art as part of their resources and attractions. We might, however, make the note that in the *Lives of the Poets* Johnson records that Cowley, having a play to write for the scholars of Magdalen and being in a great hurry to leave Oxford, gave them merely a rough draft of the acts, scenes, and of the story, and left them to supply the speeches and action themselves. This is interesting as showing that the practice, if not the actual example, of the Italian *Commédia dell' Arte* was followed in England of that date.

In Gibbon we come upon a figure very different in timber from any of the other eighteenth century littérateurs, save only Richardson —and Johnson, if you can persuade yourself to think of him as a writer and not merely as a dancing bear, growling numbers in and out. And in his *Decline and Fall of the Roman Empire* we have the one English prose work that, for its literary quality, can be named beside the great Clarendon's *History of the Revolution*, in the tale of huge and unflagging monuments of prose.

The *Decline and Fall* lacks the picturesqueness of Clarendon who really was a novelist *avant la lettre*. On the other hand, the *tempo*—the speed of the prose—of Gibbon is more calculated to let the reader travel without flagging over the immense period of time and the great territory covered by the *Decline*. We may well doubt if any other type of style would have achieved that tremendous *tour de force*. It is not merely that Gibbon's enormous industry carried him through these tracts of space, time and written pages; it is that his enthusiasm continued till the last word was written. The description of the Siege of Constantinople is as strongly maintained in the pulse of its writing as the first paragraph, and, the matter described being more lively, the words become more staccato. The fact is that the writing of Gibbon was an instrument suited for a great number of moods. Its personality, if one may use the word, remains always the personality of Gibbon; its mood changes as its owner looks at objects or scenes differing in nature or character. Let us first consider a scene from the year 1453:

Of the triangle which composes the figure of Constantinople, the two sides along the sea were made inaccessible to an enemy; the Propontis by nature, and the harbour by art. Between the two waters, the basis of the triangle, the land side was protected by a double wall and a deep ditch of the depth of 100 feet. Against this line of fortification, which Phranza, an eyewitness, prolongs to the measure of six miles, the Ottomans directed their principal attack; and the emperor, after distributing the service and command of the most perilous stations, undertook the defence of the external wall. In the first days of the siege the Greek soldiers descended into the ditch, or sallied into the field; but they soon discovered that, in the proportion of their numbers, one Christian was of more value than 20 Turks; and, after these bold preludes, they were prudently content to maintain the rampart with their missile weapons. A circumstance that distinguishes the siege of Constantinople is the re-union of the ancient and modern artillery. The cannon were intermingled with the mechanical engines for casting stones and darts; the bullet and the battering-ram were directed against the same walls; nor had the discovery of gunpowder superseded the use of the liquid and unextinguishable fire. By these arts of attack the tower of St. Romanus was at length overturned: after a severe struggle the Turks were repulsed from the breach and interrupted by darkness: but during the night each moment was improved by the activity of the emperor and Justiniani; and at the dawn of day the impatient sultan perceived, with astonishment and grief, that the ditch was cleared and restored, and the tower of St. Romanus was again strong and entire.

This writing is about as vivid as the historian on an immense scale can allow himself. He cannot use the brush as can Clarendon in his account of the murder of Buckingham not so much because, if he did, the work must become large enough to fill the Library of the British Museum and take twelve lives in the writing, but because the mind of the reader will tire at the rendering of so many emotional scenes. He must, therefore, achieve a sort of impressionism. Surely in this passage the reader sees, as much as he need, a wide landscape, city walls, engines of war at work, thousands of men rushing to the assault or the attack of redans and redoubts. If he does, then this must stand for him as the highest magic that can be achieved by style. For just as was the case with Conrad, the ambition of Gibbon was, above all, to make you see.

Let us then consider the very first paragraph of this incredible book:

In the second century of the Christian Era, the empire of Rome comprehended the fairest part of the earth, and the most civilized portion of mankind. The frontiers of that extensive monarchy were guarded by ancient renown and disciplined valor. The gentle but powerful influence of laws and manners had gradually cemented the union of the provinces. Their peaceful inhabitants enjoyed and abused the advantages of wealth and luxury. The image of a free constitution was preserved with decent reverence: the Roman senate appeared to possess the sovereign authority, and devolved on the emperors all the executive powers of government. During a happy period of more than fourscore years, the public administration was conducted by the virtue and abilities of Nerva, Trajan, Hadrian, and the two Antonines. It is the design of this, and of the two succeeding chapters, to describe the prosperous condition of their empire; and afterwards, from the death of Marcus Antonius, to deduce the most important circumstances of its decline and fall; a revolution which will ever be remembered, and is still felt by the nations of the earth.

Here obviously is the same style, the same cadence, the same mode as that which is shown in the paragraph about the most momentous siege that ever shook the world. The convolutions of the brain of no other writer could have produced the two passages. But the mood is different. One imagines Gibbon writing about the siege if not with a certain jauntiness then at least with confidence. He was aware that his glory was assured; half the world had applauded, as half the world censured—that is the exact word for the eighteenth century—what he had already done. He had only to keep up with his accustomed level and he would stand forever between—and a little before—Tacitus and Livy.

But when he wrote: "In the second century of the Christian Era, the Empire of Rome comprehended the fairest part of the earth," he was setting out on a voyage almost comparable in its results to that of the first voyage of Columbus—and lasting how much longer, and how much more solitary! A certain awe must have oppressed him as it oppresses us when we see the last rope that still unites us to land fall into the water at the dock-side in a sea departure. It is that awe that reflects itself in his words in spite of even his self-confidence.

Otherwise, Gibbon's style is almost perfection for its purpose. It has, of course, its strong savor of Latinity and many of its paragraphs might have been written by Cicero. But, for writing calling for extreme clearness in technical matter, conversational English is too vague, owing probably to the constitutional dislike that an Englishman has for giving himself away by making any direct statement. It has, indeed, been said that it is impossible to make a direct statement in English—that is to say that any direct statement in English is so shocking that it cannot be made. Thus, the Briton will never say that he is ill, he will say that he is under the weather or not up to the mark. So, the difference between Gibbon at his best and Dryden or Johnson at their worst is that the Latinisms and the linked substantives and adjectives of Dryden and Johnson and Pope were already stale in the day when they used them, whereas Gibbon, by virtue probably of his great vigor of mind, contrived somehow a prose of great vivacity. And the real difference is probably that Gibbon, though he actually went for a short time to a university, was disgusted by the curriculum and was very soon ejected for becoming a papist. So that, like Pope, being too sickly to receive an ordinary education, what instruction he did receive he got at the hands of a curate called John Kirby. And for the rest he was an insatiable reader of everything that came under his hands. Besides the *Decline and Fall*, he left behind him his *Autobiography*, which is almost as valuable a monument of prose, and from that we may learn that by the age of eleven he was "well acquainted with Pope's *Homer* and the *Arabian Nights' Entertainments*," and shortly afterwards he read Dryden's *Virgil*. "But," he states—and it is a tribute to his child's taste, "I know not how, some fault in the author, the translator, or the reader, the pious Aeneas did not so forcibly seize on my imagination; and I derived more pleasure from Ovid's *Metamorphoses*." He passed two years, 1749-50, at Westminster school, but "the violence and variety of my complaints" excused his frequent absence from the school. "A strange nervous affection alternately contracted my legs, and produced, without any visible symptoms, the most excruciating pain. . . ." Thus at school he learned neither Latin nor Greek but later he read some odes of Horace and a little Virgil under the surveillance of a clergyman at Bath. He was sent to Magdalen actually before he was fifteen; there he passed his time in what he calls desultory reading. Thus he read two universal histories one after the other, and translations of Herodotus, Xenophon, Tacitus, and Procopius. And then, says he: "From the ancient I leaped to the modern world: many crude lumps of Speed, Rapin, Mezeray, Davila, Machiavel, Father Paul, Bower, etc., I devoured like so many novels; and I swallowed with the same voracious appetite the descriptions of India and China, of Mexico and Peru." In the summer of 1751 he came across a book called *The Continuation of Echard's Roman History*, and soon after Howell's *History of the World*. They are both of them rather dismal works, but they were sufficient to inspire Gibbon at the age of fourteen with the ambition to become the historian of the world. "Mohammet and his Saracens," says he, "soon fixed my attention and some instinct of criticism directed me to the genuine sources." Before he was sixteen he had read all that was to be had in English about the Arabs, the Persians, the Tartars and the Turks and, says he: "I arrived at Oxford with a stock of erudition that might have puzzled a doctor and a degree of ignorance of which a schoolboy would have been ashamed." He had resisted with the utmost obstinacy learning Latin and Greek, because he considered those studies would be a waste of time when he could read all those authors in English. All this before he went to Magdalen. Then: "To the university of Oxford I acknowledge no obligation; and she will as cheerfully renounce me for a son, as I am willing to disclaim her for a mother. I spent fourteen months at Magdalen College; they proved the fourteen months the most idle and unprofitable of my whole life: the reader will pronounce between the school and the scholar, but I cannot affect to believe that nature had disqualified me for all literary pursuits." There, then, follows a great number of pages in which he declares that universities since their beginnings have proved the ruin of learning and the arts—an assertion with which we are not minded to disagree. Eventually: "The university forgot to instruct, I forgot to return . . . and at the age of sixteen I bewildered myself in the errors of the Church of Rome."

That is a subject to which we may return; for the moment let us make the note that he owed his conversion to two books of Bossuet—*The Exposition of the Catholic Doctrine,* and *The History of the Protestant Variations,* and owing to this conversion his father "threatened to banish, and disown and disinherit" him. He was sent, eventually, to Switzerland and installed in the house of a Calvinist minister called Pavillard. Here he was extremely unhappy because he had no knowledge of French and because: "I had now exchanged my elegant apartment in Magdalen College, for a narrow, gloomy street, the most unfrequented of an unhandsome town, for an old inconvenient house, and for a small chamber ill contrived and ill furnished, which on the approach of winter, instead of a companionable fire, must be warmed by the dull invisible heat of a stove. From a man I was again degraded to the dependence of a schoolboy."

The first result of his exile was that he learned French sufficiently well, as was the case with other authors we have mentioned, to think in French. "My pronunciation was formed by the constant repetition of the same sounds; the variety of words and idioms, the rules of grammar, and distinctions of genders, were impressed in my memory: ease and freedom were obtained by practice; correctness and elegance by labour; and before I was recalled home, French, in which I spontaneously thought, was more familiar than English to my ear, my tongue, and my pen." It would be supererogatory to labor the moral of that quotation, but the following passage as to the stylistic exercises to which he put himself will seem at least remarkable.

"In my French and Latin translations I adopted an excellent method, which, from my own success, I would recommend to the imitation of students. I chose some classic writer, such as Cicero and Vertot, the most approved for purity and elegance of style.

I translated, for instance, an epistle of Cicero into French; and, after throwing it aside till the words and phrases were obliterated from my memory, I re-translated my French into such Latin as I could find; and then compared each sentence of my imperfect version with the ease, the grace, the propriety of the Roman orator."

By the age of nineteen he had read Cicero's *Ad Familiares,* his *Brutus, The Orations, De Amicitia,* and *De Senectute*; Terence, he says, twice, and the *Epistles* of Pliny; in French, histories of Switzerland and Naples and Bannier's *Mythologies.* Above all, he says that to De Crousaz' *Logic* he owed it that he not only understood the principles of that science but formed his mind to a habit of thinking and reasoning he had never had before. In the last twenty-seven months of his stay in Lausanne, between January 1756 and April 1758, he nearly accomplished in French the reviewing of the entire body of Latin literature available at that date and he also read, and meditated on, Locke's *Human Understanding.* He also began the study of Greek, reading for himself with the aid of a dictionary half the *Iliad* and large portions of Xenophon and Herodotus—and fell in love with Mademoiselle Suzanne Courchod whose "personal attractions were embellished by the virtues and talents of her mind." But, alas, on his return to England his father would not hear of "this strange alliance," and without his consent he had no money on which to marry. And, says he, "after a painful struggle I yielded to my fate; I sighed as a lover, I obeyed as a son; my wound was insensibly healed by time, absence, and the habits of a new life." We may add that Mademoiselle Courchod, though thus losing one of the greatest men in the world, solaced herself by marrying another, becoming the wife of Necker. On his return to England he states that he had ceased to be an Englishman and he adds later that in England he was never less alone than when by himself. He, nevertheless, delighted in going to the races and, "the interruption in my studies was compensated in some degree by the spectacle of English manners and the acquisition of some practical knowledge." In spite of that he could not forget the joy with which he exchanged a bank note of twenty pounds for the twenty volumes of the *Memoires de l'Académie des Inscriptions.* We may here abandon the history of Gibbon's education, which continued indeed to the end of his life. He was about to begin his writing, his first work being the *Essay on the Study of Literature*, which he wrote with the intention of reforming France where, as he oplied, ruin was setting in because the language of Greece and Rome were neglected by a philosophic age—provoked to it by D'Alembert's *Discours Préliminaire à l'Encyclopédie*, which boldly stated that the sole merit of the classics was that they exercised the memory, and that their function in a civilized world had been superseded by the nobler faculties of imagination and judgment. This essay he finished when he was twenty-two and it may well be considered a remarkable beginning. Of it he says himself:

> Whatever may be my present reputation, it no longer rests on the merit of this first essay; and at the end of twenty-eight years I may appreciate my juvenile work with the impartiality, and almost with the indifference, of a stranger. In his answer to Lady Hervey, the Count de Caylus admires, or affects to admire, "les livres sans nombre que Mr. Gibbon a lus et très bien lus." But, alas! my stock of erudition at that time was scanty and superficial; and if I allow myself the liberty of naming the Greek masters, my genuine and personal acquaintance was confined to the Latin classics. The most serious defect of my *Essay* is a kind of obscurity and abruptness, which always fatigues, and may often elude, the attention of the reader. Instead of a precise and proper definition of the title itself, the sense of the word *Littérature* is loosely and variously applied: a number of remarks and examples, historical, critical, philosophical, are heaped on each other without method or connection; and, if we except some introductory pages, all the remaining chapters might indifferently be reversed or transposed. The obscurity of many passages is often affected, *brevis esse laboro, obscurus fio*; the desire of expressing perhaps a common idea with sententious and oracular brevity: alas! how fatal has been the imitation of Montesquieu!

In *The Decline and Fall* Gibbon makes the first and the most brilliant of all attacks on the Christian faith and the reverberations of that attack have scarcely yet died out. It is obviously not our province to comment upon this side of the work; we need merely remark that the incidence of the attack was rather against the corruptions and absurdities that crept into the creed and practice of Christianity, even before Constantine elevated the Church to power and riches . . . rather than an attack on the doctrine of the Christian revealed religion. Gibbon himself thus describes the spirit in which he approached this part of his task:

> The theologian may indulge the pleasing task of describing religion as she descends from heaven, arrayed in native purity; a more melancholy duty is imposed upon the historian:—he must discover the inevitable mixture of error and corruption which she contracted in a long residence upon earth among a weak and degenerate race of beings.*

But, such was the activity of his mind and his scorn for self-deception —or his sense of humor—that when he came to deal with that "corruption" he certainly abandoned the possibly mournful attitude of the dispassionate historian to become—and matchlessly—the ironic iconoclast. So that, from the reading of *The Decline and Fall* one comes away with the impression that Gibbon must have begun the book with the main intention of writing the chapters—beginning with fifteen— in which he exposes the beginnings of Christianity and from that drew the lesson that inspires all the rest of his enormous task: the lesson that the softness engendered by the doctrine of the Nazarene brought about the ruin of Imperial Rome. It is a doctrine with which, without being a devotee, one may disagree, common sense leading one rather to think that it was the sheer economic difficulty of administering an

---

* Controversial writings against Gibbon's attack on Christianity have been innumerable and the reader should be warned against the very many editions of Gibbon in which unscrupulous editors—Dr. William Smith, the editor of the once almost universally used classical dictionary, is amongst the worst of them—have issued editions of Gibbon from which they have not merely excised Gibbon's most telling passages but into which they have actually inserted their own apologetics. The fairest apology for Christianity as against Gibbon known to this writer is that of Dean Milman in his preface to the 1856 edition of *The Decline and Fall*. It is well worth perusal by the reader of Gibbon today.

empire so vast without means of rapid communication that finally brought down that civilization. Nevertheless—in the impossibility of here finding space to give a final estimate of this amazing writer—we must with reluctance leave him. But one might hazard the dictum that unless a man has read Gibbon he scarcely merits the name of an Englishman, an Anglo-Saxon, or even of a man at all.

It will be useful before leaving the consideration of the literature of the eighteenth century to make the note that Gibbon stood by no means alone in his day in his attack on Christian revealed religion. The only other instance of this agnostic-to-investigatory spirit that we have here been able to write about has been Pope's "Essay on Man." But Pope's "Essay" exists just because of the multiplicity of these attacks of which his poem is merely a sort of summing up. D'Alembert's phrase that we have quoted to the effect that classical studies had been superseded by the nobler faculties of imagination and judgment implied the sweeping away of Christianity by that judgment quite as much as that "imagination" would eliminate the classics.

Of this the insurgence of the cloud of, mostly German, late eighteenth century philosophers is merely another manifestation. Beginning with the gentle Leibnitz, who died in·1716, with his theory of innate ideas and pronouncement to the effect that "Sensation is a thought in process of becoming" and going on to the champion of liberal democracy, Fichte (1762-1814), who inspired the socialism of Lassalle; to Kant (1770-1804) reputed, with his transcendentalism, to be the greatest of all human thinkers; to Hegel (1770-1831) the prophet of the philosophic absolute, whose work inspired to socialism not merely Lassalle but also Karl Marx, we arrive at Schopenhauer, who has the extraphilosophic merit of being almost the only German, except perhaps Heine and Schnitzler, to write a prose really readable to non-Germans. Philosophically, he shines as one who widened Kant's transcendentalism till it included his own theory of the will to live, but for us he may be regarded as the author of *Parerga und Paralipomena*, as it were a commonplace book which includes a number of consciously exaggerated and very humorous expressions of the philosopher's dislikes.

Thus, we have *Ueber Laerm und Geraeusch* in which he denounces, with enormous professorial invectives, the carters whose whip crackings disturbed his meditations. Similarly in *Ueber die Weiber*, under the guise of denouncing all women whom he stigmatizes as the small-shouldered, broad-hipped race, he was really avenging himself on his mother for the fact that she was an enormously popular—a best-seller—novelist of the most frivolous and chattering description. He was the completely unknown philosopher, dining solitarily at a *table d'hôte* and putting down on the tablecloth and subsequently devoting to charity, a gold piece, every time that any of the army officers who sat at the same table talked of any other subject than women or horses or the like. In any case *Parerga und Paralipomena* was one of the delights of this writer's childhood and might well prove that of any other reader at any age. Indeed, one might hazard the other dictum that it is a duty to learn the German language sufficiently to be able to read Heine and Schopenhauer in the original. They both lose a great deal in translation.

But our concern here can be with none of these philosophers, any more than with the Anglo-Saxons, Bacon, Hobbes, Locke or Emerson or William James, or, indeed, any more than with the Frenchman, Descartes, the most beloved as he was the first of scientist-philosophers. It is interesting to observe the struggle that went on in Descartes between Christianity and reason, because that is, for the moment, our main line topic. But if we say that he is the basis of all our modern thought, it is almost all that we can find space to say of him. He is allied to the great Greeks in that he was rather an explorer than a dogmatist. His chief work is entitled symbolically *Meditations de Prima Philosophia*; had he been one of his German successors it would have been *De Prima Philosophia, tout court*.

For the difference between the great Greeks and their modern followers is that today we call philosophy "the love of wisdom." The patient Socrates or Aristotle considered philosophy to be the love of the pursuit of learning—or, if you prefer it, wisdom. We have to content ourselves with the small profits of dogmatic conclusions since we are so constituted that we must have quick returns. That, too, is the result of the struggle for freedom that has beset the world ever since impenetrable boredom settled on the court of Louis XIV and his even more bored and boring successors.

Whilst passing through the French eighteenth century we paid very scant attention to one of the most symptomatic—as it was one of the most brilliant—of the precursors of the modern novel. . . . That was the *Princesse de Clèves* of Mme. de Lafayette, a work that unites to the sensibility of Richardson's *Clarissa* the moral scruples in matters of love—for you could not call it passion—of a Henry James, and to them the brilliance of writing and wit of Mme. de Sévigné herself. The correspondence of those two ladies, the former of whom was, as it were, platonically united to, and house-mate of, the famous Marquis de la Rochefoucauld of the *Maxims*, overflows with interest. And, indeed, in this correspondence you here and there glimpse the maxims in the making, as when the Marquis asks Mme. de Lafayette to ask Mme. de Sévigné whether one or other of his maxims about love and jealousy would be truer to wit if it stood as written or if it were reversed. . . . The correspondence, then, of Mmes. de Lafayette and Sévigné makes the extreme hard-uppishness of these brilliant creatures as plain as the *Princesse de Clèves* makes the boredom of the royal court whose sole mental preoccupation was gossip and whose principal occupation, giving grounds for it. Mme. de Sévigné is unable to travel, to build, to give sufficiently lavish charity, or even, at the passionate entreaty of Mme. de Lafayette, to come up to Paris to see a doctor. They lived— but, indeed, the whole world lived—in a state of perpetual crisis, due to the wars, which themselves with their incessant parades and innocuous manoeuvres had become only another sort of boredom qualified by a minimum of discomfort. Nor was religion itself, even when carried, as in the case of Louis and his Maintenon, to the extremes of morose devoteeism, more than another source of boredom now that in France there were no more Protestants, and in England scarcely any Catholics, to murder, whilst, in Germany, Catholics and Lutherans had found some sort of *modus vivendi*.

That universal lack of interest in life in the upper and wealthy classes of Western Europe called almost hysterically for palliatives. It found them in the philosophy of the Germans, the agnostic speculations in England of the contemporaries of Gibbon and Pope and the rationalism and encyclopaedism of France. Searchings after—or dogmatisms about—truth, those manifestations might be for their writers, but for the great body of their readers they were indeed a literature of escape. The court ladies of Louis XV—nine years before the accession of Louis XVI who was to die on the scaffold—disturbed the wig of Diderot in crowding to look over his shoulder at the first sheets of the *Encyclopédie* in 1765; they exclaimed with excited ravishment that here they could see for the first time how things were made and wheels went round. A whole new world of the emotions and the mind seemed to open before them as they looked up the word "rouge" and all the chains of their confessors and spiritual advisers fell from their shoulders when they read that a dryad was the soul of a tree. And actually what they were doing was knocking nails into the fabric of the guillotine that a quarter of a century later was to be erected on the Place de la Concorde. The story of the *Princesse de Clèves*, though written in 1677, was the history of a struggle for freedom from, and a succumbing to, a sense of "honor" that was for all the world a Mediterranean-classical puritanism. The Princesse de Clèves in refusing even after her husband's death to unite herself to her lover, the Duc de Nemours, exactly prophesied the temperament, if not the motives, of Mr. James's Mme. de Cintré in *The American*. And, as someone said, Mme. de Cintré, though she might be a titled Frenchwoman, was nevertheless begotten within a hundred yards of Boston Common, adding wrongly that she was certainly the first Frenchwoman to be actuated by a New England conscience. She wasn't, of course; Mme. de Clèves was.

And those added restrictions to the sentimental life which persisted for at least a century at the French court merely added to the thirst for freedom that inspired the gentle bosoms of the court ladies right up to the very date of Marie Antoinette herself. . . . And do not forget that Franklin and how many of his contemporary compatriots were encyclopaedically minded agnostics, the rest being nonconformists.

And that was really the whole mental trouble with the world at the end of the eighteenth century—it had gone *fin de siècle,* a phrase that will not again have currency for another ninety years, but one that was tremendously current in the last decades of the two centuries next preceding our own. You get as good a description as any of that state of mind in the description by Jean Paul Richter of his character Roquailler "for whom there is no new pleasure and no new truth left, and who has no old one entire and fresh."

Part Two

CHAPTER ONE

I T WAS time for humanity to seek new pleasures, freedoms and truths. The movement came with the bursting on the world of the romantics—a movement that was as tremendously to influence the psychology of the world as the French Revolution itself.

In France, England and Southwestern Europe in general its operation was delayed by the quarter century of warfare attendant on the rise and fall of the French Revolution and Napoleon. But in Germany the indefatigable philosophers pullulated and the romantic novelists founded themselves on their philosophers. So they went on scratching incessantly their pens on paper, though Napoleon marched his legions under their windows and made of the Prussian capital for years a French camp. They minded that as little as did Goethe. The voice of freedom was hardly to be heard till the good Arndt came.

The bridge between the centuries and between dying classicism and newly born romanticism was furnished by the work of the great Jean Paul Richter, who lived till 1825 when Byronism had laid Europe supine at its feet. But he was born in 1763. Thus, his three chief novels, *Hesperus* (1795), *Titan* (1800-3) and *Flegeljahre* (1804-5) were written during the full tumult of revolutionary and Napoleonic days. He is classical in the sense that these novels are assemblages of characters like those of La Bruyère or Theophrastus, arranged sketchily to form a story—much as Richardson turned his letter writer's compendium into *Clarissa.*

But the voice of Richter is that of Rousseau spreading over vast landscapes with pure romanticism always brooding on their horizons. Consider this passage from the one hundred and ninth cycle of Richter's *Titan.* This is the Bay of Naples. *Kennst du,* indeed, *das Land wo die Citronen bluehn?*

A night without equal. The stars alone by themselves illuminated the earth and the Milky Way was silvern. An avenue of poplar trees climbed over and united by the tendrils of the vine led to the opulent city. On all hands we heard voices, some talking close at hand, others singing in the distance. A poor sleeping maiden whom we had taken into our coach heard the melodies even down into her dream, and sang after them; and then, when she waked herself therewith, looked round bewildered and with a sweet smile, with the whole melody and the dream still in her bosom. On a slender two-wheeled carriage, a wagoner, standing on the pole and singing, rolled merrily by. Women were already bearing in the cool of the hour great baskets full of flowers into the city; in the distance, as we passed along, whole paradises of flower-cups sent up their fragrance; and the heart and bosom drank in at once the love-draught of the sweet air.

In German this reads a little less German! And Jean Paul may be regarded as a very considerable poet in prose. He differs from the essential romantic in the almost caricaturing note with which he gets in his characters. There go to their making up at once a sentimentality and a humor that link him, however remotely, with Dickens more than with almost anyone else. And they are innumerable—Siebenkaes, Dr. Katzenberger, Leibgeber, Quintus Fixlein, Wuz, the Flutists, the angelically dying maidens, the Virtuosos, the Altruist whose dominating quality was so strong that "had he, like Christ, been crucified, he would have torn one hand from its nail to shake the hand of the centurion who was standing sentinel over him." Jean Paul himself said that he had created creatures enough to fill if not whole worlds, at least continents themselves. He is, in short, himself a very great literary "character," albeit appreciated to the full only in the few small republics of taste that find themselves isolatedly scattered through our universe and ignored by the general. That is a fate that no true writer need deplore. Nevertheless, we may say of him, as we said of Gibbon, that a man is hardly a complete man until he has read a great deal of Jean Paul. He has, as that great critic M. Léon Daudet has pointed out, no modern equivalent unless it be that master novelist, M. René Béhaine, the characters in whose enormous projection of our time are almost sufficient to people a continent that shall lie along Jean Paul Richter land. It is not necessary to read Jean Paul in the original. His

German, though not unpleasant, is nothing very special and there are several goodish translations.

The other German novelists of the *Sturm und Drang* period of romanticism are none of them of the stature of Jean Paul. And the note of their novels is mingled with that of their contemporary philosophers—most notably of Fichte. The most attractive of them is Novalis, who for long was something of a world figure and may still so remain. His *Heinrich von Osterdingen*, published in 1800, is another gathering of characters like those in the novels of Jean Paul. But they are characters drawn much more softly, inspired with a certain mysticism and overshadowed by a sort of pantheism inspired by Philosopher Schelling. This mysticism and pantheism develop gradually as the book goes on and become by degrees a sort of goblin-superstition and supernaturalism that are sufficiently trying. The book was never finished. Nevertheless, Georg Friedrich Philip von Hardenberg, known as Novalis, with his terribly early death of tuberculosis in 1801 at the age of twenty-nine, and his being pre-deceased by his agonisedly loved Sophia von Kuhn, and his passing with his great work, as we have said, unfinished—Novalis, then, had about him some of the glow of Shelley as drawn by Trelawney. He wrote in addition—to the memory mostly of his Sophia—some of the most supremely beautiful lyrics in a language not wanting in supremely beautiful lyrics. His *Nachtlieder* volume was one of the exquisite pleasures of this writer's childhood, and on a rereading very little of their night-scent seems for him to have faded. Novalis might well be more widely read.

English poetry was at its best whilst music was the breath of the country; so German literature is at its best when its lyric—and peculiarly when its folklore—stop is on. Goethe said somewhere, towards 1806, though I cannot recapture the reference: "Germany, as a whole, is nothing: the German individual is everything"* . . . and one wonders why his books remain unburned in Berlin, or his death bed with

* The writer has just been referred by a friend who prefers to remain unnamed to Goethe's *Unterhaltungen mit dem Kanzler von Mueller*, where the sentence occurs under the date of 1808.

the bowls for plants intact in Weimar. But for the non-German world the dictum will be luminous enough. The best things that Germany has given us are her lyrics and folksongs. A great part of these, along with the music of Bach who, heaven knows, was individualist enough, come from Suabia. We owe to Tieck, one of the two unpleasant German romantic novelists to whom we shall have to pay attention before leaving the subject of German romanticism for good, a debt of gratitude. He was primarily responsible for the revival in interest, in the modern world, in the work of the Suabian *minnesingers*; and he gave strong encouragement to the poets of his day to the study of those most individualistic peasant songs—the folksongs of the fourteenth and fifteenth centuries—to which we have paid already much attention. As a critic he is otherwise not highly convincing, lapsing occasionally into the purest wrong diagnoses of his world and his own self, as in the following passage from his general writings published as late as 1828:

> My youth fell in those times when, not only in Germany but in the greater part of the civilized world, the sense of the beautiful, the sublime, and the mysterious seemed to have sunk to sleep or to be dead. A shallow enlightenment, to which the divine appeared as an empty dream, ruled the day; indifference toward religion was called freedom of thought, indifference toward country, cosmopolitanism. Trivial popular observations had taken the place of philosophy, and a morbid examination of diseased mental states was heralded under the noble name of psychology. . . . In the struggle against these predominant views, I sought to win for myself a quiet place, where nature, art, and faith might again be cultivated; and this endeavor led me to hold up to the opposing party (the party of Enlightenment) a picture of their own confusion and spiritual wantonness which would in a measure justify my falling away from it.

He claims for his novel, *William Lovell,* published in 1795, that it should be the German youth's constant attendant and educator in morals. From that point of view it is a disgusting affair, beginning with a lamentable ivory-towerishness, continuing in the same for a volume and a half, as thus:

> Ah, the golden Age of the Muses has disappeared forever! When Gods full of tenderness were still walking on the earth, when Beauty and Grandeur clad in harmonious robes were still dancing hand in hand on gay meadows, when the Hours with golden key still opened Aurora's gate, and blessing Genii with horns of plenty hovered over a smiling world—ah! then the sublime and the beautiful had not yet been degraded to the pretty and the alluring.

and continuing in a genuine *progression d'effet* through a gradually increasing tendency to glorify always more and more freedom of manners and debauchery. So it goes on, à la Tyl Eulenspiegel and the Alter Deutsche Gott, to the culmination in a regular pandemonium of rape, debauchery, murder and duelling . . . a fine spectacle for youth's constant attendant to display to his charges! It is a singular development for the strain of the *Princesse de Clèves* through the *Confessions* of Jean Jacques Rousseau to attain to. And yet it is nothing else. That princess yearned to break the trammels of social "honor" but succumbed to them; in his own person Rousseau exercised himself in a bohemianism that a little *épater*'d the bourgeoisie of his day and mildly engineered a return to nature and leisured, if frugal, ease. Madame de Lafayette was Mediterranean; Rousseau Swiss-Nordic, that implying a faint shading of classicism. In full Nordic hands the faint struggle for freedom from social control and the ineffectually doctrinaire bohemianism must enormously expand its lungs and go . . . the whole hog!

And, if Madame de Lafayette, for her elegance, wit, delicacy and restraint, is at one end of the line, certainly Friedrich von Schlegel for his dullness, lubricity and license is, with his novel *Lucinde,* at the other. He is taken to be the great protagonist of the whole romantic movement; actually almost nobody but he himself could be said to stand on his party plank. Even Tieck in the worst moments of *William Lovell* is at least swift-moving beside him. *Lucinde* is a manifesto in favor of deep idleness and universal lubricity; it is coarser than the *Decameron* and infinitely heavier. It is written like this:

> Like a sage of the Orient, I was completely lost in holy brooding and calm contemplation of the eternal substances, especially thine [Lucinde's] and mine. I saw thee and myself, a gentle sleep embracing us as we were embracing each other. With the utmost indignation I thought of the bad men who would fain take sleep out of life. Oh, they never slept and never lived themselves! Why are the gods gods if not because they consciously and purposely do nothing, because they understand this art and are masters in it? And oh, how the poets, the sages and saints are endeavoring to become like the gods in this respect! How they vie with each other in the praise of solitude, leisure, and a liberal carelessness and inactivity! And they are right, indeed; for everything good and beautiful is here already and maintains itself by its own strength. Why, then, this constant striving and pushing without rest and repose?

With that we may leave the book. Otherwise Schlegel was a fair critic; it was he who first pointed out that the disadvantage of the romantic author was that, whatever he wrote, he must be himself the most important feature of his book. The Greeks, says he, observed nature and rendered it with a classic objectivism, so that the incidence of their work was on nature—and, of course, on human nature itself. But the romantic used nature merely as a mirror in which were reflected his own romantic characteristics.

But, in spite of Schlegel's manifestoes, German romanticism abandoned the course of *Lucinde* and followed rather Novalis. It became more and more sweet, more and more mystic; it identified itself more and more with German folklore and fairy tales, thus coming into its own. Non-German readers will most appreciate—as they have hitherto appreciated—the works of three authors, all curiously enough of Mediterranean origin. These are Fouqué (by his right name Friedrich Heinrich Karl, Baron de la Motte), 1777-1843, Clemens Brentano, 1778-1842, and Adelbert von Chamisso, 1781-1838 (real name, Louis

Charles Adelaide de), who was actually a French renegade and fought against his own country. The most beautiful work of Fouqué was his famous *Undine*, the delicately charming story of a wood nymph who, being immortal, could have no soul; the most characteristic in a bluff German way being Chamisso's *Peter Schlemihl*; and the most readable work of Brentano's being his fantastic tales. All these writers occupied themselves with the reinstatement of Nordic folk and fairy stories and songs. The most early important collection of these is called *Des Knabens Wunderhorn*.

But the real apotheosis of this side of the Teutonic cosmos came into its own through the labors of the brothers Ludwig Karl, and Wilhelm Karl Grimm for whom the measure of our admiration may well be marked by the fact that there is nothing in the world left to say about their collection of fairy tales. It is, on the whole, wrong to concede the brothers Grimm to the romantics. They belonged to the earth movement and are known wherever the sky covers the land. That is the real German Empire.

A completely new literature now comes upon the scene. It is that of Russia, for, until the later decades of the eighteenth century, Russia cannot be said to have had even a literary language. The task of distilling one from a variety of peasant and city dialects was begun by Mikhail Vasilyevich Lomonosov, who was born in 1711 and lived till 1765; it may be considered to have been completed by Pushkin who died in a duel at the age of thirty-eight. There are, however, those Russians who will tell you that the first person to write in the Russian vernacular, as opposed to classical and foreign languages, was the seventeenth century Old Believer, the Archpriest Avvakum, and that the person who perfected Russian in the sense of being a perfect stylist was the fable writer Krylov who survived Pushkin by seven years. The matter is unimportant, Russian having no significance or influence as a cosmopolitan tongue . . . and this writer cannot lay claim to sufficient knowledge of the language to let his advice on the matter have any value. He has, however, listened for hours to the discussion by learned and accomplished Russians as to the relative values of the styles of various Russian writers—but, as is to be expected of members of a race so politically conscious, the opinions thus uttered appeared always to be founded entirely on the utterer's shade of political thought. Thus, for the old nihilists the style of Turgenev was as commonplace as could be. But the great Prince Kropotkin—an anarchist—showed himself, in innumerable conversations, extremely kind both to the style and matter of that greatest of all Russians, and the present-day Communists regard him at least with toleration. On the other hand, the White Russians, according as in their preëxile days they were Russophils or of the Western School—who believed that Russia could only be saved by Western European contacts—despise or laud to the skies the writing of the author of *Fathers and Children.* The son of a gentleman who in his day passed for the greatest of Russian Western critics, but who for some political reason that is not very apparent wishes the writer not to disclose his name—Count X, then, declares that so exquisite was the Russian of Turgenev that he remembers his mother and father weeping with excitement whilst they read each new book of Turgenev's. . . . And the excitement was not over the story but was due to their impatience to come always to the next sentence, so beautiful did they consider every sentence to be.

The confusion is as great when you come to consider whether Pushkin—and, in a lesser degree, Lermontov—should or should not be considered romantic writers. Russophils assert that Pushkin owed nothing whatever either to Byron or to any foreign writer, and that he was a pure realist—by which they mean that the atmosphere of his writings was purely Russian. Equally they claim that because Lermontov wrote *A Contemporary Hero*, the first really considerable novel to occupy itself with common Russian life, therefore we must ignore the long poem called "A Demon," which is pure Byron, and call Lermontov also a confirmed realist.

Since, however, Pushkin's first language was French and he spoke and read nothing else until well on into adolescence, and since for some years before his return in 1826 from exile in the provinces his admiration for Byron was unbounded, and since for many hundred pages—though he subsequently became the normal oriento-fatalist Russian of renunciations and regrets—the eponymous hero of his novel in verse, *Evgenie Oniegin,* has all the gloom and irresponsibility of Childe Harold, and since for some years before his death Pushkin again became an omnivorous reader of foreign books—for all these reasons it is only logical to conclude that for some years at least he was considerably tarred by the romantic stick. No doubt his faintly negroid strain and his French upbringing may have had something to do with his poetic gifts and linguistic facility. Romanticism was in the air from end to end of Europe; and as being the very inspiration of the all-European aspiration for freedom, romanticism was the very spirit of his age. So you could only conclude that there must have been something insensible in that great poet if he had never been touched by the wing of romanticism. For it was incredible how that influence traveled back and forth. Did not Byron himself write *Mazeppa,* a Russo-Romantic pastiche of Pushkin, with its:

> The horse was brought, a fiery steed,
> A Tartar of the Ukraine breed

and its not very real landscape and projection of the manners and customs of the Steppes?

Pushkin did, however, violently react against the French influences of his childhood. His first poem, published when he had just attained his majority, is called "Ruslan and Liudmila" and is founded on Russian folk-tales told him as a child by his grandmother—in French. (He had, in the meanwhile, learned Russian in the famous Academy of Tzarskoë Selo.) And he himself has told us how, as a young man between twenty-five and twenty-seven, in the deep solitude of his father's estate in the government of Pskov, he had sat at the feet for days on end of his old nurse Arina Rodionovna and drunk in a continuous stream of legend, folksong and fairy tale. He called that process "making up for the defects in his accursed education."

At the age of twenty-seven—in 1826—he was finally recalled to St. Petersburg and became the literary ward of the tsar and by then he was sufficiently Russicized to satisfy the most extreme Russophil. *Evgenie Oniegin* he finished three years later, it having been seven years in writing. It is difficult exactly to estimate this masterpiece of a poet who, from the day when he was sixteen to his centenary a year ago, has been the unique adoration of a vast nation. . . . Few translators have, since the English sixteenth century, been anything but banal, and with one exception almost all translators from the Russian into English have been exceptionally bad. This is unusually true of translators of *Evgenie*. At any rate, all the translations of the poem or parts of it that this writer has been able to find have been extremely unfortunate—worse even than those of that other completely untranslatable poet, Heine. Even the best of them—some fragments done by Mrs. Isabel Hapgood—make avowedly no attempt to capture the magic of the versification or the quality of Pushkin's vernacular. . . . The worst specimens, by the constant employment of cliché phrases, give the verse an insupportably old-fashioned and faded aspect. They irresistibly suggest that Pushkin must have been a very minor romantic.

So that all that one can do to form any estimate is to read him in translation without, whilst reading, attempting to form any estimate at all . . . and then some time afterwards to form an estimate from one's memory . . . remembering always that according to every Russian of whatever shade of opinion the versification of Pushkin is most beautiful! They say that only Lermontov can compare with him.

The theme of *Evgenie* is that of woman's love, rejected at first and then rejecting with regret. It is spread over a vast territory of experience and emotion. In it Pushkin treats of a great number of sides of Russian everyday life which till his day had been considered by no means fit for treatment in any kind of either prose or verse. Its heroine, Tatyana, is a largely drawn and consistently developed study of Russian womanhood. She is spacious of form, vastly sincere, considerate, faithful, generous and submissive to society and to fate. Evgenie is in the beginning Byronically stern, and rejects the love of Tatyana because he considers himself mysteriously doomed to make a bad husband. Mrs. Hapgood makes him say:

> "But I for bliss was not created:
> To that my soul is foreign still.
> In vain, in vain, are your perfections;
> Of them I count myself unworthy.

Believe (I pledge my word upon it.)
Marriage for us would torture be."

So, in Byronic anger, he makes pretended love to Tatyana's sister Olga and has—prophetically—to fight a duel with Olga's fiancé. (Prophetically, because Pushkin was killed in a duel with his wife's sister's husband.) Two years later Oniegin goes to the capital. He there finds Tatyana, married to a general and one of the great ladies of the tsar's entourage. He falls irretrievably in love with her and writes her a series of letters expressing a mad passion. He comes upon her one day reading one of his letters and crying. She confesses that she loves him with a passion equal to his but insists that they must part for good.

This is of course romanticism. It is none the less real because Russian male youth is by its very race and circumstances compounded of romanticism absolutely Byronic in its irresponsible gusts of passion and of an irresolution, comparison with which would make Hamlet seem a hard man of action. If you wish to convince yourself of that you have only to read Turgenev's *Tchertop Hanov and Nyedopuhskin* and *A Hamlet of the Steppes*, which we are told are the most Russian of all Russian depictions of character. And, indeed, what character, actions or career could have been more romantic than that of Pushkin himself? It was a fairy tale.

And *Boris Godúnov*, a play founded on the story of one of the pretenders to the tsardom who kept all Russia for years in tumult and eventually dispossessed Tsar Boris of his throne, is absolutely of the essence of romance. The mere subject makes it so. It is that of the greatest of Moussorgsky's operas and the reader who will take the trouble to hear that really impassioned music will get at least something of the impression that, we are told, attends on reading the play in the original.

And, indeed, it is of the romantic in technique. All its characters except the merest groundlings seem to be eight feet tall and to stride along to the sound of tocsins, their feet a foot above the ground. . . . That too is romance, its very conception, its very essence.

Nevertheless, the Russia of *Boris* is Russia.

The fact, in short, is that Pushkin was Russian to the soul—and romantic. There was no need for Byron nor yet of *Hernani* . . . which had not yet been produced.

This poet, whilst he was yet at school and aged sixteen, was already recognized as the glorious white hope of Russian poetry. The few existing Russian poets of that day acknowledged already that he was genius incarnate; the most eminent of them, Vasily Andreïvich Zhukovsky, brought all his poems to the Academy of Tsarkoë Selo that they might be criticized and amended by that boy. His fame, founded on the brilliance at once of his verse and his epigrams—in which he scarified everyone of note—brought upon him the attention of everyone of note . . . from the tsar, fresh from the glories of after-Waterloo Paris, to the Guards' officers, the governors of provinces and all the ladies of all of them. And, for all the rest of his career, all these people acted as his dry-nurses.

They were filled with misgivings for his poetic gifts when, after his leaving the Academy, he plunged into a vortex of aristocratic dissipation. When, from the foreign office, he covered all Petersburg with his lampoons and finally committed a misdemeanor so outrageous that it became obligatory to punish him by exile, the tsar insisted that the form the punishment took should be such that he should not feel that he was punished, because any humiliation would interfere with his poetry writing. He was, therefore, promoted to a place in the suite of Count Vorontsoff, governor of Odessa. For four years he enjoyed himself in South Russia—in the Crimea and at Odessa; then among other misdemeanors he wrote—and read to—the governor such a lampoon on him that Vorontsoff, although insisting on his removal from his province, put the pretext for his removal as being solely in the interests of Pushkin's verse.

There are many people here [wrote the governor] and they display their sympathy by exaggerated laudations "of his gifts," thus rendering him a disservice since they tend to obscure his mind and enhance his opinion of himself as a great author, whilst he is really only a weak imitator of a not very respectable model—Lord Byron.*

So he was translated with all honors to his father's estate, where his father became his guardian. His father seems to have disliked Byronics almost more than the governor of Odessa. He proceeded to discipline his genius-son with such severity that in pain and bewilderment the young man appealed for succor to his friends, Zhukovsky† and Karamzin. Zhukovsky, no doubt grateful for Pushkin's improvements in his poems, and Pushkin's other very intimate friend, Baron Anton Antonovich Delvig—a delightful writer of Greek-inspired cameos—applied direct to the tsar. Pushkin *père* was then outragedly exiled from his own estate and the poet was put under the mild tutelage of the marshal of nobility of the Pskov province. Finally, in 1826, the tsar, by then Nicholas I, recalled the poet to the capital and appointed himself his poetic censor and personal guardian.

Shortly afterwards Pushkin married Natalya Anastasia Gontcharoff, a young reigning beauty of the Imperial court, and the young couple passed the rest of their days together in a round of dizzy festivities in which they dissipated not only all their own fortunes and more but all the allowances that the tsar made them . . . and more again. Nevertheless, from time to time, they retired to the country, and during these years Pushkin finished *Evgenie Oniegin* and wrote *Boris Godúnov*, as well as a number of shorter pieces, the best known of which is *The Captain's Daughter*.

But the brilliant Nemesis that waits on romantic figures finally attended to the Pushkins. Worried by the outrageous attentions paid to Mrs. Pushkin by a Baron von Hekkerens and his son—the latter being the husband of Natalya Pushkin's sister—Pushkin challenged the father to a duel. The son accepted the challenge and killed Pushkin. Thus was reversed the fate of Lensky, Tatyana's prospective brother-in-law, who fell at the hands of Evgenie Oniegin.

The outraged tsar buried Pushkin in secret for fear of popular ris-

* Slightly altered by the author.
† Vasily Andreïvich Zhukovsky, 1783-1852, a rather poor poet but a spirited translator from the English, French and German. Nikolai Mihaílovich Karamzin, 1766-1823, a historian who left two novels, *Poor Lisa* and *Natalia*, of a certain historical interest.

ings at the funeral, paid all the remaining debts of Pushkin, settled a handsome fortune on his widow . . . and was forced to provide a heavy guard of Imperial troops to protect the Von Hekkerens. . . . We have recorded the singular and admirable career of Molière. This of Pushkin's seems to have been of a purer strain of romance. His wife at least was true to him. . . . And it is, perhaps, more romantic to be killed in a duel than to die, as it were, on the stage. Or, perhaps, it is not. That is another decision that the writer must leave to his partner. . . . Because, of course, Molière died that his stage-hands might not lack their day's bread!

It now becomes our duty to travel our European territory from the extreme North to the extreme South and then to cross the literary Atlantic. And as we progress, it will become plain that romanticism was almost more a political than an aesthetic movement. In form it was a going into an ivory tower: in effect it was as if the whole earth sighed in its sleep, dreaming of shaking off bonds that cramped it. That is a somewhat romantic way of putting it, but, to come down to brass tacks, we shall see in Spain that all the romantic writers were exiles, until in 1833 Spain once more became a constitutional country and the Duke de Rivas and all the other Spanish romantics could return—mostly from London. In Italy, crushed under the yoke of the Holy Alliance and Metternich, only one outstanding romantic work was produced. And of a whole cloud of politico-romantic poets and tragedians that arose in Florence hardly one merits mention. It would hardly be unfair in a literary sense, though it would be unkind to a body of poets inspired with the ideal of freeing Italy from an atrocious bondage, to say that only three Italian writers between the birth of Alfieri and the death of Manzoni approach anywhere near to the scale of international magnitude that we have hitherto demanded of the writers of whom we have treated. They were the two named and Leopardi, and of the works of all three only *I Promessi Sposi* stands unquestioned as a universally appreciable masterpiece; and that is a romantic novel in prose.

Alfieri was born in 1749 and died in 1802, thus living till the opening days of romanticism. And, indeed, as a figure he was romantic in almost incredible proportions, a Byron with an enormous robustiousness, of a gloom terrific and resonant, a hater of tyrants, yet hating still more the French Revolution which began the removal of tyrants from the earth, claiming to be a democrat because he never struck his servants with anything but his open hand, yet stretching out his valet with a bronze candlestick because the valet pulled his hair slightly whilst combing it . . . and then sleeping—or claiming to sleep—with his bedroom door always open so that the valet might come in and, in revenge, murder him in his sleep. So, after a youth almost without education, of tragically running from end to end of Europe in search of something never to be found, he settled down to writing tragedies of great stage effectiveness and of the strictest possible classical form, which you could yet, if you wished, call romantic, because of the violence of their exclamatory language and the passionate gloom and blood-thirstiness of their atmosphere.

His plays can hardly be called literature at all. The opening of his *Agamemnon*, Act V, scene one, is as follows and is fairly representative of his methods:

Aegisthus and soldiers

Aeg. O treachery unseen! O madness! Freed! Orestes freed! Now
we shall see . . .

(*Enter Clytemnestra*)

Cly.   Ah, turn
Backward thy steps!

Aeg.   Ah, wretch dost thou arm too
Against me?

Cly.   I would save thee. Hearken to me.
I am no longer . . .

Aeg.   Traitress!

Cly.   Stay!

Aeg. Thou'st promised
Haply to give me to that wretch alive!

Cly. To keep thee, save thee from him, I have sworn
Though I should perish for thee! Ah, remain
And hide thee here in safety. I will be
Thy stay against his fury. . . .

Aeg. Against his fury
My sword shall be my stay. Go leave me
I go. . . .

Cly. Whither?

Aeg. To kill him.

Cly. To thy death thou goest!

The English is that of W. D. Howells, who does his best for Alfieri. But even in the Italian the language is not very attractive and we may say that there is hardly a word of poetry in the whole tragedy. Nevertheless, acted by merely mediocre players, the passions and agonies of the characters do get over the footlights, and the characters themselves are well-established and coherent. Alfieri is not Shakespeare, but an atmosphere something like that of Lady Macbeth does hang around his Clytemnestra, whose situation is, enhancedly, that of the Queen in *Hamlet*.

That is a fairly exact constatation and the criticism would apply fairly well to all Alfieri's tragedies. In their baldness—and they are as bald as the plays of Ibsen at their most commonplace—they achieve a sort of marmoreal atmosphere of tragic gloom. The reader need hardly give time to reading them, but he should certainly not miss any opportunity to see them played, for he will get from them something of the sensation produced by the great Greeks, with an added agitation caused by the lightning flashes of the exclamations. His literary interest today is largely historic. He served a political purpose that deserved the gratitude of those who fought for the freedom of Italy. Thus

Giudici, the mid-Victorian Italian critic, writes of him that, "though almost without education:"

> Aeschylus and Alfieri are two links that unite the chain in a circle. In Alfieri art once more achieved the faultless purity of its proper character; Greek tragedy reached the height in the Italian's *Saul* that it touched in the Greek's *Prometheus* . . . Tragedy, born sublime, terrible, vigorous, heroic. *The life of liberty* was, as it were, redeemed by Vittorio Alfieri, reassumed the masculine, athletic forms of its original existence and recommenced the exercise of its lost ministry.*

The motives for this praise are to be found in the words italicized . . . but the praise itself, though it might have been more politic not to have dragged in Aeschylus, is not politico-romantically undeserved. And, certainly, Alfieri was masculine and athletic in his life as in his dramas.

He married eventually—or perhaps he did not marry—the widow of the last of a pretender-tyrant chain, the Countess of Albany, whose husband had been Charles Edward, the last of the Stuarts. So that he could consider himself, as he did complacently, as sitting in a tyrant's shoes. His house became "the center of fashionable and intellectual society in Florence," where he lived in tranquillity till his death. Characteristically, he hastened that process by taking oil and magnesia against his doctor's orders, dying as he had lived, at once a tyrant and a rebel.

Leopardi, Count Alfred, 1798-1837, is a writer and a scholar of an extreme erudition whom it is much more difficult to define. Obscured, as it is, by a misanthropy and pessimism caused by almost fantastic and continuous ill health, his writing deserves attention only for the great beauty of his Italian and the delicacy of his versification—qualities that it is impossible to get over into English, yet without them it is difficult to consider them as poetry at all. He loved liberty and

* W. D. Howells' translation.

detested romanticism—facts rendered inevitable by the nature of his childhood. He lived for years a prisoner in the remote castle of a father who was, long before the romantics themselves, incurably romantic in his furniture and gear. Men at arms in rusty mediaeval armor guarded the castle walls; the portcullis was always down, the drawbridge up because the young poet, in the intervals of illness when he could neither read nor write, loved a peasant girl whom he had once seen at a window and whose singing came up to him on the walls. When she died of consumption—as she inevitably would—he was given again some small measure of liberty. His father wrote religious pamphlets and was passionately reactionary. So his son loved liberty.

He was given, eventually, permission to go to Rome, which he hated more than he hated his birthplace which he detested. But his father gave him so small an allowance that he had to support himself miserably by making hack translations—and he despised the Roman women more than even the male Romans, so that he lived mostly among Germans who lived in crowds in the capital of the world. He had, however, acquired such an immense erudition in Greek, that, although only twenty-two, he was considered to be the chief Hellenist in Italy, and was offered the chair of Greek philosophy at Berlin! He wandered desultorily from Rome to Milan, to Florence, home for a time, to Pisa. Finally, at Naples, he formed a touching friendship with Antonio Ranieri and his sister, and those two in a villa at Capo di Monte soothed devotedly his last years till his death. In Florence he had loved, once more unsuccessfully, and he acquired the unfortunate conviction that the Florentine ladies laughed at him. That still more embittered his life.

He had about him nothing to make them love him. He was small, his face ironic with ill health and hatred of his kind; he hardly spoke at all and was reputed to have "strange habits," dining at midnight and going to bed at dawn. As his friend, the gentle Ranieri said of him: "His whole life was not a career like that of most men; it was truly a precipitate course towards death."

He wrote a poem called *To Italy*, which earned him much popularity after his death. This writer, indeed, during part of his youth, lived in an atmosphere in which the cause of Italia irredenta was that of Heaven itself. His father and, indeed, all his relatives spat when anyone mentioned the accursed Metternich, chief author of Italian woes, and never spoke of liberated Italy without saying, "How beautiful art thou, with the stars in thy hair!" And of that heaven Alfieri and Leopardi were considered to be the chief stars—along with the cloud of names like Manzoni, Grossi, Guerazzi, Giambattista Niccolini and how many more. And this writer was told to believe that Leopardi's *To Italy*, next to the *Divine Comedy*, was the chief poem of the country of its author. But rereading it now, it seems a cold-enough compilation of Warder Street properties set down without passion and inspiration.

> My native land, I see the walls and arches,
> The columns and the statues and the lonely
> Towers of our ancestors,
> But not their glory, not
> The laurel and the steel that of old time
> Our great forefathers bore. Disarmed now,
> Naked thou showest thy forehead and thy breast!
> O me, how many wounds,
> What bruises and what blood! How do I see thee,
> Thou loveliest Lady! Unto Heaven I cry,
> And to the world: "Say, say,
> Who brought her unto this?" To this and worse,
> For both her arms are loaded down with chains,
> So that, unveiled and with disheveled hair,
> She crouches all forgotten and forlorn,
> Hiding her beautiful face
> Between her knees and weeps.
> Weep, weep, for well thou may'st, my Italy!*

And W. D. Howells here does the original no injustice, he too having been among the great lovers of Italy. . . . But as an Italian critic, quoted unnamed by Mr. Howells puts it: the poem is "without relief, without lyric flight, without a great art of contrast, without

---

* Howells' translation.

poetic leaven. . . . Despoil his verses of their masterly polish, reduce his thoughts to prose and you will see how little they are akin to poetry." . . . Mr. Howells does, nevertheless, get some poetry into his version of the "Ode on the Likeness of a Beautiful Woman Carven on her Tomb."

> Such wast thou; now under earth
> A skeleton and dust. O'er dust and bones
> Immovably and vainly set, and mute,
> Looking upon the flight of centuries,
> Sole keeper of memory
> And of regret is this fair counterfeit
> Of loveliness now vanished. That sweet look,
> Which made men tremble when it fell on them,
> As now it falls on me; that lip, which once,
> Like some full vase of sweets,
> Ran over with delight; that fair neck, clasped
> By longing, and that soft and amorous hand,
> Which often did impart
> An icy thrill unto the hand it touched;
> That breast, which visibly
> Blanched with beauty him who looked on it—
> All these things were, and now
> Dust art thou, filth, a fell
> And hideous sight hidden beneath a stone.

But the "masterly polish" of the original language certainly imparts to the whole poem a definite coldness which only becomes animated—and for Leopardi very animated!—when it touches on the topic of the "hideous sight, hidden beneath a stone." There comes at least a certain touch of human feeling into what is perhaps, except for "Risorgimento," his best known poem "To Sylvia"—to the very young girl whose singing resounded whilst

> I, leaving my fair studies,
> Leaving my manuscripts and toil-stained volumes . . .

Leaned sometimes idly from my father's windows
And listened to the music of thy singing. . . .

It may be driving censure too far if one says that the interest of
Leopardi today is mainly historic—or pathological—but the temptation to say it is very great . . . and the temptation to believe that
some, at least, of his prosaic and cruel pessimism was due not entirely
to his maladies but was innate.

It is difficult to write with any more enthusiasm of any of the other
Italian poets of that heroic struggle. But that has been almost invariably the case with nations flattened down beneath the weight of
religious and temporal intolerance and alien burdens. And perhaps
most numbing of all is the burden of exclusion from public office,
which has a tendency to silence its victim and in extravagant cases
to render his children mournfully half-witted. That was the case with
the Irish—and, indeed, the English—Catholics till the Emancipation
Act. . . . And, indeed, one should remember that the most brilliant
of modern Irish authors—Messrs. Synge, Yeats, Moore and Shaw—
were non-Irish and Protestant by descent. It was still more the case
with Poland, which for centuries produced only two writers of any
note—Krazinsky and Sinkiévich—and one other, Joseph Conrad, who
found expression only in a foreign language and in the land which
stood to the Poles as the Land of Liberty.*

And when comes the Risorgimento, the vocal poets in clouds are
apt to consider that the glory of their uprising will, all of itself, gild
the lilies of their verse. Liberty is a fine word but it is insufficient of
itself to write the plays of Shakespeare or the poems of Heine . . .
or, indeed, merely to inspire them. . . . That is why the whole Italian
literary cloud of writers of the uprising—and, indeed, the whole literature of the romantic movement—is second class. It lacks authenticity

---

* This writer finds it hard to omit here remembrance of when at the London Docks
he went down day after day to see crowds of Polish and Jewish refugees disembark.
Their unanimous first action was to fall on their knees and kiss the sacred soil. Citizens
like that we today exclude! Conrads and all. . . . You would think no country could
be rich enough to afford itself that luxury of Xenophobia.

because it has occupied only a secondary place in its author's thoughts. A Villon can write the finest poetry in the world, for he can have no thought of escape into an ivory tower from a world that was more torturing than hell. Just because he had no such hope! But a writer who aspires to place his person on a level with that of Don Juan de Tenorio, or merely with that of Casanova, and aspires, with deep gusts of the breath to attain to the *épatement* of the bourgeoisie by shocking simple citizens by the strangeness of their attitudes and the loudness of their atheisms; by rising at dawn, dining at midnight, drinking blood from a papier-maché skull and wearing slouch hats and depending ties as large as table napkins—such a writer must give more thought to inscribing his person on the pages of his books and the walls of his room than to that most difficult of all tasks: the projecting of the quintessence of the experience he has drawn from life.

That is true of all Italian prose writers of the period of the Risorgimento, save only Manzoni, and of all the poets. It is less true of the dramatists. The stage, by its very conditions, lends itself more easily to the conveyance of non-impartial or impulsive matters. It has actors to give it reality; the crowd psychology of the audience to give it quite extra-literary compulsion. The *Giovanni da Procida* of Giambattista Niccolini is a play dealing at once with an unknown-incestuous union and the expulsion from Sicily of the French garrison at the time of the massacres of the French called the Sicilian Vespers. It is written with the sort of rough and passionate patriotism that would be the death of a work of the imagination in either prose or non-dramatic verse. It reads in places rather comically—as does *Hedda Gabler*, that Nordic attempt to shake off the stifling yoke of the bourgeoisie. But it acts, like the play of Ibsen, tremendously, tearing the heartstrings of the audience, as does the *Duchess of Malfi*, and with an art every bit as legitimate. And everyone in Italy knowing that though the play pretended to show the extirpation of the French in Sicily, in 1282, it was really a passionate entreaty to the Italians to massacre all the Austrians in early nineteenth century Italy. And very properly it set all Italy in flame.

But incitements to liberty which are perfectly proper in the hot, coarse tones of melodrama are apt to lose effectiveness in prose of

the imagination or in classical odes . . . unless they are composed
by very great hands and by very composed brains. It is quite possible
to find an angle from which to regard the Malebolge sections of the
Divina Comedia as propaganda for the unity of Italy; or it is proper
to be inspired by the sound of "Avenge, O Lord, Thy slaughtered
Saints," or "Of old sat Freedom on the heights." The Italian is possessed of unparalleled powers of improvisation in verse. This may
make admirable folksongs if its topics are those of the fields, of goose-
girls and of shepherds or children. But the same powers turned to the
easier and vaguer topics of liberty or irreligion—topics easier and
more vague simply because they are ready made for the tongue of the
improviser—the same powers turned to those topics lead inevitably
to the merest clichés of phrase and imagination.

"Aux armes, citoyens, formez vos bataillons" roared by thousands
to the rhythm of their hastening feet and to the tune of the "Marseillaise" may well suffice to the destruction of impregnable fortresses.
Or the mere associations attached by the listener to the words may
quite properly bring tears to the eyes of the exile from France. Yet,
per se, it is not more inspiring than the "Fall in with your rifles. Slope
arms. Number off by the right. Form fours." of the drill sergeant. It
is the acting, or the remembrance of the acting, in that drama that
lends the supreme aspect of poetry to the words.

So it was with the Grossi's, the Guerazzi's, the Foscolo's and the
rest of the Italian poets . . . and with poets like Silvio Pellico who
had about their words the aura of their imprisonments. But, with the
glory of their day growing fainter by the recession of time, to read
their works is, as Mr. Howells put it, as laborious as to travel afoot
across the sands of deserts. Their works—whatever may have been the
case with their careers—have even no value as portraying history. . . .
But, except that the illustration is a necessity, the condemning of
politico-romantic poets is as unenviable a pursuit as that same travel.
They were strong men in their day. . . . Let us, therefore, praise Manzoni.

CHAPTER TWO

THERE are certain books, differing widely the one from the other, that are almost universally beloved and before which criticism suspends itself. They are innocent without being contemptible; virtuous without being of an insupportable puritan-hypocrisy; admirably conceived without formal perfection. And, without being amongst the great masterpieces, they are necessary to a world that would be poorer without them. Perhaps each man of taste forms his own list of such books for which, as you might say, he would die as he would die for his God, his king, his church or his republic, without being assured of the absolute impeccability of his quarrels. This writer would say as much for some of the tales of Thomas Hardy, for Mrs. Gaskell's *Cranford*, for *Lorna Doone*; for *Little Women*; for, perhaps, *The Scarlet Letter*; for many of the folk-tales of the brothers Grimm; for the story of Kohlenmunk Peter in Hauff's *Wirtshaus im Spessart*; for *Paul et Virginie*; for *Manon Lescaut*; for *Tyl Eulenspiegel*; possibly for *The Story of the Gadsby's*; the *Book of Ruth* or even *Framley Parsonage*; for Trollope, though a great—perhaps the greatest—of Victorian novelists falls under no category. He is neither romantic, nor realist nor naturalist; he just wrote—and as a countryside without marked features is "just country," he is "just novelist." Similar attributes —changing when necessary the word "novelist," would apply to all the writers of the works catalogued above. It is by no means intended to be complete. It might include the *Pickwick Papers, Vanity Fair* or the *Three Musketeers*; the *Golden Ass* or the Chinese poem, "The Undying Wrong" or the story of Sinbad or the *Death of Sir Gawain*. Such a list is the moss that we rolling stones gather as we pass through life. It will be thicker in our youths; indeed our lives will be rich according as it was thick or thin then, for to have the young mind plentifully stored with books of that type is to be sheltered from many of the griefs of age. From the masterpieces one gains strength, assurance, composure. From these others one is enriched by the memories of the days when one first read them. One renews, with those remembrances, one's youth. So when this writer thinks of *I Promessi Sposi* he remembers halcyon days he passed when the world was better. And, since he never passed halcyon days, having had a youth sufficiently troubled, and since the world was never really better—that remembrance has actually created for him today those calm seas and meadows that never were.

How it would be if one reread *Lorna Doone,* or *Cranford* or *The Story of the Gadsby's,* there is no saying. But as to how it is with rereading Manzoni's *The Betrothed,* this writer can testify. It was in his mind till yesterday a sort of dim spot of contesting bravi and agreeable young peasants. Today it is so near a masterpiece as to make almost no difference.

There must be some masterliness about a book that has given delight to a whole world for a century—*I Promessi Sposi* was written in 1827. But there is more than just some masterliness about this exuberant book; there is a real clash of passions; a real world is there reconstituted for you. Reading it as a child, if you are in the least bit sophisticated, virtuous Italian peasants, blue Italian lakes, black Italian bravi and tyrants will be apt to have, even to you, a certain air of the cliché. This writer used to question his love for the book; he does so no longer. It is written with a sort of unsleeping fire—which was, perhaps, no more than the fire of the Risorgimento. And the passion of an exciting time will every now and then so influence an author that he will be sedulous to give you always more and more exactitude in the reproduction of an unhappy time. Mrs. Gaskell's *Mary Barton,* almost dispassionate as it is, will do almost more to make you understand—and so sympathize with—the miseries of the poverty of her day than will a wilderness of Dickens' tomes. You will always feel subconsciously that, great as Dickens is, and passionate as is his desire to engage your sympathies for those of the underworld, he overdraws. He may tear your heartstrings, but *Mary Barton* will give you knowledge.

So it is with Manzoni. Like Niccolini, with his play about the Sicilian Vespers, Manzoni is intent on displaying, through the wrongs done in a past age, the tortures inflicted on the Italy of his own day by a tyranny the heaviest, the most unsleepingly cruel, the most dully insupportable that there has ever been. *I Promessi Sposi* is an historical novel and historical novels are nearly always *tours de force*—inventions of atmospheres more or less specious. But Manzoni, casting back to the eighteenth century, came upon a tyranny identical with, and only less cruel and complete than, the foreign rule that he himself saw in action under the Austrians of the unspeakable Metternich and the unthinkable Holy Alliance. In the days of *The Betrothed* Spain ruled over Italy, with the assistance of Spanish satraps, of the Holy Inquisition, of the usually connivent Italian aristocracy, who in turn were supported by the licenced assassins called "bravi." Famine swept the land; pestilences filled the lazzaretti; if you were a peasant you could trust no priest; there was no one to whom to make appeal; occasionally in thousands you poured, rioting, into the towns, seeking bread, blanketing the Spanish soldiery in such crowds that they could not use their arms. Then you died of pestilence and were thrown into the common fosses; or of starvation, when you might get Christian burial. Or you were informed against by your village mayor or the priest, and you died on a galley bench.

To Manzoni, writing from the point of view of the peasant, none of these things had changed in their effect. The Spaniards had given place to the Austrians; all the public functions were filled by the favorites of Metternich instead of those of the Private Friend of the Spanish king. The Italian nobility, filling their castles—like the father of Leopardi—with bric-a-brac, crowded to Rome and trifled in cynical degeneration in the shadow of the triple tiara. It was on the head of a good friend of Metternich's. The bravi were replaced by the dreaded *sbirri*, a secret police supported on the reports of household spies and *agents provocateurs*. Famines and pestilences swept the land; murder stalked in all the lanes. From each street went up the wail of the prisoner begging for other prisoners from behind the grille in the wall of the improvised prisons. You were imprisoned for treason; for whispered heresy; for unproven theft; for debt; for a hundred minor offences. . . . Above all, for non-payment of taxes. But the lot and conditions of the peasantry had in no ways changed. They had no better means of cultivation; no improved methods of spinning the wool for their clothes; their mayors, podestas and parish priests to whom they should have had the right to appeal were as like as not to betray them. Still, as in the eighteenth century, an occasional saintly, supercilious, or temporally powerful friar would protect you if you appealed to him. Or you could flee to a monastery for sanctuary. The weight of the state on your shoulders was a little heavier . . . and duller. It was perhaps formerly more exciting to see your betrotheds, wives, mothers, daughters or cousins abducted, raped and assassinated by picturesque bravi or romantic counts than now to see their and your bread, cattle, gear, clothing, furniture and bedding torn from under you and them by tax collectors and *sbirri* with the faces of blond morons. Or, in the alternative, to be forced to borrow money from your parish priest, who for the rest of your life would worry you with threats of the law and after your death damn you to Hell . . . though that practice, too, was common in the earlier centuries.

Thus, Manzoni could see his story enacted under his eyes and did not need to have recourse to the gloomy inventions and exaggerations that were common to the fiction of all the other true romantics. He had, in addition, something of Richardson's gift of causing the reader to feel alarm for his characters in scenes of extraordinary vividness. There is one occasion when the interest of the scene sways in an extraordinary light of storm and fear between one end of the village where the priest is ringing the tocsin because of some personal discomfort to himself, and the other where bravi appear to be abducting a pilgrim. It is a sort of lunatic effect of outcry and panic that is almost unequalled in fiction; there are amazingly managed crowd and riot effects and effects of famine, pestilence—of lazzaretti and of the tranquillity of convents.

And his characters are managed with remarkable subtlety, as well as with a great vigor and truth. Practically none of them are stock figures, nor are any of them overdrawn and static like the Pecksniffs and Heaps and Steerforths of Dickens, and the English novelists in general. His virtuous peasants are at times devious, cunning, even unscrupulous; his saintly friars exhibit moments of ill temper; his very bravi and counts feel sometimes remorse and hesitate in the midst of their exploits. Neither are his rushing crowds all of one temper; there will be a part of them moderate who keep their heads at the heights of the tumults; other numbers who exaggerate consciously their furies; others who are helplessly swept away by the movement of the whole.

Naturally, Manzoni is not without some of the defects of his day. From time to time he comments; he gives whole biographies of newly introduced characters. But the comments are, as it were, necessitated by the form. The book is supposed to be taken from the written story of a fictitious author, so that the real author finds it necessary to comment on the fictitious one. And the biographies are not introduced merely as such. Thus, the haughty, aristocratic and outrageous nun called the Signora has an important but—considering that she is a nun—an outrageous effect on the story and, since she is a singular person, her singularity has to be accounted for by a longish retrospective biography. It was an expedient that Conrad—and, indeed, the present writer—had almost too frequently to adopt. Your characters must be *justifiés*, though the skies fall.

Novels of this type are not easy to quote from. Here, however, is the aged but popular Chancellor Ferrer being drawn in his carriage through the thick of a riot. He has with him in the carriage a detested superintendent of taxes whom he pretends to be escorting to prison:

> The crowds moved onwards, before, behind and on each side of the carriage, like the mighty billows around a vessel advancing through the midst of a storm. The noise was more shrill, more discordant, more stunning, even than the whistling and howling of a storm itself. Ferrer, looking out first at one side and then at the other, beckoning and making all sorts of gestures to the people, endeavoured to catch something to which he might accommodate his replies; he tried as well as he could to hold a little dialogue with this crowd of friends; but it was a difficult task, the most difficult, perhaps, that he had yet met with during so many years of his high chancellorship. From time to time, however, a single word, or occasionally some broken sentence, repeated by a group in his passage, made itself heard, as the report of a large squib is heard above the continued crackling and whizzing of a display of fireworks. Now endeavouring to give a satisfactory answer to these cries, now loudly ejaculating the words that he knew would

be most acceptable, or that some instant necessity seemed to require, he, too, continued to talk the whole way. "Yes, gentlemen; bread, abundance—I will conduct him to prison: he shall be punished—*si està culpable*. Yes, yes: I will command: bread at a low price. *A si es. . . .* So it is, I mean to say: the King our master would not wish such faithful subjects to suffer from hunger. *Ox! ox! quardaos:* take care we don't hurt you, gentlemen. *Pedro, adelante, con juicio.*"*

The Italian being very limpid and simple, *I Promessi Sposi* must have been read by almost every foreigner while learning Italian. It has entered very deeply into the life of the transalpine world and must thus much have strengthened the hands of those who love peace and a generous humor . . . and seek to promote their cause.

The course of the romantic movement in Spain resembled that of Italy. It flowered, however, somewhat later and was thus much more under foreign influence. It resembled the German movement in that it was immensely inspired by a war of freedom. But it was far more bitter. The French invaders behaved with humanity to their German subjects, who in many districts fraternized with and, like Goethe, accepted their governors; but in Spain the invasion was conducted with a ruthless folly of despoilment and destruction. They left behind them memories so vivid in the tenacious Spanish mind that' they were, even in our own day, the prime reason that, though a Latin race, Spain did not side with France in the late war. And romanticism was further delayed by the reign of the lamentable Ferdinand VII; so that it hardly found its full voice in the Peninsula until the death of that sovereign.

The earlier outpourings of patriotic verse were, however, by no means romantic in inspiration. The great Manuel José Quintana was born in 1772 and died in 1857. The friend and disciple of the classicist, Melendez Valdés de Cienfuegos, he was himself very classicist in temperament. But very early in life he became an apostle of *"la libertad,*

* Bohn's translation.

el progreso, y la patria" and as such produced in 1797 his "Ode to Juan de Padilla":

> *de generosa ira,*
> *clamando en torno de nosotros . . .*
> *ruja el león de Espāna,*
> *y corra en sangre a sepultar su afrenta.*
> *La espada centelleante arda en su mano*
> *y al verle, sobre el trono*
> *palido tiemble el opresor tirano.*

Under French influences he became an encyclopaedist and a cosmopolitan, and later Spanish writers complain that he was unsympathetic to the men who in earlier days made Spain glorious. "Quintana," says Professor Romera-Navarro in his *Historia de la Literatura Española*, "with his encyclopaedist's ideas, all very cosmopolitan and very eighteenth century, could not rightly appreciate the ideas and sentiments of Ferdinand II, who was very Spanish and very sixteenth century." And, the Professor alleges, in his *Pantéon del Escorial* he shows the blackest injustice when dealing with the figures of Charles V and Philip II.

Nevertheless, Quintana was sufficiently non-cosmopolitan to become the very voice of the Spanish war of liberation. Trafalgar put him, therefore, in something of a quandary since it was a victory over the combined Franco-Spanish fleets, and he is forced, in his address to Nelson in "Al Combate de Trafalgar," to exclaim: *"Ingles, te aborreci, y heroe te admiro!"* ("As you are English I hate you, as you are a hero you have my admiration!").

That was in 1805. But in 1808, when the war of independence broke out—and that was an amazing struggle of almost unarmed peasantry against the finest troops in the world—then, indeed, Quintana's passion for his country burst out in his famous odes which, they say, echoed in the driest deserts and on the remotest sides of the parched mountains of Spain.

It is difficult exactly to determine in what Quintana, with his resounding odes, differed from the romantics, but the difference is marked enough to leave no doubt in the mind. It is probable that the heroic circumstances of his race, exactly observed by his classical accuracy, gave the real note to his verses. That he had some acquaintance with the English romantics—or, at least, with the English school of horror—is shown by the fact that he adapted, in 1801, Monk Lewis' *The Castle Spectre* for the Spanish stage, under the title of *El Duque de Viseo*. But the tendency seems to have gone no further than that.

The impulse towards romanticism in Spain came at first and chiefly from the works of the brothers Schlegel, of whom August Wilhelm was, as we have seen, regarded as the grand champion for all Europe of the movement: his brother Friedrich compiling a *History of Literature* which went to prove that from the earliest days everything that was good in letters was of romantic tendency. On the other hand, the current reversed itself when Herder translated into German *El Romancero del Cid* and the brothers Grimm began enjoining on their countrymen the study of Spanish fiction. The real battle between romanticism and classicism engaged itself—naturally after the fall of Napoleon in 1815—when Spain began to be flooded with the main tide of the romantic *chefs d'oeuvre*. All the novels of Scott were translated many times over; Fenimore Cooper, Chateaubriand and Byron became in the 'twenties the chief reading of all the Peninsula.

Reading, other than criticism, was however far to seek; the production of imaginative work failed before the struggles that went on over the constitution. The wretched Ferdinand VII suppressed it immediately after he had reattained his power in 1812; by 1820 constitutional agitation forced him to restore a measure of it. The king appealed for help to the Holy Alliance; Metternich lent him troops to suppress the revolters. The majority of the Spanish intelligentsia, together with all the incipient romanticists, were exiled, going mostly to London where they fell into the very whirlpool of Byronism and could see the carriages of the purchasers of *Childe Harold* block Albemarle Street before the house of Mr. Murray, the publisher.

The critics, however, continued their struggles, each claiming the priority in antiquity of their especial modes. Thus, according to the distinguished Augustìn Duran, romanticism was not a revolt from Spanish neo-classicism but a return to the methods of the picaresques and the pre-eighteenth century poets and novelists.

Actually, the curve followed by Spanish literature after we abandoned it with Quevedo had run nearly parallel with that of England; the seventeenth century was one of great dramatists and prose writers; the eighteenth degenerated into a period of exaggerated Latinity, exaggerated erudition, political pamphlets, of some dramas of distinction and of a general supineness before French tastes which ended in a prevailing neo-classicism that became almost a nothingness in the opening years of the nineteenth century.

Obviously, the early nineteenth century in Spain could in no way compare with the great age—the late sixteenth-seventeenth centuries, any more than the same period in England could compare with the Anglo-Saxon days of glory which ran contemporaneously with those of Spain. And the parallel is singularly close. In England just before and just after the accession of Victoria, you had your Scott, Keats, Shelley, Thackeray, Dickens, Byron, and in America your Poe, Cooper, Hawthorne, Irving—a period of exactly a hundred years, counting from the birth of Scott in 1771 to the death of Thackeray in 1870. It is a respectable bunch; but what is it compared with the writers of the hundred years from the birth of Shakespeare to the death of Dryden?

Similarly, the romantic movement produced a respectable body of writers: the Duke of Rivas, Gutierrez, Hartzenbusch; perhaps, above all, Espronceda, known as the Spanish Byron; de Avellaneda and Zorrilla, amongst poets and dramatists; and amongst novelists, Gil y Carrasco, Villoslava, Larra, Romanos—and a whole bee-swarm of minor names utterly unknown in the rest of Europe and only very faintly remembered in Spain herself. . . . But what were they all as against the age that produced Lope de Vega, Quevedo and the incomparable Calderón de la Barca, not to mention Cervantes and the whole host of the picaresque novelists to whom we devoted so much attention?

It is absolutely necessary here to call a halt in order to explain the omission hitherto of all mention in this work of the four extremely great seventeenth century writers just listed above, whilst the not so very great picaresque novelists were treated even with elaboration. That was because we were then considering the course of the novel from its European birth with the latter writers till the beginning of the romantic movement. To have interrupted that rather subtle story would have resulted in a solution of continuity that this writer was unwilling to risk.

It seems expedient here to say at least a word or two about them. The romantic movement is not so subtle an affair that we are likely to forget its story whilst for a moment digressing. The task is, nevertheless, one from which the present writer rather shrinks, partly because of a complete want of sympathy with Cervantes and of a sort of appallment in considering the enormous continents of the work of Calderón de la Barca justly to estimate whom a work of the dimensions of this present one would hardly suffice. Lope de Vega is a friendlier figure, partly no doubt because of his military and sacerdotal exploits, his exiles for misdemeanors, his loves, his odd erudition . . . and for the fact that whilst a volunteer on the Invincible Armada he wrote his *La Hermosura de Angelicas*, a sort of ironic continuation of the *Orlando Furioso*. Perhaps the most attractive of his works is his *La Dorotea*, a pessimistic play in prose . . . or perhaps it would be more just to call it a novel in dialogue, resembling in its form that of the *Celestina* of which we have so fervently spoken. With its innumerable moving pictures of an extreme realism (he tells us himself that *Dorotea* is written in prose, that vehicle being more sure as an imitation of truth to life, *"siendo tan cierta imitación de la verdad,"* than verse when characters are speaking); with its pictures then, with its realism which extends its wings from the rather muted virtue that the Spaniards call—after *Celestina*—"celestinesque," to the heights of the picaresque, and with the minuteness of its observation of the life it portrays . . . with all these qualities and the infinite range of emotions which the complicated psychology of the author could supply to us, and with all the characters from cardinals to Indian gentlemen and venal mothers, the *Dorotea* seems to this writer to be an incomparably varied world cinema. That, like the *Celestina*, it should have taken the form of prose dialogue rather than of a novel, was due, no doubt, to the almost immeasurable passion of the Spaniards of that day for the stage play. Spain had stage stars almost as numerous as those of the cinema today; the number of her theatres at about the date when the theatres were suppressed in England was given as three hundred; and before the first half of the century had passed, scenery and stage devices had there reached a stage that was not to be attained by the rest of Europe for a couple of hundred years or so.

Some Spanish critics prefer to the *Dorotea* a terrific melodrama called *La Estrella de Sevilla*. That, of course, is a matter of taste, and it is not for us to interfere between them and a work which they style "the masterpiece of the golden age" of literary Spain. It is certainly a magnificently engineered masterpiece of attempted rape of the virtuous heroine by the king, of other dramatic crimes, of overpoweringly pathetic interviews between hero and heroine and of the departure of the one into a convent and of the other to the wars. Various esteemed critics—Spanish, English and French—have denied that Lope de Vega was the author of this piece and doubts have been cast on the authenticity of the original existing manuscript even by those who support the De Vegian authorship. From the purely literary standpoint it would seem rather obvious that the pen that wrote the picaresque scenes of the *Dorotea* could also have given us the— in effect romantic—episodes of the *Estrella*. De Vega wrote a great quantity of lyric poetry; a *horrible tragedia* called *El Castigo sin Venganza* concerning itself with the loves of the Duchess of Ferrara and the illegitimate son of her husband. Here, as with Shakespeare, the tragic scenes are relieved with passages of comedy, but the whole ends in a sea of blood. This author wrote rustic burlesques of great heartiness after he became a priest, numerous pieces of an allegorical religiosity, and a great number of passages of theoretic aesthetic maxims—which, as often as not, he neglected to follow in his own work. They have, nevertheless, great value.

More vast in figure, in the extent of his work, and no doubt in his serious ambitions, the life of Don Pedro Calderón de la Barca occupied the first eighty-one years of the seventeenth century. During fifty of them he stood so alone in the esteem and veneration of all his countrymen that in that age of tumultuous and tortured literary jealousies not a single satirical pamphlet was written against him. He showed himself a great Christian in a long string of dramatic sacramental acta (*autos*); in a number of religious and philosophico-religious dramas. His *Devociòn de la Cruz* was as celebrated in many Protestant countries as in Spain herself. For his *El Magico Prodigioso* it is claimed in its own country that it anticipated the *Faust* of Goethe. His plays of this sort range in gamut from expressions of devotion that are almost sublime to passages of a sentimentality that most non-Spaniards and, indeed, most educated Spaniards of today esteem lamentable.

His comedies *de Capa y Espada* were spirited and titillantly naughty as a rule; though several are quite un-naughty. Their fame throughout the world was very great, so that they were the subjects of many plagiarisms. Thus, his own favorite, *La Dama Duende* was adapted by Thomas Corneille, by Killigrew in *The Parson's Wedding*, and by d'Ouville. Scarron used these comedies over and over again, the Earl of Bristol twice, and the French writers of the farces we lately described when writing of Molière, innumerably—even Mme. de Scudéry making an attempt of the sort. These plays are frequently framed with most ingenious intrigues; they are nearly always good-tempered, hardly ever cruel, the solutions of their mysteries are always artistic.

Of his philosophic comedies *La Vida es Sueño* (Life is a Dream) is another world-famous drama. It is usually compared with both *Hamlet* and Goethe's *Faust*. It is the story of a king of Poland who is also an astrologer. He reads in the stars that his son will be a sovereign of the most monstrous impiety and cruelty; he feels it his duty to kill his son at birth. The son, Sigismondo, is eventually confined in a secret place. But one day his father, doubting that he has done well to trust so implicitly to the stars, has Sigismondo brought, under a narcotic, to the palace. He comes to himself to find that he is surrounded by every sign of his being of royal birth and state. He learns his true story and, enraged and vindictive, designs vengeance on his guardian and his nurse who had attended on him when he had been imprisoned in a tower, and showers insults on his father. Thinking that Sigismondo thus shows signs that should he become king he will carry out the destiny predicted by the stars, the king takes steps to have his son shut up once more in his tower. The unfortunate Sigismondo thus believes that his interlude of royalty had been all a dream, and in a monologue as famous in Spain and most other Latin countries as that of Hamlet he laments the falseness of human greatness and the dreamlike nature of life itself.

Subsequently, being restored to his royal state by the people, to whom his story has been divulged, he is for some time uncertain whether this new state of his is not another dream and for some time meditates suicide. But, reason prevailing, he persuades himself to become a just and merciful sovereign.

This fable, if somewhat jejune in conception, is obviously an admirable frame upon which to throw philosophical and religious reflections, and to be the occasion of a great flow of most admirable poetry. Indeed, the fact that Calderón is one of the greatest lyric poets of all time is slightly obscured by the fact that nearly all his lyrics are enshrined in his plays.

His dramas—in contradistinction to his comedies—are nearly all of them not well constructed, obscured by digressions and passages of rodomontade or religious sentimentality, so that one may regret that the exigencies of his drama-mad time forced that form upon him. In it he shines most in his *autos sacramentales*, one act theological discussions which by the time of Calderón had become limited in theme to the subject of the Blessed Sacrament, the discussions being carried on exclusively by supernatural or allegorical personages. This last fact distinguishes them from the devout or saintly comedies. The *auto*, to paraphrase Fitzmaurice Kelly, has no sub-plot and no mortal characters. Several authors of criticisms or of adaptations from Calderón, including Longfellow, have considered the *Devociòn de la Cruz* to be an *auto*. It is actually a *comedia devota*.

This writer will attempt no considered estimation of the final standing of Calderón de la Barca, still less any comparison with Shakespeare, Goethe or even Lope de Vega—comparisons which have continually been made. As far as this present writer is concerned, Calderón as a figure rather marmoreal and august suggests Goethe; has no aesthetic rapport of any kind with Shakespeare, except for the slight resemblance between *La Vida es Sueño* and *Hamlet*; and differs fundamentally from Lope de Vega, in that Lope de Vega appears to stand for Spain—or, indeed, for all humanity—for all time; Calderón stands intimately for the devout, isolated Spain of the seventeenth century. To establish some sort of pattern in his own mind, this writer is accustomed to regard Calderón, as opposed to de Vega, as a literary writer of the type of Spenser, Milton, Dryden—who also made use of Calderón's comedies—or Shelley or Tennyson. On the other hand, such studies as he made having been almost purely priestly, he was by no means a great scholar of the type of Spenser or Milton and he was overintellectual rightly to belong to the category of the romantics, who nevertheless have their resemblances to him. During his lifetime he was regarded as the greatest man Spain had ever produced and so during the remainder of his century; in the eighteenth century, which in Spain resembled the classical eighteenth century of England, he passed under such a cloud that he was regarded as the author merely of some ingenious little plays. The early nineteenth century restored to him his position of the greatest of Spaniards and of one of the greatest writers of all time. Shelley read Calderón "with inexpressible wonder and delight;" Goethe wept repeatedly whilst reading him; Schlegel and Tieck and the rest of the German romantics went mad over him. Today in Spain, if poor Spain could read, the place assigned to him would be lower than that of Lope de Vega because of his priestly remoteness from life and his failure to draw characters. (Even Goethe said of him that all his characters are as alike as leaden soldiers.) On the other hand, they would say that as a lyric poet, and poet generally, he stands completely alone. The interested reader must thus read Calderón and form his own estimate.

He has been fortunate in his translators. It is true his lyrics just missed being translated by Shelley who hesitated to "throw over their perfect and glowing forms the grey veil of my imperfect words." But eight of his plays were translated by that almost greatest of all verse translators, "Omar-Khayyám" Fitzgerald, and very good translations of his lyrics have been made by Churton, Florence McCarthy, and Mr. R. C. Trench (*La Vida es Sueño*); there is a good biography by Hassell; there is a brilliant study of Calderón in James Fitzmaurice Kelly's *Chapters on Spanish Literature* and another, fuller but more conservative, in Mr. Roméra-Navarro's *Historia Della Literatura Española* published in 1928 by the University of Pennsylvania and still easily obtainable; and Cotarello y Mori's *Ensayo Sobre la Vida y Obras de Don Calderón de la Barca*, published in Madrid in 1924, will give the reader the more modern Spanish of Calderón. Other writings about Calderón have been innumerable, from the romanticisms of Schlegel to the slightly less romantic but bolder Hermann Ulrici, who in 1846 wrote a rather nonsensical work called *Shakespeare's Dramatic Art and His Relation to Calderón and Goethe*. But the above list of authorities will give the reader desirous of deepening his knowledge of Calderón as convenient a beginning of the study as will be found. The study of Spanish has of late years become so frequent that more and more readers of him in the original may form sounder and ever more sound judgments. Indeed, Spanish being still the most widely spoken language of the globe, it would seem unlikely that Calderón will ever want for readers. There follow translations from three of his poems:

Lyric from *Manos Blancos no Ofenden*

Come, death, ere step or sound I hear,
Unknown the hour, unfelt the pain;
Lest the wild joy to feel thee near,
Should thrill me back to life again.

Come, sudden as the lightning-ray,
   When skies are calm and air is still;
E'en from the silence of its way
   More sure to strike where'er it will.

Such let thy secret coming be,
   Lest warning make thy summons vain,
And joy to find myself with thee
   Call back life's ebbing tide again.*

Speech of the Spirit, *Mágico Prodigioso*

Since thou desirest, I will then unveil
Myself to thee;—for in myself I am
A world of happiness and misery;
This I have lost, and that I must lament
For ever. In my attributes I stood
So high and so heroically great,
In lineage so supreme, and with a genius
Which penetrated with a glance the world
Beneath my feet, that was by my high merit.
A King—whom I may call the King of kings,
Because all others tremble in their pride
Before the terrors of his countenance—
In his high palace roofed with brightest gems
Of living light—call them the stars of heaven—
Named me his counsellor. But the high praise
Stung me with pride and envy, and I rose
In mighty competition, to ascend
His seat, and place my foot triumphantly
Upon his subject thrones.†

Tastnia's Song in *Mágico Prodigioso*

Who that in his hour of glory
   Walks the kingdom of the rose,

* Churton's translation.
† Fitzmaurice Kelly's translation.

And misapprehends the story
    Which through all the garden blows;
Which the southern air who brings
It touches, and the leafy strings
    Lightly to the touch respond;
And nightingale to nightingale
    Answering a bough beyond. . . .
Lo! the golden Girasole,
    That to him by whom she burns,
Over heaven slowly, slowly,
    As he travels, ever turns . . .*

Don Miguel de Cervantes y Saavedra (1547-1616) did this world and our time so great a disservice that I have no intention of increasing, however microscopically, the number of his readers by writing of him. The gentle ideal of chivalry is the one mediaeval trait which, had it survived as an influence, might have saved our unfortunate civilization. Cervantes by his vulgar kick in the behind† to its departing form covered it with a ridicule that is perpetuated by every schoolboy-minded contemporary who guffaws over the distresses of the good knight of La Mancha. The real wonder is that the mind of a being such as Cervantes—good soldier, prisoner of the Moors, financial agent twice imprisoned for fraud and chronically impoverished hack author—could have conceived a figure so beautiful as that of Don Quichote. The one merit of Cervantes' masterpiece of ill taste, whose sole effect was to go towards rendering the world fit for Big Business, was that his inventions of means of discomfiture for the knight are so cheaply imagined—the windmills, the helmet of Mambrino and

* Fitzgerald's translation.
† The only serious quarrel that this writer ever had with the late Mr. John Galsworthy was occasioned by this writer saying casually to the other that Cervantes "destroyed" the spirit of chivalry in Europe. Mr. Galsworthy exclaimed with great vigor that no writer ever influenced humanity to any extent at all, and so great was his anti-Plutarchian passion that at one stage of the discussion he actually raised his hand to strike the writer whom for the moment he had come to regard as a sort of Plutarchian anti-Christ. Be that as it may, the above estimate of Cervantes' achievement would seem to be, if inelegantly vigorous, sufficiently exact.

the rest—that it is quite possible to assimilate the beauties of the Don's character and mind without paying any attention to those sillinesses . . . though, as a precaution, one should subsequently read half Mallory! When one thinks of the wide spreading of this work throughout the world and the centuries, one can only repeat, with Harpagon: *"Cela vous donne une fière idée de l'homme"* . . . and leave it at that.

It will be objected that this is not literary criticism. But that is only to be consistent with ourselves since we have determinedly refused, with a probatory exception here and there, to criticize works of propaganda as if they were works of art. Besides, human nature will come creeping in—into even the bosoms of the most exclusive of critics. To paraphrase ourselves in the words of Father O'Flynn: "Is it lave gaiety all to the laity; cannot the clergy be Irishman too?"

For the rest, Cervantes had a military good note from no less a person than Don John of Austria himself. *"Pues era hombre de meritos y servicios,"* writes that great leader in recommending him to a captaincy in the Italian wars . . . and traces of his experiences whilst soldiering in Tunis and Italy are frequent and welcome in his *novelas*, notably in *El Licienciado Vidriera* and *El Amante Liberal* from which we have already quoted.

He was otherwise no very great artist, his best work being probably his *Entreméses*, satirical and extremely observant literary *entremets*, lashing the fashionable defects of his time. The most profitable of these —and the most masterly—would seem to be, for various reasons, *El Juez de los Divorcios* (*The Divorce Court Judge*) and *El Retablo de los Maravillas*.

In the first, Cervantes invented a type of judge that was not to be found on earth until four hundred years later—and some four thousand miles to the west of Spain.

Various unhappily married couples appeared with pleas of divorce successively before this judge, the women pleading with vehemence, the husbands calmly and with good taste. The reasons for complaint were alleged and gave rise to colorful and piquant disputes between the martyred spouse and his fair mate. . . .

There follows a catalogue of the maritally unfortunate from doctors to soldiers . . . as typifying that such misfortunes assail alike those who sent their likes out of, and those who seek to retain them in, this world. Towards the end, this intermezzo justifies its definition as an "exemplary novelette." The judge is worn out by the floods of words to which he has had to listen when enter incontinently into the court two fiddlers who invite him to attend a joyful ceremony. It is that of the re-marriage of a couple whom the judge had divorced. And the *entremés* ends with the moral: The worst kind of agreement is better than the best of divorces.

It is on the *Entreméses* and the *novelas ejemplares* that, if ever an age of reason should supervene, the reputation of Cervantes will rest. They are eminent and even at times delightful because of the immense number of scenes of Spanish—usually low—life that they contain. They are narrated rather than in any sense rendered, and although at times, as if through a veil, one occasionally gets from them glimpses of scenery or of the aspect of characters, they have, like the tales in the *Decameron*, nothing but the value of anecdotes that a real writer might use in an artistic projection. Indeed, one might say of Cervantes that neither he nor the art of his day had traveled farther than had Boccaccio two centuries before. But his repertory of picaresque incident is enormous. For that we may be grateful. He was certainly no literary littérateur.

In short, if you omit *Don Quichote* from his achievements, he becomes quite a minor literary phenomenon. His other novel, *La Galatéa,* is a pastoral farrago so complicated in its involutions as to be almost incomprehensible. The present writer has at least so found it, not owing to a lack of seventeenth century Spanish, but simply because of an inability to follow the adventures of the sham shepherds and shepherdesses. On that Cervantes himself comments. His *Galatéa* is found by the barber and priest amongst the books of Don Quichote:

"But what book is that next one there?" asked the priest.
"*The Galatéa* of Miguel de Cervantes," said the barber.
"It is many years that I have held that Cervantes for a good friend of mine and I know that he is more acquainted with tribulations than with verse writing. His book exhibits some faculty of invention, but it proposes things and arrives at no conclusions. In the meanwhile let us wait for the continuation which he promises us; with better luck he may give us something that his wretched circumstances have hitherto denied him."*

Calderón died just after finishing one of his *autos* which he had come out of his religious retirement to write at the age of eighty-one at the command of the king. Thus, as comments Cotarelo y Mori, *"Murio pue, como muere el cisne, cantando."* (He died like the swan, singing.) But the unfortunate Cervantes, after he had received the extreme unction, having the certainty that he would die—of dropsy— on the morrow must set to work to write the Dedication to the Count de Lemos of his posthumous romance *Persiles y Sigismunda* in the hope that that patron would at least do something for his widow. "Thus," his last words run in that document, "adieu my jests; adieu my joyous humors, adieu my gay, sweet friends; for I feel that I am dying and have now no wish left but soon to see you again in another, happier life."

Don Quichote himself could hardly better have made the end of a very gallant seventeenth century gentleman than this poor hack writer.

It is still more interesting to observe that a considerable part of *Persiles y Sigismunda,* after it had been published by Cervantes' widow, was translated by Fletcher into his—quite filthy—*Custom of*

* Author's adaptation.

the Country, which, according to Dryden, contains more lechery than all his own plays put together.

This, taken in conjunction with the great number of plagiarisms both French and English from the comedies of Calderón should finally go to prove—and in this era of regionalism and local patriotism which asserts that no literary school ever derived from former or foreign schools, that is a thing that should be proved to the hilt at whatever risk of repetitiousness—the plagiarism of Fletcher from Cervantes, then, should go to prove that in the days of Webster, as in those of the romantics, "influences" flew as thick as bees from Gibraltar to the Quartier Latin and to the seventeenth century equivalent of Grub Street. So we may well call the age of the romantics a second renaissance in England as the age of Shakespeare and of Webster was a first one.

Cervantes has been hailed as a god and as the greatest of all Spaniards—thus ignoring Lope de Vega—by every writer, Spanish and foreign, who has ever touched upon him from Martín Fernandez de Navarrete, Bonilla y San Martín, Amezúa y Mayo to Ticknor, Hassell, Fitzmaurice Kelly and Roméra-Navarro—to Shelley, Goethe and, above all, the notorious Schlegel, the banner bearer of the romantic movement. Ticknor says that "Not even Shakespeare demands from us a sympathy so strange;" Shelley says that no other writer compares with him in awakening pity and admiration; Friedrich Schlegel calls Cervantes "godlike;" August Schlegel qualifies Cervantes' *Numancia* great poetry—a sentiment which not one other of the commentators on that work can echo.*

Nearly all of them qualify that Spanish "Undying Wrong" by saying that Cervantes really loved the Ingenious Hidalgo and his retainer, and then give various sentimental reasons which the reader

* Contrary to my usual habit—because I do not wish my carefully inculcated views of authors to be interfered with by those of other critics—I cite above the list of the chief writers about Cervantes whom I have searched for eulogies of the author of *El Ingenioso Hidalgo Don Quixote de la Mancha.* I think it only fair to the reader to give him every opportunity to see how differently the world—the less credit to it!—judges this author.

will find in one or other of the above books for casting ridicule on them. But, however it may be with his love for Sancho Panza, one is tempted as to the Don to quote the undying lines:

> Perhaps it was right to dissemble your love
> But why did you kick me downstairs?

I have even seen it somewhere declared—but I cannot recapture where—that in *Don Quichote* Cervantes was the forerunner not of the romantics but of the French literary impressionists. As who should say that he stood godlike and without favorites above his characters, as did Flaubert, who though in every way poking fun at his Emma Bovary as a watery romantic, was nevertheless in love with her as was Defoe with his Moll. . . . As who should say: "Whom he loveth he chasteneth."

It would however, I think, be more just to say that in writing that book Cervantes was trying to "get back at" not one particular fashionable of his time but on the whole fashionable world that neglected his claims and let him starve miserably as a debt collector. That world was still dimly illuminated by the rays of a candle that posterity should have very unwillingly allowed to die. Cervantes put it out. And the "revenge" theory is prophesied and confirmed. As debt collector, Cervantes traveled all Spain within hundreds of miles both of Seville and Madrid; that gave him his incomparable knowledge of that parched, formal and romantic land. But in the small place called La Mancha they set about him and would have lynched him— because they did not want to pay their debts. So Cervantes determined to bestow on that place an eternity of ridicule. He did so.

As novelist, we need not regret this digression into the Spanish past. If the writer could see an opportunity, he would here digress back too into the days of Tibullus, and you should once more see the Aegean with his girl with wearied hands and brine-heavy locks swimming always lower and lower in the sea, or once more we should hear Job curse the day of his birth and his mother's womb. Or we should stand with Rihaku and the bowmen, digging the last fern roots and gazing away from the North Wall into the lands whence come the barbarians. For when we get out of those serenities into this age of hack writers swarming like mites in Gorgonzola—and not half so well fed—the image of the great stream of thought recorded in good letters grows a little dim and we are apt to forget the streams by whose banks we walked with the philosophers. . . . So, as the novelist at the end of his story recalls, so as to give it an aspect of unity, its beginnings, so it was a good thing in the midst of the story of the rather specious romantics to return to the days of the great authentics, Lope de Vega, Quevedo, Calderón—and, if you must, Cervantes.

Of Francisco Gomez de Quevedo y Villegas, the great scholar-politician, clubfooted and half blind, who nevertheless again and again pinked his man and disarmed the most famous fencing master of his day and who, the great champion of St. Iago de Compostella, positively shamed the Pope into withdrawing his bull that was intended to make the mystic St. Theresa co-patron, with St. James, of Spain. . . . Of Quevedo, author of the great picaresque *Historia de la Vida del Buscòn*, we have said nothing at all, though we have quoted him. He was by turns poet, politician, diplomat, satirist, prisoner for four years in a cell below water level (for *lèse majesté*), and theologian. Sometimes he succeeded in one or other of these métiers, as often he failed. But for this writer at least he was one of the greatest of Spanish characters of a great age and his *Historia*, better known as *El Gran Tacaño*, one of the greatest of books.

The Spanish romantic writers, then, were El Duque de Rivas (1791-1865); Garcia Gutierrez (1812-1884); Juan Eugenio Hartzenbusch (1806-1880); and, above all, as far as this writer is concerned, José de Espronceda, and in a lesser degree Zorrilla, Larra and, to name a woman, Gertrudis Gómez de Avellaneda, a Cuban. She should make us remember that just as in the United States a literature was beginning to be born with Poe, so after the separation of Mexico from Spain in 1824 romanticists began to flower in that West also. So you had the historian Bustamante, the Indian romance writer

Altamirano, and, perhaps above all for this present writer, the novelist Covarrubias, author of a picaresque eighteenth century masterpiece called *The Itching Parrot*, which is as vivid as Quevedo himself could make his novels.

Perhaps the most interesting feature of the Spanish romantics is really the fact that they were almost the creation of the stream of romanticism sent out by Frederick Schlegel and his Germans. In turn they sent an inspiring backwash to the country of Schlegel and his friends. It is difficult otherwise to place them amongst that literature of the large scale that includes the figures of, say, Dante, Aeschylus, the writer of the Book of Job and Lao-Tsze. But as a movement, as a symptom that Spain too partook of the world unrest that resulted in romanticism, they are of interest. M. Roméra-Novarro speaking of *El Moro Exposito* by the Duke of Rivas can call it *"la mejor leyenda epica de la España moderna, la más inspirada, armoniosa y completa,"* but the effect is rather that of a small-town paper praising the quite good product of a local townsman. The most interesting part of the publication—for the non-townsman—is the preface of Antonio Alcalá Galiano. It is a discreet romantic manifesto, a watered-down version of the many efforts in the same direction of Friedrich Schlegel.

The manifesto thus issued, romanticism could go on its way. It began in Spain as elsewhere with a drama. A drama is a good thing with which to begin the shock tactics of a movement intended to disquiet quiet people. A book may make carriages block a street. But a revolutionary play, like *Álvaro la Fuerza del Sino* or *Hernani*, brings out noisy young supporters to attend first nights, to raise great public rows, to smash in the hats of opponents, to be arrested and next day to make speeches in the police courts. All these phenomena attended the first night of *Álvaro*.

It seems almost unnecessary to relate that Don Álvaro was a dashing youth, chivalrous and valiant; about his past hung a "prestigiosa" aureole of mystery. He became enamored of the lady Leonora, daughter of the Marquis of Calatrava. In face of the opposition of the father, the young couple concert an elopement. Surprised during the flight, Don Álvaro is the innocent cause of the death of the marquis, who dies cursing his daughter. Well, that is romanticism. . . .

Doña Leonora becomes *"un misterioso ermitano"* and, after innumerable duels with sons of the marquis, being denounced by the mysterious hermit, Don Álvaro *"se arroja por un precipicio."*

It seems difficult to take that sort of thing seriously today; but in its own time it was valued beyond most plays and was seriously considered by the Spanish critics: *"El drama mas celebre del Romanticismo."* And, apparently, it is still so considered, the words quoted having been written in 1928. . . . At any rate, we may well believe that, in the words of Mr. Fitzmaurice Kelly, *"Don Álvaro* by its contempt for the unities, by its alternation of prose with lyricism, by its amalgam of the grandiose, the comic, the sublime and the horrible, enchanted a generation of Spanish playgoers surfeited with the academic drama." Whether it is actually the "most celebrated" of the romantic dramas, whether it is actually more or less worthless than *Hernani, The Corsican Brothers* or *Cyrano de Bergerac*, it is difficult to say. But if we were in Spanish skins we might have no doubt.

Let us indulge ourselves with a moment's intermezzo whilst we transcribe José Maria Blanco's famous Sonnet:

> Mysterious light! When our first parent knew
>   Thee, from report divine, and heard thy name,
>   Did he not tremble for this lovely frame,
> This glorious canopy of light and blue?
> Yet 'neath a curtain of translucent dew
>   Bathed in the rays of the great setting flame,
>   Hesperus, with the host of heaven, came,
> And lo! Creation widened in man's view.
>   Who could have thought such darkness lay concealed
>   Within thy beams, O Sun? or who could find,
>   Whilst fly, and leaf, and insect stood revealed,
>   That to such countless orbs thou madest us blind?
>   Why do we then shun death with anxious strife?
>   If light can thus deceive, wherefore not life?

José Maria Blanco, Dean of Seville, became, after many sufferings, a Unitarian minister in England and is best known as Blanco White. It is interesting to quote him as a specimen of the innumerable minor poets, nearly all leading romantic and usually hungry lives in the Spain of about this period. Mr. J. C. Garcin catalogues, indeed, over seventy names of poets born between 1800 and 1820, every one of them with the exception of those here named being completely unknown to this writer and to every Spanish authority that he has been able to consult.

Larra (Mariano José de, 1809-1837) this writer will for a moment call to mind because his brilliant writing and somber humor were at one time a great cause of delight to him. This is perhaps a little arbitrary because Larra's successes were all in the department of political satires, his few attempts at the larger literature being almost ludicrous failures. He passes for the Spanish Swift and when he committed suicide—over an unhappy love affair at the age of twenty-eight—he left a gap that no Spaniard has since filled, and he had no predecessor at all. He resembled Gibbon and Pushkin in that his earliest writings were in French, a fact that may account for the unusual trenchancy and clarity of his Spanish. Nor should Zorrilla (José, 1817-1893) be entirely forgotten. He has been regarded as the dramatic counterpart of Sir Walter Scott. For the greater part of his life he was a politician and it was only when a pension relieved him of the necessity of thus earning his livelihood that he really took to literature. But his naïve plays, instinct with the sentiments of honor, patriotism and devotion have sufficed hitherto to secure him a place not merely in the hearts of his fellow citizens but behind the footlights. Certain pure hearts from time to time earn that guerdon not so much of immortality as of alms from oblivion.

With Espronceda (José de, 1810-1842), with whom we shall end this mere chronicle of Spanish romanticism, we come upon a figure of near-European dimensions. He was in his private life a continuing champion of the cause of world liberty. He organized ceaseless conspiracies against the government, fled successively to Lisbon and

London, fought on the barricades in Paris during *les trois glorieuses*—the three glorious days that got rid of Charles X—and, inspired by that success, engineered the great conspiracy of Spanish emigrados that under the leadership of Chapalangarra was doomed to complete failure. After the amnesty, on the death of Ferdinand VII, he returned to Spain and was given a commission in the royal bodyguard. But he was cashiered for writing scurrilous verses against the monarchy, led the people against the royal troops and had great part in the successful revolution in 1840. He was elected a socialist deputy, and died. He was known as the Byron of Spain, and his resemblances to Byron—whom he had known and worshipped in London—were many. He declared himself the apostle of debauchery and anarchy and was generally alien to the gravity that in the end is the sovereign quality of all Spanish work of whatever party. He had thus something of the cosmopolitan romantic in his composition and he wrote nearly as aristo-carelessly as Byron himself. Little, indeed, therefore of him remains authentic and remembered except his lyric poems and some of his longer pieces like *El Estudiante de Salamanca*, a poem which remains always in the affections of the writer since, in very early infancy indeed, he with some of his younger relations, converted it into a puppet play. The quality of its verse, its irresponsible incidents and still more irresponsible characters are of a sort that continually recur in the hearts and under the pens of romantics who, like the poor, are always with us.

It remains to say of this really great figure that, beloved in his day, he passes still amongst Spaniards for "*nuestro mayor poeta lírico del siglo*," a dictum uttered by Cascales y Muñoz in his study of Espronceda in 1914 and quoted with approbation by M. Navarro in 1928—which is near enough to our own day. And without professing to an intimate connoisseurship in Spanish prosody—for though sufficient Spanish to read *Lazarillo de Tormes* without too much stumbling has been a possession of this writer for about half a century, the proper judgment of the niceties of lyricism demands almost more appreciation of a language than is given to any stranger—yet we can well recognize the exquisite beauty of thought and the majestically cesura'd rhythm of a poem like his *Canto a Teresa*—a poem addressed to the memory of a woman who dominated his whole life. It is almost impossible to read without deep emotion, familiar though the bare thought may be, such verses as:

> *Cómo caíste despeñado al suelo*
> *astro de la mañana luminoso,*
> *ángel de luz; quien te arrojó del cielo*
> *a este valle de lagrimas odioso?*

One might say of him, as one says truly of Heine and German, that it is worth while—it is almost necessary—to learn Spanish well in order to appreciate Espronceda's lyrics in the original.

CHAPTER THREE

W E EMERGE then into the broad daylight of Anglo-French romanticism of the early nineteenth century. This was a century
more flooded with mediocre books and less furnished with authentically great literary figures than any of the cycles that have preceded
it. You could name ten thousand goodish books that you might, without any pressing necessity, noddingly know; you might name a hundred authors that cultured persons would be expected to talk about.
But you could find no one amongst either the romantics or what I
will call "straight" writers of any prime greatness of stature. There
would be none of them who would—say from 1820 onwards—be
otherwise than regionally proclaimed as great. The Russians would say
Pushkin; the English, Thackeray; the French, Balzac, or possibly
Hugo; the Germans would assert the claims of Goethe who lived
until 1832, and in 1820 was writing his *Faust* . . . and who should say
them nay. But Goethe hardly belonged to post-Napoleonic figures,
and the most marked characteristic of the eighteen twentyish literature of the world was that it burst into existence and breathed freely
because the era of the Corsican was finished. A new era against
which to protest had arrived and was to come to a head a quarter of a
century or so later. For it is impossible that the '48 when all the thrones
of the world tottered and Karl Marx—with whom we have, thank
goodness, no affair—Karl Marx, then, together with Engels, wrote
the *Communist Manifesto* . . . it is impossible to consider that the '48
was not the product of the romantic movement of the o's to 20's of the
nineteenth century. It is none the less the fact that the, as it were,
society unrest of 1820 led directly to the social struggles of twenty-
eight years later. Byron and Espronceda are no doubt turning in their
graves as we write that it was they who gave the impulse to *Das
Kapital*, but it cannot be helped. They must just turn over once again
and put themselves to sleep by humming the

Hurra, cosacos del desierto! Hurra!
La Europa os brinda esplendido botín

which was Espronceda's imitation from Byron's *Mazeppa*, which again was suggested by Pushkin.

The romantic movement was actually a protest against the bourgeois Louis Philippism that succeeded to the cuirasses and sabers of the Napoleonic era. The world's protest against that dull tyranny took itself out in imaginations of corsairs ravishing pearls, rubies and princesses; in Cossacks of the Don making Europe their booty; in dark, doomed youths standing aside in the assemblies and routs, and taking refuge either in the turban of the Levantine pirate or the dagger and the bowl of cold poison. All this discontent must come to a mob culmination—and mob culminations arrive at conclusions singularly alien from the spirit of their original impulsions. By 1849, when the rebellions were quelled, the thrones by the stupid power of Prussia reëstablished on bases duller and more stupid, an entirely different spirit had come into the world. Romanticism was finished and, gradually, under quite new pressures, literature took on a new, more grim, face.

We are, however, still in the heyday of the romantic movement. Let us make some experiments of our own. Let us first, in confirmation of the dictum that supremely great men were no longer to visit the earth, set down in enduring letters the names Homer, Aeschylus, Horace, Cicero, Arnaut Daniel, Dante, Villon, Chaucer, Shakespeare, Rabelais, Molière, Lope de Vega—and, if you will, Cervantes, Milton, Johnson and Goethe.

Let us then set down in order of birth the names of the writers whose works were available for the reader in the year 1820—five years after the Battle of Waterloo.

Let us begin by noting that Jane Austen was not among this number, she having died in 1817, though her *Persuasion*, which was posthumously published, could still be described as then a new book. Other books still new in that year, or to be published just after, were Byron's *Mazeppa* (He was about that time in Venice engaged on the fourth canto of *Childe Harold, Beppo* and *Don Juan.*); *Ivanhoe*, published in 1819; "The Ode to a Grecian Urn," published in 1820;

Pushkin's *Ruslan and Liudmila*, 1820; Hazlitt's *Table Talk*, 1821; Shelley had published the *Revolt of Islam* in 1818, and in that year he went to Italy to write *Prometheus Unbound, Adonais* and the *West Wind*. And, to strike a quite new note in the symphony, in 1820 Poe left England after five years at school there. In 1821 Fenimore Cooper published his first book *The Spy* . . . and Washington Irving, then in England and encouraged by Walter Scott, wrote and published his *Sketchbook*. It enjoyed an enormous popularity.* Thus, early began the honorable tradition that the young American author from Irving on to Stephen Crane, Pound, Dreiser and so many others must come or send his books for early recognition . . . to London. And, *per contra*, how many English writers who are names in the United States are less than the dust in the country of their birth!

Here, then, is the list of authors whose books were available and as a rule much read in 1820:

In Russia: Pushkin, d. 1837; Lermontov, d. 1841. *In Germany:* Jean Paul Richter, d. 1825; Friedrich Schlegel, d. 1829; Goethe, d. 1832. *In Italy:* Leopardi, d. 1837; Manzoni, d. 1873. *In Spain:* de Larra, d. 1837; Espronceda, d. 1844; Quintana, d. 1854. *In France:* Stendhal, 1783-1842; Chateaubriand, d. 1848; Balzac, d. 1850; Heinrich Heine, d. 1856; Musset, d. 1857; de Vigny, d. 1863; Lamartine, d. 1870. *In England and the United States:* Scott, 1771-1832; Jane Austen, 1775-1817; Lamb, 1775-1834; Hazlitt, 1778-1830; Washington Irving, 1783-1859; Byron, 1788-1824; Fenimore Cooper, 1789-1851; Shelley, 1792-1832; Marryat, 1792-1848; Keats, 1792-1821; Macaulay, 1800-1859; Hawthorne, 1804-1864.

* Let us hazard here a curious note. The writer's great grandfather, Ford Brown, R.N., a naval officer, was in Paris in 1815, after Waterloo, on duty. In his letters home he records that the most interesting thing to notice in that city was the relative sizes of the crowds that followed the great personalities of the hour. He says that the tsar's crowd was the largest of all, always. But it was sometimes matched by that of the admirers of Sir Walter Scott and sometimes nearly so by those of an American author whom he could not at the time name, saying that the crowd expected to see him dressed in feathers and a blanket as if he had been an Indian chief. Later he made a note on his letter to the effect that this must have been one Fenimore Cooper author of the *Sketchbook of Geoffry Crayon*, from which confusion one would seem to gather that it was actually Washington Irving. He had published his *History of New York* in 1809 and his Knickerbocker stories had at once attained a very great international reputation.

This writer begs that the reader will spend some time over the above list, for the sake of mnemonics, worrying out the odd coincidences that are such an aid to the memory. Thus, as we have said, Queen Victoria came to the throne in 1837 and, as if they could not face that prospect, Pushkin, de Larra and Leopardi all died in that year, being pre-deceased by Keats, Shelley, Byron, Hazlitt, Lamb, Scott, Friedrich Schlegel, Jean Paul Richter and Goethe, who all died between 1820 and 1837. But, in compensation, kindly Providence sent us, incontinently, a group of writers who, as if symbolically, being too young to write in those seventeen years, nearly all began to flourish in the year of Victoria's accession. Mark them well. They were Edgar Allan Poe, who, born in 1808 and dying in 1849 (and thus just surviving the writing of the *Communist Manifesto*), wrote his first work to attract any attention, the *Narrative of Arthur Gordon Pym* in 1837. Similarly, in 1837, Charles Dickens (b. 1812), published his *Sketches by Boz* and began his *Pickwick Papers*. But being unable to face the scotching, if not the extinction, of our Mediterranean civilization by the Franco-Prussian War, he sought another world in 1870 . . . as did Lamartine and Dumas *père*. On the other hand, in the year 1848, as if unable to face the idea of Marx and Engels, there died two very dissimilar writers: Chateaubriand and Captain Marryat, they in turn being pre-deceased between 1837 and 1848 by Lermontov in 1841 and Espronceda in 1844. The writers who were writing in 1820, and who survived the '48 were Quintana, 1854; Balzac, 1850; Heine, 1856; de Musset, 1857; de Vigny, 1873; Washington Irving, 1859; Fenimore Cooper, 1851; whilst, surely by a special dispensation, the good Manzoni lived till 1873, and thus at the age of eighty-eight was privileged to see the freeing of Italy, the establishment of an Italian monarchy and the union of all Italy, "beautiful with the flowers in her hair." For thus, whilst the Prussians were laying the axe to the root of our civilization, Pallas Athene, with Louis Napoleon as her instrument, was strengthening that civilization on the shores that had been its birthplace and home.

The battle being thus engaged and the moment of our extremity at hand, let us establish as our cardinal years for the literature of the nineteenth century those of 1820, 1848, 1870 and 1897 which was the year of Queen Victoria's Diamond Jubilee and which still more mark-edly saw the merging of Victorianism into that *fin de siècle* that saw a sort of literary revival at the hands of Henley, *The Yellow Book*, Conrad, James and the other Anglo-Saxon figures that today are most familiar to us.*

To begin with 1820. Two immense factors stand out when we again re-study the list of writers then writing. First, in face of the lack of great writers after the death of Goethe, the world of writers had indeed become a republic of letters, and its product a literature as against a world of a few great books. And, secondly and above all, in spite of wars, divisions of tongues, civil strifes, patriotisms, social divisions, internecine aesthetic hates—this whole harvest of pens, reaped between Archangel, Madrid, Gibraltar and Rome was all one litera-ture. Pushkin was merely another manifestation of Byron or Espron-ceda; Espronceda of Pushkin or Byron; Byron of Pushkin and Espron-ceda; Manzoni was merely a more documented Scott; de Larra as much applauded in Berlin as in Madrid; Schlegel as much in Madrid as in Paris or Berlin. And no man could be a proper member of any little regional republic of taste unless he was intimate with all the works applauded in all the other regional republics of taste. In a Paris crowded to overflowing with troops and citizens of every nation under our purview the author of the *Bride of Lammermoor* was fol-lowed by crowds as great as those who attended on the tsar, and Diedrich Knickerbocker by crowds nearly as great as either, and Scott saw kinships between himself and Irving as between himself and Charles Lamb . . . who might have been suckled by the same mother as Irving. And Irving learned of Granada, as did Chateaubriand of the virgin forests of America. And if you removed the snobbish gen-tlemanliness and heroics from the pages of Scott and read him in an

---

* Let us at this moment frivolously remind ourselves that the sixty-first year of a great reign was commemorated not merely by Mr. Kipling's *Recessional* but by the much more widely sung national folksong:

> Oh, dear me, that Jubilation day.
> It's only once in sixty years the people say.
> We all got drunk but we had a jolly spree,
> For we had to take the missus to the jubilee.

agreeable book like *The Antiquary*, or if you could set the story of
I Promessi Sposi in a country less tyrant-ridden, you would come on
a point of view remarkably resembling that of Jane Austen herself.

She, however, as was the way with all the more prominent woman
writers of the period, was a special case for the consideration of which
we must later find a special place.

So, if we regard ourselves as standing on a high place in time and
looking out like a later Cortez and his man, we shall seem to see an
immense delta, a huge level territory of a uniform, as if neutral hue
bounded on the North by, say, Christiania—for soon now the Scandi-
navians too will be coming in—and on the Southwest by, say, Kala-
mazoo and coming, narrowing on the East, to the Bridge of St. Louis
where Italy touches Provence. For it is as if, through the defile at
that bridge, there had poured the immense flood of the waters that
we saw, taking their rise where the Nile rises and, on the other hand,
in Cathay, and so joining in the Eastern Mediterranean to form,
flowing past Athens as past Rome, the immense delta whose flats we
are overlooking from this our height.

There is one immense difference between the great literature of the
1820's and all the little literatures, of the English seventeenth, the
French seventeenth, the German late eighteenth and early nineteenth
centuries—there is one immense difference, leading down to the general
levelness of all literature from that day to our own. That is that practically all these latter authors were hack writers. The germ of the "man
of letters" that seemed to reach earth with the hack translator, Le
Sage, author of *Gil Blas*, or the hack poet, Dryden, spread with
great rapidity in the age of Johnson and Jean Jacques Rousseau. But
by the 1820's and forever later there had and have been in the republic of letters nothing else. And it is as if the quality of monumental greatness deserted writing and the earth, as soon as the making
of money became the chief preoccupation of the writer. It was not for
nothing that the sage once wrote that literature was a good stick
but a bad crutch. It is the sad truth.

One looks from our height over that delta, and in all the stretch perceives no single mountain peak and hardly here and there more than two or three monticules. If you say *Vanity Fair* and *The Way of All Flesh*, you have exhausted the catalogue of very great English works of the imagination for all that period—but, obviously, you have a whole range of books in which Anglo-Saxondom particularly excels, from De Quincey's *Opium Eater*, to Borrow's *Bible in Spain*, Beckford's *Letters from Portugal*, Charles Darwin's *Voyage of the Beagle* to Doughty's *Arabia Deserta,* none of them however forming exactly great peaks. To the North, on the boundary, you would see the heights formed by the works of Turgenev, Dostoievsky and, if you like, Tolstoy and Ibsen. In France there would be of extremely great books only, let us say, Stendhal's *Le Rouge et le Noir*, one or other of the novels of Balzac, and, above all, *Madame Bovary*, which has been the most read novel of the whole world ever since the day of its publication. But what a literature! Chateaubriand, de Musset, de Vigny, Gautier, Lamartine, Barbey d'Aurevilly. . . . You might, indeed, go on forever. And, standing all alone, Heine, perhaps the most exquisite of all the world's lyrists since the great Greeks, perhaps the greatest of all the world's realistic-bitter romantics, perhaps, at least for his Paris days, the most tragic of deserted literary figures.

The crop of greatnesses is, therefore, not large. Nevertheless, you could not call any man even mediocrely educated who is not fairly—but even intimately!—acquainted with almost every writer on that list which begins with Pushkin and ends with Hawthorne. Obviously, one might for reasons of distaste omit one or two of them without feeling any very bitter regret. One might find it impossible to read Balzac or literary figures of fun like Byron or Dumas *père*. Indeed, it is very difficult to imagine the reader who today would seriously sit down to read either *Childe Harold* or *Don Juan*, except as a duty—and our reading list is by now so great that we have no time for duty reading. If, after a reasonable trial, the works of any writer fail to ring our bells, our duty is to throw them away and begin on someone else.

Let then this writer and this reader take hands. Descending our hillside, let us jump the little brook of time and mingle with the great creatures who are browsing amongst the asphodels of those Elysian Fields. For to us who are so small even Leopardi, who we are told was the smallest of anxious-faced scholars, must appear big, indeed. A little Brobdingnagian to us microscopic Lilliputians.

I think we shall come first upon that great nobleman, gentleman and prop of his church and king, François René, Vicomte de Chateaubriand, Minister Plenipotentiary, Ambassador to the Court of St. James, and Foreign Minister of France. In his youth he traveled far, seeking, no doubt, one ivory tower or another amongst the redskins of the then Far West; as an exile in London he began his writings with his *Essais Historiques Politiques et Morales sur la Revolution Française.* He reconciled himself to Buonaparte, returned to his country but became one of his most bitter antagonists after the murder of the Duc d'Enghien, a change of heart for which we need hardly blame him. In 1805 he published his *René,* as to which it was said academically only yesterday that it constituted him at once the greatest author of his age and country* . . . which is saying a good deal though I do not think that we need quarrel with the dictum. We must at times find ourselves ranged alongside a professor or so.

Chateaubriand's other works which it is necessary to read—but, indeed, if one wished to improve one's style in the direction of clear simplicity one should shut oneself with all the works of the Viscount until one feels that one knows the trick—are his exquisitely melancholy *Les Aventures du Dernier des Abencérages* (1826) and his *Memoires d'Outre Tombe.*

And, when one says that it is necessary to read such-and-such works that does not mean that if one has not read them one will not be able to shine—or even to keep one's place—in bookishly cultured society. It means something more subtle and personal. Thus, certain qualities are necessary to the ingredients of one's ego if one is to go through a world of unforeseen accidents with dignity and composure. It is obvious that one will hardly be a proper man unless one is acquainted with the frame of mind of, say, the Old Testament, or, let

---

* *The Columbia Encyclopaedia,* compiled and edited at Columbia University. (The Columbia University Press, New York, 1935.) A much to be commended compilation.

us add, Plutarch's *Lives* or the *Morte d'Arthur*. You will say that the majority of the world have not read those last two books—to which the reply is that the world is none so satisfactory a place. . . . In any case, if you have not read the Old Testament you will be out of touch with the majority of your fellow beings; if you have not read Plutarch you will not have made acquaintance with a sort of high courage and sense of responsibility expressed as it is nowhere else expressed, and if you have not read the *Morte d'Arthur* you will not know the quintessence of reckless adventure and the rarenesses of chivalry. You will not merely be a different man after you have read for the first time the letter of Sir Gawain to Sir Launcelot:

> I send thee greeting and let thee have knowledge, thou flower of all noble knights that ever I saw or heard of by my day, that this day I was smitten on the old wound that thou gavest me afore the city of Benwick and through the same wound that thou gavest me I am come to my own death day wherefore I beseech thee, Sir Launcelot, to return again unto this realm, and see my tomb and say some prayer more or less for my soul.

—but you will become acquainted with a fineness of approach between man and man that has vanished from our world—aided by Cervantes! . . . And you may be given the idea of restoring a little of that feeling, by your own conduct, to this world and if you are able to you will be the happier man. . . . And if a great—an enormous— many should read those words a great many of the ills that affect us would melt away. That is what literature is for.

It is necessary, then, to read Chateaubriand because he was the last of the great writers. He survived Goethe by sixteen years, and with him he had great resemblances—a sort of marmoreal calm intershot by a singularly tender sensibility. That was something that they added to the characters presented by Plutarch. You can not imagine Cicero with his eyes near to tears as he reads Calderón, nor Brutus writing: "How sad it is to think that eyes that are too old to see are yet not too old to shed tears. . . ."

That is what Chateaubriand wrote one day when he had been talking to an aged, blind Indian sachem who had passed without wincing a life of infinite hardship and courage and yet was finally moved to emotion by the news of a domestic disaster—the wiping out by enemies of a whole branch of his young family.

And it is that sentence of Chateaubriand's, read long ago, that this writer most has taken away from reading his works. It is an incentive to carry one's fortitude into the extremes of age, so it is, like all great tragic writing, a stimulant. And it is, if that were needed, evidence that Chateaubriand as traveler was more than just a coverer of waste spaces. For it is a touching little vignette from the past to think of that young French noble in tie wig, plumed hat and satin knee breeches standing in the virgin forest looking down on the ancient chief and condensing that human contact into that admirable thought. It justifies him as being the last of a line—a line of writers who were not hacks.

The ideal career for a writer was that of Chaucer. Let us return to him for a moment. As a young man he was a fighter and, as that, taken prisoner in battle, and so occupied himself in his cell with the translation of a world masterpiece. By birth he was a vintner and thus knew, not as a newspaper reporter, but as a practitioner, how trade went. Then he is a diplomat engaged in the delicate negotiation of marrying kings' sons to princesses; then a place-man in such an office as that its duties could be performed by deputies. So he had leisure to write, out of the fullness of his real human contacts, things to please. To please a widowed great princess he wrote little naughtinesses that were kept in drawers; to please the princes and knights of the court, allegories of truth, justice, prudence, chastity . . . and the knightlinesses of Sirs Palamon and Arcite. And to please the whole of humanity, of which Chaucer had such a sense, he wrote in all leisure his immortal tales which are as full of humanity as an egg about to hatch is full of the meat of the chicken it bears. And the secret of what distinguishes the great pre-nineteenth century masterpieces from the nineteenth and post-nineteenth century great literatures of near-mediocrities—for what is the good of setting up *Vanity Fair* beside the *Divine Comedy?*—that secret lies in the words "in all leisure." Think how lambent and serene this prose that you are now reading might be were it not that the writer writing it is possessed by the feeling that this work must be finished and go to the printer on . . . oh, the anniversary of the taking of the Bastille!

The extremely bitterest of all anecdotes in the annals of Grub Street has always seemed to this writer to be one told by Lockhart, the son-in-law of Scott, in his *Life of Scott*. He relates how he delayed someone in the street outside Scott's house and from the other side of the way pointed out a white hand that could be seen through an upper window. The hand holding a quill, its owner being hidden from sight, went on writing and writing, and had gone on writing and writing like that for years and years and was to go on writing for years more until it was stilled for good. That was the hand of Scott, writing some of the worst hack work that was ever written in order to pay off the creditors of his bankruptcy. And if you think of Thackeray writing also, hack work like the *Four Georges* and poor stuff about the eighteenth century humorists, in perpetual dread that his popularity should come to an end and that he would not be able to keep up the small but pompous establishment of the sufficiently commonplace house that he had built in palace gardens, Kensington, which he loved to consider is called "the royal borough;" and if you think of Gautier sitting up night after night after having written all day, to pour out criticisms of worthless plays in order just to keep himself from starvation, and groaning perpetually *"ce pauvre Théo!"* (and he the unparalleled author of *Émaux et Camées*); and Conrad writing desperately away in spite of every illness and family catastrophe so as to live just above the verge of starvation; and Hudson living with his wife in a garret with nothing to eat but a half-pound tin of cocoa and a few biscuits per week whilst he earned a few pence by disinterring from the British Museum records and genealogies for the inhabitants of the Middle West—if you think of all these things you see how true it is to say that when Johnson wrote that the lot of a writer was toil, envy, want, the workhouse and the gaol, greatness in literature went out of the window.

And observe: it is not the starvation that is the damnatory factor. Villon, the greatest of the great poets, starved and wrote matter the texture of which is incomparably tight and economical. It is the desperate haste to make deadlines, which began in the 1820's with all the paraphernalia of the commercial publication of literature. Johnson originally wrote: "the patron and the gaol," and afterwards substituted "the workhouse." He would have been more exact had he substituted the "publisher" for both, for when in the eighteenth century the whole paraphernalia of publishing and publishing seasons and the suborning of critics—or, indeed, when the critics began, like Jeffreys to be called reviewers—the disastrous element of time became all-paramount in the republic of the muses. It is not that the publisher is of necessity villainous; it is that that poor worm* is as much the victim of the late bird as the author himself. So that, since about 1820, you have to consider a sort of tide of advancing books rushing for completion towards each anniversary of the taking of the Bastille, the publishers meanwhile dancing like cats on hot stoves and wailing: "Will those fellows never be finished?" so that they may have their books out by November in preparation for a season when the public which hates books and the buying of books will find it easier to buy a few than to bother to think about more appropriate seasonal offerings.

The reader must not resent this excursion into what the late Mr. Henry James used to call the *bas fonds*, or the conditions, in which writing is produced. We are here between us compounding not a history of authors but one of literature—as if we were writing, not the history of great motor-propelled vehicles, like Mr. Howard Hughes' flying laboratory or the *Normandie*, but the history of the coal-tar product that propels them. In the less book-crowded ages that preceded the nineteenth century we had leisure to dilate on the biographies of writers like Molière or Marlowe, and the digressions were valuable because they permitted us to realize to what a great extent the life that a writer led influenced his product. It there became evident by the example of great writers that a man must have lived a full life of action, danger and even despair before he could render the life that surrounded him. For how can you estimate the real values of life unless you have fought to preserve your own with rapier or dagger, unless you have faced, like Villon, starvation, or unless you have at

* *Publisher's Note:* How true!

the very least learned the value of mere money, like Richardson, who supported himself as a printer before he ever thought of feeding the presses. There used, when this writer was a young man, to be an argument that raged perpetually in bookish circles: was it better for a writer like Browning to be possessed of means, or like Tennyson to have to make a living by writing. Browning's was a special case. There *are* instances of writers possessed of means who are, nevertheless, consumed by such a curiosity about, and sympathy for, human lives that they may actually, like the late Mr. Henry James, achieve a vicarious estimation of vital values. Such a one, indeed, was Chateaubriand, when in the Far West he stood talking to the aged and stricken red Indian chief, and from the experience distilled the sentence that we have quoted.

We must, therefore, from now on hasten through our accounts of individual writers and mistreat them in groups of two or three or under the heading of movements. . . . This not so much because our space is beginning to grow short as because the human mind will not bear a too great stressing of one same lesson in one same method. Let us then continue our consideration of the group which the reader will already have guessed to consist of Chateaubriand, Scott and Heine.

To Chateaubriand we have already devoted as many words as we ought; but let us give him more. He is the writer who writes with impunity. He is the one romantic—except Heine—who can face mockers with indifference and who can pour out romantic nonsense whilst persuading you that it is the fruits of serious observation. That is, perhaps, because the most cynical of us in his subconscious believes in the saving graces of virtue. The gloom-enveloped vices of a Childe Harold or a Don Juan Tenorio tickle irresistibly our risibilities of today. But Chateaubriand is the Christian romantic. He provides us in the René of his *René* and the Chactas of his *Atala* with two figures of such Christian virtue that you would say that you would roll on the floor with laughter as you read of them. Imagine a sachem of one of the Creek tribes on the banks of the Meschabecé delivering himself of such an oration as this:

Etrange contradiction du coeur de l'homme! Moi qui avais tant désiré de dire les choses du mystère a celle que j'aimais déjà comme le soleil, maintenant confus et interdit, je crois que j'eusse préféré d'être jeté aux crocodules de la fontaine à me trouver seul ainsi avec Atala. La fille du désert était aussi troublée que son prisonnier. Nous gardions un profond silence. Les Génies de l'Amour avaient dérobé nous paroles . . ."

Which let us translate, sufficiently diffidently for fear of rubbing off some of the bloom of the admirable style:

> Strange contradiction of the human heart! Here was I who had so desired to unfold mystery to her whom I loved already as if she had been the sun, and, lo, I was abashed and confused. I believe that I should have preferred to be thrown to the crocodiles in the tank rather than find myself alone thus with Atala. That child of the desert was as disturbed as her prisoner. The Genies of Love had deprived us of the powers of speech.

Nor would it seem possible that a French gentleman-adventurer in the early days of Louisiana could thus address himself to a venerable sachem and an adored missionary without our bursting into cacchinations:

> *Je ne puis, en commençant mon récit, me défendre d'un mouvement de honte. La paix de vos coeurs, respectables vieillards, et le calme de la Nature autour de moi me font rougir du trouble et de l'agitation de mon âme.*
>
> *Combien vous aurez pitié de moi! Que mes éternelles inquiétudes vous paraîtront misérables, vous qui avez épuisé tous les chagrins de la vie, que penserez vous d'un jeune homme sans forces, et sans vertu qui trouve en lui même son tourment et ne peut guère se plaindre que des mots qu'il se fait à lui même.*

a passage that we will leave without Englishing it because it would be

almost impossible to get it over without making it seem ridiculous
. . . which it supremely is not.

For the fact is that Chateaubriand is supremely respectable. He was
admirably good, admirably Christian, if incurably selfish, and seriously
devoted to his king and his country. His sentiments may have been
colored by too much Rousseauism in his lonely youth, which passed
always in mediaeval castles. But it is impossible not to believe that he
looked at the world seriously. His Indian sachem is not our idea of an
Indian sachem, nor his young member of a licentious and doomed
aristocracy, our idea of a doomed member of a licentious aristocracy.
But it is to be remembered that Chateaubriand was himself a young
French pre-Revolution aristocrat and that he actually did pass a number of years in contact with the Indians of Louisiana. Or again, his
description of the Mississippi may not tally with our idea of the
Meschabecé near Bâton Rouge . . . where we spent once four days.
You will find in the following description of the stream nothing about
the trembling levees almost brimmed over, the wilderness of gasoline
tanks and cranes, nor yet of the black darkness of the summer day that
for us was caused by the soil of Texas flying overhead to pour itself into
the Gulf of Mexico. But again, one should remember that Chateaubriand spent many months on the banks of the Meschabecé whilst
Bâton Rouge was in building.

> This last stream [says he—and this time in revenge, we will give
> the passage in English alone] in a course of more than a thousand
> leagues, waters a delicious country that the inhabitants of the
> United States* call *New Eden* and to which the French had given
> the sweet name of *Louisiana*. A thousand other streams, tributes of
> the *Meschabecé*—the Missouri, the Illinois, the *Akanza*, the *Wa-*
> *bache*, the *Tenasé*—enrich it with their alluvial detritus and fer-
> tilize it with their waters. When all these streams are swollen with
> the winter torrents, when tempests have laid low whole swathes
> of their forests, the trees, uprooted, amass themselves at their
> sources. Soon mud cements them into one mass, lianas bind them

---

* When Chateaubriand wrote this passage his countrymen had already aided the Colonists to throw off the alien yoke.

together, and plants, taking roots on all sides, finish the consolidation of the mass. Born on the foaming torrents, they float down to the *Meschabecé*; the river takes charge of them and drives them towards the Gulf of Mexico, lets them be caught up on sand banks and thus increases the number of its mouths. From time to time, it will raise its voice to a roar whilst passing below the mountains, and it will spread its overflowing waters amongst the forest colonnades and around the pyramids of the Indian tombs. It is the Nile of these deserts. But grace is always attendant on magnificence in Nature, and, whilst the central current sweeps down towards the sea the carcasses of pines and oak trees, one sees along the banks, floating islands of water lilies and lotus, whose yellow roselike blossoms rise up like little flags, mount upwards in all the backwaters. Green snakes, blue herons, rose-colored flamingos and young crocodiles take passage on these ships of flowers, and the fleet, spreading to the winds its sails of gold, drifts sleepily onwards to find rest in some creek retired from the main stream.

In that passage, from the beginning of *Atala*, speaks incontestably the voice of one who has seen . . . and whose purpose is, above all, to make you see. So, when you read on in these romantic pages you are a little awed by that passage and the inclination to laughter deserts you. . . . We may, indeed, confess that this very afternoon we have read right through the whole of *Atala* and of *René* without the beginnings of a smile and with a certain—if dim—conviction that we have been present at an actual scene. And, as the scene recedes in memory, it becomes more real since one forgets the strong mannerisms of the writer. And, after all, the idea of a redskin of singular virtues need not so shock us. Was it not just because of their unusual laws of hospitality that such an arch scoundrel as Boone was able to betray, outroot and dispossess whole Indian tribes?

And, when everything is said, there remains the singular beauty and dignity of Chateaubriand's writing. It is an organ that, like Gibbon's equally sedate sentences, can be beautiful over the quietest topics and agitatingly moving over *les situations fortes*. It resembles in that the verse of Corneille, the method being one singularly suited to the temperament of the French who train themselves to witness tragic or despairing situations whilst employing only the most restrained of terms in recording them. The exteriors of Chateaubriand's prose poems resemble the motives of Byron's backboneless ramblings. There is the haughty, smouldering youth whose mysterious origins may lead back to anything—to imperial birth, to hidden murder, to incestuous guilt, but never to humble ancestry. And it is odd to consider that whereas Byron decked out his incestuous commerce with his sister with verselets that would grace a lady's album, the "mystery" that Chateaubriand's René confesses to the venerable seniors on the banks of the *Meschabecé* is precisely that of a passion between brother and sister—but a passion resisted and, as you might put it, redeeming. And, as rendered at its height by Chateaubriand, you have something that stands out as a projection of passion that is, as such, unsurpassed and hardly equalled in literature. We would like to give the long passage which describes the taking of the veil by René's sister, Amélie, but its poignancy would disappear at the hands of the best translator, so different is French from English emotional writing. . . . However, let us try, here in the text, to give some of the effect in English of Chateaubriand's more contemplative prose, attempting rather a transference of the mood than an exact rendering of the words. This is René, recalling on the banks of the Mississippi, the emotion of his childhood:

> On Sundays and fête days I often heard, in the high woods, through the trees, the sounds of the distant bell that would be calling men from the fields to the place of worship. I would be leaning against the trunk of a beech and listening to that pious murmuring. Each shivering vibration from that bronze mouth made my naïve mind dwell on the innocence of rural existence, the peace of solitude, the charms of religion and the attractive melancholy of the remembrances of my first childhood. What man's heart has been so ill fashioned by destiny that it has never quivered at the sounds of the bells of his home village . . . of those same bells that once rang out in joy over his cradle, which kept time with his first heart beats, which called aloud to all the neighboring

villages of the pious rejoicings of his father, of the pains and still more of the ineffable joy of his mother? There is nothing that will not recur to the mood of enchantment that falls upon us at the sound of the church bells of our birthplace . . . our faiths, our kindred, our native land, what is past and what's to come, our cradle . . . and our grave.

This, the sophisticated reader will exclaim, is very simple stuff. It is. But so is an acorn.

We see in Chateaubriand the working of a mighty leaven. If you look back to the simplicities of *Clarissa* you catch the light that is reflected in *René*; and if you look far forward to the simplicities of psychology of a Charles or an Emma Bovary, you catch the light of Richardson's colza lamp reflected forward by the work of Chateaubriand. And along with those placidities there went the strain of sheer horror that shows in the catastrophe of Clarissa; in the taking of the veil by Amélie; in the arsenic of poor Emma . . . and, to carry the connection still farther forward into our own day, into the placid but atrocious handling of the most horrificent of all stories in English, *The Turn of the Screw*. The last words of that last absolutely authentic masterpiece, the last turn of that screw, run:

We were alone with the quiet day and his little heart, dispossessed, had stopped.

Observe how, as with Chateaubriand, the writing of that sentence is slightly mannered. That is the device of all the great writers. In great moments the convention which is a necessity for all works of art must be enhanced by just the merest motion of the screw and the language must, by the merest shade, marmorealize itself.

Let us in our browsings across the 1820 delta pause for a moment to compare with Chateaubriand, Sir Walter Scott, Baronet, Knight of the Shire, Custos Rotulorum, and Sheriff of some county that we cannot call to mind . . . Midlothian, maybe. For there is a certain marmoreal kinship between the figures of Chateaubriand and Goethe . . . and then at a certain interval between Chateaubriand and Sir Walter Scott, Custos Rotulorum and the rest. One thinks of both those non-Anglo-Saxons as standing, solitary since they were without peer, in marble, slightly age-stained, above tombs whose faces reveal just their names: "Goethe and Chateaubriand." One never thinks of either as Johann Wolfgang Freiherr von Goethe, *Staatsminister des Herzogstum Weimar* or René Vicomte Chateaubriand, *Ambassadeur et Ministre Plenipotentiaire de la France, Ministre des Affaires Étrangères Royales, Grand Cordon de l'Ordre de Saint Louis.* . . . But even in providing a tender nickname for the author of *The Antiquary*, you have to call him the "Shirra." Nor does Chateaubriand in writing of his René and his Amélie ever hint that they—like himself—belonged to an order of nobility, that of the Bretons, that with a misty and veracious tenacity traces its antiquity back to the days when the Druids wielded their sacrificial knives.

But Scott cannot introduce his Monkbarns without hinting that his mere gentility is questionable since he dates back to a mere German exile-printer of the days of the Nuremberg Bible—and is so whole streets below a semi-imbecile boor who as Sir Arthur Wardour can trace his territorial ancestry back, if doubtfully, to the days of Drust Macmorachin. And one must not omit to notice that till the last page of the book on which he becomes Lord Geraldin, the mysteriously origined hero of the work is treated very much *de haut en bas* by the doubtfully gentle Jonathan Oldbuck and Monkbarns of that ilk, because Monkbarns believes that he is a strolling player. . . . Nor, indeed, can Scott believe that even the brigands of the twelfth century were free of that particular type of snobbery; he will make them prate of birth and lineage—for all the world as if they were old maids of Cheltenham bending over Debrett's *Landed Gentry*.

It is impossible to believe that Scott lives anywhere today: he might perhaps in a doctor's dining-room in Marseilles or Tarascon, in a child's nursery in Buenos Aires, or a housemaid's pantry on Boston Hill. Or, of course, in all the *sancta sanctorum* of all the pro-

fessors of the universities of Goettingen and Jena. But his guileless-
ness is such that it is impossible to believe that any grown man could
take seriously the adventures of Ivanhoe or Rob Roy. *The Antiquary*
is a more serious attempt at novel writing, but its longwindedness is
unbelievable and its insistence on assuring the reader that Scotland
is a historically important and gentlemanly kingdom, not to be borne.

His literary merits are almost undiscoverable, and where he has
some glimmerings of how to write he exaggerates his method beyond
the verge of anyone's patience. Thus, he knows definitely that an
author's encomia of his characters carries no conviction with the
reader. So, after an inordinately discursive account of the ancestry, family vicissitudes and fortune of Oldbuck, Scott says suddenly: "The rest of his character must be gathered from the story
and we dismiss with pleasure the tiresome task of recapitulation."
But he proceeds at such length to "get in" the character of the
Antiquary—with such exhibitions of his antiquarian zeal, discoveries,
failures, absurdities, vanities, miserlinesses, generosities as thus:

> Mr. Oldbuck next exhibited thumbscrews which had given the
> Coveenters of former days the cramp.

—he gets in, then, Mr. Oldbuck's character at such length that it
takes exactly forty of the closely printed pages of the 1837 edition of
the "Waverley Novels" before anything like an adventure is so much
as adumbrated. This is a damning defect.

For it would be absurd to say that we have no time to read Scott—
or anyone else. A generation whose adult literati will read with
enthusiasm—and small blame to them—the 700 pages of Mr. Mann's
Magic Mountain, and every one of whose adolescent intelligentsia
have almost by heart the *War and Peace* of Tolstoy and *The Brothers
Karamazov*, and whose occasional readers consume by the millions such
immense works as *Anthony Adverse* and *Gone With the Wind* can
certainly not say that it has no time to read Scott. And when we
consider that in Anglo-Saxondom of today, on both sides of the
Atlantic, there are at least 52,000,000 individuals who have nothing

in the world to do with their time, the statement appears more and more absurd.

No, it is not the length of the books of authors of the type of Scott, nor is it our want of time that makes them be shrouded in oblivion. It is the tempo that the authors set. We are no longer inclined to sit four hours over a book before the author will deign to give us some idea of what his story is. We will sit up all night with a book, but the author must grip us with a line or two in his first pages. Consider how Flaubert "gets in" with the mere description of her finger nails all of the character and traits of his beloved Emma that we need to know in order to awaken our curiosity. She, being the daughter of a working farmer, if a wealthy one, Charles—in those days when farmer's daughters hoed, milked, made cheeses and, above all, knew their places—might well be surprised to see that her fingers were manicured. In those days no one beneath the rank of a countess would run to such a luxury. In addition, she did not know where her sewing things were and pricked her fingers when she was forced by an accident to sew. No wonder that young Dr. Bovary was intrigued by that detail, and that considering that the young doctor is married to a much older wife the reader in turn has his interest awakened. . . . And it is to be remembered that every detail of that amazing book, *Madame Bovary,* has been worked out with the same awareness. The most casual detail—the shouting of a beggar in the street, the operations by the doctor, the conversation of a pompous druggist—is recorded only because it inevitably carries the story forward and hangs on the inevitable tragedy of the end. Madame Bovary is, however, still half a century ahead of us, and we have not completely finished with . . . the Shirra. Nor yet with the Romantics.

The public demands, then, a rattling story . . . and has every right to get it. That the commercial novel should today be dying in face of the detective story may be matter for immediate regret. But there is this to be said as matter of literary consolation: the good detective story is—it *has* to be—as well-machined as possible. In that too, as in *Madame Bovary*, every minutest detail must have its reason. A young lady in one of those romances could no more prick her fingers without significance than could Emma Bovary herself.

That means to say that the public has done for good with the slipshod methods of amateur literary hacks like Scott. That Scott will live as a historical figure we need neither doubt nor regret. He was, like Chateaubriand and like Goethe, a good man . . . and one is tempted to say: "And don't you forget it!" His very last words— spoken to his son-in-law—were: "Be a good man, my dear, be a *good* man." A *good* man, you observe, not a good biographer or a good writer to the signet. And the proudest boast of Scott was that he had never in all the immense array of his hack scrapbag written one word that the purest maiden seated in the privacy of her bedchamber could not read without a blush. That too is historic.

And remember too that, after lunching officially in Hollyrood Palace with the lousiest—we use the word advisedly, though indeed there is no other—monarch that ever rendered despicable a throne, the Shirra sneaked away and hid in his pocket the glass from which George IV had drunk a toast in gin and water. It became forever after his proudest possession—the proudest possession of a Wizard of the North, on whose lips hung all that was noblest in all Europe and all America, waiting in ecstasy for his next, smallest word.

But still no doubt—and no doubt forever—attended by his dog, whose name we have forgotten, and having in the folds of his plaid that Pet Marjorie whom an ancestor of this writer immortalized along with another dog called Rab . . . stooping, then, forward a little and leaning on his trusty staff will stalk a stalwart figure, upwards into the mists of the low hills above Abbotsford—a jerry-built mediaeval manor which contained the worst collection of Wardour Street bric-a-brac that any house ever sheltered . . . unless it were the castle of the father of Leopardi.

But Scott will always be a historic figure and, that being so, some few people from time to time will look at his verses and a few will be found to praise him.

I suppose as much can be said for Byron, for, although he was not a good man, he was a peer and, having got as it were, a tremendous start as a peer with the carriages blocking Albemarle Street, persons will be found forever to write memoirs going to prove or disprove that he committed incest with his sister. Otherwise one may well imagine that he would today be as forgotten as "Satan" Montgomerie or "Van Artevelde" Taylor or Philip James Bailey or all of the innumerable completely and forever forgotten.

But the prodigious uproar of his name in his own day has prolonged itself at least on the continent where he still lives, foreigners being unable to distinguish between jingles and poetry in an unfamiliar language. Yes, they will recite him still up and down the Rhine and in Siena and Granada—if there is anything left of Granada—and he will continue to live as a shining Milor in Venice and Marseilles. Why, this writer has seen two old ladies in Hanover weeping together . . . because of Mrs. Harriet Ward Beecher Stowe's accusations against Byron.

They would snivel and exclaim: "But ist it bossible to dthink that one who did write:

> Mine sister, mine sweet sister, if a name
> Dearer and purer were, it should be thine? . . .

Pud id istnt bossible. . . ."

And again the writer was almost stricken to the ground by a notary of Avignon . . . for saying that if there were five lines of poetry in all Byron, that was all that there were. And the notary, as round as a cricket ball and with rolling eyes, shaking one fist at the heavens over the Rhone, and spouting:

> " 'Twas after dread Pultowa's day,
> When fortune left the royal Swede,
> Around a slaughtered army lay
> No more to combat and to bleed.
> The power and glory of the war,
> Faithless as their vain votaries, men
> Had passed to the triumphant Czar
> And Moscow's walls were safe again . . ."

And at that, fifty thousand Frenchmen every autumn take boat to Glasgow and visit the Trossachs and Midlothian—in memory of the Shirra—and, in returning, step off at Newstead and shed a tear over the grave of Boatswain, Byron's dog that went mad and would not bite its master. . . . And half as many Italians make the same journey, and there is no saying how many of the other lesser breeds. One imagines, indeed, that one would oneself stop off and take a look at Newstead if one happened to be passing within a mile or two of that Abbey. No, Byron will probably never die.

It is a misfortune because a more heartless being can never have lived. And surely no poet ever in the world wrote such a vastness of verse without manifesting ever, at any moment, the remotest scintilla of feeling . . . except occasionally for some wounded peer's vanity.

Obviously a foreigner can obtain some pleasure by spouting " 'Twas after dread Pultowa's day" in defiance and in a romantic situation. So that that much may be allowed to Byron. A poet is an international affair. Charleston, South Carolina, did not in his day appreciate Poe and does not today admire him as much as does Paris. But that is all that can be allowed to Byron.

To an Anglo-Saxon concerned for his poetry and his language, both verse and language of Byron are odious, because they are the verse and language of a nobleman who considered himself impregnable behind his rank and the fashion of the day. Poor old Scott could write:

> Why sit'st thou by that ruin'd hall,
> Thou aged carle so stern and grey?
> Dost thou its former pride recall
> Or ponder how it pass'd away?

and it has something of the tender funniness of a poorly sewn sampler. But consider this of Byron's:

> Here are the Alpine landscapes which create
> A fund for contemplation—to admire
> Is a brief feeling of a trivial date;
> But something worthier do such scenes inspire.

"Than which," positively writes the *Quarterly Review* for January 1831, "there is nothing more mournfully and desolately beautiful in the whole range of Byron's poetry."

And if you think that they are avowedly the poet's expression of his feelings of regret for going into eternal exile from his native land and—not so avowedly—of his final farewell to a sister who had been his mistress and whom he still professed tenderly to adore, you wonder what sort of being that could have been.

There are, indeed, five lines of poetry in Byron's works—or, possibly, nine if we include the first of these two stanzas:

> So we'll go no more a-roving
> So late into the night,
> Though the heart be still as loving
> And the moon be still as bright
>
> For the sword outwears its sheath
> And the soul wears out the breast
> And the heart must pause to breathe
> And love itself have rest.

And then there is the line—addressed also to Augusta:

> In the deep midnight of the mind . . .

Otherwise the thought and the language are those of a city clerk.

But just consider

> *Du liegst mir so gern im Arme,*
> *Du liegst mir am Herzen so gern!*
> *Ich bin dein ganzer Himmel,*
> *Du bist mein liebster Stern. . . .*

It is really the language of a city clerk, as the Prussians of Heine's day used to complain.

These questions of language are so confusing. Or, to be precise, they are not confusing for in one's subconsciousness they are perfectly clear. Only, it is difficult to write about them. They are, nevertheless, all-important, for the fate of the world may at any moment depend upon a phrase.

The Prussian professor, then, who made this writer dislike all the German writers of the *Sturm und Drang* period, when commanding him to write a composition on any subject would always, as it were at the starting point, fire a sort of pistol of hissing speech, exclaiming with an extraordinary hissing of sibilants: *"Ssschreib wie du sssprichst,"* which this writer found it impossible to do in a tongue where the literary language and the spoken one are so widely divorced. And, indeed, when this writer did once try writing exactly the sort of colloquial German that he spoke, the professor boxed his ears.

On the other hand, a Scottish usher at a private school was probably responsible for the immense amount of reading in all sorts of languages that this writer got through before the age of twelve. For David Watson, M.A., of St. Andrews University, used to spend every spare moment of his day and whole Sundays on end with this writer standing beside him at his pulpit and construing for him every imaginable kind of book from the *Artaxerxes* of Madame de Scudéry and *Les Enfants de Capitaine Grant* by Jules Verne, to ode after ode of Tibullus, Fouqué's *Undine*, all of the *Inferno*, the greater part of *Lazarillo de Tormes* and *Don Quichote* in the original. But for the first half of *Don Quichote* we would have the English translation by, I think, Fitzmaurice Kelly lying open beside the Spanish book on the wide desk top. In addition, Mr. Watson had this writer translate for him orally into French *The Two Admirals*, *The Deerslayer* and *The Last of the Mohicans*—which made this writer appreciate what a magnificent prose writer Cooper was.

On the other hand, Mr. Watson—he had the largest and reddest ears that can ever have been affixed to a human head, and may his soul be being read to by whole choirs of little Anglican angels!—Mr. Watson, when he had to set the writer a composition in English used to say:

"Now, Fordie, write something balanced, something sonorous . . . Johnsonian."

And after this writer had written:

> After mature consideration we find ourselves forced to arrive at the conclusion that the descent of man from the brute creation remains unproven,

Mr. Watson, with a quill pen, would strike out the words "After mature consideration we find ourselves forced to arrive at the conclusion that . . ."

Let us not apologize for the fact that in the last few pages we have cited various international instances of lingual dislikes or preferences. It becomes here our task to give an impression of a large delta of books with human beings moving amongst them. For the words "March of Literature" connote a presentation of readers as well as writers. . . .

But Byron is odious because he writes the thoughts of a city clerk in metropolitan clerical vernacular. Heine, on the other hand, writes the language of a bank employee of his day—and is in every word adorable.

Heine wrote whilst Goethe and Byron and Chateaubriand were all living. Yet there is nothing marmoreal about Heine, neither is it fitting to apply to him the word that is too often profaned by those who write about writers. Ariel is not a great figure; Puck is not a great figure. Neither are Psyche nor the being who wrote: *"Im wunderschoenen Monat Mai."*

CHAPTER FOUR

Heine's eyes must have been as many-faceted as those of a fly. He is at once romanticist, realist, impressionist, folksong folk-lore German lyricist, French lost soul, Jewish Christian, and the one man who cannot have been descended from the brute beasts. His race must have reached the earth in the days of Propertius.

In the republic of letters he is without kin or friends. Goethe gave him the cold shoulder, nor can you wonder. He felt himself pure German and wailed when he was forced to leave Paris, but declared, only half ironically, that he pined for the Northlands.

> Paris, farewell, beloved town,
> Today shall see us parted,
> I leave you in your overflow
> Of all that's joyous-hearted
>
> The German heart that's in my breast
> Has suddenly grown sickly;
> There's but one Doctor who can heal
> It certainly and quickly.
>
> He's in the Northland, there at home;
> His skill defies description;
> Yet I confess to shuddering
> Over each new prescription. . . .
>
> I'm yearning for tobacco reek,
> Professors and strong waters,
> And sauerkraut and coarser speech
> And blond-haired parsons' daughters. . . .

He was, in fact, of no place and of no race, and was to die eventually in a Paris garret in an intense aloneness of sardonically supported pain. There is no poet—there is, indeed, no other man—who resembles him. He had another otherworldliness than that of Shelley; he had another passion for nightingales than that of Keats: his nightingales ring out, confident. He had a bitter folly different from the folly ot De Vigny; his humor was a little that of Molière; he loved virtue and took it out in jeering at the official virtuous. His romantic Ritters Olaf will leave you gay at their deaths . . .

> *Ihr Veilchen Augen meiner Frau*
> *Durch Euch verlier' ich das Leben . . .*
> *Ich segne auch den Holunderbaum*
> *Wo du dich mir ergaben. . . .**

What an exquisitely right ending that is for a poem that begins necrologically:

> *Vor dem Dome steh'n zwei Maenner,*
> *Tragen beide rothe Roecke,*
> *Und der einer ist der Koenig*
> *Und der andrer ist der Henker.*

> *Und zum Henker spricht der Koenig:*
> *"Am Gesang der Pfaffen merk' ich*
> *Dasz vollendet soll sein Leben.*
> *Halt' bereit dein gutes Nichtbeil."*

* A literal translation would be:
> You violet eyes of my wife:
> Through you I lost my life.
> I bless also the juniper tree:
> Where thou gavest thyself to me.

But the German owes its charm to the fact that, prosaic German being pompous and as it were ornamented in renaissance style, poetry is obtained by taking refuge in extreme simplicity. English being normally humdrum and slipshod, the English poet has to be more dramatic. Thus, a free adaptation of the verses might run:
> For sake of my wife's eyes
> I'll wake this day in Paradise:
> I bless the elder tree
> Where thou didst give thyself to me.

The legend is that a knight called Olaf, having been too much loved by the king's daughter, is condemned to marry her and to die immediately afterwards. Before the block he blesses the earth, the sun, the trees, the birds, and ends as above.

which this writer translates as:

> Two men stand by the cathedral,
> Wearing each a scarlet mantle;
> And the taller is the monarch
> And the smaller is the hangman.
> To the hangman speaks the monarch:
> "When the priest's song ends I charge you
> That that traitor's life be ended.
> Keep your trusty saber sharpened."

This writer has been rebuked for misquoting Heine. But it is impossible to verify your quotations in his poems. You set out to look for a poem about a young knight asleep on the seashore and what the sea nymphs think of him. But it is like looking up something definite in a really amusing encyclopaedia. Your eye catches:

> *Ich halte ihr die Augen zu*
> *Und kuess' sie auf den Mund . . .*

and then you are lost. You are lost in agitated rage because for the moment—so infinitely and intimately simple the phrases are—you do not remember that they are neither English nor French. The words are there, as a soap bubble is there. They are part of yourself that you cannot express in your own language. It is impossible. Look:

> And while I hold her eyelids to
> I seal her lips with kisses;
> And now she asks the whole night through
> What sort of manner this is?
>
> From early night till morning dew
> She asks and never misses:
> "Why should you hold my eyelids to
> And close my mouth with kisses?"

I do not tell her why I do:
I seal her lips with kisses;
For whilst I hold her eyelids to
I cannot say why this is.

If you could cover those words with the iridescence of a dragonfly's wings you might have Heine.

It is impossible to write of him other than lyrically because when your eye lights on one of his pages you become as excited as if you were waiting for the spring to burst open its flowers and the first nightingale—Heine's nightingale, not the melancholy Philomela—to give tongue. His range of mood is inconceivable. He sits on the sea-shore at dusk and a mermaid comes from the waves and presses him so tight in her arms that it is painful, while the sea-mews scream and the sea complains. He passes in the morning a window from which a brown-eyed young girl leans out and asks him what his name is and what ails him. He answers:

I am a German poet
Known throughout Germany,
And when they mention the best known names
They have to talk of me.

And that which ails me, little one,
Ails a-many in Germany;
And when they talk of men's bitterest pains
They must mention my agony.

And on the far horizon, like a cloud, appears the city with its towers lost in the twilight. And the secret city has swallowed up forever his heart's beloved. And he wanders through the narrow alleys where is the house of his beloved; and in the room where she pledged him her troth and her tears fell down, snakes crawl. And he calls up the Devil and is astonished to find him, not ugly and lame, but a hand-some fellow in the best years of his life—an accomplished diplomat who talks admirably about Church and state . . . a little pale because

he is continually reading Sanscrit and Hegel. And his favorite poet is
M. Fouqué. . . . And Heine writes:

> *Du bist wie eine Blume*
> *So hold und schoen und rein . . .*

And he stands under the window of her house where there is company
and his heart breaks and she does not see it. And an amiable young
man treats him to oysters, Rhine wine and liqueurs and talks of
Heine's wide-flung fame and recites his poems at a great party where
the ladies declare his verses are divine. And he takes a night-long ride
with a beloved in a postchaise and they laugh all the way. And he is
in Salamanca, and next door to him lives Don Henriquez, known as
the Beau. And the Blue Hussars ride out through the city gate and
quite a number of them have been billeted in her heart. . . .

But even Mr. Stephan Born, the editor of the Cotta edition of
Heine, has to acknowledge that Heine said nothing to a large section
of the German people—even before 1870. They preferred Uhland,
Rueckert, Chamisso, Gentz, Adam Mueller, Zacharias Werner and
deplored that Heine had not always lived "korrekt." But Mr. Born
does make the rather penetrating remark that whereas other poets
have a shyness that makes them unwilling to reveal their inmost
thoughts "Heine thinks aloud the moment an impression strikes
him, without reflecting that the whole world is listening to him." . . .
People were not used to that in Germany!

And this must again be emphasized: Mr. Hitler burned all the
copies of Heine on which he could lay hands. But in the *Imperial
Reading Book* for German schools, accredited to "Anonymous Poet,"
you can read *"Ich weiss nicht was soll es bedeuten,"* and *"Du bist wie
eine Blume"* and *"Im wunderschoenen Monat Mai. . . ."* There was,
perhaps, never a better confirmation of the dictum that the pen is
mightier than the swastika. Indeed, the more you think about that
incident, the more extraordinary it seems.

Here is a dictator of such minute care and omnipotence that he
can eradicate a poet from his dominions—and does so. But the hearts

of his impotent lieges so need the poems of that poet that the dictator is forced to decree that the very children of his empire must have the poems of that poet by heart. This dictator can all but eradicate the Christian faith from his dominions, and priests and communicants take it lying down. But the poems must be brought back to his people by the dictator himself. They cannot live without them!

And, indeed, Heine was a necessity to the world of his day, since it is necessary that the large pompacities of one's day should be mocked by someone, and he remains a necessity to our day, since have we not, we too, our pompacities? The court jester is the most important of all the functionaries of a realm because he restores a sense of proportion to the mass-agitated. It is immensely symbolic that he should not have known why he held the lady's eyelids to whilst sealing her lips with kisses. The fuliginous heroes of Byron and Schlegel and Espronceda would each have found a hundred gloom-enshrouded reasons for the proceeding. For, remember, the hero of the *Buch der Lieder* is on the face of him as fuliginous as any of the other romantic heroes. Snakes crawl in the deserted halls, born presumably of the tears of the lost beloved. Only, from the very nature of the verse and the lilt of the words you know that that hero does not take the snakes any more seriously than anything else. . . . A Manfred would have made it plain that the snakes were part of the mysterious doom that impinged on his cloud-embowered brows. But Heine knows that he will soon be taking an all-night ride in a postchaise with an unknown beloved and that they will laugh all through the night. It is not so much that he supplies intervals of comic relief to our spleens; it is that he makes us know that, in spite of them, the world will go on. To do that he has to be forever outside our world—mocking slightly when you stand him Rhine wine and oysters and declaim his poems at fashionable assemblies. But one could write forever about Heine. The reader should make the note that it is indispensable that he should know enough German to read at least the *Wahlfahrt nach Kevelaar*. It is the simplest German in the world; a baby could understand it. And it might revive the reader's Christianity. A non-Aryan poet is, no doubt, needed to bring about that process. Was it not begun by one?

It was, perhaps, Lamartine who, in the very height of the romantic turmoil, first made the discovery that the race was no longer to the hero, the glory to any nation, and that our age, at its best, is humanitarian. He makes at least, in the foreword to *Jocelyn*, the statement that:

> *L'épopée n'est plus nationale, ni héroique, elle est bien plus, elle est humanitaire.*

That was written in 1836. Appropriately enough, for 1836 was the year that saw the real death of the hero of fiction. Next year Victoria was to be there and it was no accident that, shortly after that cosmic apparition, the most Victorian of all novelists should have written *A Novel without a Hero*. From 1837 onwards the prancing heroes of the world were to be Louis Napoleon, a parody of the Hero of Austerlitz; or General Boulanger, a parody of Louis Napoleon.

For as long as was needed for the liberation of Italy the spirit of the songs of the Risorgimento upheld a real hero-survival in Garibaldi. But once that romance was accomplished the world fell under the joint dictatorship of a widow in Windsor and a stout sagacious-eyed old fellow, who in the midst of his most impassioned orations raised to his lips a gallon tankard filled with a mixture of stout and champagne. In 1914 the name of that drink was changed to "Black Velvet." Before then it was known as "Bismarck."

You may well ask what Victoria and Bismarck had to do with literature. What indeed? On the field of Sedan, a prisoner, during all the long night, symbolically, Louis Napoleon read the last book of the last of the romantics—Lytton's *Last of the Barons* and the spirit of our Mediterranean civilization was dammed. One never heard of Bismarck or Victoria reading a book. But the one forced on the world the spirit of industrialism plus workman's insurance; the other gave us the world ideal of virtuous comfort. So literature has tended more and more to mass fiction and herolessness. For literature is at once the master and the slave of universal populations. It will force you to become what you are; but then it is forced to reflect what, in millions, you have become.

So Lamartine was forced to write humanitarian epics. Nevertheless, the fashion of his day being very strong, he had to have heroes, and, being French, his poems had to be French of the French and filled with type allegories. *Jocelyn* must begin with the heroic line *"J'étais le seul ami qu'il eût sur cette terre."* ("I was the only friend he had on this earth."), as if he were going to write of Byron or Napoleon at St. Helena. But immediately he qualifies that by adding: *"Hors son pauvre troupeau."* ("Except for his poor congregation."), so you know that the hero was only the priest of a poor village. Nevertheless, he must have been an exceptional priest to have one only friend in the world. Most priests are companionable; they like to sit in your parlor, sipping sherry and gossiping. Romanticism must come creeping in, if only by the small end of the telescope. . . . And, indeed, the eternal difficulty of the non-romantic or the proletarian epic poet or novelist is: How are you going to make interesting a central character whose circumstances and temperament are in no way interesting? For it would seem as if to be interesting you must be exceptional. . . . Even in the *Brothers Karamazov* Dostoievsky must have his beloved Alyosha.

So, going consciously about his unheroic, non-national task, Lamartine has to present you with a Death of a Hero that could only have taken place in the Frenchest of all Frances. Going to visit the parson of whom he is the sole friend, he sees no black figure telling its breviary in the orchard, no smoke rises from the parsonage chimney, no dog bays at his approach, no shepherd and no sheep are in the field. Only a mule browses on the dusty roadside grass and the cricket cries.

> I press upon the latch a finger, heavy, hard,
> And enter rapidly the solitary yard . . .
> Not solitary, no! Dear God, beside the door
> At the stair foot that leads up from the threshing floor,

Just as, at the church porch, you see a begging crone,
Crouches a woman's form, i' the shadow, black, alone.
Unmoving, with the brow bent down upon the knee,
The countenance concealed in the black drapery,
No murmur, not a groan, no solitary sigh!
Only the black o'er the visage, pulsing rhythmically,
Betrayed the silent sobs that shook the stifled breath.
I recognized in that the presence there of Death.*

The French of Lamartine is more suave than the verses above; it is almost impossible to be suave in English or to give the effect of a verse that is really a pulsation of hardly separated words . . . a hypnotic. But observe the classicism of even this romantic—the death taking place "off," the empty stage before a housefront, the long pause before the first speech. You might, if you liked, say that France—as why should she?—has never really gotten away from the classic mood of her seventeenth century. Not even in the works of her romantics is the essential basis of moderation lacking. The Frenchman of taste who upholds the most fantastic of modernist art movements will yet spend—will find it necessary to spend—whole hours in galleries hung with hundreds of monotonous canvases painted by Corot. The most advanced of today's prosateurs will all but cross himself at the mention of the name of Balzac.

So, if you wish to translate Lamartine, you must do it with a slightly stilted language. That does not mean to say that his poetry lacks tenderness or even passion. It is a matter of degree. His *Meditations* secured him not only immense applause but at a comparatively early age his election to the French Academy. That is the symbol of moderation. Yet though they contain stanzas as really sublime as

Cependant la nuit marche et sur l'abîme immense
Tous ces mondes flottants gravitent en silence
Et nous-mêmes avec eux emportés dans leur cours
Vers un port inconnu nous avançons toujours,

* *Jocelyn*, Prologue. Author's translation.

Souvent pendant la nuit au souffle du Zéphyr
On sent la terre aussi flotter comme un navire . . .*

they number also in their immense list verses as intimately tender as

Placé près de ce coeur, hélas, où tout s'efface
Tu l'as contre le temps défendu de l'oubli,
Et mes yeux goutte à goutte ont imprimé leur trace
Sur l'ivoire ammoli.

O dernier confident de l'âme qui s'envole
Viens, reste sur mon coeur! Parle encore et dis moi
Ce qu'elle te disait quand sa faible parole
N'arrivait plus qu'à toi.†

This is from *Le Crucifix*, a poem addressed by a lover to the Christ of one of those "crucifices for a happy death" which a dying person of the Catholic persuasion holds in the moment of passing and to which he whispers his last thoughts or prayers. The crucifix is still warm with the warmth of the breast of the dying woman the man loved and the man implores the crucifix to tell him what were her last dying words that were too feeble to be heard by anyone but the Christ on that cross. This is an intimacy of passion that an Anglo-Saxon would be shocked to allow himself in a public utterance, but it gives to verse of a sort that is usually marmoreal a life that is lacking in almost all English memorial poetry. Its passion resembles that of Henry King's address to the shade of his dead wife that we quoted when dealing with English seventeenth century verse.

* Meanwhile night passes; in her vast abysm
The silent worlds all gravitate with ours,
And we with it and them pursue our course
Towards the unknown haven of all stars.
Often, during the night, at the breath of the southern breeze
You'd deem our earth a ship afloat on silent seas.

† Lying upon her heart whence life and love are gone,
Thou dost defend her shade against oblivion,
And drop by drop my tears that fall unceasingly
    Soften thine ivory.
Oh, final Confidant of souls that pass away,
Lie here upon my breast; speak once again and say
What were her last faint words at passing, then, when she
    Was heard by none but Thee.

We Anglo-Saxons are accustomed to say that French poetry is not poetry because the thought expressed is clear and every French word is a hard thing, like a single tessera of a mosaic. But we omit to remember the extreme beauty of the sheer sound of the language as it goes on, continuously murmuring and always composed. It has a quality like that of the harpsichord, an instrument upon which you cannot make louder sounds by hitting the keys harder. So you have to rely on playing more and more little notes very quickly, the one after the other. Thus, in French verse you reinforce your emotion not by roughening the surface of the words but by murmuring of things that suggest more and more tense emotions.

This writer begs the reader to observe these possibly rather too technical aspects of this matter. Such intense pleasure *can* be got from French poetry in spite of the composure of its surface . . . and intense pleasures are so rare in our world! Moreover, such a technique is an admirable counsel for the conduct of one's own life —the observance of the fact that the really strong and devastating effects are produced by the most quiet range of speech and actions.

It is for the reason that that treatment would have to be too technical that we omit from these pages practically all mention of the French *symboliste* and *décadent* schools of poetry. The problems arising in the works of Verlaine, Rimbaud, or even Mallarmé, Francis Jammes, Samain, and Rodenbach are simply questions of intimate verbal technique. In a sense, these poets reached out towards misty effects that are reached by the best English poets. They aimed at broken rhythms and blurred images. They are of enormous importance because they led not only toward the non-representational works of Mr. Joyce, Miss Stein and the whole school of their imitators, but to what is non-representational, imagist and vibrating in the works of Mr. Pound and such other poets as Archibald MacLeish, Léonie Adams or the English poets Auden and Spender. But it would be useless to comment technically to an audience which cannot be expected to be deeply acquainted with the French language on, or even to attempt the translation of, such poems as Verlaine's

La lune blanche
Luit dans les bois,
De chaque branche
Part une voix
Sous la ramée . . .

O bien-aimée!
L'étang reflète,
Profond miroir,
La silhouette
Du saule noir
Où le vent pleure.
Rêvons, c'est l'heure.

Un vaste et tendre
Apaisement
Semble descendre
Du firmament
Que l'astre irise . . .
*C'est l'heure exquise!**

which may be called the high water mark of *symbolisme*.

Like Chauteaubriand, Lamartine acquired his views of the values

* The white o' the moon
Besets the trees;
And soon
The night shall be moved
With ecstasies,
Oh best beloved!

This pool awaits,
A deep mirror,
The silhouettes
Of the black willow
In wind-streams.
'Tis the hour of dreams.

A deep and tender
Astonishment
Marks our surrender,
Oh firmament
White planets light!
Exquisite night!

of life from diplomatic experiences and the sight of the barricades of revolutions. He lived quietly in one minor diplomatic post after another and after the Revolution of 1848 he was one of the founders of the Provisional Government. Thus, though his early fame died away and though his production was really extravagant, he was one of the last of non-professional French writers. In his latest days his spectacular poverty gave the greatest concern to the imperial family of Napoleon III. They worried their heads about him a great deal and made him a great many gifts. But his large expenditure was eccentric rather than ostentatious. He would receive a large sum of money . . . and then reduce himself to pennilessness by spending huge sums on the kennels of his dogs. He was, in fact, just poet!

It is usual to admire most his poems of the type of *La Cloche du Village* or *La Vigne de la Maison*. This writer has written above of those which he likes best; but the poems of Lamartine are very easy to obtain and the reader might do worse than form an opinion of his own of the works of this very distinguished man.

Lamartine had such an admiration for Byron that immediately after that peer's very creditable death at Missolonghi he wrote what he called *"Le Dernier Pélerinage de Harold,"* as it were a conclusion of *Childe Harold*. It purports to be a sort of reincarnation of Byron's thoughts and persons. It was a sufficiently flattering tribute to Byron, but it is not a very striking poem. M. de Lamartine, however, in his notes quotes Fletcher's, Byron's valet's, account of Byron's death. We may as well requote it here so as to strike amongst all these Frenchmen the note of Byron's poetry. For, indeed, if you should have listened to Lamartine and Vigny and Musset and Hugo all talking together you can be certain that very few words would have been exchanged before Byron came on to that carpet.

Byron, then, at Missolonghi during the Greek struggle for independence in which he had been taking part, had a cold, went for a long ride in the rain; fell ill; grew worse; was bled; was bled again; fainted and was a long time coming to. He had got wet on the ninth of April. On the seventeenth he said to his valet:

"I cannot sleep and you know I have not slept for a week.

I know," he added, "that a man can only go without sleep for a certain time; after that he necessarily goes mad. I had ten times rather blow out my brains than go mad: I am not afraid of death; I am more prepared for death than people think."

I do not think that my lord had any idea that his end was approaching till the eighteenth. . . . I saw that he was growing weaker hour by hour and that he was beginning to have attacks of delirium. He said at the end of one of these attacks:

"I am beginning to think that I am seriously ill and in case I should die suddenly I want to give you some instructions that I hope you will take care to have carried out."

I assured him that I could be trusted to carry out his wishes; but I hoped he would live long enough to see to them himself.

"No; it's all over; I must tell you without losing a moment."

"Shall I get pen and ink and paper, my lord?"

"Oh God, no, you would take too much time and I have none to lose. . . . Now, listen: You are looked after in my will, Fletcher."

"I beg my lord to think of more important things."

"Oh, my child," he exclaimed, "Oh my dear daughter; my dear Ada. God! If I could have seen her. Convey my blessing to her . . . and to my dear sister Augusta and her children. You will go to see Lady Byron. Tell her—tell her everything; she is well disposed towards you. . . ."

His lordship seemed profoundly affected at this time; his voice failed; I could only catch words at intervals; but he kept talking between his teeth; he seemed very grave and often raised his voice to say: "Fletcher, if you do not carry out the orders I have given you I shall return to earth to torment you."

I said: "My lord, I have not heard a word you said."

He cried: "My God; it is all over. It is too late. Is it possible that you did not hear me?"

"No, your lordship. But try to let me know once more what your wishes are."

"How can I? It is too late. It is all over."

"It is not our will, but the will of God that is done."

"Yes, it is not my will; but I will try."

In fact he made several efforts to speak; but he could not get out more than two or three words: "My daughter! My sister!" Or: "You know everything: tell everything. You know my wishes. . . ." The rest was incomprehensible.

The last words of his that I heard were: "I must sleep now." He let his head fall and never raised it again. . . . At just six o'clock on the morning of the next day, the nineteenth, I saw his lordship open his eyes and close them again without any symptoms of pain, without the movement of any of his limbs. "Oh, my God!" I cried. "I am afraid his lordship is dead."

The doctors felt his pulse and said: "You are right. It is all over!"

One may read between the lines that the hero of the world and of Missolonghi was a hero also to his valet!

To keep together the three great ones of the romantic movement let us be present at the moment when that movement was fully justified of itself by the expulsion of the bourgeois king Louis Philippe and his umbrella. Lamartine and Victor Hugo, in the Town Hall of Paris, are arranging what form the new government shall take: It was on the third of *Les Trois Glorieuses*, as they still call the three February days that saw the fall of the monarchy. Lamartine, Dupont de l'Eure, Arago, the great astronomer, Ledru-Rollin and three others had been elected—by the populace who had broken into the Chamber of Deputies. The group became the Provisional Government. Says Victor Hugo in his *Memoires*:

The seven men who in these supreme and extreme days held the destiny of France in their hands were themselves at once tools and playthings in the hands of the mob—which is not the people—and of chance—which is not Providence. . . . [Hugo was still royalist, favoring very mildly the Duchess of Orléans as regent for her son, the Comte de Paris.] But there is at this moment in France a man whose name is in everybody's mouth and the thought of whom is in everybody's mind. That man is Lamartine. His eloquent and vivid *History of the Girondins* has for the first time taught the Revolution to France. Hitherto he has only been popular; he has become illustrious and may be said to hold Paris in his hand. . . . [When, having been separated and dispersed by the violent pushing of the crowd the Seven were able to find each other again and reassemble, or rather hide, in one of the rooms of the Hôtel de Ville, they took half a sheet of paper. At the head of it were printed the words: "Prefecture of the Seine. Office of the Prefect." M. de Rambuteau may that very morning have used the other half of the sheet to write a love letter to one of his "little bourgeoises," as he called them.]

Under the dictation of terrible shouts outside Lamartine traced this phrase:

"The Provisional Government declares that the Provisional Government of France is the Republican Government, and that the nation shall be immediately called upon to ratify the resolution of the Provisional Government and of the people of Paris."

I had this paper, this sheet smeared and blotted with ink, in my hands. It was still stamped, still palpitating, so to speak, with the fever of the moment. The words hurriedly scribbled were scarcely formed. *"Appelée"* was written *"appellée."*

When these half-dozen lines had been written Lamartine handed the sheet to Ledru-Rollin.

Ledru-Rollin read aloud the phrase: "The Provisional Government declares that the Provisional Government of France is the Republican Government—"

"The word 'provisional' occurs twice," he commented.

"That is so," said the others.

"One of them at least must be effaced," added Ledru-Rollin.

Lamartine understood the significance of this grammatical observation, which was simply a political revolution.

"But we must await the sanction of France," he said.

"I can do without the sanction of France," cried Ledru-Rollin, "when I have the sanction of the people."

"Of the people of Paris. But who knows at present what is the will of the people of France?" observed Lamartine.

There was an interval of silence. The noise of the multitude without sounded like the murmuring of the ocean.

Ledru-Rollin went on: "What the people want is the Republic at once, the Republic without waiting."

"The Republic without any delay?" said Lamartine, betraying an objection by this interpretation of Ledru-Rollin's words.

"We are provisional," returned Ledru-Rollin, "but the Republic is not!"

M. Crémieux took the pen from Lamartine's hands, scratched out the word "provisional" at the end of the third line and wrote beside it: "actual."

"The *actual* government? Very well!" said Ledru-Rollin, with a slight shrug of the shoulder.

As for Hugo himself here he romantically is:

The entrance once passed, M. Froment-Meurice guided us up all sorts of stairways, and through corridors and rooms encumbered with people. As we were passing, a man came from a group, and planting himself in front of me, said: "Citizen Victor Hugo, shout 'Long live the Republic!'"

"I will shout nothing by order," said I. "Do you understand what liberty is? For my part, I practice it. I will shout today 'Long live the people!' because it pleases me to do so. The day when I shout 'Long live the Republic!' it will be because I want to."

"Hear! hear! He is right," murmured several voices. And we passed on.

With "the three glorious days" the romantic movement approached its apotheosis—and the beginning of its decay. In Hugo it had its Prince President, its King, its Emperor, its High Priest, its Bard and its God!

If there were anyone higher than God—supposing one had been, say, Swinburne—it would have been necessary to have identified Hugo with that Being.

Twenty years ago, had this writer been writing this book he would have dismissed the author of *Nôtre Dame de Paris* with five—or put it rather, twenty—words of contempt. Today he is prepared to aver that *La Légende des Siècles* is one of the monuments of nineteenth century literature . . . or say of Literature! And Hugo himself seriously considered that the city of Paris should be renamed for him. That was perhaps not so unreasonable.

You should have seen Paris at his funeral. Everything stopped in the general consternation; everything was laurel wreaths, immortelles, black or purple ribbons. The whole arch of the Arc de Triomphe was filled up by an enormous catafalque. And as the great bells of Nôtre Dame tolled for the passing of this atheist who considered that his writings were more beneficent to humanity than all the words of God and His Son—as the overtones of the great bells swept into the narrow alleys running up from the Seine—there was not a human eye in Paris—nay, in all France—from which the tears did not fall. No nation ever paid any other author so genuine a tribute of grief and consternation.

And then . . . something like a scream! Hugo, as you or I might well do, had left in his will that he was to be carried to the grave in the cheapest conveyance permitted by the law. So the body was borne through all that pomp in the hearse of a ninth-class funeral*—literally and technically ninth class. It was to lie in state under the Arc de Triomphe de L'Étoile—which had been raised to celebrate the glories of the First Empire . . . so that the reporters of the day could write:

> On the horizon, with their spring flowers, their fresh verdure, are the trees of the Luxembourg . . . but here under the catafalque that is draped as with a mourning veil by the tricolor flag—Himself, the great dead man, sleeping, in the midst of this tempest of enthusiasm, his last sleep.

* *"Un corbillard des pauvres"* ("A pauper's hearse") is the expression used by Hugo in his will.

The *corbillard des pauvres*, like a blacked packing case drawn by two spavined black horses, produced a shocking effect, really an inconceivably shocking effect of grinning hypocrisy. This writer—or the reader—might well direct that his funeral should be as inexpensive as possible for the sake of his heirs' pockets or out of modesty. But it is difficult to attribute any feeling of modesty to a gentleman who sincerely thought that Paris should be renamed after himself. And Victor Hugo knew that the people would have pulled down the Senate if they had not decreed for him a funeral at the expense of the public. So that it must have been sheer drama. Except for that—and the temptation is almost irresistible—it is difficult to be certain that any line of Hugo contains a hypocrisy. But it is as difficult to believe that he ever shed a tear of pity for any human being—except for himself on the tragic drowning of his daughter and her husband. Almost every line of Hugo's contains a careful antithesis, like the Alexandrine *"Car le jeune homme est beau, mais le vieillard est grand."* And the careful arrangement of antitheses one on another really precludes much passion on the part of the author. Great grief or great sympathy may express itself epigrammatically once in a perfectly spontaneous manner. But you can scarcely go on polishing pebble after pebble if the tears are in your eyes. Writers, nevertheless, must be judged by the effects that they produce on their readers.

The great leaders of romanticism are Byron, Chateaubriand and the Vicomte Victor Amédée Charles Hugo, *Sénateur et Paire de France*. As to the first two one may fairly call them heartless; as to the last the state of his heart may remain open to question. The effect of Byron on the young post-Napoleonic world was, according to Musset in *La Confession d'un Enfant du Siècle*, depressing in the extreme: he seemed to have robbed the heart of hope and rendered it useful only for suffering and pain.

But, as to Chateaubriand, according to Faguet (and we may very well agree with him): he was the man who renewed French imagination after the sterile influence of the philosophers and agnostics of the late eighteenth century, and after superseding Voltaire, Fontenelle, Diderot and the rest, he restored to the world not only Christianity but the belief in the virtues, and hope itself. . . . Certainly, his influence working subterraneously against the Byronic afflatus, through Mme. de Staël, George Sand and possibly Hugo himself, reappeared to some extent in Flaubert and thus reinitiated the power of imaginative literature in the modern world.

The influence of Hugo too was, if one may use so ugly a word, inspirational. In spite of the exaggerated virtue of Jean Valjean, the consistent exaggerations of style and the exaggerated vices of the police, such a work as *Les Misérables* or, *mutatis mutandis, Les Travailleurs de la Mer* undoubtedly made a great number of people think, not perhaps of what we today should call social problems, but at least, with some idea of alleviation, of those who in that day were in poor circumstances or injured and oppressed. And it is to be remembered that the "poor circumstances" of that day were such an extreme of starvation and wretchedness as would make the poorest circumstances of our own day seem nearly heaven. If that is, indeed, the case, Hugo must have contributed something to that end. So, in his one really great poem, the epic *Légende des Siècles* he caused humanity to see humanity as something of a majestic pageant as opposed merely to the inhabitants of Matthew Arnold's plain where ignorant armies fought by night. . . .

And his actual political influence on his world was perhaps greater than his social achievement.

Let us for the moment abandon the author of *Hernani* to state what seems to be common sense on the point of the imaginative writer's attitude towards social problems. Let us begin by saying that there is no objection to an imaginative author's taking whatever part he pleases in direct political actions; so long as he feels conscientiously convinced that he is a proper person to interfere in the destinies of a fellow man there is no reason that he should not—nay, there is every reason why he should—vote, write pamphlets, fight on barricades or in wars for great causes. It is his duty to be as much of a man as he can, and the mere experience of how humanity supports its vicissitudes of failure or triumph will be of the utmost service to his pen. But he should beware of—he should altogether eschew—any impulse to put his *imaginative* pen at the service of any cause whatever. Fighting on a barricade can only give him a more just knowledge of what are the real values of life; but retiring into the ivory tower of altruistic or economic idealisms will almost inevitably lead to overcoloring of shade and lighting. That at once deprives one's work of the power to carry conviction, impels to rash and afterwards regretted action and adds falsehoods to the already too many falsehoods of a suffering world. It is with that conviction at least that this work has been written.

To return then to Hugo: his direct political action on the affairs of this world was very considerable. Thus, his neglect warmly to support Lamartine's Provisional Government in declaring for a republic deprived that government of the very considerable prestige that his open support would have given it. Hugo was very conscious of the fact that Louis-Philippe had made him a *paire de France*; the new republic offered him merely the mayoralty of a Paris *arrondissement*—an offer that he rejected with the cynical and atrocious pun that he was unwilling to be made ridiculous by becoming at once *paire et maire*.

Strengthened by his authority the young government might have resisted the pretensions of Louis Napoleon, who forced it to declare him president of the Republic. Whilst president, he made a "military excursion" to Rome and restored to his temporal power Pio Nono who had been expelled from his city by his subjects. And so Napoleon the Little went on his way towards Sedan. The three glorious days that had seen the installation of the new president had prolonged themselves by another two hundred and ninety-eight sufficiently ignoble. Napoleon III was elected Prince President on the twentieth of December 1848.

But, obviously, France was not large enough to contain both Victor Hugo and Napoleon III, and after the coup d'état of 1851 the poet went into exile, so remaining until in 1870 he returned to face a greater than Napoleon—in Bismarck. And to face an entirely changed civilization in which the belief in big battalions replaced as much as had survived to us of the *Logos* of the Greeks, of St. John and of Lao-Tsze.

It is legitimate for us to consider that Victor Hugo played a very large part in bringing about the victory of the Prussians. He may or may not have been impervious to the sentiment of sympathy, but his hatred for Napoleon III was greater than any other recorded hatred of any great man for any other. It surpassed in volume and certainly in effectiveness that of Dante for the Black Guelphs who had expelled him from Florence. Without ceasing, he poured out during all his exile— from Jersey, from Brussels, from Guernsey, from London—a torrent of invective and ridicule for the emperor that undoubtedly undermined both the authority and the prestige of the empire. They are still to be read in the volume called *Les Châtiments* and are still good reading for those who like that sort of thing. There are, indeed, those who consider that book greater than *La Légende des Siècles*. It was, of course, officially excluded from France, but be sure that there was no Frenchman who did not know that the sublime Victor Hugo had called their emperor "Napoleon the Little"—and there were few members of the high society of Paris and the ruling classes of the country who did not read at one time or other a surreptitious copy of *Les Châtiments*. And thus was born that spirit of *après-nous-le-délugisme* that brought to her *débâcle* the country of Chateaubriand . . . and us to our heavy doom.

It would be easy enough to justify these statements with documents, and the task would be a pleasing and profitable one for anyone who would undertake it. But our space grows shorter and shorter and I hear readers asking what Sedan has to do with literature.

It has this to do with literature: When a Bismarck replaces a Napoleon as a world ideal, or a King of France in alliance with St. Dominic a good King René of Provence . . . the psychological tempo of the world changes from the romantic to the materialistic. And, as we have said, it is the duty of literature when it can no longer dominate the world to dance to the world's tune until it is again in a situation to set the time for the world. A Latin—a Mediterranean—civilization has a definite place for the providers of literature. A Cicero can mould the fortunes of an empire, a Lamartine those of a republic; the lightest word of a Victor Hugo will travel to the ear of the remotest peasant in the land. A Napoleon III will read a romantic novel whilst the night falls on his last battle field. A Napoleon I will define the place of music in his empire from Moscow while it is burning. A member of the French Academy has the precedence of a Marshal of France, and all the garrisons of France must turn out to salute him as he passes by; and France, believing that her books are her best ambassadors, few of her great poets have escaped the destiny of representing their country abroad. Even a d'Annunzio can play an egregious part in a materialized Italy . . . and Greece permitted Byron to lead her armies. But Prussia burns Heine, and look at any time in one or other half of Anglo-Saxondom and you will find our best writers starving.

Hugo, however, returned from exile, became after a year or so a senator and so remained till his death. As such, being not on bad terms with Freycinet, of whom no poet could be jealous, he supported that statesman's policy of railroads, roads and canals that eventually—with such unostentation that not even Bismarck observed its progress—saved France.

In his youth he had had many and loyal adherents in his battle against the classicists. In the preface to his *Cromwell* he threw down the romanticist glove to those latter combatants with such effect that on the first night of his *Hernani*, which happened on November 25, 1830, the theatre became an enraged cockpit . . . "A mêlée amongst the most outrageous that have ever figured in the annals of the stage; the theatre rocked on its base; the hisses sounded like rifle bullets; the applause like fanfares of trumpets. In the end victory declared for the innovators. . . ." *Hernani* became for the generation of its birth what the *Cid* had been for the contemporaries of Corneille. The cause of romanticism had won.

Amongst the most ardent supporters of Hugo in this enterprise were two poets and a critic, Alfred de Vigny, Gautier, and Sainte-Beuve. We have already, in writing of Corneille and Racine, seen what were the methods of the classicists—the observance of the unities, the strict use of rhymed Alexandrines with a strongly marked cesura. The romantic dramatists claimed the right, when it suited them, to break all these rules. That is not to say that they did so always. Hugo himself wrote hundreds of verses of the most impeccable regularity as against tens of broken verse, or of verse with *enjambements*—verses in which sense and sentences run over from one verse to another, a de vice which they learned from Shakespeare. Thus, in his famous soliloquy in the fourth act of *Hernani*, Hernani uses, except for one *enjambement*, perfectly regular verse. In those ten lines there is only the one *enjambement* and no broken line at all. But what gave most offence, real offence to shocked ears, were the constant ejaculations, the constant mention of blood and flame, abysses red to the base, fatal roads, *"coursës farouchës"* and the rest. And that not unreasonably. For almost any foreigner, and for any Frenchman not really enamored of the past—any past!—to attend a performance of *Hernani* or *Ruy Blas* is an almost insupportable experience. The situations are all melodramatic, the atmosphere of unreasonable gloom is interrupted only by passages of more unreasonable grotesquerie, a habit again borrowed from Shakespeare. The characters are completely static; always all of one piece, they ululate always in one tone with always the same subject, and this gives to the pieces an awful weariness of monotony.

There is, in fact, nothing at all to be said in favor of Hugo as a dramatist from the point of view of today—and very little for any of the other romantic dramatists. Dumas *père* ran a race with Hugo and a worse dramatist called Delavigne, in the invention, in each successive play, of always more and more extravagantly melodramatic situations. He may consider to have won with *La Tour de Nesle* a real debauch of blood, sorcery, chains, dungeon cells, tortures, wounds, exaggerated sexual vice, skulls. His tragedies, nevertheless, are respectable compared with Hugo's, because he at least learned from Shakespeare some rudiments of stagecraft and of dramatic construction. One could see his once all-famous *Antony* played with some interest. It is an unreasonable play with an unusually gloomy, outcast hero; but it does move to the quite unreasonable murder of the heroine by the hero with some intensification of effect and skill in construction. The plays of Vigny, who not only studied Shakespeare but translated—or rather adapted—*Othello* and *The Merchant of Venice*, are relieved by the tranquillity of his temperament and the purity of his devotion to his lyric art. Indeed, but for the absurdities of its plot, his *Chatterton* is a piece of some beauty and dignity.

Musset, too, learned very well of Shakespeare. His best plays deal with love, not infrequently with his own loves. He has a real sense of drama when he wishes to employ it, and his lyric gift is a very precious one. As may be gathered from his impression of Byron as given in his *Confessions of a Child of the Century*, he very early abandoned the Byronic tone, and what is romantic in his plays is the natural romance of the perpetual and usually unfortunate lover. His most disastrous liaison was that with George Sand. Its rupture sent him to absinthe and turned his soul to wormwood.

We arrive with these two men—and with two more that shall come immediately upon the scene—at a stage in the literary pilgrimage that exactly marks off a period. The poets and prosateurs, Vigny, Musset, Gautier and the critic Sainte-Beuve, were all—as they were the first—really students of the aesthetics of their art before they began to write. To say that no one before them studied the rules of the game as did Dryden or Pope or the French critics of the age of Corneille, would be absurd. But what they studied were exactly rules—and rules of a game the breaking of which entailed social ostracism or the frown of kings.

But these four all studied Shakespeare, Byron, Richardson, Monk Lewis and a host of other writers—all, it will surely be observed, English—in order to discover not what were the rules which they agreed to observe, but just what liberties might be safely taken. For all of them studied particularly Shakespeare and the Elizabethans in order to assure themselves that those writers observed no rules at all. And that was the definite purpose of their Anglo-Saxon researches. They did not want to observe any rules themselves and they wanted the assurances of great writers that they too were anarchic. So you had Goethe, Hugo, Dumas, all declaring that the only guide that Shakespeare followed was nature.

In a sense they were right. For Shakespeare, in common with every other great conscious artist, studied nature—and, above all, human nature—in order that he might discover what it was about nature or humanity that gave charm. They saw a charming man, woman, woodland or bird and said: "What the devil is the secret of their charm?" Then they went about trying to think out a method of throwing back on the public charms exactly similar, as a mirror throws back the reflections of the images that confront it. When they achieved that method they went on employing it. It would not, however, be either a rule of the game or a unity—it would be a personal note of how to get an effect. Shakespeare obviously followed the rules of stagecraft of his day. When he found they let him down, he jettisoned them and made others. But those rules were the infinitely unimportant ones; what mattered were his efforts to convey charm . . . or surprise or interest or tragic horror. You don't mean to say that the knocking on the door was arrived at accidentally whilst Shakespeare scrabbled off the manuscript of Macbeth. . . . No, he had observed the horror caused by some knocking at the door when the watch came to a tavern to arrest some misdemeanant—himself or another. Then he tried it out on the stage. . . . Or Marlowe may have observed something of the sort and have told him.

The trouble is that, by the days of Musset, Vigny, Gautier and Sainte-Beuve, the bloody wars were no longer, as you might say, forever knocking at the door. . . . For it is astonishing to observe how many of the great writers before that day served in the wars . . . Horace, Tibullus, Dante, Cervantes, Goethe, Chateaubriand, Stendhal—to whom we shall have immediately to pay a great deal of attention—and heaven knows how many of the young or not quite so young of the writers of today. The point is that it is an extremely quick and vivid method of coming to grips at real life. . . . You see the enemy approach; you are in danger of your life and all your life sums itself up before you: or rather you remember a great number of things and the fact that you remember them at such a moment means that they are the significant things of your life. Or seagoing in a sailing ship is a good thing; or dangerous travel; or being really on the verge of starvation in a garret.

The Gautiers, the Vignys, the Mussets, the Thackerays, Charles Reeds, Tennysons and all the rest of the writers who were to come on the scene and remain till the thunders of 1914—or 1917—resounded through the world, had none of these hard contacts with actual life. They were white-collar men with soft hands, who sat in wadded chairs, curtained to keep out the draughts. Thus, they tried to come into contact with life-that-is-near-death by writing the dreadfully specious verbal diarrhoeas that they called historical novels. It was not merely that they were providing literature of escape for the public; they were trying to escape themselves, at least into the mêlée and deeds of cape and sword in their own minds. Don't believe that Dumas in the character of d'Artagnan was describing objectively a man observed from the outside: he was telling us what he had really done— by the fireside. Don't we, indeed, know that Goethe was himself Dr. Faust, adventuring amongst magic spells, duels, seductions? . . . He has told us so.

Even Alfred de Vigny—whom one would have taken to be too serious an artist—wrote, from the depths of his ivory tower, one of those historical machines. His *Cinq-Mars*, a novel about the days of Louis XIII, is usually considered a more serious attempt at history than all the rest of the heap from Scott to Ponson du Terrail. But it is heavy, and if it is really historic enough in the episodes it selects to render, it selects historic events that are always of romantic coloring. We have Bassompierre, a little under the wine, recounting an episode of the last day of Henri IV. Le Vert Galant is entering his chariot to be stabbed in the back by Ravaillac. Here is Bassompierre describing it:

Eh, mon Dieu! Je le vois encore. . . . I see him still, in his carriage, on the very day of his death, embracing the Duke of Guise, after having told me one of his risqué and witty little tales. And the Duke said: "As far as I am concerned, you are one of the most agreeable of men; it is destiny that has thrown us together. For, if you had been only any sort of man, I should have taken *you* into my service; but since God directed that you should be born a great king, it had to be I that served under *you* . . ."

Ah, great man! How well you spoke when you said: *"When you have lost me you will recognize what I was worth!"*

That is your real romanticism. Even Henri IV has to become what is called fuliginous . . . darkly redolent of his end.

But de Vigny in his own way—like Musset, Gautier, and Sainte-Beuve—was very different from the other amateur volcanos of romance. It is true that he too served in the army, but that disgusted him so, that, a haughtily aristocratic figure, he retired, without much knowledge of human nature gained, to a retreat at some distance from the center of Paris and there shut himself up. It is true too that he joined one of the clubs of young people that had been the supporters of Hugo and *Hernani*. That *"cénacle"* had been founded by Sainte-Beuve and when he found that the young noble, in his distaste for the *tapage*, absented himself almost entirely from the club, Sainte-Beuve uttered his celebrated witticism to the effect that de Vigny shut himself up to think silver thoughts in his ivory tower: He afterwards versified the remark as:

Et Vigny, plus secret
Comme en sa tour d'ivoire avant minuit rentrait.

So now we know where *that* came from. . . . But as a matter of fact the *"turris eburnea"* is, in the Latin prayer book, one of the synonyms of the Holy Virgin.

De Vigny, however, actually retired to his suburb to study the Bible, Byron and Homer. He desired to learn from them the secret of a charm that he could find neither in the wars nor in civil life. And he succeeded so well that in his single volume of poems are to be found the only verses in modern literature that suggest both "Full fathom five thy father lies," and a little of the other worldly impishness . . . of Heine. He was, however, too proud to be self-revelatory, and his poems are little renderings of incidents to which philosophical or bitterish morals may be attached—rather than true lyrics.

No one, on the other hand, could be more revelatory of himself than de Musset. His self-disclosures run from single immortal lines like *"Je suis venu trop tard dans un monde trop vieux"* and the even more useful "My glass is not big, but I drink out of my own glass," to the almost superfluously protracted *Confessions*, in which he re-

counts the circumstances of his ruinous liaison with George Sand. . . .
But he could go further still and write little poems that were just tiny
stories, not confessions at all, not subjective. So you have the *Song of
Barberine* that, in story at least, exactly parallels some of the little
story-songs of Heine:

> *Beau chevalier, qui partez pour la guerre*
> *Qu'allez vous faire*
> *Si loin de nous?*
> *J'en vais pleurer, moi qui me laisais dire*
> *Que mon sourire*
> *Etait si doux.*

As who should say:

> And now, departing for the distant fight
> What will you do, Fair Knight,
> So far from us?
> I must go hence to mourn our parting, I, the unwise,
> Who deemed my eyes
> So glamorous.

Musset's glass was not big, but in defining his personality for us he
has left us a miniature *Portrait of a Poet*. We could turn to the wall
many other portraits of louder singing bards before we shall turn
his . . . and Vigny's . . . and, indeed, Gautier's . . . and, again,
Sainte-Beuve's.

Those four form, indeed, a group of musketeers of the art that
singularly parallel the Elizabethan group made up of Sidney, Spenser,
Lyly and some of the sonneteers . . . and the parallels are curiously
exact. Thus, the Spenser group studied foreign authors in order,
quite consciously, to give England glories as rare as their models—
Petrarch perhaps first of all, then the classics, then Marot, Ronsard,
du Bellay and all the Pleïad group. Spenser even studied Chaucer.
They left immense monuments of books that to the present writer
are perfectly unreadable. You may sit down and read a sticky jewelled

passage here and there in any of their epics or romances. But longer
you cannot sit. A sort of disgust, as if at overeating, makes you get up
with the desire to do something Philistine . . . watch a prize fight, say.
You can read this from the *Arcadia* by Sidney.

> The messenger made speed and found Argalus at a castle of his
> own sitting in a parlour with the fair Parthenia, he reading in a
> book the stories of Hercules, she by him read: but while his eyes
> looked on the book, she looked on his eyes, and sometimes stay-
> ing him with some pretty question, not so much to be resolved of
> the doubt, as to give him occasion to look upon her: a happy
> couple, he joying in her, she joying in herself, but in herself be-
> cause she enjoyed him: both increased their riches by giving to
> each other.

The image is pretty; the conceit of "in herself she enjoyed him"
arrests the attention. But what a sentence! And how could one be expected to go on reading such sentences for three months before finishing the *Faerie Queen* or *Arcadia*? And you will meet exactly that
same conceit, "he for himself and she for her in him," hundreds and
hundreds of times. Surely Sidney had studied, as we have pointed out,
the *Arcadia* of Sannazaro and the *Diana* of Montemayor, the Spanish
poet. But what a heaviness had gotten itself into his diction.

To make more exact the parallel between this group and the Frenchmen: Spenser loved beauty as perhaps only Gautier beside him did
and was, like Gautier, the very first of his race to found a school of
some sort of exact criticism of aesthetics.

Thus, Spenser, paralleling, as it is so the fashion to do today, the
technique of the painter with that of the poet, says that painters

> Blaze and portrait not onlie the daintie lineaments of beautie,
> but also round about it to shadowe the rude thickets and craggy
> cliffs, that, by the baseness of such parts, more excellencie may
> accrew to the principall: for oftentimes we find ourselves, I know
> not how, singularly delighted with the shew of such naturall rude-
> nesse, and take great pleasure in that disorderly order. Even so

doo those rough and harsh termes enlumine, and make more clearly to appear, the brightness of brave and glorious wordes. So oftentimes a discorde in musicke maketh a comely concordance.

We may add that, like Sidney, de Vigny really was a very *parfaite* gentle knight and poor Gautier was perpetually deploring his banishment into the deserts of hack journalism just as Spenser lamented that the office that Sidney obtained for him kept him all his life in the desérts of Ireland.

And, finally, with Musset, de Vigny, Gautier and Sainte-Beuve our modern literary life begins, just as with Spenser and the rest began the Great Age in England. And, as the impulsion to the Great Age in England came from France and the neighboring countries, so the impulsion towards Today in France came mainly from England.

The great influence on France came from Shakespeare, so that the light of the Shakespearean lyric seems to play about the writing of all that group. And we may add the rather queer conjunction of Scott, Byron, Monk Lewis, Crabbe, above all Richardson . . . and then Homer and the Bible. The Latin classics they seem hardly ever to have read as adults: they no doubt had enough of them in the schools. Except for Sainte-Beuve one likes all these writers with a personal tenderness that may make them seem more important than in the scale of great things they really deserve. If you insist that none of them were "great" figures, this writer will scarcely contradict you. But they were vivid ones. They wrote little and what little they wrote was exquisitely polished; not one of them sets before us a terrific wall of verbiage like the *Faerie Queen* or the *Arcadia*. They had that merit along with Lyly, whose two *Euphues* are at least brief.

No doubt the *Emaux et Camées* of *ce pauvre Théo*, had they been strung together into an "epic," would worry one to read. At times the rather close writing of *Mademoiselle de Maupin* becomes a little *"impatientant"*—impatience-making. But that only very seldom. And the picaresquely inspired *Capitaine Fracasse* one can read at a breath . . . or two. Gautier's prose is, in fact, generally limpid, with a purple patch only now and then introduced as if Gautier said to himself from time to time: "After all I *am* the author of *Emaux et Camées.*"

And the *Emaux et Camées* are really the beginnings of the sustainedly conscious writing that is the chief merit of the literature of the ages that have succeeded him. De Vigny, from time to time, thought of "technique;" Musset did so a little less often—a characteristic that we may set down to the fact that his plays were not written for stage production, so that he cared little whether they made an effect or no. But, even in his most ephemeral criticisms, Gautier very seldom wrote a careless word—which no doubt made them such a weariness to him. This is the secret of his work, expressed in an address to his fellow poets:

> *Sur l'autel idéal entretenez la flamme,*
> *Comme un vase d'albatre où l'on cache un flambeau.*
> *Mettez l'idée au fond de la forme sculptée*
> *Et d'une lampe ardente éclairez le tombeau.*

His journalistic criticisms are not very illuminating. He began by writing for *La Presse* a series of sufficiently spirited pages on Delacroix the painter, but as time went on, and as he had less and less remarkable artists to write about, his ideas became less and less illuminative, and he becomes more and more indulgent to the persons about whom he did write. He has perhaps never—or only very lately—been sufficiently highly estimated in France . . . perhaps because he was so very much loved: "*Il avait,*" as Daudet said, "*son couvert chez Brébant.*" There was always a cover laid ready for him at any place where great authors habitually dined as they do in France on a given day of the week. Always lamenting semi-humorously about the hard lot of "*Ce pauvre Théo,*" he must go away before the dinners ended to write his next day's article for *La Presse* or, after 1855, for the *Moniteur.* And just because he was *ce pauvre Théo* he excited no jealousies and no enmities.

His name appears as often in the *Correspondance* of Flaubert and the journals of Maxime Ducamp and the Goncourts as did that of

Byron in the fugitive writings of his day. Nevertheless, he achieved almost no fame and less fortune.

One joy he had. That was that from time to time he could travel in Spain. Of her he wrote: "The soul has its native country as well as the body," and, as it was for Washington Irving, the Alhambra and the general life of Granada became almost the chief note of his life as of his work. He died—as almost every real writer of merit since his day has died—in "reduced circumstances." His one good fortune was that his family survived him. And, said his sister to Ernest Feydeau: "He was all for us. He was our entire universe."

The one lesson that he learned from life is that saddest of all lessons: *"Le bien c'est l'ennemi du mieux."* He expressed that truth more extendedly thus:

> In the world of art there stands always below each genius, a man of talent, preferred to him. Genius is uncultivated, violent, tempestuous; it seeks only to satisfy itself, and cares more for the future than the present. The man of talent is spruce, well-dressed, charming, accessible to all; he takes every day the measure of the public and makes garments suited to its stature, while the poet forges gigantic armors which the Titans alone can wear. Under Delacroix you have Delaroche; under Rossini, Donizetti; under Victor Hugo, M. Casimir Delavigne!

The poor Théo had all his life a great desire to be elected a member of the French Academy: the Forty turned down his candidacy with an unchanging moroseness. But at his death the Academy broke the rule that forbids the mention, during a public session of the name of any writer not an Academician, and the President, Camille Doucet, in a speech quoted by Sainte-Beuve in his wonderful article on Gautier, paid a long tribute to the illustrious dead:

> "All literature," he said, "weeps in despair, a true poet and brilliant writer who was dear to us all. Numerous suffrages have proved his place should have been among us; all the more do we deplore the sudden stroke beneath which he has fallen."

and a number of the Academicians present declared that that day they had had the intention of electing Gautier a member of their company.

"But" as Sainte-Beuve said, "he they thus sought to honor had no need of earthly praise. The tribute had come too late."

Sainte-Beuve occupies the singular position of being the only critic of literature whose fame during his day was that of a great writer. He has preserved since then a reputation as strong and as immovable as a marble block.

He is the father of all modern "historic" criticism of literature—a process that decrees that before writing about a poet or even reading him you must know everything that there is to know about his person and history, in order to discover in his biographic details the reasons for his literary tendencies. . . . To critics of the frame of mind of this present writer, that is to put the cart before the horse and that doctrine has been anathema maranatha. Without "chatter about Harriet" Shelley would be a much-read poet; lacking Boswell, Johnson would be recognized as the greatest of English intelligences. The disinterring of *ana* about littérateurs which has been the secular preoccupation of all the universities of the world is responsible for the low estimation at which literature is held in the every-day world. Sainte-Beuve sanctified and perpetuated that process.

The process of the real critic begins with the appreciation of the work and ends there. Who need know anything about Shakespeare or Dante or Homer? But once you are really saturated in the work of a writer it is legitimate to enquire into the circumstances of his life. It is human nature—and not only that, details of an author's life may cast light on passages of his work or on the nature of literature itself. It is, thus, useful to the father of a future littérateur to know that Shakespeare was reputed a deer thief; that Marlowe really was a braggart with the sword; that Sidney died at the Battle of Zutphen; that Dante was a skillful commander of troops in small engagements; that Gibbon served with the militia; that Conrad—like today's poet laureate —was a hand before the mast, or that the writer's friend, Mr. Hemingway, served voluntarily with the Allied troops before his country took part in a late war.

Knowing that, a parent intent on having his son become a man of letters—and there are some such—will insist that his son serve in the army, the navy, the merchant marine, the grocer's store, the goodly company of tillers of the earth . . . and do it for a living. Or the budding writer may so decide for himself. The point is so important that we labor it more than máy seem reasonable. If literature is to hold its own as the great instructor of the human race, its devotees must have faced life. Whilst doing so they may read books, or they may read them afterwards—but to live a hard life and to be dependent on it is indispensable.

Nevertheless, to the writer what is of interest is the art, and the lives of his brother writers, and Sainte-Beuve lives less as a critic than as the first of his profession to make of his critical writings works of art. The writer and his contemporary friends of the late 'nineties always regarded Sainte-Beuve with suspicion and differed from almost every critical sentence that he wrote; but who could resist such a passage of description as this about Gautier? Certainly Daudet did not when he wrote *Tartarin de Tarascon*:

> In his African journey of 1845, he (Gautier) accompanied the expedition to Kabylie on the staff of General Bugeaud, who gave him a tent, two horses and a servant. Of the five civilians on the expedition, three died from fatigue or heat. Gautier returned to Paris in an Arabic costume, coifed with a fez and wearing a burnous. He made his advent into the city on the top of the Chalons diligence, a young lioness that had been confided to his care, between his knees. He had himself a leonine appearance; sunburnt, tawny, with flashing eyes, his friends recall him as he was at this fortunate epoch, in all the strength and pride of second youth, in all the opulence and amplitude of perfect manhood, breathing in life with full lungs, having his own style of dress, oriental in design and color. Two little ponies worthy of Tom

Thumb, harnessed to an elegant coupé whose body almost grazed the pavement, bore a master with a deep olive complexion who majestically filled the inside, and at each halt for a visit, was ready to mount with agile step to the suite of apartments. At this time in the flush of health and hope and worldly satisfaction, Gautier wrote his verses entitled "Fatuity." This is the first stanza:

Je suis jeune, la pourpre en mes veines abonde;
Mes cheveaux sont de jais et mes regards de feu,
Et sans gravier ni toux, ma poitrine profonde
Aspire a pleins poumons l'air du ciel, l'air de Dieu.

These are magnificent verses of their kind, verses overflowing with health and vitality. We comprehend how one may be tempted to be a materialist when matter is so rich and beautiful. Never could a meager, sickly man write such poetry. The man is matured, the real man has displaced the young man of dreams. Nature in her vigor and vivacity transports him and transforms him. This is her law. In the Goethe of Weimar, in that majestic and tranquil personage at the middle and the end of life, who would recognize Werther?"

You could not have anything much more picturesque, but it is scarcely literary criticism. Sainte-Beuve is, however, seldom so definitely picturesque. Gautier wrote a number of literary portraits that, he being a real poet, are much more intimately picturesque than any of the long string of articles published by Sainte-Beuve under the general title of *Causeries du Lundi*. But Gautier had the trick of being unknown: Sainte-Beuve contrived to be always before the public eye. His *Causeries*, as they appeared on Mondays, set all Paris a-whispering. And he was the more subtle of the two. Gautier out of a hundred pages would devote seventy-five to writing like this about the youth of Balzac:

Figure to yourself our young Honoré, his legs wrapped in a ragged coachman's overcoat, the upper part of his body protected by an old shawl of his mother's, his headgear a sort of Dantesque cap, whose cut Madame de Balzac alone knew, a coffeepot at his right, an inkstand at his left, with heaving chest and bowed forehead, laboring like an ox at the plough, the field as yet stony and uncleared of those thoughts which were later to trace for him such productive furrows. His lamp burns like a star in the depths of the somber house, the snow descends silently upon the disjointed tiles; the wind sighs through the door and window, "Like Tulou with his Flute, but less agreeably."

The remaining twenty-five would go to criticism, sometimes even to disquisitions on literary aesthetics, language, right words and the like. The more subtle Sainte-Beuve hardly ever made the mistake of writing about aesthetics and seldom, as we have said, sets down a solid wad of personal descriptions. He will touch you in traces of a personality like this passage on Massillon, the court preacher of Louis XV:

Massillon in the pulpit had scarcely any gestures: that dropping of the eye as he began, which he kept dropped habitually, till he afterward, at rare intervals, raised it, and cast it over the auditory, constituted in his case the finest of gestures; he had, says the Abbé Maury, an *eloquent eye*. In his exordiums, which were always happy, there was something that arrested the attention, as on the day when he pronounced the funeral oration of Louis XIV, when, after having silently run his eye over all those magnificent funeral trappings, he began with these words: "God alone is great, my brethren! . . ."

Or he will parallel two characters, as thus:

A man of a proud, aristocratic family, but a pupil of Rousseau, and who had hardly more than he the sentiment and fear of the ridiculous, M. de Chateaubriand, has repeated in *René* and in his *Memoirs* that more or less direct manner of avowals and confessions, and he has drawn from it some magical and surprising effects. Let us note, however, the differences. Rousseau has not the original elevation; he is not entirely—far from it!—what one calls a well-born child; he has an inclination to vice, and to low vices; he has secret and shameful lusts which do not indicate the gentleman; he has that extreme shyness which so suddenly turns into the effrontery of the *rogue* and the *vagabond*, as he calls himself; in a word, he has not that safeguard of honor, which M. de Chateaubriand had from childhood, standing like a watchful sentinel by the side of his faults. But Rousseau, with all these disadvantages which we do not fear, after him, to mention by their name, is a better man than Chateaubriand, inasmuch as he is more human, more a man, more tender. He has not, for example, that incredible hardness of heart (a hardness really quite feudal), and that thoughtlessness in speaking of his father and his mother. When he speaks of the wrongs done him by his father, who, an honest man, but a man of pleasure, thoughtless, and remarried, abandoned him and let him to his fate, with what delicacy does he mention that painful matter!"

And having thus got his installment of personalia in, he will be away in a long flood of moralizing on what he has just written. Until he thinks he has exhausted that topic and finds it time to introduce a few more personal touches. This gave the reader the idea that he was reading something much more solemn than the thumb-nail sketches of Gautier. But still real criticism is almost entirely absent from the *Causeries*. In that on Rousseau there are three lines about the verbiage employed by . . . Chateaubriand. In revenge there is a complete reconstitution of the character, moods and psychology of Rousseau and an infinity of speculation as to the habit of mind of his day.

Sainte-Beuve, in short, "initiated" the type of criticism that for fifty years or so was to become almost universal, and more particularly so in Anglo-Saxondom. It was the so-called historic method. If you read any History of Literature, English, French, Italian or German, for the next fifty years—say from 1840 to 1890—you will find almost fifty per cent of the earlier portions of the work given up to disquisitions on "The Reform Bill of 1832" or "Legislation on Child Labor," "The Arrival of Science" or the "Growth of Industrialism;" another twenty-five per cent will be given to discovering what contacts the various

writers to be considered had had with "Child Labor" (Dickens);
"Growth of Industrialism" (Mrs. Gaskell) . . . and then a lot will be
said as to what effect contact with those factors of modern life will
have had on the psychology of the writers. Finally, a few words will
be devoted to some of their books.

Before the advent of Sainte-Beuve literary criticism had limited itself
to discussions as to whether writers had or had not observed the unities
and other arbitrary rules of good taste and literary conduct. But after
Sainte-Beuve had been writing his *Causeries* for some time literary
criticism became a part of the paraphernalia of the politician, or a useful tool of the churchman as against the Darwinians. That literature
was to be considered as an art and treated as such in criticism does not
seem to have occurred to any one until Matthew Arnold came along.
And since no soul listened to Arnold with anything other than derision, it was not until the Anglo-Paris-American siege of London as
a literary center in the 'nineties of last century that any change came
over the materialist attitude that till then prevailed unchallenged.

CHAPTER FIVE

Before continuing on our way we had better devote a short interlude to British and American poetry from the days of Wordsworth to the deaths of the pre-Raphaelite poets and those, in 1892, of Whitman and Browning. It would be more convenient to dispose of the prose writers from Balzac to Hardy, who ceased writing novels in 1896; we could in that way have preserved the international note of the great estuary. But our own poets of the era mentioned are so in the foreground of our minds that, in perspective, Longfellow must seem a colossus compared to Stendhal, whose effect, nevertheless, on all literature from about 1850 onwards till today was immense and unrelenting. But that is what regionalism does to us.

It is difficult really to estimate the place in the sun of our romantic-to-Victorian poets. Where do Wordsworth, Coleridge, Shelley, Keats, Poe, Landor, Tennyson, Rossetti, Swinburne, William Morris, Christina Rossetti, Whitman, Browning and Thomas Hardy stand in a world that produced Po Chu-I, Rihaku, the author of the Book of Job, Homer, Aeschylus, Euripides, Tibullus, Propertius, Dante, Petrarch, Chaucer, Shakespeare, Donne, Pope, Ronsard, Racine, Corneille, Lamartine, Vigny, Musset and Baudelaire, not to mention Goethe, Wieland, Alfieri and Espronceda?

Naturally, our regionalists will get up and, after cursing this writer for that blasphemy, will point out that from the birth of Wordsworth to the death of Tennyson and Whitman was a mere 120 years; from the birth of Confucius in 551 B.C. to the death of Tennyson was a matter of 2,443 years. That is quite beside the point. From the birth of Aeschylus (525) to the death of Euripides in 406, both B.C., was only 119 years; and from the birth of Shakespeare to the death of Dryden was only 136 years. . . . Where would the Romantic-Victorians stand with their 122 years of production against either of those other two periods alone?

But even that is not the point. The point is that there is literature, an immense stream opening out into an immense delta; upon it huge towers, monuments, triumphal arches, Parthenons with cities at their feet. Imagine yourself regarding such a landscape. Then what space would our champions occupy; to what heights would their ceremonial buildings soar?

And the point comes more intimately home than that. We have to ask ourselves whether it would be better for our children to be first and more intimately acquainted with the *Odyssey*, Theocritus, the lyrics of Walther von der Vogelweide, the *Canterbury Tales*, the *Morte d'Arthur* and *A Midsummer Night's Dream* or with *Peter Bell* —which contains, it is true, the lovely lines

> Among the rocks and winding scars,
> Where deep and low the hamlets lie,
> Each with their little patch of sky
> And little lot of stars,

and "The Ancient Mariner" and the "Ode to the West Wind" or "La Belle Dame Sans Merci" and "Ulalume" and "The Blessed Damosel" and "The Earthly Paradise" and "Goblin Market" and "Cavalry Crossing a Ford" and "The Bishop Orders His Tomb" and "The Dynasts"?

Set down like that it would be a brave man that did not wish his children—and, in consequence, the future of civilization—to have at least the echo of all those Victorian poems in the backs of their heads. Nevertheless, one is apt to ask oneself whether, if one had to make the choice, one would not exchange the whole lot of them for, say, the *Odyssey* or the *Tempest?* Supposing some super Mr. Hitler of the future should decree that one or the other must be for good suppressed? Such a thing is possible. The Man-of-Action-in-Business is apt to detest the arts sufficiently to desire to suppress them all and, not feeling the courage to order the complete holocaust, might decide to burn only one group.

Let us approach the problem with as much courage as we may. . . . The tendency, then, of all poets and of poetry itself since the days of Prior or Gray has been to dissociate themselves from the life and language of the day. That of itself is not necessarily an "unhealthy" symptom. You will find half the youth of the Middle West of the United States today filled with the ambition to go to do pioneering work in Australia. The nineteenth century poets desired to go to mental distances to find refinements of ideals of life that were not to be found under George III and Victoria. Shelley, say, and to some extent Byron and William Morris erected that longing into a definite political doctrine. Tennyson, on the other hand, desired to make his own age definitely more chaste, more sober, more obedient to pastors and masters, or in the alternative he retired into pasts where those attributes supposedly distinguished the populaces. The pre-Raphaelite poets desired not so much ivory towers as Philip Webb-built red-brick Queen Anne mansions furnished with more mediaeval chests and gadgets than all the middle ages ever saw.

The muse was once more removed from every-day life by having, as the eighteenth century came to an end, to invent a new language— one differing altogether from the by-now-exhausted classicisms that produced the effect of having been air that had been breathed over again to the point of rarefaction. Wordsworth tried to revivify his private vernacular by reducing it to the language of a child or that of a field laborer purged of dialect and misspelling. Keats and in a less degree Shelley—and Lamb, Hazlitt and de Quincey—sought to introduce fresh air by going back to the Elizabethans, for both words and cadences. The writer's father once declared that D. G. Rossetti wrote the thoughts of Dante in the language of Shakespeare—to which this writer replied that Rossetti would have been better employed if he had written the thoughts of Rossetti in the language of Victoria. The pre-Raphaelites in general employed along with Elizabethanisms a number of mediaeval words and cliché phrases. Lord Tennyson attempted to build up a language out of Malory and Spenserian clichés, in the mood of Petrarch. Browning attempted to save himself from being stifled by using violences to almost any sort of vocabulary. Whitman tried to solve the problem by using the vernacular of the auctioneer's catalogue and the patent medicine pamphlet. He could have done worse.

For the language of every-day prose solved its problem, as the saying is, *ambulando,* and somewhat after the fashion of Whitman half a century before his day. If actually you want to find fine, nervous, expressive vernacular prose in the 1820's you must turn to the headlines in the country newspapers in England and in the larger provincial towns in the United States. Not to the metropolitan papers, whose language remained hyperclassical till a much later date. The English country, and United States provincial, presses were faced with the problem of conveying, to populaces grown politically news-conscious, exact information in a language that was clear to them and that seemed nonridiculous. Dead classicisms might still adorn the larger London papers and the extremely powerful monthly reviews; they were no longer— they never had been—acceptable to the newspaper audiences of Luton or of Philadelphia. The newspaper writers of the day turned, then, to the language of auctioneers' catalogues, local law reports and conversations in better-class alehouse parlors, and fabricated a language that was clear, simple and vernacular. A language needs, however, at least one genius to give it backbone and rigidity. English found one genius of prose in Cobbett and two or three admirable prosateurs in the essayists. And, curiously enough, Cobbett affected the American vernacular quite as much as he did the British one. His style was so extremely forcible when he was minded to be forcible that every sentence he wrote on any public matter that deeply moved him blazed like a comet. Then it was repeated from mouth to mouth by individuals not minded or not in a position to buy copies of the papers for which Cobbett wrote. He twice had to flee from England because of his too bitingly expressed and subversive opinions. In each case he went to the United States where—between the years 1792 and 1800 and from 1817-19—he spent ten years, writing so forcibly that he was assaulted by mobs and thrown out of cities by sheriffs; he established prickly gazettes in Philadelphia. In New England, where he had turned farmer in 1818, he wrote an admirable *Grammar of the English Language.* His influence on the American vernacular was as great and even more lasting than that which he exercised on the English press.

There was thus established in England on the one hand a language not at all without dignity that suited the common usage. But the dialect for the use of poets and the intelligentsia has tended further and further to alienate English literature in general and English poetry in particular from the normal layman. Thus, both imaginative prose and verse ceased as time went on to exercise any influence upon public life in either England or the United States. Power passed into the hands of a class of writers who, having no respect for imaginative literature, neglected at once to have any knowledge or to take any steps to attain to, skill in writing. Occasionally, by sheer discipline of an exactly observing mind determined to express itself with the most rigorous clarity, you found a scientist like Darwin or a lawyer like Maine who wrote a prose that was in itself a stimulation or a delight. But the majority of "serious" writing expressed itself in a language lying between the extremes of the dreadful moral rhetoric of a Ruskin or the heavy and morose dogmatisms of a Herbert Spencer.

This moroseness and that dogmatism led those, as a rule reforming, scientists, moralists or sociological writers into a sort of avocational specialism that sometimes let them express really horrifying dogmas. The whole of the Victorian utilitarian cosmogony seemed for this writer damned forever by one speech of the late Mr. John Bright in the House of Commons, the speech being afterwards elaborated and printed as a basic document of the Free Trade Party. Mr. Bright remarked with passion that the British Empire would rock to its foundations and the British workingman's material prosperity—which Mr. Bright, as tribune of the people, worked unsleepingly to promote—would forever depart from the homes of the people on the day when a child of eight was prohibited by law from working in the coal mines. The Earl of Shaftesbury—who was afterwards stoned in Whitehall—pointed out in his speech in reply that the child of eight working fourteen hours a day carried, strapped to his head, the equivalent in coal of the weight of a full-grown man twenty times a day in complete darkness up ladders of the height of St. Paul's Cathedral.

And this writer is tired of reading in histories and commentaries in every European language that the English scientific and political spirit of the Victorian day was reflected in Victorian literature. It was not. Not in Thackeray, not even in the "common or garden" novelists like James Payn or William Black. Not anywhere. Not even in the Lords and Commons themselves, Shaftesbury introducing—at first in the Peers and afterwards having introduced in the Commons—a bill abolishing child labor forever in the British dominions. And we did not lose India as John Bright swore we should, averring that it would be a tyranny that would surely be forcibly resented in the *raj*, if the Hindoo peasant were not permitted to augment the small quantity of rice that was his diet by increasing his income by the four annas a day that his infant child could earn for him in the newly established cotton mills. No, you would not have found a single imaginative writer in the England of that day to applaud Mr. Bright or let Mr. Bright's speeches influence his point of view in the direction of materialism. . . . And Dickens! And Mrs. Gaskell! And Elizabeth Barrett Browning who wrote:

> But the young, young children, oh my brothers,
>   Are weeping bitterly.
> They are weeping in the playtime of the others
>   In the country of the free.

At the same time Mr. John Stuart Mill was writing, approvingly and in support of Mr. Bright, that the child who fastened on the heads of pins performed each day 160,772 separate and distinct movements.

That utilitarian note did not even get across to such a prop of the empire as Alfred Lord Tennyson. In those days he was writing:

> While he uttered this
> Low to her own heart said the lily maid,
> "Save your great self, fair lord," and when he fell
> From talk of war to traits of pleasantry—
> Being mirthful he but in a stately kind—
> She still made note that when the living smile
> Died from his lips across him came a cloud
> Of melancholy severe from which again . . ."

And that sentence goes on for seventeen more lines.

And Queen Victoria and her lieges gulped that sort of thing down as if it had been pineapple juice. To put it vulgarly the *Fortnightly Review* paid Tennyson $100,000 for a single poem. Be sure had it contained a single word of utilitarianism the *Review* would have fined the poet $50 per word.

The writer permits himself to write with some warmth on this subject because this false diagnosis of the gradual transference of public taste and literary practice exerts even today the worst possible influence on public taste and public and private education. As we have pointed out in our earliest pages, it has always been the practice of priests to secure for their religions the services of the poets. By the middle of Victoria's reign, and for ever since, the place of the priest has been taken by the utilitarian seers—the applied scientists, the sociologists of either party, the economists. From these hierarchies there has constantly gone up the cry that the arts should harness themselves to their yoke. Every twenty years or so there goes up from them the cry that the arts should be employed in the service of their cars of juggernaut. As a rule, the net is laid in vain. To the measure of his powers, the artist should live in—and render—his own day: as a rule the great artist has done it. But, though the business of the artist is to render his own day, it is certainly none of his duty to approve or to glorify it. The artist is frequently a man of high intelligence or, at the least, he must be a man of sympathy for his fellow human beings. So, no poet has ever fully approved of his own day, not Dante, not Propertius, not Shakespeare, not Pope, not Villon, not Heine.

His duty, then, like that of every other citizen, is to persuade his day to improve itself. This he may do in two ways that are usually ineffectual and by one that, if the community in which it is practiced has any respect for the arts, is usually successful. First, then, the artist may harness his muse to the wagon of one or other of the political parties. As a rule, this is ineffectual and even detrimental, because the artist turned politician is apt to falsify his renderings of life. But Rouget de l'Isle in writing and composing the *Marseillaise* did service not merely to the French Republic but to republicanism the world over. Secondly, a poet may seek to persuade his own day to better itself by painting attractive pictures of other days or of imaginary golden ages. This is less dangerous, but as a rule more ineffectual than the artist's taking political sides in his work. It has yet to be proved that any state or portion of a state was ever led to better itself by the perusal of Moore's *Utopia*, William Morris' *News from Nowhere*, Mr. Wells' very numerous Utopian treatises or romances, or any other projection of Kissing Kindness lands. Obviously, brutal men may have been rendered more kindly by reading the *Sensitive Plant* or more chivalrous by reading the *Idylls of the King*.

The third way is simply that of the poet who, exactly observing the characteristics of his time, renders them with exactitude as did, say, Vogelweide, Dante, Heine or Villon. We have no time here to dilate upon that side of the function of the arts. It is the moral of this book and has several times already come creeping in to these pages.

The practice of the Georgian-Victorian poets was consistently to adopt the second expedient. They painted exclusively pictures of ages happier than their own or stitched tapestries of a middle ages that never existed. Wordsworth, however, did pay some attention to his own time and Browning, to archaeology when paying attention to mediaeval villains. There is not much objection to this process. In order more clearly to see his own time and place the poet must get out of them. You will see New York life in better perspective when you have learned something real about the life of Paris; you will take in better the characteristics of your own day in London when you have really studied the conditions of Rome under the Caesars. As poet, Browning became a tougher Englishman by living in Florence.

The trouble with nearly all the other poets of this group is that in turning their backs on their own day they turned always to softer times or to the softer sides of times hard in themselves. The middle ages was a tumultuous, mad, bloodthirsty, sadic affair with highlights of cathedral buildings, frescoes, handicrafts, lyrics and chivalrous rules for the conducting of single combats. It is almost impossible to read today the *Idylls of the King*, not merely because one can get cheap editions of the *Morte d'Arthur* and Browning or read Mr. Pound's projections of mediaevally incestuous, murdering mercenary princes who built the most beautiful palaces and collected Greek manuscripts with the passion of mad misers. No, you cannot read the *Idylls of the King* except in minute doses because of the sub-nauseating sissiness—there is no other convenient word—of the points of view of both Lord Tennyson and the characters that he projects . . . and because of the insupportable want of skill in the construction of sentences, the choice of words and the perpetual amplication of images.

What is the sense of requiring the reader's attention for this sort of thing

> Nigh upon the hour
> When the lone hern forgets his melancholy,
> Lets down his other leg, and stretching, dreams
> Of goodly supper in the distant pool,
> Then turned the noble damsel smiling at him . . . ?

What is the purpose of saying that it was midday, or three, or seven, in that ornithological imagery if it is not to make the reviewers go into ecstasy over His Lordship's observations of nature? And what is worse, from the writer's point of view, is that the self-indulgence engendered by the refusal to contemplate reality ended in a complete literary slovenliness. You will find nowhere in the world such a body of ill-written stuff as in the English nineteenth century poets; nor so great an inattention to form either of sentences or of stories; nor such tautology; nor yet such limp verbiage.

It makes it almost worse that nearly all of them could, from time to time, turn jewels five words long. Perfection must be set in perfections or the result is bathos. It is pleasant—nay, it is delightful—to come upon "slow-dropping veils of thinnest lawn," but it comes in a rather languid catalogue of the unusual behavior of streams in a poem decorated with too many imprecise or duplicated images. What could really be worse in the way of uncertain definition than:

> All round the coast the languid air did swoon,
> Breathing like one that hath a weary dream.

Just consider what that really means. Did the air actually **snort and** grind its teeth as do those who suffer from a nightmare?

Or consider again:

> There is sweet music here that softer falls
> Than petals from blown roses on the grass,
> Or night dews on still waters between walls
> Of shadowy granite in a gleaming pass.

The meanest short-story writer knows that you never should duplicate your similes for a very simple reason. One of your similes will be stronger than the other, so that if you use both the weaker one will weaken the effect of your image. "Petals from blown roses" is nearly perfection of a sort. Then why drag in shadowy granite and gleaming walls? They simply blur the other image and as definitions of music are simply idiotic.

Or again Tennyson will write:

> Music that gentlier on the spirit lies
> Than tired eyelids upon tired eyes.

which must be amongst the most beautiful lines in the language. But he must at once qualify it with:

> Music that brings sweet sleep down from the blissful skies

. . . a backboneless line that almost anyone could have written.

There was nothing that Tennyson touched, in fact, that he did not water down—to the very day of his death. Then he wrote

> But such a tide as moving seems asleep
>   To full for sound or foam,
> When that which drew from out the boundless deep,
>   Turns again home.

But immediately he must follow it up with eight lines of obvious images, meeting "his Pilot face to face."

Similarly, if you turn from the very end of his collected works to the very beginning and read his dedication of his life's work "To the Queen," you will find amongst a wilderness of commonplaces a verse beautiful enough almost to have justified the existence of Victoria:

> Then—while a sweeter music wakes,
> And thro' wild March the throstle calls,
> Where all about your palace walls
> The sunlit almond blossom shakes

and goes on incontinently to:

> Take, Madam, this poor book of song;
> For tho' the faults were thick as dust
> In vacant chambers, I could trust
> Your kindness. May you rule us long,

Whilst before that he has written:

> Victoria,—since your Royal grace
> To one of less desert allows
> This laurel greener from the brows
> Of him that utter'd nothing base;

which, considering that his predecessor was no less a person than Wordsworth would seem rather a grudging tribute.

Wordsworth, of course, is quite another pair of shoes. He achieved an aridity that is impressive even when set beside the bad temper of Milton. In his attempts (they must have been wearing enough to give him the right to a certain austerity of mien), in his meticulous determination to express (what he certainly saw) the poetic aspects of man and the world, he will touch our risibilities, leaving us none the less as ashamed as if we had laughed in the desert at the Sphynx. Nothing, but for the atmosphere of austerity we *know* to attach to the writer, could be much more bathotic than:

> Here on our native soil, we breathe once more.
> The cock that crows, the smoke that curls, that sound
> Of bells;—those boys who in yon meadowground
> In white-sleeved shirts are playing; and the roar
> Of the waves breaking on the chalky shore;—
> All, all, are English.

But to atone for the disrespect of quoting what must be one of the most childish pieces of regionalism ever written, let us hasten to quote the last four lines of the sonnet to Toussaint l'Ouverture:

> There's not a breathing of the common wind
> That will forget thee; thou hast great allies;
> Thy friends are exultations, agonies,
> And love, and man's unconquerable mind.

If Wordsworth had written nothing else he could claim to stand beside Aeschylus. . . . He wrote, however, a great deal more that would lead one to question his claim, and you will hear him called the most unreadable poet that ever set pen to paper. Nevertheless, there is about his best pieces an authenticity that few poets have attained. You can not really say that you cannot read even Wordsworth's longest poems once you have made the little change from the present-day tempo of your life that he has every right to claim that you should make. It is worth reading him merely to discover his jewels; but it is still more worth reading him to have his company. Few poems have much more initial beauty than the "Intimations of Immortality," say, and with the enthusiasm engendered by its beginnings you will find you have read a good way into "The Prelude," which follows it in most editions, before your satisfaction in your companion begins to slacken. And you will find that the odd priggishness of phrase in which he occasionally abounds has not the slightly nauseating effect of the ready-made phrases of poets using less bare language. The difference between reading a long poem by Tennyson and a longer one by Wordsworth has always to the writer seemed to be this: With Tennyson you eat for a long time through a joint of fat, insipid meat to come now and then on the purple patch of a truffle; with Wordsworth you wander through the empty rooms of an immense grey castle hollowed out of primaeval crags. From time to time, lying on a dusty stone floor, you will come upon a leaf from an illuminated Book of Hours, and once or twice upon a whole wall frescoed by Simone Martini.

It is true that he wrote: "Spade with which Wilkinson has tilled the soil." But he also wrote what has always seemed to this writer to be the Charter of all true poets:

> The stars pre-eminent in magnitude,
> And they that from the zenith dart their beams,
> (Visible though they be to half the earth,
> Though half a sphere be conscious of their brightness)
> Are yet of no diviner origin,
> No purer essence, than the one that burns,
> Like an untended watch-fire, on the ridge
> Of some dark mountain; or than those which seem
> Humbly to hang, like twinkling winter lamps,
> Among the branches of the leafless trees; . . .
> Then, to the measure of the light vouchsafed,
> Shine, Poet! in thy place, and be content.

Before Keats alone, of all these poets—except perhaps Christina Rossetti—the impatient prose writer must sheathe his scalpel. Before the century closed—and even in the hands of Landor—prose had become the only keen instrument of the scrupulous writer. But the verbal felicities and labors of Keats placed him not infrequently beside any prose writer that you like to name. And in words he was a perfectly conscious and perfectly self-critical artist. Thus, in the manuscript of *Endymion* you can still see how he first wrote the agreeable but not exquisitely inspiring six lines:

More forest-wild, more subtle-cadenced
Than can be told by mortal: even wed
The fainting tenors of a thousand shells
To a million whisperings of Lilly bells;
And mingle too the Nightingale's complain
Caught in its hundredth echo; 't would be vain: . . .

but he crossed them out and substituted:

'Twas a lay
More subtle cadenced and more forest-wild
Than Dryope's lone lulling of her child.

or similarly, for five rather uninspired lines he rewrites:

thou art as a dove
Trembling its closed eyes and sleeked wings
About me.

This is art.

As against Keats, Shelley is diffuse. It is impossible to dissociate
these two whose careers on earth seemed indissolubly intertwined.
The splendors, the almost supernatural beauty of the active mind of
Shelley will obviously forever gild his poems and blind one to the
mediocrity of thousands of his inferior lines. But the gold is an exterior gold; we bring it ourselves to his shrine, and his shining soul
only very seldom illuminates his poems from within. He is almost
never natural; he is almost never not intent on showing himself the
champion of freedom, the Satan of a Hanoverian Heaven. And even
when he is natural his sheer carelessness will spoil—for the impatient
prose writer—his most satisfactory poems. Take

I awake from dreams of thee
In the first sweet sleep of night,
And the winds are breathing low
And the stars are burning bright:

I awake from dreams of thee
And a spirit in my feet
Has led me, who knows how,
Io thy chamber window, sweet . . .

The poem is beautiful, but imagine the meanest short-story writer introducing into it that "who knows how?" It gives the effect of a large piece of red hot iron suddenly put into water. A writer should precisely "know how" things happen in his prose or verse. If he does not he should not write.

So, skipping Tennyson because we have had quite enough of him, and Poe and Landor because it is more convenient to treat them as prose writers, we arrive at Browning, the pre-Raphaelites, and Hardy.

By the middle of the century the utilitarians were already claiming that, in celebration of their victory, the poets were enlisting under their banner. But a more forcible demonstration than the above list of names that the poets were doing nothing of the sort it would be hard to find. It is true that Tennyson wrote an ode to the Great Exhibition of 1852 in which, out of compliment to the Prince Consort, he included a paean to papier-maché chair seats of which several cargoes had arrived from Germany.

There was about Browning a sort of "ordinary man-ishness" that marks him off from all his contemporaries. You could not call him romantic; you could not call him utilitarian. He was just Man. The others, with the exception of Hardy, were all dyed-in-the-wool romanticists. The Byronic romantics chafed against the commonplaceness of the postchaise; the pre-Raphaelites against the tyranny of the railway and the omnibus; and for the gloomy hero of mysterious origin who was the one necessary concomitant of the romantic frame of mind they substituted a general benevolence that might well have transformed the world. And certainly they believed that they were going to transform the world. They were convinced that once the world saw a Philip Webb-designed room filled with the mediaevally inspired furnishings from William Morris & Co., with a copy of the

Kelmscott Press's *Chaucer* open on a reading pulpit, the whole world would be impressed by that vision of beauty. It would at once throw out of doors all its papier-maché chair seats, burn its omnibuses and factories and incontinently set to work to fashion chairs like miserère stalls, hennins like the wings of swans, and stand all the utilitarians, crowned with fools' caps, in rows on all the schoolroom benches. Then Man should stand in his doorway gazing out over great fields of golden-growing wheat and rejoice in the coming of the mediaeval-social reform.

The writer, indeed, begs the reader not to consider that we pre-Raphaelites were the depressed beings that Gilbert and Sullivan ridiculed, or that Mr. Oscar Wilde, dining on the smell of a lily, represented us, *les jeunes* of the movement. Not a bit of it. We knew that we were getting there in spite of Mill, Lecky, Spencer, Huxley and all the Teutonic thinkers who, in the wake of Mr. Thomas Carlyle, surrounded and upheld our Nordic throne. If not King Arthur, then at least Du Guesclin and Henri Quatre should come again. The mediaevalized social revolution, like the three-horsed bus that used to run down Portland Place and had aloft a great umbrella to shield the driver from the inclemencies of the weather—the social revolution, then, like the bus, was just round the corner. We seemed to hear the very rumble of its wheels. . . . This writer does so still. . . . Alas!

No, they were not inclined to live on the smell of lilies, those robustious roarers. They each ate every morning for breakfast six eggs and half a pound of ham, had plum pudding every day for lunch, roared over the practical jokes they played on each other, covered their adulteries with each other's wives with the golden gauze of sonnet forms. . . .

Their work naturally suffered. Their sentences were nearly as backboneless as those of Shelley or Tennyson; they got more color into their similes and their similes were even more superabundant. Occasionally, Rossetti displayed a sense of words. Look at these for the loss of the White Ship in the ballad of that name:

And the ship was gone;
And the deep shuddered; and the moon shone.

Oliæi iiiipicssluiilsiii, iliai was what it was; then Swinburne and
Morris and Watts-Dunton and others would fall all over him and
insist that he write four hundred lines more of bilge, never blotting
a line. None of them ever blotted a line. . . . They were going
to cover the world with Philip Webb-built mansions, the walls
glowing golden with frescoes from the brushes of D.G.R., E.B.J.,
F.M.B.

And all the while up in the fireless top back bedroom on the
corner of the cracked washing-stand on the backs of old letters Christina Rossetti sat writing:

> Passing away, saith my soul, passing away:
> Chances, beauty, and youth sapped day by day;
>   Thy life never continueth in one stay.
> Is the eye waxen dim, is the dark hair changing to gray
>   That hath won neither laurel nor bay?
> I shall clothe myself in spring and bud in May:
> Thou, root-stricken, shalt not rebuild thy decay
>   On my bosom for aye.
>   Then I answered, Yea.

One wonders how it would have been had it been Dante Gabriel,
rather than Christina, Rossetti who sat in that bitter cold Bloomsbury
bedroom and wrote with chapped hands. He *did* have a sense of
words.

As it is, one is tempted to say that the only artists in words of all
the verse writers of the century were Christina and Browning. Browning used words with the violence of a horse-breaker, giving out the
scent of a he-goat. But he got them to do their work. And he regarded
life as a man poet should, with cynicism, with a rough optimism.

And he could write on his death bed the injunction to greet the unseen with a cheer. . . .

And all the while, in the purlieus of Philadelphia or in University Place, New York, a long-bearded man was picking words out of auctioneers' catalogues and patent medicine publicities. On the whole, the most grisly story of letters this writer ever heard was told him in the lobby of the Hotel Albert in New York—by a very old publisher who had once been young. He said that into the saloon of that same hotel once had come with rather faltering feet a large-boned old man with a ruffled beard and a sombrero. As soon as he entered that saloon every man in it raised his newspaper up to hide his face from the old man. He went depressedly out. . . . A spirit in his feet had led that very old publisher, then a young man, he didn't know why, to follow that senior. He caught him up just as he was about to cross East Twelfth Street and, catching him by the arm, said he seemed to know his face. Who was he? The old man replied:

"I am Walt Whitman. If you'll lend me a dollar, you will be helping immortality to stumble on."

He wrote not only: "Out of the cradle ceaselessly rocking," which goes on to what may seem to the impatient a good deal of faded tiresomeness. . . . But when this writer remembers those men putting up their newspapers to avoid lending Whitman a dollar, he reads on in the hope of the more confounding those men where they roast in hell . . . and gets a certain thrill out of:

> Till of a sudden,
> Maybe killed, unknown to her mate,
> One forenoon the she-bird crouched not on the nest,
> Nor returned that afternoon, nor the next,
> Nor ever appeared again.
>
> And thenceforward all summer in the sound of the sea
> And at night under the full of the moon in calmer weather,

Over the hoarse surging of the sea,
Or flitting from brier to brier by day,
I saw, I heard at intervals, the remaining one, the he-bird,
The solitary guest from Alabama.

And did not the same hand write "Cavalry Crossing a Ford"?

A line in long array where they wind betwixt green islands,
They take a serpentine course, their arms flash in the sun—hark
to the musical clank,
Behold the silvery river, in it the splashing horses loitering stop
to drink,
Behold the brown-faced men, each group, each person, a picture,
the negligent rest on the saddles,
Some emerge on the opposite bank, others are just entering the
ford—while
Scarlet and blue and snowy white,
The guidon flags flutter gayly in the wind.

Which seems to be as good a piece of impressionism as one needs.
And, after all: "When lilacs last in the dooryard bloomed. . . ." —as
to which this writer will hazard the confession that, having heard
it recited a hundred times, to and without music, he will not face
the risk of here transcribing it, for fear of becoming unable to see
the words.

Whitman, in fact, was a poet as other great poets are poets. That
he should take himself as the regional oracle of one of the meanest
ages a nation of great watchwords has even seen, or that assuming
prophetic mantles and beards he should completely misinterpret his
age's future is a very small matter. Poets have to "take it out" in
something—drink, lechery, degeneration or merely in stamp-collecting.
. . . If Whitman chose to do so with round-mouthed rhetoric, it is
rather his affair than ours.

As an interpreter of our modern day whose motto really is the

French peasant's *"La vie, voyez vous, n'est jamais si bonne ni mauvaise que l'on ne croit."** Whitman has to stand down before Hardy. Hardy, in fact, was the ideal poet of a generation. He was the most passionate and the most learned of them all. He had the luck, singular in poets, of being able to achieve a competence other than by poetry and then to devote the ending years of his life to his beloved verses. All the while he was making a living and then a competence sufficient to keep him during the closing years of his life, he was, on the side, practicing verse-writing, learning the prosodies of every nation that had ever had a prosody. He disliked novel-writing but he made a small fortune by it.

It takes a man with a determination like that to make a great poet. If he has to use that grim determination first to another end, when he is at last released he will write a *Dynasts*.

He had a peasant intelligence; so he was wise. He resembled the root of a four-hundred-year-old tree; he resembled a moss-covered rock that has lain for four hundred years in a forest. So he knew that destiny attends on chance since chance is always characteristic of the circumstances in which it takes part. Beside him, Whitman was a hysteriac. He was not wise. The essential townsman can never be wise because he cannot see life for the buildings. Whitman saw factories rise and was excited over the future of the race. Hardy saw factories smudge his rural scene, and was merely depressed. He knew that the human heart remained the essential stamping ground of the poet. Consider this:

> I leant upon a coppice gate
> When Frost was spectre-gray,
> And Winter's dregs made desolate
> The weakening eye of day.
> The tangled bine-stems scored the sky
> Like strings of broken lyres,
> And all mankind that haunted nigh
> Had sought their household fires.

* "Life never turns out to be as good . . . or as bad as one expects."

At once a voice arose among
　　The bleak twigs overhead
In a full-hearted evensong
　　Of joy illimited;
An aged thrush, frail, gaunt, and small,
　　In blast-beruffled plume,
Had chosen thus to fling his soul
　　Upon the growing gloom.

So little cause for carolings
　　Of such ecstatic sound
Was written on terrestrial things
　　Afar or nigh around,
That I could think there trembled through
　　His happy good-night air
Some blessed Hope, whereof he knew
　　And I was unaware.

When this writer looks back on his youth which was spent, as it were, between the mighty legs of the robust Victorian poets, he seems to have passed it, running for miles along a tremendous, light corridor—like the hall where all the Rubens' are in the Louvre. The walls of the corridor—for miles and years—are lined with tapestry and great high-colored pictures. They are "Felise" and "The Blessed Damosel" and "St. Agnes Eve" and "Goblin Market" and even "The Charge of the Light Brigade," the "Death of the Duke of Wellington" and "The Raven" and "La Belle Dame sans Merci" and "The Blot of the 'Scutcheon" and "Pippa Passes." Yes and "Leaves of Grass" too, because the poor dear old pre-Raphaelites just *loved* Whitman. . . . And "Endymion" and "The Cenci" and "Does the Road Wind Uphill all the Way." And "O, Wild West Wind," and "Sister Helen." . . .

So that perhaps the nineteenth century English poets deserve a special building in the vast delta of literature. It should, perhaps, be marked "For Adolescents Only," because an adolescence passed without "Felise" and "The Blessed Damosel" and the rest of them would be rather a dreary thing; and though the Arthur of the *Idylls* may look rather like a curate, he is perhaps rather better as a companion for youth than the Heroes of Big Business. . . .

And it is nice to think that, as befits great poets, the pre-Raphaelite singers all saw military service. For, in the late fifties when Louis Napoleon and perfidious France were meditating the invasion of the tight little islands that lie off the west coast of Europe, Rossetti, Morris, Ford Madox Brown and Swinburne all enlisted in the Volunteers, forming the famous Artists' Corps of the Queen's Westminsters. And they took their duties with great seriousness, forming fours daily in Hyde Park or on Brook Green, in elegant grey uniforms, with scarlet baldrics and little pink pompoms on their shakos. Becoming exhausted at the end of the days's manoeuvrings they would all have to take hansom cabs home.

And it is pleasant, too, to think that at the end of his life Whitman could write

After an Interval

(November 22, 1875, Midnight—Saturn and Mars
in Conjunction)

After an interval, reading, here in the midnight,
With the great stars looking on—all the stars of Orion looking,
And the silent Pleïades—and the duo looking of Saturn and
ruddy Mars;
Pondering, reading my own songs, after a long interval, (sorrow
and death familiar now)
Ere closing the book, what pride! what joy! to find them
Standing so well the test of death and night,
And the duo of Saturn and Mars!

Perhaps all of them could have written as much.

CHAPTER SIX

S TENDHAL also saw war and rejoiced in his nickname—*le hussard romantique.* His inherited name was Henri Beyle. He was born in 1783 and passed his youth in the neighborhood of Grenoble, a district of France that he disliked because of its frigidity. Thus, the main part of his life was passed in Italy, which was the scene of the majority of his eleven love affairs. He died in 1842.

The reader may be alarmed at coming so late in this book upon a writer born in 1783. But Stendhal, who was perhaps the greatest literary influence of modern times and remains perhaps today the greatest of literary influences, did not come into his own, as he composedly prophesied, until fifty years after he had written his *Le Rouge et le Noir* in 1831. It was in 1881 or so that his fame began to crystallize. At that date the young James, the mature Turgenev and the maturer Flaubert were all writing, and all under his influence. And by the nineties Stendhal was the Great Influence of every existing literary school—of the realists, the naturalists, the impressionists, the psychologists and of the school of the *Yellow Book* in London.

He would have called himself romantic of the romantics, and would have declared love and war to be his only passions, Napoleon and Byron his only heroes. . . . His *De l'Amour* must be the dryest book about love that was ever written; his war chapters in *La Chartreuse de Parme* must be the most dispassioned of all constatations of the purposeless and imbecile helplessness of war and of troops in action. His projections of Fabrice's ride over the field of Waterloo in the staff of Marshal Ney—on to which that stripling has got by pretending to be the lover of the wife of one of Ney's cavalry captains —is a nightmare of aimlessness. Compared with it the most depressed pages of Tolstoy's *War and Peace* read like inadequate witticisms. His two novels that count are the aforesaid *Chartreuse de Parme* of 1839 and the earlier *Le Rouge et le Noir*, of 1831.

He was the first psychological novelist, and it is difficult to be certain whether it was because of that or because of his singular handling of romantic heroes and romantic situations that he has his peculiar immortality. Both of those romances are furnished with rather fuliginous heroes of a singular selfishness of disposition that would have done credit to any hero of Byron, Chateaubriand, Hugo or Goethe. But Stendhal's heroes are all provided with real insides and are treated with as little affection by their author as if he had been the most dispassionate of realist creator-authors. Indeed, the ridiculous Pécuchet of Flaubert's *Bouvard et Pécuchet* is an agreeable and purposeful citizen as compared with either Lucien Sorel or Fabrice. Bouvard and Pécuchet in the attempt to demonstrate the folly of accepted ideas to an indifferent world, had taken All Knowledge for their province, and they pursued each department of human folly with the determination of rats clinging to the jugular veins of terriers. The famous passage which describes their investigation of literary criticism—the passage that begins *"Blair, anglais, gémit sur la licence d'Homère"*—ends, after a bewildering catalogue of the disagreements of the literary popes of all ages, with the statement that these disagreements worked so strongly on the mind of Pécuchet that it induced in him an attack of yellow jaundice. But neither of the heroes of Stendhal exhibited any perseverance at all—though it is true that in the pursuit of his ambitions Sorel "slays his first mistress when she betrays him to his second." Otherwise their determinations are muted to the end and they do desperate deeds only on sudden impulses.

The adventures and inventions of Stendhal's heroes are the most fantastic to be found in any book of adventure ever written, and they are rendered almost maddening by the light of sinister reality that plays on all his scenes. Sorel is more austerely psychologized than the Fabrice of *La Chartreuse de Parme*, but he is not, on that account, any more real. Indeed, Fabrice is so realistically and minutely selfish that he might be any valetudinarian old man living next door to one and tyrannizing fantastically over an attached and bewildered household.

It is not merely that he was fifty years ahead of his time; it was that his nature partook of all times and that he could change his aspect with the frequency of a chameleon. You catch in him glimpses of the smiling incredulity of Voltaire or of Fontenelle; glimpses of the eloquent faith of Bossuet; of the romantic fidelity to truth of the *Promessi Sposi*; of the profusion of characters and their vicissitudes of Balzac's *Comédie Humaine*, of the disillusioned optimism of Flaubert. Thackeray might have read him before determining to write a novel without a hero; he might have inspired *The Way of All Flesh, Arms and the Man, l'Histoire Comique* of Anatole France, the more cruel stories of Henry James, *Almayer's Folly* and *Heart of Darkness* of Conrad, in whom the dispassionate contempt for the selfish follies of humanity was almost more developed than in Beyle himself—or, indeed, to carry the tale one stage farther forwards, he might have inspired the frame of mind displayed in Mr. Hemingway's *The Sun Also Rises*.

To say that Stendhal did actually inspire all these writers would be to go to extremes. That he did very much inspire Joseph Conrad, at any rate during the earlier periods of his writing career, and that he at least very much impressed Henry James, the present writer is in a position to aver, and that Mr. James in his more incisive moments declared that both Flaubert and the brothers Goncourt were pale pastiches of Stendhal is also a fact. But a great writer may exercise a marked influence over other authors without their ever having read so much as a word of his works. Thus, the writer was for a long time under the impression that Stendhal must have had a direct and quite strong influence over the late—and much too much neglected—George Gissing. But, shortly before his death, Gissing assured the writer that he had never so much as heard of Stendhal.

The fact is that Stendhal was almost ignored by writers and public together until the seventies of last century. By that decade the literati began to develop an enthusiasm for him; by the nineties his name was continually on the lips of all the intelligentsia of France, Russia, Italy and Germany and even of a portion of the more advanced literary coteries of London. Thus, of the powerful clique known as Henley's Gang in the London nineties, W. E. Henley and Messrs. Whibley, Wedmore and Anderson Graham were all in varying degrees interested in *Le Rouge et le Noir* and perhaps even more in *De l'Amour*. And, according to Mr. James, Robert Louis Stevenson was almost morbidly affected by both Stendhal's romances and the book on love. He immensely admired Stendhal's dry, direct style and also the manner in which he handled incident. He, nevertheless—again according to Mr. James—deliberately avoided reading or thinking of Stendhal for fear the influence should "spoil his market."*

It is the complete equanimity with which Stendhal regards his characters that gives to his pages their extraordinary effect of reality. He will record, with the passionlessness of a Chancery lawyer commenting on an act of Parliament concerning the doctrine of redemption, how his hero, by then become an archbishop, wishing to enjoy some undisturbed days with his mistress, casually asks the prime minister of the principality that they all inhabit, to remove the extremely noble and wealthy husband of the lady for a week or ten days. The prime minister, *"qui fut attendri de cette histoire d'amour,"* says: "Certainly. When would the archbishop like the marquis removed?"

In a day or two the archbishop says: "Now is the time." And on the same day, the marquis, returning from a ride on horseback from one of his more distant estates, is politely seized by some brigands, near Mantua, confined on a barque which descends the River Pô for three days, and is then set free on an island from which, all his money and valuables having been removed from him, he finds some difficulty in returning home.

The marquis, taking the kidnapping as an "affair of private vengeance," seems to regard it as the most natural thing in the world, and we are not even told that the lovers particularly enjoyed themselves during his absence. Indeed, we know that owing to excruciations of psychological and moral scruples on the part of the lady—who had made a vow to the Blessed Virgin never to see her lover again and who in consequence would only receive him in pitch darkness—they prob-

---

* Those are Mr. James's exact words. In the writer's almost daily colloquies with Mr. James, which extended over a number of years, the literary figure of Henri Beyle, known as Stendhal, must have been the most frequent subject of their conversation as far as it concerned itself with literature. And this writer must at one time or another have heard Conrad read with enthusiasm, commenting as he went on the technique there employed, at least half of *Le Rouge et le Noir*.

ably did not have a very good time. The highest ecclesiastical authorities of the See of Rome being consulted as to the lady's rash vow, give the verdict that, in certain circumstances, the lady would be justified in seeing her lover by at least candlelight. But when the child of their union dies, the lady is convinced that that is the punishment for breaking her vow to the Virgin and so dies in the archbishop's arms.

Treated by Mrs. Ratcliffe or Monk Lewis, or even by Victor Hugo or Dumas, these incidents would seem to be of the height of improbability or grotesqueness. But knowing what we do—if only from Manzoni's *Promessi Sposi*—of the nature of Italian higher officials of that day, and drily recounted as they are in the admirably dispassionate style of Stendhal, they seem the most natural and, indeed, logical of occurrences. And we are prepared by the *Princesse de Clèves* of Mme. de Lafayette —who is another writer to whom Stendhal must have been electively related—for the moral scruples of the archbishop's Clélia. Or, indeed, we are provided by Manzoni with another instance of a girl's vowing to the Virgin that she will never see her lover again—and of her obtaining a dispensation from the vow by higher ecclesiastical authority.

But, indeed, the literary personality of Stendhal was so magisterial that, had he, instead of Swift, related the conditions of the kingdom of Laputa, we should take them to be a literal constatation of an existing, if distant, state of things.

Stendhal, in fact, reduced romanticism to the extremes of the ridiculous and, since modern conscious literature has been engaged on nothing less from the days when his star first appeared on the horizon till Mr. Sinclair Lewis wrote *Babbitt*, he is from the literary point of view the most intriguing author who wrote in the 1820's. He is this because it is impossible to think of him without giving side glances to the figures of every serious author who ever succeeded him. One thinks, say, of Bazàrof as one of the most pregnant figures of the great outburst of fiction in Russia towards the end of the last century. And at once the speculation crosses the mind: Would Turgenev have drawn Bazàrof . . . would he, indeed, have presented the whole of *Fathers and Children* if he had never read Stendhal? And the query must remain a query.

One has made for him the claim that he was the first of the psychological novelists. And, indeed, a great part of the verisimilitude of his books comes from the fact of the continuing psychological activities of his characters as they commit themselves to actions or merely contemplate the world. But we have omitted to consider that even before his day Anglo-Saxondom had produced, and that no further away than the English lush county of Hampshire—next to Kent the most sporting cricketing county of all the empire—a psychological novelist greater —or no, not greater, more delicate; but then in these matters delicacy is strength itself!—greater, then, than the author of *Le Rouge et le Noir*.

Jane Austen, the youngest daughter of an Anglican clergyman, George Austen, was born in her father's cure in Hampshire in 1775, eight years before Henri Beyle. And *Persuasion*, the last of her novels, had been published fourteen years before Stendhal wrote *Le Rouge et le Noir*.

Jane Austen was neither romanticist nor realist, she was just "novelist" as the North Star is the North Star. Almost alone with Trollope —and perhaps Mrs. Gaskell—she shared that distinction in Anglo-Saxondom until the day when the Flaubert-Stendhal influence penetrated to the British Isles and the republic across the Atlantic. . . . One might, however, make the note that Louisa Alcott died before the nineties, having published *Little Women* in 1868, and that Sarah Orne Jewett, though she survived into our own day (dying in 1919) and wrote her masterpiece, *The Country of the Pointed Firs* in 1916, yet wrote her first book, *Deephaven,* in 1877.

Jane Austen stands alone—with Christina Rossetti—as being the one consummate artist that the English nineteenth century produced . . . nay, the writer is tempted to say that you must go back to Chaucer before you will find her spiritual counterpart, and you will find no other English writer at all, before Henry James, who had her skill— her genius's delight—in drawing characters with touches as delicate as silverpoint and as impervious to the tooth of time as the statues of the

Pharaohs. And even the Master himself, except in the unrevised states of his earlier works, was heavy-handed beside her.

Her immediate predecessor, Frances (Fanny) Burney, is by no means to be despised. *Evelina. or a Young Lady's Entrance into the World* was written when Jane Austen was three, and remains as entertaining a book as you will easily find. But it is the book of a relatively coarse spirit. Mrs. Burney accepts without questioning the standards of her more than questionable day and, if she does not expressly applaud, she yet accepts without question brutalities that even today are painful to read of. And her characters have all the harsh overdrawing that is the chief—and, one is bound to say, the most applauded—defect of nearly all English fiction.

Jane Austen is free from the moral preoccupation that troubles the waters of that greatest of her predecessors, Richardson himself. She achieves thus a gayer, a more lucid reality. And although she does not either denounce or scarify the vices of her age, her continually lambent humor that plays around the weaknesses of her more socially important characters is in itself a continually flickering question mark as to the fine flower of the social products of her era.

Her "influence" upon Anglo-Saxon—and, as far as we know, any other—literature has been simply nil, though a crasser—or, at least, a less academic—public has always loved her as they love a delicious aunt. That is not difficult to understand. The academic critic despises Jane Austen because her subjects are merely domestic. He despises the novel as he dislikes most forms of art. Therefore, if the novel is to attract his attention it must be large, pretentious. He will pay attention to Balzac. Here is a man who wrote a *Comédie Humaine*, a welter of novels purporting—quite falsely—to describe a whole society.

The attraction of *Pride and Prejudice* or *Mansfield Park* for the reasonably intelligent lay public is twofold. In the first place, the stage of human society that Miss Austen projects so vividly that you feel as if you could almost touch it, is the stage of human society that, as the years of Victoria rolled on, has gradually become the cynosure of the entire world. It stood for comfort and decorum—the extremes of both.

For a century or so, the world—at any rate, the world between Rome and San Francisco—has tired of heroism, achievement, vast ideals, immense moralities. Its ideal has been the manor of the English ruling classes, its domesticities rolling on ball bearings. The very gold-diggers of Colorado demanded nothing better, though their tastes might run to bath taps of solid gold: for years the American South bought more copies of Trollope than all the rest of the world together, whilst they ignored Dickens.

The quintessence of this ideal stage of society was rendered by Jane Austen with a vividness that made the reader feel that he was actually sitting in an armchair in Mansfield Park whilst Sir Thomas made his fateful eruption on to the stage that had been erected in his own sanctum. That is it. You sit about in morning rooms with the characters; you watch Mrs. Norris prepare conserves. . . . Above all, you listen to the family gossip, in the holy of holies of the English ruling classes. And whatever pleasures the world may hold today, all of them —every single one of them—yield in attraction to that of gossip . . . when, all in a huddle, you get under way, listening to, or retailing the story of the vicissitudes of your neighbors.

The writer was once presented with a verbal picture that has for many years been one of his most treasured possessions. It is that of an elderlyish, comfortable gentleman, seated in an old-fashioned first-class railway carriage, his feet up on the cushions of the opposite seat, the brim of his top hat well down, shading his eyes. He has provided his nephew who is traveling with him with a bath bun, some acidulated drops and a copy of *The Boys Own Paper*. The train travels over Ireland. The gentleman has on his knees a writing pad. He writes and writes. What he is writing is *The Last Chronicles of Barset*. What he was writing just before, in similar trains, traveling similarly over other, similar regions of Ireland was *Framley Parsonage*. Ten years before he had written *Barchester Towers*; twelve years before—in 1855— *The Warden*.

Born in the year of Waterloo—whilst Becky Sharp was performing her masterpieces in Brussels—he was, like Jane Austen and Chaucer, before all things a snooper. That is the modern world's substitute for soldiering as far as the writer of novels is concerned. If you cannot, like Cervantes, be wounded at Lepanto and lie for five years a prisoner of the Barbary Moors, you must have a quality of invisibility, and eyes and ears that miss nothing. According to this writer's informant, the late Mr. F. M. Synge, H. M. Deputy Marshal of Ceremonies, nephew of Trollope and cousin of the Synge who wrote the *Playboy of the Western World*, a gentleman who himself wielded a nice-humored and observant pen—according, then, to Mr. Synge, Trollope was extraordinarily unnoticeable. Wherever he was, it seemed to be absolutely natural that there he should be. When he was not in trains, traveling to inspect post offices, he was in the best clubs or staying for the shooting with the best families. When he entered a club smoking-room no one interrupted his conversation; when he shot no one noticed his bag. Synge said that, occasionally, when Trollope was the last member in the lounge of the old Club, St. George's Hanover Square, the waiters would put out the lights, not noticing Trollope, although he was under their eyes.

He must, thus, have heard more gossip—and that the best gossip in the world, because club gossip is seldom malicious, its practitioners having, as a rule, a desire to know accurately where they and everyone else just exactly stands. You want to know the *exact* position and characteristics of your stockbroker, or your pocket will suffer. Trollope, then, must have heard and crystallized in his brain more gossip than anyone else who ever existed, except perhaps Jane Austen. And, except perhaps for Jane Austen, he is the greatest of all specifically English novelists. He is less of an artist than she but he is male, and that counts.

He left behind him a *Comédie Humaine*, which compared with that of Balzac—who must have been as noticeable in society as a railway engine that should have gotten into a duchess's boudoir—is like the garden of a Queen Anne manor as against a stage crowded with knockabout comedians and stage villains. Even against Dickens he is like a Civil Servant of a higher grade having his shoes shined by a bootblack. The comparison with Thackeray would take longer. Trollope had no sympathy with rogues and it takes sympathy with underdogs, bastards and the questionable daughters of ham artists, to let you go the one step further that leads to *Vanity Fair*. Trollope, in short, was an English gentleman; Thackeray was anything else you like to name under the sun. Compared with the poignant anxiety of the pecuniary straits of *Framley Parsonage*—which this writer in his private preferences places higher than any other English novel—reading of the financial vicissitudes of a Colonel Newcome is like a visit to a wax-works, and the failure of César Birotteau—though the book of that name is one of the best of Balzac's—is the *épopée* of a Marseillais Napoleon of marionettes.

Perhaps the main characteristic of writers like Jane Austen and Trollope is their complete non-literariness. Indeed, you would say that they are without the passion to write that distinguishes a Balzac, a Dickens, a Thackeray or even a genuine artist like Gautier. These all seem to be compelled to throw off literary matter as if they had a volcano in their stomachs. . . . But the writers with whom we are immediately concerned seem, like the Good Man of Marcus Aurelius—to put forth their works as the vine putteth forth her grapes and when they are gone knoweth no more of them. Certainly the last thing one would imagine of Jane Austen is that, having finished *Pride and Prejudice*, she should look round the dining table and expect congratulations— any more than Christina Rossetti when she had finished a poem would expect a torrent of praise from Mr. Ruskin and all the great shouters slapping each other on the back in her brother's studio downstairs.

One knows neither their impulses nor their aims, nor yet can one say that they belong to any school. Certainly, they are not romantics —but, then, neither are they realists nor naturalists. The style, "realism," had already been appropriated by such writers as Flaubert and the Goncourt brothers, writers who had a certain tang of disillusionment as to the motives of mankind. And "naturalism" was reserved for others who affected to observe that humanity was a very nasty beast indeed —writers like, in certain of his moods, Maupassant and, nearly all the time, Émile Zola.

Nevertheless, running mainly through Anglo-Saxondom in both its branches but with a certain tendency to deviate into Scandinavia and the Nordic lands in general, you see a sort of white lode running through the other-tinted earths of the literary delta. The torch would seem to be passed from hand to hand from Jane Austen to Trollope, and from one of the Brontë sisters in the mood when she wrote *Villette* to the Mrs. Gaskell of *Cranford* and *Mary Barton*, and, as we have already adumbrated, from Miss Alcott to Sarah Orne Jewett and so, in relatively modern days, to George Gissing, a too neglected writer, and to an even more unjustly neglected writer, William Hale White, who wrote *The Autobiography of Mark Rutherford* and *The Revolution in Tanners Lane* . . . and so to Miss Dorothy Richardson, to D. H. Lawrence* in certain of his moods, and, with immense additions of a psychological and aesthetic sort, to Miss Virginia Woolf and to various American novelists of the so-called Middle Western type, and, without any art at all, to the Mr. Sinclair Lewis who wrote *Babbitt*, and, with a certain and very effectively autochthonous art, to Mr. Sherwood Anderson, and, with tremendous personal rumblings, to Mr. Theodore Dreiser. To them one is tempted to add Mr. Thomas Hardy in his simpler manifestations like the *Mayor of Casterbridge* and *The Return of the Native*, and possibly also, though with every possible reservation, the George Moore of *Esther Waters*, the Galsworthy of the *Country House*, the Arnold Bennett of *The Man from the North*. Going then into the foreign, it is almost impossible to find anything but the rarest traces in nineteenth century France of this essentially Nordic lode. You might justly claim that privilege for Balzac's *Médecin du Village* or *Le Lys dans la Vallée* but the exaggerated benevolence of the Doctor and the almost egregious virginity of the heroine of the other book give both of those works the air of romanticism at its sentimental worst. Or, on the other hand, you might claim that the essential truth of *Le Père Goriot* gave Balzac the right to sit beside the author of *Framley Parsonage*. Or so too with the Edith Wharton who, coming for the moment out from under the aegis of the Master, wrote *Ethan Frome*.

---

* When Lawrence first came across this writer, and notably in his earliest short stories to be submitted to the writer's editorial censures, his work and indeed his temperament were as, let us call it, "uncolored" as that of Gissing or Hale White. His later developments, which occurred during the writing of *Sons and Lovers*, were injected, as it were, into him by contact with the consciously socio-moralist group of writers that at the time existed in London.

Or again *Die Ehre* of Sudermann was in its day acclaimed as a Teutonic masterpiece of the school of Zolaistic naturalism. Yet it contains whole passages between the two principal women of the book and in a rustic framework that might well come within our classification. One is, indeed, tempted to say that Sudermann, formidable Hun as he desired to appear, was actually a good simple German, colored by a wash of naturalism that he did not very skillfully apply. *Frau Sorge* of 1887—which was undoubtedly his best book—had been more of an exposition of Nordic depression, the joint product, as far as the literary coloring was concerned, of the tendencies that made possible Ibsen and Nietzsche. (The writer is not asserting that Sudermann was the disciple of either of those essential Nordics.) When later he came under the influence of Zola—and more perhaps than anything, as far as form is concerned, of Maupassant's *Une Vie*—he seemed to lose his head—as all literary Germany seemed to lose its head. The effect of the combined Nordic-naturalist stream that struck Germany at that time had on its most considerable writer, Gerhart Hauptmann, at first the effect of making him produce a number of realistic rather than naturalistic plays—*Die Weber, Vor Sonnenaufgang* and others. These were bitter protests against the sordid circumstances of the German working classes rather than the exposition of sexual irregularities which were the first fruits of naturalism in the German Empire. As stage plays they had—at any rate in those days—a very strong hold on audiences. The writer, who happened to be fairly often in Germany in the nineties, has seen whole audiences of *Die Weber* on their feet and protesting, not against, but with, that play. . . . And Germany of that day was really seething with literary excitement either with or against the Naturalists. Whole flocks of little books with titles like *Die Unbefleckte* (*Unsoiled*) covered all the bookstalls. They dealt mainly eulogistically with the careers of "soiled doves" and aroused the execration of the Lutheran clergy and the official and middle classes; they treated their themes in a staccato, sketchy manner that was taken to reproduce the effects of French fiction and effect . . . an effect that the Austrian Arthur Schnitzler (1863-1931) proved with his *Anatol* of 1893 could be very effectively adapted to the German language—by an Austrian. The general influence of Zolaism on German letters was not good; Zola himself was not light-handed and Zola-inspired German books were heavy. Ibsen was less deleterious, and Ibsen, living for a number of years in Germany, was with the advanced almost a national hero.

But in spite of that Nordic-Mediterranean contest in the upper air, the more essentially South German attributes of German literature survived and went quietly on their way beneath the pens of such writers as the Freiherr von Ompteda (1863-1931), a sort of more class-consciously aristocratic Trollope, and of Clara Viebig (b. 1860), a writer still living, whose *Schlafende Heer* still seems to the writer one of the most memorable of German novels. Both Clara Viebig and Von Ompteda are officially classed as "realists" and did undoubtedly fall in their youths to some extent under the influence of *Madame Bovary*. But they assimilated that influence in reasonable measure and successfully digested it into their own methods. *Das Schlafende Heer* (*The Sleeping Host*) in particular, a novel dealing with the attempt of the Prussian authorities to settle the Polish question by expropriating the Polish peasants from their own lands and making them work in the Westphalian coal mines and then settling peasants from the Rhine on the Polish lands—*Das Schlafende Heer,* then, is a novel told with a great humaneness of outlook. It achieves a sort of tranquil poetry from the juxtaposition of two dreadfully home-sick populations—for the poor Rhinelanders disliked the Polish plains almost as much as the Poles the Westphalian mines. The book was regarded with much official disfavor by official Germany, which made every effort to prevent its circulation.

Politics entered, indeed, a good deal into the German literary situation of that moment. For this reason: If you draw a line from the mouth of the Elbe to Frankfurt am Main, you will find that all German art and all German great men with the exception of Nietzsche, come from the regions to the South of that line—notably, of course, from the Rhenish principalities and from Suabia, which gave us Bach, Holbein, the *minnesingers* and so many more. In the nineties, for reasons no doubt sufficient to them, the Prussians adopted with a sort of grim cynicism the artistic cause of the naturalists, as being no doubt the school farthest from South German national writing. That side of the movement culminated in Nietzsche (Friedrich Wilhelm, 1844-1900), at first the passionate friend of Schopenhauer and the romantic Richard Wagner and afterwards the declared enemy of both writers and of all the arts in their South German presentations. His poem, *Also Sprach Zarathustra,* is, for instance, a glorification of blonde Nordic force against the slavish masses of Christians—or the South German populations.

Nietzsche became the voice of official Prussia. But what is artistic in South Germany swung, not so much by conscious revolution as by an instinctive nationalism, back towards the mystic supernaturalism of Novalis, Fouqué, Brentano, Freytag or the Austrian Lenau; towards the lyricism of Grillparzer, Rueckert, Immermann, Heine even, and Levin Schuecking and Annette von Droste Huelshoff who was a sort of Rhineland Christina Rossetti, and towards the Suabian-Rhine legends of Wagner. Hauptmann abandoned the bitter dryness of his *Weber* period and reacted towards the veritable South Germanism of *Hanneles Himmelfahrt* and the *Versunkene Glocke.* The younger generation of writers—with whom this writer was at one time a good deal in contact—by a queer political quirk were apt to study the French and international Mediterannean movement. But they studied it relatively platonically as being a manifestation of liberty and fraternity; they sang in private the "Marseillaise"—which was *strengst verboten*—and proceeded to evolve a sort of neutral German school of novelists who, like Trollope or Mrs. Gaskell, were just novelists. . . . Thus, this writer will not soon forget his emotion when in 1901, being at the University of Marburg—where the protest that makes so many people style themselves Protestants was signed—being then at that university for the purpose of studying, in view of a *Life of Henry VIII* that he proposed to write, certain Schmalkaldner documents of the time of that monarch, he bought quite by accident at the railway bookstall a copy of a book called *Buddenbrooks* announced as then just published.

So began, at any rate for him, the modern German literature that still pursues its course—on the Riviera, in the English shires, in the Middle West of the United States . . . anywhere other than in Germany. It has been characterized by a good many currents, from the rather maniacally mannered Scandinavianism of Wedekind (1864-1914) or the polished Mediterraneanism of this writer's late friend Arthur Schnitzler—to the Teutonically roughened historic romanticism of his present friend, Lion Feuchtwanger,* who was born in 1884, whose *Ugly Duchess* is a prevailing monument of the German School and whose political activities have made him the national hero of those who do not uphold the present German régime. And, of course, to Mr. Thomas Mann, another novelist like those others of the English school, who is "just novelist"—whose vitality, that is to say, is such that his projections of life around his story and of his story through his projections of life, outweigh his moral cosmogony and prevent his implicit adherence to any set literary school. In such masterpieces of their genre as *Buddenbrooks* and *The Magic Mountain*, as with *Pride and Prejudice* or *Mansfield Park*, the personality of the author, projecting itself through the human instances he selects to render, gives one a pleasure that, seizing upon one with the first words one reads, continues till the last page. In that pleasure one omits to notice either the writer's methods or his social or political tendencies, and his books become, as it were, countrysides or manor houses rather than bound leaves of paper impressed with printed characters.

With the name of Ibsen, which occurred some pages back in this work, a new literature impinges itself on our attention. It is that of Scandinavia. Amongst confusions of local languages and national overlappings that are difficult to follow for the non-Scandinavian, Iceland, Norway, Sweden and Denmark among them produced, between the days of the great sagas and our own time, a prodigious number of books. Even those remote and inclement northern regions were swept

---

* The writer ought to confess to the reader that this constatation of the German literature of his own day and the days just preceding it is more personal—more swayed by his own likings and the enthusiams with which he first read books whilst knowing and liking their authors—than has been hitherto usual to him. It is, however, difficult in a time when almost all the German intelligentsia are in exile, scattered over the world and without any central organ of opinion, to gather what that opinion is, so that, although hitherto he has tried to find as it were a balance between national conceptions, his own taste and the standards of wide-spread schools, he has here been forced to change his method.

by all the successive tides of literary inspiration and fashion that, rising usually in Mediterranean climes, went away like the rings caused by stones cast into a pool, to the farthest verges of the occidental world. The renaissance, the period of Racine and Corneille, the anti-classical revolution merging into romanticism, the French periods of realism, impressionism and still more of naturalism—all these periods made their mark, not unusually under the aegis of one or other member of one royal family or the other, on all those four countries. Whole hosts of regional writers made their essays in the manners of Shakespeare, Corneille, Voltaire, Chateaubriand, Flaubert or Zola, each in their due season. The results are interesting more as showing what influences can do in strongly individualized regions than as works of art *per se*. It is not, however, our province to trace the effects of the influences of the main literary stream into its backwaters so much as to trace the influences emanating from distances on the main literary stream. And it was not until the beginning of the nineteenth century that Scandinavia, in the person of Adam Oelenschläger, a Dane, made any noteworthy impression in the countries to the South. Born in 1779 in Copenhagen of a family of royal employees, he lived in poor circumstances until first his highly romantic poem *Guldhornene* and then his *Aladdin* attracted the attention of the Danish royal family and a pension allowed him to travel very widely through Western Europe. His *Aladdin* is mentioned in letters of Goethe, Byron and Chateaubriand—who welcomed his attacks on rationalism in his *St. Hansaftenspil*; both Goethe and Madame de Staël liked him personally, and Victor Hugo showed him some attentions when he visited Paris. In addition, the king, Louis Philippe, called him the Corneille of Denmark. From sheer romanticism he passed to works founded on Norse mythology and history and, with an interlude devoted to the investigation and exposition of the passion of love, he continued working in that vein till his death at an advanced age. His most impressive work is perhaps his tragedy *Hakon Jarl*.

But Hans Christian Andersen (1805-1875) is probably the best known of all the pre-Ibsen Nordic writers as he is the one who will most probably most prolong the literary fame of the Northland. It is unnecessary to dilate here upon his *Fairy Tales*. They have gone to forming the character and delighting the hearts of almost everyone now living in the European and European-descended races. He was more interested in the fate of his novels, but though faintly interesting and agreeable, they are hardly anything more than just anybody's novels.

It was, however, not until the eighties and nineties that Scandinavia really burst upon the outside world with Hendrik Ibsen (1828-1906), Björnson (1832-1910), Jonas Lie (1833-1908), the critic Morris Cohen Brandes (1842-1927), Johann August Strindberg (1849-1912), Selma Lagerlöf (b. 1858) and Knut Hamsun (b. 1859), all these having published their most impressive works by the year 1890. Later came Sigrid Undset, who was born in 1882, and since then few years have passed without one Scandinavian country or the other producing a book that has proved to be what is called a "best seller" at least in the United States. Indeed, in the present day a great many Swedish, Norwegian, Danish and Icelandic books are produced in America, mostly in the Middle West. The most noteworthy of these is probably the *Peder Victorious* of O. E. D. Rölvag, an author writing exclusively in Norwegian and highly esteemed both in the United States and his native country. He died in 1937.

It would be wanting in sincerity to say that any great literary interest attaches to these Scandinavian books, the smouldering or passionate natures of their authors really precluding much attention to their methods. Indeed, the highly distinguished Danish critic Brandes laid it down as a dogmatic axiom that the duty of the Nordic author was to attend to his ideals and let his methods, almost literally, slide. Now and then, as in the case of Björnson or Selma Lagerlöf, or indeed Esaias Tegner who wrote *Frithiof's Saga* as early as 1825, a certain beauty of temperament or buoyancy of personality will give to a work some beauty and a sense of progression that supplies to it an aspect of conscious artistry. And by dint of passion, Knut Hamsun's *Hunger* achieves a unity that disappears from his perhaps better known *Growth of the Soil*.

Otherwise from Ibsen's *Brand* to Strindberg's *Son of a Servant* and *Fool's Confession* and even, paradoxically enough, since it is a historical novel, to Sigrid Undset's *Kristin Lavransdatter*, all these works have the aspect of nearly formless outpourings of passion—or its counterpart, the inferiority complex. The Scandinavian influence, therefore, on the literary comity of regions more southerly is almost entirely temperamental. Indeed, you would not be going very much too far if you alleged that Hendrik Ibsen himself was hardly a literary figure at all. His earlier mostly historic plays are so completely set in the shade by his later modern dramas that their existence is apt to slip the memory, though his *Lady Inger of Östrat* certainly deserves not to be forgotten. But his series of modern plays from the *Doll's House* of 1879 to *John Gabriel Borkman* of 1896 are in no sense literature at all from any aspect.

This writer has frequently asked himself whether these plays are as essentially Scandinavian as the rest of the work that we are here considering. It is to be remembered that in 1864 Ibsen left Norway for Italy and that he spent the next fifteen years or so, on and off, in Germany. Now, one of the strongest of all the Nordic motifs was the almost ceaseless exploring of the Scandinavian past; it was explored merely for local color and for information or for patriotic inspiration in nations once great that had become diminished almost to disappearance. Or it was explored that it might furnish startling backgrounds for essentially modern moodinesses. Thus, *Kristin Lavransdatter,* with all its picturesqueness, is essentially a vehicle for conveying a sense of modern Nordic fornication against strong historic vicissitudes. But this note, rather robustious as it is, completely vanishes from the top-hatted frock-coated desiccations of situation and emotion of the *Doll's House* or *The Lady From the Sea.* And Ibsen's declaration of faith as regards these plays:

> Let Humanity finally discover Beauty in Liberty, let it refuse to be subject to truths which have ceased to be true and through its spirit let it return to Nature!

smacks far more strongly of the Rousseau-descended, *Sturm und Drang*-guided, Zola-Nietzschean-Prussian neo-*Sturm und Drang* period of the German eighties to nineties than of the frame of mind of Grettir the Strong, of the *Laxdaela Saga,* or even of the *Niebelungen Lied.*

That is not to say that the *Wild Duck* is not the best acting play that was ever written or that *Hedda Gabler* in the hands of actors at all capable will not cause the pulse to leap almost as spasmodically as it did in 1890 when *Hedda* was first played. But the actual writing, the dialogue, is so bald that on rereading it one raises the eyelids incredulously as if it were impossible that anything so thin, so exaggerated and so unprepared, could ever, and however presented, once have moved us. Actually, Ibsen knew supremely what he was doing.

Read in cold print, the end of *Hedda Gabler* has the grotesqueness of a faded fashion plate of a lady with elbow-long gloves and a bustle. Consider:

[HEDDA *goes into the back room and draws the curtains. There is a pause. Suddenly* HEDDA *is heard playing a wild dance on the piano.*]

MRS. ELFSTED

Oh—what is that?

TESMAN

[*Goes to the curtains.*]
But, Hedda dear—don't play dance music. Just think of Aunt Rina—

HEDDA

[*In the inner room.*]
And Aunt Julia. Yes, you're right. But after this I will be quiet.

TESMAN

It's not good for her to see us at this distressing work. You shall take the empty room at Aunt Julia's, Mrs. Elfsted, and then I will come in the evenings and we can work there.

MRS. ELFSTED

Yes, let us do that.

HEDDA

[*Calls from inner room.*]
I hear what you are saying, Tesman. But how am *I* to get through the evenings?

TESMAN

[*At the writing table.*]
Oh, I daresay Judge Brack will be so kind as to look in now and then.

BRACK

[*Calls loudly.*]
Every blessed evening, with all the pleasure in life, Mrs. Hedda. We shall get on capitally, we two.

HEDDA

[*Is heard to say.*]
Thanks for your kindness, Judge.

[*A shot is heard in the inner room.* TESMAN, MRS. ELFSTED *and* BRACK *leap to their feet.* TESMAN *throws back the curtains.* HEDDA *lies on the sofa, lifeless. Screams and cries.* BERTA *appears from the right in the inner room.*]

TESMAN

[*Shrieks.*]
Shot herself! Shot herself in the temple!

BRACK

[*Half fainting in the armchair by the stove*]
Good God!—people don't *do* such things!

Actually the moment of suspense after Hedda has gone behind the
curtain is one of the highest moments of suspense of any stage play.

Ibsen's "message" came at a moment when the world—as it will do
at times—had worked itself into a perfect fever that we used then to call
fin-de-sièclism. By it we explained every folly and excused every crime.
It was less directed than romanticism, but like romanticism it was the
protest of the individual against the shackles of a conventional society.
And it was less active than romanticism since it took the form rather of
protests against one's own inefficiency in a world that organized itself
at once to ignore one's great gifts and to prevent one's putting them to
their best uses. It affected everybody from the highest to the lowest.
The word "monstrous" was never off the private lips of Edward VII,
then Prince of Wales. He too considered himself subject to the most
villainous misconceptions and the victim of oppressions that prevented
his manifesting the whole nobility of his character. It affected still
more the artist in his garret and the dilettante on his padded sofa. The
artist so set to work that poor dear old London for the first time in her
existence became the center of an art. So perhaps she might well
have remained had not that same *fin-de-siècle* spirit prompted a half
artist called Oscar Wilde to excesses that, as in subsequent private
conversations he confessed, used to make him vomit. He was pushed
to this by his desire to "touch on the raw" a philistinism that, in spite
of his tremendous notoriety at the time, did not in his estimation sufficiently applaud his unusual gifts. His conviction killed for a number
of years the art of literature in England.

But you would not be altogether in the wrong if you regarded the
"fall" of Wilde as the effects of a breath of pine-laden breeze from the

Northern forests creeping into the fog- and patchouli-laden air of a London drawing-room. Advice to humanity to discover in a certain sort of liberty a certain sort of beauty can be very destructive to a society of a certain standard of feeding that is yet unaccustomed to any great exercise of thought. So Hedda Gablerism, though immensely recommended by the more advanced intelligentsia of the nineties as a remedy for the unthinkingness of a commonplace world, was yet too strong a medicine for the less copper-lined bosoms of the young or the not mentally very balanced. The influence of Ibsenism, however, vast as it was and influencing as it did very materially the externals of the literary life, is however a topic not strictly our own. It was a movement temperamental rather than aesthetic and was founded on things quite outside the practice of literature. It behoves us, therefore, to leave that movement without further comment. We must devote what remains of our attention to a world movement that, impinging on Anglo-Saxondom in the days of Ibsenism, has continued to manifest until today its influences on such companies of our delta as consider literature to be a conscious art.

CHAPTER SEVEN

W E HAVE, then, refined our matter down until nothing very essential remains to us but to trace that later movement in favor of conscious art and of awareness of the proud functions of our art itself in human affairs. And from now on we shall have to observe in our projection the rules of impressionism. We are writing, that is to say, no longer in any measure the biographies of writers; we must use them as if they were natural objects bringing in a touch from one here and from another there so that there may result not a picture of men, but an impression of a world movement. Centering on Paris and London, this movement radiated its effects to the very extremes of the Western Hemisphere in both Europe and America. It gave us not only the German realists, as we shall see, but the Middle Western school of a few years ago, and not only Henry James in London but Turgenev in the government of Kiev or on the Scottish moors when he chose to be there.

For the same reason we can no longer pretend to be inclusive. We must use for illustration those writers, and those writers alone, who are most useful in contributing to our impression. It may seem extreme in a work dealing with world literature to leave out all consideration of Mr. Thomas Hardy as a novelist, or of Paul Bourget and of Henri de Regnier in France and, say, Mr. Booth Tarkington in Indiana. That is not to depreciate those writers; their omission is due simply to the fact that their works do not illustrate our theme as strongly as the work of Flaubert, James or Turgenev. To atone for this, we shall later present the reader with a number of synchronized and classified tables of authors and their works; in that way the patient may minister to himself.

That process began about the middle of last century.

Until about that date men had written under varying impulsions. They wrote with the burning desire to express themselves, to impress themselves on their day, to give partial or sometimes impartial accounts of affairs in which they had been engaged, to make names, to aid their memories. Finally, came the stage when, aided by the discovery of printing, they wrote in order to earn bread.

And, eventually, the number who wrote for that purpose vastly exceeded those who had any other aim in mind. That at once changed the whole incidence of the pursuit. A man who writes for any other purpose may please himself as to how he writes; a man who writes for gain must please others—and many others. That is perfectly proper.

The real difficulties of the occupation then began. The question seemed to solve itself by the imitation of others. A man—or as often as not a woman—would write a book about ruined abbeys where stalked the ghosts of heavily armored knights, and in and out of season the owls hooted in unceasing moonlight. The book was very widely read. Immediately the literary landscape became filled with moonlight, ghosts, ivied ruins and owls. It would continue to be so decorated until the public taste palled. Then living armored knights and ladies in hennins spread all across the plains. Or learning would assert its claims and encyclopaedias became your only reading. Today in the one branch of Anglo-Saxondom the habit of reading rugged novels about hard-grained pioneers or psychological studies of youths on isolated farms in the midst of thousands of acres of wheat or corn has been superseded by a passion for sham biographies and sham scientific works. In the other branch the reading of formless and listless fiction about anything under the sun, with a slight leaning for fictitious chroniclings of families in or near cathedral closes, has given place to a reading of textbooks on almost any subject, from poultry-breeding and small farming to travel in trailers and popular psychiatry. In France analytic treatments of individual existences have largely given place to works dealing with constructive theories of life in the large, the young public which was with difficulty restrained from stoning the funeral of the late Anatole France, craving for some replacement of lost ideals. In official Germany, authority having stamped out not only the intelligentsia but all persons exhibiting any intelligence whatever, reading of anything worthy the attention of adults is almost at a standstill. But Germans in exile continue the practice of turning out historical romances or earnest studies of pre-Third Reich life . . . which, too, have become historic. In Soviet Russia the authorities, having given up the practice of insisting that all literature must be propaganda for the U. S. S. R., have permitted, for reasons apparent to themselves, the writing of hilariously cynical, fictional criticism of bureaucratic administrations. In Italy and Spain literature of the imagination is almost at a standstill.

Thus, any analysis of world literary trends is, for the first time in the history of mankind, quite impracticable. It remains then for us to trace the history of conscious literary art in fiction from its beginnings in the last years of the eighteenth century until our present chaos.

We may say that the tendency showed itself first in the works of Stendhal; or it would be perfectly proper to allege that its first traces are to be found in the first novel of Jane Austen. At any rate, it began with the—perhaps instinctive—discovery by both those artists that the juxtaposition of the composed renderings of two or more unexaggerated actions or situations may be used to establish, like the juxtaposition of vital word to vital word, a sort of frictional current of electric life that will extraordinarily galvanize the work of art in which the device is employed. That has the appearance of being a rather hard aesthetic nut to crack. Let us put it more concretely by citing the algebraic truth that $(a = b)^2$ equals not merely $a^2 + b^2$, but a^2 plus an apparently unearned increment called $2ab$ plus the expected b^2. Or let us use the still more easy image of two men shouting in a field. While each shouts separately each can only be heard at a distance of an eighth of a mile, whilst if both shout simultaneously their range of hearing will be extended by a hundred-odd yards. The point cannot be sufficiently labored, since the whole fabric of modern art depends on it.

When, then, Stendhal presents us coldbloodedly and without comment with a Fabrice racked with love but insisting in his intrigue on a course of action that can only prove—and that does prove—harrowingly disastrous to his mistress; or when Miss Austen renders for us a lady patroness feudally responsible for a whole rural district and by that whole district regarded with an awe only fitted to be bestowed upon a divine personage and when, immediately after a panegyric on the goodness of heart of that lady delivered by a minister of God—or at least of the Church of England as by law established—she renders for us, still without comment, that lady expressing sentiments and committing herself to actions of almost imbecile selfishness; or when Theodore, in *The Way of All Flesh*, on sleeping for the first time in his parents' guest-room, finds that above the bedhead is hung a framed motto bearing the words: "Be the day weary or seem the time long, at length it ringeth to even song;" or when in *Lord Jim* Conrad presents for us the old French naval lieutenant who, after expressing every kind of benevolent indulgence for the follies, the outrageous high-spirited misdemeanors verging on reckless crime, of youth—when the old French naval lieutenant hears what Lord Jim's misfortune actually was and exclaims: "Ah, monsieur, that is a matter of honor. . . . And when it is a matter of honor . . ." and then opens and closes the plump hands that had been all the while clasped on his stomach; or when, in *Éducation Sentimentale*, the miserable Cisy, overcome with all sorts of emotions because he is within a minute of crossing swords with Frédéric, sees with a sort of ghastly clearness the commonest details of everyday life *"des rares passants les croisaient. Le ciel était bleu, et on entendait, par moments, des lapins bondir. Au détour d'un sentier, une femme en madras causait avec un homme en blouse, et, dans la grande avenue sous les marronniers, des domestiques en veste de toile promenaient leurs chevaux;"** or when to trace the method quite up to date, in *The Magic Mountain*, in the middle of one of those highly-flown conversations that will arise when German meets Russ, Clavdia Chauchat kisses Hans Castorp on the mouth and nothing happens— though to be sure in this case Mr. Mann, not having fully endorsed the modern programme of technique, carries on the matter in a wealth of comment by himself—. . . when, then, we are presented with this century's growth of juxtaposed instances it is obvious that a third product results from the meeting, respectively, of each of the two elements. The immediate effect is a vitalizing of the renderings of life

---

* "A few people passed them. The sky was blue; now and then the bounding of a rabbit could be heard. At the turn of the path a woman with a banana was chatting with a man in a blouse, and, in the wide avenue beneath the chestnut trees, grooms in striped waistcoats were exercising horses."

by the author. Jane Austen's "getting in" of her portentous Lady Catherine might or might not convey a sense that in her presence we are confronting a personage in our real life; but that conviction becomes infinitely enhanced as soon as the lady opens her lips in her first egregious conversation with Elizabeth Bennet. Or the framed text in the guest-room of *The Way of All Flesh* throws, as it were, the light of a photographer's bomb on the Reverend and Mrs. Theobald; or the mere *"L'honneur, monsieur. . . . L'honneur . . ."* of Conrad's French lieutenant extraordinarily illuminates not merely the old lieutenant himself but the psychology of all male France of his generation.

The objector will here interpolate that all that is a very old story. Hypocrites have always existed and been unveiled by writers, and Miss Austen's unveiling of the moronlike qualities of Lady Catherine de Bourgh is merely the exposure of a hypocrite. It is true that hypocrites had been favorites of the writer's pen for a matter of two thousand two hundred and nine years, if we count from the birth of Theophrastus of the *Characters* to that, on the paper of Charles Dickens, of Mr. Stiggins. But till the day of Jane Austen—and later for several generations—all hypocrites had been overdrawn. You may roar over the misadventures of a Stiggins, a Chadband, a Pecksniff, a Heep or a young Mr. Blifil of *Tom Jones*. But you never really completely believe in them. If you questioned yourself whilst you roared with laughter, you would have to confess that you were doing yourself less than justice, because whilst some of their attributes and speeches are human, they partake, for the most part of them, of the exaggerated grotesqueness of marionettes.

In addition, Miss Austen is not engaged in exposing a hypocrite. She is merely contrasting the want of imagination of a moron, of a type of which the world is filled, with the reverence produced by the 'scutcheons of nobility with which she is surrounded. Lady Catherine de Bourgh, in the course of a long and meant-to-be-gracious, insolent cross-examination as to her upbringing and the resources of her family, says to Elizabeth Bennet, who is one of a family of five daughters who have never known the advantages of a governess: "No governess! How is that possible? Five daughters brought up in a house without a governess! I never heard of such a thing! Who taught you? Who attended you? Without a governess you must have been neglected. . . . Nothing is to be done in a family without steady and regular instruction and nobody but a governess can give it. It is wonderful how many families I have been the means of supplying in that way . . ." and so she goes on to discourse of her benevolences to young "persons." On the other hand, this inconsiderate and ostentatious moron is surrounded with an attitude of awe caused by the grandeur of her manor house, the deportment of her servants, and the ceaseless encomia of that man of God—the Reverend Collins. "So that, in spite of having been at St. James's Palace, Sir William [a City Knight] was so awed by the grandeur surrounding him that he had just courage to make a low bow and take his seat without saying a word. . . ."

The objector will say that there is nothing very extraordinary about all this. And, indeed, there is not—except that it is extraordinary that decent people should play up to, and connive at, such blatancies.

It is a question of, as it were, the surfaces of the works of this school. Nothing in the way of incident or character sticks far out of the story, but the effect of ordinariness set against ordinariness in a slightly different plane gives precisely the effect of not ill-natured gossip, which to the average intelligent mind is the most engrossing thing in the world, and of slight surprise which is the prime quality of art.

Still more the gaucheness, boastfulnesses and want of human imagination thus portrayed are such as, with slight changes of circumstances, are within the reach of almost anybody. We are all of us capable of talking boastfully to our just inferiors; of hanging inappropriate texts on our guest-rooms; of making of a point of honor an excuse to refuse to listen to a pitiful story. And, life being the extremely difficult thing to live harmoniously that it is, we have all come so near committing solecisms or infractions of taste that upon remembering them we seem to feel our bowels turn over.

So the interest of this type of work is both personal and impersonal.

In reading it we make better acquaintance not merely with life but with ourselves.

Let us consider Dickens, Balzac and Thackeray, three novelists all running neck and neck with one another in the matter of time and not singularly different in their approach to life and their works. You might say that all three, as far as incident goes, keep, at any rate in their best novels, within a reasonable scale of incident. They deal as a rule neither with war, conquest, passion, nor yet with crime. The most brutal incident in any of their works is the murder of Nancy by Bill Sykes and the subsequent death of Sykes himself, though actually the assault on the Marquis of Steyne by Rawdon Crawley is an affair even more startling. But they deal as a rule too frequently in coincidences that are justified by no preliminary preparation of the ground and their "characters" are all statically overdrawn. Given that a man has a cough, a hoarse voice, a black jowl and a wooden leg, not one of these novelists will let him take something to soften his voice, shave, or substitute a cork limb for the wooden peg that will stick out all over the story—*ad nauseam*. The general effect is thus one of monotony. Once you have become a fan—an *aficionado*—of any of the three you will know nearly always what he will say and do next. Thus, they sacrifice the great advantage that comes from the element of surprise in their works. The school of Jane Austen, Stendhal and Trollope, which later developed into that called "realist"—a word of disagreeable significance that one might desire to see supplanted by the term "impressionist," since their task was to convey to the world their genuine impressions of life as they saw it—that set of writers, then, relying more closely on life to give them their incidents and the timbre of their works, can get into them that element of queer surprise that life actually gives to all its affairs. This is a form of surprise of a scope infinitely more varied than could be achieved by the most inventive human brain. You always know beforehand what Dickens will do with the fraudulent lawyer on whose machinations hang the fate of a score of his characters; you always know beforehand how Balzac will deal with the million-franc financial crises with which his pages are scattered; and you always know beforehand the sort of best-club comment that Thackeray in his own person will supply for every twenty pages or so of his characters' actions. There is no surprise.

In the matter of form once they have got into the saddle none of these great writers who were not great artists is strikingly good, and Dickens at least is excruciatingly bad. From his quite early days Balzac with his elephantine vigor was so intent on telling his story that he indulged very little in purposeless digressions. His *Dernier Chouan* of 1829 is a little loose in texture, but *Peau de Chagrin* of two years later is almost what the French call *corsé*, lean and businesslike in its conduct of the story. As he goes on his way, his novels vary in texture rather as if with the spirit of his subject. Thus, *César Birotteau* is floridly leisurely in handling; the *Père Goriot* takes its time but progresses satisfactorily; and *Cousine Bette*, which is not unusually considered the greatest of all his novels, is with some exceptions as economical in its telling as a French lady doing her marketing for a large family with a small purse. The exceptions occur when Balzac gets amongst the very noble and the very wealthy, or lets the story linger over their furnishings or accoutrements. Then, indeed, it does linger aimlessly. . . . But that poor dear Balzac who has told us that his sole ideal was *"être riche et être célèbre"*—when he did get in imagination amongst the rich and the celebrated could hardly be expected to abandon too soon the blissful visions he conjures up.

Indeed, all that he knew of life and the joys of existence he had from his dream of being rich and the other one of being celebrated. Almost no other man of letters was so almost exclusively a man of letters and not of life. When he was not apoplectically turning out copy in one garret or another, to which he had fled from his creditors, he was attempting to gain his million as a publisher and losing, if not millions, at least sufficient to force him to spend year on year in turning out *romans feuilletons*. Or he embarked on other big-childishly fantastic schemes of realizing quick riches. He started gold or lead mines in distant climes; opened antiquaries' shops; tried to trade on a large scale with the Sultan of Morocco.

A volcanically constructed peasant by birth, he awakened a passion in a genuinely noble lady, Mme. de Berny. She paid his debts a number of times and would at least have enabled him to become acquainted with the life of the *salons* of the period. But his industry made him uneasy whenever he was away from his desk and his pride would not let him appear in a world of comtes and marchionesses without being at least an Academician—whose social precedence is that of a field marshal. The Academy, however, would not hear of him—because of his appearance and manners. So that it is difficult to see what avenues of approach to life Balzac had at all. And if it would not be *lèse majesté* against the French republic of letters—a crime carrying with it the penalty of imprisonment for life in the vaults of the Institut de France —one might dismiss the whole of the *Comédie Humaine* as one immense fairy tale having the merit of bringing one in contact with the titanically gasping figure of Balzac himself but totally without value as a comment on, or a projection of, life. It is usual even in the most official of French circles to admit that towards the end of his career his books were written under the influence of the "hallucinations and monomania" of his dreams of celebrity and wealth.* But one might as well go the whole way and say that, except for the very few books in which he does use the meager contacts with life that he really had, almost the whole of his work is that of the merest—if most gigantic— teller of tales, as it were a Parisian Nights' Entertainment on a vast scale. In *Le Cousin Pons* he could give you some sort of a showdown as to the world of antiques because he had once made an attempt at fortune as an antiquaire; in the *Grandeur et Décadence de César Birotteau* he could give you some idea of one who feels fortune in his grasp only to see it turn into dry leaves, because he had tried his luck

---

* The ingenuous youth of the United States are taught thus to regard this period of the life of Balzac in the *History of French Literature* by Nitze and Dargan, both professors of French at the University of Chicago: "His two chief ideals, love and creative art, were stained by the money-making ambition. Exuberant and even titanic power is his special mark. No such industry and driving force had hitherto appeared in fiction. It led him into eruptions of gaiety and egotism, in which everything had to bend to his will, and in which the world of real people faded away before the huger reality of the *comédie humaine*. It led him finally into that realm of hallucination and monomania in which he wrote his least imposing novels—*Le Cousin Pons* and *La Cousine Bette*. Numerous anecdotes show how for Balzac his visions became facts, and it is in the ultimate fusion of the real and the romantic that the secret of his spell resides."

as a printer and publisher and had for brief moments imagined himself on the verge of great wealth; in *Le Père Goriot* he could marvelously project the life of a French *pension* of the poorer order, because so many of his days had been passed in French boarding houses of the poorer order. But his budget of realities is so small as hardly to give him any claim at all to be called a "realist." Besides, the technical word "realism" implies that its writers worked within the bounds of a certain aesthetic ideal. Balzac had none; he wrote simply as cyclones blow, picking up without system here a tin roof, there a horse and buggy or again a whole swathe of forest trees.

The claim of "founder of the realistic school" might just as well go to Dickens or Thackeray, for Dickens at least had a real knowledge of the harder undersides of life and Thackeray a genius for projecting the lives and characters of the comfortable that could only have been granted to one born comfortable, and of genius. The great books of both men—and they are indeed "great" books in the sense that the *Divine Comedy* and the *Greater Testament* are great—*Vanity Fair,* then, and *Great Expectations,* are great because they are infused with the views of life of two writers who have lived intensely, who have known real griefs, and who have attained to wealth and celebrity at the expense of disillusionment. They are not, that is to say, works founded on any conventional scheme of ethics and they propound no conventional solutions of evils; they are simply records, that from time to time attain to the height of renderings, of life transfused by the light of their writers' temperaments as modified by their vicissitudes. In that sense, both of them are of the school of Jane Austen and Stendhal and both, as far as those two books are concerned, may properly be called, in the quite technical sense, realists.

In their earlier works both were influenced by the Spanish picaresque writers and their English followers—Dickens in the mere shape of his tales, Thackeray by his taste for rogues. *Pickwick* is an even more infantilely benevolent *Humphry Clinker*, servants' soirées at Bath and all, and might indeed have been called *The Adventures of Samuel Weller* quite as appropriately as the *Private Papers of the Pickwick Club*. But Thackeray's first book that, except for the quite immature *Catherine*, was not a mere reprint or remanipulation of articles from papers and magazines . . . *Barry Lyndon*, then, published in 1844, is a direct pastiche after the manner of Fielding's *Jonathan Wild*, and, since Thackeray was infinitely the more skillful of the two, it is a work much more sinister.

And though Dickens eventually made his novels somewhat more cohesive than the mere strings of unrelated episodes of the Spaniards or Fielding, it is to be doubted whether Thackeray ever got over his love for a rogue or was ever in his secret intimacy* anything other than a *homo duplex*, à la *Jekyll and Hyde*, the two sides of his brain functioning the one against the other.

It is quite feasible to say that *Vanity Fair* is the great novel that it is, just as *Madame Bovary* and *Éducation Sentimentale* are the great and still greater novels that they are, just because their authors were both in love with, and passionately intrigued by, their respective heroines.

The minuteness of illumination with which the immeasurably greater artist presents his Emma as thus:

> *Elle alla donc chercher dans l'armoire une bouteille de curaçao, atteignit deux petits verres, emplit l'un jusqu' au bord, versa à peine dans l'autre et, après avoir trinqué, le porta à sa bouche. Comme il était presque vide, elle se renversait pour boire: et, la tête en arrière, les lèvres avancées, le cou tendu, elle riait de ne rien sentir, tandis que le bout de sa langue, passant entre ses dents fines, léchait à petits coups le fond du verre.†*

---

* The author's grandfather used to relate how, traveling on the same boat as Thackeray towards the Levant, he got up early in order to make at dawn some sketches of the city of Leghorn in whose harbor the boat was anchored. Thackeray came up the gang plank from the dock and, as his feet touched the deck, struck himself on the brow and exclaimed: "I am a hoary lecher!" That same afternoon he wrote and recited to the passengers the quite charming little poem called the *Storm at Sea*. In it he recounts how his infant children at home were waking at dawn and making a prayer for him.

† "Then she went to find in the cupboard a bottle of curaçao, reached down two liqueur glasses, filled one to the rim, poured scarcely any into the other and, after having touched glasses, put hers to her lips. Since it was nearly empty she threw back her head to drink and, pouting out her lips, she laughed because she could taste

is continued right throughout the book. This is merely one of hundreds of passages of rendering the characters visually.

Yet all that Thackeray can do for his Becky is this:

> She was small and slight in person; pale, sandy haired and with eyes habitually cast down; when they looked up they were very large, odd and attractive; so attractive that the Reverend Mr. Crisp, fresh from Oxford and curate to the Vicar of Chiswick, the Reverend Mr. Flowerdew, fell in love with her.

and all through the book Thackeray has hardly more than a similar two or three words to spare for his darling. As thus:

> "Green eyes, fair skin, pretty figure, famous frontal development," Squills remarked. "There is something about her. . . ."

On the other hand, Thackeray is prodigal of records of the use she made of her eyes. . . . And prodigal too of the records he makes of her actions. If she never stands before us vividly in her physical personality there is no doubt that as a rogue she is alive to us as few rogues have ever been in literature. However duplex his homo may have been, he loved his rogue even more than he loved the soft armchairs of his club in Hanover Square or Pall Mall. He was the worst snob the ranks of great writers have ever seen, but he had somewhere concealed in his subconsciousness a spark of a gipsy nature that let him see that the social machine to which as W. M. Thackeray he ceaselessly kowtowed in public was actually an affair worthy of the contempt he as ceaselessly poured over it in his work. It is not for nothing that he suddenly breaks off his account of Becky's predatory activities in Brussels to say triumphantly:

> If this is a novel without a hero, at least let us lay claim to a heroine. No man in the British Army which has marched away— not the great Duke himself—could be more cool or collected in the

nothing, whilst with the tip of her tongue passing out from between her fine teeth she licked with little dabs the bottom of the glass."

presence of doubts and difficulties than the indomitable little aide-de-camp's wife. . . .

You see, he cannot spare even the British Army or the Duke of Wellington, for both of whom in private he had the greatest contempt. . . . You can see him at routs and parties drawing up his figure and expanding his chest, casting meanwhile glances of scorn at the back of the heavy dragoon preceding him up the grand staircase. It had to break out of him, that passage. Did he not write also of the duke's greater opponent:

> Though more than half the world was his
> And kings bowed down before his throne,
> He borrowed of his enemies
> Six feet of ground to lie upon.

Yes, that passage had to break out of him because he was trembling to make the declaration that Becky, if she had her rights, ought really to occupy positions of splendor of the world. He was not only hymning the woman he loved; he was making for exiled royalty a claim that he passionately upheld. And he does it very well. It is impossible in the scene when Rawdon breaks in upon her and the Marquis of Steyne not to feel for Becky the sympathy that one feels for any great conqueror riding overwhelmed from the scene of his final overthrow. Becky for the rest of her life was Napoleon at St. Helena. Only *she* was not such a fool as to take it lying down. She amassed a fortune; managed by its means to keep her head somewhere above the social waters, and on the last page of the book is, quite predatorily, Lady Crawley and "the object of an infamous conspiracy." The shekels with which that conspiracy was concerned go nevertheless into her poke.

English Georgian-Victorian Society bore, nevertheless, with extreme equanimity, the unceasing hail of blows from whips of scorpions that fell on it from Thackeray. For, if today you read the *Book of Snobs* in conjunction with the other masterpiece it is impossible to escape the conviction that Thackeray says to his whole society, from the Queen on her throne with Albert the Good standing beside her, down through the whole cortège of Royal Princes, Archbishops, Dukes, Marquises, Earls, Viscounts, Barons, the Right Honourables her Majesty's Ministers, the Right Honourables her Majesty's Front Bench Opposition, the Right Honourable Bench of Judges, the Right Honourable the Lord Mayor, the Courts of Aldermen and the Common Council, the city knights, the knights of all the shires, the members and the front-door porter of the Athenaeum Club and the upper servants of the nobility and gentry, that the whole lot of them are not as worth the esteem and applause of the right-seeing as that little bit of canaille, daughter of a drunken painter and a figurante from the back row of the Paris Opera ballet. But by a miracle of obtuseness Georgian-Victorian Society was completely unable to perceive the incidence of the book. It knew that it was the cynosure, it and its habits, of an awed world that stretched from the Yildiz Kiosk to Washington Square, New York. And its contempt for the mere novelist was so intense that not Goliath before the combat would have been as astonished if you had told him that a dwarf intended to launch some pebbles at him. It disposed of Thackeray, if it even read him, by the same device that permitted it on Sundays to accept the lashes of popular preachers in fashionable churches; each major general slumbering in one pew passed the buck to the field marshal snoring in the next; each viscountess to the neighboring countess. . . . So Thackeray enjoyed his club armchair to the end of his life.

But if they bore *Vanity Fair* with equanimity, the reception of *Great Expectations* was a quite other pair of shoes. The reviews fought shy of mentioning it; it was hush-hushed in such general conversations as the comfortable devoted to books; young ladies reclining on their couches to take their post-prandial reads counselled each other to avoid it. In official corners here and there it was even said, under the breath, that this was socialism.

It was not, however, socialism; but it was a product of a world-weariness that has elsewhere made socialism a practical possibility . . . of a passionate world-weariness with humanity and humanity's contrivances that might have been written by one of the troglodite eremites of the early Christian era who should have grown weary with denunciation and was set merely on depicting the failure of his efforts.

And that weariness combined with the want of enthusiasm with which the book was conceived to make *Great Expectations* the last of Dickens' considerable works. It was written ten years before his death; he contrived to finish *Our Mutual Friend* four years later, and it is a very languid performance; *Edward Drood* he did not manage to finish at all.

Great Expectations is a muted book. The usual qualities of Dickens are an immense flow of vitality; a tremendous overdrawing of characters; immense deviations for the purpose of getting in picturesquenesses that do not belong to the story—and incessant intrusion for the sake of comment. And the convolutions of his plots and subplots are so voluminous that, on the occasions when we get back to the main story, it seems as astonishing as if we were meeting an old friend.

In *Great Expectations* all these qualities are modified. There must, of course, be overdrawing of characters. Dickens cannot be expected entirely to change that technique that was part of himself. It was a quality of his eye to see things overdrawn and in recording overdrawing, he was recording life as he saw it.

And that very overdrawing came from the level at which he saw life. The ordinary Anglo-Saxon writer is usually a member of the middle classes who tries to see life as if from a superior station. He announces himself as gentleman; expects to see himself treated as "gentleman" by the hangers-on of the literary trade—the reviewers, publishers, booksellers, his fellow authors, their wives and servants. He hopes that one day he will be treated as "gentleman" . . . by gentlemen. Therefore, his sight grows dim when it is a matter of projecting the lives of those not of the gentry.

But Dickens saw life in his earliest youth from the just-above-starvation line and, though he must in the end have known all and

more of the riches and celebrity that Balzac craved, he never changed
the focus of his eyes. He never seems even to have attempted to do
so. If he draws a Lord and Lady Dedlock he draws them as if he had
never come closer to the peerage than to spy on them on their castle
terrace with a telescope. And the great quality of Dickens is not his
passion for redressing the lots of the needy and the oppressed—a loud-
mouthedness for which he is usually acclaimed, and which is usually
so loud that you never quite believe in its sincerity any more than
you quite believe in Mr. Micawber, although in drawing him Dickens
was drawing from his own father.

No, the great quality of Dickens is that his own class existed for
him till the day of his death, and that thus we have his own class as
not even Balzac gave us the atmosphere of the company in a Paris
pension of rather inferior order. That quality is so rare in literature
that one can perhaps only parallel it in the novels of the Spanish
picaresque writers. There, when you are with Lázarillo or Guzman,
you are actually in the company of rogues. They are the important
factor in life. So, when you are with Dickens, you are with a class that
normally does not bulk much on the great stage of life—yet for the
moment they are the only class that really matters.

Dickens as a man has always been for this writer far more of a
puzzle than Shakespeare. It seems to be impossible to know the real
motives of his existence. The writer in his youth lived amongst a set
of artists and writers to whom the name of Dickens was almost anathema, most of them, indeed, having known him personally well
enough to take ardent sides—usually against Dickens—in his family
troubles. They would descant without end on his "vulgarity." He apparently delighted in extravagant flowered waistcoats, extravagantly
liveried footmen, extravagantly got up barouches, tilburies, dogcarts.
But not his most bitter enemy accused him of anything that by the
most minute inquisition could be called social climbing. And the
writer's grandfather said that Dickens was a most extraordinary
"faller." He would sit at a party—say at Lady Cowper Temple's—
slumped down in an armchair as if he never meant to move again,

rather conspicuously alone, speaking to nobody and gazing over the heads of the other guests into remote distances . . . "as if he`owned the world," Ford Madox Brown used to say, employing for the sake of exactness a phrase that fifty years later was to become common American slang, "and as if nobody else literally existed for him." . . . And rather tired-looking, as if he really enjoyed the rest in the armchair. And with authoritative eyes. Like a great general.

No doubt at Lady Cowper Temple's no one really did exist for him.* Her ladyship was a woman of great charm, seriousness and interest for the artistic or intellectual sets of London of that day. If you were at all great—a Tennyson, a Carlyle, a Gladstone, a John Stuart Mill with Mrs. Taylor and all, a George Eliot with George Henry Lewes —it would be undeservedly to slight a charming and broadminded woman if you—with your Miss Hogarth, or Mrs. Taylor, or your Lewes, or whoever might be your *affiché*'d elective companion—refused to attend her parties. It was, in short, a duty for the artistic, the intellectual or the politically great of a Leftist complexion to help her to give good parties.

So that there was nothing of the *arriviste* about Dickens because from time to time he found himself in the house of that particular lady of title. Nor was it astonishing if, once there, he should think himself a great man or that the fact that he did so should appear in his distant gazing eyes. And no doubt the guests at those parties did not exist for him. In private and alone with him, George Stuart Mill or Gladstone or George Eliot might well have interested him. But in the party frame of mind, putting on the crowd psychology of an All London That Counted, they would be for him almost as nonexistent as was Stevenson for the ladies who passed him without a

---

* Robert Louis Stevenson once told the writer's father of his experiences when, dressed as a railway gangster, he sought adventure and copy in Seven Dials and other poor quarters. What, he said rather ruefully, most of all impressed him was that no well-off woman ever looked at him. He was accustomed—and apparently he thought himself to have rather a dashing air—to have ladies, when they passed him in the street, acknowledge his existence at least with a flicker of a down-turned eyelash or a slight movement aside to give him more room on the sidewalk. But when he was dressed as a workman, it was as if he had not existed at all. Such a lady's eyes would even rest on his face—which they would never have done had he appeared to be "quality;" but the glance would pass away lifeless as if over the surface of a brick wall or the face of a dog.

flicker of the eyelids. They must have been for him what a group of chattering Polish *pans* with their ladies must have seemed to Napoleon in Moscow.

And, indeed, there is no reason why he should not have thought himself one of the greatest men in his world or for all time, an epic writer of the scale of Homer; a reformer of the scale of Luther; a great man who had known the poverty of a Villon. . . . And from certain aspects it is very possible so to regard him. He overwrote; he exaggerated; he was without delicacy; his humor was the humor of a tough in a Putney barroom today. There was no literary fault that did not blaze out all over his pages all the time; the pre-Raphaelites were perfectly warranted in having their teeth set on edge by his vulgarities.

On the other hand, like Homer he gave us a world and his writings were epic because his illustrations of life came from the commonest popular objects. And it is impossible not to see that Anglo-Saxondom was a better double world because he had passed through it. You could not be in the company of Dickens and his books for twenty-seven years without becoming more benevolent, without developing some sort of sympathetic imagination as to your fellow men in this tragic world.

If before he existed you had gone down to some riverside hotel at Greenwich to eat whitebait at its best, and if the waiter who served you had had a be-pimpled scarlet nose, an alcoholic sniff, a greasy red toupee, disgustingly shabby dress clothes, a smear of fat across his shirt front, and if, as a crowning offence, he had paddled about you in enormous walking shoes that he told you had come a fortnight before from the body of a merchant shipping mate washed up on the gravel below the hotel terrace . . . well, you would have felt yourself justified if you had told the host of the place that you would never again dine there nor bring your friends, in spite of the exquisiteness of the whitebait and the beefsteak, oyster and kidney pudding, if he did not get rid of that fellow. But after you had read a good deal of Dickens that living caricature would have become a man to you; you would realize that a pair of large shoes from a washed-up corpse would, indeed, to that poor fellow with his flat feet and bunions, be such a gift from heaven that it would be ungrateful not to mention it with exulting thankfulness. And you would go on to speculate on the desperate poverty of a being to whom his feet were his life and his daily bread and who could yet not afford supportable footwear, so that his only light from heaven and hope must come from the feet of a drowned corpse. So your imagination, working à la Dickens, might provide the poor man with a tubercular daughter and other pathetic circumstances, and in the end you would substitute a half crown for the shilling you had intended for his tip and so secure for yourself a permanent seat at the table d'hôte of a kingdom where there are many mansions.

That type of influence on the world is not strictly literary, but it is not necessary for us to be too strait-laced. The influence of this great man was secured by his books and that influence was exercised enormously for the good of humanity.

The point that it is, nevertheless, necessary to make is that Dickens was in no sense a systematizer or a political or sociological theorist. It is true that he advocated or denounced with fire certain measures intended to benefit the poor and a great many measures of prison reform and the like. But they were specific measures that had been suggested to him by his passionate recoil from the effects of poverty or unimaginative tyranny on individuals. What he practiced was, therefore, not exactly individual charity but the rendering of individual cases of hardships so that they undoubtedly produced on large numbers of the public a similar effect of recoil from the harshness of its own day. He showed you an innocent small child being refused sufficient food by a Bumble and thousands of his readers wondered if there were not thousands of innocent children being victimized by Bumbles all over Anglo-Saxondom.

It is possible that could he have observed the effect of his books on his countrymen—could he have had any means of measuring it —he would have been spared the deep pessimism that inspired him at first to the writing of *Great Expectations* and then to the gradual laying down of his fine pen. But he had none and the spread of the black blight of industrialism across his country gave to the world an aspect of darker and darker cruelty. It should not be forgotten that as a boy he had known the mental and the lesser physical horrors of child labor, standing for eighteen hours of the day, the whole support of his shiftless family, washing labels off bottles whilst his little brain ran races with all the horrors of a monotonous world. So the sweeping across the world of conditions that set grown men to work in circumstances exactly similar to those of his martyred childhood impressed him with a deep sadness. And the phenomena of widespread individual ruin caused by the introduction of machines into hand-industries caused the number of individual cases of hardship that came before his eyes to seem innumerably increased. Thousands of dispossessed and homeless artisans—combmakers, bitmakers, cobblers, nailmakers and similar workmen—wandered half the country over, their starving children hanging to their hands, their feet dragging, their faces emaciated. So that to Dickens it well seemed that the greater part of what he had written had proved of no effect. Dickens was forty-eight when he wrote *Great Expectations* and fifty-eight when he died . . . and there is no man at all thinking who has lived to attain the age of fifty-eight in the last hundred years who has not passed ten years in thinking—and not without warrant—that world conditions have steadily and irresistibly deteriorated. For the greater part of his thinking life Dickens had lived in days when individual liberty and human contacts were the main note of the world. The tyrants in his day were the Bumbles and the Lords of Chancery and the great landlords; those who made life brighter were the brothers Cheeryble or the Mr. Jarndyces. He lived to the verge of an age when the tyrannies were "conditions" and the benefactors were wars on other parts of the globe that caused the commodities that you mass-produced for the time to rise in price. Thus *Great Expectations* is the muted book of a man for whom most of the savor has left life.

It is as if the long illness that prostrates Pip for the great part of the end of the book permeated the whole work from its very inception. And its inception is in a graveyard and its end takes place in an old property that had been laid waste so that a factory may occupy the place where the hero and heroine had played in childhood. And the hero is no hero and the heroine, no heroine; and their hands are not in the end united; and there is no immense fortune to be chanted over by a triumphant Wilkins Micawber; no conspiracy is unveiled; no great wrong righted. The book is, in fact, one of those works, rare in the English language, that can be read by a grown man without the feeling that he is condoning childishness and would be better employed over John Stuart Mill.

And it should never be forgotten that, hopelessly inartistic as he was in his other aspects, Dickens had one quality of his art in a very high degree—and that the almost sole essential quality. The style of Thackeray was so-so; he wrote correct English; did not use too many periphrases; was never offensively exuberant with his words; displayed sometimes a little vivacity; but was as a rule not offensively pedestrian. His style was, in fact, what grocers call "a good household article." As for Balzac . . .

He, like Dumas *père*, has been accused of writing like a cabdriver and the charge is true enough of the author of *The Three Musketeers*. But Balzac . . . heavens, he writes like a cab itself—an old cab, jolting, lumbering, vibrating to the trot of a most aged horse, so that you would swear it could never reach its earthly close. His sentences are too long to have any quality of drama or surprise; too short to achieve any resonance or cadence. They are never relieved by the short statements of fact that awaken somnolent readers; they are completely without any picturesqueness of rendering. They go on from the inception of a book to its close in a perpetual *train-train* . . . but exactly like the tinny rhythm of the hooves of an old cab horse on a hard macadam road. As thus—and remember that this is one of the most pathetic moments of a whole book:

La jeune femme, avertie par Louise que tout était prêt, parcourut lentement le jardinet, la chambre, le salon, y regarda tout pour la dernière fois. Puis elle fit à la cuisinière les recommanda-

tions les plus vives pour qu'elle veillât au bien-être de monsieur, en lui promettant de la récompenser si elle voulait être honnête. Enfin, elle monta dans la voiture pour se rendre chez sa mère, le coeur brisé, pleurant à faire peine à sa femme de chambre, et couvrant le petit Wenceslas de baisers avec une joie délirante qui trahissait encore bien de l'amour pour le père.

La baronne savait déjà par Lisbeth que le beau-père était pour beaucoup dans la faute de son gendre, elle ne fut pas surprise de voir arriver sa fille, elle l'approuva et consentit à la garder près d'elle. Adeline, en voyant que la douceur et le dévouement n'avaient jamais arrêté son Hector, pour qui son estime com-mençait á diminuer, trouva que sa fille avait raison de prendre une autre voie.

which the writer translates thus:

The young woman, having been informed by Louise that everything was ready, went slowly through the little garden, the bedroom, the sitting room and looked at everything for the last time. Then she gave explicit instructions to the cook to take care of the well-being of her master, promising to make it worth while if she proved trustworthy. At last she got into the carriage to go to her mother, her heart broken, crying enough to excite the pity of her *femme de chambre* and covering the little Wenceslas with kisses and a delirious joy which betrayed sufficiently the love she still had for his father.

The baroness knew already from Lisbeth that the father-in-law counted for much in the fault of his son-in-law, she was not surprised at the arrival of her daughter, she approved of it and agreed to keep her with her. Adeline, seeing that her sweetness and devotion had never checked her own Hector for whom her esteem was beginning to diminish, found that her daughter was right in taking the other way.

And it is all narration without thought of rendering anything at all. Consider as against it a not exceptional passage of Thackeray:

He was a fine, open-faced boy, with blue eyes and waving flaxen hair, sturdy in limb, but generous and soft in heart; fondly attaching himself to all who were good to him—to the pony—to Lord Southdown, who gave him the horse—(he used to blush and glow all over when he saw that kind young nobleman)—to the groom who had charge of the pony—to Molly, the cook, who crammed him with ghost stories at night, and with good things from the dinner—to Briggs, whom he plagued and laughed at— and to his father especially, whose attachment toward the lad was curious too to witness. Here, as he grew to be about eight years old, his attachments may be said to have ended. The beautiful mother-vision had faded away after a while. During the next two years she had scarcely spoken to the child. She disliked him. He had the measles and the whooping-cough. He bored her. One day when he was standing at the landing-place, having crept down from the upper regions, attracted by the sound of his mother's voice, who was singing to Lord Steyne, the drawing-room door opening suddenly, discovered the little spy, who but a moment before had been rapt in delight. He was listening to the music.

The long opening sentence is a little spineless; but it goes on conveying minute surprises and little images and one feels that the author has it pretty well under control. The little group of six short sentences are well contrasted and, as it were, designed. And the long sentence beginning "One day," has a real cadence that it imparts to all the preceding sentences of the paragraph. It is not Flaubert, of course, but it is a designed paragraph and has a certain unity. It has that effect of a ball, running over slightly ruddled surfaces, until it comes to the top of a slow long incline. There it seems to pause for a moment with the words "One day" and so runs smoothly and without haste or the surmountings of any obstacles, straight to its predestined close. It is, in short, the "type" paragraph of the modern writer. It might, as far as construction goes, have been written by Mr. Hemingway or Miss Virginia Woolf; the late Mr. Galsworthy or Conrad.

But consider how Dickens, with the real hand of the master stylist, gets in a landscape, some generations of dead, the note of a whole book and its masterly opening. These are the third, fourth and fifth paragraphs of *Great Expectations*:

> Ours was the marsh country, down by the river, within, as the river wound, twenty miles of the sea. My first distinct impression of the identity of things seems to me to have been gained on a memorable raw, damp afternoon toward evening. At such a time I found out for certain that this bleak place overgrown with nettles was the church-yard; and that Tobias Pirrip, late of this Parish, and also Georgiana, wife of the above, were dead and buried; and that Alexander, Bartholomew, Abraham, George, and Robert, infant children of the aforesaid, were also dead and buried; and that the dark, flat wilderness beyond the church-yard, intersected with dikes and mounds and gates, with scattered cattle feeding on it, was the marshes; and that the low leaden line beyond was the river; and that the distant savage lair from which the wind was rushing, was the sea; and that the small bundle of shivers growing afraid of it all and beginning to cry, was Pip.
>
> "Hold your noise!" cried a terrible voice, as a man started up from among the graves at the side of the church-porch. "Hold your noise, you little devil, or I'll cut your throat!"
>
> A fearful man, all in gray, with a great iron on his leg. A man with no hat, and broken shoes, and with an old rag tied round his head. A man who had been soaked in water and smothered in mud, and lamed by stones, and cut by flints, and stung by nettles, and torn by briers; who limped, and shivered, and glared, and growled; and whose teeth chattered in his head as he seized me by the chin.

We come then to Flaubert, Henry James and Joseph Conrad.

The objector will object that that is to leave out a tremendous number of writers. It is. It is to leave out Disraeli, Charles Reade, the Brontës, George Eliot, Wilkie Collins and whole hosts like James Payn, William Black, Blackmore, Mrs. Lynn Lynton, Mrs. Humphry

Ward, Edna Lyall who were all best sellers and seriously regarded in their day and are now, it is to be imagined, less than names. Or possibly the author of *Lorna Doone* is just remembered. It is to leave out in France too a number of considerable names: Dumas *fils*, Daudet, the brothers Goncourt, Zola, France, Loti, Bourget, Barrès. . . . It is like leaving out Paris for a Frenchman, for what would Paris of the last hundred years be without those names of men that were all day on every Parisian's tongue—the very background of that *tout Paris* that is the most glamorous of all social organizations? For this trait is the distinguishing line between the Mediterranean and the Anglo-Saxon tradition. In London—in New York, too—no doubt the names of Reade, the Brontës, George Eliot, Wilkie Collins would be just known in the drawing-rooms and still more the boudoirs of the wealthier classes, and outside them hardly at all. But on the Boulevards, Dumas *fils*, Daudet, the Goncourts, Loti, Bourget would be figures as familiar to every soul as the Emperor, his consort, Morny, MacMahon, Garibaldi, or the Prince of Wales. Their latest *bons mots* or their latest ill-natured speeches would be on the lips of every concierge and of every fiacre driver before they were a day old . . . as would the latest developments of the affair of Flaubert and La Muse. So that obviously we cannot leave them out integrally—nor all the poets—for to leave out that rustling side of Paris life would be to leave out a whole side of the history of literature.

We have, as we have said, to treat them as a movement, not as individuals to whom we can devote even the tiny monographs that we have been giving to several authors hitherto. For the sword wears out the sheath and it is very problematic whether we—this writer and the reader—could stand any more projections of literary figures beyond the three principals that we have already mentioned. It is also a matter of scale. It would be wanting in humor to devote, in a work that has been able to give no more than a page or two to Cervantes, much more than a line or so—picturesque as Daudet was—to the inventor of *Tartarin de Tarascon*.

And again, a fact that sharply divides Anglo-Saxondom from almost any of the other European civilizations, the other nations all have literatures; we have only some great—some very great—books. When you talk of Daudet, the Goncourts, Flaubert, Maupassant, Turgenev, France, Bourget, Barrès, Henri de Regnier, you are talking of what we may call a box where sweets compacted lie—they had contacts physical and mental—all those men. They dined together *chez Brébant*; they had their *soirées de Medan*; and not only were their meetings national events but when they sat at dinner they shouted continually about technique—about style, cadences, progressions of effect, the aloofness of the author, the handling of conversation in novels, their architecture, their scale. . . . And at other humbler restaurants —*quaeque ipse miserrima*—notably at the sea-food grill at the corner of the rue Monsieur le Prince and the Boulevard Saint Michel, there met the poets Mallarmé, Hérédia, Verlaine, Rimbaud, Verhaeren, Maeterlinck . . . even occasionally Edmond Rostand.

In Anglo-Saxondom—since the great centuries—we have almost never had literatures to write home about. You had in America the Concord group—which was in effect an English provincial ethical debating society with almost no literary products save for *Little Women* and *Walden*. Or for a short lustre you had in London the *Yellow Book* Group . . . Harland, Beardsley, Le Gallienne, Beerbohm, Davidson, Moore, Dowson, Stephen Phillips, poor little Crackenthorpe who was drowned in the Seine, with in the air, as it were around them, Henry James, Conrad, the infant H. G. Wells, the infant who was then this writer, and Gissing and Hale White and that great figure Dorothy Richardson, and more remotely Meredith, Hardy and the still young Kipling. Those were times such as London had never seen since the Mermaid Tavern closed its doors for the last time on the retreating form of Webster. They died of the trial of Oscar Wilde and were swept off the carpet for good by the South African war.

They had a short, once more Parisio-Anglo-American revival in London in the 13's and 14's under the aegis and the powerful impulsion of Mr. Ezra Pound . . . and Marinetti. Then the streets round Campden Hill rustled with all the accents of all the forty-eight states of the North American Union and H. D., and Robert Frost, and Mr. T. S. Flint, and Katherine Mansfield, and (Percy) Wyndham Lewis, and Norman Douglas and how many others!—held high the banners of vorticism, imagism, futurism, and paraded those respectable streets in trousers of green billiard cloth and Japanese foulards. So that for the instant it looked as if the conquest of London were, indeed, at hand. But August 1914 blew all that out of existence, except for some few representatives of vorticism who were blown to West Eighth Street, New York. The sacred spark of that divine fire was, indeed, kept just alive on that downtown street, aided by blasts from the breath of Mr. Pound who had to leave London because the Metropolitan Police liked Milton and Mr. Pound did not. That is to say that Mr. Lascelles Abercrombie, having written in the *Times Literary Supplement* a front-page eulogy of the author of *Lycidas*, Mr. Pound very properly challenged Mr. Abercrombie to fight a duel with him in Hyde Park. And to challenge anyone in London to fight a duel is to commit an offence carrying with it capital punishment.

So the Divine Fire, kept alive in its Eighth Street tinder—the Flaubert-Maupassant-Rimbaud-Mallarmé-James-Conrad-impressionist fire—burst out, once more in Paris, once more Anglo-Americanly and once more under the aegis of Mr. Pound who had made that city his home. About him grouped themselves, with a quite considerable adhesiveness, Mr. Joyce, Miss Stein, Mr. Ernest Hemingway, Mr. Glenway Westcott, Mr. E. E. Cummings and a whole Middle Western American group, as a rule from the University of Chicago, an educational institution differing from all the other universities of Europe and America in that it really has fostered imaginative writing and at least one movement*—that of the Middle Western novelists and poets.

---

* This writer would like to make the following statistical note. In 1924 he started in Paris a review that was open to contributors from all over the world and in all European languages. Of the contributions that he received, at least eighty per cent came from the American Middle West, and these contributions were astonishingly level. The writer selected from amongst them for publication Mr. Ernest Hemingway, Mr. Glenway Westcott, Mr. Carlos Drake, Mr. D. H. Jowett and some others. But the actual level of a great number of the contributions that he did not print was astonishingly near that of those that he published, and a very large percentage of them would have been publishable by any review in the world. One may add that that writing current is by no means exhausted at the present day.

That movement was remarkable not solely for the excellence of its products but because it assumed almost the aspect of a folk literature, so nearly without exception did the younger generation of the lonely farmhouses and millions of acres turn its attention to writing in the early twenties of this century. It deserves this note because it is, as far as this writer is concerned, almost the only instance of a similar tendency anywhere discoverable in modern literary history . . . and because, with its later Southern extension, it has kept alive almost the last traces of a conscious literary art in a world everywhere so driven to distraction that the pen as a weapon has grown almost as obsolete as the stone arrowhead. So, indeed, we stand today with realism that once agitated a world, rearing its head, alone and breathing the last words of the Flaubertian message somewhere on the course of the Mississippi.

It is probable that those chief ornaments of Southern writing, Misses Elizabeth Madox Roberts, Katherine Anne Porter and Caroline Gordon would raise their voices in the most emphatic Dixie protests should one declare that the blood of the sage of Croisset flowed in their F.F.V. veins—just as the author of the *Tentation de St. Antoine* would probably declare himself, if ravished, also astonished at the thought of having had such descendants. It has, indeed, been one of the most singular features of this writer's long career of literary contacts to observe with what vituperative animation almost every author will deny his absolutely obvious origins, declaring with accompanying blasphemies that he has never read a word of, say, Flaubert or Conrad or Henry James. Thus, the late Stephen Crane once with extreme violence declared to this writer that he had never, either in translation or in the original, read a word of any damn French writer of the realistic school. It is true that a little later he declared that he had been moved to write the *Red Badge of Courage* by finding that Zola's *La Débacle*—which as a detail, in answer to some comment of this writer on the style of Zola, he said that he had read in French, along with most of Maupassant and at least the *Education Sentimentale* of Flaubert—he had found then that *La Débacle* was such a rotten projection of war that he had determined—at the age of twenty and never having been nearer a battlefield than the city of Elizabeth, New Jersey—to show the world what war really was like. He was the first really American novelist.

It will be useful, by way of clearing up the literary scene, to strike here the note of the singular penetration of the American Eastern states by the Flaubert-Turgenev-Jamesian literary motif. It is quite astonishing to take up the—then—seriously literary monthly reviews, of the late eighties and nineties, like *Harper's, Scribner's* or *The Atlantic Monthly* and to observe what a great extent of their space is given up to discussion of the "techniques" of, precisely, the latest works of those three writers. Emerson, Holmes, Alcott and even Thoreau seem by then to have been almost forgotten. And it is as if the Eastern states, losing that intimately English contact, felt nevertheless the necessity for some European cultural connection and found it with enthusiasm in that Russo-French-Paris-American conjunction. And having, as they Americanly must, an immense curiosity to know how all sorts of wheels go round, and finding, as they intelligently and brightly did, something completely different in literary tempo and texture from the slipshod English work of the type of George Eliot's that had hitherto formed their chief literary pabulum, every delicately cultured young lady from the Hub itself to the Baltimore Monument . . . And isn't it astonishing how, at the mere mention of the Master's—the American not the French one's—name, one's style at once takes on bewildering involutions! . . . So that we had better perhaps drop that sentence and begin again.

From all this, it results then that the impressionist school had its place prepared for it on the Western side of the Atlantic in at least the Western republic of taste—the reading classes. So that it is not astonishing that the first American novelist should before twenty have read quite a sufficiency of impressionist literature to make his style and his approach to his subject astonishingly Gallo-impressionist. Or that when, half a century later, a specifically realist-impressionist literature should swim to the surface in the great plains it should find almost immediately an enthusiastic home on Fifth Avenue and wherever the influence of Fifth Avenue permeates.

And that last speculation brings us to something of importance. It would not be astonishing that the three lights of Southern letters whom we lately mentioned should patriotically declare that they had never heard of a single French writer. And it might well be true, for the engrossments of life in the Old South are manifold and world-excluding. But there is a literary factor that we writers do—and shouldn't ever—forget. Behind all literary movements and techniques stands the reading public, and if we do not write to the taste of the intelligent reading public not only shall we not last but we shall know no public existence.

Between us and the reading public are the filters of two formidable trades, those of the publisher and those of the bookseller whose knowledge of the tastes of the reading public is purely empirical. They are, nevertheless, our arbiters of life and not infrequently of death. Thus, never in his career has this writer been without the distressing knowledge that there exists at least one—and not infrequently two or three—masterpiece or work of real imagination and authenticity that has been unable to get past that brazen double wall. Not infrequently —or, indeed, usually—this has later become a matter of bitter regret to the practitioners who turned those works down. That, as has been said, has always been the case, in England, France and the United States; it is peculiarly the case today and so it will be till this writer's career closes, and for other lovers of writing, forever into the hereafter.

It is peculiarly the case today because the novel is dying—and very properly—in face of the romance of crime. The fact is that the reading public is more intelligent—and more useful to literature—than is usually acknowledged by the practitioners of the arts. It is the public that from the beginning has made new art forms triumph—and it has done it in the face of the violent opposition of the critics, professors, clergy, publishers and dilettante cognoscenti and the serious and comic papers. It knows what it wants. It upheld Shakespeare and his fellows against the classicists of the *Ferrex and Porrex* school; the classicists of the eighteenth century when the freer art forms of the sixteenth and seventeenth had lost their impetus; the romanticists; and, in due course, the realist-naturalist-impressionists. Tomorrow we may well see a neo-romantic school sweep the world—but it will be at the public desire.

Today's craving for the romance of crime is perfectly healthy, proper and aesthetically justifiable. If you will take up a good—and that means a popular—detective story you will see that its construction is admirable; its style fluid; it will of necessity employ the modern aesthetic device called the "time shift," which the established critics of the more pompous journals still find esoteric. And it gives information as to the workings of life that is certainly of value—much as the historic romance in its heyday supplied the public with all the information as to history that ninety per cent of us ever had.

On the intellectual side, it is perhaps to seek, and its values of life are apt to be very conventionally estimated. That is because the superior intelligences of the day do not usually—and they are quite wrong—apply themselves to the mystery story. Yet the great novels of the world, whether of the romantic, the classical or the realistic modern schools, have all—and this is no paradox—been mystery stories. *Vanity Fair* is a mystery story, worked from the inside instead of from the out. So is *Madame Bovary*; so is Conrad's *The Secret Agent*; so, for the matter of that, is *Tom Jones* with its working up to the triumphant exposure of young Mr. Blifil; so is *The Vicar of Wakefield*; so, substituting psychological for material values, is almost every novel of Henry James.

It is true that the writer of the greater fiction works as a rule from the inside—with the criminal—instead of exteriorly with the detector of crime. That is because, keeping company with the criminal, you have a better opportunity for following the psychological involutions of that character, and to the reflecting writer the psychological developments of his characters, or his affairs, is his reason for writing. Just imagine *Madame Bovary* worked from the outside, a psychologically acute investigator of crime being called to Emma Bovary's bedside the moment after her death and having to unroll, from all the data given by the author, the history of poor Emma's gradual deterioration from her gentle but indomitable romanticism, through sordid intrigues and peculations to her inevitable suicide. What a *roman policier* that would be!

And let that Gallicism serve to remind us that in France the considerable psychological romancers have already turned their attention to the esoteric psychology of crime. The most distinguished of the younger Gallic *romanciers* is M. Georges Bernanos—a writer most admirable in his construction, his writing, his progression of effect and the poetry of his outline. And his *Sous le Soleil de Satan* is an immense theological argument around a perfectly bloodthirsty murder. It passes, nevertheless, for a great product of fictional imagination. Or consider the *Pendu de St. Phollien* or the *Ombres Chinoises* of M. Georges Simenon, the one, precisely, a solution of a perfectly psychological murder mystery in which the whole story turns on the effects of a hyper-romantic econovo-political crowd brainstorm on an impoverished group of intellectuals attached to a provincial university; the other being an analysis of an impulsion towards crime of a French bureaucratic household under the impulsion of the insupportable poverty that is the lot of so many French minor officials. It is Dostoievsky . . . and Dostoievsky, *corsé,* constructed, economized and filled with the poetry of pity. . . .

All this brings us again to the main consideration with which we set out in this section of this chapter. Let us use the image of a pond with dimpling waves on its surface. The air above those wavelets receives exactly their reversed form—as exactly as wax receives the impression of a seal. It would, nevertheless without doubt, violently deny that it was in any way influenced by anything so petty as the wavelets on a pool. This may illustrate the fact that writers obviously influenced by other writers will deny that they ever read or heard of those fellows. In this case the public is the pool. Having become accustomed to writing of a certain efficiency through reading the works of writer A, it will refuse to read the works of writer B unless they are projected with at least as much skill as that of writer A. We shall provide shortly, as being typical impressionism, an imaginary paragraph. It would be impossible to imagine that once they have become used to that quick and picturesque method of presentation—which you will find today imitated in all the popular magazines of at least the United States—the public would wish to return to the comments, digressions and narrative style of the paragraph that we shall provide as being non-impressionism. Therefore, the aspiring writer, to have any chance of public hearing, must adapt himself to using the latter method. He may not arrive at this by the study of Flaubert, James, Conrad, Turgenev or the Goncourts. It may be absolute truth that he has never even heard of those fellows, but he has got either naturally to write like them or to have been impressed by writing similar to those, of other writers. And the further that by native genius or by the study of the works of his colleagues he can carry the manner, the better he will succeed. We might say that the most prominent conscious Anglo-Saxon writers on either side of the Atlantic today are Mr. Hemingway and Miss Virginia Woolf. We don't happen to have any means of knowing whether either of these writers has much studied the work of their impressionist predecessors but we can assert with the greatest confidence that had their books not been in tone with those of the great writers who preceded them they would not only not now occupy their enviable positions, but in all probability they would have found no one ready even to publish them. The process, indeed, is one of natural selection; the air above the pond being the world writers, and the pond, the world where without something lively to read, *l'on s'ennuie*.

Flaubert was born in 1821 in Normandy, so that his intellectual awakenings were to Louis-Philippism and its decline, and his intellectual prime passed to the tune of the rise and fall of Louis Napoleon. The point is important because so much of his intellectual activities went to revolting against those differing but equally imbecile Louis-isms. He fought primarily against accepted ideas and the vested interests of the intellect, and in no period of the world has any government, without being one of physical brutality, exercised such an insupportable, such a stifling tyranny as that of those two bourgeois monarchies. Tyrannies of tsars may have been even more obscurantist in motive—but no tyrant had such brilliant figures to attempt to stifle, the intellectual era of Napoleon III having been one of the most brilliant and certainly the most crucial that the civilized world has ever seen.

James, on the other hand, was born in the Washington Square district of New York in 1843. The son of an, as it were, unorthodox pope of an unusually refining religion, his father was the intellectual-hospitable center of New York cosmopolitanism at a date when tides of European intellectual celebrities flowed almost unparalleledly through that city. Thus, Mr. James used to say that in his babyhood and young youth he must have sat on the knees of more of the intellectually great than in his late manhood he could possibly believe to have existed. At the same time the Concord school was spreading the New England conscience in an unequalled unparalleled tide all down the Eastern seaboard and even, under the insufferable Teuto-reactionism of Thomas Carlyle, over other Easts. And nowhere did that tide find a deeper porthole than in the Greenwich Village household of Henry James, Senior, and nowhere did the Conscience find more impressionable ground to impress than in the heart of the Junior who became for many of us the Master beyond all masters. As a result, his young intellectual tree took a slant in the direction of a taste for the society of the great, of an absolute craving for material delicacy, and a passion for disentangling psychological convolutions such as can never have beset any other writer. In addition—and this is a tremendously strong note —he inherited from his father a disposition so profoundly religious that at times he dreaded for his own mental stability and feared to approach at all whole fields of metaphysical speculations.

Conrad, on the other hand, was before anything, personally, a constructive—but not a Utopian—politician. He constructed whole republics in his books; gave fantastic politico-cynical bodies politic to the mightiest cities in the world; and in what is for this writer the greatest of his books, *Under Western Eyes,* he analyzed the nihilist opposition to the tsarist régime of his own day in a manner which, impassioned monarchist though he was, cast almost unequalled disdain on the whole Imperial system.

That is not singular when you consider that he was born in Poland in 1856 and that the earliest sight his eyes could remember was of a Siberian prison yard in which Cossack guards rode slowly up and down through the falling snow amongst women and children, in furs, in woollens, in rags or half nude—the wives and widows and orphans

of the survivors of the leaders or of the rank and file of the Polish
Revolution of 1863.

Misfortune, in the shape of exile and a romantic temperament, took
him to sea and did not much let up when his destiny dictated that he
should pass the greater part of his maturity as a man of letters in England. It would, indeed, be ingratitude on the part of his advocates to
deny that England received him with hospitality and, towards the end,
with comprehension and sympathy for his more obvious literary ex-
cellences. For he was the most consummate, the most engrossed, the
most practical, the most common-sensible and the most absolutely
passionate man-of-action become conscious man-of-letters that this
writer has ever known, read of or conceived of. You might come upon
him, almost inarticulate, plunged in those tremendous fits of Slav-
Oriental despair that at times deprived him even of the power of
motion. And you might mention some minute—or some large—problem of literary technique. He would spring up from his deep armchair, the color would return to his face, he would gesticulate energetically to return the blood to the extremities of his limbs and with
his passionate Marseilles-accented intimate jargon plunge straight into
the problem of finding the *mot juste* for the frame of mind of a woman
whose foreign husband has become suddenly insane and is incapable
of speaking her language any more. Or he would spring from another
state of gloom of a different origin and, having run once or twice up
and down the room, would exclaim: "Look here, Fordie; look here ma
dear falla: we've got to settle that form for the author-as-narrator-
without-comment right away. Right now. Here. *Pronto et plus vite
que ça. Car tu sais aussi bien que moi que si nous n'y arriverions nous
reterions pour tout jamais dans le ventre insondable de nos sacrées
misères. . . ."*

These preoccupations with the "how" of literature which to the
average Anglo-Saxon seem so puerile, have nevertheless puzzled the
minds of grave persons of all sorts of races and climes for many, many

centuries. Thus, the following passage was written almost exactly a thousand years ago off the eastward coast of the Cathay of Confucius and Lao-Tsze:

"I have lately," said Genji,* "sometimes stopped and listened to one of our young people reading out loud to her companions and have been amazed at the advances which this art of fiction is now making. How do you suppose that our new writers come by this talent? It used to be thought that the authors of successful romances were merely particularly untruthful people whose imaginations had been stimulated by constantly inventing plausible lies. But that is clearly unfair. . . ." "Perhaps," she said, "only people who are themselves much occupied in practicing deception have the habit of thus dipping below the surface. I can assure you that, for my part, when I read a story, I always accept it as an account of something that has really and actually happened."

So saying she pushed away from her the book which she had been copying. Genji continued: "So you see, as a matter of fact, I think far better of this art than I have led you to suppose. Even its practical value is immense. Without it what should we know of how people lived in the past, from the Age of the Gods down to the present day? For history-books such as the Chronicles of Japan show us only one small corner of life; whereas these diaries and romances which I see piled around you contain, I am sure, the most minute information about all sorts of people's private affairs. . . ." He smiled, and went on: "But I have a theory of my own about what this art of the novel is, and how it came into being. To begin with, it does not simply consist in the author's telling a story about the adventures of some other person. On the contrary, it happens because the storyteller's own experience of men and things, whether for good or ill—not only what he has passed through himself, but even events which he has only witnessed or been told of—has moved him to an emotion so passionate that he can no longer keep it shut up in his heart. Again and again

* _The Tale of Genji_, by the Lady Murasaki, translated from the Japanese by Arthur Waley. Page 501. (2 vols., the Houghton Mifflin Co.)

something in his own life or in that around him will seem to the writer so important that he cannot bear to let it pass into oblivion. There must never come a time, he feels, when men do not know about it. That is my view of how this art arose.

"Clearly then, it is no part of the storyteller's craft to describe only what is good or beautiful. Sometimes, of course, virtue will be his theme, and he may then make such play with it as he will. But he is just as likely to have been struck by numerous examples of vice and folly in the world around him, and about them he has exactly the same feelings as about the pre-eminently good deeds which he encounters: they are important and must all be garnered in. Thus anything whatsoever may become the subject of a novel, provided only that it happens in this mundane life and not in some fairyland beyond our human ken."

The Lady Murasaki—for no doubt that authoress is really expressing her own doubts when she makes her Prince Genji speak—the Lady Murasaki was obviously preoccupied with technical problems of literature, for in the six volumes of her immense and famous romance such questions appear very frequently—mostly in the form of queries as to verse writing.

Japan stood, in that day, *vis à vis* China, much as Anglo-Saxondom stood towards France in the days when Conrad, in England, was worrying his head over the problem of the formal convention of the novel. China was an immensely old, intellectual civilization to which was attached a relatively new, almost entirely materialistic race who felt, nevertheless, some craving for literary aesthetics, and, in some instances, an ambition to carry literary form a stage farther than it had been carried in the spiritual motherland.

The problem of realism versus whatever the other thing is had been solved for France on the day when Flaubert sat on the bench of a criminal and was acquitted. Official France—the government of Louis Napoleon—had decided to prosecute him for having written *Madame Bovary* not so much because they considered the book lecherous as because it was new in its approach to life. A government consisting of a semi-Corsican adventurer, some exceedingly dissipated dukes, some priests and some nearly imbecile cavalry officers almost automatically considered that a new literary form must be subversive to a status quo which they found agreeable and even essential to their existences. But a court consisting of officials of their own appointing having decided that there was nothing subversive in tendency in the adventures of poor Emma, official France turned its attention to other matters. The public, never having had any doubts in the matter, went on reading the book with complacent avidity and Flaubert, the Goncourts, Maupassant, *ce pauvre Théo* and Turgenev, and later the infant Henry James went on discussing literary problems with ferocity. They were joined later by Zola and his supporters, who introduced the newer note of naturalism but remained on amicable terms with the realists. . . . This writer once picked up on the Quai Voltaire a copy of *Pot Bouille* which is inscribed: *"Emile Zola . . . à Gustave Flaubert, qui est bon bougre."*

In effect, realism is a frame of mind reinforced by the new literary technique of impressionism, with an increased attention to the quality of words, which gave to its products a singular vividness. The frame of mind of realism was founded on a basis of relatively gentle cynicism or, as in the case of Flaubert, of disillusionment. For, essentially, Flaubert was an optimist—a believer in perfectibility who was disappointed that humanity, with all the opportunities it had had, had never got any farther on the road to sanity, reasonable behavior and altruism. But it was possible to belong to his school without being cynical at all: thus the young James regarded the world with eyes merely of wonder; Gautier with rather joyful curiosity; Turgenev with a tremendous benevolence together with a really constructive passion for bettering Russia. Thus the real *trait-d'union* between all these authors and modernity in general was the technical one which this writer prefers to call Impressionism.

At various times this writer has been called by authoritative but too sanguine critics the "last of the pre-Raphaelites," which is rather absurd, and "the father of impressionism," a term applied to him only yesterday by a distinguished speaker on a public literary occasion in the United States. It is at once too much honor and very unjust to other writers. It would be just feasible, considering that we did a little enlarge the technical scope of the movement, to say that Conrad, this writer aiding him, introduced impressionism to Anglo-Saxondom. But it would be much more just—as witness the contributions of Ernest Dowson in particular, and George Moore and several other writers to the *Yellow Book* which dominated literary Anglo-Saxondom from 1894 to 1897—to say that impressionism, coming from Paris, struck London in a sort of literary folk-wave in the early nineties.

This writer published his first, quite unnoticed, novel in 1893, and as far as it faintly went it was a piece of impressionism. Conrad published his first novel—*Almayer's Folly*—in England in 1895. But the book was begun—and the coincidence is one of the most curious in literary history—on the margins and end papers of *Madame Bovary* whilst his ship was moored to the dockside in Rouen harbor, and the portholes of his cabin there gave a view of the house which Flaubert described as being the meeting place of Emma Bovary and Rodolphe. That would be in 1893. In that year W. D. Howells published in New York his *Imperative Duty* and Henry James was beginning his *Princess Casamassima*, which may be described as the last of his novels to have a distinctly cosmopolitan and Latin flavor. It was not published till 1896 and in certain moods Mr. James used to attribute the delay to the fact that he was distracted by the claims made on him by Henry Harland for assistance in editing the *Yellow Book*. Harland himself, another Paris American, was like Dowson an impressionistic novelist of great and delicate skill, both being now much too much forgotten. In *Yellow Book* days he was extremely young, physically delicate and beardedly nervous. In moments of agitation he would break like Conrad into rather passionate and gesticulatory French. But it is only fair to say that, in 1873, George Moore published a volume of poems called *Flowers of Passion*, which was eminently Baudelairean in inspiration, and in 1883 and 1885, respectively, *A Modern Lover* and *A Mummer's Wife*. So that if anyone has to be called father of Anglo-Saxon impressionism it should be he.

The main and perhaps most passionate tenet of impressionism was the suppression of the author from the pages of his books. He must not comment; he must not narrate; he must present his impressions of his imaginary affairs as if he had been present at them. Thus, the following—imaginary—passage from *Vanity Fair* would not be impressionism.

> Disgusting as we may find it, on crossing to the window our heroine—whom the reader must acknowledge to be indeed a gallant little person—perceived Captain Crawley and the Marquis of Steyne engaged in a drunken boxing bout. . . . But such things must be when to the moral deterioration of illicit sex passion is added the infuriating spur of undue indulgence in alcoholic beverages.

But it would have been impressionism had the author written:

> In the street the empurpled leg-of-mutton fist of a scarlet heavy dragoon impinged on the gleaming false teeth of a reeling bald-headed senior. Becky screamed as a torrent of dark purple burst from the marquis' lips to dribble down his lavender silk waistcoat. That ended, as she spasmodically recognized, her life of opulence. The dragoon, an unmoving streak of scarlet, lay in the gutter, one arm extended above his unshako'd locks.

That would be an impressionist paragraph. It will be noted that here the author is invisible and almost unnoticeable and that his attempt has been, above all, to make you see. It is presented rather than narrated because all that you get are the spectacle of the affair and the psychological reaction of one of the characters. It is unnecessary to narrate the fact that Becky, who had previously been reclining on a silken divan, got up, went to the window, threw up the blind and, looking out, saw the affair we have presented. . . . The reader, being a person of normal common sense, will know that she could not have seen the blood dribbling from the marquis' jaws unless she had gone through all those processes, and to record them would lengthen the passage and render the presentation of the affair much more dull.

Similarly, moral-drawing comment would take away from the vividness and entirely destroy the verisimilitude of the scene. The moral drawing is all done with the words "That ended . . . her life of opulence." For, even did the reader know nothing of the affair till that moment, he would be astonishing for naïveté if he did not realize that a lady, seeing two intimate friends indulging in fisticuffs under her window and making the mental comment that that meant a future shortage of money—that such a lady must be the mistress of at least one of the intoxicated contestants, and that one the marquis, because he would probably be the wealthier of the two. And the reader can be left to draw the extremely obvious moral that an impecunious adventuress—for she must be impecunious or she would not anticipate ruin and she must be an adventuress or she would not have been kept by a wealthy member of the British aristocracy—that, then, an adventuress who attached herself to a marquis given to overindulgence in alcohol, whilst having a husband—for no officer of His Majesty's Fourteenth Cavalry would indulge in the public street in fisticuffs with anyone at all unless he had been a deceived husband—whilst having, then, a husband with the same failing . . . that, considering all these things, that adventuress must be guilty . . . of imprudence, or of hideous moral turpitude, according to the temperament of the reader.

Thus, the drawing of a moral is unnecessary; and the introduction of himself by the author in order to draw the moral would have the effect of completely destroying the reality of the scene for the reader. The reader would say to himself: "Hullo. I really thought this was something real I was looking at. But here's that wearying old W. M. T. bucking in, broken nose and all. . . . So that it's really only a silly novel."

The paragraph—the reader will be good enough to examine it again —is for two reasons not very good impressionism. Impressionism demanded of its writers not only a vivid style but one sort or another of agreeable and flowing cadence. Thus, that paragraph insistently demands for its completion a minute statement, three or at most four syllables long, to give it unity and to settle finally its significance.

Thus, after "unshako'd locks," the writer should have added something like: "The die was cast."

The paragraph is also bad, from the point of view of style, because it is verbally overvivid. Flaubert and all his horde spent half their lives in the pursuit of the *mot juste*—and the other half in making sure that the word chosen was not too *juste*. A too startling epithet, however vivid, or a simile, however just, is a capital defect because the first province of a style is to be unnoticeable. When Stevenson—who spent an immense amount of his time in finding too just words, and jewels five words long that on the stretched forefinger of Old Time sparkle forever—when Stevenson, then, wrote the famous imagery: "With interjected finger he delayed the action of the timepiece," meaning merely that his character put back the clock, he was woefully delaying the action of his story . . . and giving at once the impression of the intrusion of the author that the impressionist so carefully avoided.

When Flaubert wrote one of the most perfect passages of prose that was ever written, presenting with an extraordinary conciseness and vividness the life of a mediaeval knight from his beginnings to high command . . . as thus:

> *Il s'engagea dans une troupe d'aventuriers qui passaient.*
>
> *Il connut la faim, la soif, les fièvres et la vermine. Il s'accoutuma au fracas des mêlées, à l'aspect des moribonds. Le vent tanna sa peau. Ses membres se durcirent par le contact des armures; et comme il était très-fort, courageux, tempérant, avisé, il obtint sans peine le commandement d'une compagnie.*
>
> *Au début des batailles, il enlevait ses soldats d'un grand geste de son épée. Avec une corde à noeuds, il grimpait aux murs des citadelles, la nuit, balancé par l'ouragan pendant que les flammèches du feu grégeois se collaient à sa cuirasse, et que la résine bouillante et le plomb fondu ruisselaient des créneaux. Souvent le heurt d'une pierre fracassa son bouclier. Des ponts trop chargés d'hommes croulèrent sous lui. En tournant sa masse d'armes, il se débarrassa de quatorze cavaliers. Il défit, en champ clos, tous ceux qui se proposèrent. Plus de vingt fois, on le crut mort.*

which the writer renders as:

> He enlisted in a band of adventurers who were going by. He made acquaintance with hunger, thirst, fevers and vermin. He grew accustomed to the tumults of pitched battles, to the look on the faces of the dying. The wind tanned his skin. His limbs became hardened by contact with armor and, since he was very strong, courageous, temperate and sagacious, he had no difficulty in obtaining the command of a company.
>
> At the beginning of battles he led his soldiers on with a great sweep of his sword. Upon a knotted cord he ascended the walls of citadels, at night, swung about by hurricanes whilst flaming clots of Greek Fire attached themselves to his cuirasse and boiling resin and melted lead fell in showers from the crenellations. Often the impact of a rock broke his buckler. Bridges too weighted with men crumbled beneath him. With one swing of his mace he got away from fourteen knights. He challenged in the lists everyone who offered. He was left for dead more than a score of times.

the language is so soft, the key so low that it is as if a flight of the feathers of eiderdown passed across your consciousness, leaving you forever that sight of the citadels, the night, the hurricane and the young soldier clinging to the rope whilst the blazing clots of Greek Fire streaked down from the crenellations above him.

Or when Conrad, as this writer has elsewhere pointed out, begins a story with this passage:

> This could have happened nowhere but in England where men and sea interpenetrate, so to speak—the sea entering into the life of most men and the men knowing something or everything about the sea . . .

and thus ends it:

> "We have lost the first of the ebb," said the Director suddenly. I raised my head. The offing was barred by a black bank of clouds

and the tranquil waterway, leading to the uttermost ends of the earth, flowed sombre under an overcast sky—seemed to lead into the heart of an immense darkness.

the language is again so low-keyed, so of the vernacular, so just, so fluid that when you read you have again no sense of reading. The tempo is set and the whole contemplative tone of the story is at once set sounding by the first words of the first paragraph. And before you have been reading a few minutes it is as if great moods swept across your consciousness, and you are left again with the image of a great estuary, a great distant river, an immense continent with a solitary and imbecile battleship emptying shells into it . . . and the prophecy of a great darkness that has since descended on the minds of the world. For, indeed, Conrad might have claimed, like Flaubert, that if humanity had really read *Heart of Darkness*, we might very well have been spared the horrors of our mondial débâcle.

It would be to become too technical in a work of this description to go farther into the developments of the impressionist technique effected by Conrad. They were founded on nothing but common sense— and surely the reader must have noticed that the technical rules of the earlier impressionists were founded on nothing but the common sense observation of effects of writing on the reasonably intelligent reader. . . . They were founded on common sense, then, and they have been so generally accepted, knowingly or unknowingly, by the successors of those great men, that they are no longer, as it were, anything to write home about. Even the "time shift" device which in the early days of the century drove the then established critics to utter paeans of fury . . . even the time shift has been perforce adopted by every writer who has since sat down to concoct a detective story. He cannot avoid it. He has to begin with a murder; the intelligent detective on arriving has at once to begin going back into the history of the corpse. The story returns into the present tense in order that the detective may tell what he has learned of the past of the corpse to a number of characters who plunge back out of that present into the pasts of a half-dozen suspects. They, in turn, return to the present to report—and in order that the story may be carried forward. And so it goes on until, in the end, a dazzling ray from the past illuminates not only the past murder with which the story began, but every subsequent episode of the story proper—of a past which was once the present. . . . But if you said that that was the mental technique of a long short story of the impressionist Guy de Maupassant or of the Russo-impressionist-realist Tchekov, you would be told that all that "technique" was esoteric, affected, arbitrary.

The importance of impressionism lies in the fact that it provided the first "technique" that was within the reach of everybody, and relied on no arbitrary rules. It was fought into existence in the tumultuous discussions of the men we have lately principally mentioned, and it met with almost no opposition, what opposition was aroused being devoted to naturalism, a technique that was again rather a matter of a frame of mind, than any literary rules. Naturalists were realists whose temperaments, rather than any deep implanted despair of humanity, impelled them to illustrate their subjects with only the gloomiest, as well as—where practicable—the most repellent actions and materials that their notebooks allowed them to present. The process was carried out with a tenacity that always seemed to the present writer to imply a certain underlying zest; indeed, to the present writer the conversation of M. Zola during his exile in London over the Affaire Dreyfus almost seemed to imply a deep-seated sense of humor. Thus, having an appointment to meet the author of *Pot Bouille* in Hyde Park, the writer found him seated on a park bench almost in tears over the quantity of hairpins that with the end of his cane he was counting on the ground beneath his nose. This seemed to M. Zola to imply that the female population of London was so wanting in care and so wasteful that only the gloomiest speculations could be entertained concerning the fate of a nation of whom the late owners of the hairpins were the mothers or instructresses. And, on returning to France, the last words of that naturalist chief to the writer were, after a couple of melancholy head-shakings and a deep sigh: "Those hairpins! Those hairpins!"

And when one thinks of all that boisterous and vital crowd one is at first inclined to sigh and quote the melancholy words of Pushkin: "A hundred years went by and what was left of that haughty and proud people, full of free passions? They and all their generation had passed traceless away."

Flaubert has been dead fifty-eight years and is under a deep cloud in his own country; Henry James, twenty-two and is disregarded in his native land; Turgenev, it is true, has already in Russia reached his period of resurgence and is said to be more read than any other Russian author of his generation, his fame approaching that which this writer would accord to it—that of being the greatest poet in prose who ever used the novel as the vehicle for his self-expression. Maupassant died in 1893 and is as discredited as his master Flaubert in the city of the Grands Boulevards; Zola died in 1902 and is today remembered chiefly as having been a rather unsatisfactory friend to Cézanne—the greatest of the French impressionist painters; Jean Karl Loris Huysmans—who was a greater artist than Zola—left the cathedrals and highways of this world in 1907, and I do not suppose that once in any year you will hear his name mentioned where people talk of books. Daudet died in 1897 and his *Tartarin* and still more his *Lettres de mon Moulin* are still read, rather contemptuously. Conrad died in 1924 and has already had a large measure of the herb oblivion strewn on his grave. Loti died in 1923 and is still, one imagines, read in suburban homes and young ladies' academies of the more advanced type. And finally, in 1924, amidst an execration that can hardly ever have been paralleled, died Jacques Anatole Thibault, who wrote—and that was one of the reasons for the detestation in which he came to be held—as France.

It has always seemed to this writer that the term "realist" could be fittingly applied to a little English group which began with George Gissing and Hale White and whose most distinguished exponent, Miss Dorothy Richardson, is still writing, though abominably unknown. The chief characteristic of this group is an extreme, an almost Flemish, minuteness of rendering of objects and situations perceived through the psychologies of the characters and not, as it were, motivated by the temperament of the writer. Proust carried this tendency to almost the limits of profitable elaboration and was rewarded with a measure of world fame. That the work of Miss Richardson, less wilfully elaborate and much more verbally beautiful, should meet with a complete world neglect is an amazing phenomenon, though one of a type sufficiently un-rare to fill one with despair of one's fellows. I will permit myself to express the hope that every one of my readers will at the earliest reasonable opportunity procure himself a copy of Miss Richardson's *Pointed Roofs*, a beautiful book which, published in 1915, was drowned under by the reverberations of the late war, but which was followed by nine others all linked together in subject under the general title of *Pilgrimage*. I will take this opportunity of making the same plea for the French novels of M. René Béhaine, a novelist as to whom far from only I have pledged their words that he is the greatest of French living writers.

The reason for the literary discredit that has fallen to the share of the realists in France, the country of their origin, is not a literary one. It arises from the depths of depression in which the war left the country of the lilies even in the hour of its triumph over the Nordic foe. In France, as in the rest of the world, the great words "honor," "chivalry," "religion," "self-sacrifice," "loyalty" and the "spirit of the forlorn hope" were dead. But in France alone was that extinction of the spirit of the past bitterly mourned and intensely regretted—more even by the young than the old. Thus, every negational utterance will make the young French writer shiver as if you had touched in him an open wound. Even Flaubert whose pessimism was, as we have said, really a disillusioned optimism, is included in one ban with Anatole France who was a really Satanic denier of virtue. So young

France, like Chateaubriand before the "viperisms" of Voltaire, desires, unconsciously enough, a new romanticism and, as all France has traditionally done, a man . . . of letters. Another Hugo! The man may come or the mood may very well pass. But, for the moment, if—as this writer did only a month or so ago—if you talk enthusiastically of Flaubert to a young Frenchman making his way difficultly along the slopes of Parnassus, he will draw in his teeth with a hiss and exclaim: "Never mention him, monsieur. The man was an old vulgarian. His humor is insupportable." But, nevertheless, if you should compare favorably Dostoievsky to Flaubert, he will draw himself up and exclaim darkly: "Never mention the two in the same breath, monsieur. Flaubert was at least a Frenchman, which is to say, the same thing as an artist." All the same, the sky is gloomy for the renown of the impressionist.

Delacroix, however, who is more and more recognized not merely as a romantic painter of an enormous *envergure*, but also as a *faiseur de mots*—an epigrammatist of the most acute kind—makes in his *Journal* under the date of 1859, the following deposition that is astonishingly true as a comment on a history of literature. He says:

> Real beauty is eternal and would be accepted at all periods; but it wears the dress of its century; something of that dress clings to it and woe to works which appear in periods when the general taste is corrupted.

Nevertheless, real beauty is eternal, the corruption of one generation's taste being the delight of generations hundreds of years in the future. The humorousnesses of Shakespeare and the bitternesses of Dante set on edge the teeth of the generation immediately succeeding each of them—because the humor was a hundred times twice told, and the bitternesses directed to dead men who, public parties changing, had become heroes. Today we ignore alike the witticisms and the reasons for the bitterness, as if both humor and bitterness were a little dust on the marble of the "Victory of Samothrace." So it may well be with this writer's dead friends and their great masters.

Let us finally say a word about Dostoievsky, who is the man who, man of letters though he was, must be considered to be the greatest single influence on the world of today. He has the aspect of greatness of an enormously enlarged but misty statue of Sophocles; he has the aspect of a Flaubert whose disillusionment has covered a whole universe; of a Zola who, having been born a great genius, makes the bottomless abysses of his epileptic fatalism color the mentality of continents. . . . But indeed his *Brothers Karamazov* stands as a fragment beside—but there is no work of literature with which you could parallel it. We have just mentioned the "Victory of Samothrace." . . . Well, if the mind of Villon and the hand of a pre-Periclean Greek could have hewed out of the rock of Golgotha a statue called the "Downfall of Hellas," you might parallel it with the work of Dostoievsky.

It would be absurd to claim him as a realist because his literary equipment is that of the romantics; but it would be absurd not to call him a realist, because the images he calls up are more real than life, and as visions have outlasted the lives of generations of men. The multitude of his characters is that of the crowds you will see pulsing into and out of vast industrial works; as a psychologist he surpasses anyone who ever delved into the human mind.

We might prophesy, then, that the "great" work of art of the future will come from the fusion of the genius of Dostoievsky with the art of the impressionists. Both tendencies are living bacilli in the world of today. . . . We may imagine it, that "great" work, psychologized as only Dostoievsky could psychologize; with a crowd form that only the genius and patience of a Flaubert could supply; with the mental subtlety of a James; the kindliness of a Turgenev; a touch of the panache of a Conrad and the minute observation of the author of the *Shepherd's Life.* . . . Why, yes, it will come because all those things have been put into the world by our art and because all the peoples of the earth demand nothing else, if only that they may have a little rest from their fears and the leisure to sit down and read. And what the Master shall command the hand of the slave shall contrive.

APPENDIX

SYNCHRONIZED TABLES OF NINETEENTH AND
TWENTIETH CENTURY AUTHORS*

To HAVE a real knowledge of the literature of
these centuries all the works here listed should
be read. Ford Madox Ford has indicated with
an asterisk the names of authors that it is indispensable to read in order to grasp the main
literary currents of this era. The books scheduled
are not necessarily the best known works of their
authors but those which in the opinion of
F. M. F. most markedly display their personalities.

* Prepared by Olive Carol Young for Ford Madox Ford's
The March of Literature.

ROMANTIC AUTHORS[1]
(Names Italicized Not Strictly Romantic)

SPAIN	FRANCE	ENGLAND
Quintana, Manuel José (1772–1857)	Mirabeau Victor Riqueti (1715–89)	*Wordsworth, William (...)* 1850)
Ode to the Invention of Printing (1800)	L'ami des Hommes	The Prelude (1805)
Ode to the Battle of Trafalgar (1805)	Bernardin de Saint-Pierre, Jacques Henri (1737–1814)	Poems in Two Volumes (1807)
Saavedra, Angel de (1791–1865)	Études de la Nature (1784) Paul et Virginie (1788)	Scott, Sir Walter (1771–1832) Antiquary (1816) Ivanhoe (1819)
El Moro Esposito (1834)	Mme. de Staël [Staël-Holstein, Anne Louise Germaine, Baroness de] (1766–1817)	Coleridge, Samuel Taylor (1772–1834)
Don Alvaro (1835)		
De Larra, Mariano José [essayist] (1809–37)	Delphine (1802) Corinne (1807)	Lyrical Ballads (1798) Sybilline Leaves (1817)
Espronceda, José de (1810–1842) ["Spanish Byron"]	Chateaubriand, François René (1768–1848)	Kubla Khan (1797) Byron, George Gordon (1788–18)
Estudiante de Salamanca Canción del Pirata	A'ala (1801) Les Aventures du Dernier des Abencérages (1826)	Childe Harold (1812)
Zorrilla y Moral, José de (1817–93)	*Stendhal [pseud. of Marie Henri Beyle] (1783–1842)	Prisoner of Chillon (1816) Don Juan (1819–24)
Poniard of the Goth (1814)	Le Rouge et le Noir (1831)	Shelley, Percy Bysshe (1792–1822)
Don Juan Tenorio (1844)	Chartreuse de Parme (1839)	Alastor (1816)
Becquer, Gustavo Adolfo (1836–1870) [Talewriter, poet "Spanish Poe"]	Lamartine, Alphonse Marie Louis de (1790–1869)	Prometheus Unbound (1820) Adonais (1821)
	La Cloche du Village Raphael Graziella	Keats, John (1795–1821) Ode on a Grecian Urn (1820) Ode to a Nightingale (1820)
	Michelet, Jules (1798–1874)	Endymion (1820)
	Histoire de France Love The Sea	Macaulay, Thomas Babington Lays of Ancient Rome (1842) History of England from the Accession of James II (1849–61)
	De Vigny, Alfred Victor (1799–1863)	
	Poésies Antique et Modernes Eloa	Bulwer-Lytton (1803–73) Last Days of Pompeii Rienzi
	Balzac, Honoré de (1799–1850)	Ruskin, John (1819–1900)
	La Peau de Chagrin La Comédie Humaine	Seven Lamps of Architecture (1849)
	Hugo, Victor Marie (1802–85)	Sesame and Lilies (1865)
	La Légende des Siècles (1859) Les Misérables (1862)	Crown of Wild Olive (1866) Arnold, Matthew (1822–88)
	Dumas, Alexandre [Dumas père] (1802–70)	Strayed Reveller and other Poems (1852)
	The Three Musketeers (1844) Count of Monte Cristo	Merope: A Tragedy (1858) Collins, Wilkie (1824–89)
	Sand, George [pseud. of Amandine Lucile Aurore (Dupin), Baroness Dudevant] (1804–76)	The Woman in White (1860) The Moonstone (1868) Stevenson, Robert Louis (1850–94)
	Indiana (1832) Elle et Lui	Treasure Island (1883) Kidnapped (1886)
	Musset, Alfred de (1810–57)	Dr. Jekyll and Mr. Hyde (1886)
	Contes d'Éspagne et d'Italie (1829)	
	Premières Poésies (1833)	
	Gautier, Théophile (1811–72)	
	Émaux et Camées Mlle. de Maupin Le Roman de la Momie	

[1] *Note:* All the authors scheduled as Romantics should be read to obtain a reasonable knowledge of the Romantic Movement. F. M. F.

ROMANTIC AUTHORS
(Names Italicized Not Strictly Romantics)

RUSSIA	GERMANY	ITALY
M. V. Lomonosov 1711–1765 ["father of Russian literature"]	Richter, Jean Paul (1763–1825) *Hesperus* (1795) *Titan* (1800–03) *Flegeljahre* (1804–05)	*Alfieri, Vittorio* (1749–1803) Niccolini, Giambattista (1782–1861) *Giovanni da Procida*
Karamzin, Nikolai Mihailovich (1766–1826) [historian and novelist] *Poor Lisa* *Natalia*	*Arndt, Ernst Moritz* [inspirer of German national revival] (1769–1860) *Geist der Zeit* (1806–18)	Manzoni, Alessandro (1785–1873) *I Promessi Sposi* (1827)
Zhukovsky, Vasily Andreïvich (1783–1852) [poet, modern trans.]	Novalis [George Friedrich von Hardenberg] (1772–1801) *Heinrich von Osterdingen* (begun 1799, unfinished at death)	Grossi, Tommaso (1791–1853) *Foscolo, Ugo* (1778–1827) [classical poet]
Batyushkov, Konstantin Nikolaievich (1787–1855) [poet, classical trans.]	Schlegel, Friedrich von (1772–1829) *Lucinde* (1799)	Leopardi, Giacomo [Count] (1798–1837) *Alle Pressamente alla Morte* (1816)
Delvig, Anton Antonovich (1798–1831)	Tieck, Ludwig (1773–1853) *William Lovell* (1795–96)	Guerrazzi, Francesco Dominico (1804–1873) *L'Assedio di Firenze*
Pushkin, Alexander (1799–1837) *Ruslan & Liudmila* (1820) *Boris Godúnov* (1828) *Evgenie Oniegin* (1822–29)	Fouqué, Friedrich Heinrich Karl [Baron de la Motte] (1777–1843) *Undine* (1827)	
Lermontov, Mikhail Yurevich (1814–41) *A Hero of Our Times* (1836)	Brentano, Clemens (1778–1842) *Fantastic Tales, passim*	
	Chamisso, Adelbert von [real name Louis Charles Adelaide de] (1781–1838) *Peter Schlemihl* (1813)	
	Brothers Grimm [Jakob Ludwig Karl 1785–1863, and Wilhelm Karl 1786–1859] *Maerchen, passim*	
	Rückert, Friedrich [pseud. of Freimund Raimar] (1788–1866) *Sonnets in Armor* (1816) *Springtime of Love* (1823)	
	Droste-Hülshoff, Annette Elis., [Baroness von] (1797–1848) *Walther*	
	Lenau, Nikolaus [pseud. of Nikolaus Niembsch von Strehlenau] (1802–50) [Austrian] *Savonarola* *Faust* *Die Albigenser*	

POST-ROMANTICS

ENGLISH

NOVELISTS	POETS	OTHERS

NOVELISTS

Marryat, Frederick (1792?–1848)
Peter Simple (1834)
Mr. Midshipman Easy (1836)
Disraeli, Benjamin (1804–81)
Virginia Grey (1826)
Captain Popanilla (1828)
Lever, Charles James (1806–72)
Charles O'Malley (1841)
*Gaskell, Elizabeth Cleghorn (1810–65)
Mary Barton (1848)
North and South (1855)
*Thackeray, William M. (1811–63)
Vanity Fair (1847–8)
*Dickens, Charles (1812–70)
Tale of Two Cities (1859)
Great Expectations (1860–1)
Reade, Charles (1814–84)
The Cloister and the Hearth (1861)
Jack of All Trades (1858)
Brontë, Emily (1814–48)
Wuthering Heights (1847)
*Trollope, Anthony (1815–82)
Doctor Thorne (1849)
Small House at Allington (1864)
Brontë, Charlotte (1816–55)
Jane Eyre (1847)
Kingsley, Charles (1819–75)
Hypatia (1853)
Westward Ho! (1855)
Eliot, George [pseud. of Mary Ann Evans] 1819–80
Mill on the Floss
Silas Marner
De Quincey, Thomas (1822–88)
Confessions of an Opium Eater (1821)
Meredith, George (1828–1909)
Ordeal of Richard Feverel (1859)
Diana of the Crossways (1885)
*White, William Hale (1830–1913)
Autobiography of Mark Rutherford (1881)
Revolution in Tanner's Lane (1887)
*Butler, Samuel (1835–1902)
Erewhon (1872)
Erewhon Revisited (1901)
Way of All Flesh

POETS

*Browning, Elizabeth (1806–61)
Sonnets from the Portuguese (1847)
Aurora Leigh (1857)
Fitzgerald, Edward (1809–1883)
Rubaiyat of Omar Khayyám (1859)
Rossetti, D. G. (1828–82)
Dante and His Circle (1874) [trans. from Italian]
Ballads and Sonnets (1881)
*Rossetti, Christina (1830–94)
Verses (1847)
Morris, William (1834–96)
Defence of Guinevere and other Poems (1858)
Earthly Paradise (1868)
Swinburne, Charles Algernon (1837–1909)
Atalanta in Calydon (1865)
Poems and Ballads (1866)
Wilde, Oscar (1856–1900)
Lady Windermere's Fan (1893)
Housman, Alfred Edward (1859–1936)
A Shropshire Lad (1896)
*Yeats, William Butler (1865–)
Poems and Ballads of Young Ireland (1888)
Plays for an Irish Theatre (1911)
Robinson, Edwin Arlington (1869–1935)
Collected Poems (1921)
Man Who Died Twice (1925)
Masefield, John (1878–)
Collected Poems and Plays
*Pound, Ezra (1885–)
Cathay (1915)
Selected Poems (1928)
Brooke, Rupert (1887–1915)
Collected Poems (1819)
*Cummings, Edward Estlin (1894–)
Enormous Room (1922)
Collected Poems (1926)
*Adams, Léonie (1899–)
High Falcon
*MacLeish, Archibald
*Tate, Allen
Spender, Stephen
Auden, W. H.

OTHERS

Beckford, William (1760–1844)
Letters from Portugal (1780)
Vathek (1782)
Carlyle, Thomas (1795–1881)
Sartor Resartus (1836)
French Revolution (1837)
Borrow, George Henry (1803–81)
Bible in Spain (1843)
Romany Rye (1857)
Darwin, Charles Robert (1809–82)
Origin of Species (1859)
Huxley, Thomas Henry (1825–95)
Man's Place in Nature (1893)
Collected Essays (1894)
Stubbs, William (1825–1901)
Constitutional History of England in its Origin and Development (1874–78)
Gardiner, Sam Rawson (1829–1902)
A History of England from the Accession of James I to the Outbreak of the Civil War (1883–84)
History of the Commonwealth and Protectorate [unfinished] (1894–1901)
Green, John Richard (1837–83)
Short History of the English People (1874)
History of the English People (1878–80)
Doughty, Charles Montagu (1843–1926)
Travels in Arabia Deserta (1888)
Cunninghame Graham, Robert Bontine (1852–1936)
Mogreb el-Acksa (1904)
Shaw, George Bernard (1856–)
Arms and the Man (1898)
Man and Superman (1903)
Saint Joan (1923)

POST-ROMANTICS—ENGLISH *(Concluded)*

NOVELISTS *(Continued)*

*Alcott, Louisa May (1832–88)
  Little Women (1868)
*Hardy, Thomas (1840–1928)
  Jude the Obscure (1896)
  Collected Poems (1919)
*Hudson, W. H. (1846–1922)
  Purple Land (1885)
  Green Mansions (1904)
*Jewett, Sarah Orne (1849–1919)
  Deephaven (1877)
  Country of the Pointed Firs (1896)
*Moore, George (1852–1933)
  Esther Waters (1894)
*Conrad, Joseph (1856–1924)
  Romance (1903)
  Nostromo (1904)
  Lord Jim (1906)
*Gissing, George (1857–1903)
  New Grub Street (1891)
  Whirlpool (1897)
Barrie, Sir James (1860–1937)
  A Window in Thrums (1889)
  Little Minister (1891)
*Wharton, Edith (1862–1937)
  House of Mirth (1905)
  Ethan Frome (1911)

NOVELISTS *(Continued)*

Kipling, Rudyard (1865–1936)
  Barrack Room Ballads (1892)
  Kim (1901)
Bennett, Arnold (1867–1931)
  Old Wives' Tale (1908)
  Clayhanger (1910)
Galsworthy, John (1867–1933)
  Man of Property (1906)
  White Monkey (1924)
Wells, Herbert George (1868– ——)
  Tono-Bungay (1909)
  Outline of History (1920)
Belloc, Hilaire (1870– ——)
  Verses and Sonnets (1895)
  The Path to Rome (1902)
Chesterton, Gilbert Keith (1874–1936)
  The Man Who was Thursday (1908)
Maugham, Somerset (1874– ——)
  Of Human Bondage (1915)
*Anderson, Sherwood (1876– ——)
  Winesburg, Ohio
  A Story Teller's Story (1924)

NOVELISTS *(Concluded)*

*Joyce, James (1882– ——)
  Portrait of the Artist as a Young Man (1916)
  Ulysses (1922)
*Woolf, Virginia (1882– ——)
  Mrs. Dalloway (1925)
  To the Lighthouse (1927)
Young, Francis Brett (1884– ——)
  Deep Sea (1914)
Walpole, Hugh (1884– ——)
  Fortitude (1913)
  Dark Forest (1916)
Lewis, Sinclair (1885– ——)
  Main Street (1920)
  Babbitt (1922)
  Arrowsmith (1925)
*Lawrence, D. H. (1887–1930)
  Sons and Lovers (1913)
  The Rainbow (1915)
  Love Poems and Others (1913)
*Richardson, Dorothy M.
  Pilgrimage (novel in 8 volumes)
  Oberland (1927)

POST-ROMANTICS

FRENCH

NOVELISTS	POETS	OTHERS

NOVELISTS

Gautier, Théophile (1811–72)
Émaux et Camées (1842)
Le Capitaine Fracasse

*Flaubert, Gustave (1821–80)
Madame Bovary (1857)
Salammbô (1862)

*Goncourt, Edmond de (1822–96)

*Goncourt, Jules (1830–70)
Renée Mauperin (1864)

Dumas, Alexander [Dumas fils] (1824–95)
Camille (1852)
La Question d'Argent

Zola, Émile (1840–1902)
Le Roman Expérimental (1880)
La Terre (1887)

Daudet, Alphonse (1840–97)
Lettres de Mon Moulin (1869)
Tartarin sur les Alpes (1885)

France, Anatole [Jacques-Anatole Thibault] (1844–1924)
Le Jardin d'Epicure (1894)
L'Île des Pingouins (1908)

*Huysmans, Jean Joris Karl (1848–1907)
Là-Bas (1891)
En Route (1895)

*Maupassant, Guy de (1850–93)
Des Vers
Boule de Suif

Loti, Pierre [pseud. of Julien Viaud] (1850–1923)
Pêcheurs d'Islande (1886)
Madame Chrysantheme (1887)

Bourget, Paul (1852–1936)
Cruelle Énigme (1885)
Le Disciple (1889)

Barrès, Maurice (1862–1923)
Sous l'Oeil des Barbares (1888)
Le Roman de l'Énergie Nationale (1920)

*Regnier, Henri de (1864–1926)
La Cité des Eaux
Les Jours Rustiques et Divins (1897)

Rolland, Romain (1868– ——)
Jean-Christophe

*Béhaine, René (1872– ——)
Les Nouveaux Venus (1899)
The Survivors [trans.] 1938

POETS

Lisle, Leconte de (1818–94)
Mûll

*Baudelaire, Charles (1821–67)
Les Fleurs du Mal (1857)

*Mallarmé, Stéphane (1842–98)
L'Après-Midi d'un Faune (1876)

Hérédia, José-Maria de (1842–1905)
Les Trophées (1893)

*Verlaine, Paul (1844–96)
La Bonne Chanson (1870)
Romances sans Paroles (1874)

*Rimbaud (1854?–91)
Le Bateau Ivre (1895)
Sonnet des Voyelles (1895)

Verhaeren, Émile (1855–1916)
Les Forces Tumultueuses (1902)

Maeterlinck, Maurice (1862– ——)
La Princesse Maleine (1889)
L'Oiseau Bleu (1909)

Rostand, Edmond (1868–1918)
Cyrano de Bergerac (1897)
L'Aiglon (1900)

Fort, Paul (1872– ——)
Ballades Françaises (1897–1920)

OTHERS

Sainte-Beuve, Charles-Augustin (1804–69)
Vie. Poésies et Pensées de Joseph Delorme (1829)
Causeries du Lundi (1851–62)

*Renan, Ernest (1823–92)
Souveniers d'Enfance et de Jeunesse (1883)

Sarcey, Francisque (1827–99)
Quarante Ans de Théâtre (1900–99)

*Taine, Hippolyte (1828–93)
Histoire de la Littérature Anglaise (1864)

Paris, Gaston (1839–1903)
Histoire Poétique de Charlemagne (1865)

Brunetière, Ferdinand (1849–1906)
Études Critiques sur la Littérature Française (1880–1907)

Lemaître, Jules (1853–1914)
Les Contemporains (1885–99)
Impressions de Théâtre (1888)

Lanson, Gustave (1857– ——)
Histoire de la Littérature Française (1880–1907)

*Gourmant, Remy de (1858–1915)
Promenades Littéraires (1914)

POST-ROMANTICS

GERMANS

NOVELISTS	OTHERS[1]
Immermann, Karl Leberecht (1796–1840) *Epigonen* (1836) *Münchhausen* (1839)	Freytag, Georg Wilhelm Friedrich (1788–1861) [translated Arabic works]
*Sudermann, Hermann (1857–1928) *Frau Sorge* (1887) *Song of Songs* (1908)	Grillparzer, Franz (1791–1872) [Austrian] *Der Traum, Ein Leben* (1817–34) *Der Arme Spielmann*
Viebig, Clara (1860– ——) *Schlafende Heer*	Nietzsche, Friedrich Wilhelm (1844–1900) *Thus Spake Zarathustra* (1882) *Will to Power* (tr. 1909–10)
*Hauptmann, Gerhart Johann Robert (1862–?) *The Weavers* *Sunken Bell* *Atlantis*	Wedekind, Franz (1864–1918) *Spring's Awakening* (1891) *Such is Life* (1907)
Ompteda, Georg (1863–1931) *Sylvester von Geyer* *Eysen* *Cäcile von Sarryn*	Schücking, Walther (1875– ——) [critic]
*Schnitzler, Arthur (1863–1931) [Austrian] *Anatol* (1893) *Green Cockatoo*	
*Mann, Thomas (1875– ——) *Buddenbrooks* (1901) *Magic Mountain*	
Feuchtwanger, Lion (1884– ——) *Ugly Duchess* (1923)	

[1] Dramatists, critics, historians, philosophers.

POST-ROMANTICS

SPANIARDS

NOVELISTS	POETS	OTHERS[1]
Valera, Juan (1824–1905) *Pepita Jiménez*	Nuñez de Arce, Gaspar (1834–1903) *Battle Cries* (1875) *Shoemaker's Bill* (1859) *The Faggot* (1872) [drama]	Moratín, Leandro Fernandez de (1760–1828) *The Maidens' Consent*
Pereda, José María de (1833–1906) *Pedro Sánchez* (1883) *The Taste of the Earth*		Echegaray, José (1833–1916) *Madness or Sanctity* *The Great Galeoto* (1881)
Alarcón, Pedro Antonio de (1833–91) *Diary of a Witness of the War in Africa* *Three-Cornered Hat*		Guimerá, Angel (1849–1924) *Martha of the Lowlands* *La Pecadora Daniela*
*Pérez Galdós, Benita (1845–1920) *Doña Perfecta* *Episodios Naçionales*		Menéndez y Pelayo, Marcelino (1856–1912) *History of Aesthetic Ideas in Spain* *Calderón and his Theatre* (1881)
Pardo Bazán, Emilia (1852–1921) *Mother Nature* *Mystery*		Benavente y Martinez, Jacinto (1866– ——) *Saturday Night* (1903) *The Passion Flower* (1913)
*Palacio Valdés, Armando (1853– ——) *The Fourth Estate* *Papeles del Doctor Angélico*		Alvarez Quintero, Serafin (1871– ——)
Unamuno, Miguel de (1864– ——) *Life of Don Quixote and Sancho Panza* *The Tragic Sense of Life*		Alvarez Quintero, Joaquin (1873– ——) *The Women Have Their Way* *A Hundred Years Old*
Blasco Ibáñez, Vicente (1866–1928) *Four Horsemen of Apocalypse* *The Mayflower*		Martinez Sierra, Gregorio (1881– ——) *Cradle Song* (1917) Poetry *Love Magic* (drama) *Anna Maria* (novel)
*Baroja y Nessi, Pío (1872– ——) *Struggle for Existence* *Memories of a Man of Action*		Madariaga, Salvador de (1886– ——) *The Genius of Spain* (1923) *Englishmen, Frenchmen and Spaniards* (1928)
*Perez de Ayala, Ramon (1881– ——) *A.M.D.G.* (1910) *Belarmino y Apolonio* (1921		

[1] Dramatists, critics, historians, etc.

POST-ROMANTICS

ITALIANS

NOVELISTS	POETS	OTHERS[1]
*Amicis, Edmondo de (1846–1908) *Cuore* *Fogazzaro, Antonio (1842–1911) *Malombra* [novel] *Il Santo* [novel] *Miranda* (1874) [poem] Serao, Matilde (1856–1927) *Conquest of Rome* *Desire of Life* *In the Country of Jesus* *Svevo, Italo [pseud. of Ettore Schmitz] (1864–1928) *Zeno's Conscience* (1921) *The Hoax* *Deledda, Grazia (1875– ——) *Elias Portolù* (1903) *Reeds in the Wind* (1913)	*Marinetti, Filippo Tomaso (1878– ——) [Founder of futurism] *King Bombance* *Mafarka the Futurist*	*Pirandello, Luigi (1867– ——) *Right You Are if You Think You Are* *The Late Mattia Pascal* (1923) [novel]

[1]Dramatists, critics, historians, etc.

POST-ROMANTICS[1]

SCANDINAVIANS

NOVELISTS	POETS	OTHERS
Oelenschläger (1770–1850) [Danish]	*Tegner, Esais (1782–1846) [Swedish]	*Ibsen, Henrik (1828–1906) [Norwegian]
Guldhornene (1802)	Frithjof's Saga (1820–25)	Peer Gynt (1873)
Aladdin (1805)	Axel (1822)	Wild Duck (1884)
Hakon Jarl (1807)		Doll's House (1899)
Almqvist, Karl Jonas Ludwig (1793–1866) [Swedish]		Hedda Gabler (1899)
Book of the Thorn and the Rose (1832)		Brandes, Georg Morris Cohen (1842–1927) [Danish]
Andersen, Hans Christian (1805–75) [Danish]		Main Currents of Nineteenth Century Literature (1871–90)
Fairy Tales (1835 et seq.)		
*Björnson, Björnstjerne (1832–1910) [Norwegian]		
Synnöve Solbakken (1857)		
Anne (1858)		
Beyond Human Power (1883)		
*Lie, Jonas Lauritz Edemil (1833–1908) [Norwegian]		
Family of Gilje (1883)		
The Commodore's Daughters (1886)		
*Strindberg, Johann August (1849–1912) [Swedish]		
The Son of a Servant (1866)		
The Fool's Confession (1878–8)		
*Lagerlöf, Selma (1858– ——) [Swedish]		
Jerusalem (1902)		
The Ring of the Löwenskölds (1931)		
*Gösta Berling (1890–1)		
Hamsun, Knut (1859– ——) Norwegian]		
Hunger (1896)		
Growth of the Soil (1917)		
Rolvaag, Ole Edvart (1876–1931) [Norwegian-Amer.]		
Giants of the Earth (1924–5)		
Peder Victorious (1928)		
Undset, Sigrid (1882– ——) [Norwegian]		
Kristian Lavrans Datter (1920–22)		
Burning Bush (1930)		

[1] A very useful work, the first attempt to co-relate all the Scandinavian literatures has lately been published in America by The Dial Press: The History of the Scandinavian Literatures, based in part on the work of Giovanni Bach, additional sections by Richard Beck, Adolph B. Benson, Axel Johan Uppvall, and others; compiled, translated in part, and edited by Frederika Blankner.—F. M. F.

POST-ROMANTICS
RUSSIANS[1]

NOVELISTS	POETS	OTHERS
Gogol, Nikolai Vasilyevich (1809–52) *The Cloak* *Dead Souls* Turgenev, Ivan Sergeyevich (1818–83) *A Sportsman's Sketches* (1852) *Smoke* (1860) Dostoievsky, Feodor Mikhailovich (1821–81) *Poor Folk* (1844–5) *The House of the Dead* (1870) Tolstoy, Leo Nikolayevich (1828–1910) *War and Peace* (1864–68) *Anna Karenina* (1875) Chekhov, Anton Pavlovich (1860–1904) [short stories and plays] *The Cherry Orchard* *The Bet* Sologub, Feodor [pseud. of Feodor Juzmich Teternikov] (1863–1927) *The Little Demon* (1907) Andreyev, Leonid Nikolayevich (1871–1919) *The Seven Who Were Hanged* (tr. 1920) *He Who Gets Slapped* [drama] (1916) Artzybashev, Mikhail Petrovich (1878–1927) *Sanine* (1907)	Tolstoy, Aleksey Konstantinovich, Count (1817–75) [poet, dramatist, novelist] *Boris Godúnov* *Ivan the Terrible* Nekrasov, Nikolai Alekseyevich (1821–78) *The Pedlar* *Who Lives Happily in Russia* Aksakov, Ivan Sergeyevich [Slavophil poet] (1823–86) Akhmatova, Anna [pseud. of Anna Andreyevna Gorenka] (1895– ——) [Head of Acmeist (anti-symbolist) School]	Krylov, Ivan Andrevich (1786–1844) *Fables* Ostrovsky, Aleksander Nikolayevich (1823–86) *The Bankrupt* (1847) *The Snow Maiden* (tr. 1872) Gorki, Maxim [pseud. of Aleksey Maximovich Pyeshkov] (1868–1936) *In the Depths* [drama] *The Mother* [novel] Shklovski, Victor Borisovich (1893– ——) *On the Theory of Prose* (1929)

[1] All the above must be read to obtain merely a superficial knowledge of Russian Literature since 1800

Index

Realizing that in a work of this scope an imaginatively prepared index is a very necessary working tool for the reader, the publishers have carefully indexed the book in such a manner as to make it as utilitarian as possible.

In using this index, the reader should note:

(a) All words set in *italics* in the index are the actual titles of literary works, such as novels, plays, biographies, histories, long poems, etc.

(b) All words set in Capitals and Small Capitals in the index are the names of writers.

(c) The titles of short poems, orations, etc., appear in quotation marks in the index.

(d) All words set in upper and lower case in the index are general index matter.

INDEX

865